THE BOLD RIDERS

The Bold Riders

Behind Australia's Corporate Collapses

Trevor Sykes

ALLEN & UNWIN

First published in 1994 by
Allen & Unwin Pty Ltd
9 Atchison Street, St Leonards, NSW 2065 Australia

National Library of Australia
Cataloguing-in-Publication entry:

Sykes, Trevor.
  The bold riders.

  Includes index.
  ISBN 1 86373 702 2.

  1. Business failures—Australia—History—20th century.
  I. Title.

338.71

Set in 10/12 Palatino by DOCUPRO, Sydney, NSW 2066
Printed by Australian Print Group, Maryborough, Vic. 3465

10 9 8 7 6 5 4 3 2 1

'Over the Mountains of the Moon,
Down the Valley of the Shadow,
Ride, boldly ride,
The Shade replied,
If you seek for Eldorado.'

Edgar Allan Poe
'Eldorado'

DEDICATION

To Daya, who endured this book for three long years.
And to Mandalay for keeping her company.

Contents

Contents

Figures and tables

Figures and tables

Preface

They were bold riders, all right. The corporate cowboys of the 1980s rode our financial landscape as none had done before. They used tiny equity holdings as the basis for huge empires built on mountains of debt. They took the savings of Australians, entrusted to our banks, and channelled them into takeovers on a scale that had never been seen before. The bold riders took over our brewing industry and most of our media and textiles. They rode out boldly across the world, raiding the international brewing industry, seizing the West End theatre district, invading the United States, Hong Kong and even Chile. In the Central Business Districts of Australia, they built glittering towers of glass and concrete which in the next decade would stand empty as monuments to folly.

The Eldorado they sought came in many shapes. A mansion with rich furnishings and an art collection was de rigeur. It was usually supplemented by a country estate with equally rich fittings. There were private jets and luxurious boats, strings of racehorses and sleek, high-powered cars. Their wives wore big diamonds and—in many cases—so did their girlfriends and mistresses. When the crash came, some of the riders went bankrupt but managed to retain a vestige of their Eldorado in overseas bank accounts, perhaps enough to finance fresh empires. The investors who had financed their delusions of grandeur were left high and dry.

This book tells the bold riders' story. It was not an easy book to write. The Australian legal system proved to be an enormous stumbling block. Court cases which should have taken at most a year to be finalised dragged on for five or six years or—in cases such as Bond and Estate Mortgage—even longer. No full official report was made public into some of the collapses, Spedley being a notable example. Several court cases were still incomplete at the time this book went to press. However, waiting for them all to have been completed could have taken until the next Ice Age. As the book's primary purpose is to explore the causes of large business failures it does not much matter if the final details of some court cases remain unknown. The message is that corporate justice works very slowly and badly in Australia in both the civil and the criminal jurisdictions. Readers can assume that, unless I have stated otherwise, all criminal charges and civil suits are being defended. Given the lags of the publishing industry, some cases may be settled or concluded before this book is published. Where cases are unresolved I have often indicated the position at the time of writing. I need hardly remind readers of the great precept of British justice that we are all innocent until proven guilty.

Complexity of the subject was another problem. The bold riders of the 1980s constructed corporate structures of a complexity we had not seen before. Nobody, for example, has an accurate count of the number of entities involved in the Linter collapse, which included public companies, private companies, trusts and even individuals. Transactions were difficult to follow, particularly in such interwoven groups as Rothwells and Spedley. If this book went into full detail of all these highly complicated matters it would become an unreadable eye-glazer. However, without some understanding of these transactions in several cases the reader would not know how frauds were committed, how accounts were falsified, how accounting standards were prostituted and how investors were misled. I have tried to simplify transactions as far as possible and to go into detail only on key transactions, eliminating any that did not seem relevant to the core reasons for a group's failure. Believe me, for every complex transaction described in this book there were at least twenty more that have been omitted.

A third problem was the scale of the subject. It soon became apparent that a detailed study of every sizeable crash of the 1980s could not be fitted into a single book. It would also have kept the author occupied well into the 21st century. So some collapses were arbitrarily omitted. As the Fairfax media group had been covered in four books—including one by me—it was left out, although the reader will find references to it. The New Zealand cowboys were left out because exploring their history and downfall would have involved the expenditure of time and money across the Tasman. So such disasters as Equiticorp, Ariadne and the Bank of New Zealand get only passing references. The Elders/Fosters group was omitted because it didn't collapse. John Elliott's buyout vehicle Harlin did collapse, but the available facts were rather scanty and digging up more would have been an international exercise which neither the author nor the publisher would have found worth financing. Some of the medium-size groups such as Interwest and Hartogen also had to be omitted.

All these omissions amount to a charitable gesture. If any other authors want to write on the same subject, I have left ample material for them to explore. I doubt whether their conclusions will be substantially different, however.

My thanks to all of those who helped with this book. As some did not want to be named, it would be rather invidious to list the others. My special thanks, however, to Mark O'Brien, Ian Ferrier, Tony Hodgson, John Harkness, John Murphy, Peter Allen, Geoff Hill, Lindsay Maxsted and Paul Wright. A number of others helped greatly by reading chapters, providing documents or pointing me in the right direction. They know who they are and so do I.

Finally my thanks to my gallant bride Daya, who lived with this book for three years when we could have been doing something much more enjoyable.

1
The seeds

*Nothing has changed about understanding credit in a hundred years.
Someone has money, someone needs it and you either structure it
properly or you don't do the deal.*

David Ryan

The corporate booms and busts of the 1980s were the greatest ever seen
in Australian history. The boom saw a bunch of corporate cowboys
financed to dizzy heights by greedy and reckless bankers. Large sectors
of Australian industry changed hands. Ownership of the major brewing
and media companies changed completely. The nation's largest company,
Broken Hill Proprietary Company Ltd, became a shuttlecock in a game
between Robert Holmes à Court and John Elliott. Alan Bond built an
enormous empire on debt and creative accounting.

The ensuing bust saw awesome destruction. The collapses included
Australia's largest industrial group (Adelaide Steamship); the ninth
largest enterprise in the nation, measured by revenue (Bond Corporation);
nearly half the brewing industry (Bond Brewing); all three major commercial television networks (Bond Media, Qintex, Channel Ten);
Australia's largest car renter (Budget); the second largest newspaper
group (Fairfax); Victoria's largest building society (Pyramid); and
Australia's largest textile group (Linter). Severe problems were faced by
Australia's largest company, as measured by revenue (Elders), its largest
media group (News) and the other half of the brewing industry (Fosters).
The former Premier of Western Australia, Brian Burke, was charged after
a Royal Commission into his government's role in promoting the corporate cowboys of that state.

The devastation was equally great among the financiers. Total write-
offs and provisions by banks and financiers amounted to $28 billion.[1]
Australia's three largest merchant banks (Tricontinental, Partnership
Pacific and Elders Finance) had to be rescued by their parents. Two of
Australia's four state banks (State Bank of Victoria and State Bank of

1

South Australia) suffered devastating losses and were investigated by Royal Commissions. The SBV was taken over by the Commonwealth Bank. The other two state banks, the Rural & Industries Bank of Western Australia and the State Bank of New South Wales, were deeply scarred. The four major trading banks (Westpac, National, Commonwealth and ANZ) had to write billions of dollars off their loan books, the suffering being particularly heavy in Westpac and ANZ. The losses of foreign banks operating in Australia were even higher proportionately, some of the worst being those of HongkongBank Australia, Standard Chartered, Security Pacific and Bank of New Zealand.

At the end, investors were left excoriating corporate cowboys such as Alan Bond, Christopher Skase and Laurie Connell. While these and other men deserved blame, it should have been spread more widely. Australia, after all, is no stranger to corporate cowboys. The country has had them in almost every decade of its existence. What was truly abnormal about the 1980s was the extent to which they were able to lay their hands on money. Never before in Australian history has so much money been channelled by so many people incompetent to lend it into the hands of so many people incompetent to manage it.

The banks financed the takeover of old, stodgily managed businesses by new, often unsound managements. Backed by debt from the banks the corporate cowboys drove up asset prices, in particular the prices of businesses, property and equities. The paper castles they built were increasingly vulnerable to any harsh wind. The first cyclone to blow came on 20 October 1987, when the world's share markets lost one-quarter of their value in a single trading session. An overrelaxation of monetary policy then allowed a false boom to continue for more than another year, particularly in the property market. Then renewed high interest rates busted the property market too and plunged Australia into a recession. Before studying the case histories of the collapses, it is necessary to understand the background of how and why the boom grew and the forces that punctured it.

The banks

The key factor underlying the crashes of the late 1980s was the prostitution of the banking system. The breakdown of the Australian banking system was both financial and moral. It did not happen in isolation from the rest of the world, as episodes such as Banco Ambrosiano, Penn Square and Morgan Grenfell illustrate. But to keep this book within bounds we shall examine only what happened in Australia. Here, some $20 billion was lost in unsound lending by banks, which are normally perceived as the guardians of the conservative monetary faith. Where did the banks run off the rails and cross the line that separates sound from unsound lending? The answer is that there were several factors which snowballed in the heady boom of the mid-1980s, but that the progressive weakening of lending criteria began in the 1970s and the real origins dated back to the 1960s.

The bankers of the 1980s forgot the lessons of history. In the 19th century, Australia suffered a wave of bank collapses in almost every decade, culminating with the banking crisis of 1893 when two-thirds of the nation's banking assets were frozen by wholesale suspensions of payments.[2] As a protective measure, the Commonwealth Bank was established in 1911 as the central bank of issue. This ushered in a half-century of relative tranquillity in Australian banking, interrupted only when three banks went to the wall at the depths of the Great Depression in 1931. Banks operated under strong controls during World War II, with the central bank dictating overdraft rates and, later, statutory reserve deposit ratios and liquid asset ratios. By the 1950s, when the Reserve Bank of Australia took over central banking functions from the Commonwealth Bank, Australians banks were tightly controlled, but safe. However, a new force was appearing. The post-war boom had proved fertile ground for a fringe banking industry to arise as finance companies flourished, untrammelled by central banking controls.

Finance companies

The banks quickly expanded into this new and more profitable market. Between 1953 and 1957 every major bank acquired a stake in a major finance company. The Bank of New South Wales had Australian Guarantee Corporation (AGC); the ANZ had Industrial Acceptance Corporation (IAC); the National had Custom Credit; the Commercial Bank of Australia had General Credits; the English, Scottish & Australian had Esanda; the Commercial Banking Company of Sydney had Commercial & General Acceptance (CAGA); and the Bank of Adelaide had Finance Corporation of Australia (FCA). The finance companies began in hire purchase—financing cars, refrigerators and even food mixers.

The long, stable prosperity of the 1950s and 1960s brought high profits to the finance companies, encouraging them to become more entrepreneurial. They began financing property speculation in association with the corporate cowboys of the day. FCA financed Alan Bond's first land speculation at Lesmurdie Heights in 1960. CAGA helped Bond make his first million in 1967. A huge block of already subdivided land was up for sale at Kardinya, on the southern fringe of Perth, for $1.2 million. Bond didn't even have the deposit, but he flew to Sydney and borrowed the entire amount from CAGA. He immediately resold the land. CAGA took a share of the profit on top of its customary 12 per cent interest and they both made a killing. In Bond's early days he is also known to have used IAC and Custom Credit.

There was a natural affinity between the finance companies and the cowboys. A speculator who is expecting to make 100 per cent on a deal is not too fussy about whether he is borrowing at 10 per cent or 20, and will cheerfully pay the lender a fee on top. As long as asset price inflation continued, therefore, the finance companies loved lending to the cowboys, whose big fees and high rates swelled their profits. So although the banks extended relatively little credit to the embryonic cowboys, their finance companies extended a lot. Each trading bank was like a stiffly respectable hotel which insisted that guests could not take ladies to their rooms. The desk clerk could always, however, give you a reference to the wholly owned whorehouse next door.

Merchant banks

Merchant banks also began competing for business, notably Martin Corporation, formed in Sydney in 1966 by a consortium which included Baring Brothers, United Dominion, Cater Ryder, Mercantile Mutual, Mutual Acceptance, The Chartered Bank, A.B.S. White and later Wells Fargo. The fact that there were so many shareholders in Martin Corp meant that none of them was in control. The executives, under managing director Harold Abbott, seized the initiative and began doing some adventurous deals.

Martin Corp would acquire notoriety when it hit the wall a few years later, but in its infancy it was regarded as an exciting place to work for smart young men eager to break out of the staid mould of Australian banking. Early recruits included Laurie Connell, Peter Joseph, Malcolm Irving and Brian Yuill.

Weakening loyalty

Another factor at work was the loosening of traditional loyalties. For two decades after World War II, Australian companies, and especially the larger ones, were one-bank companies. The National Bank, for example, had all the business of the Herald & Weekly Times. Big corporates rarely moved their accounts from one bank to another (it caused a mild sensation in financial circles if they did) and banks competed for big clients only with great discretion.

It began to occur to some bankers that the raiders represented more profitable business than the old, staid companies they were attacking.

4

Raiders borrowed more money and so paid more interest. Raiders were happy to pay high fees. Raiders were more active, taking over fresh companies and selling assets, and thus generated extra business. They were much more lucrative than some stolid business generating an unexciting 10 per cent per annum and keeping its debt low. If you were a banker to a Mr Ten Per Cent, it paid to sell him out to a raider. An early example of this was the takeover of the sleepy old jam merchant Henry Jones IXL by John Elliott's team in 1972. Henry Jones' banker was the Commercial Bank of Australia. One of the financiers of the takeover raid was the Commercial Bank's finance subsidiary, General Credits. This caused some mutterings around the clubs of Melbourne.

Hostile takeovers

Traditionally, the Australian trading banks and life offices had looked askance at financing of hostile takeovers. In the mid-1970s this attitude began to change as market raiders such as Ron Brierley, Alan Bond and Robert Holmes à Court began to attract support. At first the support, like the raiders themselves, was diminutive. The raiders could only attack small targets and their finance was mostly derived from the fringe-dwellers of the Australian banking system.

The first institution to take them seriously might have been the National Mutual, which together with the Bank of New York in 1974 set up a merchant bank named Citinational Holdings. The chairman, Keith (later Sir Keith) Campbell, chose as his chief executive a banker named Nick Dawe, formerly of the Commercial Bank of Australia and Martin Corp. Dawe was typical of the restless breed of the early 1970s. 'I could see where I was going', he said. 'I didn't fancy staying in the bank till I was 65 and then retiring.'[3] Dawe began financing the fledgling entrepreneurs of the day. Citinational's first Christmas party in 1974 featured such fledglings as David Bardas, Ron Brierley, Peter Hutchins, Christopher Box and Peter Yunghanns. The message was clear: if they had a deal that needed finance, come and talk to Nick.

A few months later Nick financed the first takeover bid of the then smallest fledgling of them all—Christopher Skase. The vehicle was what might be called a venture capital company named Team Securities Ltd. Team's first bid was for Victoria Holdings Ltd, a small listed company which ran the old unlicensed Victoria Hotel in Melbourne's Flinders Lane. Citinational financed the bid and National Mutual tried to give it a flying start by immediately selling its 17 per cent holding in Victoria Holdings to Team. The bid ran into heavy weather when it was resisted by small shareholders; but to market observers the most interesting aspect was that one of Australia's great life offices had actively tried to help a raider take over a listed company.

Banks increasingly began to back raiders. A notable example occurred in 1981 when Robert Holmes à Court's Bell Group bid for the old pastoral group Elder Smith. The bid sparked a short, fierce contest involving several players before Elders was taken over by John Elliott's Henry Jones IXL. One point to become evident was that several banks were prepared to lend large sums to finance a hostile takeover.

The crash of '74

Prime Minister Gough Whitlam introduced a credit squeeze in September 1973. Long bonds went to 8.5 per cent that month, the highest they had been for a generation. The squeeze really bit the following April and May, when bank bill rates blew out to 17.5 per cent and FNCB-Waltons was borrowing at 22 per cent, then considered an astronomical rate.

July 1974 saw the first property collapses, the most prominent victim being Sydney-based Home Units Australia, run by Sidney King and Gary Bogard. Its lenders had been three finance companies: CAGA, IAC and FNCB-Waltons—an offshoot of First National City Bank, which later became Citibank. In Home Units Australia, therefore, two of the major Australian trading banks and the largest foreign bank operating in Australia had received painful first-hand experience of what happened when loans were made on overvalued properties.

The lesson was to be ignored repeatedly by nearly all the banks over the next fifteen years.

September saw the collapse of Mainline Corp, whose main financier had been the ANZ. Another victim was Cambridge Credit Corp, whose tangled affairs embroiled several finance companies. It owed IAC $30 million. The Cambridge collapse also spotlighted another trend. The finance companies had enjoyed such lucrative fees lending to the property developers that some of them had taken the next step and become principals. CAGA, FCA and IAC featured as joint venture partners with Cambridge in many properties. This may have increased profits in good years, but it left the financiers fully exposed to the risks of a market collapse.

September 1974 also saw the near-collapse of Alan Bond, who was in Newport at the time on his first America's Cup challenge. His major financiers were IAC ($35m.), CAGA ($10m.) and Patrick Intermarine. The banks—under considerable persuasion from Bond—decided they could not put him out of business while he was fighting for the Cup and Bond survived one of his greatest crises.

hese property crises were followed by further waves in 1977 and
which saw:

- The liquidation of Parkes Development (major lenders IAC and
  CAGA).
- The receivership of Associated Securities Ltd, a subsidiary of Ansett
  Transport Industries. Ansett let it sink rather than fund further
  losses, fearing that it might imperil Ansett as well.
- The collapse of FCA, forcing the takeover of the Bank of Adelaide
  by the ANZ under orders from the Reserve Bank.
- The near-collapse of Hooker Corp.
- The near-collapse of CAGA, which so badly crippled the 180-year-
  old Commercial Banking Company of Sydney that it fell easy prey
  to a takeover bid by the National Bank a few years later.
- The rescue of IAC by its foreign parent Citibank.

The finance companies involved in these disasters—IAC, CAGA, FCA
and ASL—were four of the eight largest finance companies in Australia
at the time. In terms of size they ranked respectively as the second, fifth,
sixth and seventh largest. The failure of FCA brought down the Bank
of Adelaide and the troubles of CAGA very nearly brought down
the Commercial Banking Company of Sydney—the two smallest of
Australia's seven trading banks.

Even without much benefit from hindsight, it is amazing that the
banks and other financiers learned so few lessons from this long and
quite traumatic string of failures in the second half of the 1970s. Almost
every error of lending that was committed in the 1980s had been committed—and punished—in the 1970s. The memory of them was expunged
very quickly.

Negative pledge

By 1989 these had become the two dirtiest words in modern banking. It
took an effort of memory to recall that negative pledge was hailed as a
creative breakthrough when it first appeared in a loan to Pioneer Concrete
Services in 1978.

After the corporate collapses that followed the Menzies credit squeeze
of 1961, the major Australian life offices imposed tight borrowing restrictions on companies. To a modern businessman it would seem odd that
it should have been the life offices rather than the banks which set down
the terms for trust deeds. But at the start of the 1960s both institutions
were vastly different from what they are today. In 1961 life offices were
the major lenders to the corporate sector. The property and share portfolios held by the offices were small compared to their commercial loan
portfolios and their lending departments were larger than their share

departments. By contrast, banks then tended to provide shorter
capital and overdrafts to the corporate sector or secured loans on spe
assets.

These lending patterns were more rational than those which prev
from the early 1980s. The life offices, whose major liabilities were poli
which might take decades to mature, could afford to lend long tern
companies. The banks, whose liabilities mostly comprised call deposi
could avoid having any serious mismatching of assets if they restrict
themselves to offering companies overdraft and short-term facilities. Th
companies borrowed by issuing debentures, which normally gave lenders
a first and floating charge over the company's assets. The debenture
were issued under trust deeds approved by the life offices, which becam
standard trust deeds for all raisings.

By the late 1970s Pioneer was finding its trust deed particularly
irksome. Sir Tristan Antico had built Pioneer into one of Australia's first
modern multinational success stories, having expanded into several countries. In some of them such as Spain and Italy the operations were
marginal, but Pioneer was making good profits in Britain and Hong Kong
and wanted to expand.

The trust deed specified ratios of assets to liabilities. A breach of those
ratios would put Pioneer in default, which was regarded seriously in
those days. Under the terms of the trust deed Pioneer had to include its
foreign liabilities but could not offset this by including its foreign assets.
Banks were none too sophisticated in those days and had relatively poor
overseas links. Bob Thomas, former chief of the Australian Industry
Development Commission (AIDC), said: 'No one trusted assets outside
Australia because you couldn't get a charge over them'.[4]

Nor did the deed allow revaluation of assets. For example, Pioneer
might have been restricted to borrowing only 60 per cent of the value of
its assets. Let us say Pioneer had a quarry in its books which had cost
$5 million but had since been written down in the books to $3 million.
The market value of the quarry might have appreciated to $6 million, but
unless it were formally revalued Pioneer would still be able to borrow
only $2 million against it.

In the United States companies were overcoming this problem by
using negative pledge. Essentially negative pledge means that a lender
does not get security over any assets of the company. Instead the lender
gets a pledge that no other lender will rank ahead of him in the event
of a liquidation. 'Eventually Pioneer went to the Bank of New South Wales
and asked it to arrange a negative pledge loan', said Thomas. 'The Wales
was not willing to do the work to establish the arrangements but if
someone else did the work they were willing to be lead lender.'

The AIDC was willing, because it was government policy at the time to encourage Australian companies to expand overseas and the trust deed requirements of the day were an obstacle. Arthur O'Sullivan, later to become chief of AIDC, did a lot of the work. Others involved included Hambros Australia and David Block, who was an advisor to Pioneer. Under its trust deed Pioneer had issued $12 million in debentures and had another $16 million in bank lines secured by debentures plus a few other loans. Under the negative pledge covenant which succeeded the trust deed in November 1978, Pioneer had $10 million from the Wales and $15 million from the AIDC while Hambros in Australia and the United Kingdom underwrote a $US25 million Eurodollar raising. The negative pledge loans were under a covenant which still imposed restrictions upon Pioneer, although they were not as irksome as those of the old trust deed. The company still had to conform to borrowing ratios, for example, but they were to be determined by counting its assets and liabilities on a world-wide basis.[5]

After the Pioneer raising, several major industrial companies began following the same route. Under managing director John Leard, Australian National Industries Ltd had already been pursuing the same path, lifting its borrowings under revolving credit facilities from $10 million to $29 million in 1978.

These early negative pledge covenants contained several safeguards. One safeguard under the Pioneer covenant was that all subsidiaries of Pioneer had to guarantee the borrowing. This meant that wherever the money went in the Pioneer group, the lenders had a claim against the relevant subsidiary.

Later negative pledge covenants were to omit this safeguard with disastrous results. Money lent to Linter Group, for example, was passed on to other subsidiaries and associates whose names were not even known to the original lenders. The National Australia Bank's syndicated negative pledge loan to Bond Brewing Holdings did not prevent BBH funds being transferred to associates against whom the syndicate had no claim, and it was only late in the day that the NAB began plugging the holes by amending the covenant.

The life institutions had maintained an iron grip on the terms of trust deeds. A dissatisfied corporate could shop around looking for better terms but was unlikely to gain any significant advantage. The banks showed no such discipline. The introduction of negative pledge hit the Australian banking system with all the force of the discovery of fire. There was now a new way of lending money and it gave banks access to the corporate sector on a larger scale than ever before. Banks began competing to lend on negative pledge. Fundamentally, there are only two ways banks can compete on lending. They can either cut rates or weaken their security requirements. They did both, and from then on the road would lead remorselessly downhill.

Stamp duties acted as a further incentive to negative pledge lending. Any registered charge over an asset had to carry stamp duty, which in a big loan could amount to hundreds of thousands of dollars, with the borrowers footing the bill.

Property valuations

One dubious amendment to the Pioneer trust deed concerned asset valuations. The effect was that if the value of an asset rose Pioneer would be able to borrow against the asset's market value without having the revalued amount formally written into the books of the company. Pioneer appears never to have misused this freedom, but others did.

Indeed, the property boom of the early 1970s had already provided plenty of evidence that this could be dangerous. If financiers of the day were prepared to lend only two-thirds of the sworn value of a property, a developer might buy a property for, say, $1 million, then have it revalued to $1.5 million. The developer could then borrow the whole $1 million purchase price. In many instances developers revalued a property so high that they managed to borrow more than its purchase price.

State banks

The State Bank of New South Wales (formerly the Rural Bank), the State Bank of Victoria, the State Bank of South Australia and the Rural & Industries Bank of Western Australia all emerged as significant players in the corporate lending market. This was partly at the imperative of their governments. Neville Wran, as Premier of New South Wales, was always eager to turn the Rural Bank into a competitive commercial bank so that its dividends could become a valuable source of state revenue. In the west Brian Burke treated the R&I as part of the confederacy between the government and a group of corporate cowboys, later known collectively as WA Inc.

Given the fact that competition for corporate business was already becoming keener because of the foreign and merchant banks—as well as the increasing cowboy spirit of the old trading banks—this meant the state banks had to cut margins finer and take greater risks to get business. The SBV's wayward subsidiary Tricontinental was almost throwing money at bad risks by the end of the 1980s.

Multiple bank lending

Traditionally, Australian corporates had dealt with only one or two banks. As their cash needs grew for expansion (sometimes soundly based, sometimes not), bank lending began to be syndicated with a lead bank spreading the loan between itself and several others. This was followed by multiple banking, in which the corporation borrowed separately from several banks. In the late 1970s this meant a corporation might have loans or standbys from nine or ten different banks under a negative pledge arrangement. Sometimes the banks were unaware of the corporate's exposure to each other. By the late 1980s this kind of lending had exploded to the point where in Hooker and Linter Group there were 30 or 40 banks involved.

This type of lending carried several inherent risks. One was that the difficulty of getting lenders to agree in a crisis increased in proportion to the number of them. Bob White, former chief executive of Westpac (as the Bank of New South Wales had become), said:

> That is where the real danger was because there was no real coordination between the lenders and when something went wrong there was no obvious leader. Tiddlers tried to get out as soon as they smelt trouble and that was the single most damaging aspect. Also the banks ranged from someone who came in last week to someone who had been in for four or five years. The possibility of getting some agreement is very difficult in the early stages and the longer it takes to get agreement the higher the risk of loss.

Foreign banks

Three foreign banks had always held licences in Australia. They were the Bank of China (which was dormant for a long time after 1949), the Banque Nationale de Paris and the Bank of New Zealand. The first two played little or no role in the explosion in corporate lending of the late 1970s and 1980s but the BNZ was a big player, being a prominent backer of the wave of New Zealand cowboys who came to Australia.

In the 1970s exotic names began to appear on the pieces of paper in front of Australian corporate treasurers. In pre-deregulation days foreign banks were limited in the amounts they could lend to Australian corporates, but the limitations were more theoretical than practical. 'They would have a representative office here and do business by telex', said White. 'We used to call it "lending out of a suitcase".' Before deregulation, the only thing the foreign banks really could not do in Australia was book loans. So they booked them in Singapore or California or somewhere and could still write business with all the customers of the Australian banks.

Tricontinental Corp

One of the leaders in the drive towards more aggressive lending was Tricontinental. In its early days Tricontinental was under the chairmanship of Sir Ian Potter and was funded by equity issues to foreign banks looking for an entry into the Australian market, such as Security Pacific of California and Mitsui Bank. As early as 1972 Trico was stirring up the trading banks by doing significant fund raisings for blue-chip industrials such as Dunlop Australia. By the early 1980s Tricontinental's struggles to win market share had made it a sizeable force. Its 1985 annual report said that it had 'significantly broadened its futures market trading capacities'. This may have been an understatement. According to other merchant bankers, Trico was the heaviest single player in the bill futures market. It would have as many as 1000 contracts open at a time, leaving its rivals wondering at the risks it was taking.

After Ian Johns became general manager, Trico's exposure to corporate high-fliers also increased. Chris Corrigan, former managing director of BT Australia, said:

> At BT we would have had five meetings with the State Bank of Victoria during the early 1980s. Each time we had a review of Trico we would get very uncomfortable because it was at the extreme risk end of the spectrum. The SBV would pledge support and say they were completely aware of what was going on. We would ask them to guarantee Trico but they wouldn't.

Another former rival says: 'If you go through carefully and look at the sort of businesses they were in, they were always going to hit the wall'.

To his credit, Johns never made any secret of his penchant for fast-track clients. In an interview with *Australian Business* in 1987 he said:

> We have for some years targeted a lot of smaller clients, shying away from the top 100 or so companies. Previously these were people not well known and respected by the market, but now many of them have grown impressively and we've grown with them. We used to be criticised for doing business with some of these people, but now our competitors are in there after their business.

Johns's 'people' included Christopher Skase, Alan Bond, Bob Ansett, Joe Gandel, Solomon Lew, George Herscu and Marc Besen. Not all of them turned out to be bad risks, but too many were.

Credit control

Theoretically, a bank should have a credit and a lending department, so that any loan proposed by the lending team is analysed by the credit team, and a credit committee that adjudicates if there is a difference of opinion. Corrigan said:

> Bank management is supposed to establish the balance, but in the 1980s the credit function ended up buying the dream. In BT in 1986 it became quite intense when we were refusing to back people, not so much in pure lending as in swaps. There might be some semi-credible company with a swaps deal involving millions and we would have a blanket 'No' on the deal.

BT's credit committee was headed successively by Corrigan and Rob Ferguson, which may explain why it emerged from the bust with a clean loan book. But as another banker said sourly: 'BT didn't lend anything because it didn't have anything'.

Harvey Garnett, Westpac's chief general manager, group credit policy and control, recalled that around 1983 every corporate account manager in Westpac attended a three-week course on 'relationship management', as it was called. 'However, the driving force was marketing thrust rather than credit analysis', he said. 'The course was aimed at how you should go out and sell yourself. Also we took the view that there was nothing wrong with the top 200 companies in Australia, if you took out the ASLs and Mainlines. They were above reproach.' This attitude had a self-fulfilling element, because if a bank lent a cowboy enough money he would graduate into the top 200 anyway. Bond, Elliott, Holmes à Court and Spalvins were all comfortably within the top 200.

Perhaps worse, the banks structured staff incentives poorly. Garnett said: 'We had very material rewards for business written that gave very little focus on the quality of the credit'. This practice, common in the banking industry, meant bank officers were rewarded in proportion to the size of their deals. This unbalanced the banks internally, because it was impossible to give bonuses to a credit officer who rejected deals.

As the lending teams in banks began collecting fat bonuses and flash cars their arrogance rose. After all, they were the people who had been out last night with Alan Bond or John Elliott. They were not going to take any negative nonsense from the credit analysts, who were grey people from the backroom. Understandably, the credit people were often trying to get on the lending team.

Competition

According to a widely held economic theory, competition is an absolute good which can somehow be relied upon to produce the most desirable result. This certainly did not happen in some important aspects of the Australian banking system in the early 1980s.

The major trading banks were facing increasing competition for their large corporate customers. Merchant banks, foreign banks, state banks and their own finance companies were all trying to get a bigger share of the corporate lending market. In the words of one merchant banker:

> Banks competed on margin until there was nowhere to go. Then they competed on loan structure until there was nowhere to go. And then they competed on documentation. Some of them arrived at the stage where they were almost saying: 'Come in. There's the safe. Take the money and give it back to us when you feel like it'.

People

The explosion of the banking industry during the early 1980s was not accompanied by any similar explosion in the number of highly qualified bankers. All that happened was that the existing pool of talent was spread more thinly among many more banks. Bidding for skilled and semi-skilled staff became intense and salary packages shot up vertically for anyone with even a modest acquaintance with corporate banking. The going salary for a foreign exchange dealer suddenly became $100 000. As no merchant bank could afford not to boast a forex desk, they all had to pay these rates even though in several cases the size of their forex book was too small to ever cover their dealers' salaries.

As the prime goal of each bank was to hold or increase market share, the main quality sought in bank chief executives was aggression. In several of those who were appointed aggression may indeed have been their best characteristic, because prudence certainly wasn't. Many of the banks were run by second-rate people, as the subsequent postmortems would show.

Price

When a bank lends money its price is represented by the interest rate. In the boom of the 1980s banks had two principal sources of income—fees and the margin between their borrowing and lending rates. Normally (not that there was much normality in the 1980s) banks lend money to corporations at a set margin over the prevailing bank bill rate. That margin should be at least half of one per cent—or 50 basis points—just to cover its administration costs on a loan. Half of one per cent on a $50 million loan (a reasonable size, but not uncommon) was not a lot of money. The $250 000 could be quickly spent on a bank's marketing officers, credit committee, documentation and the like. So if the bill rate was 15.5 per cent the bank needed to lend at 16 per cent just to break even.

By the early 1980s banks were shaving their margins to 10 or 15 points. This meant that if the bank bill rate was 15.5 per cent they would be lending to corporates at 15.6 to 15.65 per cent. Any loan done on these margins would almost automatically lock the lender into a loss, which was justified on the grounds that the bank had to maintain market share.

After capital adequacy ratios were imposed on the banks by the Reserve Bank of Australia in the late 1980s, the minimum margin effectively increased to about 75 basis points.

Loan structure

Once the old-fashioned trust deeds and secured loans were abandoned in the late 1970s and early 1980s, most loans to the corporate cowboys were on negative pledge. In essence this meant the loans were unsecured but no other lender ranked ahead of them, although a loan covenant ought to have tied the borrower to certain conditions, such as prudential ratios that had to be observed.

One important condition—missing in later years—was that any loan to a holding company or group should be guaranteed by all asset-owning and borrowing subsidiaries. Otherwise a situation could develop in which a loan made to the holding company had a covenant covering the holding company alone. The holding company might be showing $100 million in assets, but $10 million of that might be inventory and the other $90 million loans to subsidiaries or, worse, shares in subsidiaries. The subsidiaries owned the assets. If these subsidiaries then borrowed heavily on the security of their assets, the original lender to the holding company would be gravely disadvantaged. In any liquidation of the subsidiary, the assets would be sold and the lenders on the assets would have to be paid out before the shares in the subsidiary (the only security of the original lender) could recoup anything. If the assets were sold for less than the loans on them, the shares would be worthless and the original loan would be lost.

This situation arose in Bond Brewing Holdings, where a staggering $1.5 billion from Bell Resources was secured only on the shares of BBH. At the same time BBH had raised $800 million from a syndicate led by the National Australia Bank and an equivalent sum from US bondholders. Until these latter amounts could be discharged the security that Bell Resources held on BBH's shares was worthless. Worse, for a time Bell Resources had only a third mortgage on the shares, the first two being held by the Hong Kong & Shanghai Bank.

Banks tended to analyse a group on a consolidated basis and to forget exactly which company in the group they were lending to. This happened in several cases, most dramatically in Abe Goldberg's Linter Group. Money lent to Linter often went through to an associated company named

15

Gibraltar Factors, and from there to any one of several dozen companies, trusts and other entities.

Documentation

Over the decades, guarantees which accompanied any bank loan to a company group had developed into long and complicated documents. Every time case law set a new precedent or revealed a defect in guarantee documents a fresh clause was added to them. In the 1980s, under the pressure of competition and the sheer volume of deals being done, documentation suffered. Younger bank employees became contemptuous of what they considered red tape. Documentation became an area where more aggressive banks could compete. Documents which had previously covered fifteen pages of dense legalese became truncated to a single page.

Letters of comfort

Competition in documentation produced a legal bastard called a letter of comfort. Broadly, this is a letter written by someone of substance (usually a parent company or major shareholder) to comfort a lender to a subsidiary without actually guaranteeing its debts. Here, as an example, is a letter of comfort written by I.S. Slogett, company secretary of Dalgety Farmers Ltd to Oakminster Ltd. At the time, Dalgety was a shareholder in Duke Securities and Oakminster was lending Duke money.

> Dear Sir,
>
> We confirm that we are aware of all facilities which are presently made available by your company to Duke Securities Ltd (hereinafter referred to as the Company) and that you have our assurance that we will use our best endeavours to not permit the company to enter into liquidation (whether voluntary or compulsory) or to enter into any arrangement with its creditors without its liability to your company being completely discharged.

The amount of comfort this letter ultimately imparted was slight indeed. Duke Securities went into liquidation despite whatever efforts Dalgety made, with Oakminster owed $2 million.

One merchant banker recalled:

> The best piece of 'security' I ever saw anyone take was an unsigned photocopied letter of comfort with a notation at the bottom that the bank officer had spoken to the company treasurer, who had confirmed that but for the shortage of time he would have been able to get that letter signed and the borrower's parent would have felt bound by it. On another occasion a lender had a problem and the borrower said: 'We can

arrange a merchant bank guarantee for you'. The merchant bank turned out to be Duke.

Deregulation

Federal Treasurer Paul Keating deregulated the financial system in fifteen months between late 1983 and early 1985. The move was almost universally applauded at the time by financiers, economists and commentators.[6] Keating's moves followed recommendations of the highly lauded Campbell Report on the financial system. Almost the only critic of deregulation was former Treasury Secretary John Stone, and he was widely discredited at the time for his handling of the economy under Malcolm Fraser. But even if Stone had still been at Treasury, some degree of deregulation would have been inevitable in the mid-1980s because it had become an irresistible international trend.

Keating, in typically unrestrained fashion, embraced deregulation wholeheartedly; in hindsight it would have been wiser to pursue a more moderate course. But Keating cannot be much criticised. Deregulation is probably best viewed as an unavoidable mistake. Nearly everyone overseas was doing the same thing and nearly everyone in Australia approved of it.

The timetable on deregulation ran as follows:

- December 1983, Keating floated the $A
- June 1984, foreign exchange licences were granted to 40 applicants
- February 1985, Australian banking licences were granted to 16 foreign banks

This puts deregulation into chronological perspective. All the major flaws in banking practices in Australia, which led to the massive bad debts being recognised in the late 1980s and early 1990s, existed before deregulation. The competitive pressures from merchant banks and foreign banks, the introduction of negative pledge and the erosion of lending standards were all happening before February 1985 or even before the Hawke–Keating Government was elected in 1983.

Deregulation was not responsible for starting the undesirable trends in corporate lending but it certainly exacerbated them. Deregulation of banking in 1984–85 was the financial equivalent of throwing a bucket of kerosene onto a house that was already blazing.

Open slather

Bob White said: 'After deregulation it was complete open slather'. Chris Corrigan said: 'We came out of the 1970s accustomed to rapid inflation in which asset prices rose and borrowing costs stayed negative in real terms. If you borrowed against assets, they would be worth more in a few years and you couldn't lose'.

Corporate advisor Mark Burrows of Baring Brothers Burrows said:

> We had a sort of lemming environment in which if Holmes à Court said a share was worth $2, then to the bankers it had to be worth more. Provided someone stood up who had some credibility it was all ipso facto bankable. Nothing adverse came to light because with the creation of value the ability to put things under the bed to hide the crook deals was unprecedented. If you were a critic no one dealt with you. Who was going to deal with someone who stood up and said, 'This is all bullshit'?

Prudential ratios

Throughout the whole period under discussion, the Reserve Bank of Australia imposed a rule that no bank was to lend more than 33 per cent of its capital in any single transaction. Loans of more than 10 per cent had to be reported to the Reserve Bank, and loans over 25 per cent had to be approved by it. This rule inhibited the Australian banks but the foreign banks could drive a horse and cart through it. Mark Johnson, a director of Macquarie Bank and former managing director of the Australian Bank, said: 'The foreign banks were under no limitations until banking licences were granted. Then they came under the same ratios as anyone else, but if they had a big deal the bank would organise direct participation by head office. This meant they could do deals others could not'. The Hong Kong & Shanghai Bank and its subsidiary Wardley Australia were particularly aggressive, financing Bond, Skase, Elliott and many other entrepreneurs.

The rule became attenuated in the 1980s as banks raised their capital bases. One way of doing this was by the quite legitimate route of large equity issues. Another way was by introducing quasi-equity that was accepted by the Reserve Bank as part of the capital base. There were also other devices.

An interesting example was provided by Westpac. Even after the share market crash, managing director Stuart Fowler was eager for Westpac to be the first bank in Australia to chalk up a $1 billion profit. The theory of Westpac's then strategists was that as operating costs would not rise with extra assets any additional business brought in would go straight to the bottom line, even if margins had to be shaved. However, assets (loans) could not be increased unless equity were increased. So in 1988 Westpac had a rights issue which raised $743 million. Simultaneously, Westpac's head office in Martin Place, which had been in the books at a paltry $20 million, was revalued to $1.1 billion. The combined effect of these two moves was to raise Westpac's shareholders' funds by nearly $2 billion. As the bank could gear at 20 to 1, this meant it could lend another $40 billion. Westpac came close to doing this, increasing total assets from $70.3 billion to $108.6 billion between 1988 and 1990.

Unfortunately this was exactly the wrong time to be lending money, especially to Westpac's high-flying corporate cowboys and property developers.

Raising their capital bases enabled the banks to raise more in borrowings and to lend more. The higher capital bases also meant that the amounts that could be lent to a single borrower could be raised. When the ANZ, for example, raised its shareholders' funds from $3.1 billion to $3.9 billion in 1988, it automatically lifted its maximum lending ability for a single borrower (under the 33 per cent rule) from $1 billion to $1.3 billion.

Lending lost sight of fundamentals

In the case of Hartogen Energy valuations of oil and gas leases were done according to formulae. This resulted in a group of banks lending a total of $200 million to Hartogen, including Westpac ($60 million, of which $35 million was secured), Commonwealth ($29 million) and Natwest ($35 million, of which $10 million was secured). But they were lending on assets, rather than earnings. Warren Panzer, liquidator of Hartogen Energy, has estimated that by the time it crashed Hartogen had $10 million in net cash flow, which was dramatically less than its minimum interest bill of $16 million. Negative cash flow by itself is not necessarily fatal for an oil company, but in Hartogen's case it had reached abnormal proportions.

Abe Goldberg's Linter group provides another example. The group wound up with bank loans totalling $925 million on a profit and loss account that could hardly have supported more than $250 million. (Its best projection of earnings before interest and tax was $75 million for calendar 1990.) Manifestly, none of the football team of banks who lent money would have done so if they had been fully aware of Linter's exposure to the rest. Another problem was that banks were not always aware of what other members within their own group were doing. Thus, after Linter's collapse, Westpac discovered that not only did it have an exposure, but so did its subsidiaries AGC, Bill Acceptance Corp and Partnership Pacific. The group's total exposure was not $100 million, as Westpac had first thought, but $150 million.

There was a 'me too' effect in lending. Corrigan says: 'In the banking area a lot of people are followers, who say: "If so and so is doing it, I'll be in the syndicate". And it got beyond credit analysis. People were lending on visions'.

Commitment fees became skimpy compared to the size of the facility. When René Rivkin's Oilmet bid for QBE Insurance it paid a fee of only $50 000 for a $400 million commitment from New Zealand Insurance.

Castlemaine Tooheys

Banks began lending in bigger licks. Probably Alan Bond's best deal ever was in 1985, when he took over the big brewer Castlemaine Tooheys Ltd. Funding of $900 million was provided equally by the Hong Kong & Shanghai Bank, Standard Chartered and State Bank of New South Wales. This was the biggest lick lending Australia had seen at the time. Previously a loan of $900 million would have had to be syndicated by a dozen or more banks. Bond was perceived (wrongly) by the investment community to be paying too much for Castlemaine, so Australian bankers backed away from the deal with the exception of the State Bank's then managing director, Nick Whitlam.

'Castlemaine was a watershed deal for Bond and this bank', said the State's subsequent managing director, John O'Neil. 'Our capital was $427 million and we put up $300 million. Fairly good anecdotal sources said Anheuser Busch was prepared to pay $3 billion and Bond had not bought Heileman at that stage. So we were comfortable with a package of $900 million.' However, this meant the State Bank was committing more than two-thirds of its capital to a single deal—way above the Reserve Bank's maximum permitted exposure of one-third. It was always the State Bank's intention to sell its exposure down to the prudential level, even though it was a state instrumentality and could argue that it was not obliged to conform to Reserve Bank guidelines. In any case, when the Reserve's Governor, Bob Johnston, demanded that the State Bank offload its holding, the bank complied.

Whitlam and O'Neil were convinced that some other banks played dirty pool by starting a 'whispering campaign'. O'Neil said the placement was difficult because other banks had taken the attitude 'let's teach the State Bank' and refused to participate. Ultimately the State Bank funded a letter of credit from the HKSB for $300 million which effectively transferred the risk to the HKSB. But it was a good deal for the State Bank, which took a fee of $5 million.

And, as Bond had bought well, it was a good deal for the other banks too. The effect of the deal—at a time when the stock market boom was really gathering steam—was to legitimise both lending to Bond and lending in big licks. O'Neil said: 'I think we believed that big lick deals were there to do and you could take a big risk in some. The NSW

Government was interested in profitability and our only way of getting rich quick was to do pretty big licks'.

Refinancing Castlemaine

Bond merged Swan Brewery and Castlemaine to form Bond Brewing Holdings (BBH) and the whole deal was refinanced in 1986. Westpac had put together a syndicated facility of $1.2 billion, which the banks were going to lend to BBH secured. This deal got right to the wire but was stalled at the last minute when Westpac's general manager corporate banking, Phil Deer, refused to sign. It is not clear who initiated the breach, but Bond Corp had hinted that they had a better alternative. This turned out to be the syndicate led by the National Australia Bank which lent to BBH on negative pledge.

There was deep irony here. In 1989–90 the NAB syndicate was to suffer great angst while trying to appoint a receiver to BBH. If the NAB had not competed for BBH's business in 1986 the brewing group may well have had to accept the Westpac offer, which would have been under a secured charge and presumably have given the banks no great difficulty in appointing a receiver. To that extent the NAB was the architect of its own misfortune. But this is said with some advantage from hindsight. O'Neil, whose State Bank was the only other Australian in the NAB syndicate, said: 'We have gone back to the BBH deal. On what was presented to us and our knowledge at the time, we would do this deal again'.

Enormous deals were done with amazing speed

April 1986 saw the greatest market raid in Australia's history, as Elders bought 19 per cent of BHP for $2 billion. The main financing was arranged in a matter of three days from Chase, Citibank and Paribas. Even more astounding, in 1987 the ANZ Bank agreed in a space of five days to fund Warwick Fairfax in a $2 billion bid for John Fairfax Ltd. At the time they hardly knew Warwick and most of the arrangements for the giant loan were made by telephone by Bert Reuter, who carried a lot of clout because the bank had known him as Holmes à Court's right-hand man.

Other fringe institutions got into the act. In Perth the WA Teachers Credit Society suddenly blossomed as a bank. From making modest loans to teachers, the credit union became a large-scale commercial lender. One result was that its four largest borrowers owed a total of $100 million, or seven times the society's capital base. The collapse of any of them would therefore pose a mortal threat to the society. As a further act of imprudence it had lent $19 million to Rothwells. The society's exposure to its four largest debtors increased from $50 million in mid-1986 to $106 million a year later. One of the four was Laurie Potter, whose chain of health clubs was collapsing. Another was Robert Martin, whose relationship with the Superannuation Board chairman Len Brush was attracting unfavourable publicity at the time.[7]

The society took losses on all four of the big debtors and in 1987 the society had to be taken over by the R&I Bank. (If it had been allowed to collapse, 30 000 teachers would have had their assets frozen.) The society had been shockingly run. The auditor found that one group of borrowers had been advanced $51 million, although their formal loan limits totalled only $18 million.[8] The society's losses seem to have been somewhere north of $125 million.[9]

Smarter corporates

While the competition between banks was mushrooming, the corporate clients were getting smarter. Corporate treasurers rapidly learned to take advantage of the fine margins on interest rates and currencies being offered. Any treasurer who wanted the best overnight rate on the $A, for example, could ring around the banks and shop for the lowest quote. The dealer who made that quote would then find that he or she could not lay off with another bank. But the corporate treasurer might be able to lay off with whoever had quoted the highest rate and make a riskless few thousand dollars for his company at a bank's expense.

Clients played banks off against each other in several ways. Don Argus, managing director of the National Australia Bank, said:

> The merchant banks were fee-based institutions and all they wanted to do was write big deals. Your corporate customers would say: 'If you don't do this deal, that other bank will'. That became a pretty self-fulfilling exercise. The corporates had begun to divide and rule. For example, the proliferation of standby lines began to appear in about 1985 with a fee on each line. Then the corporate treasurer got smart. He would not pay a fee for a line. He started to fund day to day cash needs off the interbank market.

The chase for market share

The foregoing were the main factors underlying the unprecedented boom in credit creation in the 1980s. Creative accounting also deserves a mention. The rest of this book will deal extensively with creative accounting, so we need not go far into the subject here. Suffice it to say that the nature of the profits and assets claimed by the corporate cowboys became increasingly detached from reality as the 1980s progressed. The fallacies in their accounts may not have been apparent to ordinary investors, but they should have been obvious to the banks, who had large stakes in their enterprises and should have had the skill and diligence to analyse their accounts. In the event, very few banks pulled the plug before the market did. As will be apparent in the following chapters, most of the cowboys were in deep trouble well before October 1987.

During the boom very few of those involved in the banking scene were able to step back and keep what was happening in perspective. It is now evident that, from the mid-1970s, the Australian trading banks drifted into a position where their concern to maintain market share led them to bid increasingly for business that was not worth having. Banks were providing increasing amounts of capital to businesses such as Bond Corp, Westmex, Estate Mortgage, Qintex, Linter and Hooker at a time when the equity base of those businesses was shrinking or in fact negative.

The historical rule of thumb had been that non-financial institutions should not be funded more than 50 per cent by debt and that the rest should be funded by equity, in the form of either subscribed capital or retained earnings. At some point of debt, arguably 80 per cent but certainly by 90 per cent, the lender has effectively become the equity holder in the business. Failure to recognise this led to a fundamental error on the part of the banks. They were accepting debt returns on equity risks. Whenever this practice is indulged in long enough, the iron laws of risk and reward will ensure that the returns on the good loans are inadequate to cover the losses on the bad ones.

The second fundamental error made by the banks was to give inadequate weight to their credit analysts and committees. The deal makers were allowed to rule and the banks reaped the whirlwind. Negative pledge, with sensible safeguards, is a defensible form of lending. As Leigh Hall, manager of the AMP Society's investments division, said: 'There's nothing wrong with negative pledge as long as you're dealing with honourable people. Unfortunately there weren't enough honourable people'.

Big upfront fees were exciting, but should have been written into the profit and loss account over the length of the loan. If appropriate provisions were then raised against the loans, it would quickly become apparent that the value of some of them was really negative to the bank. According to one apocryphal story, the National Australia Bank at the end of the 1980s did an evaluation of its corporate lending for the decade. After adding in all the big fees and subtracting the subsequent provisions, the bank is supposed to have worked out that it made a loss on the corporate sector over the ten years. As the National was probably the best run of the major banks, the implications for its rivals were even worse.

It also became clear that many of the bank-owned finance companies should be strongly controlled by their parents. Otherwise the more adventurous ones would keep biting their owners on the ankle. This was a lesson Westpac took an amazingly long time to learn with AGC.

There was a double failure of regulation. The Reserve Bank of Australia (RBA) failed to regulate the banks and the banks failed to regulate their offshoots. Admittedly, the RBA had power only over the licensed banks and much of the growth in dubious corporate lending originated outside that area. But a vigorous central bank could have exerted more power. In the event the RBA was largely content to watch from the sidelines, particularly after deregulation. How, after all, was the RBA supposed to regulate a deregulated industry? One of the few effective actions taken by the RBA was its demand that the State Bank of New South Wales sell down its Castlemaine exposure. Yet that was one of the more successful and defensible deals of the era.

The moral of the decade was perhaps best summarised by David Ryan of BT Australia, who said: 'Nothing has changed about understanding credit in a hundred years. Someone has money, someone needs it and you either structure it properly or you don't do the deal'.

Black Tuesday

On 21 September 1987 the all ordinaries index hit an intra-day high of 2312. That was the peak of the Australian share market. Over the next four weeks it eased 160 points, closing on Friday 16 October at 2145. While the market looked a little softer, there had been no cause for panic. Then on Monday the 19th it slumped a frightening 81 points to 2064.

The London Stock Exchange had been knocked out by a freak hurricane on the Friday. Power and water supplies were cut off in large areas of London, and roadways were blocked by fallen trees. On Monday the 19th the London Stock Exchange opened in chaotic conditions, with most brokers more concerned with sheer physical survival than with the stock market. The Financial Times 100 index plunged to 2052 for a loss of 250 points on the Thursday close.

Next in the time sequence came New York, where the size and speed of the falls were exacerbated by computerised trading. In a single trading session the Dow Jones plunged a whopping 509 points—more than its gains of the past year—closing at 1738.

Australian traders watched the overnight Dow on their screens in horror. The global tidal wave was sweeping towards Australia as sunrise crept remorselessly around the globe, but there was absolutely nothing the traders could do about the impending disaster. What had been Black Monday overseas would be Black Tuesday in Australia. On that unforgettable Tuesday, 20 October 1987, the All Ordinaries Index lost 500 points—one-quarter of its value. Almost the whole of the loss occurred at the instant of opening. Bids fell vertically for blue-chip stocks and for anything of lesser quality there were often no buyers at all. If anything, the 25 per cent fall was an understated figure because it only measured those stocks where sales had occurred. Many had become unsaleable. In the absence of bids they were marked into the indices at offer prices, which were often hypothetical.

For the corporate cowboys the crash was terminal, although Holmes à Court was the only one who recognised it clearly at the time. John O'Neil says: 'The deterioration in the quality of assets only really became visible after that. Those people who relied on asset sales rather than cash flow found themselves coming up short'. The crash represented a massive writedown of price–earnings multiples. The balance sheet of a cowboy typically had a number of investments on the asset side, supported by generous gearing on the liabilities side. Now the investments had to be written back to market values. The debt stayed the same (indeed it increased with accruing interest), so the equity shrank convulsively.

As the cowboys fell over, the banks began to relearn a number of lessons their forebears knew. Among other things, banks rediscovered the difference between private and public companies. O'Neil said: 'Girvan, for example, did not behave like a public company'. The ghastly messes in Hooker and Linter were made worse by the fact that there were no lead banks to organise a workout or receivership. But even where there were syndicates, lead banks were criticised. O'Neil said:

> Don't take comfort from the fact that the lead major is a big international or Australian bank and therefore must be smarter than you. A lot of us learned that you should not just rely on the lead major. You have to be doing all your own due diligence. Worse, a lead major could sell out and not even inform the other members of the syndicate.

There was also an inevitable diminution of competition. Three of Australia's largest merchant banks—Elders Finance, Tricontinental and Partnership Pacific—were more or less absorbed into their parents. Many of the foreign banks retreated into niches. O'Neil said: 'A lot of the pain we got afterwards was really the price we paid for the fare for foreign banks out of Australia'. The first victim of Black Tuesday looked like being Rothwells, which was saved by the combined efforts of Alan Bond, Wardley Australia (wholly owned by the HKSB), the WA Government, the National Australia Bank and a listing of Australia's heaviest corporate hitters which included Kerry Packer, Robert Holmes à Court and John

Elliott. The RBA, fearing that a money panic might follow the share market crash, eased interest rates. In hindsight, the action was probably correct but rates were eased too far and too much money was pumped into the system.

This encouraged some deluded cowboys and their financiers to play one last round in 1988. An amazing number of cowboys and their bankers failed to recognise that the game had changed. Alan Bond did three of his biggest and worst deals—the takeovers of Heileman and Bell Group and the attempted takeover of Lonrho—after October 1987. Many of the cowboys plunged into the commercial property market, oblivious to the lesson of history that a share market collapse is usually followed a year or two later by a property collapse. The financiers were equally blind. Tricontinental and the State Bank of South Australia were still making bad loans in 1988 and even 1989.

Interest rates

The RBA, having relaxed rates too far in 1987–88, did a backflip and tightened them too far and for too long in 1988–89. Any appraisal of financial behaviour in the late 1980s must start with interest rates. When Paul Keating deregulated the financial system, he abandoned one of his key tools for controlling economic activity. In the 1960s and 1970s the Federal Government and the RBA could fine-tune bank lending by manipulation of the LGS and SRD ratios. The LGS was the ratio of liquid assets and government securities to total assets. The SRD was the statutory reserve deposit which banks were required to lodge with the RBA at nominal rates of interest. By raising or lowering these two ratios the RBA could turn the money tap on and off.

The system worked tolerably well, the major problem being that the RBA only had power to apply these ratios to banks; it was unable to control the burgeoning fringe banking industry among finance companies, merchant banks and the like. In 1974 Treasurer Frank Crean tried to extend these powers to the fringe banking area under the *Financial Corporations Act,* but although the legislation was passed the relevant schedule was never proclaimed which meant that the Act was effectively a dead letter.

In his sweeping deregulation of the financial system in 1983–84 Keating effectively went in the opposite direction. Henceforth no attempt would be made to regulate banking activity through quantitative controls on the amount of money banks were injecting into the system. After deregulation, the government and the RBA could only control money by manipulating its price: the interest rate. The result was high and jagged interest rates throughout the 1980s, as illustrated in Figure 1.1.

Figure 1.1 Interest rates 1980–1992

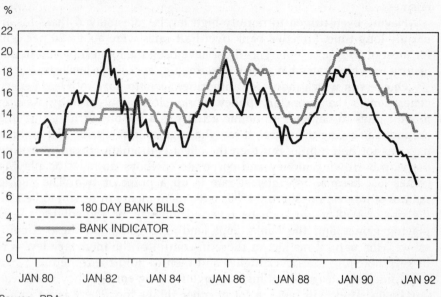

Source: RBA

The first point worth making from the chart is that by historical standards interest rates were high throughout the 1980s. They also swung wildly. They did not vary from low to high so much as from high to extortionate. When looking at the bank indicator rate it should be remembered that this was a basis rate. Towards the end of the 1980s banks were commonly charging a premium of 4 per cent above it. During the extended high interest rate period of 1989 bank overdraft rates of 25 per cent were not uncommon.

These high rates were due to a number of factors, but the corporate cowboys were a not insignificant cause. The big lick borrowings of Bond, Hooker, Adsteam and their ilk tended to be pacesetters for the rest of the business spectrum. Their insatiable demand for funds was a powerful force keeping the price of money high. It is at least arguable that the corporate cowboys and their cowboy bankers raised the cost of doing business for everyone in Australia during this period.

For the purposes of this book the most important period is from October 1987 (when rates were comparatively low) to the end of 1991. The chart shows the relaxation in rates after the crash as monetary authorities tried to avoid a money panic. This was a legitimate fear, but rates were eased too far. This led to a corresponding overcorrection in the second half of 1988 when rates began to climb again. Between April 1988 and May 1989 bill rates rose from 11.7 to 18.4 per cent, representing a rise of more than 50 per cent in one of the most basic costs of Australian business.

Having been driven to unduly high levels, rates stayed there for an unduly long time. Effective bank overdraft rates were above 20 per cent for most of 1989 and 1990. This must have been the longest period in our history in which rates have been sustained at such high levels.[10]

One lesson which monetary authorities seem to have to relearn every generation is that monetary policy works slowly but brutally. Raising interest rates to dampen economic activity is a bit like turning the QE2 around. You swing the wheel, throw the engines into reverse and nothing happens for half a mile. But then the effect is dramatic. Businessmen do not stop borrowing money and corporate cowboys do not stop playing games just because the interest rate is up a point or two. The zigzag pattern of interest rates in the 1980s gave them plenty of reason to believe the rise of 1988 might soon be reversed anyway. So the cowboys kept playing games and the banks kept lending to them. In these circumstances, the natural instinct of those in control of the monetary levers is to keep notching rates ever higher and then to hold them there.

If interest rates are kept high enough for long enough they will break any boom. They will break a lot of other things too. There is no picket fence dividing interest rates paid by speculators and corporate cowboys from those paid by small and legitimate businesses. The same rates also flow through, usually in slightly ameliorated form, to homebuyers and farmers. The heavy-handed use of interest rates in 1989–90 was a prime cause of the recession that afflicted Australia for the following three years. A great deal of misery was caused by the men who set the rates shown in Figure 1.1. At least part of that misery could have been avoided by a better sense of timing in the use of high interest rates and by more direct controls on bank lending to selected client groups. But the latter, of course, would have been contrary to the spirit of deregulation.

The property crash

With the share market dead on its feet in late 1987, the surviving cowboys swung into the property market. Many of them, such as Bond and Hooker, had been in it for a long time anyway. The relatively low interest rates of early 1988 encouraged them to believe that they might escape their troubles in the equity market by gearing up in Central Business District (CBD) property.

What happened is best shown by Figures 1.2 and 1.3 from Jones Lang Wootton Research. The cowboys who were borrowing in 1988 and 1989 to build high-rise CBD office blocks, and the banks who were lending to

Figure 1.2 Construction and vacancy, Sydney CBD

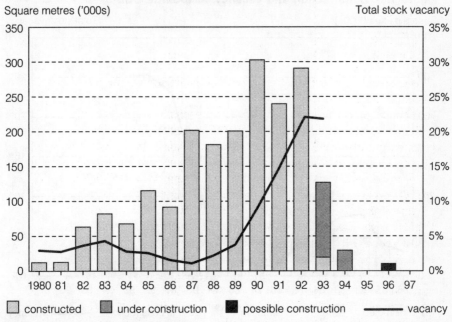

Square metres ('000s)   Total stock vacancy

constructed ▢   under construction ▨   possible construction ■   vacancy ——

Source: Jones Lang Wootton Research
Note: 1993 figures are as at June

them, were looking at history rather than the future. Vacancy rates in the
Sydney CBD had been below 5 per cent throughout the 1980s and had
been particularly low in 1987. As a rough rule of thumb, as long as
vacancy rates are below 5 per cent the landlords of the office blocks can
dictate the rents. But when vacancy rates rise, the balance of power shifts
to tenants. Landlords get lower returns on their buildings because real
rents fall. Sometimes buildings cannot be let at all. Where this crossover
point occurs would make a useful academic study, but from observation
the tenant holds the whip hand when more than 10 per cent of the office
space in a city is vacant.

The cowboys and their lenders who stampeded into office block
construction in 1988 and 1989 showed woeful lack of experience. History
tells us that a share market crash is frequently followed within a couple
of years by a property crash. In 1987 the 25 per cent markdown of equities
on 20 October must have injured a great many investors. Some would
have to quit their office space. There was bound to be rationalisation in
the broking industry and probably among merchant banks. The corporate
cowboys would have to shorten sail. These groups were among the most
expansive occupiers of office space. So there was reason to believe that
demand would fall, or at least not expand as quickly.

Simultaneously, an unprecedented amount of space was coming on

Figure 1.3 Construction and vacancy, Melbourne CBD

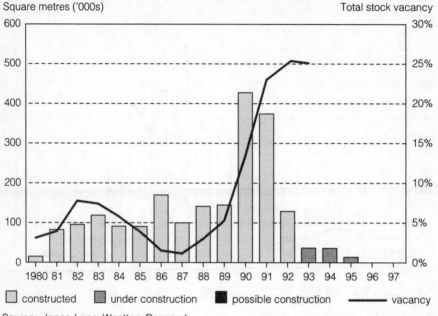

Square metres ('000s)   Total stock vacancy

constructed   under construction   possible construction   —— vacancy

Source: Jones Lang Wootton Research
Note: 1993 figures are as at June

stream. Between 1982 and 1986 the amount of office space built in Sydney had been around 80 000 square metres a year. From 1987 to 1989 (inclusive) it would average just under 200 000 square metres. This should have been enough to cope with any tightness of supply in 1989. Instead, capacity soared again. Office block construction would reach 300 000 square metres in 1990, followed by 250 000 square metres in 1991 and nearly 300 000 square metres again in 1992.

By that time the property market was well and truly dead and liable to stay so for several years. The Sydney CBD vacancy rate soared from less than 5 per cent in 1989 to 22 per cent in 1992 and the city was dotted with see-through buildings.

Melbourne was in even worse state. New space had been coming on the market at around 100 000 square metres a year up until 1987, rising to 150 000 in 1988 and 1989. But 1990 and 1991 saw in total an extra 800 000 square metres dumped on the market at a time when Melbourne was suffering its worst economic downturn since the Great Depression. The vacancy rate shot to 25 per cent and was likely to stay high for a long time.

Not only was the supply of space excessive but demand went through the floor. The long, bitter recession led to an unprecedented wave of retrenchments that eventually took toll of the service industries which

Figure 1.4 Gross prime office rents, Sydney CBD

Per square metre

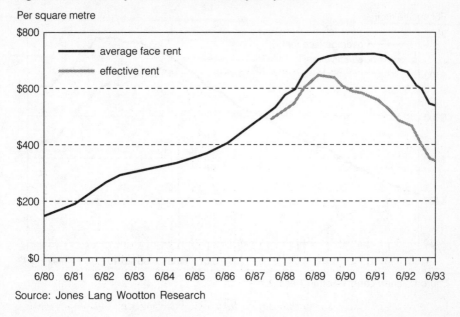

Source: Jones Lang Wootton Research

had been the major space takers. As sharebrokers, banks, institutions, accountants and even lawyers began cutting back on staff, demand for space dwindled. Electronic innovations such as the mobile telephone and laptop computers also meant that an increasing number of workers and consultants could operate outside the CBD or had only limited need for desks.

The glut of office space broke the commercial property market in every capital city except Canberra. Real rents collapsed as desperate landlords—sometimes receivers—found they had to offer increasing incentives to fill their expensive new buildings. By the start of 1993 landlords were wooing tenants with incentives that included free fit-outs of their offices, rent-free periods, cash and (a really desperate move) the assumption of tenants' obligations on their previous office space. Jones Lang Wootton reported in mid-1993 that effective rents had declined by 5.3 per cent from the previous year to $337 per square metre, while incentive levels for a major tenant on a long lease had increased to around the equivalent of 56 months rent free.[11]

As real rental income shrank, so did the value of buildings. Many buildings became worth less than the value of the loans raised to build them—as was the case with No. 1 O'Connell Street, Sydney. Banks and institutions which had been lenders to office blocks found themselves installed as owners, often with no buyer in sight. Any sale at realistic

Figure 1.5 Gross prime office rents, Melbourne CBD

Per square metres

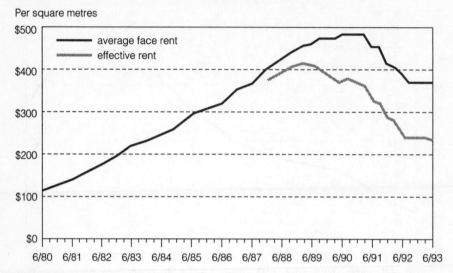

Source: Jones Lang Wootton Research

prices would have crystallised ghastly losses, so owners tended to hang on. Many buildings probably had a negative real net worth. In the Melbourne CBD there was hardly an arm's length sale of a major CBD office block between 1990 and 1992. Some proposed buildings were never constructed at all, Westralia Square in Perth being an example.

The new buildings were usually beautifully engineered and equipped with state of the art electronics. The incentives offered to tenants meant that they filled slowly, albeit at low effective rents. The real victims became the owners of slightly older or second-rate CBD buildings or fringe CBD buildings, who lost tenants in droves to the gleaming new CBD towers.

Most of all, the commercial property market had lost the free-spending corporate cowboys who had always treated themselves to lavish offices with money that was never theirs. The era of the opulent offices of Christopher Skase and Alan Bond had gone. The property boom had been their last hurrah. When it crashed, so did they—and their financiers.

2
The first trustee company: TEA

You are receiving a set of papers which is about the nearest to reality that we have been able to obtain for a long time.

Alex Oglivy to TEA board, April 1983

The collapse of Trustees Executors & Agency Co Ltd (TEA) in May 1983 was tinged with scandal. It was the first trustee company ever to fail in Australia. It had an establishment board headed by chairman Alex Ogilvy, who sat on the BHP board, and Sir Robert Norman, the former chief executive officer of the Bank of New South Wales. TEA's sudden closure caused a profound shock in financial circles, because its image had always been that of a dull, dusty but eminently safe and respectable pillar of the Melbourne establishment. The company's 1982 accounts had shown net assets of $7.79 a share, yet eleven months later it closed its doors without a word of explanation to shareholders or clients. It took years for the truth to emerge, and it is still not certain that we know the full truth.

Trustees Executors & Agency Co Ltd was the first trustee company to be formed in Australia. It was the brainchild of William Templeton, who had been born in Glasgow in 1820 and was brought to Australia by his family at the age of ten. During the rush to Victoria in 1851 he joined the Gold Escort Corps and later became a warden and a magistrate. His experiences in the courts brought home to him the difficulties faced by wealthy people—and even those of moderate means—who sought someone to act as their executor after their death.

A trustee company was the logical answer. After conferring with several advisors, Templeton issued a prospectus for Trustees Executors & Agency Co Ltd in 1878. Its float was delayed because a special Act of Parliament was needed to incorporate it. Some members of parliament were reluctant to give the company the powers that until then had been the prerogative of individuals.

After an inquiry by a select committee TEA was allowed to float

33

provided that it raised £25 000 capital, that no individual was allowed to hold more than 500 shares and that at least £10 000 of its funds was invested in Victorian Government securities. TEA raised the capital and began life at the end of 1879 in a single room in Flinders Street, opposite the Hobson's Bay Railway Station. After several changes of address (at one stage it bought the Mitre Tavern but fortunately never converted that historic hostelry into a trustee office), it settled in 1938 into a head office at 401 Collins Street.

If Templeton had returned to the company on its ninetieth birthday he would have found much of it familiar. The head office had a reassuringly ornate facade, more in the style of the 1870s than the looming 1970s. The company was still engaged almost entirely in its traditional trustee business—acting as an executor, administrator and trustee and assisting with wills and estate planning. Its capital had stayed cosily small, amounting to only $280 000 in 1970, although shareholders' funds had grown to $1.6 million. No individual was allowed to own more than 0.5 per cent of the company. Business growth looked good, with trust funds under administration rising from $110 million to $184 million between 1960 and 1970.

This structure masked hidden weaknesses. Shareholders were, because of their small shareholdings, held powerless in the company. One result was that the board and management had tended to become self-perpetuating. Another was that TEA was undercapitalised and its margins were declining. The assets managed by a trustee company—and the earnings generated on them—belong to the beneficiaries. A pure trustee company's only source of income is its fees for management. With computers still in their relative infancy in the early 1970s, maintenance of the records was labour-intensive. This could be tolerated in the low inflation and low wage growth decades of the 1950s and 1960s. But, as inflation began to rise in the 1970s, TEA's chronically low margins came under increasing pressure from costs. The effect can be seen in the 1972 profit and loss account (Table 2.1).

Expenses were eating heavily into revenue with the result that net

Table 2.1 TEA profit and loss account

Year to	June 1972	June 1971
Revenue	$1 264 282	$1 167 409
Expenses	(1 117 310)	(1 029 285)
Profit	146 972	138 124
Tax	(58 500)	(54 000)
Net profit	88 472	84 124
Dividends	(53 200)	(50 400)
Retained profit	35 272	33 724

Table 2.2 TEA balance sheet, June 1972

		(All figures in $000)
Freehold property	1 540	
Other fixed assets	175	
Investments	1 158	
Current assets	77	
TOTAL ASSETS		2 950
Bank overdraft	190	
Other liabilities	343	
TOTAL LIABILITIES		534
CORPUS COMMISSION		718
Paid capital	280	
Reserves	1 418	
SHAREHOLDERS' FUNDS		1 698

profit was only around 7 per cent. The net profit also looked low compared to shareholders' funds, which by then totalled nearly $1.7 million. Profit had shown no growth between 1971 and 1972 because extra revenue had been matched by rising expenses. Finally, it was a dog of a result considering that TEA had nearly $200 million under management. The company was going nowhere.

The first solution proposed was to develop a money market operation. Until then, temporary funds held on behalf of TEA's trustee clients had been placed in trust or bank accounts. When considering ways of expanding its business in 1972 TEA's board decided to accept interest-bearing deposits from clients.[1] TEA could offer clients, say, 5 per cent on client interest-bearing deposits (CIBs) and relend the money at 5.5 per cent in the professional market on bonds, bills or inter-company loans.

In itself, there was nothing wrong with this idea. One snag was that if TEA actively solicited funds, it would have to issue a prospectus. So the board decided it would accept CIBs only 'if requested'. When the board took this decision in 1972 TEA was conservatively geared. Its brief balance sheet is shown in Table 2.2.

Corpus commission is an item peculiar to trustee companies. It is uncharged commission on estates and trusts under administration. To a lay observer it would appear to be more properly reckoned as an asset, or contingent asset, than as a liability. But whichever side of the ledger it is counted, TEA was conservatively structured. Debt was confined to a $190 000 bank overdraft, its freehold property was its head office and the investments were primarily shares, debentures and Commonwealth and semi-government securities. Borrowing money from clients would raise its gearing, but as long as the funds were reinvested safely at a margin above the borrowing rate there would be little risk and TEA's bottom line should be enhanced.

When deciding to create CIBs, the board noted that the provisions of the *Companies Act* barred TEA from advising clients of the facility unless they requested the information 'but it is in order to suggest that certain improved facilities are available'. Trust officers were urged to begin immediately making suggestions to clients. The line between soliciting deposits and suggesting to clients that they should seek information about deposits is a very fine one. Morally, TEA ought to have issued a prospectus but the cost would have greatly eroded its profits from the CIB operation.

Essentially, clients were being asked to lend money unsecured to TEA. A letter to clients said:

> As part of the professional handling of clients' money which has stemmed from our large trust business, the company maintains extensive and sophisticated money market operations . . . Our philosophy is based on the need for a satisfactory return with safety of capital. Having been entrusted with other people's funds for over 100 years, our benchmarks for investment in the short-term money market are very conservative.

Property investment was not mentioned.

The board originally approved a CIB investment program that would have put about half the CIB funds into mortgages, on the basis that they were a relatively high-yielding and reasonably liquid security. This again would have been a sound enough strategy. But it went off the rails when the CIB funds were used to finance speculative property developments.

How CIB funds came to be used to finance property has never been properly explained. The board had specifically vetoed such a use of funds in a resolution in September 1980. Yet within a few months CIB funds were being used to finance property ventures and frequently with the board's concurrence. Even where the board may not have authorised this use of funds it should have known they were being so used. Each monthly board meeting was presented with the group financial services report which included detailed and categorised information on all loans made from CIB funds. This report included the borrowers' names and the amounts and terms of loans made by TEA to joint venture partners. Although the figures were staring them in the face for the two years that it took TEA to fast track down the road to ruin, the directors apparently did not recognise the significance of the information.[2]

The move into property

How did TEA become so committed—and eventually overcommitted—to property? The subsequent report by the National Companies and Securities Commission (NCSC) inspectors, Trevor Beasley and Michael Adey, said the initiative for TEA's diversification into property development came from

Peter Bunning, who joined the company in July 1974 as manager, administration and development.[3] Tall, intelligent and persuasive, Bunning seemed the ideal new manager to breathe life into the fusty old TEA. As one developer who dealt extensively with Bunning later said: 'He was pretty impressive'. Bunning became a director in May 1980.

It is inherent in any money market operation that the liquidity of the assets should match the liquidity of the liabilities. If clients call more cash than the operator can raise immediately by liquidating securities the operator may borrow to bridge the gap, but such borrowings should be essentially temporary to allow an orderly liquidation of securities. Property is one of the most illiquid assets, particularly uncompleted development property.

The growth in CIB funds was spectacular. Between the balance dates of 1974 and 1982, total client deposits held by TEA exploded from $5.1 million to $133.6 million. At first they were reinvested, as intended, in the professional money market. Net profit had moved up to $505 000 by 1978. The accounts give no clue as to how much of this was derived from the money market, but deposits by that time had grown to $52 million.

TEA first dabbled in property investment in 1976 with the Melbourne Clinic, a psychiatric hospital.[4] Its second project, two years later, was Staghorn Court, a home unit block at Surfers Paradise. Both projects were relatively small and returned a profit for TEA. Its appetite whetted by these two ventures, TEA suddenly launched into a string of property developments in 1980. Table 2.3 shows the abbreviated accounts of TEA in June 1980, just as this expansion was beginning.

By June 1980 TEA had assets with a total book value of $108 million. The table shows that these were funded $102 million by borrowings and other external liabilities, and $6 million by the equity which shareholders had built up in the company over its 102 years. In financial jargon, the company was geared 17:1 (102:6), or more than 94 per cent.

Gearing measures the extent to which a company's activities are being financed by debt, as opposed to equity. Gearing is the ratio of external liabilities to shareholders' funds, and can also be expressed as a percentage.[5] As gearing will feature heavily in our later discussion of corporate collapses, it is as well to explain it briefly here. A company which has $12 million in assets, financed by $6 million in borrowings and $6 million in shareholders' funds, is 50 per cent geared. In other words, its assets can diminish in value by 50 per cent before its shareholders' funds have been eliminated and it becomes—for most practical purposes—bankrupt. A company which is 94 per cent geared will be wiped out after only a 6 per cent diminution in its assets.

But all companies are not equally vulnerable. A mining company, exposed to the hazards of commodity prices and exploration results,

Table 2.3   TEA accounts, June 1980

(All figures in $m)
BALANCE SHEET

Fixed Assets	3.5
Current Assets:	
Short Term Investments	67.4
Other	3.4
Investments:	
Debentures, loans, mortgages	32.0
Other	1.8
TOTAL ASSETS	108.1
Current Liabilities:	
Deposits	97.2
Other	3.9
Non-Current Liabilities	0.9
TOTAL LIABILITIES	102.1
Paid Capital	0.3
Reserves	5.7
SHAREHOLDERS' FUNDS	6.0

PROFIT & LOSS ACCOUNT
Year to June 1980 (All figures in $000)

Pre-tax Profit	1 777
Tax	(699)
Net Profit	1 078
Dividends	(420)
Retained profit	658

should carry very low gearing. For an industrial company the historical rule of thumb has been around 50 per cent, on the grounds that a company which has no debt is not trying hard enough to maximise its opportunities. For a bank or financial institution gearing levels of 90 per cent or more are not uncommon, on the grounds that they lower their risk by matching their liabilities and assets.

In TEA's case, the liabilities largely consist of the $97 million in deposits which purportedly had been placed on the short-term money market. Obviously the risk would rise if TEA's assets were not as liquid as its liabilities.

In practice few financial institutions ever manage a perfect match of their assets and liabilities, and it has always been impossible for any institution indulging in mortgage lending. A 25-year home loan can hardly be matched by a 25-year deposit.

TEA's gearing looked high in 1980 but provided that its affairs were being prudently managed there should have been no cause for alarm. But the net profit of barely $1 million represented a threadbare return on total assets of $108 million. TEA needed to improve its earnings.

It was in this context that TEA suddenly launched into property on a larger scale in 1980. Table 2.4 shows the projects it undertook between then and its demise.

Table 2.4   TEA's two-year property splurge

Project	Approx. date of TEA's entry	Initial Commitment by TEA ($000)	Profit/(Loss) ($000)
Cliveden, Sydney	March 1980	4 500	($3 000)
Holiday North, Surfers Paradise	June 1980	1 400	120
The Resort, Surfers Paradise	Sept. 1980	5 000	(250)
Cosmopolitan, Surfers Paradise	Sept. 1980	1 700	(1 800 est.)
72 Pitt St., Sydney	Sept. 1980	n.a.	n.a.
Scottish House, Sydney	Oct. 1980	3 100	(2 000+)
Goode House, Melbourne	Nov. 1980	1 000	(6 650)
The Quay, Sydney	Dec. 1980	1 000	n.a.
Beaconlea, Surfers Paradise	Jan. 1981	2 720	(200)
Lahaina, Mooloolaba	March 1981	94	(340)
Riverside, Surfers Paradise	May 1981	1 000	(1 000+)
Seahaven, Noosa Heads	August 1981	900	(100)
Olderfleet, Melbourne	Sept. 1981	500	(2 500)
Reef House, Cairns	Nov. 1981	1 150	n.a.
Trinity Beach, Cairns	Nov. 1981	525	n.a.
The Resort, Cairns	Feb. 1982	550	(45)
Total		25 889	(16 965)

The table is almost sufficient explanation by itself for TEA's collapse. A financier with only $6 million in shareholders' funds suddenly committed itself to nearly $26 million in property ventures over two years. The first four deals alone created a commitment equivalent to double its shareholders' funds. And these were only the initial commitments. In almost every case TEA's commitment blew out to a far larger sum. Its exposure to The Quay, for example, totalled more than $8.5 million by the time the receivers were appointed. When TEA went into receivership its advances to its own property projects totalled $46 million, of which $30 million was from clients' deposits.

It is worth emphasising that these were not liquid investments. Few things are more difficult to sell than an uncompleted building project. Any funds invested in property development should be regarded as a medium-term investment. Thus TEA's rapid expansion into property was tying up ever greater sums which would only be released upon completion and sale of the projects. In these circumstances it was vital that TEA's exposure should be limited and that projects should be finished on time and on budget. In the event, TEA drifted into the position where it was frequently the sole financier, project deadlines were not met and cost overruns dramatically exceeded the original estimates. These were the factors that combined to kill TEA.

Timing is the key to successful investment in any field. This is particularly true of property, where prices tend to move in long cycles lasting several years. When TEA began taking the plunge into property

39

in 1980 the market was very buoyant. A series of property company collapses in the late 1970s had resulted in a virtual cessation of Central Business District (CBD) construction. Office vacancies shrank, rentals rose and developers began to recognise that the market was undersupplied. This led to a strong upward trend in property prices and falling yields in 1981.[6] As Table 2.4 shows, TEA launched on to this wave enthusiastically, rapidly expanding its property projects in the booming market. But, in surfing parlance, the wave was a dumper. By the second half of 1982 Australia was suffering a short but severe recession. Interest rates rose, gross domestic product (GDP) growth was negative for the first time in 30 years, and unemployment peaked at 10 per cent. The buoyant property market suddenly receded. Higher interest rates forced commercial property yields up, with a concomitant fall in property prices. TEA was caught badly exposed.

But TEA's property investments were conducted in such a feckless manner that the group would probably have been brought down even if the 1982–83 recession had not happened. The board at no point formulated any policy on property investment. Peter Bunning was left to make ad hoc decisions as and when opportunities arose. In May 1980 the board resolved to delegate authority to Bunning and one director to buy investment property when time did not permit referral to the board. The authority was subject to the purchase price not exceeding a sworn valuation and satisfactory reports being obtained on the structure and equipment of the building. This resolution, however, implicitly referred to established buildings rather than refurbishments or property developments.

In October 1980 the board decided to liquidate TEA's equity portfolio, raising $2.3 million 'for various other purposes'. It is not clear what the board had in mind, but Bunning clearly wanted to reinvest the money in property. In November he presented a paper to the board recommending the extent to which TEA should invest in real estate. The paper was never considered or approved by the board, but in retrospect it is interesting because Bunning proposed three safeguards which would later be broken by TEA with disastrous results. He recommended that TEA should (a) invest a maximum of $2 million in real estate projects, (b) only commit itself to projects where the developed real estate had been presold and (c) obtain fixed price contracts so that TEA was not exposed to cost overruns. Had these safeguards been followed TEA would still be alive, but they were being breached even before the board paper was written.

Management of the property investments devolved heavily on Bunning, who initiated many projects and carried them through with little or no reference to the board. 'Much of the failure of the company's management to prepare reports on the property projects in the manner sought by the other directors can be attributed to [Bunning's] authoritarian managerial style and his encouragement of a regime in which property development projects were regarded as a confidential and discrete business activity', the NCSC inspectors said. 'One consequence was that the overall scope and details of the property development projects were poorly comprehended even by the few staff, other than Mr Yeo, who were directly involved.' The company secretary, Malcolm Reid, was concerned because cash flow forecasts which he prepared for Bunning were not shown to the board. Reid told the chairman, Alex Ogilvy, of his concerns. But Ogilvy merely spoke to Bunning and Bunning told Reid the chairman did not want to be worried about these things.[7]

Nor were there any internal checks and balances. The first report of the internal auditor, Alan Lane, was written in January 1982 and criticised the state of accounting records in the property area. Bunning refused to show the report to the audit subcommittee on the grounds that Lane did not comprehend the overall situation and that his report was misleading. TEA was operating without procedure or policy manuals in the property area. A consultant had been employed to write procedure manuals but the project had been delayed by Bunning because he believed it was 'a lot of crap', according to Lane.[8] No machinery existed to ensure that reports by the internal auditor came to the notice of non-executive directors who were not members of the audit subcommittee. These structural weaknesses meant that TEA was peculiarly reliant on its managing director to keep the board fully and accurately informed. But a vigilant board could have ensured that it got the information it needed anyway.

Bunning became heavily involved with Melbourne and Sydney projects while Michael Yeo, the only other full-time executive in the property division, was mainly concerned with those in Queensland.

TEA property deals had several common characteristics. No matter what its original intention, TEA always tended to stray into becoming the main or sole financier, sometimes for sums well beyond its ability to fund. Almost invariably the projects ran over budget in both time and cost and sometimes by a large factor. Its first project, the Melbourne Clinic, was presold and therefore almost riskless but later projects were built 'on spec'. Usually a trust was created to own the building. Although TEA often provided all the finance it rarely owned 100 per cent of the equity.

Parcels of equity were taken by partners, sometimes in return for little risk or work. Several of the deals involved the same partners. One which appeared in several deals was the Citicentre group of private companies, run by David Atkin and Tjeerd La Grouw. Another was Lenlord Nominees, the family company of Bunning's tax accountant Leigh Jamieson. Yet another was Stirling Properties (formerly the Jaguar distributor

Bryson Industries), a public company which was controlled by Aberdeen Assets. The relationship between Jamieson and Bunning was particularly close, with payments running to thousands of dollars being made by Jamieson to Bunning's family company Petane Holdings. The payments were described as consulting fees. As Bunning was by then the chief executive of a public company which was the major financier of many developments in which Jamieson had an interest, it was clearly inappropriate for him to be receiving payments from Jamieson.

Stirling Properties was a total contrast to TEA, being a textbook example of intelligent property investment. It was started by Charles Abbott, a lawyer in the blue-blooded firm of Blake & Rigall, who joined a few of his Carlton neighbours—including stockbrokers John McIntosh and Chris Hamson—in forming a property syndicate. Each put in just $800. They bought and sold houses profitably, with the syndicate being transformed into Aberdeen Assets with a financier as 15 per cent partner. They backlisted via the shell of the former Jaguar distributor Bryson Industries and moved into CBD properties at the bottom of the cycle. Their technique was to pick up old buildings cheaply, refurbish them and sell at a profit. They appear to have been a lot smarter than the people at TEA, taking lower risks while the trustee company provided the finance. Years after TEA bit the dust, Aberdeen Assets would be sold to Garry Carter for $22 million.

TEA's short journey to obliteration is best illustrated by detailing one of its major deals: The Quay.

The Quay

One of the most striking apartment blocks in Australia is The Quay, which stands at the eastern end of Sydney's Circular Quay and looks at the splendid vista of the Opera House and the Harbour Bridge, its residents disturbed only by the ceaseless traffic on the Cahill Expressway below. Looking at this luxury building today, a tourist could hardly guess the financial turbulence in which it was constructed.

The proposal to build The Quay on the site of the old First and Last Hotel was brought to Bunning by Citicentre. After considerable internecine dealing between the potential partners in this project, two buildings were acquired at Nos 2 and 4 Albert Street for $1 million each, then the adjoining First and Last for $1.5 million. A prime concern of the joint venturers was to knock the old hotel down before it might be classified by the Historic Buildings Preservation Council. The publican held a farewell party on the night of Saturday, 22 May 1981. The demolition team moved in next morning, only a few hours after the drinkers had cleared the bar. The publican and his wife were awoken (with severe hangovers) by a worker battering down the wall of their bedroom. 'It was hilarious', said Michael Yeo, manager of TEA's mortgage and lending department. 'They didn't even get the stock out before the demolition team moved in.'

Funding of this project was a constant problem. TEA initially provided $1 million; then part of this was replaced with a bill line of $3.5 million from the venturesome Melbourne merchant bank Tricontinental Corp. From the day the hotel was knocked down TEA was seeking a financier for the site.

The construction plans were also alarmingly loose. The properties were bought without any plans or specifications for their replacement. All that existed was an idea for a building to cost around $12 million. The site was purchased, the buildings were demolished, the initial design was prepared and approved and construction began before the final design had been done—a procedure known as 'fast tracking'. Sydney City Council approved in principle the rezoning of the site for residential purposes in November 1981—six months after the First and Last had been knocked down.

By January 1982 the joint venturers had spent $5 million and were seeking funding of $29 million. The TEA board had approved only limited expenditure on the original properties and was most unlikely to commit further unless a substantial number of the apartments were presold. But not a single apartment was sold before TEA went into receivership.

Insofar as there was a plan, The Quay emerged as a 29-level apartment block, of which six levels would be car space, one level shops and one level a restaurant. The rest of the building would contain 57 luxury apartments at prices ranging from $215 000 for a one-bedroom unit up to $2.5 million for a penthouse. Again, the ownership of the building was through a unit trust structure. This deterred investors—including potential buyers in Singapore and Hong Kong whom Bunning canvassed during a fortnight's visit in mid-1982—so the trust scheme was replaced by conventional strata titles.

After demolishing the old buildings and excavating foundations, Concrete Construction poured the first concrete on the site in August 1982. In the subsequent investigation Citicentre and Bunning blamed each other for starting construction before funding had been arranged. In the absence of any agreement (and any sales) the bills were paid by TEA. By April 1983, when the slab for the fourteenth floor was being poured, TEA had spent $9.3 million on the project. This money, which included the site purchases, was all drawn from CIB funds. According to Sir Robert Norman: 'The advances to The Quay were not authorised by the board and nor were the proposals to finance it approved by the board'.[9]

The Quay did, however, serve the purpose of generating a paper profit for TEA. In June 1982 Citicentre purported to buy half of TEA's 60 per cent interest in The Quay for $2 million, enabling TEA to record a profit of $1.4 million on the transaction. TEA lent Citicentre the money for the purchase. This transaction also meant that TEA did not have to consolidate The Quay into its 1982 accounts. On 7 June Bunning reported to the TEA board that agreements in principle had been reached with Citicentre and Concrete Constructions for one of the companies to buy half of TEA's interest. There had been no agreement with Concrete Constructions and the board was unaware that the whole $2 million paid by Citicentre was provided by TEA. Howarth Peterson, one of the directors, said mildly afterwards: 'I suppose it would have been wise to obtain the board's approval but the whole investment (apart from land purchase) was made without board approval so I do not suppose the sale of an interest without board approval is very much different'.

In October Bunning told the board that discussions were being held with Tricontinental on the future funding. The board noted that this was the first TEA venture to be undertaken without significant preselling. Bunning did not tell the board that construction had already begun (a fact which must have been noticed by half a million Sydneysiders at the time). One director, Max Mainprize, said the board had been assured that construction had not begun. Mainprize believed the board was strongly opposed to construction proceeding until The Quay had been substantially presold.

For the February board meeting Yeo prepared the most comprehensive statement made to the board until then on TEA properties. The report said that The Quay building was proceeding on time under a fixed price contract for $21.5 million. This was the first time the board was formally notified that construction had begun. Peterson said: 'The decision to start was not a decision of the board of TEA—suddenly this block of concrete appeared'.[10] Yeo's report also said that Tricontinental wanted a guarantee from TEA of up to $30 million before it would take over the financing. The board would not agree to such a guarantee, which one of the directors, Edward Harty, labelled 'ridiculous'. The guarantee was out of all proportion to TEA's shareholders' funds, even though these had been raised to $16 million (mainly by asset revaluations which would later prove over-optimistic). Financing had still not been arranged, nor The Quay completed, when TEA went into receivership.

The board's continuing ignorance on this project was remarkable. The Quay was one of the most visible construction jobs in Sydney at the time, being smack alongside the Cahill Expressway. Several hundred thousand motorists, office workers and tourists saw it every day and it was frequently the subject of newspaper comment and speculation. (On his return from Singapore in July 1982 Bunning was interviewed by the *Australian Financial Review* and quoted as saying that ten units had been sold, which was untrue.) Yet the board managed to remain in ignorance of the fact that they were funding The Quay's construction and that the sale of their interest to Citicentre was bogus.

Perhaps this was a manifestation of the very Melbourne nature of the TEA board and the Collins Street syndrome that regards Sydney as a foreign country. Yet even this hardly explains the fact that over the eight months of construction from August 1982 to April 1983 the *Financial Review* seems to have taken more interest in The Quay (and to have spent more time interviewing Bunning on the subject) than the board did. Sir Robert Norman lived in Sydney and observed the construction. The chairman, Alex Ogilvy, visited the site in February 1983. He said: 'I satisfied myself that the projects were where they were supposed to be and that they were, in fact, progressing. It did not take me much further than that'.[11]

No report on The Quay was given to the board for its meeting in March 1983. Mainprize asked for a statement to be prepared detailing the company's individual property projects and their valuations. This report was presented to the board's next meeting on 11 April 1983. This time Bunning proposed that TEA authorise three loan approvals totalling $17 million on the project, but the board jibbed. When TEA went into receivership the following month, construction work on The Quay had reached the 15th level and the project had cost $12.8 million, of which $8.5 million had come from TEA's CIB funds.

The revaluations

There was a similar pattern in TEA's other property developments. The result was that, in the space of two years, Australia's oldest trustee company was brought undone by overreaching itself in property investments. Shareholders were left in the dark as the 1981 and 1982 accounts painted a picture of rising profits and shareholders' funds. This misleading picture of financial health was achieved with the aid of creative accounting.

This trend began in the accounts for the year to June 1981. The accounts subcommittee of the TEA board met on 10 August 1981 and resolved to revalue the group's properties from $3.1 million to $11.4 million. They approved the accounts and declared a dividend and a one-for-two bonus issue of shares. Present at this subcommittee meeting were three directors—Ogilvy, Bunning and John Nave—and the financial controller, Malcolm Reid. On the next day TEA announced that it had made a $1.5 million profit for the year, up 39 per cent on 1980. It also announced that, thanks largely to capital gains and a revaluation of property interests, its shareholders' funds had risen from $6 million to $16 million.

This cheerful picture was the result of considerable artifice. Neither in the press release announcing the company's results nor in their subsequent annual report did the directors disclose to the market or shareholders that investment in property developments was now a significant element of TEA's business activities. Yet the company was involved in at least ten projects at the time. The NCSC inspectors' report concluded that the growth of shareholders' funds and profits for 1981 'was achieved in part by improper revaluations of property assets and by the overstatement of profit on a particular property project'. The inspectors estimated that the revaluation of property in the 1981 TEA accounts, and the consequent expansion of shareholders' funds, had been overstated by $3 million. One block of land at Riverside in Surfers Paradise had been bought for $3.2 million and revalued to $7 million only six weeks later.[12]

The question that arises is how much the board knew about TEA's property dealings and exposure. It is a question that has never been satisfactorily answered. Perhaps the board was comforted by the fact that TEA's auditors, Arthur Young & Co, gave an unqualified audit report.

The board might also have been disinclined to look too hard at the numbers for other reasons. TEA's group accountant John Box, when examined by the inspectors, said an extremely high base of profitability had been established in 1981 for a specific purpose. Asked about the specific purpose, he said: 'At the time there was consideration of a merger between Trustees Executors and Perpetual Trustees'.[13]

Table 2.5 records the directors who held office through TEA's big plunge into property.

In November 1981—nearly three months after the profit statement—a paper was presented to a board meeting by the company secretary and financial controller, Malcolm Reid, warning that a serious cash deficiency might develop after February 1982, partly because of amounts lent to the company's property projects. The amounts at that point totalled $4 million. The board asked for projected balance sheets to be prepared for December 1981 and June 1982 so that appropriate action could be considered. The board also instructed that cash flow projections and a report on property investment projects should be included in the directors' board papers each month.

A fortnight later, on 18 November, the board asked for the reports to include agreements covering mortgage loans and other contingent commitments. But the property reports subsequently presented to the board each month were essentially operational summaries and contained little

Table 2.5   TEA board from 1975

Name	Appointed	Retired
Sir Thomas Webb	Before 1.1.1975	25.4.1983
E.P.M. Harty	"	*
J.L. Nave	"	5.10.1981
G.W. Ramsden	"	30.6.1982
A.W. Ogilvy	4.10.1978	*
Sir Robert Norman	1.4.1980	*
P.R. Bunning	21.5.1980	*
H.E. Peterson	1.3.1982	12.5.1983
M.S. Mainprize	5.7.1982	*
Chairmen		
Sir Thomas Webb	1.1.1975	25.4.1978
G.W. Ramsden	26.4.1978	4.8.1980
A.W. Ogilvy	from 4.8.1980	

* In office when receivers and managers appointed 13.5.1983

financial data. However, the board did receive a monthly financial services report on CIB funds which was quite detailed and categorised all loans made, including those to joint ventures in which TEA was involved. 'Some directors clearly did not recognise the significance of the information', the inspectors said.[14]

However well or dimly the board understood the position, it took no action to follow up its November instructions.

Yet there were enough danger signs if the board had been vigilant enough to notice them. Little more than a month after Reid's warning in November, the board met on 7 December 1981 to consider another paper prepared by Reid. This showed that TEA had made a loss of $155 000 in the September quarter because of tighter margins in money market operations. Most subsidiaries had been operating at a loss, and Reid said it was necessary 'to produce a profit of $750 000 from property investments' by the end of the year to achieve the budgeted profit of $960 000 for the December half. The sinister connotations of the verb 'produce' do not seem to have struck directors.

The result was almost achieved. In February the board announced a pre-tax profit of $944 000 for the December half. This was achieved after booking the fees and income shown in Table 2.6.

TEA's accountant for property projects, Ken Scott, told the inspectors that Reid had instructed him to write a memo setting out the list of fees summarised in Table 2.6. Scott described the fees as 'based on the concept of Mr Bunning of emerging profits'.[15] As Table 2.4 shows, none of the projects ever made a profit, so TEA's interim profit for December 1981 was bogus. Yet, when the board met on 17 February to approve the

Table 2.6 Sources of the December 1981 TEA profit

The Resort, Surfers Paradise:	
Finance establishment fees	200 000
East West site, Surfers Paradise:	
Finance & administration fees	100 000
Scottish House:	
Sales commission	55 000
Finance & administration fees	400 000
Olderfleet:	
Management fee	<u>185 000</u>
Total	940 000

interim statement, Sir Robert Norman was recorded as saying that the labour-intensive operations of a trustee company would not normally permit profit growth and that the property division was making an important contribution to the profits. Indeed, it contributed almost the entire profit of $944 000.

In the interim statement directors said: 'Despite reduced margins in money market activities due to market conditions and increased competition, the group has improved its performance in several other areas'. The statement did not mention property investments, although the entire profit was derived from property—or, more accurately, from creative accounting of property investments.

July 1982 saw a meeting of the audit subcommittee of the board attended by Ogilvy, Harty, Bunning, Reid, TEA's internal auditor Alan Lane, and representatives of Arthur Young & Co. Lane made a report to the board on the funding of six of TEA's twelve current property developments. His report disclosed some significant shortcomings in TEA's management of its property developments. Among others he noted that the cost of The Resort apartment block at Surfers Paradise had escalated from $22 million to $33 million and that the likely loss on it was now about $1.5 million. The directors present took no action on Lane's report. It was not disclosed to the full board of TEA, which remained ignorant of the internal auditor's misgivings.[16] One of the many flaws in TEA's organisational machinery was that there was no requirement for the audit subcommittee's proceedings to be reported regularly to the full board. However, this does not explain why neither Ogilvy, Harty nor Bunning saw fit to alert the board to Lane's report.

The directors declared that profit for the year to June 1982 was $3.1 million before tax and $1 655 000 after tax, representing a 10 per cent rise on 1980–81. Shareholders and the investing public had no way of knowing that TEA's traditional business had been unprofitable for the year and that the profit would have been a loss but for $3.4 million purportedly derived from three property transactions which had taken place on 18 June:

- a profit of $1.4 million from the sale of half of TEA's interest in The Quay
- a profit of $500 000 on the sale of half of TEA's interest in the Olderfleet project
- the taking of a $1.5 million fee from the Scottish House joint venture

The NCSC inspectors said that Bunning was determined to achieve an increasing profit trend for the company in accordance with a five-year profit projection he had made in 1981. Bunning had told Reid and TEA's group accountant John Box early in 1982 that he was seeking a $2.5 million profit contribution from the property division.[17] In other words, it seems to have been more important for the results of TEA to comply with Bunning's five-year forecasts than with reality. This policy was particularly unwise because by mid-1982 Australia was in recession. In the circumstances the announcement of the true result—a small loss— would have been excusable. Instead, TEA's statements were diverging even further from reality. Scott, and particularly Box, argued with Bunning on this point but were overruled. Scott said that Bunning 'simply wouldn't make any comment on those sort of things—he would just remain stony-faced'.[18]

The inspectors discovered that in each of the three deals mentioned above the sale had been to a purchaser which had been financed by TEA. The entire 1982 profit was therefore manufactured. The only cash received by TEA was from payments financed by itself. These were the figures that came before the audit subcommittee on 30 August 1982. That meeting was attended by Ogilvy, Harty, Bunning, Reid, Lane and two partners of Arthur Young & Co.

The subcommittee appears to have understood the basis upon which the profit had been calculated. The inspectors said that the subcommittee reviewed the accounts in detail. In The Quay deal TEA had indemnified the buyer, Citicentre, against loss.[19] The auditors and TEA agreed that the accounts should include a note setting out TEA's contingent liabilities. Reid drafted a note but, before the board met a week later, Bunning had prevailed upon Citicentre to waive the guarantee. So when the board met on 6 September it approved the directors' report and the accounts.[20]

The inspectors could not discover the extent to which the proceedings of the two audit subcommittee meetings were reported to the full board on 6 September. This was despite some questioning by the inspectors of Ogilvy and Harty—the two directors on the subcommittee apart from Bunning. 'Although he had been chairman of the company, Mr A.W. Ogilvy's stated inability to recall significant matters was disquieting', the inspectors said.[21]

The annual report of TEA for 1982 was duly released. Shareholders were given no indication of the artificiality of the group's profit. The accounts also showed shareholders' funds at $16.4 million. Net tangible assets represented $7.79 a share.

The unravelling

Despite this rosy picture, Sir Robert Norman was becoming concerned about the lack of comprehensive information. Rumours had begun reaching him in Sydney about the state of some of TEA's projects. On 23 November he wrote a confidential note to Ogilvy saying he was concerned by the 'total lack of real information' the board was receiving about the company's property dealings. He asked that at the next meeting the board be presented with the following information about each property on which TEA was carrying a financial risk:[23]

- TEA's partners and its share of the partnership
- the total agreed commitment for TEA
- TEA's present exposure
- the estimated completion date and expected date of repayment
- the formal security given to TEA
- the source of funds used by TEA to finance its share
- the rate of interest being paid by TEA on those funds
- a management opinion on each property
- a recommendation for board decision

'You may be more closely informed about what is going on', Sir Robert wrote to Ogilvy. 'I hope so. In the present climate I believe all directors should be fully informed regularly in regard to our property dealings. If all is satisfactory, so be it. If they are not, they present a very real problem for the board . . . I have the highest regard for P.B. [Bunning]. At the moment I wonder whether he is fully seized with the extreme seriousness of the present national economic recession.'

To an outsider the most amazing aspect of Sir Robert's list is how the board had managed to function for so long without such essential data. Howarth Peterson, who had joined the board only in March 1982, was also concerned about the scanty information possessed by the board on its property investments.

On 6 December the board saw a report from the property executive, Michael Yeo, summarising the progress of property projects. The board asked for a more comprehensive report for its next meeting. A further memorandum was produced for a board meeting on 11 February 1983 but the board was seriously disturbed by the lack of specific detail. In particular, directors wanted to know whether CIB funds were being advanced on property projects. The board had still received no satisfactory detail by March, when it approved the interim result. This was a consolidated loss before extraordinary items and after tax of $416 000—the first loss in the group's history. The board's lack of touch with reality is demonstrated by the fact that it nevertheless approved a dividend of 10 cents a share.

On 11 April a further report listed the individual property projects and detailed the basis of their valuations. The board asked for further financial information on those projects and a draft profit and loss account and balance sheet for the year ended June 1983 setting out the assumptions made for each property project, together with a statement of ongoing commitments and future options. To get the data the board bypassed Bunning. Harty said the board 'almost stepped into the management role to try to find out what the correct position was'. The board had 'lost confidence in its chief executive as a director of the company', Harty said.[23]

The next report was prepared by the financial controller, Malcolm Reid, and submitted to the board on 26 April with an accompanying memorandum from Ogilvy. In his memorandum Ogilvy said: 'You are receiving a set of papers which is about the nearest to reality that we have been able to obtain for a long time'. It is no tribute to Ogilvy, as chairman and one of the three directors on the audit subcommittee, that it had taken so long for this vital data to reach the full board. By 26 April TEA had only seventeen days to live.

Ogilvy's letter canvassed three options. The first was to continue in the hope that the sale of The Quay and other properties could be achieved quickly. This, however, would expose the board to the possible legal consequences of borrowing money without a clear ability to repay. The second option was to seek the appointment of a receiver. The third, which Ogilvy thought the most desirable, was to seek a merger with Perpetual Trustees, which had discussed such a move before. 'Perpetual are very worried about a trustee company failing and more restrictions being placed on their money market activities', Ogilvy said; which indicated that Perpetual's management may have known more about the state of TEA than the TEA board did.

Reid's report estimated that, by June, shareholders' funds of TEA would be reduced by losses or writedowns from $16.3 million to $11.9 million. If TEA had to quit its property projects on a fire sale basis, shareholders' funds could be reduced to two or three million dollars. Ogilvy suggested that there was real doubt whether the directors would be able to make the statutory statement that there were reasonable grounds to believe that the company would be able to pay its debts as and when they fell due.

A shocked board met on 2 May to discuss its options. Directors received an independent report on The Quay, Olderfleet and Goode House from Brian Baker of Baillieu Allard Real Estate. Directors agreed on several steps: to seek repayment of $9 million in CIB funds lent on Scottish House; to try to raise the necessary finance to complete The Quay; to try to get more standby finance; to try to sell the trustee business to another trust company; and to seek funds from the National Australia Bank.

On the following day Bunning asked executives of Hill Samuel Australia, a merchant bank of which Ogilvy was an Australian director, to assess TEA's overall financial position. A report was delivered by Graeme Samuel to a board meeting on 10 May. The bottom line was that TEA's shareholders' funds were somewhere between $2 million and minus $5 million. On a worst case basis it could be minus $8 million. The immediate problem was that the company held $98 million on call or on less than seven days notice, backed by standby facilities of less than $10 million. A further $16 million was on 30 days notice or less. If market rumours should trigger a run on the company's funds it would be unable to meet the calls. Too many of its assets were in property which was illiquid.

The directors agreed with Hill Samuel's assessment. They decided to continue trading in the absence of definite facts showing the company was unable to meet its debts. As a precaution they decided that any new deposits should be accepted in one of the company's common funds or on a secured basis. They instructed Hill Samuel to complete its assessment of TEA and sought urgent talks with Perpetual and two other companies that had expressed interest in a merger. Finally, they decided to advise the Corporate Affairs Commission of the situation. Ogilvy and Bunning were appointed as a two-man committee with full authority and power to take whatever decisions were necessary. These were the two directors most responsible for the mess.

Two days later Ogilvy and Bunning received a further report from Samuel, aided by John Gerahty (another Hill Samuel employee who would later rise to fame as chairman of AFP Group plc). Samuel told the committee that a more detailed investigation into TEA's affairs had indicated that there was clearly a net deficiency in shareholders' funds and that the company might be unable to balance its money market book the next day. Samuel said TEA was insolvent and recommended that a creditors' scheme be proposed. Acting on this advice, the board appointed receivers the next day. The job went to David Crawford and James Poulton of Peat Marwick.

TEA's last board meeting was held on 30 May. The only directors who attended were Ogilvy, Mainprize and Bunning. They accepted the formal report from Hill Samuel, which estimated that TEA had a net deficiency of $8.3 million. Ogilvy said that this agreed with his own calculations. Crawford and Poulton were appointed as provisional liquidators the following day.

The closure of Australia's oldest and one of its most respected trustee companies was performed with great secrecy. No meaningful statement was made to the shareholders or investing public about the causes. The fact that Ogilvy and Norman stood high in the Australian business establishment lent a tinge of scandal to the episode. Scraps of the truth emerged during subsequent court cases against Bunning and Jamieson (who had been his tax accountant), but the full story was not unveiled until the inspectors' report was tabled by the Victorian Attorney-General, Jim Kennan, in 1990.

Bunning was convicted in the Victorian Supreme Court in June 1987 on secret commissions charges and was sentenced to nine months jail, fined $1800 and ordered to repay bribes totalling $27 225 to the liquidators. On 4 September 1987 he pleaded guilty to four charges of falsifying TEA's accounts and was sentenced to three years jail with a minimum of six months, to be served concurrently with the earlier sentence. Jamieson was convicted with Bunning on the secret commissions charges and was sentenced to nine months jail plus $30 000 in fines. A number of other charges were laid against various parties on insider trading and falsification of documents but were either dismissed or withdrawn.

Should the board have shared some of the blame? The inspectors thought so. With some qualifications, they said that 'each of the directors in office from 1980 onwards failed to exercise adequate care, skill (consistent with his knowledge and experience) and diligence in the performance of his duties'.[24] Peterson and Mainprize carried less responsibility because they were in office for a relatively short period before the crash and had been, together with Sir Robert, the first directors to become concerned about TEA's state of affairs. Nave and Ramsden had retired at times which meant they had little influence on the financial reporting for the year ending June 1982 and subsequent periods.

After making these qualifications the inspectors said the board had had an ongoing obligation to consider, comprehensively and systematically, the extent to which it wished TEA to be involved in property, to define the limits on managerial authority, and to say what reports it needed from management. 'While the board agreed from time to time that it was necessary to set parameters for investment in property development it failed to do so and failed to discharge adequately the duties noted above', the inspectors said. 'This failure constituted a lack of an adequate degree of care, skill and diligence of the directors in the discharge of their duties.'[25]

The inspectors also criticised the board for failure to supervise the use of CIB funds, failure to monitor TEA's money market operations, and failure to give adequate consideration to the maintenance of prudent capital ratios. They felt that the directors ought reasonably to have known that the profits for 1981 and 1982 were overstated. On property, the inspectors concluded:

> The board of TEA did not at any time consider in any comprehensive or systematic manner the extent to which it wished the company to be involved in property development; the risks entailed for the returns required; the scrutiny and selection of projects suitable for investment; the company's ability to negotiate and manage large-scale property investments; the limits of equity and loan participation acceptable for individual projects; the selection and suitability of joint venture partners and other associates; the conditions and terms under which loans might be made to those joint venture partners; the extent, availability and cost of the resources (financial and human) necessary; the procedures for approval of commitments and expenditure; and the managerial, fiscal and reporting controls and documentation standards which would be required.

Considering that the directors were charging $67 000 a year for their services, they might have attended to a few of these details.

Nor did the auditors escape a blast. The inspectors said that Arthur Young & Co had made inadequate inquiries and obtained insufficient information (both externally and from their own previous audit records) to establish the true character and financial significance of the transactions of 18 June 1982.

Bunning received the most criticism in the report. The inspectors said that, when examined, his answers to many questions were perceived to be either false or intended to mislead. They criticised him on several grounds, including those upon which he was convicted. The inspectors' opinion was that Ogilvy had failed to exercise adequate care, skill and diligence in not informing other board members of material matters, particularly relating to the audit subcommittee's information on the sources of the 1982 profit. The same criticism was levelled at Harty.

After TEA's collapse all the trustee business was taken over by the ANZ Banking Group. These funds, administered on behalf of 'widows and orphans', had never been put at risk. However, those widows and orphans who had been induced to deposit money at call with TEA were at risk because they now became unsecured creditors. As such, they eventually recovered 94 cents in the dollar, which is a very good return by liquidation standards. But shareholders—whose last audited accounts had shown their net tangible asset backing to be $7.79 a share—were wiped out, as usual.

I have a personal bias. Where a company's operations plainly involve a degree of risk—as is inherent in mining, for example—then investors should be aware they stand a chance of losing and perhaps even of losing everything. Investors should not be exposed to the same risks in a company that projects an image of a high degree of security, as in a bank or a trustee company. Admittedly, the widows and orphans whose funds were administered by TEA were never at risk unless they were induced to put money on deposit with the company. Nevertheless, investors were taking a higher degree of risk than the century-old facade of the company indicated. Its affairs were run with a degree of recklessness never reflected in the accounts.

The law under which companies are run was in a state of change during the period covered by this chapter. However, it always included a provision that directors should act honestly and diligently in the discharge of their duties. On the balance of probabilities (as opposed to the degree of certainty necessary to sustain a charge under the Companies Code), it is doubtful whether all the directors of TEA can be said to have acted with sufficient diligence over the final two years of TEA's life. They gave too much latitude to the chief executive and made little effort to ensure that they were properly acquainted with the facts.

On the court's assessment, Bunning's personal profits from his dealings were relatively small. They would not have paid the interest on some of the defalcations we shall see in later chapters. Bunning's prime motivation appears to have been to enhance the performance of TEA (and thus his own status). But it must have become apparent to him by early 1983 that the end of the game was in sight, because there was a large and growing gap between the reported state of TEA's affairs and reality. Bunning's conviction made him the only businessman of any substance to go to jail in the 1980s for a company offence. This always looked an undeservedly lonely distinction.

3

The birth of WA Inc

He had a vision of turning Western Australia into some sort of Camelot where people would share and get on well together.

Bob Maumill on Brian Burke

In the classic television series *Upstairs, Downstairs*, the family lawyer once observed: 'Most of the harm in this world is caused by people who are trying to do more good than they can achieve'. Well, Brian Burke tried to do more good than he could achieve. Burke came from a deeply Catholic and Labor family. His grandfather Peter was a staunch Labor man on the Ballarat goldfields and his father Tom was Federal MHR for Perth. Tom's maiden speech was about the declining birthrate. When Brian became a Western Australian parliamentarian his maiden speech was a eulogy of his father. Tom Burke at one point had challenged Dr Evatt for leadership of the Labor Party, but his career was destroyed by Labor's left-wing czar, Frank ('Joe') Chamberlain. Brian never forgave the Left and he showed great organising ability while still a student to help the Right regain control of the WA party: a story well told in John Hamilton's biography, *Burkie*.[1] In pursuit of his political career Burke made several personal sacrifices, giving up food (he had been noticeably fat as a reporter) and cutting back on booze after a drunken driving charge.

And he genuinely cared. Radio broadcaster Bob Maumill, who knew the future Premier during Burke's larrikin days as a reporter, recalled:

> He could preach to people about love and caring. There was an earnestness about him, but he could put people at ease. He had a vision, you know, of turning Western Australia into some sort of Camelot where people would share and get on well together. A sort of Camelot with him as King Arthur.

Burke's Camelot was at heart a clannish place. Later dubbed 'WA Inc', it centred on a handful of Catholic and ALP mates, many of long standing. But although the term WA Inc was coined in the 1980s, the concept goes back to the dawn of governments. As long as there have been governments, there have been businessmen seeking to profit by providing goods or services to them at high margins. One of the chief duties of a government is to ensure that such goods and services are fairly priced.

As Western Australia is one of the most geographically isolated regions in the world, the government was bound to be thrown into a symbiotic relationship with much of its business community. Nor was the relationship without justification. A government's primary duty is to care for its citizens. By employing local suppliers and contractors, a government keeps wealth circulating within its own community. In the course of providing jobs and wealth, the government naturally hopes also to win the affection of its prospering voters. Pork-barrelling can be a benign community process as long as the government is not being overcharged and its favours are distributed equally among competent contractors.

At the core of the scandals that were to surround WA Inc was the implication that the government had been unduly enriching a chosen few within the business community. It was also questionable just how far the government's largesse was passed on by those few to the community at large.

Historically, state governments have also felt the need at times to prop some tottering local business that would otherwise fail. This too can be justified where the government support is small or short-term or where the benefits in terms of jobs saved and wealth created more than offset the costs. In practice, however, state governments have rarely indulged in even a primitive cost-benefit study before conferring such support. Too often support has been granted reflexively and to those businessmen who have the ear of the government, rather than according to any set of impartial criteria.

The career of Robert Holmes à Court, for example, might well have perished in its infancy when he bought control of Western Australian Woollen and Worsted, had an anxious Liberal Government not decided to throw its support behind his major asset, the uneconomic Albany Woollen Mills. The Albany works was the largest employer in that electorate, so political as well as economic considerations prompted the Minister for Industrial Development, Sir Charles Court, to aid the enterprise. This was the starting point for a lifetime friendship between Sir Charles and Holmes à Court.

The bail-out of Alan Bond was less justifiable. In 1975 Sir Charles, as the Liberal Premier, solved one of Bond's most serious problems: the Santa Maria deal. Santa Maria was a block of land on the northern outskirts of Perth which Bond had been trying to have rezoned from rural to urban for years, despite the insistence of the Metropolitan Regional Planning Authority that it should remain open space under the authority's corridor growth plan. The previous WA Labor Government had planned, in conjunction with Gough Whitlam's Federal Labor Government, to build a satellite city named Salvado in the northern growth corridor. The relevant Federal body was Tom Uren's Department of Urban Development (DURD), which allocated $13 million to Western Australia to buy land for urban development. Court took the Federal money and bought Santa Maria for $4.6 million, of which Bond got half and his joint venture partner, Hanover Holdings, got the rest. The deal did not give Bond the bonanza he wanted but it got him and his financier, IAC Holdings, off the hook. Court said that his Urban Land Council planned to use the space as a green area to preserve underground water supplies. As one of Court's critics at the time said, this amounted to buying—for open space—land that was already open space.[2]

Sir Charles said that Bond was angry with him at the time, but the anger appears to have dissipated quickly. Bond donated $20 000 to the Liberals' 1977 election campaign. In turn, Sir Charles put together a syndicate to raise $250 000 when Bond's challenge for the America's Cup was almost bankrupted that year. Court also leaned on the managing directors of Bond's major financiers, warning them that any institution that wanted to do business in Western Australia in future had better not be known as the one that put Bond under.[3]

The creation of WA Inc by Labor leader Burke was therefore not without Liberal precedents. However, Burke's concept appears to have been for something more systematic than the eclectic pork-barrelling and occasional bail-outs that had preceded the 1980s.

A rough parallel can be drawn between Brian Burke and Gough Whitlam's Minister for Energy and Minerals, Rex ('The Strangler') Connor. Burke seems to have been fascinated by the alleged glamour of big business, and particularly the glamour of company promoters and raiders who were allegedly making fortunes by the day. This was the era when the old business establishment of Perth was about to be engulfed by a new wave of brash young wheelers and dealers who were beginning to rise in Western Australia. One was the tall, urbane Robert Holmes à Court, who operated very much by himself. His antithesis was the loud young property lair Alan Bond, who was at the centre of a very loose fraternity comprising the rest of the new breed.

At the same time Burke was suspicious about what he perceived as the business establishment of Perth. Ross Louthean, head of the Resource Information Unit, says: 'Burke gave the impression he would have loved to tweak the tails of the establishment by showing them that the up-and-comers of the day were better at doing deals'. This is the syndrome that led Connor to Tirath Khemlani and enmeshed the Federal Labor Party of 1975 in the Loans Affair. The same syndrome seems to have led Burke to Laurie Connell. If so, it was a manifestation of paranoia. The grey suits in the Central Business District may always vote Liberal but they will always do a business deal with the government of the day, whatever its complexion. In the classic phrase (unfortunately from Bernie Cornfeld of the notorious Investors Overseas Services): 'They may be schmucks, but they're the government'.

The economic background also helps to understand Western Australia in the early 1980s. Two decades of Liberal rule had roughly coincided with two decades of triumphant development of major mineral projects, notably the great Pilbara iron ore mines and the emerging North West Shelf. From being a backwater state, Western Australia had become internationally bankable. But when Burke came to power in February 1983 the state was suffering—along with the rest of Australia—from a short but severe recession. It is now forgotten that one of his first acts in office was an enforced slash in public service salaries—an act which wounded the compassionate Burke and compelled him to cast about for solutions.

The idea of a partnership with the business sector was not new. Three years before Burke's election one of his lieutenants, Julian Grill, had approached Harold Abbott, general manager of Kia Ora Gold and Phoenix Oil & Gas, and asked him how the Labor Party could 'get alongside' businessmen. Abbott prepared a report of some 100 pages for Grill, which he took back to Burke.

But the Godfather of WA Inc was a large, overweight fringe businessman whose brilliant intellect and promising career had been undermined by his addiction to alcohol and racehorses. This was Jack Walsh, whose father Joe had been a close friend of Tom Burke and a fellow Catholic. Joe Walsh founded Walsh's menswear stores in Perth. Jack Walsh and Brian Burke had known each other since childhood.

When young, Jack was a champion swimmer (something hard to imagine in his later life, when booze and good living had plumped him out to 160 kilograms or more). After a brilliant scholastic career at Melbourne University, he did an apprenticeship in retailing at Harrods and Macys before returning to become managing director of the family business. In 1964 he left the post in favour of his brother Maurice. From contemporaries one gets the impression that Jack may have been a better businessman than his brother, but was sacked because he had been running up heavy gambling debts. From Walsh's Jack went to General Development Agency (GDA), a real estate business run by Don O'Sullivan, the scion of another wealthy family of Perth Catholics.

GDA was the biggest residential real estate agency in the state, developing whole subdivisions at Mandurah, Whitfords Beach and Forrestfield. O'Sullivan held the equity but left the management largely to Walsh, who rose to the post of managing director. GDA expanded into bigger property deals, not all of them successful.

As a businessman, Jack Walsh seems to have had strengths and weaknesses. Mining promoter Peter Briggs, who knew him well, said: 'Jack was a terrific guy. He was smart. He had a very good mind and understood business'. Walsh would get up at 4 a.m. to go into the office, but at lunchtime would head for a pub and the working day would be over. He was also a heavy gambler. 'Jack Walsh was the biggest punter in Western Australia', Bob Maumill told the Royal Commission that later inquired into WA Inc. 'He had everyone terrified. I think he broke half a dozen bookmakers.' But in the long run the bookies always beat the punters and Walsh was no exception.

O'Sullivan and Walsh set up the WA Bloodstock Agency—acquiring the Tibradden training complex on the Great Eastern Highway and dealing in thoroughbreds. Naturally—given the compact nature of Perth society—Walsh was well acquainted with another big racehorse owner and punter, Laurie Connell.

By mid-1982 GDA had built up a 43 per cent stake in Hawkestone Investments, thereby also controlling its associate, Abrolhos Oil and Investments. O'Sullivan became managing director of Hawkestone and Walsh joined the board. This led to a loose but interesting grouping. The chairman of both Hawkestone and Abrolhos was Perth's former Lord Mayor, Sir Ernest Lee-Steere. Sir Ernest was chairman of the WA Turf Club and a friend of Walsh. Sir Ernest was also chairman of a company called Phoenix Oil & Gas, which was controlled by Peter Briggs who had installed Harold Abbott as managing director. Walsh's office around this time was close to Briggs's on the 15th floor of Elder House.

During his formative years as a merchant banker at Martin Corporation, Laurie Connell had been a protégé of Abbott. In the intimate world of Perth finance, Walsh and Connell had more than one connection. Walsh began spending an increasing amount of time working for Connell. This was prompted by two factors: Connell wanted to strengthen his Labor links; and secondly GDA, having over-extended in property and investments, was beginning to strike financial trouble. Walsh's personal affairs must have begun going downhill by this time and he would eventually die with few assets. But this was not apparent to those who met him. Walsh made no secret of his good political contacts. He made a habit of cultivating journalists, particularly young ones, in the bar of the Palace Hotel. In those days the Palace, on St Georges Terrace, was the great drinking haunt of West Australian Newspapers and Walsh could be found in the bar from 11 a.m. He bought rounds generously, exuded an air of authority and gave many a cadet tips on political and business stories. As a friend of Burke and his family, and a middleman in the business–journalistic–political milieu, there seems little doubt Walsh guided Burke to Connell.[4]

Another mutual contact was radio broadcaster Bob Maumill. As we have noted, Perth society was fairly small by eastern standards. Much of the subsequent WA Inc Royal Commission centred on the alleged impropriety of dealings between various people who all knew each other fairly well. In Perth of the early 1980s you could meet nearly half the movers and shakers in the city during a leisurely lunchtime stroll along St Georges Terrace. The Perth racing scene was correspondingly intimate and Walsh, Connell and Maumill were three of its more prominent members.

Maumill ran a bloodstock business while leading an itinerant career as a radio broadcaster, mainly in Perth but interspersed with stints in Sydney and Melbourne. Maumill was an uninhibited character with the disconcerting habit of saying exactly what he thought, which won him a reputation—and some following—as a wild man of radio. In 1975 Maumill's name was linked with Connell's in the Kalgoorlie Sting. The scandal hardly dented the irrepressible Maumill, whose evidence was a breath of fresh air in the turgid hearings of the Royal Commission. A few samples:

- 'I must have bought over the years a hundred horses from Laurie, all his slow ones.'
- 'I did a lot of horse deals for Jack Walsh. He lost money on every one of them and everyone he ever dealt with in the horse business that I know of took him for a ride.'
- 'The first time [I worked for Laurie] was when he called me at the radio station and said that he and Alan Bond had put a fair amount of money into show jumping in Western Australia and the people of Western Australia were doing their absolute utmost to avoid going along to watch it.' (Maumill's solution was to invite Princess Anne to the show jumping and to a memorable party at Connell's house.)
- 'Brian Burke named 10 people he took advice from and I was flattered to see that I was one of them, but as events unfold before the commission I see the close circle of confidants was about two or three thousand at last count.'[5]

Maumill also featured in a classic piece of repartee when describing Connell's office to the Commission. 'I once met a Lord of the realm in there. On one wall he even had a picture of the Queen.' When it was pointed out that pictures of the Queen were not uncommon, Maumill replied: 'Yeah, but in this one Laurie was standing next to her'.

Maumill was close enough to Burke to talk him into going partners in a horse named My Fair Share, with the aim of educating Burke in the racing business. Also, Maumill's daughter worked as Burke's electorate secretary. As Leader of the WA Opposition in 1983, Burke knew he had an excellent chance of winning office from the tottering Liberal administration. He needed funds and he wanted to start forging an alliance with business. But not with Perth's old business brigade, who were Liberals to a man. Perhaps Burke's greatest flaw was that his mind stayed grooved in class distrust of the WASPs who ran the main Perth companies. Burke saw the rising entrepreneurs as more flexible in their political alliances and brighter than the old guard. On Walsh's advice, Burke rang Connell and asked for a donation.

The telephone call was a great misjudgement that Burke would live to regret. Burke should have known better at the time. To understand why, we need to retrace Connell's history to that point.

'All I ever wanted to do was go out and earn a dollar', Laurie Connell once told a reporter. Connell was always proud of his humble beginnings. Born the son of a bus driver from the Perth suburb of Tuart Hill, Connell left school at the age of fifteen to start as a lunch boy at the WA Department of Industrial Relations. He was always a natural sportsman. He made his first dollar as a golf caddy while at school. In his youth he is reported to have been an occasional tent fighter. Looking at his stocky build and cheerfully rugged grin, one could well believe it. He looked like a man who could either take punishment or hand it out. Later he became an A Grade hockey player. He always carried the air of pugnacious self-confidence of a man who had proved himself physically. He worked his way up to the financial section of the department, studied accountancy at night school, qualified, then in 1968 went to Sydney to work for the newly formed investment bank, Martin Corporation.

When it was founded in 1966, Martin Corporation was an exciting new venture. In the days before merchant banks multiplied to the point of absurdity in Australia, Martin Corporation acted as a magnet to rising young financiers. It promised to be run along more adventurous lines than its counterparts and at the same time boasted respectable parentage. The team of bright young men who assembled at Martin Corporation included several who would later become famous or notorious in their own right. The managing director was Harold Abbott, who went on to take over a group of mining and investment companies from the highly adventurous Ian Murray ('The Sunshine Kid'), and then on again to become a protégé of Peter Briggs in Phoenix Oil & Gas. Another staffer was Peter Joseph, later to be on the boards of Australian National Industries and Dominion Mining. Yet another was Brian Yuill, whose Spedley Securities will feature in a later chapter.

In its first four years, Martin Corporation reported two small losses followed by two modest profits. But in 1970–71 its capital was wiped out when it incurred huge losses after the collapse of Australia's 1969 nickel boom. Martin Corporation's overseas shareholders injected new capital and purged the bank through a wave of sackings. The purge was overseen by Harry Beardsmore from United Dominion, who had been appointed deputy chairman of Martin Corp.

Announcing the 1971 loss, Beardsmore said that it had been partly due to a falling share market but also to some bad banking decisions. Some 50 staff were sacked following the loss. 'Those currently on our staff, I would consider, would not make those mistakes again', Beardsmore said.[6] This was over-optimistic. Two of the staff still in place were Brian Yuill and Laurie Connell. Yuill, who had been running Martin Corporation's money market book, was promoted to associate director in July 1973. Another executive appointed associate director at the same time was the divisional head of corporate finance, Peter Joseph.

Connell had moved back to Perth by the time the collapse became public. His ability at wheeling and dealing had so impressed his seniors in the bank that they had given him free rein in Western Australia. Connell had negotiated his own terms of employment with Martin Corporation in what must have been one of the first modern profit-sharing contracts in Australia. On his own estimate, he was probably making more money than anyone else in the bank.

As Martin Corporation would later become notorious as the kindergarten for financial ne'er-do-wells, it is perhaps worth making the point that neither Connell nor Yuill appear to have been responsible in any way for its early disasters, nor for any other wrongdoing there. 'Connell ran the money market desk in the Perth office and he reported to Brian Yuill', Joseph said.

> Both of them were good at figures. Connell was ambitious. He was a young tearaway in every sense, whether it was driving a car or the way he went about the money market. He was a relatively junior figure hunting deposits for Martin Corporation in Perth and he did some lending, as I recall. 'Cavalier' is the word and even then one instinctively was careful about him. His background was modest: there was no affectation about him in any way and it was that Australian 'mates' thing that made him popular. Yuill had an excellent name. He was putting together deals with BHP on steel bills, which was a big event at the time and one side of the business that was going quite well. Yuill was always on the money market side and very meticulous, very straight up and down. You felt here was a guy who had it all together and even when Laurie was being headstrong, Brian—who obviously liked him—would always control Laurie and make sure he didn't venture too far from the straight and narrow.[7]

Martin Corporation now fades from our story. It continued under its old name for another decade, then was taken over by the Canadian Imperial

Bank of Commerce and became CIBC Australia in 1984. Leaving Yuill to a later chapter, let us follow Connell, who left Martin Corporation in the mid-1970s to strike out on his own as L.R. Connell & Partners, taking with him several of his clients from Martin Corp.

The Kalgoorlie Sting

Connell's links with Bond appear to have begun when he sold some land for Bond in the 1960s, according to one report.[8] When Connell set up on his own, one of his first new clients was Alan Bond, who was just getting his act back together after almost going broke in 1974. Bond was grateful for Connell's assistance and the two would be connected in many deals in future. In 1978 Connell helped Bond in the purchase of Santos, which would turn into one of the most profitable deals in Bond's career. This forged a close personal link between the two men, whose business empires were both based in Western Australia and who shared a similar outlook on life and business. But the incident which thrust Connell most prominently into the limelight in these years had nothing to do with business. It was called the Kalgoorlie Sting.

The Kalgoorlie Sting has been described in detail elsewhere.[9] Briefly, a horse named His Worship won the Bernborough Handicap at Melbourne's Sandown course on 3 September 1975. The race broadcast was relayed to a race meeting at Kalgoorlie via station 6IX in Perth. Connell, who was at the Kalgoorlie races, backed His Worship, forcing its price down from 9/2 to 2/1 on. Connell said he bet $750 and collected $2135 from on-course bookmakers. Immediately after the race, bookmakers protested that the broadcast from 6IX had been delayed and Connell's bets had been placed after the race had finished. The allegation was that Connell could have had access to the race result through a press phone at the racecourse. The announcer on the 6IX program at the time was Connell's friend Bob Maumill.

On 5 October, after a lengthy inquiry in which evidence was taken from illegal bookmakers as well as field bookies, the West Australian Turf Club stewards disqualified Connell for two years. Two appeals by Connell were lost. The disqualification was later waived by the WATC but the episode marred Connell's reputation in racing for a long time afterwards, even though he became one of Australia's biggest stake-winning owners. To an outsider the evidence against Connell seems circumstantial. He had a very tight time frame in which to act, with only a few minutes to discover the result and place his bets. Even if the sting had been arranged in advance it would have been complicated by the fact that the race started several minutes late anyway. Further, the amount involved seems derisory compared to the effort which organising the sting would have taken. The most damaging aspect of Connell's behaviour was his refusal to testify to the steward's inquiry. A statement giving his version of events was not released until six weeks after his initial disqualification.

The Kalgoorlie Sting had by no means been erased from Perth memories when Connell launched Rothwells as a merchant bank. The catalyst was a minor entrepreneur of the day named Rodney Cake. A former journalist who had become a fringe player in Western Australian mining and finance, Cake had become aware that a cashbox on the other side of the continent was up for sale. A cashbox is just that—a company which has cash and nothing else. The cashbox in this deal was a quiet, stodgily respectable public company called Rothwells Outfitting Ltd, which ran a menswear store of the same name in Brisbane.

Rothwells had been incorporated in 1926. As an open register company, where nobody had a dominant shareholding, it had been eyed by various raiders over the years. In October 1981 Rothwells—now controlled by a group of investors led by Bill Gunn (the son of the former chairman of the Australian Wool Board, Sir William Gunn)—sold off its traditional menswear business, goodwill, plant and leases to a Papua New Guinea company. Having stripped the company of all assets except cash, the directors planned to begin a new incarnation as an investment and financial services company. At the time, the Queensland Premier, Sir Joh Bjelke-Petersen, was publicly considering removing death duties in Queensland. As the Queensland State Government Insurance Office held a 10 per cent stake in Rothwells, the possibility was that Rothwells could become a merchant bank with de facto state government backing. It was in this atmosphere that Cake began trying to negotiate a takeover in 1982.

In the negotiations Cake was using the services of Kalgoorlie solicitor Don McManus and Perth accountant Tom Hugall. But in 1982 Australia was still weathering a short, sharp recession and Cake hit the perennial problem of small entrepreneurs: he couldn't raise enough cash. Cake says Hugall arranged to set up the financing from Connell. 'I kept asking Tom and he said: "It will all be done soon" ', Cake recalls. 'Then Connell did the deal for himself and Hugall joined Connell.'[10]

Through a subsidiary named Craybell, Connell bid $1.91 a share for Rothwells. This attracted yet another predator in the shape of Christopher Skase's Qintex Ltd, but Craybell lifted its bid to $2.06 and won the day. Given the sort of competition that arose, Cake would probably have lost the prize even without Hugall's defection. Meanwhile, historians are left to toy with the fascinating hypothesis of what might have happened if Rothwells had been run by Skase instead of Connell.

Connell finished up owning 60 per cent of Rothwells for a little over $3 million. The company's tangible assets comprised $2.7 million net cash.

However, it had a couple of large intangible assets. Until this date, Connell had been operating through two main entities. The first was L.R. Connell & Partners, owned by himself and his wife Elizabeth. The other was Oakhill Pty Ltd, his family company. While Connell could trade and do deals through these entities, they had relatively little corporate status. By acquiring Rothwells, he gave himself a listed public company which he could proclaim as a merchant bank. Even better, it was eligible for trustee status.

Many organisations, including charities and government bodies, can only invest their funds with institutions that have trustee status. To become an authorised trustee in those days, a company had to have a minimum of $2 million issued capital and to have paid dividends continuously for fifteen years. Rothwells fulfilled those criteria. The fact that its old business had been sold off and that it was under completely new management and was embarking on a completely new line of business was immaterial. Rothwells would have qualified for trustee status if Ned Kelly or Saddam Hussein had just taken control. Rothwells immediately began soliciting deposits from investors.

Craybell's successful bid for Rothwells was in September 1982. In October Rothwells began business as a merchant bank with its head office in Perth and its registered office in Brisbane, which accounted for the bulk of the business until late 1984. L.R. Connell & Partners was appointed the general manager of Rothwells with full authority to implement the money market and investment policy of the company, which pretty well meant total authority. On 13 October 1982 a new board was appointed, including Sir Joh's close friend Sir Edward Lyons as chairman and Connell as deputy chairman and managing director. There were three other directors, Bill Burgess, Peter Gallagher and R.T. Whitby, the last being a remnant of the old board. Although not a director, Tom Hugall was made company secretary and attended the initial and later board meetings by invitation.

Queensland has the third largest state economy in Australia. By 1982 some 30 merchant banks had set up branches in Queensland, hoping to attract some of the rich flow of state treasury into their money market books; but to that point none had received preference. Sir Edward was a powerful political and financial figure at this stage of Sir Joh's long reign. Taking him aboard was the price Connell had to pay for Queensland Government backing. Rothwells received the first money market dealer's licence issued in Queensland in 120 years. Rothwells publicity referred to this, somewhat inaccurately, as a merchant banking licence.

The official launch of Rothwells as a merchant bank must rank as one of the most remarkable in Australia's financial history. At a lavish party at Rothwells' plush new head office, the bank was declared open by Sir

Joh. Those attending included the power elite of Queensland. Apart from Sir Edward there were the Police Commissioner, Sir Terence Lewis; the Chief Justice, Sir Walter Campbell; and the Under-Treasurer, Sir Leo Heilscher, often regarded as Australia's most powerful public servant. During the party the cream of Brisbane's sharebroking fraternity watched enthralled as a spirited argument broke out between Sir Joh, who was keen on abolishing stamp duty on share transactions, and Sir Leo, who doubted whether any net benefit would accrue to the state as a result. Sir Joh subsequently removed the duty. By association, Connell was credited with having somehow been influential in the decision, and Rothwells attracted large sums in brokers' deposits.[11]

Indeed, throughout its career Rothwells would be a favourite resting place for brokers' deposits. This was at least partly because Rothwells was also prepared to accommodate brokers with loans whenever they required short-term funding. Connell won the nickname 'Last Resort Laurie' because brokers, speculators and corporate financiers who could not raise money anywhere else (or anyhow not without a tiresome amount of time, effort and paperwork) could usually get funds from Laurie.

Rothwells had taken no deposits in 1981 and by July 1982 was holding only $443 000. In 1983 deposits soared to $50 million at balance date, all short term and $46.4 million of it secured. How did Rothwells achieve this remarkable rise?

The answer is that it offered some of the highest interest rates around. It also offered high commissions to investment advisors, who in the early 1980s controlled a great deal of small investor money. There was always a temptation for these investors to put their clients' money with which-ever financier was offering the highest commissions. They may well have been encouraged to think it was sound by Rothwells' apparent imprimatur from the Queensland (and later the WA) Government. When Rothwells collapsed five years later and the liquidation was begun by the staff of Ferrier Hodgson, they found that many small investors had been prompted to place their cash with Rothwells at the suggestion of brokers and advisors. Small Queensland investors were the launching pad for Connell in Rothwells and when the bank went broke they were still the largest single class of investor.

Another factor was that the Queensland Totalizator Administration Board—of which Sir Edward was also chairman—began making deposits with Rothwells. Despite reports to the contrary, the Queensland TAB appears to have placed only a few million at a time with Rothwells, and always fully secured. Also, the deposits did not begin until late in 1983.[12]

In hindsight, it was all very simple. Connell had taken over a midget financial institution. By getting Sir Joh to his launch and Sir Edward on his board, he was able to project an image of government backing. He then offered top interest rates to depositors, and top commissions to advisors to encourage them to direct their clients to him. The spectacular jump in deposits would enable him to promote Rothwells as a rapidly growing and highly successful merchant bank.

So when the then Western Australian Opposition Leader Brian Burke made his first phone call to Connell in early 1983, Connell was looking like the latest boom colt from the west. He had just managed the takeover of Rothwells. He had a reputation as a man who could do a deal. And if he could work closely with Sir Joh Bjelke-Petersen perhaps he could work closely with Brian Burke, although their politics were poles apart.

The phone call was the first contact ever between Connell and Burke.[13] Until then Connell's sympathies, as an unabashed capitalist, had been with the Liberal Party. His father-in-law had been a longstanding Liberal politician. Connell knew the incumbent Liberal Premier, Ray O'Connor, and was supporting him in the campaign. Just before election day, Burke rang Connell at his beach house and asked for a donation. Connell was surprised by the call, having never met Burke and having no idea how the Opposition Leader had come by his beach house telephone number. Connell later testified to the WA Inc Royal Commission:

> The thrust of it was that he had been endeavouring to get to know and meet people in business and that people in business shouldn't be afraid of his election to office. It was his intention that he'd create a healthy environment for business and that it was really in the interests of people in business to see him come to office rather than the other point of view. He made a strong case out as to why he would win office and that there should be a close relationship between business and his new government.

Connell immediately donated \$25 000 to the Labor campaign, having earlier given a like amount to the Liberal Party's. It must have seemed a reasonable price to any businessman to win the ear of a potential Premier who was promising to develop close links with business. And as soon as Burke won the 1983 election the ever-opportunistic Connell decided it was time to develop the contact. Connell was helped by his old mate Bob Maumill, whose relations with Burke ran hot and cold. They were warm enough a day or two after the election, when Maumill arranged a meeting between Connell and the new Premier at the home of Burke's brother Terry.

There is an interesting difference in emphasis between Maumill's and Connell's account of the way the meeting was set up. According to Connell the invitation was at short notice, and inconvenient to him, but he attended anyway. According to Maumill, Connell came to 6PR and asked him to arrange the meeting. Maumill told the Royal Commission:

> He said the town had been to sleep for too long, that there was a chance

to bring it alive, that if Brian Burke had the willingness to take on board the views of the new business community, then he believed it would be in the best interests of the state. He was anxious to meet him because he wanted to do business.

Maumill rang Burke and gave him a brief character reading of Connell:

> I told him he was bad-tempered. I told him that from what I knew of it, from working in his office, he was the biggest commercial game in town. I said there was a succession of lawyers, politicians, stockbrokers, everyone in town that wanted to do business, made their way to Laurie Connell's office. I said 'There's more traffic through his office than St Georges Terrace', and Burke responded that he needed a conduit to the business community.

Maumill told Burke that he thought Connell could be the conduit, so Burke agreed to meet him 'on neutral ground'.

Asked at the inquiry if Connell's reaction might have been that it was inconvenient and he would have liked to postpone the meeting for a few weeks, Maumill replied: 'It would have taken something of absolutely monumental proportions—like an earthquake—to keep him away'.

Terry Burke's home at the outer northern suburb of Churchlands was the venue chosen for a small party. Apart from Burke and Connell (who didn't know where Churchlands was until then), those present were Jack Walsh, Terry Burke and his wife Lucy, Michael Naylor (a senior member of Burke's staff and later executive director of Goldcorp) and Burke's press secretary Ron Barry.

Maumill said that Connell was quite excited about the meeting. He added:

> After everyone had shaken hands and met, Brian Burke assumed the statesmanlike pose that he was so good at when he reclined in a chair in Terry Burke's lounge room and said: 'Laurie, let's lay the ground rules. Anything we talk about has got to be in the best interests of the people of the state'.

That was all the history Maumill got to see, because he was then asked to leave the meeting. But he was so struck by Burke's remark that he wrote it down on a parking ticket (any reporter will sympathise with the extemporisation) and later used it in a radio broadcast.

After the meeting, Connell told Maumill he liked Burke's style. Burke told Maumill he thought Connell a real dynamo who would have to be kept under control. 'He wanted to travel at a million miles an hour. I think he wanted to get everything done the next day. Laurie was impatient and headstrong. Brian Burke recognised that early in their relationship, even from that first meeting', Maumill said.

Burke was the sort of young, warm, moderate politician that Labor voters—and particularly journalists—adore. He had been anti-Vietnam, he was against the business establishment and he wanted to do good for the people of Western Australia. He genuinely wanted to work together with the business community for the good of the state. However, his judgement of people was mediocre. The coterie of mates who had been with him from the early days and taken him to power were given important jobs in the new government, but not all of them were good administrators. Picking Connell as his conduit to the business community was his worst mistake. Connell had the drive to muster financial support for Burke—a task made considerably easier when the carrot of government rewards could be dangled before them. But Connell had also been involved in enough scandals to make a warier politician pause. As mentioned earlier, the Kalgoorlie Sting had been a sensational affair and had certainly not been erased from Perth memories by the time Burke made his phone call to Connell. And there had been a more recent scandal.

On 13 January 1983 Connell had a horse named Saratoga Express running in the AHA Cup at Bunbury. Before the race the main danger seemed the favourite, Strike Softly, ridden by Danny Hobby. On the day of the race Saratoga Express was backed from 6/4 against to 7/4 on. Then, soon after the race started, Hobby jumped off Strike Softly. Even with its main opposition removed, Saratoga Express still could not win, running second to the 6/1 chance Rowella. It looked like an attempt to fix the race. The stewards held an inquiry and five days later disqualified Hobby for two years. The stewards added, ominously, that they were continuing their inquiries. The AHA Cup was run only four weeks before Burke made his first phone call to Connell.

The ultimate blame for the relationship must rest with Burke because, in fairness to Connell, it must be said that at no time did he make any secret of the fact that he was after money. It was Brian Burke himself who coined the phrase 'I'd hate to stand between Laurie and a bag of money'. Burke even seemed to recognise his mistake. Maumill testified that when he won office Burke did not like what he knew about Connell, but he was still prepared to listen to him. Connell's support for the Labor Party looked smart after Burke had won and even smarter in March, when Bob Hawke won a historic election that swept the Labor Party back into Federal power.

Mates and associates

Not only was the Australian Labor Party buoyant, so was Perth. On 26 September Alan Bond won the America's Cup with *Australia II*. He was the first foreigner to wrest the Auld Mug away from the New York Yacht

Club. Perth, watching the historic race on television sets in the middle of the night, went berserk. Prime Minister Hawke, half-intoxicated with joy, declared that any employer who did not give his staff the day off was 'a bum'. Hawke's Treasurer, Paul Keating, was at the Newport dock celebrating with Bond, Rupert Murdoch and what seemed like a million delirious well-wishers. The Cup came to Perth amid a boisterous round of celebrations. At one of the parties Bond derided a table of WA Liberals, saying they had always helped overseas investors in the state but not the local entrepreneurs. Under Labor, Bond claimed, entrepreneurs such as himself would be given the mandate for any new projects. Then overseas capital would be invited to finance the projects and the local entrepreneurs would wind up with a free ride. The Liberals laughed, but the formula Bond enunciated was almost exactly what would happen.

Burke was closer to Connell, his main conduit to the business community, than he was to Bond. Indeed, Connell's contact with Burke started a stampede by nouveau riche businessmen to change their political allegiance. Dallas Dempster, Tony Oates and Alan Bond had previously been identified more with the Liberal Party. Burke also had contact with Holmes à Court (who showed a canny ability to play both sides of the political fence), John Horgan, Connell's friend John Roberts and—when in Australia—Lord Alistair McAlpine.

Having gained power, Burke appointed several old mates to key positions in the WA Government's financial structure. Len Brush had been the 26-year-old president of the Northcote branch of the ALP in 1970 and his wife Brenda was branch secretary.[14] They moved to Perth in 1971, where Brenda eventually became Burke's electorate secretary. After Burke became Premier, Len joined his policy secretariat in 1983 and was executive chairman of the Superannuation Board from 1984 until it became the Government Employees Superannuation Board (GESB) in 1987. Brenda was Premier Burke's secretary and ministerial officer. From 1982 to 1984 the executive director of the Superannuation Board had been Richard Yorg. Then Yorg was shunted to one side by Burke, ostensibly because of a joint venture deal done by the board with Kevin Parry at a property called Hall's Head. The deal had been channelled through a shelf trust to overcome a prohibition on the board investing in property. The deal had also been structured so as to give tax advantages to Parry. On the grounds that he was outraged by these manoeuvres, Burke shifted Yorg out of the board and appointed Brush as full-time chairman. Brush would later do an almost identical deal with Parry—with Burke's approval as Treasurer. However, by then the joint venture had donated $150 000 to the ALP.

Brush's suitability for the job of chairman was not evident to everyone. Denis O'Hara of Price Waterhouse noted:

Our prior experience with Len is that when briefed he tends to jump to conclusions and head off in tangents . . . We must be aware that Brush has direct access to the Premier and is prone to jump to conclusions with only half facts. The potential problem is that Brush may misrepresent the situation in his dealings with the Premier, by only having half the facts and a warped view of those facts.

These observations were later confirmed by the WA Inc Royal Commission, which found that Brush should never have been placed in a position of trust. 'He has been discredited and we have found that his evidence on any material matter should not be accepted unless corroborated by cogent evidence.'[15] Brush was charged with receiving a bribe from a property developer when the Superannuation Board invested in the Fremantle Anchorage development. Brush was found not guilty.

Tony Lloyd and Kevin Edwards were university students with Burke. They helped him organise anti-Vietnam demonstrations and the push against Frank Chamberlain. At one early stage they even ran a trotting form guide together. Lloyd was to become director of the policy secretariat in the Premier's Department. He was Assistant Under-Treasurer from 1984 to 1987 and in 1987 he was chairman of the GESB. Edwards was the most powerful of Burke's advisors, possessing considerable negotiating ability. A veteran of trade union infighting, he was labelled a member of the Broad Left. One of his achievements was to bring the WA Teachers Union into the Trades and Labor Council. It was Edwards who soothed the teachers after the new Premier had to cut their salaries by 10 per cent. Edwards was appointed executive director (policy) of the Department of the Premier and Cabinet. In 1986 he became deputy chairman of the State Government Insurance Commission (SGIC) and in 1988 served as a board member of the GESB. Edwards wielded substantial power under Burke, sometimes being described by public servants as the de facto Premier. A nuggety figure with a greying moustache and sunken eyes, he was described by one businessman as 'having a mind like a steel trap'.

These appointments of party members and old mates were significant in the light of Burke's 'whole of government' attitude to the role of statutory instrumentalities such as the GESB and the SGIC. Edwards and Burke regarded them as arms of government which existed to fulfil the government's policy aims and objectives. In the final analysis the 'whole of government' concept would mean to Burke that, if he wanted to rescue Rothwells, it was justifiable to use SGIC or GESB funds to do so, regardless of whether it was a financially prudent use of the money. The concept also disregarded the rights and interests of the policyholders and superannuants who had their money invested with those instrumentalities.

The first of the 'WA Inc' deals was unveiled on 10 October 1983, a bare fortnight after *Australia II* crossed the line at Newport. The WA

Government bought a 5 per cent interest in the Argyle diamond mine in the Kimberley from a Bond Corporation subsidiary, Endeavour Resources, for $42 million.

The previous Liberal administration had insisted that the Argyle joint venturers should build a town at the mine, which would then have cost some $70 million to $100 million. In 1983 the joint venturers—CRA, Ashton and Northern Mining—were jibbing at the requirement and asking to be relieved of it. Endeavour had just acquired Northern Mining, which held 5 per cent of the project. Endeavour had financed much of its purchase with debt (Bond had a habit of gearing up his mining companies as heavily as he did industrial companies) and could not meet the interest payments. Bond Corporation, as frequently happened, was strapped for cash after an expansionary phase. Alan Bond also began to realise that he had paid too much for Northern Mining. Bond Corp's managing director, Peter Beckwith, discussed the cash shortage with Connell just before Bond's balance date in 1983. Connell suggested selling Northern Mining to the WA Government. In its final form, the deal involved the government taking $50 million from the joint venturers in return for releasing them from their commitment to build a town.

Simultaneously, the government bought Northern Mining for $42 million, from which Connell took a $5 million fee.[16] Connell sold the deal to the government on the basis that they would get Northern Mining for nothing. When Connell put the deal to Burke, the Premier's first question was 'What's in it for you?'. Connell said he would get a fee from Bond, but did not reveal how much. The joint venturers agreed only grudgingly. They had spent $100 million on exploration and preliminary work and one government official had boasted 'we had them over a barrel'. Progress on the mine had been suspended for several months while the negotiations continued. The mining industry was upset by the government's tactics and even more concerned by statements from Burke that he was keen for the government to take equity positions in mines, particularly gold.

The Northern Mining purchase was valued for the government by L.R. Connell & Partners and Price Waterhouse. The valuations may have been independent but they were difficult to perceive as such, because of Connell's close association with Bond and the fact that Price Waterhouse was Bond Corporation's auditor. Price Waterhouse had already audited the Bond Corporation accounts in which Northern Mining was valued at $42 million. Having not qualified those accounts, Price Waterhouse could hardly say a few months later that $42 million was an excessive value.

Bond Corporation, through its subsidiary Endeavour Resources, had paid $52 million for Northern Mining in 1981 and at first tried to sell it to the government for $50 million. Burke cut the price back to $42 million, and after Connell's fee the price received by Endeavour was only $37 million. In other words, Endeavour was taking a $17 million loss on an investment it had held for only two years. The WA Inc Royal Commission later commissioned a report by Resource Finance Corporation which calculated that Endeavour had paid $20 million to $25 million more for Northern Mining than its realisable value. This was not an isolated occurrence in the Bond empire. Bond's buying enthusiasm often carried him away. Getting rid of such overpriced purchases generated some of Bond's most questionable deals.

Even though Bond was taking a loss on Northern Mining, the price paid by the government was widely criticised as too high. One who had trouble with the valuation was Jack Walsh, whose job was to give Burke an information memorandum justifying the price. In a letter to Martin Rowley at Bond Corporation, Walsh wrote:

> We appear to have a problem which, if we were associated with lesser mortals than our respective beloved leaders, could be of considerable concern. Specifically, L.R. Connell & Partners have recommended to the Premier of Western Australia the purchase of a specific asset from your group for $42 million cash. Our recommendation was accepted and your managing director has shaken hands with the Premier on this basis. Our advice was based on information provided to us by Bond Corporation which unfortunately has required significant amendment over recent weeks. The latest information supplied to us would not support a purchase price of $42 million and is in a form which is hard to follow. We have no doubt that the investment is in fact worth $42 million and that we will be able to demonstrate this from the new information to be supplied today.[17]

Nevertheless, enough data was supplied for Burke to justify the deal to his taxpayers. The final justification was that the government then sold its interest to the WA Diamond Trust, which was floated publicly by Hill Samuel Securities and the AMP Society on a valuation of $65 million. The government reaped a quick $3 million profit on the deal. So at the end of the day the joint venturers were relieved of their obligation to build a town, but at the cost of some future royalties. Bond relieved his balance sheet by selling Northern Mining. The government made a profit. The end cost was borne by subscribers to the WA Diamond Trust float. Seven years later the $1 units were trading at between 80c and 85c and had almost entirely been absorbed by the remaining joint venturers, CRA and Ashton Mining. Investors in the trust were the end victims of a string of over-optimistic valuations, some carrying the imprimatur of government.

Under questioning in parliament about the Northern Mining deal, Burke said: 'It was the government's policy that local firms with superior commercial knowledge, expertise and experience would be engaged by the state where possible. The firm of L.R. Connell & Partners fulfilled all these criteria'. Burke also said that L.R. Connell & Partners had recognised 'the entrepreneurial initiative and direction of the new government . . . and made submissions to the government in relation to business opportunities that would benefit the state'.[18]

It is worth pausing for a second to reflect on whether this deal fulfilled the goals Burke had in mind for WA Inc. His concept of WA Inc was, broadly, that the deal-making abilities of favoured businessmen should be harnessed to the advantage of the government and, accordingly, the people. The government had gained a quick $3 million on this occasion, but Bond had gained a greater benefit by unloading Northern Mining for $42 million. The Argyle area was the poorer for the lack of infrastructure. Burke saw criticism of the deal as being political and appears never to have looked more closely at the business implications.

Burke also seemed capable of closing his eyes to any unsavoury aspects of a deal. In the case of Northern Mining, the original acquisition of 33 per cent control by Endeavour had been branded by the National Companies and Securities Commission with the first 'unacceptable conduct' declaration in Australia's history. Soon after the government had bought Northern Mining, Alan Bond was convicted on two charges of having failed to disclose a substantial shareholding in Northern Mining in 1981. The shallowness of Burke's outlook would ultimately ruin his reputation.

Burke went even further the following February when he provided a testimonial to L.R. Connell & Partners. It is worth reproducing in full.

To Whom It May Concern.

I have pleasure in introducing the firm, L.R. Connell & Partners as a reputable Australian financier established in Perth.

Mr L.R. Connell and his associate Mr J.P. Walsh have acted as my financial advisors in several major assignments over the past 12 months.

In particular, L.R. Connell & Partners successfully completed one of the state's most complex and unique negotiations to vary the Diamond (Argyle Diamond Mines Joint Venture) Agreement Act resulting in substantial capital savings to the joint venturers and restructured royalty payments amounting to $50 million to the advantage of both the companies and the government. The firm was also instrumental in the state's acquisition of Northern Mining Corporation and the 5 per cent participating interest in the Argyle Diamond Project.

The firm's knowledge of and expertise in the finance industry especially in Western Australia has enabled them to bring to the marketplace finely tuned expertise based on local needs for investment and corporate finance.

In conjunction with Mr Connell's major interest in the highly successful Australian merchant bank, Rothwells Ltd, the firm is accorded good standing with the Government and the business community in Western Australia.

(Signed) Brian Burke,
Premier of Western Australia

This is an extraordinary letter to be written by the Premier of a state, to the world at large, endorsing a local businessman. It carries the clear implication that anyone wanting to do business in Western Australia would be well advised to retain L.R. Connell & Partners. A businessman reading the letter might also be forgiven for assuming Burke had assured himself that Rothwells was financially sound, when he had done no such thing.

But Connell and Walsh had done Burke a favour. In 1984 Burke, Walsh and Connell worked on the establishment of the John Curtin Foundation, set up to give the WA Labor Party a financial base. It was a last hurrah for Walsh, who died a few weeks before the foundation was opened in September 1984. The patrons were Burke and three former Labor Premiers, John Tonkin, Frank Wise and Bert Hawke (Bob's father). The vice-patrons read like a Who's Who of WA entrepreneurs, including Alan Bond, John Horgan (Metro Industries), Ric Stowe (Griffin Coal), Kevin Parry (Parry Corporation), John Roberts (Multiplex) and Sir Ernest Lee-Steere (Phoenix Oil & Gas). The only self-evident Labor man among them was Kim Beazley senior. By October the foundation had raised more than $1 million—mostly from its vice-patrons—to give the WA Labor Party unprecedented financial muscle. The Liberal Party was stunned and angered by the presence of so many prominent businessmen as Labor Party fundraisers. The question was whether those businessmen who raised funds for the Labor Party received in return undue preference from the government.

It used to be popularly said in Perth that every important deal in the state in this era went across Connell's desk. Given Connell's close association with the Premier and the financial sinews of the Labor Party, it would not be surprising. Burke's dream of harnessing entrepreneurial talent for the benefit of the people looked like being of at least equally great benefit to the chosen entrepreneurs.

Burke had also enlarged his WA Inc strategy by the formation of the WA Development Corporation (WADC). This had been specifically promised in his election campaign, which envisaged a WA Development Bank. The bank, in partnership with private enterprise, was supposed to increase the amount of risk capital available for investment in the state and also to increase the share of investment going to WA.

For chairman of the WADC Burke chose John Horgan. Yet another Catholic, Horgan came from a respected WA business family and had met Burke casually at Belmont Park races just before the 1983 election. Strolling the trackside by himself after the third race, Horgan had come upon a lonely figure sitting in the old grandstand. The businessman was uncertain at first about approaching the Leader of the Opposition, but the two men were soon in amicable conversation. Not long after the election Burke called upon Horgan to reorganise the finances of the WA Football League, which Horgan did in collaboration with a number of other businessmen. Their only reward for this task was a dinner in the Cabinet Room, after which Burke approached Horgan to become chairman of the WADC.[19] Although Horgan received nothing for his work on the WA Football League, he was better compensated for his role in the WADC and in another ill-conceived Burke venture called Exim Corporation. According to documents later tabled in the WA Parliament, Horgan's fees totalled $3.6 million for his chairmanship of WADC and Exim, including a termination fee of $750 000 when the WADC was wound up in March 1989.

Exim was in hot water from its inception when Burke had hired Keith Gale to set it up. Gale had only just been released from prison after serving four years of a thirteen-year sentence for defrauding Gollin & Co. This had been a notorious and highly publicised case. Gale's appointment appeared bizarre. Apart from anything else, the Gollin case had raised considerable doubt about Gale's financial acumen as well as his honesty. Predictably, the appointment raised a storm of outrage in Western Australia. Burke's Camelot was becoming populated by some odd knights.

But Connell was going from strength to strength. As one Perth businessman said later: 'People liked going to Laurie for money. They could go in at 9 a.m. and have their money by 9.15 with very little paperwork. The interest charge didn't matter in a bull market because they were making so much on the stock market with the money they got.'[20] Connell's fees were high too. The record may have been set in 1987 when Rothwells arranged an $11 million loan plus $4 million in lines of credit for Povey Group Holdings Ltd, the family company of yet another Western Australian entrepreneur, Mark Povey. Rothwells charged $4.5 million for the facility.

Between 1983 and 1987 Connell had frequent discussions with Burke. As Connell described them, the talks were usually wide ranging on issues such as the future of the state-owned R&I Bank, resource development, the creation of the WA Development Corporation and a host of other topics. Connell's clout with the government reached legendary proportions. When Connell's friend Dallas Dempster was part of a consortium tendering for the development of Burswood Casino, Dempster paid Connell $2 million not to compete.[21]

Over these same years Connell would become one of the most exuberant entrepreneurs of his generation, spending money lavishly on bloodstock, parties and friends. Prosperity meant that Connell was able to indulge his passion for horses. He was one of the largest racehorse owners in Australia and, for a while, one of the most successful. By the start of 1984 he owned 150 horses, most of them kept at his Bedfordale property south of Perth and the rest at his stately manor at Stow-on-the-Wold in England.

Connell was noted for his betting plunges, winning nearly $1 million when his Phizam won the 1985 Perth Cup. After the last race Connell announced that he would buy drinks until the bar closed—a generous offer considering there were still some 500 drinkers present and closing time on a racetrack is often defined as when the last person leaves. On another occasion, Connell chartered a train and took 200 friends to the Bunbury Cup. When the trainload arrived, they discovered that Connell had a marquee full of crayfish and champagne as well as Gerry and the Pacemakers for entertainment.

At the age of 30 Connell had taken up show jumping for a bet. A friend recalled that he fell off a lot because he always attempted harder jumps than he could manage. But he collected $3000 in wagers when he won an event at Perth's Royal Show. With typical energy, he was largely responsible for Western Australia's show jumping circuit becoming the richest in the southern hemisphere. His reward was to be appointed manager of the Australian equestrian team for the Los Angeles Olympics in 1984. Connell personally financed a five-month overseas tour for the team in the lead-up to the Games. He studied and filmed American courses and built replicas at his Cotswolds manor for training. The exercise is estimated to have cost him $300 000.

A hard look at early accounts

In this roseate scenario there was only one jarring problem. Rothwells was losing money and nearly broke. This fact was being hidden from the public by extensive falsification of its accounts. This would not become evident until well after Rothwells collapsed and accountants from Deloitte did an extensive re-examination of its books. Deloitte[22] established that Rothwells accounts were fraudulent for at least 1984, 1985, 1986 and 1987. Details were published in the report of the official inspector, Malcolm McCusker, QC, which refers repeatedly to sham transactions. As it would have served McCusker's investigation little purpose to trace the accounts back further, nothing was ever published on the accounts for 1983, the first issued under Connell's control.

Some unpublished investigatory work was done, however, which indicates that Connell probably began borrowing funds from Rothwells for his own private purposes almost as soon as the deposits began arriving. By July 1983 he owed Rothwells some $12 million. The bulk of this debt was erased from the books before balance date. Note 3 to the 1983 accounts merely showed that $3.1 million of the commercial bills were from a director. The unidentified director was Connell. This was the residue left after a shuffle whose mechanics are unknown but were probably similar to those in later years. The brief, bare Rothwells accounts for 1983 hinted at none of this. All they showed was the huge increase in deposits from $443 000 to $50 million, accompanied by a jump in profit from $200 000 to $770 000.

From the start Connell ran Rothwells as though it were his personal bank. Transactions by his partnership L.R. Connell & Partners tended to be processed through the same channels and by the same staff as transactions by Rothwells. Several of the prime accounting documents of Rothwells were interchangeable with those of LRC&P. A single accounting document might produce an entry into either the manual or the computer book and the staff simply ticked at the top of the sheet to indicate whether it was a Rothwells or an LRC&P entry. Mentally, Connell appears to have had trouble distinguishing between his personal finances and those of the public company in which he held an office of stewardship on behalf of others. To give Connell the benefit of the doubt, the way the entities were confused was probably due to sloppiness rather than a deliberate intent to deceive, but it contributed to the eventual massive deception of the public.

Whatever the intention, the net effect at the end of each year was that Rothwells had been funding Connell's private affairs. The confusion was never great enough to produce the opposite result. Each year the cross-funding had to be unravelled at balance date, but each year the tangled skein that had to be unravelled was greater.

In the year to July 1984 Rothwells showed deposits soaring from $50 million to $97 million. The so-called bank declared a jump in net profit from $770 000 to $2.2 million. Pre-tax profit was stated as $3.1 million. It would take six years and extensive reconstruction of its books before Deloitte could estimate that Rothwells' actual result for the year was a loss of $4 575 000.

Deloitte's main investigations were into the results declared for 1985, 1986 and 1987, but their researches also reached back to 1984. Unfortunately there are some gaps in their report, as reproduced by McCusker, of the 1984 Rothwells result. Nevertheless, it is worth trying to comprehend what happened to the Rothwells accounts in 1984, because it set the pattern for what happened on a greater scale in later years.

The core problem was that Rothwells was acting as Connell's private bank. Connell was siphoning off huge sums which he was unable to repay. McCusker's report in 1990 said:

Numerous aspects of the affairs of Rothwells require investigation, but none more so than that thrown up by the following irrefutable facts: In the course of each of the years 1985, 1986 and 1987 Mr Laurie Connell, the former chairman of Rothwells, through either L.R. Connell & Partners or Oakhill borrowed huge sums from Rothwells. No hint of these borrowings appeared in the published annual accounts, or in the annual report of Rothwells, for any of those years. At year's end, Connell's indebtedness to Rothwells was removed from the books of Rothwells by journal entries based on transactions which were either totally or substantially fictitious.[23]

To understand what happened, let's start with Table 3.1, which shows Rothwells' abbreviated balance sheet for 1984.

The picture looked simple. Enhanced by its trustee status, Rothwells had attracted $97 million in deposits from the public. This had mainly been invested in $18 million worth of bank NCDs and $69 million in commercial bills. This was misleading. There was nothing to indicate that loans to the managing director were equivalent to half the bill portfolio. Just before balance date Connell and his companies had owed Rothwells $34 million. Table 3.2 summarises how those debts—and, importantly, other amounts owing—were removed from Rothwells' books at balance date of 31 July in 1984.[24]

Thanks to a series of transactions on the eve of Rothwells balance date, all debts of L.R. Connell & Partners were wiped out and Rothwells was left owing some $87 000 to Connell. This feat was accomplished by financial legerdemain. Hardly any of the transactions could have been

Table 3.1 Rothwells' balance sheet, 31 July 1984

	($000)	($000)
Current Assets:		
Negotiable certificates of deposit	18 236	
Commercial bills	69 054	
Deposits at call	12 723	
Commonwealth bonds	420	
Other	3 392	
Total Current Assets		103 805
Investments (shares and trust units)		4 541
Other Assets		196
Total Assets		108 542
Current Liabilities:		
Deposits	97 571	
Other	2 528	
		100 099
Deferred Tax Provision		673
		100 772
Shareholders' Funds:		
Share capital	2 560	
Reserves	5 210	
		7 770
Total Funds Employed		108 542

countenanced by any company which was concerned for the interests of its public shareholders. To understand what happened we need to look more closely at the three big adjustments in Table 3.2: cashbook transactions, transfers between accounts and the sale of commercial bills to Rothwells.

The two major items in the cashbook transactions were two payments by LRC&P to Rothwells of $7.9 million and $22.8 million. Both were actually financed by Rothwells itself. In the first, Rothwells made out a cheque on 26 July for $7 873 803 to Brian Yuill's merchant bank, Spedley Securities Ltd (Rothwells books showed the amount going to a Spedley subsidiary named Aldershot Pty Ltd). Spedley, in turn, made out a cheque for $7 873 803 to Rothwells to be applied against the LRC&P debt.

A device such as this, where a series of cheques for the same amount go around in a circle is called a round robin. The round robin may have been invented by Stanley Korman, who used it to great effect in his Stanhill group in the 1960s. The Rothwells/Spedley (Aldershot)/LRC&P round robin was a primitive one. In the hands of a maestro round robins can achieve intricate beauty. Connell's were fairly ordinary but, as we shall see, there were a lot of them. The 1984 solutions to his debt problem look as though they were cobbled together energetically and hastily at the last minute, relying heavily on mates such as Alan Bond and Brian Yuill.

The second cheque of $22.8 million was paid by round robins through six entities. Table 3.3 shows how the money flowed.

Here are half a dozen round robins, where Rothwells pays a sum to a company in the Yuill or Bond groups and the company applies the same amount (or an almost identical amount) to the reduction of LRC&P's debts to Rothwells. In a nutshell, Rothwells has financed the reduction of Connell's debts to itself.

One point worth noting in passing is how obliging the Spedley group was to Connell. Spedley was a privately owned company at this time, with the industrial group Australian National Industries as its major shareholder. However, it was the custodian of large deposits of public

Table 3.2 The disappearing act of 1984

	($000)
LRC&P debt to Rothwells at 30.7.1984	34 223
Adjusting Entries:	
1. Routine journals (net)	(235)
2. Cashbook transactions (net)	(29 207)
3. Transfers between accounts (net)	16 198
4. Corrections	75
LRC&P debt after adjustments	21 054
5. Sale of LRC&P commercial bills to Rothwells	21 141
Balance	(87)

Table 3.3   The round robins of July 1984

Rothwells pays to:	Rothwells' books $	LRC&P books $	LRC&P receives from:
Spedley	4 063 897	4 063 897	Spedley
Swan Brewing	8 000 000	8 000 000	Swan Brewing
Mid-Western TV	120 000	305 000	Mid-Western TV
Broadlands	2 000 000	2 000 000	Broadlands
Sogeri	902 298	900 000	Sogeri
Spedley	7 188 602	7 000 000	Spedley
	22 274 797	22 268 897	

money. Its depositors never had an inkling that in the 31 July transactions it had incurred debts totalling more than $18 million to Rothwells and had made loans of the same magnitude to Laurie Connell's private company. Spedley's clients never knew the details and would have been horrified if they had. The sum involved, $18 million, was equivalent to the shareholders' funds of Spedley Securities at the time.

The $22 million raised by the six round robins and the Aldershot round robin cleared all but $5 million of the $34 million LRC&P debt from Rothwells' books. Item 3 in Table 3.2 shows that another $16 million now arose, entitled 'transfers between accounts'. These transfers represented an attempt to balance the books between Rothwells' interests and Connell's. As far as Deloitte could ascertain, the adjustments fell into the following categories:

- LRC&P having repaid money to Rothwells' depositors on Rothwells' behalf.
- LRC&P having advanced funds to Rothwells' clients on Rothwells' behalf.
- Debts, previously recorded as being due to Rothwells, now taken to belong to LRC&P.
- Rothwells having made various payments on behalf of LRC&P, including repayments of LRC&P's customers' deposits.
- Other significant adjustments which were not well enough documented for Deloitte to trace.

From these transfers we can draw three conclusions: (a) Rothwells and LRC&P's business interests were intimately entwined, with each at times servicing the other's debts and customers; (b) that as the result of the transfers was a further credit of $16 million to Rothwells, Connell's total debt to Rothwells was not $34 million, as previously stated, but $50 million; (c) that the bulk of the funds depositors put into Rothwells were routinely diverted into funding the operations of LRC&P.

Connell's original $34 million debt to Rothwells had been reduced to $5 million by alleged repayments (the round robins). The recognition of the $16 million net due to Rothwells from the transfers meant the total debt had gone back up to $21 million. Table 3.2 shows that this was eliminated by 'asset sales' in which LRC&P sold $21 million worth of commercial bills to Rothwells, all on 31 July.

This was a very large purchase for Rothwells to undertake at short notice, amounting to nearly one-third of its entire (purported) bill portfolio. Any ordinary bank run with diligence and prudence would have submitted the bills to close scrutiny. There is no evidence that Rothwells did any such thing. The parts of Deloitte's examination of the 1984 records that have been made public give some detail on only $13 million of the bills. Of these:

- There was no evidence in the ledger cards to suggest that bills totalling $7 845 000 were ever repaid.
- One bill for $300 000 from a company called Harsav Pty Ltd was paid in full.
- Bills totalling $1.4 million were from Bond Corp but because of the extensive transactions between Bond Corp and the Connell group it was not possible to say whether this had been repaid or not.
- Bills totalling some $3.2 million were repurchased by LRC&P at its next balance date of 31 July 1985.

The first item is worrying enough by itself. Out of a sample of $13 million in bills, apparent bad debts totalled more than $7.8 million. But the situation may be worse than this. On the evidence of what happened in later years, it may be that some of the 'commercial bills' sold by LRC&P to Rothwells were not genuine bills. In later years, testing by Deloitte revealed that several of the bills sold by LRC&P to Rothwells at each balance date were denied by the alleged debtors. This carries the implication that the bills were fictitious debts, invented for the purpose of giving LRC&P a purported 'asset' to sell to Rothwells at balance date to get the ledgers square. Some of the $7.8 million may not have been repaid because it was never owed. The least that can be said about this transaction is that no due diligence was done by Rothwells on the bona fides of the bills they were accepting in cancellation of the LRC&P debt.

The fourth item in the above list also carries some sinister implications. Of the $13 million Deloitte tried to trace, $3.2 million was sold back to LRC&P at the following balance date of 31 July 1985. It looks as though the $3.2 million represented bad debts. Consequently, when the *next* balance date arose these would have formed part of the 'transfers between accounts' that would have to be reconciled between Rothwells and LRC&P. This implies in turn that unless some of the bad debts miraculously came good the 'transfers between accounts'—representing the amounts LRC&P owed Rothwells—were bound to snowball each year. Indeed, the size of the $16 million 'transfers between accounts' for 1984

(Table 3.2) indicates that similar transactions may have been made in 1983. This is another reason to believe that Connell's borrowings from Rothwells may have begun almost as soon as he took over.

And it goes further than that. Rothwells never made any provisions in these years for bad debts. Nor did they show any non-accrual loans (loans on which the borrowers were not paying interest). Therefore every loan on Rothwells books had to be shown as accruing interest. This increasingly fictitious interest that was never paid went to swell Rothwells' reported revenues and profits in subsequent years. It also meant that there was a large and growing fictitious asset in Rothwells' accounts.

The annual report of Rothwells for the year to 31 July 1984 also contained a strong element of fiction. The accounts stated that:

- total assets were $108 million
- net assets were $7.8 million
- pre-tax profit was $3 061 000, after crediting interest received and receivable of $13 679 000

In the light of the Deloitte findings presented in the McCusker Report, we can draw the following inferences:

- Connell had borrowed, in one form or another, some $50 million from Rothwells, or half the bank's total assets. There was no indication of this anywhere in the accounts.
- The figure of $7.8 million in net assets equates to the amount of commercial bills sold by LRC&P to Rothwells on balance date and which appear never to have been repaid. Recognising these alone as bad debts would therefore have wiped out the shareholders' funds of Rothwells. Recognition of any other bad debts, of course, would have meant the bank had to report a deficiency.
- The profit was achieved after crediting $4.7 million in interest from LRC&P. Of this, only $3.5 million was actually paid (on 31 July, 1984), but significant repayments of cash were made by Rothwells to LRC&P in the first two weeks of August. In addition, any significant bad debt writeoff would of course have wiped out Rothwells' profit. If the $7.8 million in bad debts had been recognised as such, and the $1.2 million unpaid interest not credited, Rothwells $3 million profit for 1984 would have been shown as a $6 million loss, which seems closer to the truth.

Basically the same formula of round robins, transfers between accounts and sales of commercial bills would be followed at every future balance date of Rothwells to remove Connell's increasing debts from Rothwells' books. But the debts would grow larger each year and so would the gap between appearance and reality. The accounts became increasingly bogus as Rothwells struggled to hide the fact that it was essentially acting as

Connell's private bank. But the public never had any inkling of this until well after Rothwells finally collapsed.

One job done by Rothwells for the government in 1984 was a report—compiled with Price Waterhouse—on the reconstruction of the Motor Vehicle Investment Trust. It was as a result of this report, completed at the end of 1984, that the MVIT was turned into the State Government Insurance Commission of Western Australia. The SGIC would be involved in some of the most questionable of the WA Inc deals.

Fremantle Gas

Another deal that would later involve Connell concerned Perth CBD property. In early 1985 the State Superannuation Board entered into a joint venture agreement to develop the David Jones site in St George's Terrace. As a result, the SSB took a 50 per cent interest in this site with the remaining 50 per cent held by Midtown Property Trust. Midtown was owned by Bond Corp and Spedley, but Spedley would sell its stake to Connell in October 1987.[25] Shortly after the David Jones deal the WA Development Corporation sold the Perth Technical College site in St George's Terrace to the same joint venturers for $33 million. The SSB funded the purchase.

The first WA Inc deal in 1985 was the warehousing of Fremantle Gas & Coke Co Ltd. The State Electricity Commission of Western Australia (SECWA) was the monopoly gas supplier in Perth except for Fremantle Gas, which had the right to supply an area of five miles (eight kilometres) radius around Fremantle. It was common gossip that one day SECWA would have to take over its small but strategically placed competitor. Fremantle Gas was a public company in which Robert Holmes à Court and Wesfarmers each held about 13 per cent. Holmes à Court had, as usual, given himself several options. He held an interest in the Dongara gasfield north of Perth and appeared to be manoeuvring a deal of his own with the Fremantle board. Or he could bid for Fremantle Gas and hold SECWA to ransom on the price. At the end of 1984 Holmes à Court made a takeover bid, offering the shareholders no cash but scrip in one of his subsidiaries, J.N. Taylor Holdings.

According to Connell, Burke rang him in January 1985, said he didn't want the Holmes à Court bid to succeed but wanted SECWA to acquire Fremantle Gas and that the Deputy Premier, David Parker, would contact Connell about the matter. (Asked later whether he had a direct line to the Premier, Connell said: 'I think it would be fair to say he had a direct line to me'.) At that time, a bitter enmity had developed between Holmes à Court and Alan Bond. Connell was identified closely with Bond.

Connell realised that if he were to bid for Fremantle Gas, a personal dimension would be added to the takeover battle and Holmes à Court would only sell very dearly, if at all. Connell needed a front man who was neither identified with Bond nor threatening to Holmes à Court.

For this task, Connell chose Yosse Goldberg of Western Continental Corporation. At a subsequent meeting between Parker, Connell and executives of SECWA, Connell indicated that Western Continental Corporation could bid for Fremantle Gas and hold it for a time before selling it to SECWA. The proposal appears to have been adopted without anyone bothering to discuss the proposed prices, except for a rather vague proposition that Western Continental should buy the stock at $4.80 and sell it to SECWA at $5.20. Certainly it was generally understood that Connell and Western Continental would not be doing it for their health.

Western Continental was then controlled by Yosse Goldberg and Dr Ron Wise. They ran it on the surprisingly free-form basis that either of them could do his own thing within Western Continental. In the risk spectrum of Western Australian enterprises of its day, Western Continental would have been placed at the hairier end, having led a perilous financial career for several years. Even in the tolerant ambience of Perth in the mid-1980s, there was no way that Western Continental could have mustered the funds for an assault on the old gas company.

The Royal Commission's findings summarised above may be wrong in one important respect. On anecdotal evidence, it appears that Goldberg took the Fremantle Gas deal to Connell, rather than the other way around. The WA Inc Royal Commission report gives little of Goldberg's background and does not indicate how long he had been interested in the gas industry. Goldberg and Wise held a controlling interest in Strata Oil when it first discovered gas at Dongara, and sold for a nice profit. Through a vehicle named Eastern Petroleum they then tried to retake a 50 per cent stake in Strata, but dropped out and lost $5 million when their underwriter reneged. Goldberg had been interested in Fremantle Gas, as the distribution end of the Dongara field, for some time. He tried to take out Holmes à Court's stake in early 1983, before Burke was even elected. Goldberg believed SECWA would at some point force either a Liberal or Labor Government to take over Fremantle Gas. What was not predictable was the price. Goldberg disliked Connell, but Connell was the conduit to Burke and Connell would do a deal. This version of events would be consistent with the evidence of Burke, who said that Connell first approached him about Fremantle Gas. The Royal Commission rejected this evidence and accepted that of Connell, who said Burke had rung him in January 1985. Goldberg refused to face examination by the commission, leaving Australia for several years. Whichever way the deal went, the size of the government's proposed takeout price came as a delightful surprise to Goldberg in March 1985. His banker, David Hurley of the Western Australian branch of Standard Chartered Bank, recalled that Goldberg called at his home at 7 a.m., virtually babbling. Hurley said:

> He was very excited and very keen to talk to me at length and depth about the financing of the takeover. Unfortunately he was so excited that I couldn't get too much sense out of him, so I said 'We've got to go and talk to the person who has the details', which was Laurie Connell.

Hurley could not take the risk of backing Goldberg until he received Parker's personal assurance that a resale was guaranteed. Asked if he would have financed Western Continental without Parker's guarantee, Hurley said: 'Not in a million years'.[26] Western Continental duly mounted the bid. After some haggling, Holmes à Court agreed to sell in May at $5.20 a share and the rest of the shareholders followed suit, leaving Western Continental the owner of Fremantle Gas for $24 million. Originally, the plan was for Goldberg to on-sell Fremantle Gas to SECWA within six months, but then it was pointed out that he would be liable to capital gains tax on the profit. So the sale was deferred, at considerable expense to WA taxpayers. The deferral also entailed some risk to Goldberg because there was a State election in February 1986. However, the Labor Party won comfortably. In September 1986 Parker instructed SECWA to buy Fremantle Gas from Western Continental for $39.75 million, despite the objections of the commissioner and a deputy commissioner of SECWA.

Connell and Goldberg made a number of payments while the transactions were in train. In June 1985 L.R. Connell & Partners paid $300 000 which went into the No. 1 Advertising Account of the WA Labor Party. The intermediary in this transaction was Brenda Brush.

The circumstances of Connell's June 1985 payment of $300 000 were unusual, to say the least. Connell had been told by Burke some time before that he would be expected to make a big donation to the ALP. But the demand was made suddenly, while Connell was out of the office. Mrs Brush rang Connell's office and spoke to an employee named Paul Quinn, demanding $300 000 in cash. Quinn naturally had to get Connell's approval, which was difficult because Connell was flying to the eastern states on a chartered jet at the time. Quinn eventually contacted Connell's party at a refuelling stop in the middle of the Nullarbor. He spoke to Rothwells director Peter K. Lucas, who had never heard of the demand. Lucas spoke briefly to Connell, who approved the payment. As Connell's bank did not have that much cash available the money had to be delivered by an armoured car company. When Mrs Brush called to collect the cash Quinn demanded that she count it in front of him before taking it away. Mrs Brush then put the money into a satchel and took it to the Town & Country Building Society, where she deposited it in a newly opened account. In evidence before the subsequent Royal Commission Mrs Brush had remarkably little recollection of the entire event.

The immediate approval by Connell is ample evidence that he was expecting a levy. Connell said that Burke had earlier told him that he expected the business community to raise $4 million to $4.5 million for the ALP. Connell said:

> It was put to me that the Labor Party was looking to restructure its finances so that there wouldn't be the type of requests, if you like, that he made of me just prior to the '83 election, which is a fairly undisciplined, I suppose, sort of request. This was part of the exercise that the Labor Party was going through to restructure their finances and the position was squarely put that a healthy business environment had been developed by Labor, would be continued to be developed by Labor and therefore it was in our interest to contribute to this fund that was being established to enable them to continue to stay in office.[27]

Connell—used to living in a world of mates, fees, charges and various sophisticated forms of kickback—does not seem to have been too bothered by the ethics implicit in such an approach. He duly took the hat around to fellow spirits such as Alan Bond, Brian Coppin, John Roberts, Yosse Goldberg and Dallas Dempster, putting the bite on them for a quarter to half a million dollars each.

In July 1985 another $300 000 was donated to the party by Western Continental, although the payment was routed through L.R. Connell & Partners and Connell's lawyer Leon Musca. (Goldberg could spare the sum. As soon as the takeover was completed he had invoiced Fremantle Gas for $2 million for 'administrative services' and paid Western Continental, as the owner of all the shares, a dividend of $1.2 million.) Goldberg's $300 000 was split into two parts, $200 000 being paid into the No. 1 Advertising Account and $100 000 in cash being retained by Burke. By the time the transaction was investigated, Goldberg had fled to London and had refused to return to answer questions. Musca said that Goldberg had told him he had been summonsed to see Burke who had got 'straight down to the point' by asking for money. 'Leon, it is like dealing with the Mafia', Goldberg told Musca. Goldberg told Musca that he was astonished by the request, because he was by no means in the habit of making political donations. Musca, who had to put the money through his trust account, said he checked the arrangement by ringing a number which Goldberg gave him. The telephone was answered by Mrs Brush, who told him that the payment was urgent and that $100 000 had to be in cash.

Mrs Brush was rather vague about the donation when she gave evidence to the WA Inc Royal Commission. Brian Burke thought the donation had been anonymous. The Royal Commissioners thought

Burke's version 'quite implausible'. They observed: 'There was no reason for Mr Goldberg to conceal his substantial donation from Mr Burke. On the contrary, there was every reason for his desiring it be brought to Mr Burke's attention'.[28] Musca gave Mrs Brush two cheques, one for $200 000 payable to the No. 1 Advertising Account and the other for $100 000 payable to cash. For some reason never explained, Mrs Brush took the $100 000 cheque to Canberra to cash it. 'Mrs Brush, as became normal for her, had no useful recollection of the matter', the Commissioners said.

Once in charge of Fremantle Gas, Goldberg increased its revenue, and hence its profits, by raising gas prices. Fremantle Gas was pregnant with undistributed profits, but Goldberg could not increase the dividend it paid without the approval of the relevant Minister, David Parker. As soon as the Burke Government was re-elected in February 1986 (thanks partly to a well-funded advertising campaign) Goldberg began badgering Parker for permission to increase the capital of Fremantle Gas. In May, Parker allowed Goldberg to treble the authorised capital of the company. Its issued capital was raised from 4.7 million shares to 15 million. Fremantle Gas, whose dividend was restricted to $375 000 in the previous year, when it had been a public company, was suddenly able to pay Western Continental a dividend of nearly $2.8 million, of which $2.4 million came from pre-acquisition profits. In a further burst of generosity, Fremantle Gas paid Goldberg management fees of $2 million.

In August, Parker, Connell and Goldberg met at Connell's house. After lengthy negotiation, Parker agreed to buy Fremantle Gas from Western Continental for just under $40 million. Even after allowing for interest, political donations and other costs, this gave Western Continental a profit of well over $10 million on the deal. Over a bottle of whisky afterwards, Parker said that Goldberg should put something back into the community and suggested he make a donation to the Spare Parts Puppet Theatre, a marionette theatre in Parker's electorate and run by a friend of his. Goldberg donated $125 000.

In the long run, the puppet theatre and the ALP were the only ones to benefit from these transactions. Goldberg's high-rolling career came to an abrupt end fourteen months later when the share market collapsed. The profits from the gas company deal slipped through his fingers like grains of sand. Connell invoiced Western Continental for a $5 million fee, which he never collected.

But the biggest losers were the former shareholders in Fremantle Gas & Coke. As the owners of the enterprise, the shareholders should have been the ones to benefit if the government felt compelled to pay an outrageous price for the utility. But they were fobbed off with $24 million and the government instead paid almost $40 million to Western Continental. The government also allowed Goldberg to rip a quite unjustifiable dividend and management fees out of the company. At all times during the negotiations the government had the statutory power to compulsorily acquire any gas-making utility in the state. Why this power was not exercised to acquire Fremantle Gas at a fair price to shareholders was never satisfactorily explained.

The advertising account run by Burke was a slush fund. The Labor Party has long had slush funds of this sort, controlled at the leader's discretion, but in Burke's case the details were destined to become more public than ever before. Burke does not seem to have taken any of the money for himself. He invested $87 000 on rare stamps, which were put into albums with his own collection. Only Burke knew which stamps were his and which belonged to the Labor Party. Burke was an expert stamp collector but showed poor timing in his investment, because the stamp market collapsed a few years later and the stamps were sold at heavy losses. Burke seems to have put some $40 000 of his own stamps into the party funds to make up for the losses.

One other matter probed by the WA Inc Royal Commission in relation to Fremantle Gas concerned an odd coincidence. On 20 November 1986, less than a month after selling Fremantle Gas, Goldberg raised a loan of $35 000 from Western Continental. On the following day Parker bought a house at 12 Knutsford Street, Fremantle, paying the deposit of $12 980 in cash. A month later Parker opened a Commonwealth Bank account, depositing $11 100 in $100 notes. The Royal Commissioners were curious about the source of these funds, because they could not be traced to any prior bank account or other investment operated by Parker. When asked to explain, Parker said it was money that he had saved over a long time. Parker said it had not been in a bank account because he had kept the money in a satchel in his office. The Royal Commissioners rejected Parker's explanation, but said they were unable to find that it had been given to him by Goldberg. And by that time Goldberg was in London and had refused to return to testify.

Rothwells' 1985 accounts

Rothwells' 1985 annual report was a slim but glossily beautiful document promoting more strongly than ever the company's image as a prosperous and exciting merchant bank with the Midas touch. Deposits were shown to have leaped another $100 million to $197 million. Profit was claimed to have doubled to $4.4 million. Shareholders' funds were stated at $21.3 million. Sir Edward Lyons stepped down from the Rothwells board. Sir Edward had recently resigned as head of the Queensland TAB after a long and bitter feud with Queensland's formidable Minister for Racing,

Russ Hinze. Connell became chairman of Rothwells as well as managing director.

The figures were dazzling, but the reality was even more sharply different than in 1984. On balance date eve, 30 July 1985, according to Rothwells' books, L.R. Connell & Partners owed $60 million to Rothwells. The debt was extinguished by the same series of manoeuvres as in 1984 but the sums were larger, as shown in Table 3.4.

Once more, Rothwells obligingly financed round robins to enable LRC&P to repay its loans. Once more, Rothwells obligingly bought a portfolio of commercial bills from LRC&P without checking on whether the drawers could pay their debts or whether they owed the money at all.

The bulk of these deals could not have withstood inspection. To take one example, under a deed of assignment dated 31 July 1985 Connell's private company Oakhill Pty Ltd purportedly assigned to Rothwells debts with a face value of $35.9 million. Oakhill's accounts for 30 June 1985 showed that it had total assets of $14.5 million, of which debtors accounted for less than $1 million. How could this company have had $35.9 million in debtors to assign to Rothwells a month later?

The hectic rate of transactions on 31 July may have confused their authors, because the notation in Rothwells' journal states that the debts being assigned were from L.R. Connell & Partners (although the deed bore Oakhill's company seal and the signatures of a director and secretary). However, a subsequent search by McCusker showed that at 31 July 1985 only $8.4 million of the debtors on the list were debtors of LRC&P. Whether one chooses to believe that the debts were assigned by Oakhill or by LRC&P, McCusker's report implies that at least $27.5 million of them were phantoms.

The LRC&P books contain a journal entry on 1 August 1985 crediting LRC&P with $35 million. The notation says that this was a reversal of the previous debit to Rothwells 'raised in error'. So, in the books of LRC&P, the assignment of debts to Rothwells was extinguished the day after it was made, on the grounds that it was in error. However, the day

Table 3.4 The disappearing aot of 1985

	($000)
LRC&P debt to Rothwells at 30 July 1985	60 366
Adjusting Entries:	
1. Routine journals (net)	264
2. Cashbook transactions (net)	(58 544)
3. Transfers between accounts (net)	32 703
4. Corrections	299
LRC&P debt after adjustments	35 088
5. Sales of LRC&P/Oakhill loans and advances	(35 088)
LRC&P debt to Rothwells after all entries	Nil

in between had been Rothwells' balance date and no correcting entry was ever made in the Rothwells annual report for 1985. If it had been, of course, Rothwells would have had to show that its chairman owed the bank $35 million. Rothwells shareholders were kept in ignorance of the situation even though $35 million represented more than one-fifth of the $163 million securities held by Rothwells at balance date.

One might fairly ask how the auditor managed to declare Rothwells' 1984 or 1985 accounts true and fair. The same question was asked extensively by McCusker. The auditor was Louis Carter from the Brisbane office of KMG Hungerfords, which later became KPMG Peat Marwick. When McCusker asked why an auditor was not employed from Hungerfords' Perth office, he was told that members of the Perth firm at the time were considered too 'entrepreneurial'. McCusker said: 'An alternative reason suggests itself, when one considers the perfunctory and tolerant manner in which the audits were carried out by the Brisbane team'.[29]

Carter's notes indicated that he was aware of the assignment of the $35 million in debts on 31 July. He even made a selection of the thirteen largest debtors assigned to Rothwells to verify the debts, but he never proceeded to seek confirmation from them that the debts existed. McCusker later established that, if letters had been sent, Carter would have discovered that none of the thirteen owed money to Oakhill.[30] In other words, there would have been a deficiency of $21.5 million in Rothwells books. This discovery alone would have almost wiped out Rothwells' shareholders' funds. In addition, the chairman of the company would have had to explain how and why his company had sold non-existent assets to Rothwells.

Carter had received the list of the $35 million purported debtors only two days before he was due to sign off the Rothwells accounts. Given that the $35 million represented 21 per cent of all Rothwells' securities and given the suspicions that ought to have arisen when such a large transaction occurred on balance date, Carter should have postponed signing the accounts so that he could make an adequate investigation. McCusker said:

> It is quite extraordinary that this unusual balance day transaction should have been given such scant treatment . . . The revelation of the fact that the $35 million entry was a sham, which would have flowed from the responses to the confirmation letters, would have obliged the auditors both to qualify their report, stating the true position [as to Connell's debts], and to report the entire matter to the Corporate Affairs Commission.

If this had happened, Rothwells' collapse would have occurred in 1985 instead of 1987, and would have involved far smaller sums.

This was not the only flaw in Rothwells' 1985 accounts. At balance date it was showing $162 million in receivables, of which $101 million was in commercial bills. These comprised loans to the higher risk end of the market, as Carter seems to have been aware.[31] Yet Rothwells announced its profit without providing for any possible bad debts, and Carter endorsed this judgement by issuing an unqualified audit report. A subsequent examination of Rothwells' 1985 accounts by Deloitte estimated that a provision of at least $17 million should have been made for bad debts at 31 July 1985. That, of course, would have converted the stated $7 million profit into a loss.

Carter's relaxed attitude is harder to explain given the fact that he had recognised deficiencies in Rothwells' accounting systems. Following the 1985 audit, he wrote Connell a letter saying that problems he had noticed during the 1984 audit were still in existence. He wrote:

> . . . The bill register had not been reconciled regularly with bills on hand and the general ledger was not being agreed with the register. The general ledger was not being kept up to date and the important control provided by having a regularly balanced set of books was not functioning. Because of these shortcomings, one could not be completely satisfied that the bill register represented all bills on hand or that, indeed, all bills had been properly controlled.

Carter's excuse for not qualifying the Rothwells accounts was that in 1983 Connell had told him that he 'stood behind the debts of Rothwells'. Carter claimed that two other Rothwells directors, Tom Hugall and Peter K. Lucas (not to be confused with Peter Lucas of Bond Corporation), had repeated the assurance. Carter told McCusker: ' . . . we were comforted by the fact that Connell had another merchant banking operation in existence and it was quite feasible for him to sell a loan from Rothwells into his own organisation to ensure that Rothwells suffered no bad debt'. McCusker observed:

> Despite the claimed reliance by Carter on the belief that Connell 'stood behind Rothwells' debts', he never sought clarification of precisely what that meant, nor did he seek or see any written confirmation of such alleged undertaking by Connell, even in the form of a minute; nor did he take any steps to satisfy himself that such an undertaking had substance. Connell has denied, in evidence, that he ever gave such an undertaking.

A point that arises here is that if Connell had said he would make all Rothwells' bad debts good, then that still did not exculpate Rothwells from non-disclosure. The correct disclosure would have been for bad debts to be assessed in accordance with normal practice and a statement made that Connell had guaranteed them. The guarantee—if it was made—was a material piece of information which Rothwells' shareholders were entitled to know. For the guarantee to be valid, it should have been in writing and backed by some confirmation that Connell was worth at least $17 million or whatever the bad debts totalled.

Carter's endorsement of Rothwells' accounts was more an act of faith than a statement of fact. Questioned by McCusker, Carter agreed that the debtors' files gave little assistance, because the records were scant and unsatisfactory. 'We relied more on in-depth discussions with directors . . . rather than looking at files', he said. When McCusker pointed out that major banks such as Westpac and the National Australia Bank made provisions of 1.4 and 1.5 per cent for bad debts, Carter said: 'Well, I don't accept that as a valid comparison because Westpac and National are in a completely different banking scene than what Rothwells were'.

From here on the gap between appearance and reality at Rothwells grew to astounding proportions. McCusker later said that the management of Rothwells was facing a continuing liquidity crisis from August 1985. The bank had three fundamental problems which would haunt it for the rest of its career.[32] The first was the ever-increasing demand for funds by Connell and related entities to finance his private interests. The second was the mismatch of Rothwells' loan portfolio to depositors' funds. The fact that call deposits were being plunged into long-term, illiquid investments (often irretrievably bad loans) meant that a relatively small spate of withdrawals could cause a liquidity crisis. As the number of bad loans grew larger, the amount of withdrawals needed to trigger a crisis grew proportionately smaller. The third problem was that Rothwells capitalised fees and interest due from borrowers into their principal loan balances. This practice swelled reported profits and the size of assets (i.e. loans) but meant that over time the amount of interest received as actual cash was dwindling. The gulf between actual cash paid in interest to depositors and actual cash received from interest payments widened inexorably. Often the withdrawal of a deposit or payment of interest could only be met by raising fresh deposits. In banking, this is the road to ruin. Yet Rothwells for the next two years managed to project an image of expansion and success.

To the outside observer Rothwells was expanding apace in the longest, strongest share market boom in living memory. High technology floats were all the rage in 1985–86 and Connell was not a man to resist a trend. In September 1985 Rothwells underwrote the $9.9 million float of Vital Technology Australia Ltd, which had patents to high-tech components for information and data systems. Another high-tech float was Protective Research Industries Ltd, which was developing a rust and paint remover for steel surfaces. Connell was also a major shareholder in a consortium formed to bid for Perth's third television licence. This consortium was headed by Darcy Farrell, a Perth public relations consultant who later joined the Rothwells board. Connell's links with the government were further strengthened by his appointment as chairman of the Meat Marketing Board.

Carter's criticisms had resulted in a study of Rothwells' accounting and financial systems by Harry McGranger, Connell's former boss at Martin Corp. In June 1986 McGranger wrote a report identifying a number of problems including non-collection of interest, non-repayment of overdue loans, inadequate security, poor documentation of security and bill rollovers, and liquidity problems arising from a lack of cash flow.

Later Connell would claim that he had not been 'hands on' at Rothwells after 1984.[33] This denial of his involvement strains the credulity of those who remember the close public association between Rothwells and Connell during the mid-1980s. And whether he was 'hands on' or not, the evidence is overwhelming that he was aware of the problems. McGranger made his report to Connell in June 1986. Paul Harris, another former Martin Corp employee who had been appointed to Rothwells' Sydney office, also became disturbed about Rothwells' financial position. In late 1985 he sent several memos to Rothwells, three of which were directed to Connell, seeking information on key financial data so that he could approach banks for lines of credit. Oliver Douglas, who joined Rothwells in April 1986 as treasurer, gave a vivid picture of the group in those days.

> The major task of money market staff was to find the funds to cover sizeable daily transactions. It seemed that Connell and Lucas were doing most of the deals and it fell on treasury to find the funds to cover those deals at the end of each day . . . As far as I could tell many of the deals being done for third parties were transacted in such a way that L.R. Connell & Partners received upfront fees for arranging the deal and Rothwells provided the finance. Most of the deals were loans to companies associated with management and friends so they could acquire shares and other assets. Increasingly over my time at Rothwells it seemed that Connell just went out and spent the dollars and Peter Lucas and the treasury were called upon to cover it. The level of spending was such that it was like having to put out a bushfire each night.

The result was even higher debts when July 1986 arrived, and an even bigger reshuffle. Rothwells' 1986 annual report was a glossy selling document, in which piles of golden coins were used to show Rothwells' profits leaping from year to year. Pre-tax profit for 1985–86 was stated at $18.6 million. A Deloitte reconstruction of the accounts later estimated that, instead, Rothwells should have shown a loss of around $81 million.

On the balance date shuffles of 1986, Douglas said:

> Tom Hugall was most certainly the instigator of these adjustments made

95

to the balance sheet of Rothwells Ltd. Tom Hugall spent a lot of time with Mal James giving him instructions on what to do and what they were proposing to do to manipulate the balance sheet. Further, Tom Hugall used to get into a huddle with Connell and Lucas concerning this matter.[34]

The core problem was the proportion of deposits in Rothwells which were being siphoned into Connell's private interests. By the end of July 1986 the combined indebtedness of L.R. Connell & Partners and Oakhill to Rothwells had reached the breathtaking total of $138 million. Once more, Connell and his executives were facing the familiar problem of eradicating his large private debts from the Rothwells books. The solution was also familiar, adhering to the pattern established in 1984.

Part of the solution was a purported consignment to Rothwells of $138 million of debts owing to Connell. Rothwells was given a list of the debtors, but a substantial number of those named later denied owing any debts at all. McCusker dismissed the list as a deliberate fabrication.[35] In some instances the debt *was* owing, but to Rothwells. Apart from anything else this meant that when the debt was 'sold' to Rothwells, the same asset was being counted twice in its books.

This shuffle again enabled Rothwells to produce an annual report which boasted about the group's progress without revealing that Connell's private interests were the bank's largest debtors. If the debts of $138 million had been disclosed, shareholders might have begun wondering how solvent the fabled Connell was. The answer would have been jarring. A subsequent investigation by Deloitte estimated that, at July 1986, L.R. Connell & Partners had a deficiency of partners' funds of $70 million and Oakhill had a deficiency of $31 million. How LRC&P and Oakhill managed to run up these quite impressive deficiencies, largely in 1985–86, is the great unanswered question of the Rothwells saga. Not a dollar was provided for possible bad debts in Rothwells' 1986 accounts. Any realistic provision for bad debts on the Connell accounts would (once again) have wiped out Rothwells' shareholders' funds. McCusker said:

> Depositors [of Rothwells] would surely have been alarmed had they known that they were, in reality, lending largely to Connell, on an unsecured basis, to finance personal acquisitions such as racehorse stables and art; and even more alarmed had they been informed that Rothwells, the company to which they believed they were lending, was effectively insolvent.

No hint of this tainted Rothwells' glossy 1986 annual report. Although the $138 million comprised some 40 per cent of all Rothwells' commercial bill portfolio of $324 million, once again auditor Carter signed the accounts as true and fair. This action puzzled McCusker, leading to the following interrogatory gem:[36]

McCusker: Are you saying that you simply did not notice that this loans and advances account had gone from zero to $138 million in the space of a month?
Carter: No, I didn't notice that.

McCusker concluded: 'At best, it is difficult to avoid the conclusion that Carter engaged in a course of deliberate blindness to avoid being told what in fact was the truth, and which would have been readily discoverable from reasonable enquiry: the list provided to him to support the item 'Loans and Advances—other' of $138 million was a fiction'.

4

Rothwells: the three collapses

Really the only thing that was keeping Rothwells going was the fact that more people wanted to put money into it than wanted to take it out, and that if that ever changed [Connell] would have a problem.

Jonathon Pope, Price Waterhouse

By late 1986 Connell looked bigger and better than ever. Rothwells accounts painted the picture of a booming bank. Connell also looked to have fearsome political clout. The Leader of the Opposition, Bill Hassell, had been a vocal critic of the Fremantle Gas & Coke deal. In October 1986, with petty arguments over the Rothwells accounts out of the way, Connell wrote a letter of complaint to the Liberal Party. As a result he was invited to ventilate his complaints at a party committee meeting— held in Connell's office—which Hassell refused to attend. A few days later Hassell was sacked as Opposition Leader and replaced by Barry MacKinnon, but MacKinnon would do Connell few favours.

Perth had barely recovered from this sensation when the Perth Cup was run in January 1987, embroiling Connell in the first of another series of turf scandals. The two-mile Cup was won by his Rocket Racer, which had never won over more than ten furlongs before and had still been eligible to run in graduation stakes races only two months earlier. Connell plunged on Rocket Racer in the Cup, backing him into favouritism at 2/1, and Rocket Racer scored a runaway win by nine lengths. But, on returning to scale, Rocket Racer began staggering and was obviously distressed. WATC veterinarians immediately injected the horse with a corticosteroid and an anti-inflammatory. After that, it would have been pointless to swab him. Stewards pointed out that he had been swabbed on five previous occasions and had returned negative results. Rocket Racer's ailment was later diagnosed as severe heat exhaustion. He ran one more race, then died of a heart attack.

This was sensational stuff. Connell was by then the biggest racehorse owner in Australia with some 400 thoroughbreds estimated to be worth between $20 million and $50 million. He was Australia's biggest stakemoney winner of the season after Robert Sangster's Swettenham Stud. Perth racing circles were still speculating on the causes of Rocket Racer's amazing form improvement when it was announced in February that traces of the drug etorphine, colloquially known as 'elephant juice', had been found in swabs of three Perth racehorses. The swabs involved two horses trained by George Way and owned by Connell and his close friend John Roberts, chairman of Multiplex Constructions and also chairman of the WATC. Etorphine was originally developed as a tranquilliser for large animals such as elephants, hence its nickname. In tiny doses, however, it can be a stimulant to racehorses by enabling them to run at their peak for a longer period without pain. After an inquiry Way was disqualified for fifteen years by the WATC. Connell and Roberts were not implicated in the incident. Later a strapper confessed to having administered the drug to Way's horses.

The incidents hardly dented Connell's social career. While the elephant juice cases were being investigated, Connell played host to the world's most noted horse lover. During a Royal Tour through Western Australia Princess Anne partied for a night at Connell's Narbethong country home. As the party wore on, the pianist tired and was threatening to quit. Connell solved the problem by slapping $1000 into his hand.

By this time an executive director of Rothwells named John Hilton had suggested to Connell that he should consider a public float. The plan was to sell most of his assets into Oakhill and sell Oakhill shares to the public. Connell's main interests by then comprised shareholdings in Rothwells and a number of public companies, including Paragon Resources, Central Kalgoorlie, Hannan's Gold, Katanning Holdings, Beltech Technology, Intellect Electronics and Vital Technology, plus his equity in Perth CBD properties. Price Waterhouse was chosen to advise on the proposed float, which meant that one of their accountants, Jonathon Pope, had to check Rothwells' debtors. Pope soon discovered that security for many debts was nil and that the whole bank was unsound. 'Really the only thing that was keeping Rothwells going was the fact that more people wanted to put money into it than wanted to take it out, and that if that ever changed [Connell] would have a problem', Pope said.[1]

Pope's reports were made only to Connell, but after his initial ones Pope began to discover difficulty getting details of accounts, particularly those relating to L.R. Connell & Partners and Oakhill. 'He must have said "Well don't bother going any further" ', Pope concluded. Pope and his team had been keeping a private tally of what they considered bad and doubtful debts. It became obvious to them that Rothwells' entire share capital and reserves had been effectively wiped out. It should be emphasised that this was *without* counting Connell's debts to Rothwells through L.R. Connell & Partners and Oakhill. Pope had been forbidden to look at those accounts. Rothwells' debts exceeded its assets. Pope also said that Rothwells should cease treating unpaid interest on bad debts as income. Adopting this recommendation, however, would have revealed to the world that Rothwells was broke.

Instead, Rothwells' image as a successful bank was being promoted. The public relations department of the City of London put out a stockmarket letter recommending investment in Rothwells, praising the quality of Rothwells' loan portfolio as 'typically well secured commercial bridging loans'. In April the *Australian Financial Review* published a long article on Rothwells and Connell, saying: 'The bank itself takes no principal positions as Connell does not believe the risk is appropriate'—a statement that could hardly have been more inaccurate.

The *Financial Review* did not know it, but by then Connell was plotting its takeover. As four books have so far been devoted to an exhaustive description of the takeover of John Fairfax Ltd, it will be mentioned here only insofar as it affected Rothwells.[2] In early 1987 Warwick Fairfax, the younger son of the former chairman, Sir Warwick Fairfax, was planning a takeover of the family empire in conjunction with his mother Mary. Warwick, obsessed by the need to avenge his father in a family feud, had tried to recruit a number of financial advisors for the mission. He did not succeed until June 1987, when he promised Connell the quite outrageous fee of $100 million for the job.

As we've noted, Premier Brian Burke once said that he would hate to stand between Laurie Connell and a bag of money. This quote is invariably trotted out when discussing Connell and doubtless has its roots in truth. But Connell's treatment of the Fairfax fee was almost dismissive. Connell worked only in spasms on the bid. He promised $10 million of the fee to Sydney public relations consultant Martin Dougherty and another $45 million to Bert Reuter, who worked as strategist.

This fabulous fee turned out to be a curse and Connell might in hindsight have regretted taking the assignment. It distracted Connell heavily at a time when he needed to concentrate on saving Rothwells, although it was probably beyond redemption by then. The $2 billion Fairfax takeover was a marginal proposition at best. It was based on a number of fallacious propositions—one was that the family would support Warwick, another was that the superannuation fund would be able to reinvest the proceeds from its share sales back into the business—which exposed Connell to derision and a lawsuit when they unravelled. The bid focussed intense and unfriendly media attention upon Connell, whose finances were in no shape to stand deep scrutiny. Rothwells' other problems became so pressing that the bank had to discount the fee to Bond

Media and then Warwick reneged on payment, finally settling for $27 million, less the substantial legal costs which accrued after a bitter court case. Given that Rothwells must have been beyond redemption by early 1987, Connell's efforts on the bid might be viewed as a voluntary contribution towards his bank's creditors.

Rothwells' 1987 accounts

The concept of the Oakhill float having been dropped, Connell was faced with an even more massive paper shuffle when Rothwells' next balance date loomed in July 1987. By this date Connell's indebtedness to Rothwells had reached the heroic total of $324 million. This represented more than three-quarters of the $418 million deposits held by Rothwells at the time. Hugall proposed that the $324 million debt be dealt with as shown in Table 4.1.

The first point about this table is that it shows what was proposed to happen, not what actually happened. Many of the deals were never completed, and later led to litigation. However, Rothwells' 1987 annual report was prepared on the basis that these deals had happened and was verified by the auditor as though they had. As these accounts would later cause considerable anguish, the deals of Table 4.1 are worth exploring in a little detail. Once again, an enormous debt of Connell's was purportedly extinguished by various deals which had the effect of replacing loans to Connell by some other form of asset in the Rothwells accounts.

Musca. Four days before balance date, Hugall asked Connell's solicitor Leon Musca if he would buy for $12 million a parcel of debts from Rothwells with a face value of $14 million. Hugall offered a loan from Rothwells for the whole $12 million. The debts were to be bought by a $2 shelf company called Quintex Pty Ltd (not to be confused with Christopher Skase's Qintex group) and were to be the entire security for the $12 million loan. The loan would be guaranteed by Oakhill and there would be no personal recourse to Musca. Musca, being exposed to no personal liability and a possible profit, agreed and selected a list of $14 million of Rothwells' debtors. However, the debts were never assigned to Quintex although Musca tried unsuccessfully for some months to have them transferred. Musca could not get details such as the security offered by the debtors, nor even their addresses. One point worth noting is that Rothwells derived no benefit from this deal. Instead of being owed $14 million by various debtors, it was now owed only $12 million plus interest from a $2 company which could renege at any time. And if Oakhill's guarantee for this amount was good, then why not leave Oakhill on the

Table 4.1 The disappearing act of 1987 (all figures in $m)

Debts to Rothwells at 15 July 1987:

L.R. Connell & Partners			112
Oakhill Pty Ltd			46
Loans from 1986			<u>166</u>
Total			324
Less:			
1. Transfer of deposits		39	
2. Transfer of loans			
L. Musca	14		
Austasia	15		
K. Walsh	15		
TFH (AILMIC)	15		
Total		59	
3. Transfer of shares			
Beltech	59		
Rothwells	14		
Watrain	12		
Total		85	
4. Settlement Bow Investments		3	
5. Spedley advance to Oakhill		50	
6. Transfer of property			
Katanning Surfers Royale	8		
" CBD	45		
" Lucky Bay	1.5		
" Oakhill	2.5		
Total		57	
7. Unlisted shares		7.85	
8. Hi-Tech ventures		0.7	
9. Petrochemical Industries		<u>21.45</u>	
Total transfers		323	<u>323</u>
Balance (owing by Oakhill)			1

books as a debtor instead of going through this elaborate exercise to remove it?

Austasia Finance. This was a member of what became known as the Pier Street group of companies, which were effectively satellites of Rothwells. Connell did not control the Pier Street group, but Hugall held posts on many of the companies. Pier Street companies often collaborated with Connell and Rothwells on deals, as will be seen.

Austasia's directors included Hugall, Lucas, Joseph Sacca and Michael Dorsey. Hugall told the Austasia board on 29 July that the company would be buying a parcel of Rothwells' debts, which would be financed by a loan from Rothwells. The transaction was then shown as having happened although the Austasia board never approved the deal. Nor were they even told which debts they were buying, let alone the prices. Two independent directors, Malcolm Brown and Edward Brunton, were surprised to receive an audit confirmation letter in August to acknowledge a debt of $15.8 million to Rothwells. Brunton was still seeking details of the deal in late October, by which time the share market collapse had made his inquiries an even lower priority for Rothwells' executives. The fact that the whole transaction was bogus was evidenced by Connell himself. Realising that the assignment of the debts would mean paying stamp duty, Connell's solicitors wrote to the State Taxation Department saying 'no written directions concerning the debiting and crediting of the accounts with Rothwells Ltd were given by either Austasia Finance or L.R. Connell & Partners'.

Walsh. Kevin Walsh was Lucas' accountant and the hurried deal done with him was also never completed by Rothwells. Rothwells purported to lend $15 million to a small company owned by Walsh so that it could buy alleged debts from LRC&P.

AILMIC. Australian Index Linked Mortage & Investment Co Pty Ltd was a $2 company whose directors were Hugall and Dorsey. AILMIC was supposed to have bought $15 million in book debts from LRC&P on balance date of 1987. Dorsey, an actor whose previous fame had been in the steamy soap opera *Number 96*, was operating as a director under considerable handicaps. He had extremely limited vision and said he relied heavily on Hugall, in whom he had complete confidence. Dorsey later testified that he had been unaware of the $15 million debt purchase until he was interviewed by Corporate Affairs Commission investigators two years afterwards.[3] Many of the debtors on the list prepared by Hugall denied that they owed any money to LRC&P. Nor were any of them advised that their debts, whether real or fictitious, had been transferred from LRC&P to AILMIC.

Beltech. This purported transaction comprised a sale of shares by various Connell entities to Beltech for $59 million, with the proceeds being credited to Rothwells. Beltech was one of the Pier Street group, its directors including Dorsey and Sacca. Sacca told the Beltech board on 30 July that the company was going to buy the parcel of shares, without being able to tell the board such fundamental details as the names of the vendors or the shares they were buying. But he did tell them that Beltech would be buying the shares at 10 per cent below market value. To be fair, Sacca had made a similar purchase from Connell for $38 million at the previous balance date and generated a profit for Beltech.

The deal was financed by a bill line from Rothwells, which Sacca signed for on 2 August, but there were still no details of which shares Beltech was buying or from whom. Beltech, a listed company with its own shareholders, never got the shares. (According to McCusker the portfolio included one block of Paragon shares which had been sold three

103

times.) Beltech was still trying to get the scrip when the market crashed in October, slashing the value of the purported portfolio. The problem was solved in classic Rothwells fashion by Beltech selling the portfolio to a $2 company called Devoncove, which was financed by another loan from Rothwells. This so-called deal was heavily criticised as soon as it was announced.

Rothwells. The sale of a $14 million parcel of shares in Bond Media and BDC Investments to Rothwells by Oakhill and LRC&P was equally cavalier. A parcel of $13 million worth of shares in BDC Investments was supposed to have arbitrarily changed hands, although theoretically the transaction should have been approved by shareholders because more than 5 per cent of issued capital was involved and several directors had a material interest. However, this was a real transaction and Rothwells made a profit on it.

Watrain. This was a $2 company which Rothwells purported to lend $12 million although there was never any meeting of Watrain directors to authorise the transaction. McCusker's investigation could not discover what assets Watrain was supposed to have bought from Connell with the money.

Bow Investments. This company had agreed with Connell to buy a parcel of shares in Protective Research Industries for $3 million from L.R. Connell & Partners. Rothwells financed the transaction with a $2 million loan to Bow. The transaction was genuine but not completed until November, which meant Connell should have been shown as a debtor for the $3 million at balance date.

Katanning. McCusker described these purported property deals as a sham, saying Katanning directors at the relevant time were unaware of any such transactions.

Petrochemical Industries. The $21.45 million allegedly arose from Connell assigning his interest in this venture, although Connell subsequently denied having assigned it. The transaction was not completed, and was in any case reversed after balance date, so Connell should have been shown as a debtor for this amount in the Rothwells accounts. If the interest had been assigned, of course, Connell could never have done the notorious Petrochemical Industries (PICL) deal later.

When audit time came, Louis Carter saw the adjustments and knew their purpose was to remove Connell's debts from the Rothwells accounts. He made no attempt to verify that the $59 million in debts supposedly assigned to the four $2 companies (item 2 in Table 4.1) had in fact been assigned, or even existed. His explanation to McCusker was 'We weren't auditors of L.R. Connell & Partners', overlooking the fact that the assigned debts were supposed to be Rothwells' security for the loans, together with Oakhill's guarantees. With unconscious irony, Carter said that he considered these loans were 'in the ordinary course of Rothwells' business, which is a rather unusual business'.[4]

Carter told McCusker that he still felt comforted to know that Connell stood behind Rothwells' debts. He did not accept that people reading the Rothwells balance sheet would not have realised the extent to which Connell was using Rothwells' funds. That Connell would be doing so, Carter told McCusker, would be obvious, 'a matter of commercial common sense'. The fact is that none of Rothwells' balance sheets from 1984 to 1987 gave the slightest hint that Connell was a borrower of its funds, let alone on such a huge scale. Indeed, the whole point of the lengthy machinations which fill this chapter and the previous one was to hide the fact. People reading Rothwells' annual reports may have suspected that Connell had his hand in the till, but they had no way of knowing it. A lay observer might have thought that as auditor it was Carter's duty to see that investors knew the extent of Rothwells' exposure to Connell.

There were other flaws. In 1986 Rothwells had included in its income a fee of $5 million charged to Western Continental for corporate advice on the Fremantle Gas takeover. Yosse Goldberg never paid. Nevertheless, Rothwells again raised a fee of $5 million in its 1987 accounts. Again Goldberg didn't pay. Rothwells' 1986 and 1987 income—and pre-tax profit—were therefore each overstated by the same $5 million. Even if Carter had taken the view that Goldberg would eventually pay (a view that would not have been universally shared by those who had dealt with Goldberg around October 1987), the $5 million could still only have been part of Rothwells' income and profit in one of the two years.

The accounts were signed on 11 September 1987. Six weeks later, on 19 and 20 October 1987 the whole wild party of the 1980s would end and all the pianists in the world couldn't get it started again. The deposits held by Rothwells were genuine debts. Many of the loans on its books were not, because there was inadequate underlying security. Such security as existed was often in the form of shares whose prices had been propped by buying from friendly associates. After the share market Götterdammerung of October 1987 the prices of these shares dropped vertically and many were unsaleable at any price. Rothwells' liabilities greatly exceeded its assets and it would need massive help to survive.

The first rescue

The share market crash was described in Chapter 1. Its impact on the financial community was akin to a tidal wave. Old hands had seen some pretty rough water before on the financial markets, but nobody had ever seen one-quarter of the market's value wiped out before trading had even started. Confusion was the order of the day. As the battered investors and their brokers emerged on 21 October it was evident that there was danger that the financial panic might be followed by a money panic: that there could be a run on the banks.

Any corporate cowboy who had borrowed heavily to buy shares would have been wiped out by the crash. Ergo, the bank that lent him the money would be suffering losses. The immediate reaction of investors after a devastating crash is a flight to quality and security, which means— among other things—that they take their money out of adventurous banks and put them into stodgy ones. Simultaneously, as 21 October dawned, many of the brokers with large sums on deposit at Rothwells had an acute need for cash.

Stockbrokers had been one of the largest sources of funds for Rothwells. By offering top short-term rates, Rothwells had attracted large deposits. Brokers had also been enticed to deposit money at Rothwells by the prospect that if they supported Connell he might return some business whenever one of his deals was coming together. The relationship was open-eyed, however. The brokers sensed that Rothwells was a boom-time phenomenon and might be vulnerable whenever conditions changed. If the ship ever began taking water, the nimble-footed professionals would be the first to run for the lifeboats. It was also a matter of stark necessity. In the market cascade of 20 October stockbrokers throughout Australia had sudden need of large funds to plug the yawning holes that had appeared in their own portfolios and those of their clients. So, as soon as the market crashed, the brokers began calling back their substantial deposits with Rothwells.

So the professional money stampeded for the lifeboats. The other large class of depositors with Rothwells comprised small investors, shire councils and similar bodies in Queensland and Western Australia, who had been lured innocently into Rothwells on the grounds that it enjoyed trustee status and was offering high rates of interest. This might be called the amateur money. These depositors were slower to move and were left without lifeboats when Rothwells quickly ran out of cash. The rescue of these marooned passengers became a major preoccupation for the WA Government.

Before the share market crash, Connell had been savouring the triumph of the takeover of John Fairfax Ltd. By jacking the price up to $2 billion—borrowed from ANZ—Warwick Fairfax had bought out his family and also such fearsome greenmailers as Robert Holmes à Court and Kerry Packer. Against all odds Warwick had won, together with his advisors Laurie Connell, Marty Dougherty, Bert Reuter and Aleco Vrisakis. But it was a deeply flawed victory. Connell had got the shares of Packer and Holmes à Court by selling them Fairfax assets, but none of the deals had been stitched up and all would have to be redone later. Warwick had paid too much for the family empire and this would result in its receivership three years later. Much of the takeover planning had been based on false assumptions, particularly in regard to the family's willingness to stay behind Warwick. The reputation of nearly everyone involved in the takeover would suffer during its outworkings. Connell would become one of the most vilified merchant bankers in Australia's history; Dougherty would be sacked by Warwick and become involved in a public slanging match with Warwick's mother, Mary; Warwick would be categorised as a nerd; Vrisakis would face a long fight before clearing himself of criminal charges relating to later behaviour in Rothwells; Lady (Mary) Fairfax would be regarded as greedy and power-hungry; and ANZ's approval of a $2 billion loan to Warwick, when none of its senior officers had even met him, would become the prime example of feckless banking for the era.

But all this was in the future. In October 1987 Connell took a short celebratory holiday in Hawaii and returned only a few days before the 20th. When the market collapsed he bunkered down in the Sydney office of Rothwells to deal with the emergency. The rest of the Fairfax takeover team, who normally used Rothwells' office as their headquarters, transferred to the palatial comfort of Bert Reuter's penthouse suite at the nearby Regent Hotel.

The run on Rothwells began on Wednesday the 21st. Rothwells was issuing cheques drawn on its account with the National Australia Bank, but the National began bouncing Rothwells' cheques. News of this quickly spread among the brokers. By midday on the 22nd Connell realised that Rothwells was in deep trouble and would need major reconstruction. He rang David Hurley of Standard Chartered Bank in Perth. Harley thought a rescue would be too hard and advised receivership. In hindsight, this would have been the best solution and saved a great deal of subsequent angst and losses, but Connell was not giving up without a fight. He rang his close friend Peter Beckwith, managing director of Bond Corporation. Connell also phoned Burke to say that the bank was under pressure. Failure of the bank would be catastrophic for Burke, who had associated himself publicly with Connell. The bank held deposits from small investors all over Western Australia as well as from several WA shire councils and the Catholic Archdiocese of Perth. They would surely blame Burke for encouraging them. Also, if Rothwells' funds were frozen several of the depositors such as the councils would automatically turn to the government for funds. Burke was in the moral position of Dr Frankenstein. The biggest single problem for Burke was probably the Catholic Education Commission, which had $40 million invested with Rothwells. If these funds were frozen by a Rothwells closure, the Catholic education system in the state would also have to close down or be bailed out by the government.

Burke referred Connell to Tony Lloyd, who arranged for the Government Employees Superannuation Board to buy $5 million of Rothwells' commercial bills from the bank. The WA Inc Royal Commission later found that both Burke and Lloyd had acted improperly. 'In an extremely uncertain financial climate, [the purchase] was effected urgently, without proper advice, to assist an ailing merchant bank which was not well regarded by Mr Lloyd', the Royal Commissioners found.[5] The State Government Insurance Commission bought Connell's share of the Midtown Property Trust for $30 million, protected to some extent by an option to put the trust to Bond Corporation six months later for $40 million. In December and January the SGIC borrowed $25 million from the WA Treasury so that it could buy more bills from Rothwells. When the Royal Commission subsequently sought details of this transaction the SGIC claimed professional legal privilege for all advice it had received, thereby blocking access to some of the truth about its dealings. The SGIC also told the Royal Commission that its filing system had been reconstructed, so that it no longer existed in its original form. 'This exercise was, of course, inimical to the concept of accountability', the Commissioners observed.[6]

On the Thursday following the crash Beckwith rang James Yonge, managing director of Wardley Australia Ltd in Sydney, and asked him to see Connell. Wardley was the Australian merchant banking arm of the Hong Kong & Shanghai Bank, the largest backer of Alan Bond. Yonge had helped Bond raise $1.2 billion for the takeover of the brewing group Castlemaine Toohey in the previous year. Wardley had no previous dealings with Rothwells but Yonge realised that its failure, hard on the heels of Black Tuesday, could precipitate a banking panic. Yonge was an Englishman, blond, confident and with a touch of arrogance. He had taken over Wardley Australia after the sacking of Michael Bato (described in a later chapter)—an event which must have imprinted the importance of the Bond account on the minds of all HKSB managers. Yonge agreed that Connell could come along to his office and brief him. When Connell arrived he said that Rothwells had so far issued $43 million in cheques which the National was refusing to honour. This first meeting between Connell and Yonge went badly, apparently because Connell took an aggressive line with Yonge's officers. According to Yonge, Connell was distraught. For much of the meeting he was trying to raise a personal loan from Wardley secured on some land that he and his wife owned, but Yonge refused. When Connell insisted, Yonge said: 'If you push us, you'll get nothing'. Asked later if this were the way Wardley normally treated customers, Yonge said: 'No, but then we don't often meet people like Connell'. Mainly as a favour to Beckwith, Yonge got Wardley's people to put together a loan offer on the land and also to look at how much they could lend on Connell's stake in Paragon. Later Yonge agreed to lend $7.5 million. Connell thought it inadequate because he needed more funds for his contribution to Rothwells. At this point Yonge was barely lukewarm about rescuing Connell.

On Friday Connell flew to Melbourne with Yonge and John Dickinson of Wardley. Together with Tony Oates of Bond Corp they spent the afternoon with National Bank senior executives including managing director Nobby Clarke. The National executives told Connell that they would not increase their exposure to Rothwells and would not even continue their existing level of support unless more capital was injected. After the meeting ended, Connell's team went to Essendon Airport where they held a further conference in one of the lounges. Then Connell, joined by Aleco Vrisakis, flew to Perth in his private jet. Vrisakis—grey-haired, bow-tied and regarded as one of Australia's top corporate lawyers—had now been seconded from the Fairfax takeover team to work full-time on the Rothwells rescue. Earlier that day in Sydney, Vrisakis had met the Wardley team and at their suggestion had rung Larry Adler, the shrewd, wheeler-dealer chairman of FAI Insurances. Adler was a client of Vrisakis and the two men knew each other reasonably well, but Adler offered Vrisakis no comfort when the lawyer suggested a bail-out of Rothwells.[7]

The Wardley men returned to Sydney. Yonge, under the impression that the deal was hopeless, thought: 'Thank goodness this is over. We don't have to worry about Rothwells any more'. But in Sydney Yonge received a phone call from Beckwith, who said he had just been talking to Burke. Beckwith painted a dire picture of how the WA financial world could unravel if Rothwells were allowed to collapse. Yonge saw clearly that his own interests would suffer if the panic flowed on to Bond Corporation, and agreed to bring his top men to Perth on Saturday.[8]

In Perth, Connell was at Rothwells' office at 8 a.m. with Vrisakis, Beckwith, Oates and various Rothwells executives. They were joined early in the afternoon by Brian Yuill, Yonge and top Wardley men John Dickinson and Kerry Roxburgh who had flown in from Sydney on Bond's private jet. At about the same time they were joined by Alan Bond, who had flown in from Rome. Bond had strong ideas about what should be done and took control of the meeting. According to Deputy Premier David Parker, who arrived a little later, Bond did most of the talking and the second most vocal person was Yonge. Connell was relatively subdued. The first task was to work out how much cash Rothwells needed. The estimates were large and vague, starting at $70 million and rising to around $300 million. The meeting appears to have been concentrating on

109

the liquidity needed by Rothwells to replace deposits, rather than on the fundamental position of Rothwells. If those present had concentrated on the fundamental position they should have seen quickly that Rothwells was a basket case with an enormous deficiency thanks to all its bad loans and investments.

The first suggestion of the Wardley team was that Rothwells should be taken over by the WA Government–owned R & I Bank—as later happened with Tricontinental and the State Bank of Victoria. This idea had been discussed by the Wardley team on the flight over, but it was rejected on the grounds that the sums were too large and that it would not resolve the immediate problems of Rothwells. Instead, it was decided to make a preference share issue for $150 million, underwritten by Wardley and with the biggest names in Australia as sub-underwriters. Those present began making phone calls to see what support they could muster from corporate heavyweights.

Earlier—around midday, before the arrival of either Bond or Yonge— Connell had phoned Kerry Packer, with whom he had developed a rapport during the Fairfax negotiations. Packer said he was prepared to commit $10 million to a rescue package and would be prepared to increase the sum to $20 million if necessary. Connell said that Packer also wanted him to run the company as long as Packer's money was involved. Beckwith proposed that the issue be underwritten by Wardley but Yonge was still lukewarm about the commitment.

Yonge, Dickinson and Roxburgh left the room to confer. Although the issue would be fully sub-underwritten, the risk would revert to Wardley should any of the sub-underwriters be unable to meet its commitment. The Wardley men decided that the risk was too great. Yonge returned to the room to tell the meeting the bad news. Roxburgh figured that that was the end of the ball game as far as they were concerned. He also figured that he wouldn't be getting a ride back to Sydney on the Bond jet, so he booked a ticket on a commercial airline. But inside the room the game was still in play. According to Yonge, Bond pulled him aside and said: 'You're not being very helpful'. Yonge said: 'I can see no reason why we should take a risk in relation to Rothwells'. Bond said: 'Don't worry about it, James. You, Wardley, will suffer no pain'. Yonge got Bond to repeat the promise in front of Dickinson and Roxburgh[9]—who were furious about the deal but were now stuck with it. Yonge still needed to confirm his commitment with the head of the Hong Kong & Shanghai Bank, a link which took some time because when Yonge rang Hong Kong on Sunday the chairman was in church.

Encouraged by Packer's backing, Connell rang Paul Morgan of Morgan & Co in Brisbane and Peter Falk of McNall Hordern in Sydney. These brokers had enjoyed business from Connell in the past and both now indicated support. Canvassing by phone in this way, the team secured pledges for an amazing $135 million between 1 p.m. and midnight from a list of the biggest names in Australian business at the time—including John Elliott of Elders-IXL, Sir Tristan Antico of Pioneer Concrete, Larry Adler of FAI, Dick Pratt of Pratt Group, Brian Coppin of Western Underwriting, Bill Lowenthal of Industrial Equity and even Alan Bond's arch-enemy Robert Holmes à Court.

Holmes à Court agreed to back the rescue, although it took several phone calls from Burke and Parker to persuade him. Holmes à Court only pledged $5 million, but he gave the rescue enormous credibility. And this may well have represented an opportunity for the supreme opportunist. Holmes à Court's empire had also been mortally shaken by the share market crash. While other corporate cowboys such as Bond, Elliott, Connell, Skase and Spalvins still believed they could keep playing the same games, Holmes à Court—almost alone amongst his peers—recognised quickly that the game was over. He would be the first to liquidate his empire and the most successful. He succeeded thanks only to massive support from the WA Government. When Burke called Holmes à Court seeking support for Connell, Holmes à Court may well have been thinking of the next move and agreed to support Connell in return for the WA Government supporting him. Holmes à Court was no stranger to government support, having made his first million largely from the government's subsidies of the Albany woollen mill.

During that Saturday Connell, Yonge and Dickinson had been on the phone to the National Bank's managing director Nobby Clark, trying to persuade the National to keep cashing Rothwells cheques. Connell did not know Clarke, but Dickinson was a former National Bank officer and Yonge could speak to Clarke on the common ground that while the Hong Kong & Shanghai was the lead banker to Bond Corp, the National was lead banker to Bond Brewing. Clarke was impressed by the pledges Connell was getting but said that Connell would need to have them documented before Monday morning. Connell was also keeping Burke informed. Burke said that the WA Government could not take equity in Rothwells. Bond suggested that it guarantee the bank facility.[10] Burke, also impressed by the size and names of the corporate pledges, promised to provide guarantees of up to $150 million to cover the balance, provided that the government ranked ahead of the preference shareholders in the event of a liquidation. This gave the National the comfort it needed.

Connell undertook to commit $70 million of his own funds to Rothwells. In addition, a debt subordination agreement was made between Connell and the preference shareholders in regard to $50 million which Connell claimed he was owed by Rothwells. The terms of this agreement were later the subject of a lengthy court case, but in effect they provided that if Rothwells went into liquidation Connell's $50 million would be held in trust by Connell to make up any shortfall in distribution to the preference shareholders. When the shareholders ultimately claimed the $50 million Connell sought to have a share issue made by Rothwells for $50 million and to set the subscription money off against his debt.

Burke insisted that the rescue talks be kept secret because he hoped to talk the WA Opposition Leader Barry MacKinnon into bipartisan support for the rescue. It was not until 4 a.m. that the meeting in Rothwells' office broke up, and by breakfast the team were in the office again seeking further sub-underwriters and preparing documentation. They got enough further sub-underwriters to lift the rescue package to the $150 million target. That morning there was an attempt to recruit the backing of the Liberal Party at a meeting at Bond's house at Dalkeith. Those present included Bond, his financial director Tony Oates (a leading Liberal Party fund-raiser), MacKinnon, his deputy Richard Court and Bill Hassell, the former leader who had been sacked after a confrontation with Connell. The three Liberals heard the pleas of Bond and Oates and adjourned to consider their decision. They did not back the deal. Burke held a meeting of Cabinet that afternoon and it decided to back the deal anyway.

The rescue was announced in an offhand, almost accidental manner. Burke held a regular Sunday press conference, a practice that he knew as a former journalist would assure him of headlines in the Sunday night television news and Monday's *West Australian*. On Sunday the 25th the main interest was in the results of three by-elections where the government had done poorly. As the press conference dragged to a close one journalist asked what was happening with Rothwells. Burke, seeing the chance to salvage some favourable headlines, announced the rescue package. It was the big news in the press the next morning. As the news of the big names underwriting the preference issue was announced the panic on Rothwells subsided.

Ultimately, a total of $164 million would be raised. There was a one-for-one issue of ordinary Rothwells shares at $1.75 and a two-for-one issue of 12.5 per cent cumulative redeemable convertible preference shares with a par value of 50 cents but also issued at $1.75. There would be 31.3 million ordinary shares issued and 62.6 million preference shares. As Rothwells ordinary shares were trading around 30 cents—having crashed from a boomtime high of $3.25—the shortfall was bound to be almost total.

Standing back from this package for a moment we can see that the National Bank agreed to join the rescue because it had the government guarantee, and that the government guarantee was provided by Burke because he was impressed by the big corporate names who had given underwriting pledges. The big corporate names were therefore the foundation stone of the rescue. These big corporates had one thing in common: they all thought that Rothwells was fundamentally sound. None of them had had the opportunity or time to do their own due diligence on Rothwells. The only evidence they could have had was the 1987 accounts of Rothwells released two months earlier and the assurances of those involved. The accounts, as we have seen, were wrong in three major respects: they showed Rothwells making a profit when it should have reported a loss, they showed it had substantial shareholders' funds when they should have showed it with a huge deficiency, and they did not show the size of Connell's debts to Rothwells. As these three factors were the overwhelmingly important ones in assessing Rothwells' financial health, the accounts were misleading and useless to any investor or lender. It is inconceivable that any of the rescuers would have invested if they had known Rothwells' true position. During the weekend of 25–26 October Connell had had little to say. Such assurances as were given about Rothwells' soundness seem to have come mostly from Beckwith, Bond and Yonge.

David Parker said that when he arrived at Rothwells' office in the middle of the Saturday afternoon Bond and Yonge went through the affairs of Rothwells in some detail, describing the situation in terms of a need for liquidity. Giving evidence eighteen months later, Parker said that he could not remember who said what but both of them had stressed that:

> . . . the problem at Rothwells was not a problem of capital deficiency; that there hadn't been a major defalcation of funds or other problems of a similar type. They went through in some detail the mismatch between the nature of the deposits in Rothwells, which were largely at call or on a very short term basis, and the loans out, which were largely on a longer term basis.[11]

On the Sunday afternoon Yonge was called before the Cabinet meeting which was discussing the proposed guarantee to Rothwells. Joe Berinson, who was State Treasurer, questioned Yonge closely about Rothwells' financial viability. Parker testified later that Yonge had been 'very dismissive' of Berinson's concerns and had behaved in a 'superior' manner, as though Berinson did not understand high finance. Parker also testified that both Bond and Yonge had said that 'contrary to some rumours that were around, Mr Connell himself was not a substantial borrower from the bank'. Assurances that Rothwells would be in a stable condition after the proposed capital injection were also given by Beckwith. At the Monday press conference announcing further details of the rescue package, Yonge certainly made some very bullish statements about the soundness of Rothwells after the rescue. He later said that he had relied on the audited 1987 accounts.[12] Yonge also assured Nobby Clark that the rescue would be successful.

Yonge's private company, Mirfield Holdings, had borrowed $750 000 from a Rothwells subsidiary earlier in 1987, but apart from that neither Yonge nor Wardley had any connection with Rothwells until the beginnings of the rescue. There was no way that they could have carried out any thorough independent check of the bank. In asserting Rothwells' soundness Yonge was making a statement (aggressively, according to Parker) when he did not know whether it was true or not. Yonge, and Wardley, were at this time regarded with some awe for their success in such coups as the financing of the Castlemaine Tooheys takeover. Yonge's views and recommendations would have carried weight with the sub-underwriters, the National Bank and the WA Government. Wardley was not acting altruistically. It would charge a $4.5 million fee for its part in the rescue and was also protecting its relationship with its biggest client, Bond Corporation. McCusker accepted that Yonge had been relying on the 1987 accounts and the assurances of others when he put his own prestige behind the deal. However, it was irresponsible of Yonge, and the fact that Wardley was only prepared to risk $2.5 million in the final underwriting indicates that Yonge was not prepared to put his money where his mouth was. Whether he intended it or not, Yonge played the role of the Judas sheep in the Rothwells rescue, leading others to invest money while his own bank took no risk.

In the rush and heat of the deal nobody stood back and asked one question: why did this so-called bank suddenly need so much money? Rothwells' 1987 accounts had shown total assets of $724 million and bad debt provisions of only $4 million. The ink was not long dry on the auditor's statement that this was a true and fair view of Rothwells. Yet now a package totalling $370 million ($150 million from the preference issue, $150 million from the government-guaranteed National Bank loan and a purported $70 million from Connell) was necessary to rescue it. Even after allowing for the fact that it was facing a run and that some of its investments might have been wiped out by Black Tuesday, this was a very large sum in proportion to its total funds and should have cast grave doubt on the accuracy of its accounts. The package of $370 million also represented more than 80 per cent of its total deposits of $418 million.

But, in times of high drama, people often get carried away by the excitement of events and neglect to ask basic questions. The government asked Tony Lloyd—as finance director of the WA Development Corporation—and Kevin Edwards to carry out an independent examination of Rothwells' receivables. Yonge had suggested that the bad debt provision should be raised to $40 million. In the short time available Lloyd and

Edwards came up with a guess that this should be increased to $100 million. This would still have left the government's guarantee well covered.

The press conference on Monday was held in an atmosphere of self-congratulation by those involved at having stopped a panic. The brotherhood of Australia Inc had shown its power and loyalty to a troubled member. One who added to the congratulations was myself, writing in *Australian Business* that financial history showed that the best course of action in a panic was to defend the first sound bank that was being attacked. It did not occur to me that so many titans of finance could have been persuaded to back Rothwells without adequate assurance that it was sound. Thus does error multiply. As the truth slowly emerged in later years it became clear that Rothwells should have been left to sink. Even if the government had had to bail out the depositors, it would have been cheaper than the PICL deal.

Neither Wardley nor Bond put much of their own funds at risk in the underwriting. Wardley collected a fee of $500 000 from Rothwells, plus another $250 000 from Connell. In return it agreed to underwrite the $150 million preference issue only after $147.5 million of it had been assured. Connell described this as a 'Clayton's underwriting'. On the Saturday afternoon of the rescue Yonge demanded a worthwhile fee for Wardley from Rothwells and, after some haggling with Connell, agreed on $4.5 million. This represented 3 per cent of the capital raising. As Yonge said: 'We never do anything for nothing'. Bond Corp sub-underwrote $17.5 million of the preference issue, but Bond then persuaded Connell to pay a fee of $16 million for its part in the rescue. The other sub-underwriters were annoyed when they learned of this fee a few days later. Bond had grabbed the glory for the rescue while taking only $1.5 million of the risk. Burke doubted whether the government would have backed the rescue if it had known that Bond Corp intended to charge a fee. In recruiting sub-underwriters Bond had not hesitated to sell the line that the rescue was in the national interest. According to his longtime friend Brian Coppin, Bond said that Coppin would be personally responsible for the collapse of Rothwells and possibly several other businesses in Western Australia if he did not commit to the deal, forcing Coppin to commit $6 million unconditionally to the sub underwriting. Coppin said he would not have gone into it if he had known that Bond intended to collect a fee.

Coppin's version of this incident was denied by Bond but, whatever happened, Coppin's treatment was in interesting contrast to that of another Bond mate, Dallas Dempster. In January 1988 Dempster was asked to meet his sub-underwriting commitment for $7.5 million. He got a loan from Rothwells to Dempster Nominees, which on-lent the money to Dempster Holdings, which took up the sub-underwriting—all on the

115

same day. In Rothwells' books, the Dempster Nominees loan went down as 'working capital for Petrochemical Industries'. This transaction underwent considerable subsequent alterations, but effectively was never repaid. Adding these numbers together, the $150 million subscribed by the corporate heavies was reduced by $26.25 million by fees and defaults.

The Catholic Education Commission emerged as possibly the best judge of the situation, withdrawing all its funds from Rothwells in the few weeks after the rescue. It later resisted substantial government pressure to redeposit the money with Connell's bank.

The rescue had one other side benefit for Connell. Since March 1987 the National Companies and Securities Commission (NCSC) had been investigating Rothwells for share market manipulation and warehousing, particularly in connection with Vital Technology. The size of the rescue operation persuaded the NCSC that it should not plunge the markets back into panic by pursuing the investigation, which was reaching its final stages. The NCSC agreed to terminate the investigation provided that (a) Connell stepped down as chairman of Rothwells; (b) Lucas left the company; (c) Rothwells handed back its dealer's licence; (d) Tony Lloyd, Aleco Vrisakis and Darcy Farrell joined the board, with Lloyd becoming managing director; and (e) a new business plan was submitted under which a new corporate direction would be adopted and no further deposits solicited. The business plan[13] provided that Rothwells would:

- not deal in securities nor act as an investment advisor
- not make any invitation to the public to deposit money or subscribe to debentures except through a registered prospectus
- establish and maintain a match between the maturity of borrowings and assets
- seek investment in hard assets and cash flow
- use the talents at its disposal to generate substantial fee income
- ensure that L.R. Connell & Partners would be a passive investor

These terms were accepted by Connell and Rothwells. The NCSC wrote a letter to Rothwells in December 1987 saying that, provided the undertakings were implemented on a continuing basis, the NCSC would not continue or open investigations of any events that had occurred before 27 November. Connell would later claim that this was an indemnity, but in truth the NCSC had left itself a proviso. As a final clincher, the NCSC informally 'fined' Rothwells $1 million. Rothwells paid the money, purportedly to cover the costs of the NCSC investigation until then, and the payment remained secret for nearly four years.

In November Rothwells ran a newspaper advertisement headed: A Message From the Chairman of Rothwells Ltd. The advertisement claimed that Rothwells was now stronger than ever, with a capital base of $280 million and a ratio of liabilities to capital of only 2.4:1. 'This makes

Rothwells one of the most conservatively geared financial institutions compared to the industry average', the advertisement said. 'We are now in a position to resume profitable growth and retain our place among the best performed financial entities in the country.' The advertisement was misleading. Rothwells' alleged profits of the past had been dubious at best and it was still in deep trouble.

Why PICL happened

Following the rescue the WA Government seconded two officers of the R & I Bank, Peter Roberts and Michael Hurst, to check Rothwells' portfolio of receivables. They started work just before Christmas and soon found some disturbing facts. A mere 29 borrowers had accounted for 81 per cent of Rothwells' loan portfolio. The top 20 shareholders in Rothwells were prominent among them. The pair sent letters to debtors of less than $5 million seeking recovery, but found they received few replies. They were not allowed to send similar letters to those owing more than $5 million. A bank file on a borrower normally contains such basic data as how and when the loan was made, its purpose, the terms of repayment, the security and formal approval. Roberts and Hurst estimated that 60 per cent of Rothwells' files contained no such documentation and some were downright vague. Roberts told Lloyd that about 70 per cent of the debts could be doubtful. Hurst thought the whole portfolio ought to be considered doubtful. Independently David Hurley of Standard Chartered Bank, who had joined the Rothwells board in 1987, had come to the same conclusion, saying: 'I've never seen such a great portfolio of nonsense in my life'.[14]

In a further exercise Hurley tried to age the debts. At first glance, the problem did not seem too bad because the debts did not appear to have been owing long. But further investigation showed that a number of the bad and doubtful debts had been converted from term liabilities to on-demand debts, which meant they were really older than they appeared. He discovered that all of them had been picked up by the computer system about eighteen months before. In truth, they dated back three to four years. Hurley suddenly realised that he was on the board of a financial time bomb. Worse, roughly two-thirds of the debt was owed, in one form or another, by Connell companies.

Hurley told Vrisakis and Lloyd. 'Vrisakis nearly went pale when he saw it', said Hurley. 'I'm going to go home', Vrisakis said; and in the light of subsequent events that was perhaps the best thing he could have done. Vrisakis then went to Connell and said: 'I've got a very bad heart and I can't cope with this'. The next time Connell met Hurley he said sarcastically: 'Thanks, mate'. According to Hurley, this led to a directors' meeting at which Connell and Vrisakis attacked the competence of Roberts and Hurst and voiced concern that if their views got out to the public it could bring Rothwells down. Connell urged that copies of their papers should be withdrawn and destroyed. Most were, and Roberts and Hurst were quietly returned to the R & I. Hurley accused Vrisakis of character assassination. Vrisakis said there were errors in the Hurst and Roberts report, but denied that he had been responsible for the destruction of copies.[15]

Nor was this the only disturbing report circulating within Rothwells at the time. Two employees, Rod Hare of Rothwells and John Selwood of LRC&P, had reviewed the bank's exposure to the Pier Street group of companies in December 1987 and concluded that those companies had a combined deficiency of at least $137 million. Hugall, who was company secretary of several Pier Street companies, claimed the Hare–Selwood assessment was too bleak. Connell ordered John Hilton to edit the report before passing it on to other directors.

This was the state of play in February 1988. The directors had reason to believe, following the investigations by Selwood, Hare, Roberts, Hurst and Hurley, that a substantial proportion of the group's receivables comprised bad and doubtful debts. By this time, Rothwells' interim report for the six months to January was looming and in the circumstances only an audited report was going to be satisfactory to the investors. How severely would the auditor treat the bad debts?

They need not have been concerned. The Hungerfords team for the half-year audit was again led by Louis Carter. Carter took the view that the values of the underlying assets were not adequately reflected by the current market. One of Rothwells' heaviest exposures, totalling $264 million in loans, equity and hybrids, was to the Pier Street group of companies, which had been hard hit by the crash. As we have seen, Hare and Selwood had concluded that the Pier Street group had a combined deficiency of at least $137 million. While holding that the Pier Street share prices did not reflect their underlying values, Carter made no attempt to assess those values himself. Instead, he relied upon assurances by the directors.[16] Carter's opinion of Rothwells' solvency stands in splendid isolation. Every other person who had conducted an investigation of some sort into Rothwells' affairs—Harris, McGranger, Pope, Hurst, Roberts, Hare, Selwood, Hurley—had quickly concluded that the bank was in grave trouble. Carter preferred to rely on directors' assurances.

When examined by McCusker, Carter also claimed that the half-year audit was not a report to the shareholders and not for publication, but simply for the directors. His grounds for this belief are not apparent, especially as he relied heavily on assurances by the directors in making his assessments. The logic of this position would appear to reduce to the proposition that Hungerfords were being paid their audit fee to tell the directors what the directors told them. The overwhelming fact of the situation was that Rothwells had just undergone the most heavily publicised rescue in Australia's history. Corporate subscribers, a major bank and the WA Government had put $300 million dollars into it and were anxious to know how it was faring. So were the public who were still trading its shares. As a public company, Rothwells had to make its interim report public and the audit statement was part of that report. And not the least interested party would be the NCSC, which had only recently been persuaded to suspend an investigation into the company.

Lucas did most of the dealing with Carter, telling him that Rothwells' assessment of its bad debt position was $70 million. Carter, after an investigation, thought $127 million but agreed ultimately to provisions totalling $114 million. In fact, the paucity of Rothwells' records was such that it was not possible to reach any definite figure and the auditor's report should have said so. Carter conceded the inadequacy of Rothwells' files and said he had relied on the directors, who were in a better position than the auditors to have an intimate knowledge of the accounts.[17] This position could be reduced to a *reductio ad absurdum*: if a company is so badly run that an auditor cannot tell its position from its accounts, then it is okay to rely on what the directors say it is worth. Rothwells got an unqualified audit certificate for its report for the six months to January 1988, which showed an operating loss of $20 million for the half year after a doubtful debt provision totalling $114 million. The press release added: 'The directors took the unusual step of having the accounts for the period fully audited, confirming their validity'. Rothwells had bought another reprieve.

The market was reassured but appearance and reality were as far apart as ever. Rothwells was now in a serious position financially. It was receiving virtually no income. Depositors were still demanding their money back. Most of its outstanding loans were non-performing. It was keeping its doors open thanks to government support from the SGIC and similar bodies.

The WA Government's support went to amazing lengths. This was shown in February 1988 in the Bell Group deals. The empire of Robert Holmes à Court had been mortally wounded by Black Tuesday. Over the previous twenty years Holmes à Court had built, from scratch, an enormous empire. Starting as a lone lawyer, he took over the tottering Albany-based WA Woollen Mills. Through government subsidies and some shrewd but ruthless dealing in the nickel boom he climbed to the point where he could take over the earthmoving business of Bell Group. He then formed a share-trading subsidiary named Bell Resources. Tall, supercilious and urbane, Holmes à Court played the greenmail game to the hilt, making fortunes by his shrewd positioning in takeover battles for Ansett, John Fairfax and the Herald & Weekly Times. At his zenith, Holmes à Court was the biggest force in the British cinema industry, owned strategic holdings in US Steel, Texaco and Standard Chartered Bank, and almost took over BHP singlehandedly.

Holmes à Court's family company Heytesbury Holdings held 43 per cent of Bell Group, which in turn held 46 per cent of Bell Resources which controlled the bulk of the assets. All three companies had borrowings at what appeared adequate security levels. But Black Tuesday made nonsense of formerly adequate levels. Suddenly share prices fell to or below the level of the debts and Holmes à Court, from being the nonchalant, cigar-smoking tycoon who always mocked the misfortunes of others, became a deeply worried man as his empire headed for the rocks.

The riches of the empire were in Bell Resources, but the way to control them was by acquiring Bell Group. Connell, ever the opportunist, met Holmes à Court in late 1987 to discuss a possible rescue. His idea was that Rothwells should find a partner for a joint takeover of Bell Group. The jarring difficulty here was that Rothwells was in even deeper trouble than was Bell Group, as even Connell recognised. Connell approached Kerry Packer, first with the idea of a joint venture and then with the concept that Packer should take over Bell Group and pay Rothwells a fee of $50 million for the idea. This was a very high price for an idea and the fee was dumped when Packer instead teamed up with corporate raider Ron Brierley for a foray in Bell Resources shares. As Connell said later, Brierley was a New Zealander, and not noted for his generosity.

Connell then approached Bond with the same idea, including the $50 million fee. The trick was to get Holmes à Court's stake in Bell Group without having to buy out the public shareholders. Under stock exchange rules at the time, any buyer acquiring more than 19.9 per cent of a public company had to make an equivalent offer to the remaining shareholders. After some discussion Connell and Bond hit on a plan whereby Bond would buy 19.9 per cent of Bell Group from Heytesbury, and another 19.9 per cent would be bought by the WA SGIC. This would get Holmes à Court out of nearly all his Bell Group shares while avoiding the need to make any offer to the public, who held 55 per cent of Bell Group. This meant that a government body would have to connive in a scheme to outflank the Companies Code and to bar the public shareholders from a chance of selling out at the same price as their chairman would be getting.

Three days before Christmas 1987 Burke had retired. A biography of him had been quickly sponsored by Connell, who claimed to have paid $67 000 towards the book. The new Premier was Peter Dowding. On 15 April 1988 Alan Bond met Dowding. Just three weeks earlier, Bond's chief lieutenant, Peter Beckwith, had contributed $200 000 on behalf of Bond Corporation to Dowding's campaign funds. Bond proposed to Dowding that they should each take over 19.9 per cent of Bell Group. Connell said that Bond and Dowding personally agreed to put the deal together, which meant that Rothwells' fee was again dumped. He said: 'Where the decision was finally made was at a meeting in Peter Dowding's office that Alan Bond attended and laid the deal out on a whiteboard in the office'.[18] Dowding always denied this but the Royal Commission found that an agreement was reached between the two men, and it is difficult to envisage the deal being done without Dowding's consent. It may have been that the SGIC was not bound by the takeover code. Indeed, such an opinion was prepared by lawyer Peter Wiese at Aleco Vrisakis's request. But the opinion was never tested in court and even if it were legally correct it was morally outrageous for a government instrumentality to be evading a key element of takeover law. The Commissioners found that it was improper for Dowding to have acted in a manner clearly contrary to the spirit of the takeover code.

According to Connell, the SGIC's offer to Holmes à Court was typed by Connell's wife Elizabeth at home one Sunday. Kevin Edwards then dropped it in to Holmes à Court, who lived just around the corner. On his return Edwards joked with Connell about Holmes à Court receiving it 'like a letter out of the blue', even though the deal had already been done. The then WA Minister for Finance, Joe Berinson, later said that part of the reason for the government's involvement in the purchase of Bell Group shares was to ensure that Bell Group and Bond maintained their large deposits with Rothwells.[19]

This was a very poor rationale for being involved in such a financially and ethically dubious deal. However, it is consistent with another government action at the time. As part of the WA Government's rescue package for Holmes à Court, the SGIC had acquired the Westralia Square development site in the Perth CBD. In February 1988 the government was negotiating to sell the site to a joint venture between Kerry Packer's Consolidated Press Holdings and property developer Warren Anderson. As part of the deal, Dowding insisted that the joint venture put $50 million on deposit with Rothwells. This was ultimately borne by Anderson, and was a key factor in his subsequent downfall. It was an extraordinary condition for a government to attach to a property deal supposedly for the benefit of the SGIC.

The Bell Group deal smacked of collusion as soon as it was announced. The NCSC held an immediate hearing. The first witness was Kevin Edwards, who, as Chief Executive of Burke's Department of the Cabinet and deputy chairman of the SGIC, had implemented the government's policy of trying to save Rothwells. Edwards, who disliked having his photo taken, left the hearing with a briefcase in front of his face to frustrate photographers. The tactic was successful, but at the price of making Burke's former chief executive look like the suspect in a bank robbery. It did nothing to help the slumping reputation of the WA Government and its business associates.

These measures smack of a desperate determination by the government to save Rothwells. Incredibly, it was not matched by any determination to monitor Rothwells' affairs. The government had provided its $150 million guarantee without setting up any formal reporting requirement from Rothwells. Lloyd appears to have briefed various members of the government broadly and informally of the situation. The size of the problem only began to emerge in March or April, when Rothwells' director John Hilton told Burke that some $500 million of the bank's debts might be irrecoverable. A more modest estimate was made in June, when Beckwith told the WA Mines Minister, David Parker, that $290 million of Rothwells' loans might be bad. This was at a meeting attended by Parker, his fellow minister Julian Grill, Kevin Edwards from the WA Government, Peter Beckwith and Peter Mitchell of Bond Corp, and Lloyd, Vrisakis and Hilton from Rothwells. The ministers were told that depositors were still withdrawing funds from Rothwells, which needed a further injection of funds. Beckwith suggested that the problem be solved by the PICL deal.

Petrochemical Industries Co Ltd was jointly owned by Connell and Dempster. Its assets comprised a deposit on a block of land at Kwinana, the right to build the state's first petrochemical plant (planned to produce vinyl chloride monomer, ethyl dichloride and caustic soda), a fixed price contract for its construction and some heads of agreement for sales. But the project was not viable at the proposed sales prices and Dempster had been unable to raise finance for it. Except for the government mandate, there was nothing much in PICL that could not have been duplicated by anyone who had a suitable piece of real estate and who said: 'Hey, I've got a great idea! Let's put a petrochemical plant here!'. The project was announced by Parker in January 1987, when he said the PICL partners— Connell and Dempster—had an exclusive mandate from the government to undertake a feasibility study.

In early 1988 the PICL project was going nowhere. But however unviable the project was, Connell's half-interest was almost the only asset he had left that could get him out of trouble. The PICL project was the subject of many discussions in early 1988 between Dempster, Connell, Bond, various representatives of the WA Government and prospective financiers. The idea of selling PICL to the government seems to have emerged from discussions between Connell, Lloyd, Edwards and Hilton.

The PICL deal put a price on the project of $400 million, which could have been anywhere up to 100 times the value of its tangible assets. McCusker said:

> The price fixed for the project was, essentially, decided upon by the buyers and was contrived so as to be sufficient both to buy out the hard core of non-performing debts, which were understood to be in the vicinity of $300 to $400 million, and to be sufficient to enable Rothwells to discharge its liability to the NAB, of $150 million, as well as to repay deposits which Bond and related companies had with Rothwells.

This view is reinforced by the evidence of Hilton, who by May 1988 had come to the conclusion that the bad debts in Rothwells totalled some $500 million. He told Burke that to bail Rothwells out the PICL price would have to be increased to this figure. But Burke backed Lloyd, who refused on the ground that he wanted to be sure Connell derived no net benefit from the bail-out. On all evidence, the price and terms for the deal were set by the government. Grill, a minister involved, said that three reasons for the government's decision were (in order): to allow Rothwells' bad debts to be disposed of; to inject additional funds into Rothwells; and to help a desirable project get off the ground.

Like so many deals in Rothwells' history, PICL had to be consummated urgently because balance date of 31 July was looming. Dempster agreed to sell his half-interest in PICL for $50 million and Connell agreed to sell his for $350 million. The disparity in prices alone indicates the artificiality of the deal, because there was no reason why the two half-interests should have differed in value. The $400 million was contributed by Bond Corporation ($225 million) and the WA Government ($175 million). Dempster picked up his $50 million and bowed out, making no attempt to get the same settlement as Connell even though he was more truly the founder of the project. Connell's company Dalleagles Pty Ltd, which owned his half of PICL, received $350 million and simultaneously paid the same amount to Rothwells in return for $350 million of its bad debts. Thus another $350 million cash was pumped into Rothwells.

Incredibly, again, the government made no attempt to supervise the details of the deal. Rod Hare was told to select $350 million worth of Connell-related debt to be dumped into Dalleagles. He did so in consultation with Hugall and Hilton, having some trouble keeping the total down to that figure.

Rothwells immediately discharged the debt of $150 million to the NAB, thereby releasing the WA Government from its guarantee. Rothwells also repaid deposits of $125 million to the Bond group and $50 million to Bell Resources—the same deposits the WA Government in February had been so anxious to keep in place. This cynical deal was therefore structured to get the government, the NAB, Bell and Bond out of Rothwells while leaving other investors such as the preference share-holders still stuck in the bank.

Parker said that the deal was structured so that the government's exposure to the $150 million guarantee to Rothwells would be swapped for a more palatable and useful investment in a petrochemical plant. He also subsequently estimated that the government had paid $300 million too much. Other estimates would put the overpayment higher. The PICL deal aroused incredulity as soon as it was announced. It was obviously a jerry-built deal to get Rothwells out of a further financial scrape.

The deal also put Bond and the WA Government on an uneven footing. Bond had gained 50 per cent of the project for a net investment of $100 million ($225 million invested less $125 million which could not otherwise have been retrieved from Rothwells). Bond would still be the operator of the project. The WA Government had got itself into a stupid position under the deal, because it had undertaken to provide sufficient support and guarantees to enhance the value of PICL to $400 million. The $400 million already pumped in did not do this, because it had gone to the vendors. Therefore the WA Government was still committed to pump in more support to bring the project's value up to $400 million. This was tantamount to an open-ended guarantee to a project over which it had no control.

Worse, Rothwells was still not saved. In fact it was looking like a bottomless pit. In broad terms, the first and second rescues of Rothwells had pumped a net $570 million into the so-called bank before the repayment of money owed to Bell and Bond. Table 4.2 summarises the position.

As it subsequently turned out that parts of Connell's $70 million donation were in fact financed by Rothwells, the bottom figure in the table could be reduced to around $530 million. This was still an awful lot of money to pump into a bank whose audited accounts had claimed assets of $800 million. Surely Rothwells must now have been sound?

The answer was 'No'. Rothwells was still collapsing. After some further haggling between the government and Bond, the PICL deal was

Table 4.2 Rothwells' two rescues (all figures in $m)

First rescue, October 1987	
Preference shareholders	150
National Bank	150
Connell	70
Second rescue, July 1988	
WA Government and Bond	350
	720
Less NAB repayment	(150)
	570

completed on 17 October 1988. As outlined above, Rothwells immediately made payoffs to the NAB, Bond and Bell. The net result was that within hours of receiving the $350 million, Rothwells was broke again and asking its creditors for a $200 000 overdraft. Indeed, according to director John Hilton, those inside Rothwells had been aware for months that the $350 million would be insufficient to save it. Originally the deal was supposed to have injected a net $50 million into Rothwells, but the conditions imposed by Bond for his support rendered the deal of no net benefit.[20] Another big problem was that Connell was still draining money out of the bank. Between April and October 1988 Connell's debts to Rothwells rose by more than $40 million.[21]

The PICL deal was supposed to have been settled at the end of August, but dragged into October. Parker provided some support for Rothwells through the R&I Bank, but by mid-October Kevin Edwards— negotiating on behalf of the government—had made a firm recommendation not to proceed with settlement of the PICL deal unless the government had some assurance that Rothwells would remain liquid. Nevertheless, Parker and Dowding pressed ahead. 'Mr Parker's dominating concern was to ensure that Rothwells did not collapse, thereby embarrassing the government', the Royal Commissioners said. 'If Mr Parker paused to consider the wider interests of the public, which must have been clearly evident to him, he did not consider them long.'[22] The PICL deal was settled on 17 October with exchanges of cheques between the parties.

The great PICL deal kept Rothwells alive for only two days.

The bottomless pit

On 19 October Lloyd, as Rothwells' managing director, was facing a demand from a depositor for repayment of $4 million. Rothwells could not pay. Worse, Standard Chartered had $20 million in bills falling due the following day and was not going to renew them. Rothwells would be unable to pay them out. Late that afternoon Lloyd, Connell's solicitor Leon Musca, Edwards, Grill, Hilton, Harc and Peter K. Lucas had met to discuss the latest crisis. In the evening they were joined by Peter Wiese, a solicitor representing the government. They phoned Beckwith and asked if Bond Corporation could supply funds. Beckwith suggested that Connell should supply the money, referring to paintings worth some $20 million on the walls of Connell's home. It was not until after 9.30 p.m. that Grill rang Dowding at home. The Premier was in bed ill and his temper was not improved by the news.

Dowding rose from his sickbed and joined the meeting in Rothwells' office. Musca, Hilton, Hare and Lucas left Lloyd's office and sat in an adjoining room while Dowding was briefed by Edwards, Grill, Lloyd and Wiese. Dowding was irate, slamming doors and kicking furniture. His shouting could be clearly heard in the next room. 'We have just paid $400 million for a petrochemical plant worth nothing', Dowding shouted angrily. 'Now we're back to where we started. I am surrounded by liars and cheats. Now you want more money. Who are we saving from going to jail this time?' Musca took a note of the words, which seem a fair summary of the situation.

Dowding's anger would have been more constructive if it had been vented before the PICL settlement. He had received enough warning signals. The deal had been widely criticised as shady and overpriced. It was bad enough that the government had been heavily besmirched by the deal, but now Dowding was learning that it had all been for nothing because they still hadn't saved Rothwells. And there was even worse news.

Under insolvency law, a liquidator may inspect all payments made by a company in the six months before it went into liquidation. If undue preference has been shown to any creditor within that period, the creditor can be forced to repay the money to the company for distribution to other creditors. In Rothwells' case this meant that if the company went into liquidation within six months of the payback to the National Australia Bank, the bank might be forced to refund its $150 million. In that case it would certainly call upon the government to honour its guarantee for the same amount. In addition to the $350 million the government had pumped into PICL it would have to find another $150 million for the NAB and then take its chances in the list of Rothwells' creditors. The government's position would be more indefensible than ever, particularly as Rothwells now appeared to be a bottomless pit of bad debts.

Over the next 24 hours Dowding cooled down, but only a little. On the 21st he attended a breakfast meeting at 6 a.m. at Bond's home with Bond and Grill. They discussed a further rescue package of $150 million, but Dowding refused to put any more government money in unless Bond and Spedley also contributed. Rothwells' immediate problem was that it needed $15 million. This was met by the State Electricity Commission of Western Australia paying Rothwells $15 million in advance for coal supplies from Rothwells' wholly owned subsidiary, Western Collieries. SECWA's commissioner, Norman White, refused to make the purchase until ordered to do so by Grill. The cheque was drawn by SECWA to Western Collieries, but was banked—well after normal banking hours—to the account of Brian Yuill's Spedley Securities. The immediate liquidity problem of Rothwells, which had occupied the Premier, ministers and the top brass of SECWA for several days, turned out to be that Spedley was

Table 4.3   SGIC and R & I support for Rothwells

		($000)
SGIC		
Purchases of Rothwells-accepted bills	17 300	
Rothwells promissory note	48 300	
Endorsement of bills bought by CIBC	9 000	
Deposits	16 500	
		91 100
R & I		
Bill facility (Paragon)	10 000	
Overdraft	7 512	
		17 512
SGIC Deposits with Spedley & PICL		
Spedley deposit on-lent to Rothwells	30 500	
PICL deposit on-lent to Rothwells	5 000	
		35 500
		144 112

under pressure from one of **its** creditors. Lloyd was subsequently convicted of having used his position as a director of Western Collieries improperly in appropriating the cheque to Spedley, but the conviction was later quashed.

When Dowding consented to the $15 million advance purchase, he told Bond that the government was 'doing its bit' towards Rothwells' third rescue. In fact the government had done much more than its bit. In addition to the PICL deal and the guarantee, the State Government Insurance Commission and R & I Bank had been heavy supporters of Rothwells. By November 1988 these two bodies had pumped $144 million into Rothwells. Table 4.3 shows the items involved.

But all this support was inadequate. The brutal truth was that Rothwells was unsalvageable and had probably been in that condition for years. Government support was already at ridiculous levels and no further support could be justified. The total support given to Rothwells was, indeed, approaching the level of its alleged total assets. The government's long tolerance and deep pockets had both run out. And there was trouble on another front. The PICL deal had basically been done, although not completed, on 29 July so that Rothwells' bad debts could be removed before the 1988 balance date. But this time the Peats audit team would be headed by Steven Scudamore, and he took a radically less friendly view of Rothwells than Carter had. By the end of October 1988 it was becoming apparent that the accounts for that year would never be signed off, because Rothwells' management could not satisfy the auditor's queries. Without audited accounts, Rothwells had no chance of survival. The end had at last come.

Ian Ferrier, of Ferrier Hodgson & Co, was appointed provisional

Table 4.4   Rothwells' accounts reconstructed

Year ended 31 July	1984 ($m)	1985 ($m)	1986 ($m)	1987 ($m)
Stated pre-tax profit	3.1	7.2	15.6	28.7
Adjusted pre-tax profit	(4.6)	(9.9)	(81.1)	(108.0)
Shareholders' funds	7.8	21.3	54.3	65.6
Adjusted sh. funds	1.0	7.0	(37.9)	(58.4)
Debt of LRC&P/Oakhill before 'clear-outs'	34.2	60.4	142.0	322.2

Note: Figures in brackets indicate losses or deficiencies.
Source: Deloitte.

liquidator in November. It was just six years since Laurie Connell had taken over Rothwells. In that time the bank had managed to lose perhaps $600 million. On Deloitte's reconstruction, the accounts had been extensively falsified for years. Deloitte redrew the accounts, adjusting them for all the bad debts that were never paid. The results, as shown in Table 4.4, were a growing gap between the group's appearance and reality.

What happened to $600 million?

The immediate reaction to the table is to ask what happened to the money. The answer is less immediate and none too clear. Over a space of six years Rothwells lost some $600 million, of which more than half went to Connell in one form or another without being recovered.

Where the money went is a question that has never been satisfactorily answered. It ranks as the greatest unsolved mystery of the crashes of the 1980s. The segments of the McCusker and WA Inc Royal Commission reports that try to answer the question are brief and uncertain. The following attempt is therefore speculative, and gleaned from such few clues as were available.

There would appear to be three main categories of losses: those on investments in Connell-related entities, those in Pier Street companies, and those in other areas. Taking the last of these categories first, it would appear from the various reports into Rothwells that the bank made relatively few investments that could be described as arm's length. The reports concentrate on the bank's investments in its extensive ring of associates, which seem to have used the bulk of its funds.

The most incestuous investment of all was in itself. Rothwells indirectly funded the purchase of its own shares. McCusker traced a series of 1986 and 1987 deals in which various friends of Rothwells bought heavily into the bank. About $16 million of these purchases appear to have been ultimately funded in one form or another by Rothwells. The buyers included Holidays Pty Ltd (controlled by Robert Pearce, the managing director of Alan Bond's private company Dallhold Investments), Pioneer Nominees (controlled by Leon Musca), Dalbrit Nominees (controlled by H.W. Daly, a friend of Connell), Media Portfolio (one of the Pier Street group) and Beverage Holdings (controlled by P.K. Lucas).[23]

Rothwells also funded the Pier Street group of companies. By mid-1988 it had poured $264 million into them and they had a combined deficiency, according to the Hare–Selwood report, of some $137 million. The group was administered from Hugall's office at 19 Pier Street, Perth. The companies were linked by common directors and shareholdings, with control being exercised by Hugall in conjunction with Michael Dorsey, Joe Sacca and Peter K. Lucas. They included Beltech, Watrain and Austasia.

Beltech had loans to Oakhill of $32.6 million, which were assigned by Connell to Rothwells. Beltech also had a bad debt of $28.6 million comprising the shortfall on the Devoncove deal mentioned earlier. That debt was finally returned to Rothwells. Austasia had $21.7 million in bad loans to L.R. Connell & Partners that was assigned to Rothwells. Watrain had another $20 million in bad loans. All these bad loans were cleared out of Rothwells in the PICL/Dalleagles deal. Other small companies named CWB, Ritson Nominees and Telbase (owned by Hugall and Dorsey) owed Rothwells another $10 million.

Beltech went into receivership. Joe Sacca claimed that it still owned Connell's half-share in PICL that had been assigned to it in the 1987 debt reshuffle, and was therefore entitled to the $350 million. As the $350 million had already gone up in smoke this looked a forlorn claim, but was an indication of the relationship between Rothwells and the Pier Street group. The transactions between Rothwells, the Pier Street companies and Connell entities were so extensive—and sometimes so inadequately documented—that it will probably never be possible to specify with any accuracy who owed Rothwells what.

Rothwells had investments in many companies that were linked with Connell, Hugall or Lucas. The investments had been carried at inflated values in the books, disguising the fact that the companies depended heavily on Rothwells' support. The failure of Rothwells was quickly followed by the collapse of several of these companies. Katanning Holdings had bought $17.5 million worth of Rothwells shares from Bond Corporation in October 1988 and saw the lot go up in smoke a few days later. Another public company associated with Connell was Intellect Electronics, a videotape maker which hit the wall in 1988 with a deficiency of some $34 million. Rothwells had invested $29 million in this high-tech speculation, and lost about $25 million net. Media Portfolio and Vapac were two more Pier Street companies to go into receivership. Most of these companies had invested heavily in Rothwells and each other.

But the biggest question mark is how much was lost by Connell and his related entities. These included the partnership of L.R. Connell & Partners and private companies such as Oakhill, Dalleagles and Turfcutter. One point worth recognising is that a substantial proportion of the final debt was illusory, in that it comprised unpaid fees and interest that had been compounded, sometimes over years. This interest bill finally totalled more than $60 million.

A great deal more was spent on the high life. There were the 400 racehorses, the manor in the Cotswolds, the train to Bunbury, the show jumping circuit and the bloodstock studs in Western Australia and New Zealand. The Connell family was known to own a number of valuables. He had a silver collection valued at $3 million and a fine collection of Australian paintings, all of which were sold in 1989. The family jewellery collection at one time included a magnificent diamond necklace valued at $1.2 million, a $192 000 diamond and pearl ring and a $95 000 string of pearls. It required eleven closely typed pages to list the family jewellery for insurance purposes.[24]

When the crash arrived Connell was planning Australia's most luxurious home. He had bought seven expensive houses on a one-hectare block on millionaires' row in Victoria Road, Dalkeith, and had demolished them to make way for one grand house. Even by Perth's standards of conspicuous consumption this was a lavish property. The land cost (including the former houses) was $2 million. Philip Cox & Partners, who designed parts of Sydney's Darling Harbour, were the architects. The Connell mansion was to have some 80 squares under cover, excluding the 25-metre swimming pool with a retractable roof. It was to be built in a series of interconnecting blocks around courtyards and gardens, a tennis court, a squash court and garage space for the Rolls Royce and seven other cars. There were gallery spaces for Connell's collection of art including Robertses, Streetons and Turners. There was a salon where twenty people could dine while listening to a grand piano. There were a library, billiards room and five bedroom suites. As two full-time staff would be needed to manage the estate there were servants' quarters. Gina, daughter of the iron ore magnate Lang Hancock, exaggerated only slightly when she said that these quarters alone were larger than her father's house just down the road. Cox's design was inspired mostly by the Alhambra at Granada, and he persuaded Connell—who had better taste than many of his contemporaries—to shun the ostentatious interior fittings so beloved of the Perth *nouveau riche*. Connell told reporter Ben Hills: 'I wanted to build something that was going to be there in 100 years time so someone wouldn't do to it what I'm doing and run a bulldozer through it in 20 years time'.[25]

This scale of consumption gets rid of substantial money, probably around $40 million in Connell's case. He reportedly lost greatly on racehorses, possibly around $20 million. This seems a staggering sum, but Connell was Australia's biggest racehorse owner in the mid-1980s, with a stable of more than 400 at its peak. The bloodstock market crashed spectacularly in 1989, when the sale prices of yearlings often failed to cover their sires' stud fees. This would have wounded Connell's finances deeply. He had also plunged into the Australian art market, buying around 100 Australian paintings during the 1980s. His taste generally seems to have been good but, when the corporate high flyers crashed, so did art prices and the portfolio must have been sold at considerable losses. Connell's family trust managed to hang on to the family's luxurious home in Peppermint Grove, as well as his beach house near Busselton. As at one point they had mortgages totalling $2.7 million they were valuable assets.

One of the biggest drains on Connell's empire seems to have been the need to support the share prices of his satellites. The largest drain was Paragon Resources. Oakhill's acquisition of control of this mediumweight gold miner cost more than $100 million, which was ultimately funded by Rothwells. Connell wanted to establish a price of $1.50 for Paragon shares before he floated Oakhill and tried to achieve this through a wave of buying by himself and his friends. However, as it became apparent that Pope's report on Rothwells would be adverse, the plans for the Oakhill float began to fade. This left Oakhill holding a lot of high-priced Paragon stock. Then the share market crash of 20 October arrived and Paragon shares nosedived to $1, despite more friendly buying from Spedley and the Sydney broking firm of McNall & Hordern. The stock's biggest supporter was Geoffrey Lord's Elders Resources, which had paid $30 million for 22 million shares on a no-loss guarantee from Oakhill. Post-crash the value of these shares dived to $16 million, while simultaneously it became apparent that Oakhill could not honour its guarantee. Finding a home for this parcel became a matter of urgency. Despite lengthy and convoluted negotiations with Connell and Hugall, Elders Resources was unable to shake itself free of this parcel. When Paragon shares slid to 2 cents Elders Resources lost virtually the whole $30 million.

The portfolios of Connell and Rothwells were littered with bad investments. A high-tech company called Vital Technology Australia Ltd was formed to develop and market information technology including a system known as IBIS, standing for Image Based Information System. IBIS was a paperless office system based on computerised management of microfiche. Under the underwriting agreement, Rothwells was obliged to exercise nearly five million options at $2 each for a total of $9.9 million.

Table 4.5 Where the money went (all figures in $m)

Personal assets and lifestyle	50
Racehorses	25
Phantom interest and fees	60–70
Paragon	105
Rothwells	16
Pier Street	137
Vital Tech	15
Smaller investments	25
	433–443

Rothwells also lent Yosse Goldberg's Western Continental $5 million to support Vital's share price. Vital was ultimately worth very little.

Adding all these elements together, the rough picture is given in Table 4.5.

This is a lot of money, but a large amount is still missing. As we have seen, the various Connell entities owed Rothwells a total of $324 million at July 1987. If the first rescue of October 1987 had not occurred and Rothwells had gone into liquidation, a liquidator would have had an obligation to pursue Connell for these enormous debts. The first rescue not only forestalled that but enabled Connell to borrow more from Rothwells afterwards. The WA Inc Royal Commission's consulting accountant Stephen Mann calculated that $62 million had flowed out of Rothwells to Oakhill and L.R. Connell & Partners between October 1987 and November 1988.[26] McCusker estimated that by June 1988 Connell's debt to Rothwells had reached at least $350 million and could well have been more like $500 million.[27]

After the PICL deal, which was Rothwells' second rescue, Connell managed to clear $350 million of his direct and indirect liabilities to the bank. But even that was not enough to clear up the entire Connell-related debt. Connell still owed substantial sums. When Ian Ferrier moved in as liquidator he calculated the debts owing by Connell's companies to Rothwells at $16.7 million. In addition there were guarantees on a further $97 million, making Connell's entire exposure, including contingencies, $113.7 million. Ferrier believed the realisable value of these claims by Rothwells was $75 million. Most of this $75 million must have been represented by the assets of the debtors whom Connell had guaranteed.

However, Connell was claiming offsetting debts totalling $115.2 million from Rothwells. Ferrier and Connell struck a deal under which Connell relinquished all his claims. In addition he bought back a debt owed by Rothwells of $25 million, assigned Rothwells a claim of $14 million against Katanning and agreed to pay $12 million cash over three years. It should be remembered that Ferrier, as a liquidator, had to strike the best deal he could for creditors and was not conducting a criminal investigation. Ferrier did, however, try to satisfy himself that $12 million was all that was available. Ferrier, one of Australia's hardest-nosed liquidators, made inquiries in Australia and overseas and was confident that Connell had no significant assets left. McCusker later said:

> Although there are a number of matters giving rise to possible claims, the greater part of the Connell-related debts to Rothwells [in the vicinity of $500 million] which might have been the subject of a recovery action was cleared off the slate first by the PICL transaction, and then (though to a lesser extent) by a deed of settlement with the liquidators, foreclosing any substantial claim against Connell/Oakhill by the liquidators on behalf of Rothwells and its shareholders and creditors. When one considers the very large amounts involved, there was surprisingly little examination of Connell's real financial position.[28]

So the mystery of Rothwells' missing millions (all told, perhaps $100 million which vanished in Connell-related entities) may never be solved. They weren't in Oakhill which reported a deficiency of $65 million in 1988, rising to $74 million in 1989. Dalleagles had net assets of just $2. The fact that Connell over the next few years sold most of his personal assets, such as the paintings, the silver collection and the studs, indicates that Ferrier might have been right. The money from these sales presumably was needed for the time payment of the $12 million. But, from the viewpoint of the wider public interest, it is regrettable that there was never any satisfactory public accounting of the hundreds of millions that were lost in Connell's private empire. Because of the nature of the commercial settlement, his private companies such as Oakhill did not even go into liquidation. Finally, it is difficult to believe that the $350 million bad debts he took from Rothwells in the PICL deal were totally worthless. Anything Connell managed to realise from them would have been pure gain.

Burke's shoddy Camelot

It took years to sort out the political and financial mess created by Burke's vision of WA Inc and his chosen agent, Rothwells. Malcolm McCusker, QC, appointed to report on Rothwells' collapse, revealed for the first time Connell's massive borrowings from the bank and the fact that its finances had been unsound for years before the crash. A select committee of the WA Legislative Council was appointed to inquire into the PICL deal and a Royal Commission of three judges was appointed to inquire into the whole of WA Inc. Ferrier, as provisional liquidator, conducted investigations, as did the National Companies and Securities Commission and its successor, the Australian Securities Commission. A civil action was fought to determine the ranking of the preference shareholders and various creditors. Several criminal charges were laid against those involved in Rothwells. The bank's affairs were thoroughly ventilated although Connell's personal finances were not.

Whereas McCusker unravelled the financial affairs of Rothwells, the Royal Commission into WA Inc unravelled the political connections. This showed that Burke's vision of Camelot had degenerated in practice to a system where selected businessmen were given favours by the government in return for political donations. In principle, Camelot did not seem far removed from Tammany Hall.

However, there was one backfire in the direction of the Opposition, involving the former Liberal Premier Ray O'Connor, and Bond Corporation's Observation City Hotel on Scarborough Beach. For years, some members of Stirling Council had been trying to encourage a high-rise development on this beautiful beach. After Alan Bond won the America's Cup in 1983 he announced that he would defend it off Fremantle. Bond had a strong interest in developing a high-rise hotel in the area, but the project was opposed by the Scarborough Ratepayers Association. Laurie Connell was retained by Bond as a consultant, Jack Walsh interviewed several councillors and Ray O'Connor was retained to approach the Liberal councillors. In March 1984 the proposed hotel was approved by ten votes to three at a meeting of the council. As the dirty linen of WA Inc began to receive its airing an allegation was made that councillors had been bribed. O'Connor was on a retainer of $500 a week. Bond Corporation also drew a cheque for $25 000, designated 'Cash—Mt Lawley Campaign Fund', which Walsh passed to O'Connor. The cheque was deposited in O'Connor's bank account where it helped reduce his overdraft. The WA Inc Royal Commission found that the $25 000 was intended by Bond Corporation to be distributed by O'Connor in bribes for Stirling City councillors, but that no bribes had ever been paid. Instead, O'Connor had misappropriated the money for his own use.[29]

Despite this Liberal Party sideshow, the Burke Government took the bulk of the damage. Substantial favours, such as the exclusive mandate for a petrochemical plant, the windfall profit on Fremantle Gas and the indefensible use of public funds to bail out Rothwells, were granted to a small clique of businessmen who gave big donations to Burke and his party. It should be pointed out that quite large and legitimate donations were given to the ALP by other businessmen, such as iron ore magnate Lang Hancock. However, the scale of political donations made by the WA Inc clique rose substantially after Burke's election in 1983. The Royal Commission attempted to list the relevant donations, but its records were incomplete and it may have missed some. The totals of some which it traced between 1983 and 1989 are shown in Table 4.6.[30]

With the exception of Holmes à Court, who was notoriously stingy,

Table 4.6 Donations to the WA Labor Party, 1983–89

Warren Anderson	$366 000
Alan Bond	$2 038 000
Laurie Connell	$860 000
Dallas Dempster	$512 000
Yosse Goldberg	$425 000
Robert Holmes à Court	$30 000

they donated substantial sums. But then each of these businessmen derived, or expected to derive, very substantial benefits from the WA Government. Apart from the $100 000 cash from Goldberg which went into Burke's office safe, these and other donations were paid into the No. 1 Advertising Account and were, in Burke's words, 'the property of the party'. The Royal Commission was unable to trace all the donations to this account because Mrs Brush had destroyed all the records—an act she was never able to explain to the Commission's satisfaction. The Commission was able to trace the cheques drawn on the account. Most were for legitimate party purposes, but some were unusual.

The Balga Soccer Club in Burke's electorate received $44 000 between 1985 and 1987. This may have been a justifiable use of ALP funds, but the club treasurer had always been under the impression that they were personal donations by Burke. When Mrs Brush was out of a job in 1987 she received $80 000, of which $55 000 was an advance for work to be done. Burke also punted the gold market through his friend Michael Naylor, who was an executive director of WADC and an executive of the WADC subsidiary Goldcorp. The gold trading was done under fictitious names and totalled some $200 000. 'Mr Burke was prepared to use what were ordinarily regarded as campaign funds for most unusual purposes', the Royal Commission report observed.

Most unusual of all was Burke's use of the $100 000 cash to invest in stamps. Burke said he invested some $87 000 of the money in stamps and the Royal Commission was unable to prove or disprove the figure. 'Mr Burke's entire evidence about the extraordinary retention and expenditure of cash was most unsatisfactory and totally lacking in credibility', the Royal Commission found.[31] 'We are satisfied that Mr Burke deliberately diverted the funds from this particular donation with the intention of using those funds for his own purposes. Such purposes may have included, but certainly were not limited to, an intention to assist candidates of his choice.'

The Royal Commission had been appointed by the new Labor Premier, Carmen Lawrence, in November 1990. By this time Peter Beckwith and Jack Walsh—two important witnesses—had died. One early star witness was Laurie Connell. In evidence, Connell named other donors to the ALP as Robert Holmes à Court, Dallas Dempster, John Roberts of

Multiplex, Ric Stowe of Griffin Coal, media owner Kerry Stokes, fishing magnate Mick Lombardo, Brian Coppin of Western Underwriters and Jack Bendat. The way Connell was prepared to drop names in his evidence to the Royal Commission gave his statements the impression of candour.

The most embarrassing disclosure in Connell's evidence to the Royal Commission concerned a party fund-raising lunch in June 1987, where the guest speaker had been Prime Minister Bob Hawke. The ALP was short of funds at the time, with a Federal election approaching. Connell claimed that Hawke had agreed to postpone a proposed tax on gold in return for donations totalling $950 000. In a whip-round at the lunch Connell, Dempster and Bond had each put in $250 000 and John Roberts $200 000. In parliament, Hawke denied the allegation, but was later forced into an admission that he had discussed a gold tax before the lunch. This was the first of an embarrassing series of errors which led to Hawke's having to apologise twice to parliament in three days. While Hawke was trying to distance himself from WA Inc, it was revealed that in August 1987—just two months after the notorious gold tax lunch—he had gone on a fishing trip with Bond, Connell and the Federal ALP's chief numbers man, Senator Graham Richardson. A video showing three of them huddled together in a small dinghy appeared on national television. Bob Hawke had managed the near impossible: for a while, his credibility looked lower than Connell's. The Leader of the Opposition, John Hewson, said: 'There is an enormous stench which has emerged out of the activities in Western Australia that has carried through to the very highest position in this government, to the Prime Minister'.

Burke was a heavy casualty of the Royal Commission. A grateful Hawke had earlier appointed him Ambassador to Ireland. Burke was recalled from Dublin to give evidence, a balding, furrowed man who hardly seemed related to the self-confident youngster who had won the 1983 election. He was eventually forced to quit his post after evidence revealed that he had continued to operate the Leader's Account from Dublin. Burke's former deputy, David Parker, also became a target. Connell alleged that Parker had asked for $1.75 million to launch himself as 'an international deal maker'. Connell said: 'He was aware that Robert Holmes à Court, who was a friend of his, was going to spend a lot of time in London. He thought that he'd like to do similarly: to go and live in London and put deals together'.[32] According to Connell, the request was made in 1988 after Parker had supported a scheme to have the WA Government pick up a $17.5 million bill owed by Connell. As Cabinet never supported the scheme the whole proposal fell through, Connell said. The allegation was vigorously denied by Parker.

Connell's name-dropping would have been more convincing if he had not tried to save his own skin in the process. He told the Royal Commission that he had left the running of Rothwells to others and did not know the extent of the problem loans. As most of the problem loans were to Connell entities this was difficult to accept.

The WA Government, which bore much of the responsibility for Rothwells growing so large, spent several months after the crash trying to welch on the indemnity it had given to the National Australia Bank. Exhaustive negotiations by liquidator Ian Ferrier resulted in the NAB and the WA Government making net contributions of $10.5 million and $12 million respectively. This was enough to ensure that Rothwells' depositors were repaid in full. Unsecured creditors and preference shareholders— after much haggling—received around 50 cents in the dollar.

The Rothwells collapse was a bonanza for lawyers. Bond Corp sued the WA Government for abandoning the PICL project, Connell issued 250 libel writs against journalists and Ferrier spent time in court before getting his settlement with the NAB and the WA Government.

There were also criminal prosecutions. The first victim, ironically, was not one of the prime movers in Rothwells but Tony Lloyd, who had been installed as managing director after the bank's first collapse. He was convicted of fraud for his involvement in the $15 million Western Collieries deal, sentenced to two years' jail and fined $5000. The sentence was later quashed by the WA Court of Criminal Appeal and Lloyd was instead fined $15 000. Later again, a retrial was ordered. Vrisakis was convicted of failing to exercise reasonable care and diligence while a director of Rothwells, but the conviction was overturned on appeal. Hugall was found guilty of stealing $8.5 million from Katanning Holdings in a Rothwells-related deal and was sentenced to three years' jail. He served a year before being released with a brain tumour and died in early 1992.

Kevin Edwards was fined $10 000 for being knowingly concerned in the Western Collieries loan. An appeal against the conviction resulted in its being quashed and a retrial ordered. Edwards left Western Australia for Vietnam, where he worked as a banking consultant. One of his regular visitors was David Parker, who was living in Hong Kong. Another visitor was Tony Lloyd—making Hanoi something of a haven for WA Inc refugees.

Connell was charged with conspiring to defraud investors in Rothwells. He fought the charges vigorously, claiming that he could not get a fair trial. To support this claim, his legal team commissioned a telephone survey of 400 people and found that 49 per cent of them thought he was guilty of falsifying accounts. Respondents described Connell as 'dishonest, a crook, corrupt, a shyster, a liar and not a nice man', according to Connell's lawyers.[34]

Charges were also laid against Louis Carter for conspiring with

Connell. KMG Hungerfords issued a statement saying: 'The firm strongly rejects any suggestion that the audit was inadequate and will vigorously defend its position. Our legal advice is that in no way do the matters raised in [the McCusker] report justify the laying of charges against Mr Carter'.

Then in January 1992 Connell was charged with race fixing. The allegation was that he had not allowed the horse Strike Softly to run on its merits in the 1983 AHA Cup at Bunbury. The story was sensational, even though the fix had been bungled. Strike Softly's jockey in the Cup had been a 20-year-old apprentice named Danny Hobby. When the Cup field started, Hobby resorted to the desperate and rather obvious expedient of jumping off Strike Softly soon after it left the stalls. The stewards suspended Hobby for two years.

After the suspension, Hobby was made 'an offer too good to refuse' (his own words) of a two-year trip around the world with his girlfriend, $30 000 cash and an allowance of $3000 a month. In 1986 the money ran out and he returned to Australia and threatened to tell his story. He was paid $10 000 and a further $300 000 to leave the country. Eventually, Hobby spent eight years abroad, moving from London, to Europe, to North America, to New Zealand and finally settling in Kuala Lumpur. He had to keep moving to dodge Australian police, who had never forgotten the incident and were still chasing him for race fixing. He had also received a few threats. By 1991 Hobby had received a million dollars, but Connell had run out of money. Then the WA Police, on speculation, went to see him in Malaysia. Hobby came back to Australia and told his story.

Newspaper readers who thought they had seen the worst of Laurie Connell were treated to a fresh bout of lurid allegations. One was that a hit man had contacted Connell and offered to silence Hobby and trainer Bob Meyers for half a million. Hobby pleaded guilty to race fixing and was sentenced to three years jail. Meyers received two and a half years. Judge Rob Viol said that Hobby's sentence would have been nine years except for mitigating factors, notably that Hobby had agreed to give evidence in any further case. Connell was charged with conspiring to fix the AHA Cup. The charges relating to Rothwells were deferred while the race-fixing case was heard. After the case had been going a month, the judge said he thought it would last six months. Then he had a heart attack and the whole trial had to start again, with a fresh jury empanelled. Australians were left contemplating the thought that fixing a horse race (on which Connell was alleged to have bet $30 000) was being given precedence over a trial that might have shed light on how Rothwells came to lose some half a billion dollars.

The evidence was rivetting, particularly from Meyers, who described how Connell had driven into Meyer's yard in a Rolls Royce. Connell had allegedly asked Meyers to approach Hobby to pull Strike Softly and $3000 was suggested as the price. When Meyer rang back to say Hobby wanted $5000, Connell said: 'Sweet, set and bet'. Connell said that under no circumstances was Hobby to know who had initiated the approach.[34] Meyers had kept silent for eight years, but finally told his story after police arrested him on other charges. Under cross-examination by Connell's QC, Alec Shand, Meyers agreed he was 'a thoroughly degraded person, an absolute scoundrel and a crook in the most calculated way'. Meyers also told the court that about 90 per cent of WA trainers used 'electric boots' to spur horses. A trainer without an electric boot was like 'a carpenter going in without his hammer', he said. 'There was nothing wrong if you didn't get caught.' Meyers had been jailed for five years in 1989 for having conspired with others to break into the homes of associates and have others bash them with baseball bats and pick handles.

Not only was Meyer's character open to attack, but so was his evidence. Connell claimed to have been at Busselton on the day Meyer alleged he had driven into the stables to fix the race. The trial lasted until May 1994 and the jury deliberated for five days before reaching their verdict. At first glance, their verdict seemed bizarre because they found Connell not guilty of fixing the race but guilty of perverting the course of justice by paying Hobby to stay out of Australia afterwards. But the verdict was not illogical. Connell had enough alibi to raise a reasonable doubt that he might not have been in Meyer's Belmont stables on the day Meyer stipulated. But there was certainly evidence that he had paid Hobby to stay away. As this book went to print, Connell was planning an appeal against the verdict.

If McCusker is correct that Connell spirited some $500 million from Rothwells, it ranks as one of the largest depredations upon a company in Australia's history. As we have seen, it was carried out with no great sophistication. Rothwells offered high rates of interest to the public and high commissions to advisors, who deposited hundreds of millions with the bank in the flush 1980s. Connell took most of the money out and appears to have lost it in bad investments and an extravagant lifestyle. As long as more money was flowing in through the front door than Connell was taking out through the back, the depositors never noticed. They were encouraged to believe the bank was sound by Rothwells' glossy annual reports showing ever-increasing profits and assets. They were also encouraged by the implicit support of the Queensland Government and the tacit support of the WA Government. In each case, the support was obtained through Connell making generous donations and plugging into the government's network of cronies. Neither government made any investigation of the affairs of Rothwells to check whether the bank warranted their imprimatur. Such an investigation should in particular have been ordered by Brian Burke before writing a glowing testimonial to Rothwells in 1984.

The perception of Rothwells' health was reinforced by an unqualified audit certificate. An audit which does not tell investors that the chairman of a bank has borrowed more than half its assets is not worth having. Nor would it have taken much digging to bring the unsound condition of Rothwells to light. The internal inquiries by Harris, McGranger, Douglas, Pope, Hare, Selwood, Hurley, Roberts and Hurst all detected the truth quickly—or as much of the truth as they were allowed to see. Carter's replacement, Scudamore, also seems to have needed little time to discover the true nature of Rothwells.

Looking at the Deloitte reconstruction of the books, it is clear that Rothwells never made a profit from 1984 onwards. If its results had been reported accurately it would have lost its trustee status in 1985 and would probably have been in liquidation in 1986. The disaster would have been greatly lessened. Instead, it was kept alive.

In hindsight, Connell was not a brilliant financier. If profits or losses are the index, he was a disastrous financier. His main skill seems to have been that of overcharging for his, or Rothwells', services. The high fees charged by Rothwells for finance were in many cases illusory because the loans were bad. It's bad business to collect a 20 per cent fee on a loan if the loss on the loan is going to be more than 20 per cent. In far too many cases Rothwells' loan losses approached 100 per cent. Normal commercial prudence would dictate that a financier should satisfy itself of each borrower's credit quality; and that not too high a proportion of the loans were concentrated on any borrower or group of borrowers. In Rothwells, credit assessment appears to have been non-existent and the loans were heavily concentrated amongst Connell and his cronies. Connell could hardly have run Rothwells worse if he had a death wish for the bank.

Nor does Burke emerge from the story as a brilliant politician, despite his reputation at the time. He allied himself with a bunch of opportunists and get-rich-quick merchants with no substance behind them. When they fell apart so did Burke's vision of WA Inc and his aspirations to become Prime Minister. Although Burke appears personally to have made little, if anything, out of the whole episode his reputation was buried under allegations of corruption.[35]

The concept of WA Inc was of a partnership in which businessmen would make money and the people of the state would benefit. The concept was defensible, but the implementation and the choice of players was not. The riches generated by WA Inc went to a chosen few within the business community. It is also questionable just how far the government's largesse was passed on by those few to the community at large. The vision descended into a grubby story of greed. Such was Camelot.

5

Spedley: the paper castle

My unenviable task is to seek to distil from this morass of confusion created intentionally by persons once thought by some to represent leaders of the Australian business and financial community, the true nature of the dealings between Spedley Securities and Bond Brewing Investments. The circumstances of this case show that those involved had scant, if any, regard for the law, and equally little regard for proper standards of corporate behaviour.

Mr Justice Cole

[Warning: Many of the transactions described in this chapter are mind-numbing. Readers without high powers of concentration are strongly advised to go straight to Chapter 6.]

The deceptions practised by Rothwells would not have gone far without the assistance of the Spedley and Bond groups. Whenever Rothwells needed to repaint its accounts at balance date, Spedley usually lent a hand. During all this time Spedley was run by Brian Yuill, the young man who 'had it all together' at Martin Corporation. Acquaintances from his early days speak of him having a mind like a computer. His dealing abilities in the bill market impressed all who knew him. In conversations he never needed to take notes. His memory was phenomenal.

Yuill was ambitious to be rich. Born in 1945, he grew up on a Maitland dairy farm. His father was a prisoner of war in a Japanese camp and died of his wartime privations while Brian was still a teenager. Yuill started work early as a messenger for Supervised Discounts Pty Ltd in Sydney. There he found a mentor in Jack Land, who had formerly run the Mines Pension Fund in Broken Hill.[1] Yuill became a money market dealer and in 1968 he and Land agreed to join the fledgling Martin Corporation. Land died of a heart attack before making the switch and Yuill found himself running Martin Corporation's money market operations.

By all accounts, Yuill was brilliant at the job. His colleagues included Jamie Craven and Ken Hawkins (who would later move with him to Spedley), Peter K. Lucas (later a director of Rothwells), Willie West (who would become the London partner of Potts West Trumbull) and Peter Joseph (later a director of ANI then chairman of Dominion Mining).

141

Yuill—young, charming, capable and impressive—formed bonds with these men, who would each play a role in the Spedley saga. The strongest personal bond was with Laurie Connell, who came to Sydney to be initiated into merchant banking and hit it off with Yuill immediately. Connell and Yuill both wanted the good life: big houses, fast horses, fine wine and all the other trappings. Both were capable of great generosity to their friends, generating strong loyalties which in some cases would even survive the collapse of their empires.

The fledgling Martin Corporation of the 1960s had more than its share of those who would later become notorious as corporate cowboys of the 1980s, but it had also recruited some very bright financiers such as Peter Joseph and Malcolm Irving, who headed Martin Corporation when it became CIBC Australia. Two others were Ian MacFarlane and John Strickland, who had both worked in the London money market. In 1968–69 the London bill market was greatly more sophisticated than the Australian, which was still in its infancy. A company needing short-term money would draw up a bill for $100 000 for 30 days at a set rate. It would then be endorsed by a bank and offered on the money market, but frequently the market was so thin that banks wound up holding their own paper. Another reason for the bill market being slow was that banks tended to offer bill facilities mainly to their lower quality customers.

Martin Corporation had established good links with BHP, which was interested in giving the almost non-existent bill market a shot in the arm. At that time BHP was selling steel to its customers on the basis of payment within seven days of invoice. As BHP sold its steel in very large minimum lots this practice caused periodic hardship and ill will among its steel merchants. MacFarlane and Strickland conceived a scheme whereby the merchants could accept bills of exchange to the value of the invoice, due in 90 days and drawn by BHP, with the merchant meeting the cost of the discounting. Martin Corporation became the arranger and discounter.

This suited everyone. BHP got its money, the steel merchants got their steel at a slightly higher price in return for extending their payment period out from seven days to a more manageable 90 days, Martin Corporation made fees and bill buyers were given a thicker and much higher quality market to trade. This was an important step in the growth of the Australian bill market.[2] Yuill did not devise the bills, but he arrived at Martin Corporation when they were being introduced and quickly seized the opportunity to sell them into the bill market.

Yuill survived the Beardsmore purge at Martin Corporation, but that was not enough for his ambition. Yuill dreamed—as did many rising young financiers of the day—of having his own merchant bank. His opportunity came from a rather unlikely source. Australian National

Industries (ANI), formed soon after World War II, was a solid but rather sleepy steel merchant and heavy engineering business headquartered above its forging plant in the western Sydney suburb of Lidcombe. In the late 1960s it became more dynamic thanks to its thrusting finance director, John Leard. He wanted to expand and diversify the old engineer and was the driving force behind ten takeovers by ANI between 1969 and 1972. In 1972, while Martin Corporation was still recovering from its horrors, the ANI board appointed Leard managing director. Leard was a dynamic character, with tight dark curly hair and an intense manner. He was also prepared to be unconventional. He must have been one of the few chief executives to wear a safari suit to work, but he was unconventional in other ways too. He was always exploring new methods of financing, being one of the first to adopt negative pledge lending in Australia, and was noted for his strong political views. He had an equally strong belief in himself.

Leard was determined to make ANI more entrepreneurial. He expanded through further takeovers and drove up the profits of the old engineering group. Old Australian companies traditionally retained strong ties with a single banker, but Leard shopped around for the best advice and terms. Soon ANI had a dozen bankers and one was Martin Corporation. Leard was always interested in innovative financing techniques and was attracted to bankers with bright ideas. As a steel merchant, ANI would naturally have been attracted to the man who had made the market in steel bills.

Leard had for some time wanted to form his own merchant bank. ANI became progressively involved in fringe banking in the 1970s, mainly through its holding in a financier named Aldershot Ltd. The formation of a merchant bank had been discussed periodically by Leard and Yuill since at least mid-1975. At one meeting in December 1976, attended by several executives who would later play a leading role in Spedley, a document was laid down setting out the principles upon which the proposed merchant bank would grant credit. Credit would only be granted after the board had approved of the client and the exposure. Management would only be able to lend within credit limits that had been approved by the board. These principles seem to have been laid down by representatives of the M.W. Marshall group (referred to below), who had strong views on credit facilities. If the principles had been followed the Spedley disaster would never have occurred.[3] Early in 1977 Leard took the plunge. He asked his principal legal officer, Christopher John Spedley Cutler, to find a suitable name for a bank. After discovering that the more resounding names had been taken, Cutler used one of his middle names and formed Spedley Holdings Ltd. In February 1977 ANI announced the formation of Spedley with an initial capital of $2 million in equity and shareholders' loans.

ANI took a 45 per cent direct stake in Spedley Holdings. Aldershot, in which ANI had a 49 per cent stake, took another 20 per cent (see Figure 5.I). By structuring the holding this way Spedley did not have to be consolidated into the ANI accounts, although for all practical purposes ANI was the controlling shareholder. Yuill and Ken Hawkins held 12.5 per cent each, for which each had contributed $125 000, and the M.W. Marshall group took the remaining 10 per cent. The Marshall group had a few years earlier been a subsidiary of the London broking house of Cater Ryder & Co, which was one of the shareholders of Martin Corporation. In 1972 directors and staff took over Marshall and now they were investing in a bank to be run by a former Martin executive. It is worth making the point that both Marshall and ANI were well acquainted with Yuill's work at Martin Corporation, and obviously they were impressed enough to back him as chief executive of a merchant bank in which they and he would be almost the only stakeholders. Leard was chairman, Yuill was managing director and Hawkins ran the Melbourne office. Spedley Holdings had a wholly owned subsidiary named Spedley Securities, which was the group's main operating company.

ANI always had a strong presence on the Spedley board. Apart from Leard, ANI representatives included ANI's managing director Neil Jones and its finance director John Maher. David Gray, another senior ANI executive, became a director of Spedley and remained as Spedley's chairman after he had resigned from ANI.

In hindsight, Spedley received curiously little attention in ANI's ensuing annual reports. Admittedly, ANI's equity was just under half, which meant it did not have to be consolidated into the group accounts. One could also argue that it was a minor diversification from ANI's mainline business in steel and engineering and that the amount invested was petty cash by ANI's standards, so it could be ignored in the annual report. This is not entirely convincing. A merchant bank's capital commonly forms only a fraction of its total liabilities, the bulk being provided by deposits.

The ANI accounts of the late 1970s and early 1980s never listed any contingent liabilities in relation to Spedley, implying that ANI never guaranteed its offspring. This implication is not entirely correct because ANI certainly issued letters of comfort to Banque Brussels Lambert to support a letter of credit facility which originally stood at $US5 million, and another letter of comfort to the Commonwealth Trading Bank for general bill endorsement facilities of up to $2 million. The letter of comfort to Banque Brussels Lambert, issued by ANI in 1982, said ' . . . It is our practice to ensure that our affiliate Spedley Securities Limited will at all

Figure 5.1   Spedley, 1977

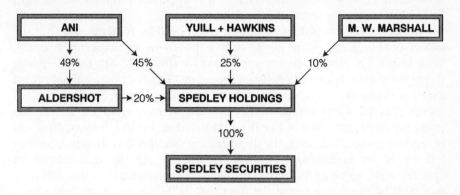

times be in a position to meet its financial obligations as they fall due'. One reason for ANI giving BBL a letter of comfort, as opposed to a guarantee, was specifically to avoid having to show it as a contingent liability in the ANI accounts. However, after Spedley failed, Mr Justice Rogers of the NSW Supreme Court found that it was enforceable, so for all those years the letter of comfort was—for all practical purposes—an undisclosed contingent liability.[4]

Even without a letter of comfort, ordinary depositors would have been reassured by ANI's presence as a parent of Spedley with directors on the Spedley board. In the event of Spedley failing, those depositors might have sought recourse against ANI (as in the event, they did), so Spedley had the potential to become a substantial liability for ANI. Yet in Spedley's first seven years it never received more than a couple of sentences in the annual report and in some years was not mentioned at all. Considering that ANI's annual reports were among the best in Australia during those years, in terms of disclosure, the silence about Spedley was a curious lapse.

The Spedley group could be considered a private bank. Members of the public could deposit money with Spedley Securities, but it did not solicit them. Spedley Securities took deposits almost exclusively from within the professional market, having facilities with a large range of domestic and overseas banks. It reinvested the deposits in such securities as government bonds, semi-government issues and commercial bills. In addition, Spedley earned fee income from underwriting and corporate lending.

As Spedley had no public shareholders and made no public offerings of notes or debentures, its affairs were of little interest to analysts or journalists. Any of them who did pry would have emerged little wiser because the Spedley accounts were skeletally brief and, as the years went by, increasingly misleading. Although the Spedley group would not collapse until 1989, when John Harkness was appointed liquidator, it might have been insolvent since at least 1986.[5]

In reviewing the history of Spedley it should be remembered that the affairs of this group were never fully exposed in an inspector's report. Glen Miller, QC, the inspector appointed by the NSW Attorney General, Gerry Peacocke, delivered one brief report in 1990. No other official report ever became public. Miller illuminated some aspects of Spedley but the report was far from comprehensive. Other details emerged in various court proceedings, notably the liquidator's case against former directors of Spedley and ANI and the liquidator's Section 541 hearings. What follows is an assemblage of these fragments. As the transactions in Spedley were some of the most complex and convoluted of the 1980s we may well be missing some of the finer details. However, enough has been revealed for us to be confident that the big picture is fairly accurate.

Extending the foundations

Spedley Securities' first full-year accounts for 1978 showed that it had attracted deposits totalling $67 million, an impressive figure for a fledgling bank to attract in such a short time. Spedley's net profit was a modest $178 000, not much to earn on deposits of that order.

In that year Spedley took over Aldershot Ltd, an incestuous deal which meant that Spedley for a time owned 20 per cent of itself. This was straightened out—after a fashion—by Spedley placing 10 per cent with Yuill and another 7.5 per cent into an ANI executive superannuation scheme whose beneficiaries included Leard, Maher and Gray.[6] This holding was later sold to an associated company, GPI, but as long as it remained in the superannuation scheme there would have been an argument that Spedley should have been consolidated as a subsidiary of ANI. It never was.

Aldershot was only one of a series of takeovers and investments by Spedley in the early 1980s. In 1980 Spedley took a 20 per cent holding in another Sydney financier, Bisley Investment Corporation Ltd. In 1983 the group further expanded when Spedley Securities took over the UK-based Kirkland-Whittaker group, one of the twelve companies licensed by the Bank of England to deal in the interbank foreign exchange and Eurocurrency deposit markets. Later Kirkland-Whittaker, too, was transferred to the control of Spedley Holdings. One of the most successful investments was a joint venture with the North Carolina National Bank, named NCNB Spedley, which specialised in trade financing of capital items for the resources industry. The NCNB bought Spedley out of the venture in 1986.

Spedley Securities had two primary activities. The first was money market operations, in which it took deposits from financial institutions (and occasionally the public) and re-lent the money in the form of bills. The second activity was trading securities, principally negotiable certificates of deposit (NCDs), bills and shares. During these early years Spedley Securities, while exuding the image of a professional and expanding banking house, was returning only paper-thin profits. Although reported profits rose every year they were tiny. In 1982 pre-tax profit was stated at $1.3 million. In 1983 it rose to $2.2 million, a meagre return on total assets of $176 million. Banking profits are typically small in relation to turnover, but 1.25 per cent for Spedley Securities was pretty low. Nevertheless, Spedley's image was of a merchant bank with growing profits and a steadily strengthening balance sheet. It was essential that this should be so, because the deposits from financial institutions would have quickly dried up if Spedley began showing losses. Also, losses would imperil its dealer's licence.

It may be that Spedley Securities never in fact made any profits at all. On later evidence Spedley actually made a loss in 1982 and 1983 and announced a profit only after ANI helped it dress the books each balance date. In 1982 ANI paid $1.4 million to Spedley on 29 October, two days before balance date. This was described as fees receivable for consulting to ANI on various deals over the past five years. Those 'fees' turned what would have been a loss of $100 000 into a profit of $1.3 million. Without this sudden recognition of a backlog of five years' fees, Spedley Securities could not have maintained its unbroken run of increasing profits. An undated memo from Leard to David Gray around this time referred to the necessity to write down some bonds, but said that this would be cushioned by a fee from ANI for the same amount. Then, after balance date had passed, Spedley would pay ANI a dividend equal to the after-tax amount of the fees, restoring the status quo.[7]

In 1982–83 ANI took over another engineering company, Comeng Holdings Ltd. ANI paid Spedley a secret $4.3 million fee for consulting on the takeover. This was despite the fact that it had retained BT Australia as its consultant for the takeover and BT was named on all the documentation. However, the fee turned a $2.1 million loss into a $2.2 million profit for Spedley, again enabling its results to show an unbroken upward trend. In ANI's annual report, Leard mentioned Spedley's unbroken profits but did not tell shareholders they had paid the so-called bank such substantial fees. In those days $4.3 million ($5.7 million counting the 1982 fee) would have bought a lot of consultancy.

In 1984 Spedley Securities increased further in size by taking over the merchant bank Group Holdings Ltd, which had formerly been two-thirds owned by the Melbourne sharebroking firm of A.C. Goode & Co. Spedley

outbid the Melbourne broking firm F.W. Holst & Co and Goode accepted
very quickly. Potts West Trumbull were Spedley's brokers. One asset
acquired in this takeover was an aura of increased respectability, because
Group Holdings included 100 per cent of First Federation Discounts, one
of Australia's nine authorised money market dealers. These institutions
operated in the arcane world of bonds, Treasury notes and bank bills.
Their growth had been fostered by the Reserve Bank of Australia when
it was keen to create a secondary market in government paper. The nine
dealers were guaranteed by the RBA, putting them at the pinnacle of
financial status in Australia but carrying the corollary that they had to
be monitored by the RBA. The affairs of First Federation appear to have
been managed impeccably, but RBA monitoring did not extend to the
affairs of its parent and associates.

As long as Leard stayed on the ANI and Spedley boards, Yuill appears
to have been more or less under control; but in June 1984 Leard stepped
down as managing director of ANI. In October 1984 he left the ANI board
and in February 1985—before the Group Holdings restructuring—he
resigned from Spedley too.

Before stepping down from the Spedley board Leard wrote a seven-
page memo to his successor at ANI, Neil Jones. The memo contained
recommendations about how Spedley Securities should be directed and
operated. He suggested areas where Jones and ANI's finance director John
Maher should concern themselves. Leard criticised the managers of
Spedley. He warned Jones to keep ANI's interests in mind when acting
on Spedley matters. 'ANI should take the view that Spedley is now a
large investment requiring closer ANI monitoring than in the past', he
said. This memo would later acquire fame as the 'smoking gun' in the
Spedley/ANI case.[8]

Having written this memo in January 1985 Leard retired and became
a political polemicist, airing some rather radical views and writing books
about his travels around the world. Commentators often considered Leard
a right-winger, but Leard did not. 'I was always middle of the road', he
once told the author. 'But somewhere along the years, the road shifted.'
Up until Leard's departure, the fudging in the Spedley and ANI accounts
was relatively small. Afterwards, the Spedley accounts became increasingly misleading and ANI appears to have become tied to Yuill's chariot
wheels, unable to check his dealings then finally forced to increasingly
desperate measures to cover them up and bail him out.

The restructuring of Group Holdings was an important turning point
in the Spedley story. Spedley Holdings paid $7 million to acquire the
capital of Group Holdings (see Figure 5.2). Then a complicated series of
deals occurred. Group Holdings sold its main businesses—First Federation and a money market company named Security Deposits—to Spedley

Holdings for $9.5 million. This was an odd arrangement because Spedley had already acquired 98 per cent of Group Holdings. In buying the official and unofficial dealers from it, Spedley was virtually buying the same assets twice. If a public company had done such a deal, eyebrows would have been raised and questions asked. But as Spedley was a private company it could do as it wished.

Then some 60 per cent of the shares in Group Holdings were sold back to the public through Potts West Trumbull and McNall Hordern, another Sydney broking firm linked to Spedley. This float recouped for Spedley the $9.6 million it had paid for the two money market companies. The net effect was that Spedley had now laid out $7 million for First Federation and Security Deposits. This roughly equated their assets, which comprised a couple of million dollars tax losses in Security Deposits, $4 million funds in First Federation and First Fed's dealer's licence, which the takeover price had valued at an historic high of $1.7 million.

Everything else in Group Holdings was now owned by others. This included its listing, the $9.5 million just injected by Spedley and a couple of million dollars cash from before the takeover. Investors who picked up the Group shares were buying into a listed cashbox with $11.4 million. (One small shareholder which came aboard at this time was Rothwells.) In a separate deal Brian Yuill, who had previously held 20 per cent of Spedley, swapped that shareholding for 40 per cent of Group Holdings (see Figure 5.3). The combined effect of these deals was to confer advantages on Yuill at the expense of the shareholders of Spedley. Before the takeover of Group Holdings and the subsequent deals, Yuill was managing director of Spedley and held 20 per cent of it. After the deals Yuill was still managing director of Spedley, but now he owned 40 per cent of Group Holdings, which owned 22.5 per cent of Spedley and $11.4 million cash (of which Spedley had put in $9.5 million). And Yuill had achieved this without having to spend one dollar of his own. The sale to Spedley, incidentally, enabled Group to book a $5.3 million extraordinary profit, giving Group a brilliant start.

It is by no means clear why the ANI board should have allowed this deal, because it meant that the managing director of their merchant bank now had an inherent conflict of interest. If Brian Yuill came across a good deal in future, would he put it into Spedley or Group? Although Yuill retained his post at Spedley, Group Holdings would increasingly become his personal bank. Indeed, from about this date he treated *both* of them as his personal banks. Large commitments would be made by both Spedley and GPI with little or no reference to the boards. Large risks and exposures would be undertaken to suit the needs of Yuill and his mates, rather than with any regard for the risks to the banks' creditors and shareholders.

Figure 5.2   Spedley after Group Holdings takeover, 1984

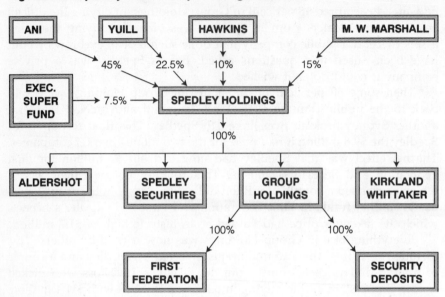

Group Holdings made a one-for-one bonus issue, then split its shares, effectively quadrupling the number on issue. Its name was changed to Greater Pacific Investments, commonly known as GPI. In June 1986 GPI raised $41 million with a one-for-one rights issue at $1.50. This meant that Yuill would have to pay $16.5 million to maintain his equity at 40 per cent. He did this with money that was entirely borrowed from Spedley Securities. Figure 5.4 shows how the money was funnelled through Oakhill and Beverage Holdings, the private companies of Laurie Connell and Rothwells' managing director Peter K. Lucas, and then through a Yuill company named Nodrogan Pty Ltd to another Yuill company named Hapeni Pty Ltd which held the GPI shares. Hapeni then extinguished the debt to Nodrogan by issuing preference shares in satisfaction. Nodrogan never repaid any principal or interest to Oakhill and Beverage. Oakhill and Beverage made several later attempts to reverse or undo these transactions and also to account for interest that was supposed to be paid on them, but the loans continued to dog all the parties until both Rothwells and Spedley collapsed.[9]

From the formation of GPI in 1985 the core Spedley group was fundamentally complete, although there would be constant minor changes and some major additions over the years. Referring again to Figure 5.3, a reorganisation by Marshall's would result in its 15 per cent holding in Spedley being transferred to Alexander Laing & Cruickshank of Britain, but these alterations had little practical effect. Yuill, with his fellow executives, controlled the day to day business of Spedley Holdings, Spedley Securities and GPI. GPI in turn held 20 per cent of Bisley Investment Corporation. Brent Potts was chairman of Bisley and senior partner of Potts West Trumbull, a broking firm which benefited from getting a large chunk of the business generated by Yuill's group. McNall and Hordern, another firm which dealt extensively for the confederation, was 50 per cent owned by Bisley. Another professional link was with the law firm Baker & McKenzie, whose senior partner Jim Beatty played a prominent role in the group's affairs. Baker & McKenzie did all Spedley's legal work. Beatty was chairman of Group Holdings/GPI and would be chairman of GPI Leisure and Tulloch Lodge when they were formed later. Spedley and GPI had extensive dealings with each other. Although these companies had separate owners and creditors, Yuill behaved as though their funds comprised one big ball of money which could be rolled around the confederation at will, regardless of the risks involved for the outside shareholders.

This attitude is typical of boomtime promoters throughout history, and was widely shared during the 1980s in Australia by such bold riders as Alan Bond and Laurie Connell. The trouble is that, when the boom stops, it is never possible to get the money back into the places where it belongs. The effect is the same as a game of musical chairs. When the music stopped at the end of the 1980s, shareholders found there were hardly any chairs left at all.

In Spedley's case, many professional depositors must have been reassured not only by the affable and brilliant Yuill but also by the names surrounding him. ANI was a solidly respectable engineering company with a long, unbroken history of rising profits. First Federation was part of the Reserve Bank's charmed inner circle of authorised dealers. Brent Potts was regarded as one of the most brilliant and successful sharebrokers of his generation, with a genius for securing large parcels of stock during takeover raids. Potts was chairman of the associated company BT Insurance, a director of GPI Leisure and Bisley Investment and also a director of the Australian Stock Exchange. James Beatty, a senior partner of the internationally respected law firm Baker & McKenzie, was chairman of the associated companies GPI Leisure and Tulloch Lodge. The association with Bond and Connell was a worry, but the brief, uninformative accounts issued by Spedley gave no reason for significant concern.

Life in the castle

Like his great mate Laurie Connell, Yuill was able to survive for an

Figure 5.3 Spedley after Group Holdings reconstruction, 1985

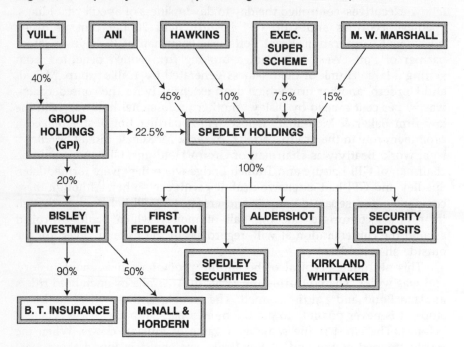

amazingly long time on the basis of misleading accounts. Also like his great mate Connell, Yuill was a high liver. Yuill was always a racegoer, although not as flamboyant as Connell. Yuill had owned horses and backed them since his Martin Corporation days. At first this was a relatively modest hobby. Yuill was quietly spoken and not ostentatious at the track. As Spedley's apparent success grew, Yuill's purse deepened. His horses were trained by Les Bridge. He was also a friend of top bloodstock dealer Reg Inglis, who said: 'He'd buy a horse this week, give us a cheque next week. There was never any problem. Brian loves racing and he liked a bet. He was a quiet and very likeable character'.[10] Yuill became the first outsider to buy a stake (13 per cent) in the old family bloodstock business of William Inglis & Co.

Yuill and his wife Elisabeth bought the Edgecliff mansion Fenton, formerly the home of Dr Lorimer Dods. Classified by the National Trust, Fenton has seven bedrooms, four bathrooms, two kitchens and a front porch flanked by Doric columns. Through his company Bondoro Pty Ltd Yuill bought a country estate, Guntawang, where he bred horses. The Guntawang homestead, near Gulgong, was an 1860s colonial home listed with the National Trust. It was restored at a cost of $1 million. It has seven bedrooms, a swimming pool, billiard room and children's rumpus

Figure 5.4   Financing GPI rights issue, 22 July 1986

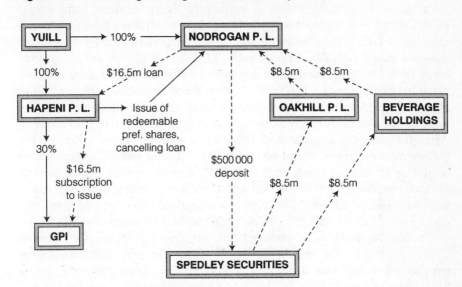

room. Two 17th century fireplaces were imported from England. The carpet was also imported from England, along with the carpet layer, who complained of jet lag as he put them down. 'It makes Milton Park look like a Travelodge', said one frequent guest. The Yuills frequently hired a Lear jet to take their guests to Guntawang for weekends. In mid-1989, when Spedley's troubles were at their height, Elisabeth bought the adjoining Thornbury station.[11] According to Glen Miller, QC, the Guntawang purchases had been funded by Spedley and GPI, through Bondoro. By mid-1990 these loans had grown to $6 million including interest.[12]

Yuill bought a boat so that he could watch the America's Cup defence when it was sailed off Fremantle in 1987. *Anastasia* was a 17-metre launch with a full-time skipper and engineer. After the race *Anastasia* was brought east and moored at Rushcutters Bay. In London, in the same year, Yuill bought a four-storey terrace house in Carlyle Street, Chelsea. Spedley lent £1.1 million to Willie West, the London representative of Potts West Trumbull, who bought the five-bedroom mansion on Yuill's behalf. Spedley also financed an $88 000 Bentley for Yuill's use in London.

Yuill and Spedley projected an image of expertise and easy affluence. In the luxuriously appointed office the main business would be done in the morning. Yuill was a forceful character who did most of the talking at meetings. The executive who carried out most of his orders was Jamie Craven. Craven was corporate manager of Spedley Securities and was the alternate director on the Spedley boards to ANI's finance director, John Maher. Yuill bullied Craven frequently. Every morning Yuill would meet Craven and other close associates. One was John ('Jake') Corner, a director of GPI, Bisley Investments, Bisley Properties and BT Insurance. Another was Jim Beatty. Craven said: 'Mr Beatty's offices are 30 seconds away from Mr Yuill's and not a day goes by that a meeting does not take place between him and Mr Yuill'.[13] Often there would be a phone call to Hawkins in Melbourne. But, whoever Yuill talked to, in truth nobody appears to have been much inclined to question the assured Yuill anyway. After the morning's deals had been done and positions taken in the money markets, there would be lunch in the dining room. Perhaps a beer to start with around noon, then fine food, top wines and a good port to finish. Frequently Yuill would eat out at the better restaurants of Sydney and the eastern suburbs. He wore a well-tailored, pin-striped grey suit and an air of quiet affluence as he chainsmoked through a meal.

Yuill's memory was phenomenal. So was his persuasive ability. Craven said: 'He was like Rasputin. He could persuade quite intelligent people that a deal was in their interests'. Yuill in these years also had a high degree of self-discipline. He was capable of giving up smoking and alcohol for long periods.

A great deal of postmortem investigation was conducted into how much each of the key executives knew about various deals. Yuill was certainly the ringmaster who knew all about all of them. Perhaps the most important point is that substantial deals were frequently done without the knowledge or approval of the relevant boards, such as those of Spedley and GPI. One striking similarity with the Bond empire is the way Yuill bonded executives to him through personal favours. In Spedley one mechanism was 'top hat' loans. These were no-interest housing loans made by Spedley to six executives, totalling some $2.3 million. Other Spedley loans were made to executives from time to time. For the 'top hat' loans there was never any documentation. If they had been recorded and fully accounted for their opportunity cost after tax, these loans would probably have created an extra negative of about a million a year on Spedley's profit and loss account. But being undocumented they were never seen.[14]

So Spedley executives always had money and good houses, reinforcing the image of a successful bank. In the words of Peter Joseph, Yuill looked as though he had it all together. In fact, the image of wealth and mastery was bogus. Spedley had to falsify its accounts to survive. Behind the facade of affluence the brute reality of Spedley was that it never made money. Its bread and butter business should have been its money market, but it was a consistent loser. In February 1986, for example, it was borrowing money at an average rate of 17.63 per cent and lending it at an average of 13.27 per cent. This is what is called a negative lending margin of 4.36 per cent. The whole idea of a money market operation, of course, is to lend money at a higher rate than you can borrow it. In practice, this can never be done all the time. Clients who make big deposits may be offered higher rates to keep their business. On the lending side the market may be awash with funds for a day or longer periods, forcing the available rates down. Or the operator may take the view that interest rates are about to rise and will deliberately take lower rates on short-term paper to avoid being locked into longer term paper. But after allowing for all these factors a money market operation should in the long term make at least enough money to cover its operating costs. Otherwise it is hard to find a good reason for being there.

For so-called professionals, Spedley's money market performance was dismal. It had negative lending margins (that is, it was lending money at a loss) throughout 1986. In 1987 it had a positive margin of 2.44 per cent in April, traded slightly above break-even in a few other months, but was otherwise negative throughout the year. John Maher said that Yuill's usual explanation was that lending and borrowing were part of a total business and that they produced other business which was profitable.[15] This was a dubious justification. In any business the core operation should make money or at least wash its face. In Spedley's case the profits produced in other areas such as share trading appear never to have been adequate to offset the losses on the money market, and this pattern continued for several years. Maher himself conceded in the Section 541 examination that there was no justification for a merchant bank lending at lower than cost in the longer term.

So Spedley had to window-dress its accounts with manufactured profits. This became a bilateral arrangement. At various times Spedley and Rothwells helped window-dress each other's balance sheets, with Bond Corporation occasionally chipping in to assist. This was easier because their balance dates were staggered. Bond balanced at the end of June, along with most Australian companies, but Rothwells balanced in July and Spedley in October. A bad debt in Rothwells' books, for instance, could be sold to Spedley for an inflated price on 31 July and bought back next day. It would never appear in the Spedley books. This does not appear to have happened in any planned way. On the contrary, it seems that every balance date for Spedley and Rothwells was an emergency which had to be met by all sorts of last-minute, ad hoc devices with friends being called in as a last resort.

Readers will recall from Chapters 3 and 4 that by 1984 the Spedley group was helping to fudge Rothwells' accounts for the year. Rothwells' July 1984 balance date was greatly alleviated by two devices. In the first, Aldershot borrowed $7.9 million from Rothwells and lent it back again.

But when the loan returned to Rothwells it was credited against Laurie Connell's account with Rothwells instead of being credited to Aldershot. This helped Connell to avoid appearing as a debtor in Rothwells' books that year. In the second device, Spedley participated in a round robin in which third parties borrowed $22 million from Rothwells and lent the money to L.R. Connell & Partners, which repaid $22 million in debts to Rothwells. The money had thus gone around in a circle and indeed went back again in the next two weeks as all the deals were unwound. Spedley's share in this round robin was $7 million. Thus the Spedley group committed itself to a $14.9 million exposure to Connell. The exposure was admittedly for a brief period but tacitly it was made to a man whom Yuill either knew, or at least should have had reason to suspect, could not pay his debts. At the time, $14.9 million comprised the bulk of the shareholders' equity in Spedley.[16]

Spedley often fell back on good old ANI. One of Spedley's longstanding problems was a parcel of 1996 Commonwealth bonds. Because of the high interest rates that prevailed throughout Spedley's life, these bonds at all times had a market value well below their cost and avoiding a writedown on them became a perennial problem. On Spedley's balance date in 1985, for example, the bonds were sold to ANI for $5.6 million, which was well above their market value. Spedley bought them back immediately afterwards.[17] It is difficult to think of a valid reason for paying rates significantly above market for bonds, whose prices are a function of the prevailing interest rate. In a separate deal on its 1985 balance date, Spedley sold 7.5 million shares in Bond Corporation to Allan Hawkins' Equiticorp Australia. Equiticorp sold some of the holding, but the rest were sold back to Spedley in April 1989 under the terms of the agreement. Spedley made an apparent profit of $10 million on the deal. Without it Spedley would have had to report a loss in 1985, but instead managed to report a $1.7 million profit. Equiticorp was promised 20 per cent interest while it held the shares.[18]

The loose, easygoing confederacy continued between Bond, Spedley and Rothwells. In 1985 Spedley again came to Connell's rescue when Rothwells' July balance date loomed and Connell's increasing borrowings from Rothwells had to be hidden. This time Spedley participated in round robins for a total of $24 million, effectively taking that exposure to Connell overnight to help reduce his debt to Rothwells.[19] And just before Bond Corporation's June 1986 balance date, Spedley paid Bond Corporation $1.1 million which was used to eradicate loans of that amount owing by Bond director Tony Oates. It should be recognised that, until this point, the Spedley group had operated entirely in the financial services industry. It ran no factories, mines or cash flow businesses apart from some in Bisley. Spedley's assets were pieces of paper and dealing skills. Although the group projected an image of expertise and profitability, subsequent examination of its books suggested that in real terms it probably made operating losses in every year from 1984 onwards. It may very well have run out of money earlier if it had not been for the float of GPI Leisure.

Austotel and GPI Leisure

In 1986 Bond Corporation was looking, as ever, for a way to raise cash. Following the takeovers of Swan, Castlemaine and Tooheys, the three old-established companies became parts of Bond's wholly owned subsidiary, Bond Brewing, which owned nearly half of the brewing industry in Australia. Thanks to history, it also owned hundreds of tied hotels. Although legally these pubs had been owned by the breweries, by custom the goodwill of each business had belonged to the publican. This was because, although a hotel could be owned by a company, the licence to run a hotel could only be held by an individual. This gave an individual the opportunity to add value to the licence. Typically, a young man might learn the trade as a cellarman and barman, saving some money. Then he would borrow more and buy the licence for some rundown hotel for, say, $50 000. He and his wife (the trade suited married couples) could work hard to build the business up by improving the liquor and food service, hiring jazz bands for lunch and night trade, and—in the pre-TAB days— having an SP bookie in the corner of the public bar (he always sat next to the phone). After a couple of years of hard work and long hours the couple could with luck sell the business for $100 000. With this lump sum they might retire or move on to a bigger pub and make an even bigger killing. All the brewery did was consent to the change. The arrangement worked well because the brewery's turnover improved. No employee works harder than one who has the incentive of a lump sum.

But although the arrangement was sanctified by custom, it was not established by law. Bond Corporation now decided to capitalise on the accumulated goodwill of the 267 hotels it owned by selling them into a trust called Austotel for $323 million. There was an immediate and highly vocal outcry from publicans who with one legal swoop had been deprived of their nest eggs. Those who had worked hard to build their pub's goodwill now saw it snatched by Bond Corporation. For many publicans, the goodwill represented their life's savings. As Alan Bond was reputedly one of Australia's wealthiest men at the time, the bitterness against him ran high. The outcry was largest in New South Wales and Queensland, where the majority of the Austotel pubs were. The NSW publicans raised a fighting fund and started a legal action which dragged on for some time and was ultimately unsuccessful.

Austotel Trust was owned 26 per cent by Bond Corporation, 25 per cent by Melbourne hotelier Bruce Mathieson and 49 per cent by GPI Leisure, a public company floated by GPI for the purpose. Austotel had total funds of $350 million, comprising $323 million for the hotels and the balance for refurbishment and the possible purchase of new hotels. Of this $350 million, $200 million had been borrowed from a syndicate headed by Lloyds Bank NZA and the State Bank of South Australia. The other $150 million was subscribed in equity. Bond Corporation paid $39 million for its 26 per cent share (it could afford to, having just collected $323 million), and Mathieson paid $37.5 million for his 25 per cent. GPI Leisure paid $73.5 million for its 49 per cent (see Figure 5.5).

GPI Leisure was floated by GPI in August 1986 as a public company with 100 million shares paid to $1 each. The seven directors included Beatty, Yuill, Potts, Craven and Corner, the managing director of Bisley. Readers will note that, although the Austotel stake cost only $73.5 million, GPI Leisure raised $100 million. After deducting the costs of the issue it had $22 million spare cash. The prospectus stated that this would be used for working capital and proposed investments in other leisure-related activities. With an independent board, GPI Leisure might have fared well. But GPI held some 30 per cent of its capital and Yuill and his GPI colleagues dominated the board. The Bond group held another 7 per cent. GPI had to put up $30 million for its 30 per cent stake in GPI Leisure. This $30 million was raised by GPI's $41 million rights issue of June 1986.

The short, brutal history of GPI Leisure is one of the most disgraceful episodes of the 1980s. GPI Leisure was floated to the public as a tourism and leisure stock. It raised $100 million in equity capital on the grounds that this would finance its stake in Austotel and that it would pursue other high-quality investments in tourism, leisure and entertainment. Its real destiny—as we shall see—was to be raped.

By now Spedley and Rothwells were becoming tied to each other's chariot wheels. As they were known to be friends and business associates a loss by one of them would cause a drop in confidence in the other. They were becoming bound to support each other and, as noted, the staggered balance dates made it easier. So Spedley again helped Connell when Rothwells' balance date came around in July 1986. This time, however, the assistance was a relatively modest $13 million.

The 1986 accounts for Spedley Securities showed that it had total assets of just over $400 million and net assets of $27.8 million. It declared a profit of $3.6 million for the year. Glen Miller, QC, the inspector appointed by the NSW Government, would later estimate that window-dressing had enhanced this profit by $17.9 million. In other words, Spedley Securities should have declared a $14.3 million loss for the year. 'If these stated apprehensions as to inaccuracy of the accounts are

158

established with certainty, Spedley Securities was in dire financial straits from at least 1986 to the date of its demise', Miller said.[20] Two points worth noting here are that Spedley's losses apparently increased between 1985 and 1986, and that a $14 million loss would have wiped out half the shareholders' funds in Spedley and caused a considerable loss of confidence in the company.

Spedley Securities expunged the 1986 loss with several devices. The Bond shares (which were actually owned by Spedley Securities' sister company, Aldershot) were pressed into service again. This time they were sold to GPI for an apparent profit of $12.1 million. GPI had bought the shares with money borrowed from Spedley.[21]

So the facade was still intact. In February 1987 Yuill launched one of the high-profile floats of the boom, Tulloch Lodge Ltd. The public sub-scribed $15 million to Tulloch Lodge, whose main asset would be the services of leading racehorse trainer Tommy Smith, the little magician whose success with two-year-olds was legendary. Apart from Smith's talents, the assets of Tulloch Lodge comprised a five-year lease on his Tulloch Lodge stable and some rural agistment properties. The five directors included Beatty as chairman, Smith and Yuill. The five under-writers included Potts West Trumbull, McNall & Hordern and Spedley Securities. Tulloch Lodge was a glamour float, but it must have marked some sort of apogee of the share boom that $15 million could be raised on the talents of a racehorse trainer and little else. Naturally, Tommy Smith was delighted with Yuill. 'He's a lovely bloke to do business with', Tommy said. 'So straightforward about things.'[22] Professional investors were wary of the float, being sceptical of the value of some of the assets. But the bloodstock industry was also booming at the time and punters rushed to subscribe. They would have got better odds from the book-makers, because the destiny of Tulloch Lodge—like that of GPI Leisure—was to be raped.

One point in favour of Tulloch Lodge was that investors were clear from day one that they were taking a gamble. Their shares would have value only if Smith could buy and train winners. This was a risk, but nobody in Australia had a better track record than the little man from Randwick. He scored the quinella in Australia's richest two-year-old race, the Golden Slipper, with Star Watch and Comely Girl. These factors would enable Tulloch Lodge to post a maiden profit of $730 000 pre-tax in 1988. But, while horses were obviously a risky investment medium, it was not the hazards of the track that would prove lethal to Tulloch Lodge. Its big risk was the man who had created it, Brian Yuill.

In July 1987 Spedley made its biggest contribution yet to a Connell round robin. This time it lent $50 million to Laurie Connell's private company Oakhill in return for a $50 million deposit from Rothwells. This enabled Connell to extinguish $50 million of his debt to Rothwells at balance date.[23]

For at least three years the management of Spedley had been unable to *trade* the group out of trouble. This period covered the longest sustained share market boom in Australia's history—a boom that was bound to end some time. Whenever it did, Spedley's position would go from bad to desperate.

Spedley insecurities

The music stopped on 20 October 1987. After the great market crash Spedley had a severe and immediate problem. Having reached its limits with its traditional lending sources (many of which were withdrawing money from the group), Spedley was forced to seek support from its major shareholder. On Black Tuesday ANI had $34 million on deposit with Spedley. ANI was only a reluctant lender. On 21 October—the day after the crash—Maher gave an instruction that any surplus funds of ANI were to be placed elsewhere in the market than with Spedley.[24] A few days later, ANI decided not to lend to Spedley except on a secured basis.

A crucial board meeting of ANI was held on the 27th. Board papers at this meeting gave Spedley's figures for the eleven months to September. The papers showed that, over this period, Spedley had lost $737 000 on the money market. However, the board was told that a profit of $5 million would be achieved in October.[25] This probably stayed the board's hand from any drastic action. Nobody would have wanted to be carried away by panic and withdraw support from Spedley if it still looked viable. However, there was enough to worry about. Spedley's September balance sheet showed an excess of current liabilities over current assets (known as an adverse current ratio). It was a condition of Spedley Securities' dealer's licence that it must maintain more current assets than current liabilities.

There was another factor. The Rothwells rescue had been announced only the day before. It looked as though corporate Australia was pulling together. With some reluctance, ANI decided to support Spedley. One deal was a piece of window-dressing. ANI bought a parcel of shares from Spedley for $26.7 million although their market value was probably half that (the portfolio included such gems as seven million Bond Media shares at issue price of $1.55). ANI had put and call options ensuring that the portfolio would revert to Spedley. But $26.7 million was only a first step. The amount of support Spedley needed turned out to be massive. By the 30th ANI had lent Spedley another $61 million, taking its total exposure to $95 million.

160

Figure 5.5   GPI, GPI Leisure and Austotel, August 1986

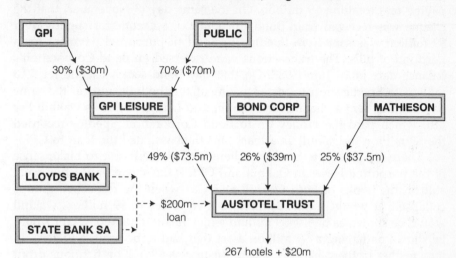

Several ANI directors thought the company should consider the sale of its Spedley stake. This was probably not a practical option at the time, given the general withdrawal of buyers in the wake of Black Tuesday. However, Maher did threaten to increase its lending rates to Spedley substantially. The objective was to give Spedley a strong incentive to look elsewhere for funds.[26] As an incentive it was a total failure. By 20 November Spedley had borrowed $126 million from ANI and by 10 December ANI's total exposure had reached $149 million.

The prime responsibility for these loans would later be taken by Neil Jones and John Maher, as ANI's two representatives on the Spedley board. Outside directors of ANI would complain that they did not know until much later of the level of loans being pumped into Spedley from ANI. The syndrome seems to have been that if they could support Yuill temporarily he would come good in the long run. If directors had been alert they should have been aware of Spedley's deteriorating financial position. For at least two years before the market crash, Spedley had been making its profit in deals just before balance date—a danger sign. The ANI directors in particular should have been aware of this, because sometimes the balance date transactions had involved their company. One such deal in 1987 was a put and call option taken by ANI over a parcel of Spedley bills with a nominal value of $26.7 million.

In 1987 the problem of window-dressing the Spedley accounts was acute because its balance date fell just eleven days after Black Tuesday. Spedley managed to report a profit of $4.5 million, close enough to its promise of $5 million. This time Bond Corporation came to the rescue by paying fees totalling $9 million. On the same day (3 November) that the cheque was received from Bond Corporation, a cheque for slightly over $9 million was sent from Spedley to Bond in purported payment for a portfolio of bills. The transactions were reversed on Bond Corporation's balance date of 30 June 1988. On that day Bond sent a cheque for $9.3 million to Spedley in purported payment for the bills and on the same day Spedley sent a cheque for $9 million to Laurie Connell's Oakhill Pty Ltd, which paid the money on to Bond Corporation. Spedley recorded the $9 million to Oakhill as a loan, and then assigned the loan to GPI.[27]

There is a lesson to be drawn here for anyone trying to make sense of the purported losses in Oakhill and GPI. If the above transaction were still on the books of both Oakhill and GPI when the respective groups collapsed, it would have appeared as two losses of $9 million. Oakhill would be shown as owing $9 million which it could not repay. GPI would be shown as having a $9 million asset that had to be written to zero. In fact, neither of them had lost a cent. Instead, a $9 million fictitious profit of Spedley's had been shuffled into the accounts of two other companies. Transactions such as these must have greatly inflated the reported losses of several of the companies involved in the Rothwells/Spedley groups. The instance also illustrates that some losses could have been counted twice, or even more often.

A separate problem was the need to increase Spedley Holdings' capital. This was to have been financed through an issue of convertible notes to Broadlands, the finance subsidiary of New Zealand Insurance, in a genuine arm's length deal. But Broadlands backed out at the last moment. As several banks had been told that Spedley's capital was to be increased and were expecting it, Yuill deemed it imperative that the capital raising proceed. But to do so he had to resort to a device.

Spedley Holdings expanded its capital by issuing convertible notes totalling $27 million. The notes were issued to a $2 shelf company called Pluteus (No. 152) Pty Ltd. This investment was actually financed by Spedley Securities, after a round robin (see Figure 5.6) in which Spedley Securities lent $27 million to GPI Leisure which on-lent it to Pluteus.[28] Spedley Holdings then used its $27 million of extra capital to subscribe for further shares in Spedley Securities. So the capital of both Spedley companies was artificially enhanced. At a later stage, GPI Leisure was eliminated from this round robin.

The machinations enabled Spedley to report the $4.5 million profit. This stopped the run which had developed on Spedley, and Yuill had bought a year's grace. Spedley's true situation in 1987 could have been far worse than shown. After his post-crash examination of Spedley Securities, Miller estimated that the $4.5 million profit had been overstated by $57.6 million. That meant Spedley Securities really made a $53 million loss for the year.[29] Apart from anything else, Spedley's provision for bad debts at October 1987 was a mere $1 million. It was later estimated that $30 million to $40 million would have been closer to the mark, but any such provision would have reduced profit accordingly.

If these estimates were anywhere near accurate Spedley should have stopped trading on the spot, but instead over the next year it increased its book.

The crash caused severe problems for Spedley's offshoots, GPI and Bisley. Bisley Investment admitted to losing $55 million on share price index (SPI) option contracts. The story that emerged was that a subsidiary named Bisley Options Management had been writing call options on SPI contracts and was caught badly. While the physical market had fallen 500 points on Black Tuesday, the SPI had plummeted 674 points and at its worst was down 780. Although Bisley had a computer selling program in place, it had been unable to sell in a market where buyers did not exist. Bisley was busted. The loss had wiped out its shareholders' funds which at June 1987 had been $50 million, excluding minorities. To survive, Bisley needed an immediate capital injection of $37 million. This was provided through a rights issue which was ultimately funded by Spedley Securities.[30]

GPI had even bigger problems. GPI withdrew a $20 million deposit from Spedley immediately after the crash, making GPI one of the biggest contributors to the run on Spedley. A significant proportion of the money injected into Spedley by ANI immediately after Black Tuesday was on-lent by Spedley to GPI. Over the next twelve months GPI would borrow from ANI the staggering total of $170 million.

By Christmas 1987 ANI was pressing Yuill to sell some of Spedley's receivables so that ANI could retrieve its then outstanding loan of $147 million. ANI had at this point two representatives on the Spedley board: Maher and chairman Neil Jones. In addition, ANI's former chairman David Gray was a director of Spedley. Jones and Maher seem to have been remarkably uninformed about the activities of Spedley. It was only after Black Tuesday that they received a list of Spedley receivables. Maher said he was concerned at the level of exposure to some related companies, including $40 million at that point to GPI. He was also concerned that many large exposures had been entered into by Spedley without any reference to the board. But having become concerned—and having pumped so much money into Spedley—ANI would take little effective action until the following October. Maher told Yuill that many loans should not have been advanced. He also told Yuill—on 13 November—that all credit risks which had not previously been approved were to be submitted to the board for approval. That never happened. Yuill continued to defy and ignore the board.[31]

In the midst of these dire problems Yuill was still not stinting himself on luxuries. In December 1987 he authorised payments by Spedley totalling $82 000 to buy himself a Cobra sports car. Also, Spedley continued to help Rothwells. On 29 February 1988 the State Government Insurance Commission of Western Australia lent $10 million to Spedley which Spedley on-lent to Rothwells the same day.[32] For the next few months things appeared to be correcting and Spedley repaid ANI some $75 million by mid-1988. But in truth Spedley was robbing Peter to pay Paul. Peter was GPI Leisure.

After the public float GPI Leisure quickly showed profits. In the year to June 1987 it showed a net profit of nearly $4 million and paid a $2.5 million maiden dividend. The hotel business was fine. As GPI Leisure had no interest bill to service and no substantial overheads its cash flow was strong. Suddenly in early 1988 it went on a debt binge. In April 1988 GPI Leisure announced that it would raise $100 million by a pro-rata issue of $1 convertible notes to shareholders, with the books closing on 12 May. The notes bore interest at 11.5 per cent. As far as the public was concerned the issue went smoothly, but beneath the surface it was sticky. The underwriters—Potts West Trumbull and Alexander Laing & Cruickshank—insisted that GPI take $40 million, which was $10 million more than its entitlement. This was funded by yet another round robin. GPI Leisure deposited $40 million with Spedley, which lent it to GPI, which subscribed for the notes. The net cash effect was zero. Craven says the shortfall on the note issue was considerable, leading to several other 'mates' getting soft loans from GPI Leisure/Spedley to take up the issue. Craven reckoned that after these devices had been employed the note issue raised only about $40 million in real cash, although it was publicised as $100 million.[33]

How GPI Leisure was going to fund the $11.5 million interest bill on these notes each year and still pay any dividend was a question that was never answered. It could have been said that the $100 million could be deposited at higher rates and the margin would be profit. In fact, the money was deposited with Spedley, which Yuill must have known— although no outsider knew it—was under water at the time.

Just before the issue closed, Yuill did an even more indefensible deal for GPI Leisure. On 6 May GPI Leisure borrowed $100 million from Standard Chartered Bank, agreeing to pay bank bill rates on the loan. GPI Leisure immediately invested the money in 10 per cent preference shares in Spedley Holdings. This deal was entirely masterminded by Brian Yuill as a way of pumping $100 million equity into Spedley Holdings' balance sheet. However, it was a disastrous deal for GPI Leisure and its shareholders. GPI Leisure had incurred a very large debt which would have to be repaid, but on the other side of its balance sheet its asset was illiquid equity in a private company. Yuill's justification of the deal was that it would enhance the income stream of GPI Leisure because the dividend on the shares would be greater than the interest rate on the loan. This was a deeply dubious proposition. Accountants Arthur Young & Co later calculated that as long as the dividend on the preference shares was fully franked (i.e. tax rebatable) it equated to an interest payment of 16.4 per cent. Therefore Yuill had exposed GPI Leisure to a $100 million debt on the assumption that (a) bank bill rates would not go above 16.4 per cent and (b) Spedley Holdings could maintain a preference dividend of 10 per cent. Both assumptions rapidly proved untrue. Federal Treasurer Paul Keating drove interest rates up at the end of 1988 to halt what was perceived as an inflationary boom in the economy. By March 1989 bank bill rates had reached 17.6 per cent. And by that time Spedley Holdings was not only unable to pay preference dividends, but had declared an $8.5 million loss for the year to October 1988.

On a worst case, Spedley Holdings could go broke and GPI Leisure would lose its $100 million. Any financial expert with full access to the records would probably have concluded that Spedley was already broke at the time it did this deal in May 1988. And if anyone was in a position to know, it was Yuill. This potentially lethal commitment by GPI Leisure was undertaken without any reference to the shareholders. It was only in the following March, ten months afterwards, that Yuill grudgingly put it to an meeting of GPI Leisure for approval. Despite the misgivings of shareholders the deal was then approved, largely because Spedley would have collapsed immediately otherwise.

GPI Leisure shareholders had other grounds for objecting to the deal. GPI Leisure had floated in August 1986 on a prospectus which said its aim was to seek out high-quality investments in the leisure, entertainment and tourist industries. The investment in Spedley Holdings could by no stretch of the imagination be described as any of these things. Therefore GPI Leisure had undertaken a major shift in its objectives and had kept the shareholders uninformed for the best part of a year. Also, the shareholders did not know that their previously ungeared company now had a debt of $100 million. If the convertible notes were counted as debt— which they rapidly became—the debt/equity ratio was now 2:1.

Worse, GPI Leisure endorsed $165 million of Spedley Securities bills which had been taken by ANI. In the event of a default by Spedley Securities, ANI would have recourse against GPI Leisure. From being a debt-free investor in the tourism industry at its birth in 1986, GPI Leisure by the end of 1988 had become a high-risk financier with a total debt and risk exposure of $390 million to the Spedley group: $100 million in

Figure 5.6   Round robin of October 1987

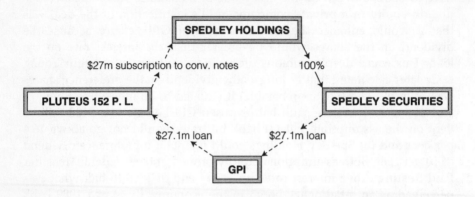

Spedley Holdings preference shares; $165 million in endorsement of
Spedley bills; and $125 million in deposits with Spedley. As if this were
not enough, in January 1989 GPI Leisure would go even further by
guaranteeing $100 million of Spedley receivables, taking its total exposure
to Spedley to $490 million.

The market knew of the convertible note raising by GPI Leisure but
not of the rest. These deals would be kept hidden for another half a year.
Every balance date now represented a fresh bushfire for Yuill and had to
be put out or covered as well as possible.

The next place the flames were due to be seen was in GPI. A collapse
of this company would be an immediate personal disaster to Yuill, who
owned 40 per cent of it. Yuill had borrowed $17 million from Spedley to
maintain his stake in GPI during its rights issue two years earlier. This
in turn had funded GPI's subscription to GPI Leisure, which had now
been hollowed out to finance Spedley. A collapse of GPI—which owed
huge amounts to Spedley—would bring down the whole row of domi-
noes.

GPI's balance date was elastic. Originally it was 30 June, but in 1986
Yuill pushed it back to July to enable GPI's accounts to reflect the impact
of the rights issue. The company reverted to a June balance in 1987. For
the half year to December 1987 GPI reported a seemingly sound $3.24
million net profit—a good result considering that this period included
the share market crash. However, this profit would have been a loss
except for Yuill's decision to drop equity accounting of GPI's stakes in
Bisley, Spedley and GPI Leisure. Announcing the December result, GPI
said it would 'be bringing to account the full 12-month equity accounted
profits of these companies as at June 30, 1988'. This indicated—mislead-
ingly—that all companies were making profits. But there never was a

166

year to June 1988. On 7 June Yuill announced that he was going to privatise GPI by bidding 50 cents per share for the ordinary shares he did not already own and 70 cents for the preference shares. In August 1988—weeks after GPI was supposed to have balanced—the company announced that it had pushed its balance date back to November 1988. The bid was extended a number of times until Yuill was able to proceed to compulsory acquisition in December. That being done, the 1988 accounts were never published. The buyout cost around $35 million. It was borrowed from the Bank of New Zealand, which would lose the lot. Public investors in GPI who sold out to Yuill had reason to be grateful, because he was pouring money into a black hole. GPI was worthless: a fact which would have been revealed if its accounts had become public.

October 1988: the great round robin

But the takeover bought time until the next fire, which was the October 1988 balance date of Spedley. This time the solution was elaborate. Yuill masterminded a round robin which had the effect of removing GPI and Pluteus (No. 152) as debtors of Spedley Securities and replacing them with GPI Leisure.

When the share market crashed on 20 October 1987 GPI had $20 million on deposit with Spedley Securities. The deposit was withdrawn that day, doubtless to plug holes which had suddenly appeared in GPI's investment portfolio. GPI then began borrowing heavily from Spedley. By 20 October 1988 GPI owed Spedley $147 million. It will be remembered that ANI had pumped $147 million into Spedley. ANI could be viewed as having invested in GPI via Spedley. One question never answered was why a private investment company such as GPI needed such enormous borrowings to plug the hole in its accounts.

This loan by Spedley Securities was neither prudent nor ethical. It was unethical because the professional money market people who placed funds on deposit with Spedley would have expected it to use the money buying bonds or bills. They would hardly have expected Spedley to on-lend $170 million to a private company controlled by Spedley's managing director. It was imprudent because the borrowings represented more than a quarter of Spedley Securities' total assets.[34] Yuill had made these loans to GPI without board authority. The board had laid down stringent guidelines on credit, often putting meagre limits on quite strong companies. To give a few examples, CSR was limited to $2 million and Woolworths and Consolidated Press were limited to $1.5 million each.[35] Lending $170 million to GPI was off the planet.

To solve his problems in October 1988, Yuill resorted to a five-step round robin which is illustrated in Figure 5.7.

Step 1: Spedley Securities advanced $250 million to GPI Leisure. The first $113 million of this represented repayment of deposits which GPI Leisure had made with Spedley. (Many of these deposits may have been to finance round robins such as GPI's $40 million subscription to GPI Leisure notes.) The remaining $137 million was an unsecured loan to GPI Leisure. It must be remembered that GPI Leisure was a public company. While repayment of the deposit would undoubtedly have been welcomed by the shareholders of GPI Leisure, there was no good reason for their company to have incurred a further debt of $137 million when it already owed $100 million to Standard Chartered. The most disgraceful aspect of the Spedley affair is the cavalier way in which the funds of GPI Leisure were manipulated—often by huge transactions—in ways that were of no conceivable benefit to its shareholders.

Step 2: GPI Leisure lent $186 million to GPI. No disinterested shareholder of GPI Leisure could have supported such a huge loan to a private company. GPI Leisure would have been better off leaving its funds on deposit with Spedley Securities, because in the event of failure there may have been some recourse against Spedley's major shareholder, ANI.

Step 3: GPI Leisure lent another $83 million to Pluteus (No. 152). In any contest for the most unconscionable transaction in Spedley's career, this would probably rank as the winner. Pluteus 152 was a $2 shelf company, which had by then borrowed $30 million from Spedley Securities and invested $27 million of it in convertible notes in Spedley Holdings. Pluteus 152 had no other assets.

Step 4: GPI—thanks to the loan from GPI Leisure—repaid all but $1.9 million of the $147 million it had owed Spedley Securities.

Step 5: Pluteus 152 repaid the $30 million it owed Spedley Securities and bought a portfolio of shares from Spedley Securities at book value of $54.5 million. The market value of these shares was at least $10 million less.[36] The shares included ordinary and preference shares in Rothwells at a face value of $17 million. At this point Rothwells was headed for liquidation. Its ordinary shares would become worthless and the preference shares would become worth only half their face value.

This round robin had three main effects. First, it shifted the debts of GPI and Pluteus 152 from Spedley Securities to GPI Leisure. Second, it turned GPI Leisure from a creditor of Spedley Securities to a debtor. Third, Spedley Securities avoided the necessity of declaring a loss on its share portfolio, or at least having to show the difference between book and market values in its 1988 accounts. This loss had been effectively transferred to GPI Leisure via Pluteus 152. GPI Leisure and its shareholders were heavily disadvantaged by these transactions. After accountant

John Harkness became liquidator, GPI Leisure was given the right to reverse the round robin. However, as several of the companies concerned had by then gone broke, all this effectively gave GPI Leisure was the right to sue for the return of money.

Readers will note that, although GPI owed $147 million to Spedley, GPI Leisure lent it $186 million. Why did GPI need the extra $39 million? The answer was that Spedley took the opportunity to clean up some old Rothwells transactions. Of the $39 million, GPI lent $26.5 million to Oakhill Pty Ltd, Beverage Holdings Pty Ltd and Austin Morgan Pty Ltd. Oakhill was Laurie Connell's private company and Beverage Holdings was associated with Peter K. Lucas.

In a subsequent court hearing, Spedley director Jamie Craven said that the loans owed by GPI had been moved to GPI Leisure because 'there was a belief that GPI would not have qualified as an eligible asset for the purposes of Spedley's dealers' licence' because of its association with Yuill. Craven said that Yuill had given instructions for the round robin, after which the company solicitor, James Beatty, 'would sprinkle holy water on them'.[37]

So the accounts of Spedley Securities were window-dressed again. They showed total assets of $595 million, net assets of $92 million and a loss of $10.6 million. Glen Miller, QC, estimated that the loss was closer to $170 million.

Ross Levings, Spedley's company secretary, took one look at the 1988 accounts and resigned. He had contemplated resigning earlier, but Yuill had persuaded him to stay. The manipulations of 1988 were the last straw because they had been caused by problem areas which Levings had long been nagging Yuill to rectify. Also, Levings found it had become 'frustrating and impossible' to record many of the transactions accurately.[38]

Word was beginning to leak around the marketplace about Spedley's true condition. The ANZ Bank was now getting very twitchy about Spedley's exposure to Rothwells. Spedley was reassuring about the exposure, but it appears to have been at least $60 million. On 2 November— just two days after Spedley's round robin—corporate lending manager Karl Mizens met Yuill and was assured that Spedley was not facing liquidity problems. But at last the grand confederation was being broken. On the following day, 3 November, Rothwells went into provisional liquidation. In the face of Spedley's links to Laurie Connell the ANZ did not remain convinced for long. From the close of business on 8 November the bank began dishonouring all cheques presented for payment to Spedley accounts in Perth and Sydney. The ANZ subsequently refused to provide Spedley with temporary overdraft facilities and withdrew all credit facilities on 14 November.[39] And Spedley's affairs had attracted the attention of the regulators. On 10 November the NSW Commissioner for

Corporate Affairs, Barry French, met Yuill but was assured that the maximum exposure of Spedley Securities to Rothwells was $11.8 million.

This was not quite true. The State Government Insurance Commission of Western Australia, having already pumped large sums into Rothwells in its own name, had begun using Spedley as a conduit for back-to-back loans. When Ferrier and Tuckey were appointed joint provisional liquidators of Rothwells in November 1988, they discovered that SGICWA had lent a total of $30.5 million to Spedleys, which had on-lent it to Rothwells. By this time, of course, Rothwells was hopelessly insolvent. When SGICWA called back the loan of $30.5 million from Spedley on 3 April 1989, Spedley defaulted on the repayment and went into provisional liquidation eight days later.

While Yuill was reassuring the ANZ in November 1988, ANI was handing out some reassurances of its own. At the time ANI was bidding for the British engineering company Aurora plc. Aurora's merchant banker, N.M. Rothschild, wrote to ANI asking for details of ANI's exposure to Spedley. ANI's chairman Neil Jones rebuffed the query dismissively. 'If that's all Aurora has got, then it must be really desperate', he said. In a later court hearing, Jones would testify that he had been woken by a phone call in the early hours of the morning of 10 November. The call was from ANI's finance director, John Maher, telling Jones that Spedley needed $20 million from ANI urgently. As ANI already had an exposure of $75 million to Spedley, Jones' response was a short Anglo-Saxon word.[40]

Spedley was in worse shape than ever and ANI was more exposed than ever. To shore up Spedley after the Rothwells collapse, Yuill again approached ANI. Maher requested a list of Spedley receivables that might be recovered—the same request he had made when Yuill came seeking support a year earlier. Maher again discovered that Yuill had been lending money without any reference to the board. Nevertheless, ANI poured another $150 million into Spedley between November 1988 and April 1989.

Creative accounting had enabled Yuill to hide these disasters for a remarkably long time. But the end began drawing near in November 1988. ANI's concern with Spedley had become more active. In November ANI set up a four-man executive committee to try to protect ANI's investment, sort out ways to reconstruct the group and find some way of extricating ANI from Spedley. The committee comprised Maher, ANI's deputy chairman Ron Johnson, and directors David Gonski and Howard Stack. Craven said:

> Brian Yuill was constantly asked to sit in on meetings and talk about Spedley's receivables. He just refused belligerently. Gray and Maher were terrified of him and wouldn't confront him. They would send me out to get him and he'd say, 'They can get fucked', and pour himself another whisky. It was a terrible time.[41]

At the same time ANI installed Greg Robinson, divisional controller of ANI's subsidiary Steelmark, as an unofficial manager of Spedley. Spedley staff had to obtain Robinson's approval before they could write cheques and he oversaw payment and distribution of money at Spedley.[42]

The ANI executive committee laboured for some time in the belief that Spedley was viable and could be rescued. In truth, it was a financial snakepit. Priestley & Morris' team of auditors, headed by Graham Launders, had been uncomfortable with several aspects for some time. As far back as 1986, the auditors had been worried about the inadequacy of Spedley's loan documentation. However, Yuill had made it plain that he was not prepared to change his ways. His comment, recorded in a note of the auditors of October 1986, was that the company had always done business without formal documentation in many cases and he was not prepared to change. In December 1987 the auditors had sought information about $200 million worth of receivables, where interest seemed to be in arrears or unpaid. Maher eventually concluded that many of the records of the company were in Yuill's head and the collectibility of the receivables might be in the same place. He was the only one who knew the terms and conditions of many loans. One example was a loan made via Potts West Trumbull to a company named Oakridge Pty Ltd in the Caribbean island of Nevis, where company law restricted information about owners and controllers of companies.[43]

How much of this had been realised by the executive committee is uncertain, but their optimism about restoring Spedley to viability waned over the weeks. The coup de grâce was the discovery of previously undisclosed futures losses in Spedley. Not only were these losses large, but they had been hidden by deliberate forgery. The losses seem to have been uncovered by Graham Launders, a partner with Priestley & Morris with responsibility for the Spedley audit. Launders had been put on his toes by the increasing concern about Spedley and its links with Connell and Bond. In the course of his audit over the years, Launders had often checked the group's futures trading by inspecting documents from the International Commodities Clearing House (ICCH). Carrying out the same check in 1988, he realised that what he had been seeing were photocopies. The original documents must have been photocopied, tampered with, then photocopied again. The only reason for doing this must have been to hide losses. Launders subsequently testified that futures losses could have been disguised in this way as far back as 1985. When Launders discovered the forgeries in 1989 the futures losses totalled $35 million.[44] These were separate from the 1987 futures losses in Bisley.

The forgeries appear to have started as far back as 1984. In that year the audit papers included a photocopy of a letter from a Mr Pieterse of the futures clearing house, the ICCH, confirming the existence of a debt.

Figure 5.7   Round robin of October 1988

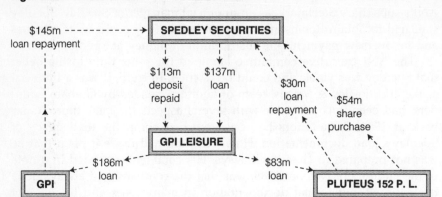

However, in a subsequent investigation Pieterse denied signing such a letter although the signature was his. Some deft hand with a photocopying machine had put Pieterse's signature on a letter on ICCH letterhead. In 1985 the ICCH owed Spedley $1.1 million at balance date but a forged photocopy increased it to $3.3 million. The effect of this was to inflate Spedley's profit by $2.2 million that year. The problem with this scam was that, unless the group could make some windfall profit which would wipe it all out, Spedley had to keep the forgeries going each year. Spedley not only perpetuated the forgeries but increased them. By October 1988 the balance owed by the ICCH was still only $1.1 million but the forgery showed it as $36.1 million.[45]

From being a castle, of a sort, Spedley had become a bottomless pit of Rothwells' dimensions.

For ANI, which had endured much angst over the years thanks to Yuill and Spedley, this was the last straw. According to Craven, Maher was 'shaken, shocked and horrified' when he learned of the losses and had promised that 'heads will roll'.[46] Launders would have qualified Spedley's audit statement, but the directors presented a guarantee from GPI Leisure that it would cover all receivables of Spedley up to $100 million. Launders signed an unqualified audit report, unaware that the board of GPI Leisure had not even met, let alone agreed to any such guarantee.[47] According to Craven the guarantee had been given by two directors—himself and Beatty.

On 23 November there was a confrontation between Jones and some of the outside directors of ANI. The directors had just learned that the exposure of ANI to Spedley had reached $170 million. They were reassured, and some of them believed as late as January that a commercial solution might be found to Spedley's troubles. On 15 December the ANI board passed a resolution ratifying the actions of Jones and Maher. The majority of ANI's directors now wanted to quit Spedley. The last day of January 1989 was the deadline for closing off the Spedley accounts for the year to the previous October. That day saw a series of meetings and decisions within the group. The events can be summarised as follows:

- ANI agreed in principle to sell its Spedley holding to BT Insurance.
- Jones and Maher resigned from the Spedley board.
- Potts and West agreed to sell their 16.5 per cent stake in Bisley to GPI at 20c a share.
- Potts and West resigned from the Bisley board and Potts resigned from the BT Insurance board on 1 February.
- Peter Beckwith, managing director of Bond Corporation, sent Spedley a letter purportedly confirming the existence of a $7 million loan from Spedley to Bond Brewing Investments.
- Yuill sent a facsimile message to Beckwith offering an indemnity for any claim arising under Beckwith's letter.

The letter sent by Beckwith was false. No such debt existed. But Spedley had to show enough assets to convince the auditors that it was solvent and, in the absence of real assets, Yuill had to invent them. If the letter had not been sent by Beckwith, Spedley's auditors would have qualified the accounts and Spedley's money market licence might not have been renewed.[48]

Despite many subsequent denials, the rest of the actions that day look to an outsider very much like the stampede to leave a sinking ship. ANI had launched Spedley, nurtured it with capital and helped window-dress its accounts several times over the years. Now it was quitting. Potts and West were also heading for the hills.

The Kitool episode

Spedley's reputation suffered further damage when the Kitool affair became public. In 1988 Bond Corporation had declared a profit of some $400 million. In late February 1989 the ABC screened a 'Four Corners' program researched by English journalist Paul Barry, which explored two deals that had contributed to Bond's 1988 profit. One was a deal in which Bond Corporation had acquired 260 hectares on the outskirts of Rome in late 1987 through a Cook Islands subsidiary. Bond Corporation then sold 49 per cent of the company for $110 million and claimed a $73 million profit as part of its 1988 result. When details of the deal emerged they immediately strained credulity for two reasons. The first was that the land could not possibly have appreciated so much so quickly. The second was that the purchaser was a $2 company named Kitool Pty Ltd.

Who owned Kitool—and who financed it—became great mysteries. Kitool had reportedly paid $50 million down on the Rome land and still owed $60 million. Manifestly, Kitool was in no position to finance such a purchase from its own resources. It had two directors, merchant bankers Ross Grant and Bruce Watson. Grant said that Kitool had been acting for either Bisley Investment Corporation or Bisley Properties. Watson said that Kitool was a completely separate entity from Bisley. Bisley issued a statement to the ASX (Australian Stock Exchange) saying that Kitool was not a subsidiary of Bisley, that Bisley had not entered into put and call options with Bond Corporation and that Bisley had no actual or contingent liability in relation to Kitool.[49] These statements left the situation as clear as mud. Bisley had defined what Kitool was not, but not what it was. Clearly someone at Bisley knew more than they were saying, and were keeping the market uninformed. And by now the credibility of all those connected with Spedley and Bisley had sunk to the point that many traders may well have disbelieved whatever they said anyway.

One fact that did emerge was that Tulloch Lodge had lent Kitool $10 million. Given that Tommy Smith had been buying enthusiastically at the Auckland and Trentham sales, Tulloch Lodge certainly did not now have $10 million in cash. This sparked an automatic question. What in Hades was a company supposed to be in the racehorse business doing lending $10 million it didn't have to a $2 company to buy what looked like crazily overpriced land in Italy? When the question was put by a reporter to Tommy Smith, as joint managing director of Tulloch Lodge, he said:

> I don't know anything about it. I only run the racing bit. It's the first I've heard of it. It's all above my head. Beatty would be the bloke to talk to. I wouldn't think we would have the money. We did have quite a bit of money but we spent $12 million on horses. So I wouldn't have thought we'd got $10 million.[50]

Beatty, as Tulloch Lodge's chairman, refused to comment on the deal saying that all would be revealed in the company's interim report at the end of March.[51] It turned out that Tulloch Lodge owed several million to bloodstock agencies, while its cash reserves comprised $3.2 million on deposit with Spedley Securities.

End of Spedley

ANI quit Spedley in March 1989, selling its 45 per cent of Spedley Holdings to BT Insurance (Holdings) Ltd for $12.6 million. BT Insurance was a listed company (unrelated to BT Australia) and was owned 63 per cent by Bisley and 20 per cent by GPI with the balance held by the public.[52] The deal appears to have been financed unwittingly by FAI

Insurances Ltd, which lent $12.6 million to Spedley in early March. Spedley on-lent the money to BT Insurance. The effective price to ANI was actually higher, thanks to a secret deal in which GPI bought Greater Mid Western Insurance Co from ANI for $8.5 million although it had net assets of only half a million dollars. The effect was that ANI got out of Spedley for $8 million more than had been announced.

The formal end of the Spedley empire can be dated 11 April 1989. On that day GPI Leisure requested that both Spedley Holdings and Spedley Securities be put into provisional liquidation. Simultaneously, Brian Yuill and Jamie Craven resigned from the GPI Leisure board. John Harkness of KPMG Peat Marwick was appointed provisional liquidator of Spedley Securities by the NSW Supreme Court, and became official liquidator on 25 May. This appointment had one awkward aspect. Peat Marwick was auditor of Consolidated Press Holdings which by then had taken a controlling interest in ANI, creating a potential conflict of interest if Spedley Securities were to take action against ANI. This problem was solved when Peter Allen of Arthur Andersen & Co was appointed additional liquidator of Spedley Securities on 15 May 1991. Allen was responsible for the liquidation in respect of the litigation between Spedley Securities and ANI.

Ripples spread quickly from the Spedley collapse. The day after Yuill and Craven left the board, four associated companies—Bisley, GPI Leisure, Tulloch Lodge and West Coast Holdings—were suspended from trading on the stock exchange. The Reserve Bank ordered First Federation to close out its $800 million money market book, which it did quickly and efficiently. Shares in ANI came under attack. Formerly regarded as a blue-chip industrial, ANI was driven from $1.58 to $1.06 on the market in a few days. At this price ANI was vulnerable to a takeover raider. Precisely such a predator appeared when Consolidated Press Holdings stepped into the market and eventually acquired 45 per cent of ANI.

On 27 April the NCSC set a precedent by appointing a receiver to GPI Leisure and GPI. Normally a receiver is appointed by a secured creditor, but the NCSC exercised a previously unused power to protect investors. The NCSC action was taken in the Supreme Court of Victoria on an affidavit from one of its investigators, William Crosby. This revealed that Jamie Craven had made what looked like a full disclosure to the NCSC, giving details of round robins, losses and manipulations. The receiver of GPI and GPI Leisure was Tony Hodgson of Ferrier Hodgson. At the end of April, the Reserve Bank decided to withdraw authorised dealer status from First Federation. The dealer had wound up its affairs in good order. It was the first time the Reserve Bank had ever exercised its authority to close down an authorised dealer.

The fact that Spedley was another paper castle dawned slowly on the

Sydney financial markets. The realisation was accompanied by a sense of horror. Connell and Bond had always been tolerably recognisable as Wild West cowboys, but Spedley had been a well-connected player in the Sydney money markets. Nearly everyone who mattered had dined luxuriously in Yuill's boardroom or had met him in the Members' at Randwick. First Federation was an authorised dealer; ANI was one of Australia's blue-chip industrials; Potts West Trumbull was a respected broking firm whose senior partner was a director of the ASX; Baker & McKenzie was a leading law firm. Sydney financiers were shocked as the extent of Yuill's manipulations became apparent.

Outside directors of ANI had also become active. On the evening of Harkness' appointment three directors—Howard Stack, Peter Joseph and David Gonski—went to ANI's city office to confront Jones and Maher. The three directors asked Jones to stand down as chairman and Maher as a director on the grounds that the two ANI representatives on the Spedley board should step aside until the matter could be cleared up. They told Jones that the deputy chairman, Ron Johnson, was prepared to take over as chairman at least for the time being. According to those present, Jones' reaction was 'ferocious'. Over the next fortnight, outside directors began to realise that ANI's large exposure to Spedley dated back to Black Tuesday. They also began to realise that the bulk of the directors had not been told of the size of the Spedley exposure in October 1988.

Brent Potts was also concerned. Potts wrote to the GPI Leisure board expressing his concern at GPI Leisure's action in endorsing $165 million worth of Spedley bills held by ANI. As a director, Potts claimed never to have known of GPI Leisure's endorsement of the bills. It was Potts who convened the GPI Leisure board meeting on 11 April, resulting in the resignation of Yuill.

Rodney Adler, who had recently succeeded his late father Larry as chairman of FAI Insurances Ltd, predicted that the ramifications of the Spedley collapse would be greater than those of Rothwells'. 'Rothwells was always a disaster waiting to happen', said Adler. 'But Spedleys was associated with names like ANI and Brent Potts. It built up a picture of an organisation with the right contacts and the right direction. This has destroyed the respect ANI had in the market. It has taken down established people and established businesses.'

In September 1989 the NSW Attorney General, Gerry Peacocke, appointed Glen Miller, QC, as an inspector into the affairs of Spedley and its associates. At the end of 1990 a progress report from Miller was tabled in the NSW parliament. By the standards of such reports Miller's was brief, covering only 49 small pages. It made no pretence of covering the full history of Spedley's affairs. However, it did not mince words on the main point. Miller reported that Spedley's profit reports had been falsified since at least 1986 and probably 1983 or even earlier. He said it had made losses, instead of its reported profits, in every year from 1986 onwards. 'Investigation has revealed that loans were consistently advanced with little or no supporting documentation, with no apparent review as to the creditworthiness of the borrower or as to the borrower's capacity to repay', Miller said. 'From 1983 onwards it appears that creative accounting practices were widely used by the group.'

Legal action—and inaction

The labyrinthine dealings of Spedley meant that after it collapsed there was a spate of lawsuits by injured parties seeking recovery. Claiming that the company had been insolvent, Harkness took preference actions against 32 parties which had withdrawn money from Spedley in the six months before the crash. The actions were defended by the clients, who claimed that they had made the withdrawals in good faith and in the ordinary course of business. One of Harkness' actions which succeeded was against Potts West Trumbull, who were ordered to repay $15 million. Potts West Trumbull had not only been Yuill's main broker but had helped him with little comforts, such as organising his house in London and trying to get him a Cobra sports car. By the time the court order came down in May 1993, Potts West Trumbull had been absorbed into Prudential-Bache Securities. Potts West Trumbull appealed the verdict.

Spedley Securities, under Harkness, sued Spedley's former auditors, Priestley & Morris, for $300 million. Standard Chartered Bank and GPI Leisure, trying to get their $100 million back, sued Spedley Securities and ANI. Spedley Securities sued the Bank of New Zealand for the alleged sale of $29 million of receivables which had been granted to it as security for a loan. Spedley sued its former directors Jones, Gray, Yuill and Maher for alleged breach of fiduciary duty. Spedley also claimed that ANI, as an employer of certain Spedley directors, was vicariously liable for some breaches. ANI, as a major creditor, claimed that Spedley was using money owed to ANI to pursue actions against ANI.

The air was thick with flying writs. ANI sued in an attempt to have GPI and Spedley Securities honour put options over a share parcel bought in November 1988. ANI lost its case, then won an appeal. A $22 million payment by Spedley Securities to the Bank of New Zealand in February 1988 in connection with the Bisley rights issue resulted in a court case between Yuill, Maher, Jones, Gray, GPI and the Bank of New Zealand.

The best summary of the difficulties in this complex litigation was given by Mr Justice Cole when commenting on a lawsuit mounted by

Spedley in seeking to recover $5.6 million from Bond Brewing Investments. His Honour said:

> This comparatively simple set of circumstances masks a tangle of conflicting fact, inconsistent documents, convenient and inadequate memories and outright fraud. My unenviable task is to seek to distil from this morass of confusion created intentionally by persons once thought by some to represent leaders of the Australian business and financial community, the true nature of the dealings between Spedley Securities and Bond Brewing Investments. The circumstances of this case show that those involved had scant, if any, regard for the law, and equally little regard for proper standards of corporate behaviour.

He added: 'I have little doubt that the reason the transaction is not fully documented is because such documentation would establish, beyond argument, breach of the law'. Spedley Securities won the case.

Banque Brussels Lambert sued ANI over its letter of comfort, which had stipulated that the bank would have 30 days to get its money refunded if ANI ever intended to sell out of Spedley, as it had in January 1989. The bank won.

Harkness ordered a Section 541 hearing to explore Spedley's affairs. The hearing, conducted by NSW Supreme Court deputy registrar Tania Sourdin, took a year to complete. Evidence revealed amazing sloppiness in the conduct of Spedley. Millions of dollars in loans were circulated between Rothwells, Bond and Spedley with inadequate documentation and sometimes none at all. Yuill commonly did things without a board meeting. He borrowed $110 million from ANI in the seven weeks following the October 1987 market crash without holding a board meeting because 'it would have been a bit like talking to yourself'.[53] The Section 541 examination also showed that Yuill's once fabulous memory had suddenly lapsed. He was unable to remember details, for example, of a transaction in which two directors of Standard Chartered Bank, John Stone and Max Carling, had been given non-recourse loans by Spedley of $100 000 each to buy shares in GPI Leisure. As the only security was the shares these loans amounted to gifts.[54] Most deals between the Spedley, Bond and Rothwells groups were done on a wink and a nod. When documentation existed, it was usually misleading.

A major problem of the Section 541 hearing was its location. As the city courts were full the hearing was held at the small, seldom used courtroom in Paddington Police Station. When the courtroom was full witnesses had to wait on hard wooden benches in the corridor. During breaks in the hearing, sworn enemies and their solicitors were crowded together in close proximity. The one thing which united them was a distaste for the press, who used these breaks to take photographs of the principals. Some sought refuge in the Light Brigade Hotel across the street and some stayed too long. On one memorable day, Yuill's answers were so vague and useless that he was ordered to leave the court. On another, Sourdin declared that Yuill was 'trifling with the inquiry'.

Another problem was locating Neil Jones, who was missing. Harkness hired a private detective to find Jones, who eventually appeared before the hearing at the end of May.[55]

The Spedley liquidators filed a lawsuit in March 1991 claiming more than $300 million damages from Yuill, Maher, Jones and ANI. ANI was claimed to be vicariously liable because Maher and Jones had represented ANI on the Spedley board and had failed to supervise Spedley's lending policies under Yuill. With interest, this claim eventually totalled $750 million.

This case was delayed for ages while a court battle was fought over who should hear it. The Chief Judge of the Commercial Division of the Supreme Court, Mr Justice Rogers, had indicated that where possible Mr Justice Cole should hear matters relating to Spedley. ANI, John Maher and Brian Yuill applied for Cole to disqualify himself from hearing proceedings where they were defendants, on the grounds that he had already made a finding against them in the Bond Brewing case. Cole refused to stand down and the case went to the Court of Appeal, which eventually found by a majority of three to two that there would be an appearance of bias if Cole heard the case because of a previous adverse finding by him (quoted above) about the conduct of Maher and Yuill.

This decision by the Appeal Court was a major setback to plans to streamline hearings of corporate cases. By having one competent judge hear all the cases, he could build up a knowledge of the complexities and be more likely not only to understand the issues and reach the correct decision, but to do so relatively quickly. The Appeal Court decision, taken to its logical conclusion, meant that every time a judge made an adverse finding about a corporate cowboy he would have to be replaced for the next case, and some unfortunate new judge would have to start unravelling the whole messy story from scratch. If a lot of charges were being heard separately against the same defendant it would be possible for New South Wales to run out of judges before the prosecution ran out of charges. Mr Justice Cole commented wryly: 'the law does not lightly or readily yield to the intrusion of efficiency'.

Mr Justice Giles took over the case briefly, but upon protest from Yuill he also disqualified himself. The third judge was Mr Justice Rolfe. Yuill applied to him for the civil case to be deferred until the criminal charges against him could be heard. Mr Justice Rolfe refused. Yuill appealed to the NSW Court of Appeal, which upheld Mr Justice Rolfe's decision. The civil case then went to mediation before the former Chief Justice of NSW, Sir Laurence Street. In September ANI reached a settlement with Spedley.

ANI dropped its claims of $240 million against Spedley and agreed to pay $22 million cash. Of the $240 million, about $200 million was 'hurt money'—real cash that ANI had pumped into Spedley to support the group and which was now gone forever. ANI's legal bills were said to have totalled $35 million. The effect of the settlement was that ANI had absorbed $240 million of Spedley's losses. Spedley's unsecured creditors received a return of 67 cents in the dollar, considerably better than they first expected.

In a separate action the receiver of GPI Leisure, Tony Hodgson, claimed up to $100 million damages from ANI in relation to GPI Leisure's subscription for 11.1 million preference shares in Spedley Holdings in May 1988. This lawsuit was filed in March 1991 but, typical of the delays in Spedley cases, did not begin in earnest until August 1992. This case was notable for one memorable exchange when the former chairman of ANI, Neil Jones, was being examined by Francis Douglas, for GPI Leisure. Jones told Douglas that he did not think it important that directors of public companies understood financial accounting principles. The following dialogue ensued:

> Douglas: You say they don't have to understand financial accounts?
> Jones: I didn't.
> Douglas: But you could not understand a balance sheet of Spedley Securities?
> Jones: That is so.

Shareholders in ANI were left pondering the evidence that their former chairman was unable to read a balance sheet.

For a long time it seemed that Brian Yuill would survive. He lived high on the hog for a while. Four months after Spedley collapsed he was spotted in a fashionable London restaurant with his old mate Laurie Connell, eating caviar and lobster and drinking Krug. After the meal they were picked up by a black Rolls Royce. It took another couple of years before a NSW judge restrained Yuill from selling or dealing in his assets and limited the income he could pay himself to $500 a week. Yuill avoided bankruptcy, but his private company Bondoro Pty Ltd was put in liquidation. Bondoro's assets included Guntawang, which was sold for $3.3 million; Yuill had paid $3.1 million for it and spent another $1.8 million renovating it. The rest of Bondoro's assets were sold and Yuill settled with his creditors after paying in $600 000 cash. His deprivation was not great. He had retained Fenton. He had also retained his house in Chelsea, although Harkness had obtained an injunction preventing him from selling it. He was no longer seen at the racetrack, but his wife Elisabeth raced a few horses with Randwick trainer Les Bridge.

For all the losses and questionable deals in Spedley it seemed that nobody would be convicted of a serious criminal offence. By the end of

1991 the reports and court hearings into the Spedley affair had resulted in the conviction of only one small fish. Peter Dawkins, a money market manager, had pleaded guilty to twelve charges of improperly using Spedley funds for his own purposes and to falsifying Spedley accounts to deceive the public and others as to Spedley's true financial position. Dawkins had run up an internal loan account totalling $614 000 and then drew cheques from Spedley accounts to extinguish the debt. Such practices were common among Spedley employees. Dawkins was sentenced to two years' weekend detention. He said that Yuill had told him to doctor the books and not to let other Spedley directors know about it. Yuill denied the allegation.

It now seemed that the Australian Securities Commission and the Commonwealth Department of Public Prosecutions (DPP) were so desperate to land a conviction that they turned on the easiest target available: their best informer. The early investigation and proceedings had been greatly helped by the evidence of Jamie Craven, who had started giving evidence within a week of the collapse. The New South Wales Corporate Affairs Commission and Department of Public Prosecutions had assured Craven orally that, as long as he told them everything he knew and was not guilty of any major crimes himself, they would 'keep him safe'. However, from 1 January 1991 corporate law came under the administration of the Australian Securities Commission and the Commonwealth Department of Public Prosecutions. Craven did not have a written indemnity and, in legal terms, the ASC owed him nothing. In March 1993 he was charged with four criminal offences. Three charges related to procuring Spedley to enter into agreements for fraudulent purposes, and the other related to procuring a loan of $22 million from Spedley for the advantage of GPI. The ASC might well have been within its legal rights to charge Craven with these offences, but it seemed an immoral way to behave towards someone who had been of great help to the prosecution. Craven had cooperated fully until then in the belief that he would be protected. He had gained little or nothing for himself out of the transactions to which the charges related and was by then bankrupt and divorced. It also seemed a stupid action by the ASC, because it would naturally discourage any informers from coming forward in future cases.[56]

Criminal prosecutions moved at a snail's pace. It was not until February 1993—four years after Spedley's collapse—that four charges were laid against Jake Corner for making improper use of his position as an officer of various companies. Corner was committed for trial in October.

But the delays were not always the fault of the ASC and the Department of Public Prosecutions. Brian Yuill fought one of the most determined rearguard legal actions of any of the bold riders. Between the end of 1990 and the start of 1993 Yuill was charged with various offences. Then some charges were dropped and fresh ones introduced. In the finish there were two main batches of charges. One batch involved three transactions in the October 1988 round robin. Yuill was committed for trial on this batch of charges in July 1993.

The second set of charges related to four personal dealings by Yuill for which Spedley footed the bill. They involved the following transactions:

- The Cobra sports car which Yuill had tried to import, but which was sent back to England. Yuill said he had never seen the car.
- Yuill's purchase of 13 per cent of William Inglis, which had been paid for by $1.7 million from Spedley.
- A payment by Spedley of $3.3 million to Triton Investments, a private company controlled by Jake Corner, Yuill's friend and business partner. Triton had then lent the money to Yuill's private company Nodrogan Pty Ltd, which had used the money to 'repay' a debt of $2.8 million owed by Yuill to Spedley.
- A payment by Spedley of $375 000 to B.R. Yuill Holdings Pty Ltd to pay financial and legal expenses related to the privatisation of GPI.

Yuill was committed for trial in October 1991. This trial did not begin until two years later. When it opened, some of the most damaging evidence came from Yuill's former partner Kenneth Hawkins, who had been deeply disturbed when an auditor drew his attention to Yuill's unauthorised use of Spedley funds. Hawkins said that he first saw the letter from the auditor in 1988. In a later court case, he said: 'I think I made my questioning known via Yuill's secretary and Yuill phoned me and abused me. [He said] "Keep your f . . . ing nose out of the business. This is my company and I'm running it the way I see fit. If you don't like what you see, get out" '. Hawkins said he had raised no more objections because 'had I pursued the matter, I would have been unemployed'.

The trial also highlighted the plight of Jamie Craven, who refused to answer 150 questions on the grounds that they might tend to incriminate him. He would not even say what his duties were at Spedley. Mr Justice Shadbolt threatened Craven with contempt of court proceedings. Craven responded with an affidavit in which he accused the DPP of doublecrossing him.

Yuill was no longer the dominant figure of his heyday. The man who had once been described as a 'Master of the Universe' (from Tom Wolfe's *Bonfire of the Vanities*) was nervous as he made an unsworn 55-minute statement from the dock. 'If I appear to be nervous, it is because I am', he told the jury. He described how he had built Spedley from a small start. 'It was something that was of great pride to me', he said. 'It was my life. It was the thing apart from family that I treasured most of all. In no way would I have acted improperly. It's just not the way it was.' The jury found him guilty on all seven charges and he was sentenced to eight years' jail. Yuill appealed against the conviction, claiming the judge had misdirected the jury. Yuill served seven months jail before the conviction was quashed by the Court of Criminal Appeal. At the time of writing, Yuill was also defending further charges relating to GPI Leisure.

Final accounting

ANI had injected around $200 million into Spedley and GPI Leisure had subscribed for $100 million in preference shares. After deducting the $39 million shortfall from the October 1988 round robin, Spedley Holdings and Spedley Securities had received a net $260 million—and they still collapsed. To this should be added some $120 million in shareholders' funds which were wiped out. Taking all this into account, along with several smaller sums which other parties had lent Spedley, the total size of the loss must have been at least $400 million. For years after the Spedley collapse there was never any public explanation of how Yuill the mastermind had managed to lose such impressive sums.

More than half of these losses had to be made up by ANI, which paid a high price for its failure to police its erring associate. While Yuill may have been the master of the Spedley universe, ANI always had the ability to pull the plug on him if they had enough information and backbone. The $200 million injected by ANI was roughly equivalent to the level of receivables that the auditors believed could have been non-performing. (These did not include the ICCH forgeries totalling $35 million which were discovered only late in the piece.)

ANI shareholders who footed the bill for the losses had the right to expect greater diligence from their directors. The fact that Spedley had been window-dressing its accounts at each balance date was known to at least some ANI directors. The put and call options on Spedley bills, the bond sales at balance date and other transactions should have given alert directors a strong enough whiff of smoke to start them looking for the fire.

Where was the money lost? On the evidence available, Spedley's money market book was usually unprofitable. These losses were only partly covered by investment profits. Black Tuesday was a disaster. Spedley lost about $10 million in the share market crash. In addition, the loss by Bisley of $55 million on futures appears never to have been really plugged. Millions more went in 'top hat' and other loans to Yuill and executives. The accounts were successfully window-dressed each year, but in the absence of genuine profits this meant that the hidden black hole in Spedley grew larger each year. The losses were disguised as receivables in the form of loans to entities such as Oakhill or off balance sheet companies such as Pluteus 152: fictional assets which were the legacy of round robins. Every time Spedley papered over a loss a fresh bunch of these fictional assets had to be manufactured and the only way of getting them off the balance sheet was to dump them out into GPI. As long as Spedley was receiving more money in deposits than it was losing in operations it could continue to look healthy. But the run that set in after Black Tuesday was mortal.

Rob Macfarlan, QC for the Spedley liquidators, once referred to GPI as Yuill's graveyard for corporate cadavers. This does not seem an unfair description. Maher had been concerned in 1987 to learn that GPI had borrowed $40 million from Spedley. Over the next twelve months its debt to Spedley increased by another $107 million (possibly including some interest) and it had additional debts of $39 million to Connell and Bond associates.

The losses of GPI—the largest single drain in Spedley—were not explained until September 1990 when the liquidator of GPI, Tony Hodgson, lodged a statement of its affairs. GPI had assets with a book value of $327 million, which were estimated to be realisable at only $66 million. This left a yawning deficit after liabilities of $150 million.

Some of GPI's so-called assets were the result of the round robin which was subsequently reversed. But as Hodgson sorted through the mess a lot of familiar names began to appear. GPI was owed $10 million by L.R. Connell & Partners, $18 million by Oakhill Pty Ltd (Connell's private company) and $7 million by Beverage Nominees (Peter K. Lucas' company). It held $19 million in Rothwells shares, which were worthless. There were $30 million in GPI Leisure shares and $40 million in GPI Leisure notes whose value was wrecked by Yuill himself. Another $16 million was invested in the associated company West Coast Holdings, which was under official management. There is almost a pattern in GPI's losses. Every time ANI had to be called in to prop up Spedley, Yuill seemed to have to hide another body in GPI.

When looking at these numbers we should remember the example explored earlier of the $9 million debt by Oakhill to GPI that resulted from the Bond Corporation fee payment of October 1987. This debt—or asset—was fictional. It also showed up in at least two sets of accounts. Doubtless there was triple counting (and perhaps even more) of such fictional assets, which might be uncovered if any diligent analyst could ever work through all the accounts of Spedley, Rothwells and their associates. Given the lack of a full official report into Oakhill, GPI or Spedley we shall probably never know all the facts, but the true losses of the two groups were probably considerably smaller than those the headline figures shouted. Nevertheless there were significant losses. They were operating losses that had been accumulating from year to year. The real tragedy is that they would have been less if they had been exposed several years earlier.

The relationship between Yuill and Connell was sometimes described as 'seamless'. This is a good description, because when we look at the losses suffered by their private and public companies it becomes apparent that sometimes losses which started in one camp wound up in the other. Both sides tried to move the corpses back into their home graveyards, but this became increasingly difficult as both empires creaked towards their collapses. The relationship between Connell and Yuill stayed as seamless in corporate death as it had been in corporate health.

6

Bond: the ultimate
bold rider

*These men are being paid millions of dollars to refrain from competing
against Bond Corporation when, in fact, they should have all been
sacked. But far from there being any suggestion of sackings because all of
Bond Corp's shareholders' funds have been lost, those executives, plus
Alan Bond himself, are still being enriched at a staggering rate by their
smoking ruin of a company . . . There have been a few disgraceful
episodes in Australia recently, but the ruination of Bond Corporation is
about the worst.*

Alan Kohler, *Australian Financial Review*, November 1989

Alan Bond was Australia's ultimate bold rider of the 1980s. Nobody else
took the country so high or brought it so low. His victory in the America's
Cup of 1983 was celebrated as a national triumph. He struck a chord
with the ordinary man, because his origins were as humble as anyone's.
Starting as an apprentice signwriter in Perth he built a global empire. He
controlled the world's largest privately owned gold mining company and
the world's fifth largest brewing group. Bond Corporation became the
ninth largest enterprise in Australia. But critics pointed out that the
empire had shaky foundations from the start, and they were proved right
when Alan Bond became derided in the 1990s. His name became synonymous with the excesses of the 1980s.

When the boom was in midstride in 1986, *Australian Business* magazine ran an article exploring the psyches of the great American corporate
raiders of the day.[1] It quoted Abraham Zaleznik, a psychoanalyst who
taught at Harvard Business School, as saying: 'To understand the entrepreneur, you first have to understand the psychology of the juvenile
delinquent'. Zaleznik's theory was that entrepreneurs were always the
bad boys in the class because they refused to accept anyone else's rules.
They were chronically incapable of working as employees because they
had to march to the beat of their own drums.

This profile fitted Alan Bond like a glove. It took an English-born boy
to become Australia's biggest corporate larrikin. English journalist Paul

Barry spent some time trying to research Alan Bond's childhood for his biography *The Rise and Fall of Alan Bond*, apparently with little help from his subject. The picture that emerges is of an incorrigibly naughty boy from infancy, playing truant from school and being a tearaway in class. He seems to have been a chronic rebel against authority from an early age, and suffered little punishment for it either at home or school.

He could only have been eight years old when he made his first foray into business. Jam jars were scarce in England immediately after the war and Alan made a few shillings collecting them and selling them to local shopkeepers. He quickly realised that he needed to operate on larger scale and got his mates to start collecting for half the shopkeepers' rates. His sister Geraldine said: 'I don't know that he wanted to be rich but I think he liked the fun of wheeler-dealing. He also liked what money could buy, and he liked to outmanoeuvre people.'[2]

Alan's father Frank lost part of his lungs after his ship was torpedoed during World War II. Frank's doctor predicted that he would die unless he lived in a dry climate. As the Bond family was poor anyway it took little incentive for them to try their luck by migrating to Australia, a move largely organised by Alan's formidable mother Kathleen. They disembarked from the P & O liner *Himalaya* in Fremantle in 1950. On Barry's account, Bond's schooling seems to have been less remarkable for any academic distinction than for his truant escapades. One time when Alan ran away from school he got as far as Queensland—no mean feat for a child in 1950s Australia. A former schoolmate, Gordon Doohan, told Barry of the time Alan 'got his first ten shillings'. The two boys were walking past a dry cleaning shop when Alan noticed it was empty and that the cash was just kept in a drawer. According to Doohan Alan dived in, pinched a ten shilling note from the drawer, and the two boys ran around the corner to another shop and bought cigarettes with it.[3] The young Alan seems to have indulged in a bit of petty thievery, such as stealing oranges. This is not uncommon in boys and we should not read too much into it. Perhaps it is more important that he seems to have been rarely caught and never punished.

Leaving school at the then minimum age of fourteen, young Bond became an apprentice signwriter under a painter named Fred Parnell. Bond suffered the severe handicap of having indifferent spelling, but Parnell took him on because he had a bright personality. Other workers at the painting shop later remembered him as cocky and an upstart. He was an unruly employee and took a few too many days off, so Parnell eventually terminated his apprenticeship by mutual agreement. Bond left the business after three and a half years, not completing his five-year apprenticeship. Parnell was the first and last person who ever employed Bond. For the rest of his life Bond would be his own boss and do as he wanted.

Bond set up a signwriting business called Nu-Signs. Because he used to collect Parnell's invoices he knew what the going rates were and began undercutting. He was energetic and soon attracted a lot of business. The short, tubby teenager who gave a lot of lip to everyone could also attract girls. He won the heart of the red-haired, happy-go-lucky Eileen Hughes, daughter of prominent Fremantle businessman Bill ('Doozer') Hughes, even though he had to convert to Catholicism to marry her. The wedding was a rather tense affair. Frank Bond, as a Freemason, disagreed with his son becoming a Catholic. Kathleen disapproved of Eileen. The Hugheses—a leading Catholic family in the suburb—could hardly have been delighted that Eileen was pregnant when Alan had asked Doozer for her hand.

Nu-Signs won a lot of contracts by undercutting, but this often meant the firm lost money on a job. Bond stayed one jump ahead of creditors by using the proceeds of the next job to pay off the last one. He would go anywhere and do anything. He claims to have painted half the railway stations in Western Australia, and may well have. To make ends meet he would skimp on the job, cutting coats here and there and thinning the paint. Dave King, an early Nu-Signs partner, told Barry: 'We did the Esplanade Hotel down at Busselton. We started off with a forty-four gallon drum and finished with forty-three gallons left'.[4]

From the very start, Bond was prepared to do anything to make a quid. As well as painting anything anywhere, Nu-Signs dabbled in a variety of other businesses. It sold television sets and washing machines and even tried fattening sheep. But while painting signs for real estate agents Bond quickly realised that the big, fast money was in property. This would be the main business of his career. In June 1960 the 22-year-old Bond bought five acres at Lesmurdie for £13 000, borrowing the entire amount from Finance Corporation of Australia. The land was 25 kilometres east of Perth—a long way out to live in those days. The neighbourhood was dry and some of the blocks were steep. But Bond imaginatively named it Lesmurdie Heights, advertised it heavily and offered the blocks at double the prices of similar land in the neighbourhood. On the day of the 'land sale' Eileen sat out front under a beach umbrella, stuffing cash into a bookmaker's bag as she was rushed by eager buyers. All the money was repaid within three months and Bond had made his first killing.

Bond plunged into further real estate speculation, financing it partly with borrowed funds but partly by using whatever cash flowed into Nu-Signs. This meant that Nu-Signs' creditors were not paid. When one harassed employee asked Bond whether he would pay Nu-Signs' debts he cheerfully replied: 'No, it's cheap money.'[5] Bond would stretch creditors to their limit, waiting until they summonsed him and then paying a little of what he owed. That meant the creditor had to issue a new summons and the game could be played again. From his very earliest days debt never seems to have bothered Bond, particularly interest-free debt from trade creditors. Any money he owed he seemed to regard as his and he made almost a sport of not repaying it. Instinctively, he also realised that debt is cheap during a time of asset price inflation. For the rest of his life he would never be out of debt.

If the business world worked the way it is supposed to, Bond would quickly have run out of credit and been bankrupted. In practice, the professional lenders (and particularly finance companies) loved him and were happy to push money at him. Why this should be so takes us to the core of Bond's modus operandi, which never changed throughout his career. Throughout history, corporate cowboys have been attractive to lending institutions because they are prepared to pay whatever price is necessary to get money. Bond was prepared not only to pay the top going rate for money but to pay establishment and other fees as well. The interest and fees boosted the lender's revenue spectacularly and won plaudits for its manager. In fact, the fees and interest were often not paid but merely book entries. Let us say a speculator borrowed £100 000 at 12 per cent for one year and incurred £5000 in fees. The interest and fees could simply be added on to the principal to make a total debt of £117 000 to be repaid in twelve months. Meanwhile the finance company had booked £17 000 to its own revenue. If the speculator were snowballing his business the interest and fees might never be paid, but be continually rolled up into larger and larger loans while the finance company reported larger and larger revenues and profits. If the speculator then went bust, these revenues would turn out to be phantoms and would have to be written off the finance company's accounts. Bond dealt with all the finance companies. Bank-backed ones such as FCA (Bank of Adelaide), Commercial & General Acceptance (Commercial Banking Company of Sydney), Industrial Acceptance Corporation (ANZ) and Custom Credit (National Bank) all helped him at critical points. Bond must have been one of the largest Western Australian customers of the finance companies in these years.

The finance companies were encouraged to gamble on Bond and his ilk because in the 1960s land values around Perth were rising quickly from very low levels. And because Bond was a large customer and helping to inflate their profits the finance companies were prepared to shut their eyes to his land valuations. Usually finance companies lent money not on the basis of the cost of land but of its valuation. The normal maximum percentage was 90 per cent, but brave lenders sometimes went to 100. Bond might buy a block of land for, say, £40 000, intending to get a residential rezoning and do an elementary subdivision by scraping a few gravel roads across the land with a bulldozer. Typically, he would not put a penny into the deal. Instead, a friendly valuer would revalue the land to, say, £50 000. If the finance company were lending on 90 per cent of valuation, Bond had just increased the amount he could borrow from £36 000 to £45 000, or £5000 more than it had cost him. It became a standing joke among his associates that whenever Bond was in trouble his solution was to buy something.[6] If he revalued it quickly he could borrow more than it had cost and have funds to pay, say, the wages at Nu-Signs for the week. Pretty obviously his financial position was vulnerable to any setback, such as a rezoning not being approved or a subdivision failing to sell. Whenever that happened the lenders just had to whistle for their money for a while. Bond never worried.

Nu-Signs changed its name to Lesmurdie Heights Pty Ltd, then to Bond Corporation. It was controlled by Bond's private company Dallhold Investments. Bond Corporation rapidly became a force in the Perth property market, building Exchange House for the Perth Stock Exchange in 1968. In 1970 he went public with the float of WA Land Holdings.

Bond was a compulsive dealmaker. In December 1989 the *Australian Financial Review* published a précis of his deals since 1960. They covered four pages in solid type. In these 30 years Bond's empire grew to a massive global conglomerate with hundreds of subsidiaries. Let's look at the more important deals.

Three decades of wheeling and dealing

1968 Bond Corporation bought nearly 20 000 acres of land at Yanchep, north of Perth, in partnership with Taylor Woodrow of Britain. Bond Corporation bought out Taylor Woodrow in 1971.

1973 Bond bought 46 per cent of Robe River Ltd from the collapsed Mineral Securities Australia Ltd for $19.6 million on time payment. Bond took board control of Robe River Ltd, which held 35 per cent of the Robe River iron ore mine.

Tokyu Corporation of Japan became a 40 per cent partner in Yanchep, which was being developed as a marina and township. Bond challenged for the America's Cup in 1974 and was planning to make Yanchep the home of the Cup if he won.

1974 Amid a chain of property crashes, including Mainline and Cambridge Credit, the Perth Stock Exchange queried Bond Corporation following reports that it had liquidity problems. Bond attacked 'sensational reportage' for causing a lack of confidence and said that Bond Corporation had the support of its financiers. Bond Corporation then had $90 million in debts and a disturbingly small margin of assets over liabilities.

1976 After Bond struggled for three years to make periodic payments to the Minsec liquidator, Engelhard Industries of the United States and Burns Philp bought Bond's Robe River holding. The remaining shareholders had to agree that the offer would not be extended to them. Bond Corporation had been reporting losses for two years.

1977 Bond Corporation sold its remaining interest in Yanchep, which had been a dog, to Tokyu.

1978 Bond Corporation completed a long asset sale—including International House, its Perth headquarters—which had raised between $60 million and $70 million over two and a half years.

Leaner and with less debt, Bond Corporation acquired 25 per cent of Endeavour Resources Ltd; then did a joint takeover of Burmah Australia Exploration, which owned oil and gas leases in the Cooper Basin. The Burmah deal was also on time payment. The acquisition gave Bond Corporation 37.5 per cent of Santos Ltd. Santos contested the deal but eventually reached a settlement in which Bond became deputy chairman of Santos. A month after Bond Corporation bought Burmah, Santos announced a major Cooper Basin oil discovery and its shares soared.

1979 The South Australian Government passed a law decreeing a limit of 15 per cent on holdings in Santos. After a bitter fight, Bond sold to below 15 per cent. Profits on the sale paid off Burmah.

1979–80 Bond Corporation and Endeavour made various raids and share plays. At the end of 1980 Bond Corporation bought 10 per cent of Swan Brewery and Bond joined the board.

1981 Bond Corporation bought 70 per cent of the struggling Sydney retailer Waltons, then sold some properties to it.

Endeavour bought 35 per cent of Northern Mining. Endeavour then bid for the rest of the shares in Northern; the offer being subsequently revised. The National Companies and Securities Commission (NCSC) declared the way Bond had acquired the initial 35 per cent to be unacceptable conduct—the first unacceptable conduct declaration in Australia's history. In 1983 Alan Bond was convicted on two charges of having failed to provide substantial shareholder notices in this takeover.

Alan Bond personally bid $121 million for the 80 per cent of Swan Brewery not owned by Bond Corporation. The bid was the largest private bid ever made in Australia, and was made by him as an individual to avoid the requirements of the Trade Practices Act.

The renamed Waltons Bond bought a shopping centre and Bond Corporation's Taylor's Lakes residential development on the western fringe of Melbourne.

1982 Bond Corporation sold the rest of its Santos holding, making a total profit of maybe $100 million on the deal.

Bond Corporation bought 9 per cent of Grace Bros and for several months fought a takeover war with other parties interested in the old

Sydney retailer. In the process, Grace Bros sold 58 per cent of retailer Norman Ross to Waltons Bond.

Bond Corporation acquired 40 per cent of the troubled property development Austmark.

Bond stepped down as chief executive but remained chairman, with Peter Beckwith as managing director.

1983 Bond Corporation quit Grace Bros by accepting a takeover offer from Myer.

Bond won the America's Cup on 26 September.

Bond Corporation sold its 5 per cent of the Argyle diamond mine to the WA Government.

Bond Corporation posted a disappointing profit, under $9 million, while Waltons Bond and Austmark reported heavy losses.

1984 Bond Corporation acquired Winthrop Investments, which held controlling interests in Mid-East Minerals and Petro Energy and 34 per cent of Metals Exploration.

Bond Corporation acquired 31 per cent of the UK blimp maker Airships Ltd.

Bond Corporation acquired the Australian franchise for Hyundai vehicles from Korea.

Bond Corporation bought Swan Television for $40 million.

1985 Bond Corporation made a successful $1.2 billion bid—the largest until then in Australia's history—for Castlemaine Tooheys. With Swan, Bond then had nearly half the Australian beer market. A huge advertising campaign was launched to promote Bond beers.

1986 Bond Corporation bought Pittsburgh Brewing Co of the United States for $80 million.

Bond Corporation bought Screen Entertainment of Britain for $200 million, then reportedly sold it to the Cannon Group five days later for $365 million.

Metals Exploration bought Hampton Gold Mining Areas for $73 million. After this takeover Dallhold bought 59 per cent of Mid-East Minerals, which in turn owned 44 per cent of Metals Exploration. Metals Exploration then became the vehicle to take 38 per cent of North Kalgurli Mines which in turn held 68 per cent of Gold Mines of Kalgoorlie. Through this chain of substantial shareholdings Dallhold controlled all these gold mining companies.

Kumagai Gumi of Japan joined Bond Corporation for a proposed $300 million redevelopment of the Waltons site opposite Sydney Town Hall, planning Australia's tallest building. It was never approved. Waltons Bond, which had lost $34 million for the year, sold all its remaining property to Bond Corporation.

Bond announced that he would build Australia's first private university on the Gold Coast.

1987 Bond Corporation floated Bond Corporation International Ltd on the Hong Kong Stock Exchange. BCIL then bought the local television station HKTVB for $190 million.

Bond Media bought the television stations TCN-9 in Sydney and GTV-9 in Melbourne from Consolidated Press Holdings for $1.05 billion, comprising $800 million cash, $200 million in Bond Media convertible notes and $55 million in options. The deal made Bond Australia's biggest television operator but carried the seeds of disaster. Bond Media also launched Sky Channel. Bond Media's public float later in the year was a flop, with a 40 per cent shortfall and the shares listing below issue price of $1.55. Bond Corporation also agreed to take 22.5 per cent of British Satellite Broadcasting, one of two groups aiming to introduce satellite television into Britain.

Waltons Bond retail outlets were sold to the Venture group for $120 million.

BCIL bought Bond Centre in Hong Kong, then sold half of it to Japanese property developer EIE.

Bond Corporation bought the Sydney Hilton from the AMP Society for $160 million.

Dallhold bought 90 per cent of St Joe Gold Corporation, one of the largest gold miners in the United States, for $700 million.

Bond Corporation bought the US brewer G. Heileman & Co for $US1.2 billion.

Bond Corporation made a restraint agreement with its key directors under which they would receive $41 million for their exclusive services.

Dallhold took over Gold Mines of Kalgoorlie for $375 million.

BCIL paid $US262 million for a controlling stake in the Chilean national telephone company.

1988 Bond Corporation bid $46 million for the remaining shares in Waltons Bond.

Bond Corporation paid $306 million for the Chifley Square site in Sydney and planned a $1 billion redevelopment.

Bond Corporation sold the Sydney Hilton for a purported $300 million to an unidentified buyer who subsequently proved to be Singapore businessman Ong Beng Seng.

Bond Corporation bought 19.9 per cent of Bell Group from Robert Holmes à Court. Simultaneously, the State Government Insurance Commission of Western Australia bought an identical parcel. Faced with another unacceptable conduct declaration by the NCSC for acting in concert with the SGIC, Bond Corporation made a takeover offer for all minority holdings in Bell Group except those held by the SGIC. The bid resulted in Bond Corporation getting 68 per cent of Bell Group and thereby effective control of Bell's 40 per cent–owned Bell Resources Ltd.

The Australian Broadcasting Tribunal called a hearing to establish whether Bond was a fit and proper person to hold a television licence.

BCIL increased its holding in Chilean Telephone Co to 53 per cent.

BCIL acquired an option to buy a 49 per cent interest in a large parcel of land on the outskirts of Rome.

Bond International Gold was floated in the United States, with Dallhold retaining 62 per cent.

Bond Corporation reported a profit of $355 million for the year to June 1988.

Bond Corporation bought a 20 per cent stake in Lonrho of Britain.

Bond Corporation sold the Emu Brewery site in Perth to FAI Insurances for $130 million.

Bond Corporation bought the St Moritz Hotel in New York for $US180 million.

1989 Bond Corporation took over BCIL.

A story screened on the ABC's 'Four Corners' program alleged that Bond Corporation's 1988 profit had been inflated by booking proceeds from the sale of the Sydney Hilton and the Rome land although neither deal had been completed.

Bond Corporation was forced to quit Lonrho at a loss of $110 million.

The Bell Resources accounts revealed that it had lent $1 billion to Bond Corporation and associates. Bond Corporation tried to wipe out the debt by selling Bond Brewing to Bell Resources for $3.5 billion. Eventually 50 per cent of Bond Brewing was sold to Lion Nathan of New Zealand and the other half went to Bell Resources in part satisfaction of the amounts owing by Bond Corporation.

Australian Ratings downgraded Bond Corporation to CCC.

BCIL sold the remaining half of Bond Centre to EIE for $364 million.

The NCSC announced an inquiry into Bond Corporation, particularly the Emu Brewery deal and the removal of $1 billion from Bell Resources.

The SGIC tried to enforce an agreement under which it could sell its Bell Group stake to Bond Corporation at $2.70 a share. After negotiations the SGIC failed and had to dump the stock on market at far lower prices, then sue Bond Corporation for the balance.

Bond Corporation announced a loss of $980 million, the largest until then in Australian history. The loss wiped out shareholders' funds, leaving a deficiency of $200 million.

Consolidated Press, still owed $200 million of the consideration for its television stations, began moves which eventually resulted in it taking control of Bond Media and restructuring it as Nine Network Australia.

Understanding Alan

Exploring all these deals would fill a much larger book than this with

194

forbidding detail. To understand Bond it may be more fruitful to consider the main characteristics of the man and his empire.

The use of time payment

Even in the abbreviated list above a few Bond characteristics stand out. One is that many purchases were made on the basis of a dollar down and the rest to come. The most notorious of these was the Robe River deal. The Mineral Securities liquidation was potentially one of the most complex in Australia until then. The creditors were divided into secured and unsecured, but it was well understood that some of those claiming security might not be able to stand scrutiny. If the liquidator, Jim Jamison, could not pay out both classes in full the liquidation was liable to dissolve into a welter of lawsuits as unsecured creditors tested the security of the others.[7] To pay them in full it was crucial that Jamison should be able to sell Minsec's largest single asset—its stake in Robe River—but the only buyer who would agree to the price he needed was Bond. The only way Bond could pay was by putting a fraction of the price down as a deposit and promising to repay the balance on a six-monthly schedule.

This generated some moments of high farce. As each scheduled payment date approached, the financial press would begin speculating whether or not Bond would make the payment. On at least two occasions Jamison sat in his office until midnight waiting for a cheque that didn't arrive until a few days later. Jamison found himself being likened to Cinderella. But Bond knew what he was doing. Jamison could not pull the plug on Bond without unstringing the entire Minsec liquidation. Bond's financiers were in a similar bind. They did not want to keep bankrolling him into Robe River, then perceived as a marginal proposition, but nearly all of them had a stake of some kind in Minsec and they could not afford to let the liquidation collapse either. The Robe River stake was not finally bedded down until it was taken over by Engelhard Industries and Burns Philp. But in the interim it had bought Bond four years of survival.

The ultimate use of time payment came when Bond bought Van Gogh's famous painting 'Irises' for $79 million. The price was one of the most astronomical of the art boom of the 1980s. It was not revealed until years later that Sothebys had sold the painting to Bond on terms.

Taking control on the cheap

A second point which is evident from the list is that Bond frequently tried to gain control of a company—and particularly the ability to deal with its cash and other assets—without extending a takeover offer to the rest of the shareholders. This brought him into frequent collision with the law and won him Australia's first unacceptable conduct declaration in the manoeuvres over Northern Mining. For most of the period we are considering the takeover law required that anyone who bought 20 per cent or more of a company should make an equivalent offer to the remaining shareholders. However, the law did not apply where the shareholding was acquired along with a parcel of other assets, as happened when Bond acquired Burmah Exploration, which owned Cooper Basin leases and 37.5 per cent of Santos. Bond used this technique frequently. Another way of evading the law occurred in the Bell Group takeover, where Holmes à Court unloaded a 39.9 per cent shareholding in equal tranches to Bond Corporation and the SGIC—a deal which reflected no credit on Holmes à Court. Bond never had any intention of making a similar offer to the outside shareholders in Bell Group and did so only under severe prodding by the NCSC. Forcing Bond to make that bid was perhaps the most notable achievement of the NCSC in its controversial conduct of corporate law during the 1980s.

Rights of minorities ignored

The rights of minority shareholders received scant regard throughout Bond's career. He always treated assets as his own, regardless of what stake others had in them. The worst example of this was in Bell Group's 40 per cent–owned associate Bell Resources. More than a billion dollars was ripped out of Bell Resources, with no regard for the fact that other shareholders owned 60 per cent of it. One Bond Corporation accountant, Ron Nuich, said:

> There appeared to me to be a 'group philosophy' throughout the place. There was no delineation between Bell Resources, Bond Corporation and Bell Group Ltd. Therefore, although it may seem unusual, it was quite usual for a Bond Corporation person to give instructions to people who were solely responsible for Bell Resources matters. It was extremely rare, if it ever happened at all, that Bell Resources personnel would determine what was to happen in the company. The group philosophy principle basically was that Bond Corporation owns everything and there was no such thing as a minority shareholder.[8]

Fees

Management and other fees were paid to directors or their associates for what most people would have thought were their normal duties. When Bond launched WA Land Holdings in 1969 as a public company one of its first acquisitions was a block of land known as Santa Maria. Shareholders in WA Land could have been excused for thinking that one of the duties of their directors, for which they were paid, was to find and develop properties. But when Bond bought Santa Maria for WA Land he charged the company a $100 000 finders' fee. Given the amount of trouble WA Land would have trying to develop this land, the company should have charged Bond. The land had not been rezoned from agricultural to residential at the time, and in fact never was. In another early move Bond pocketed a $250 000 profit selling WA Land a Perth office block that he had bought less than a year earlier.

To take another example, in December 1987 Gold Mines of Kalgoorlie (GMK) bought from Poseidon Ltd the 50 per cent of Kalgoorlie Lake View Pty Ltd that it did not already own. The purchase price amounted to an effective $375 million, to be paid on terms and involving a mixture of cash, gold and convertible notes. To finance the deal GMK made a two-for-one share issue to raise $168 million; the rest of the purchase was to be funded by loans. GMK's letter of offer to shareholders said:

> The transaction was negotiated on behalf of GMK by Dallhold Investments Pty Ltd over several months . . . [that] company also assisted GMK in negotiating third party security support for the gold delivery obligation involved in the transaction. In recognition of Dallhold's assistance GMK's board of directors resolved on February 23, 1988 to pay Dallhold a fee for its services of 2.5 per cent of the effective purchase consideration of $375 million, subject to the transaction being completed.

This was very generous of the GMK board. The fee amounted to $9 375 000. In addition, the GMK board agreed to pay Dallhold a fee of $5 million for 'assistance in obtaining the underwriting commitments in respect of the original proposed issue and assisting in arranging the underwriting agreement for GMK's two-for-one rights issue'. Alan Bond had a conflict of interest because he was chairman of both GMK and Dallhold. The public shareholders of GMK ought to have been able to assume that their chairman was working in their interests rather than for his private gain. They ought to have been able to assume that if the chairman of GMK saw an opportunity for a favourable deal it would be part of his normal duties to do the deal for them, not to charge them for it. While the deal was rather fancy it ought to have been within the normal capacities of the GMK board and management.

One justification for the $9 375 000 fee was that the deal took several months to negotiate. Some elements of it may have; but the main deal with Poseidon itself was negotiated in a couple of days according to Poseidon's chairman, Robert de Crespigny. The fees totalling $14.4 million were excessive in view of GMK's financial position. In the year to June

1988 GMK's net profit was only $13.4 million and it fell to $8.8 million the following year.[9]

Finally, judged by the outcome of the deal, Dallhold deserved no fees at all. As a result of the deal GMK was strategically placed to develop Kalgoorlie's superpit, but also had to face large capital expenditures while burdened with heavy debt. GMK had paid too much and was never able to complete the project. The underwriting hit heavy weather, with the gold index falling from 2104 at the start of 1988 to 1556 by 18 February. As the original issue price of $2.50 for GMK shares became increasingly unattractive it was slashed to $1.50. This was a brutal rather than a complicated solution and, while it undoubtedly caused some angst, it was certainly no stroke of genius deserving a fee.

Intra-group dealings

A corollary of the preceding Bond characteristic is that the group was marked by heavy internal dealing. Bond companies typically sold assets to each other. There were also extensive dealings between Bond's public and private companies. The outside shareholders in the public companies usually came off worst in these deals.

In the mid-1980s, for example, Dallhold, through its controlling interest in Metals Exploration, acquired control of the public companies Gold Mines of Kalgoorlie and North Kalgurli Mines. While they were under Dallhold's control, those two companies lost some $80 million in a myriad of dealings with other Bond group members.[10] The money drained out in service fees and sales of assets. After getting control of GMK and North Kalgurli, Bond had hit shareholders with heavy rights issues which raised $380 million. Some of this had to be contributed by Metals Exploration. But simultaneously—and largely unknown to the shareholders—money was flowing back the other way.

The ownership structure of Bond's gold companies changed over time, but by July 1988 Dallhold owned 59 per cent of Mid-East Minerals, which owned 44 per cent of Metals Exploration, which owned 38 per cent of North Kalgurli Mines, which owned 50.1 per cent of Gold Mines of Kalgoorlie. Through this string of shareholdings Dallhold controlled the entire group. On 1 July 1988, just before the Bond International Gold (BIG) float, Metals Exploration sold three gold properties to GMK for $50.75 million. The consideration comprised cash of $42 million plus five million 5c par shares in GMK issued at a premium of $1.70 each. The three properties were:

- 55 per cent of the Forrestania gold deposit in Western Australia
- a group of gold interests in central Victoria including Bailieston, 60 per cent of Rushworth and 95 per cent of Graytown

- the Mingela prospect near Townsville

The proposed deal was recommended by the directors of GMK and approved by its shareholders. The areas did nothing to enhance GMK but turned out to be almost worthless. In its 1989 annual report a year later, GMK wrote $43 million off its exploration interests. As it had few other exploration properties of note on its books, nearly all the writeoff must have related to those it had bought from Metals Exploration the year before. Shareholders in Metals Exploration—notably Dallhold—had benefited to the tune of $42 million at the expense of GMK and in the process had tightened their hold on GMK. Shareholders in GMK had just been clobbered for $100 million in a big rights issue. This deal lost them some 40 per cent of the money in one hit.

Debt

Any company run by Bond was always hocked to its eyeballs. If he took over a company with low debt its gearing was soon increased. Even his private company Dallhold, which owned 54 per cent of Bond Corporation, was a heavy borrower. The 1988 accounts stated Dallhold's total assets at $824 million but total liabilities ran to $538 million—a gearing of 1.9:1. For a company whose main assets were gold and nickel mines this was definitely unhealthy.

Australia's greatest salesman

Alan Bond was Australia's greatest salesman of his time, and perhaps ever. He was exuberant, cheerful and persuasive. Any conversation with Bond rapidly blossomed into a world of limitless opportunities and exciting new horizons. The writer's standing advice to anyone meeting Bond for the first time was: 'Carry your right arm in a sling, so you can't sign anything'.

Bond was also Australia's best marketer. In his early days of subdivisions he would give some unremarkable piece of land a fancy name, put big signs up, advertise it heavily and sell it for twice as much per block as the land on sale next door.

Bond was an eternal optimist, always looking for an opportunity and trying to take others with him. He really does seem to have envisioned a Sun City on the wastelands of Yanchep. Only a visionary would buck a century of history to challenge for the America's Cup, showing great determination to keep trying until he won it. Bond University was at base a property exercise, but it was visionary nonetheless. Like all the corporate cowboys of the 1980s, Bond was fearless. The thought of failure appears never to have crossed his mind.

Bond's greatest talent was his ability to foresee trends. He foresaw the great future for network television and satellite broadcasting. His entries into gold and oil were ahead of his time. He had a particularly good eye for property, picking Chifley Square, Bond Centre and St George's Hospital. But he also believed he could finance these assets by debt and hold onto them until their time arrived.

Put succinctly, Bond believed his own bullshit. This attitude lured him into many a disaster. As he believed he could see value and opportunity where others could not, he was always prepared to pay more for an asset. Sometimes he was right, as in Santos, Castlemaine Tooheys, Bond Centre and the Chilean telephone company. On the bigger plays, particularly towards the end of his career, he was often wrong. His payment of a billion dollars for the two Channel 9s was at least 30 times earnings and probably more like 50 times. But at least the stations had earnings. He bid more than a billion dollars for Heileman at a time when its core brewing operations were probably losing money. It was the worst single deal of Bond's career and, more than any other, the one that killed his empire.

Generosity

Bond's most attractive characteristic was his personal generosity, even in the days when he had very little. One of his earliest cars was a flashy Oldsmobile—a car that made heads turn in Perth in those days. Bond would happily throw the keys to any mate who wanted to drive it. As a schoolmate observed, Bond was always generous with his toys. When he unveiled 'Irises' in his head office in Perth Bond spontaneously said that, if any of his guests ever wanted to show the painting to their friends, they were welcome to bring them around. And the promise was honoured. Friends of Bond could always impress their friends by showing them the masterpiece.

As the Bond group became a big pot of jam Bond was happy to let key executives dip into it too. The best example of this was the Palace Hotel deal. The Palace was an ornate hotel on St George's Terrace, for generations the drinking hole of newspapermen from West Australian Newspapers, whose headquarters was just opposite. Several property men had considered redeveloping the site but were deterred by the National Heritage listing which required them to retain the hotel intact. Bond Corporation acquired 45 per cent of the hotel for $5.5 million in 1978. The other 55 per cent was held by various entities, including 10 per cent in a $4 company named Rowdore Pty Ltd. Rowdore's four $1 shares were held by Alan Bond and his three principal lieutenants: Peter Beckwith, Tony Oates and Peter Mitchell. Four dollars was the only money they ever put into Rowdore. Bond Corporation guaranteed its debts and paid all its bills. Two years later Rowdore sold its 10 per cent to Bond Corporation for $3.6 million, which meant that each of the four pocketed a profit of $900 000—less $1.[11] These profits would otherwise have gone to Bond Corporation—and accordingly to its shareholders.

Another example of Bond's generosity is the story of the three Ferraris. Bond was in England in the mid-1980s and wanted the latest lair's toy, a Ferrari Testorossa. The retail price of these cars was just under £80 000, but delivery took months and there was such a waiting list for them that a black market had developed and new ones were selling as high as £200 000. Bond—as usual—was impatient. After a jovial argument with one of his top executives, Ken Judge, Bond made a bet. If Judge could get him one within two weeks he'd buy one for Judge and one for another executive, Simon Farrell. With such a large incentive Judge made sure he delivered in time to win the bet, as Bond knew he would.

The story illustrates the airy disregard the men at the top of Bond Corporation had for money. The corporate world was a big money tree and Bond was enjoying it to the hilt. Australian finance has always had a few cheerful rogues, who are great company with a fund of good stories and a zestful attitude towards life. If there were a Society of Cheerful Rogues, Alan Bond would have been its life president.

Toys

The Oldsmobile was only the first of a string of big toys. The cost of them tended to be borne by companies in which public shareholders still held a stake. By the end of Bond Corporation's career there was what came to be known as a 'Toys facility', totalling some $50 million. This included a Falcon 900 corporate jet, the beautiful four-masted schooner *Jessica* (which had been renamed *Schooner Fourex*), and property at San Diego where Bond was planning a challenge to recapture the America's Cup. The jet was originally ordered by Laurie Connell. When Rothwells hit the wall Bond took the jet off him and put it into North Kalgurli. When the shrewd, thrifty Robert de Crespigny took over the gold companies he insisted that he was not taking over any planes, boats or other toys. Bond sold the jet at cost to Bell Resources, which already held the rest of the toys. Neither North Kalgurli nor Bell Resources ever derived any benefit from these 'assets'.[12] (This policy boomeranged on Bond in 1990. When he lost control of Bell Resources, and an angered John Spalvins appointed merchant banker Geoff Hill as chairman, the company applied for the liquidation of Bond Corporation. Bell Resources claimed that Bond Corporation owed it $3 million in bills relating to the corporate jet. This claim developed into a winding-up application that became a grave threat to Bond Corporation.)

Bond's big splurge was in the twelve months after the stock market collapse of October 1987. He bought 'Irises' only three weeks after 20 October, paying a record price for art while the rest of the investment world was still reeling in shock. In late 1987 he bought the Rome land. In July 1988 he bought the beautiful but isolated Cockatoo Island off Australia's north-western coast as a potential tourist resort. In September 1988 he bought the 16th century Glympton Park estate near London for $22 million; the estate included a mansion and village in a thousand hectares of farmland. Three days later he paid $7.8 million for the 62-metre *Jessica*. In October 1988 he bought New York's St Moritz Hotel from Donald Trump for $US180 million, and the Kona Kai Club resort in San Diego for $US40.5 million.

Women

The marriage of Alan and Eileen ('Red') Bond was an open one in which Alan enjoyed a number of extramarital dalliances. Two of the most durable were with women named Diana Bliss and Tracey Tyler, both of whom received a number of expensive presents from Bond. Eileen retaliated with heavy spending on jewellery and lifestyle.

Chutzpah

The Yiddish word 'chutzpah' translates roughly as insouciance or impudence. It is probably closest to the slang word 'cheek'. Bond had chutzpah by the gallon. One of the best stories is told by Barry and concerns the days when Bond was stuck with Yanchep. Even Australia's best salesman never managed to persuade enough buyers to invest in building blocks on this scruffy bunch of sandhills. One day Bond drove John Bertrand, the helmsman who won the America's Cup, to the putative resort. As they approached, Bertrand was amazed to see that the barren coast had suddenly turned green. 'Christ!', Bertrand exclaimed. 'Have you put in irrigation?' 'No', replied Bond. 'I've painted the sandhills to make the brochures look better.'[13]

Luck

Bond had audacity and was able to attract financial backing. He always kept trying and managed to survive disasters such as Yanchep that would have sunk lesser men. Sooner or later he was bound to get lucky, especially in an era of asset price inflation.

Bond's lucky strike was Santos. In 1978 Burmah Oil of Britain was in trouble and selling off assets worldwide. Several local parties put together offers for Burmah's local holdings but Bond's was at least $10 million higher than any of them. Bond bought Burmah Australia Exploration for $36 million in August 1978. Burmah held 30 per cent of Basin Oil, 67 per cent of Reef Oil and 37.5 per cent of Santos, all of which had their major assets in the Cooper Basin. Looking at it another way, his holdings amounted to 46 per cent of the oil and 60 per cent of the gas and condensate reserves. The purchase was actually made by a consortium headed by Bond Corporation, Dallhold and Endeavour. This was mainly because Bond Corporation could not raise the money by itself, even though only $11 million of the price had to be made as a down payment. The rest, of course, was on terms. Santos was producing cash flow from its gas and oil wells, but the company had only just paid its maiden dividend of two cents and future payouts looked thin and unreliable. The dividends would therefore be unlikely to cover the interest expense on Bond's borrowings.

But, while Bond was haggling with the stock exchanges over whether he should bid for the outstanding shares, he got lucky. Just a month after he had bought out Burmah, Santos literally struck oil. The Strzelecki No. 3 well in the Cooper Basin recorded the biggest onshore oil flow rate in Australian history. Santos had a 35 per cent stake in the lease, so Santos shares soared more than 50 cents to over $2. A few months later, dividend was lifted to five cents. Even so it would have been worth only some $870 000 a year to Bond, while his interest bills would have been running at around $3 million.

The SA Government then passed legislation barring any group from having more than 15 per cent of Santos. This legislation was fiercely contested by several parties, including the then Federal Treasurer John Howard and the Australian stock exchanges. But the government was determined that Bond—who had already developed a considerable reputation for his freewheeling tactics—should not control one of South Australia's few remaining substantial companies. The South Australians were widely criticised for their actions, but in hindsight they were better judges of Bond's character and motivations than were several vaunted bankers, finance journalists and businessmen of the day. The SA Minister of Mines and Energy, Hugh Hudson, analysed Bond Corporation's accounts, pointing out its high gearing and lack of profitability. He said that the empire had suffered significant financial difficulties over a number of years and was then in a very weak financial position. He pointed out that one of Bond Corporation's first moves had been to charge Santos $50 000 a month in consulting fees and that only the independent directors had stopped the amount being $100 000.

'The Bond Corporation does not have the financial competence (if one examines the record), or the knowledge of hydrocarbons to be in control of a major energy company', Hudson said. Referring to the SA Government's experience in dealings with Bond, Hudson said: 'If Mr Bond feels in a position of strength, he will threaten and attempt to govern by fear. Once he knows the cards are stacked against him, he will plead and give assurances without limit.'

Hudson said that Bond was using Santos to solve his own empire's financial problems. Hudson also noted that Bond had proposed that Santos should make a share placement to Spedley Securities. 'The money raised by Santos was to have been re-lent to Spedley with no indication being provided of the use Spedley would make of the money returned to them', Hudson said.

> However, as Spedley Securities is the merchant bank employed by Bond Corporation it was confidently expected that the money would end up being used to finance the payments to Burmah. The history of this matter indicates to the government very clearly that the Bond Corporation has not yet solved its financial problems and that should the Bond Corporation gain complete control of Santos that control could well be used to rectify any problem arising from the Bond Corporation's obligation to Burmah.[14]

Hudson's analysis of Bond's modus operandi was criticised by several commentators at the time, but later seemed much closer to the mark than those of many other allegedly professional investors and financiers.

Bond contested the legislation fiercely before selling down his Santos stake—and eventually selling all of it—under protest. As the market was rising, he profited handsomely. The sale of his first tranche, getting Bond down to 15 per cent, produced an $8 million profit. It was not until 1982 that Bond quit the rest of his Santos shares, together with Basin and Reef. He cashed the shares in to finance his takeover of Swan Brewery. His total profit on the deal is hard to estimate because the holding costs were never disclosed, he did some buying and selling over the years and Santos expanded its capital by issues during the period. However, analysts estimated that he had made a profit of at least $100 million on the whole deal. It was his first big successful deal and one of the best in his career.

Roots in property

Bond made his first big money in property and was involved to some extent in property dealing throughout his career. It was always an important part of the Bond empire. Property dealing essentially involves buying real estate and either holding it until it can be sold at a profit or changing it through rezoning or building to make a profit. Over time, property has been Australia's best investment. However, there is a cost involved in holding it as interest charges, rates and other costs accumulate. As time goes on they accumulate at a compound rate. If the price does not rise quickly enough to cover these costs the profit will turn into a loss. If the price goes down, as not infrequently happens, the loss will be large. If the property was purchased by borrowing money, the lender must be held at bay until the property comes good. If it cannot be sold for the right price in the open market, then a sale to an associate must be arranged.

Bond never lost the property mentality. He dealt with his assets continually as though they were property, to be bought and sold for big capital gains.

Limited expertise in running businesses

Until he bought Swan Brewery with the proceeds from Santos, Bond had never owned a significant cash flow business. At Swan Brewery he was immediately struck by the novelty of running a business where cash poured in every day after he opened the doors. This led him to put a high premium on cash flow businesses as he began bidding high for breweries and media companies. But, of course, while cash flow businesses are highly desirable they can be overpriced like anything else. Bond certainly overpriced the Channel 9s and Heileman.

Amazing ability to charm bankers

The most amazing aspect of the Santos deal was how Bond financed it. At the time he bid $36 million for the Burmah stake Bond not only didn't have the money but seemingly had no prospect of raising it. The 1970s had seen him struggling to make $2 million payments on Robe River and also stuck deep in the sands of Yanchep until he persuaded his partner, Tokyu Corporation, to bail him out. No Australian bank would lend him significant money. In 1978 WA Land Holdings had not paid a dividend for five years and had been reporting profits of the order of a million or two a year compared to an interest bill of more than $30 million. To this point Bond had done some 100 per cent borrowing from finance companies on land plays, but $36 million was out of the finance companies' league.

In December 1978 (well after he had signed up for Santos) Bond flew to China for three weeks and negotiated a new source of finance from the Hong Kong & Shanghai Bank. He persuaded that bank not only to finance him into the Santos play but also to help raise a $600 million consortium loan to finance pipelines for the company. Apart from the Hong Kong & Shanghai Bank the other major participants were the Canadian Imperial Bank of Commerce and the Republic National Bank of Dallas, with a minor role being played by the Australian Resources Development Bank. Two of the people who helped Bond in this were Talbot Beckwith, the former ANZ Bank chief manager for international business whose son Peter was now Bond's right-hand man, and Laurie Connell, through his old Martin Corporation connections with the Canadian Imperial Bank of Commerce. The links forged between Connell and Bond from this deal would last until the collapse of Rothwells.[15]

The other important link forged was between Bond and the chief executive of the Hong Kong & Shanghai, Michael Sandberg, who was affectionately nicknamed 'Uncle' by Bond's executives. Sandberg was greatly impressed by Bond over their lunches at the top of the bank's Hong Kong headquarters, overlooking the harbour. Without Sandberg, Bond might never have expanded beyond Western Australian property development. It was the Hong Kong & Shanghai that financed him successively into the Santos, Swan Brewery and Castlemaine Tooheys takeovers. These all turned out to be good deals, but it should not be forgotten that Sandberg personally played a large role in the promotion of Alan Bond.

Bond was still holding his 15 per cent of Santos when he wanted to take over Swan Brewery. He tried to finance the deal through the Hong Kong & Shanghai's local subsidiary, Wardley Australia. Wardley's then chief executive, Michael Bato, agreed to finance the Swan takeover, which would ultimately cost $135 million. However, Bato was concerned about Bond's balance sheet at the time and was trying to restrain his borrowings. Bato insisted that Bond Corporation sell various assets to improve its gearing ratio. So the money for Swan was advanced only as a bridging loan. As 1982 wore on, the assets were not sold and Bato became increasingly concerned about his client. The short, sharp recession of 1983 was looming, interest rates were rising and Bond was looking overgeared. Undaunted as always, Bond was making a play for the old Sydney retail chain of Grace Brothers and buying into Simplicity Patterns.

As long as Bond did not repay the loans or sell down the assets Wardley found itself committed to providing general funding for the group, which had never been Bato's intention. He had become a captive financier. 'Either you have confidence in a client or you don't deal with him', said Bato. 'I found I couldn't deal with Bond.' So Bato got tough and demanded repayment. But Bond had more highly placed contacts in the bank, notably Uncle Michael. Bato's demand on Bond was followed by a big board meeting in Melbourne attended by Bato and the chief executive of Wardley Hong Kong, Ewan Launder. After that meeting Bato was summoned to Hong Kong, where Launder told him: 'I want you to resign. You're not being entrepreneurial enough'. Bato resigned. His career was ruined. He found it difficult to get a job over the next eleven years—a fact which hardly reflects credit on the Australian banking industry. The story of his fate could hardly have been lost on later executives of Wardley Australia, which became Bond's main bank.[16] Bato's successor, James Yonge, would work very closely with Bond over the next two years.

Not a detail man

Bond could always see the grand sweep of a deal, but did not bother with details. This was always left to others, notably the reliable Peter Mitchell, who wound up as a director of 600 companies in the Bond empire. Indeed, there were even whispers about Bond's basic literacy. He had left school with atrocious spelling ability which was no small impediment to his early career as a signwriter. He was good with numbers, although he seems to have had the typical short attention span of corporate cowboys and was too impatient to slog through the notes to the accounts. But he was without peer in seeing the possibility of making a dollar.

This meant that Bond's subordinates spent considerable time straightening out deals which Bond had done conceptually. When he bought the St Moritz Hotel from Donald Trump the deal was done without any reference to Bond's executives and was sealed by Bond giving Trump a cheque for the $1 million down payment. However Bond had only his personal chequebook on hand, so he crossed his name off the bottom of the form and wrote in Bond Corporation's. Next day puzzled executives from Trump contacted equally puzzled executives from Bond Corporation saying they were unable to bank the cheque and could they have a real one please. It was duly sent.

A good dealer, but not a great dealer

Wheeling and dealing was in Bond's blood. His weakness was that he was a compulsive dealer and could not let a deal go once negotiations had begun. He hated to think that someone else might do the deal instead. The simplest (and often silliest) way to close any deal is to offer a bigger dollar, and Bond did this constantly when faced with a reluctant seller. This often left Bond Corporation saddled with a badly overpriced asset. Some of the company's worst transactions were those that subsequently had to be made to somehow get rid of the asset—often by shoving it on to a related company where the public shareholders wound up absorbing much of the loss.

Sometimes Bond got it right. Frustrated by the haggling with the then chairman, Lloyd Zampatti, to buy Swan Brewery in 1981, Bond clinched the deal by suddenly adding $17 million to his bid. This caused a problem because he did not have the money. However, he raised it by ringing the head office of the Hong Kong & Shanghai Bank and telling them he was committed to the purchase.[17]

When matched against really tough dealers Bond came off second best. The two most vivid examples were his negotiations with Kerry Packer and Robert de Crespigny.

The sale of the Consolidated Press Holdings (CPH) television interests to Bond was negotiated in January 1987. The Channel 9s in Sydney and Melbourne were the main asset of Consolidated Press, put together by Sir Frank Packer. After Sir Frank's death his second son Kerry Packer privatised CPH in 1983, becoming executive chairman. The 9's were regarded as the jewel in the CPH crown and a family heirloom. For both financial and sentimental reasons Packer was a reluctant seller when Bond tried to buy the stations. But when Bond wanted to buy an asset he went after it like a shark after red meat. And, like a feeding shark, Bond often failed to notice the concealed hook.

The financial world was shocked when Packer and Bond announced the deal. Nobody had ever thought that Packer would sell. But, as soon as they saw the price and terms, shrewd heads around the market reckoned that Bond had just borrowed the stations. The price was an enormous $1055 million. Bond combined them with his own television stations in Brisbane and Perth to create an Australia-wide Channel 9 network; then floated them, together with some minor television interests, in a company called Bond Media Ltd. The Bond Media information memorandum showed that the stations were making perhaps $25 million after tax. Bond had therefore paid a price of something like 50 times earnings. A price/earnings multiple half that size would have been considered on the high side, even in the boom.

The multiple was bad enough, but Bond had not completed the deal. The terms were $800 million cash, $200 million in convertible redeemable Bond Media preference shares and $50 million in options. The preference shares could be converted by CPH into Bond Media ordinary shares at $4.65 per share at any time before 31 March 1991. Alternatively, CPH could redeem them for $200 million cash at 31 March 1991. Both the $200 million preference shares and the $50 million options could be put back to Bond at that date. It was fairly obvious from day one that CPH would go for the cash, because there was never any hope that Bond Media shares would reach $4.65 in the four years. To help finance the deal, Bond Media

208

raised $400 million in a public float in March 1987 at $1.55 a share. This was a heavy issue, which listed at a discount. After the issue Bond Media was very heavily capitalised with 528 million ordinary shares.

Even though CPH had collected $800 million it had at all times the potential to reclaim the stations if Bond couldn't redeem the preference shares for $200 million. Also, the preference shares carried a six per cent fully franked dividend, requiring a payout of $12 million a year. But to make the dividend fully franked Bond Media needed to generate a profit of at least $20 million. To put it another way, the first $20 million of any profit was committed to CPH and the ordinary shareholders had to rely on the surplus for theirs. The preference shares became a timebomb for Bond.

Even after the share issue Bond Media was saddled with a debt too big for the network to service. In the information memorandum to attract subscribers to the issue, Bond Media directors said they expected revenue growth in the order of 15 per cent per annum for the years 1986–87 and 1987–88. Profit was forecast to increase because Bond Media claimed that there had been a reduction in program costs, a significant reduction in overheads and lower capital expenditure which would cut depreciation charges. These forecasts would turn out to be quite wrong, because the costs of Bond Media would run wild over the next two years. The revenue expectations were fulfilled. By 1988 Bond Media's total revenue was $450 million and by 1989 it hit $518 million. Net profit, however, could only reach $30 million in 1988, or less than six cents a share, and in 1989 the company made a loss of $2.8 million. Costs were out of control. Net interest soared from $41 million in 1988 to $57 million as rates climbed in 1989. Depreciation and amortisation were not curtailed, rising from $20 million in 1988 to $23 million in 1989. And operating costs—calculated by deducting other revenue, operating profit, interest and depreciation from total revenue—jumped from $322 million to $396 million. A media network pulling in half a billion dollars a year through the front door was unable to hang on to enough of it to make a profit. Bond Media was so overburdened with debt that it never had much chance, but lack of cost control sealed its fate. Packer repossessed his network. When people congratulated him later, and asked what the next big bonanza deal would be, he mused: 'You only get one Bond in your life, and I've had mine'.

Bond made essentially the same mistake when dealing with Robert de Crespigny, a shrewd accountant who had started from scratch and by tenacious dealing had put together the Normandy Poseidon group of mining companies. The negotiations with de Crespigny centred on the Kalgoorlie superpit. This was a visionary idea, not originated by Bond but most enthusiastically developed by him, of combining the entire Golden Mile at Kalgoorlie into one giant open cut mine. The resulting hole would be one of the few manmade structures on earth that could be seen from the Moon.

Dallhold, through GMK, bought half of Kalgoorlie Lake View Associates from de Crespigny's Poseidon for $375 million. The price comprised $200 million cash, 214 000 ounces of gold over six years and a $25 million note payable in seven years or convertible within two years into five million GMK shares. This deal was done in December 1987, some eleven months after the Channel 9s deal, and for Bond it contained the same fatal flaws. Bond burdened GMK heavily with debt, a very risky tactic in a mining company. If GMK could not deliver the gold or redeem the $25 million note, control could revert to de Crespigny. This timebomb went off in August 1989, when de Crespigny effectively gave back the gold obligation and the note in return for a controlling 20 per cent interest in GMK. Further, the controlling interest was in a GMK much larger in size than the assets de Crespigny had sold to Bond. It was also heavily encumbered; de Crespigny's first action was to begin reducing its debt. De Crespigny was generous in victory, saying that Bond's development of the superpit to that date was 'a Cecil Rhodes effort'. But to no avail. Bond had outlaid a total of $1 billion in cash in the Bond Media and GMK deals, and wound up being tossed out of them with almost nothing.

Bond at his zenith

Upon these strengths and weaknesses Bond built a mighty empire which reached its zenith around 1988. By then Dallhold had become the world's largest privately owned gold miner, as well as having just over 50 per cent of Bond Corporation. Bond Corporation was the seventeenth largest enterprise in Australia, as ranked by revenue in the *Australian Business Top 500*. In 1989 it would rise to ninth largest.[18] At 30 June 1988 Bond Corporation reported total assets of $9 billion, net assets of $2.6 billion and revenue of $5 billion. Net profit was $400 million. Let's look at Bond's main areas.

Brewing. Bond Corporation had become the world's fifth largest brewer. In Australia it owned Swan, Castlemaine and Tooheys. It had half the beer market in New South Wales, 80 per cent of Queensland and 90 per cent of Western Australia. In the United States it owned Heileman, that nation's fourth largest brewer, and Pittsburgh.

International. Bond Corporation held 66 per cent of Bond Corporation International Ltd, which was building the huge Bond Centre in Hong Kong and held 36 per cent of the Compania de Telefonos de Chile and 30 per cent of station HKTVB Hong Kong.

Media. Bond Corporation held 52 per cent of Bond Media, which owned Australia's top-rating television network comprising TCN-9 Sydney, GTV-9 Melbourne, QTQ-9 Brisbane and STW-9 Perth. Bond Media also owned nine radio stations around Australia, the nation's only satellite television broadcaster Sky Channel, half of Media Niugini and 15 per cent of the British TV-am. Bond Corporation owned 22 per cent of British Satellite Broadcasting, which was trailing Rupert Murdoch's Sky Channel to introduce satellite television to Britain. Through its control of Bell Group, Bond Corporation had effective control of West Australian Newspapers.

Energy. Bond Corporation had interests in the Harriet oilfield on the North West Shelf and oil exploration areas in Western Australia, New Guinea and China's Hainan Island. It had coal mines in the Hunter Valley and at Ipswich. Through its indirect shareholding in Bell Resources, Bond Corporation had a stake in the Weeks royalty on the Bass Strait oilfields, still Australia's largest oil province.

Property. Bond Corporation was building Chifley Square in Sydney and the R&I Tower in Perth, and trying to get planning permission to redevelop the Waltons site in Sydney as Australia's tallest building. Bond Corporation had bought 260 hectares of land just north of Rome and was still selling residential property at Taylor's Lakes, outside Melbourne. Bond University was being built on the Gold Coast and St George's Hospital on Hyde Park Corner in London was being redeveloped, both as a joint ventures.

Bond's family company. Dallhold Investments Pty Ltd owned 51 per cent of Bond Corporation and had huge interests in its own right. It was the world's largest privately owned gold miner through its controlling interest in Bond International Gold (BIG), which owned a string of US and South American mines. Through its holdings in Mid East Minerals Dallhold controlled large gold properties in Australia, including a half-interest in the Kalgoorlie superpit and the Greenvale nickel mine in Queensland. Dallhold also had extensive property interests.

Alan Bond had become larger than life. He was Australia's best known businessman. He had won the America's Cup and—as a gesture to Australia's Bicentenary—had donated $12 million to build an exact replica of Captain Cook's *Endeavour*. He was the world's fifth largest brewer and largest private gold miner. He had plans for the world's first global communication network, with satellites over Britain, Australia and South America. In a quarter of a century Bond had risen from apprentice signwriter to head of a global enterprise that ranked among the giants of Australian industry. In his chairman's review Bond declared that 1988 had been 'another year of momentous achievements' in the group's history.

The group's planned and systematic building of operating businesses

211

with strong, recession-proof cash flows and quality assets, its concentration on efficiency and profitability, its development of superior
management at all levels, and the globalisation of interests, are the
wellsprings for Bond Corporation's ongoing success.

The downturn in global stock markets which commenced in October
1987 severely shook the confidence of investors and business managers
and many companies of previously high repute faltered. However, Bond
Corporation emerged from this period stronger than ever and with its
capacity for continued development unimpaired, ready to take advantage
of the opportunities which would follow.

The men at the top of Bond Corporation may have been in the grip of
delusions of grandeur. At the annual meeting in November 1987, shareholders had approved a proposal that key executives should be bound
to the company by being paid for the exclusive right to their services
over the next five years. A staggering total of $41 million was to be paid
to the executives, including $10 million to Beckwith, $6 million to Mitchell
and $2.5 million to David Aspinall, Bond's general manager of media and
communications. These payouts were unprecedented by any Australian
company. As Alan Kohler later pointed out in the *Australian Financial
Review*, shareholders would have been better off if they had paid the same
amount *to get rid* of the top men. 'These men are being paid millions of
dollars to refrain from competing against Bond Corporation when, in fact,
they should have all been sacked', he fumed.[19]

What was wrong

What could have been wrong with this glowing picture of corporate
health? The answer is that quite a number of things were wrong; some
of the clues are given in the 1988 outline above. The biggest mistake was
strategic. The share market crashes of October 1987 were the clearest sign
possible that the investment world had changed, but Alan Bond turned
a blind eye. Bond Corporation was continuing to expand apace. Two of
its biggest and worst judged expansions—into Bell Group and Lonrho—
were made after October 1987. The takeover of Heileman had been
announced only a month before the crash, but no opportunity had been
taken to negate it or even to reduce the price. Bond would have had
a better chance of survival if he had consolidated and liquidated
immediately after 20 October. It may well be that he was technically
insolvent even before October 1987; a liquidation would only have proved
that more quickly. Given the tangled state of Bond's dealings and records,
we shall never know. His arch-rival Robert Holmes à Court, read the 1987
storm signal correctly and began liquidating his empire immediately in
a desperate race to survive.

Another clue is the relationship of total assets at $9 billion to net assets at $2.6 billion. This meant that liabilities totalled $6.4 billion, or two and a half times shareholders' funds. Bond was still very highly geared at a time when it looked increasingly dangerous. He was still playing last year's game. Indeed, as Bond traditionally took a highly optimistic view of his asset values, the real gearing was much higher and shareholders' funds may well have been negative. There was some faint recognition of this point. Tony Oates told the 1988 annual meeting of Bond Corporation that the group was planning $1 billion to $2 billion in asset sales during 1988–89 to reduce debt.

Bond's biggest single mistake was the purchase of Heileman, and the reason for the mistake appears to have been sheer incompetence. According to managing director Peter Beckwith, Bond Corporation undertook eight months of 'meticulous preparation' before launching its bid for Heileman.[20] Either this preparation did not disclose that Heileman's core beer operations were trading at a loss or the meticulous planners chose to ignore the fact. Bond Corporation paid $US1.25 billion ($A1.75 billion) for Heileman. As soon as Bond Corporation took over it sold Heileman's non-core assets in baking, snackfoods and machine products. These divisions had generated profits of some $A52 million. Without them, Heileman made a $A95 million loss in the first eight months under Bond control and another $A70 million loss in the first full year, 1988–89. Heileman did not have a brand capable of taking on the big names such as Budweiser, Schlitz and Coors. Its top brands were Lone Star in Texas, Old Style in the Midwest and Colt 45 nationally. It operated ten breweries in nine American states and had sales greater than those of the entire Australian beer market. But its costs were even higher. Heileman became a bleeding wound in the accounts. Peter Coors later reckoned that Heileman was worth only $US350 million in 1988—less than one-third of the price Bond paid.[21]

Bond's Australian breweries were in better shape, but deteriorating. After the takeover of Castlemaine Tooheys, Bond had put Tooheys former managing director Bill Widerberg in charge of Bond's Australian brewing division. Widerberg had the vision of creating a single national beer brand. Brands such as Tooheys in New South Wales and XXXX in Queensland would still exist, but the national brand would be Swan Premium. This grandiose concept was the sort to appeal to Alan Bond. Beckwith, and to a lesser extent Oates and Mitchell, disagreed with the idea but Bond backed Widerberg and the national beer was born. This was a mistake. A lot of expert comment was later voiced by marketing people saying the mistake should have been foreseen, but it may well have been a concept that could only be proved true or false by trying it. An enormous national advertising campaign was swung behind Swan

Premium. Whatever Bond's other faults, no marketing idea ever failed for want of backing. The aim was to get 5 per cent of the market outside Western Australia.

Market shares for beer, although always arguable, appear to have been fairly static before 1985. In the next five years the market shares of Bond brands slipped in their home states. In Western Australia Swan had historically enjoyed 95 per cent of the market, but was eroded to 90 per cent—a loss that could be excused on the grounds that any such dominant market share can only go down. Elsewhere was worse. When Bond took over Tooheys it was the market leader with a 52–53 per cent share in New South Wales. Five years later its arch-rival Carlton & United (CUB) was claiming 52 per cent in New South Wales and Tooheys had fallen to 42–43 per cent. In Queensland, Bond made a small but insensitive marketing mistake. Fiercely parochial Queenslanders were galled to see the fine print on the XXXX labels changed to show that the beer was now brewed at Canning Vale in Perth. The result was catastrophic. When Bond took over Castlemaine it commanded three-quarters of the Queensland beer market, with CUB holding only 22 per cent. Five years later CUB's share was still 22 per cent, but the newcomer Power Brewing had captured 14 per cent from Castlemaine through drinkers' discontent with Bond. A better idea of the impact may be gained by talking litres. In 1985 the Bond beers sold more than 800 million litres a year in their home states. By 1990 that figure had dropped by 130 million litres to below 700 million. In any market a loss of such a share is a disaster. Bond executives tried to put a good face on it by saying that they had deliberately shed some unwanted market share—a statement greeted with derision by beer market veterans who had seen bloody battles for every percentage point.[22]

Bond Brewing Holdings also poured millions into an invasion of CUB's stronghold, Victoria. BBH bought Melbourne's most famous pub, Young and Jacksons, opposite Flinders Street station, so that it could mount an enormous neon sign on top advertising Swan Premium. Another huge sign was erected at St Kilda Junction. A beautiful and expensive three-minute television commercial was made, starring Australian idols such as golfer Greg Norman, artist Ken Done and motorcycle champion Wayne Gardner. But although the marketing was beautiful and backed by big dollars, and although the product was good (his worst enemies never criticised the quality or flavour of Bond's beers), it didn't work. Swan remained perceived as a Western Australian beer. Most Australians had tried it and liked it, but were not about to switch from their favoured local brands to Swan Premium.

Particularly strong parochial factors were at work in Victoria and Queensland, states notoriously suspicious of outsiders. Also, Bond had outraged publicans by pirating their businesses' goodwill into Austotel for the GPI Leisure float. The world's best conceived advertising campaign can be sabotaged if the distribution outlets have been rendered hostile. Swan's 5 per cent target for the non-WA market was never achieved. The most open market, New South Wales, achieved 4 per cent briefly but Victoria never achieved 3 per cent. Ironically, the best marketing successes in these years were dry beers produced under the labels of Tooheys and Castlemaine.

Bond Media, too, was digging itself into deep trouble by 1988. Its net profit of $30 million before extraordinaries boiled down to less than six cents per share on this overcapitalised and overindebted company. It was also a disturbingly small profit alongside Bond Media's net interest bill of $41 million (which would grow to $54 million the following year). The balance sheet revealed that creditors and borrowings of Bond Media totalled $731 million. The network was getting top ratings, but not translating them into a strong enough bottom line. Bond Corporation's 51 per cent holding in Bond Media was carried in the accounts at a value of $414 million, although there was widespread scepticism whether it was worth that much. Bond accounts were recognised as putting the most optimistic possible valuations on assets and profits.

Bond committed one other highly visible folly in April 1988. Holmes à Court had been trying to liquidate his empire, including his 43 per cent controlling stake in Bell Group Ltd. Bell Group then owned a range of assets including the Bell transport and earthmoving group, West Australian Newspapers and 15 per cent of the Standard Chartered Bank of Britain. The most significant asset was its 40 per cent stake in Bell Resources Ltd, which in turn held 20 per cent of BHP and a number of other valuable interests. In the wake of the October crash Bell Group shares had slid to $1.30. This was an unappealingly low price to Holmes à Court, but he was unlikely to get a much higher bid. Under company law, anyone buying 20 per cent or more of Bell Group would have to make an equivalent bid for the rest. The solution was for Holmes à Court to split his holding into two parcels of 19.9 per cent and sell them simultaneously to the SGIC of Western Australia for $2.50 and to Bond Corporation for $2.70.[22] By making the sales at different prices it was hoped to avoid the allegation that the buyers had been acting in concert.

This was a tawdry deal by Holmes à Court because he got a price for his shares under terms that denied the same price to his public shareholders.[23] Worse, he had left the shareholders to the mercies of Alan Bond, who now had effective control. Another deplorable aspect of the deal was that the SGIC, a state government instrumentality, should have abetted it. Nor was the SGIC investing soundly, because the $160 million outlay would have blown its balance sheet out beyond any prudential limits. Bond's game plan was to seize control without making any equivalent bid for the outside shareholdings, but in this he was thwarted by the National Companies and Securities Commission and its tenacious chairman Henry Bosch.

Bosch insisted that Bond Corporation bid $2.70 a share for all outstanding stock except that held by the SGIC. For a while, Bond pushed an alternative plan under which Bell Group would take over Bond Media and Bell Resources would take over Bond Corporation. Shareholders in both Bells were horrified by the prospect. Under severe prodding, Bond agreed to Bosch's demand. Bond Corporation bid $2.70 for the rest of Bell Group in July 1988. The offer stayed open only for the minimum period of a month, and Bond wound up with 68 per cent of Bell Group, at a total cost of $545 million. Those Bell Group shareholders who grabbed the bid were the smart ones. The others would watch their shares become worthless, with Bell Group going into liquidation in 1991.

The timebombs

Bond Corporation's 1988 accounts had been signed off in mid-September. Despite Bond Corporation's apparent prosperity there were timebombs ticking away throughout the empire. By then Heileman and Bond Media were sliding further into the pit and Bond had been forced to make the bid for Bell Group. Within weeks the whole empire began disintegrating as the bombs started to explode.

The first bomb was the most damaging. For some time Bond had been on cordial terms with Tiny Rowland, chief executive of the UK conglomerate Lonrho. Despite an intimacy generated at Antibes, where they had met several times because their boats had neighbouring moorings, Bond somehow completely underestimated the intensity of Rowland's attachment to Lonrho and the underlying ferocity of his nature. Bond and Rowland liked each other, and had discussed possible joint ventures. Bond had raised with Rowland's wife the possibility of helping defend Lonrho from possible raiders by buying a few shares. Rowland told him it would not be necessary. Bond did not get the message.

Rowland had an odd background. His father had been a proud German businessman named Furhop and his mother a Dutch liberal. They were living in India when World War I broke out, which resulted in the mother being confined in an internment camp near Darjeeling. While there she bore a son, Roland Walter Furhop. Roland was raised in Germany between the wars. He joined the Hitler Youth, as was common among teenagers, but there is no evidence that he was a serious Nazi. He spent World War II in England, serving as a medical orderly and being interned towards the end of the war. Changing his name to Roland

Rowland, he set about building a business empire in Africa. In his later years he returned to become one of the rogue bulls of the City of London and to acquire the *Observer* newspaper. By 1988 he was a tall, lean, suntanned seventy-one. With his greying hair, charming manner and well-cut suits he looked the sophisticated London businessman, but not far below the surface lurked a street fighter. He had come up the hard way and was renowned for being a tough businessman and a dangerous enemy. His business duels frequently escalated to become personal feuds.

The merest reading of his history should have indicated that he would react violently to any hostile attempt to take control of his flagship, Lonrho. How Bond managed to miss all the clues will probably remain a mystery, but the most probable explanation is sheer arrogance. On 26 September Bond sprang a buying raid on Lonrho, acquiring 20 per cent for an outlay of $655 million. This made Bond the largest shareholder. Bond then rubbed salt into Rowland's wound. Rowland's yacht *Hansa* was moored next to the quay at Antibes. Bond's *Southern Cross III* was three berths away. As soon as Bond became Lonrho's largest shareholder, the captain of *Southern Cross III* asked *Hansa*'s captain when his yacht was going to be moved so that Bond's boat could go alongside the quay. Rowland was furious. 'It was so embarrassing', he said. 'It's such a small community down there, everyone must have heard about it. It was then that I decided to destroy him.'[24]

Until this point there had been widespread recognition among analysts and financial journalists that the profits and asset values in Bond's accounts were over-optimistic, but public criticism had been muted. Analysts are really in the business of finding buy recommendations for their firm's clients, not of attacking companies—and particularly not one of the largest groups in Australia. Any analyst who really distrusts a company tends to resort to a code when writing his or her report. Instead of saying 'dump this dog', the report might say that the stock is 'a hold at best'. Add a few phrases such as 'heavy gearing' and 'treatment of asset values is questionable', and the message is easily perceived by professionals. And in any case some analysts were working for firms which had a vested interest in keeping Bond shares up.

Journalists were inhibited by the laws of defamation. Criticism of Bond had therefore been generally clothed in technical language and had attempted to give an objective viewpoint. After all, Bond had survived so far by pulling one rabbit after another out of a hat. Who was to say that he could not survive longer yet?

Tiny Rowland suffered no such inhibitions. With his creation Lonrho under threat, he went directly for Bond's jugular. He knew that Bond would have to borrow to fund the bid. The most direct way of thwarting the raid, therefore, was to cut off Bond's borrowing capacity by attacking his financial credibility. Rowland launched a full-scale, broken bottle attack on Bond's accounts.

A stream of documents and circulars attacking Bond began emerging from Lonrho. They circulated throughout the City in London and to financial journalists. The biggest report, in November 1988, ran to 93 pages. On the opening page the document stated baldly: 'Bond group companies are technically insolvent, the commercial existence of which is through extraordinary bank support'. The syntax was slipshod but the message was clear. Lonrho estimated the Bond group had total borrowings of $14 billion and that its net worth was negative by a startling $4.2 billion. Lonrho estimated that instead of a profit in 1988 the Bond group had made a loss of $300 million. Worse, this loss would rise to an annual $650 million in future under an annual interest bill of $1.1 billion.

Peter Beckwith's response was that the Lonrho allegations were nonsense and Bond Corporation would not dignify them with a reply. This was nowhere near good enough. The ship had been torpedoed below the waterline and the first mate was denying that anything had happened. Lonrho's allegations went into considerable detail. If they were not refuted by equally detailed argument they would be regarded as correct. In the event they certainly proved more correct than Bond's own accounts. In the six months after November 1988, when the Lonrho attack was launched, Bond Corporation shares halved from $2.25 to $1.12. Other factors were at work, but Lonrho was the most powerful.

Amazingly, some stockbrokers were still prepared to recommend the shares. Greg Matthews of Merrill Lynch had put out a circular in May 1988 headed 'Strong Growth Predicted' and recommending Bond Corporation as a buy. The share price was then $1.70, but Matthews estimated that net tangible assets of the group were worth more than $3.90. At best this was injudicious at a time when Bond was battling with the NCSC over whether he would have to bid for the rest of Bell Group. However, Matthews' recommendation was eclipsed in January 1989 when Roger Colman of County NatWest Securities Australia put out a buy recommendation on Bond Corporation, calculating that the current net asset value of the shares was around $5.65. The recommendation did Bond shares no lasting good as they continued sliding. Even without the benefit of hindsight it was clear that the only recommendation worth making on Bond shares from October 1987 onwards was to sell.

Then the next bomb exploded. In March 1989 the ABC's 'Four Corners' screened perhaps its best program ever. It was an investigation of Bond, led by Paul Barry. The program disclosed that the 1988 Bond Corporation profit had been inflated by the inclusion of two deals which had not been completed by June 1988 and were still not completed nine months later. As previously noted, Bond Corporation had declared a profit of $402 million for the year to June 1988.[25] Nobody reading the accounts would have guessed that more than a quarter of this figure was derived from two transactions which rated only a paragraph each on page 44 of the annual report.

The first deal was the sale of the Capital Centre in Sydney, which included the Hilton Hotel. This sale was supposed to have occurred in December 1987 for a purported profit of $80 million. Again the buyer proved elusive, but was supposed to be Singapore businessman Ong Beng Seng. Tracing this deal was difficult, because the centre was owned through a chain of companies sited in exotic tax havens. Much subsequent investigation showed that Ong had paid a deposit of $16.7 million in December, but the deal was then renegotiated and a formal agreement was not entered into until just before Bond's 1988 balance date. The agreement was subject to a number of terms and conditions, the key one being that Bond Corporation was responsible for procuring the necessary finance for Ong. The agreement was the subject of further negotiation after June 1988, and Bond never procured the necessary finance. Settlement did not occur until late in 1989 and then for a lower price than Bond had claimed. So the profit was not as large and was much later. Mr Justice Beach of the Victorian Supreme Court said:

> The Ong transaction is one of the more mysterious transactions I have ever been called upon to investigate during the course of my legal career. In some respects it has been like dealing simultaneously with a slippery eel and a large and very active octopus. When one feels one is making some headway towards gaining an understanding of the true nature of the transaction one suddenly finds oneself up a blind alley and obliged to start afresh.

The second deal was the Rome land sale. The 1988 annual report noted that Bond Corporation had acquired about 260 hectares of land nine kilometres north of Rome during the year and had sold a minority interest for 'a significant profit'. Barry revealed that part of the land had been sold to Kitool Pty Ltd for $110 million, generating a profit of $74 million for Bond Corporation. This deal aroused scepticism as soon as the facts were ventilated on television. It was incredible that a block of land could have more than doubled in value within a few months. It was even more incredible that $110 million could have been paid by Kitool, a $2 shelf company. As we saw in Chapter 5, Kitool had no obvious source of funding and its two directors could not even agree publicly on who owned it.

The transaction had been accompanied by put and call options to Bond Corporation's 60 per cent–owned subsidiary, Bond Corporation International Ltd (BCIL). The automatic question was why BCIL did not simply take a stake in the land from its parent, rather than dealing through the mysterious Kitool. The only sensible answer was that a sale to a subsidiary could not have been recognised as a profit, whereas warehousing the transaction through an alleged third party could. The transaction therefore appeared to have been designed to inflate the 1988 profit and raise the valuation of the Rome land remaining in the books.

Admittedly, Bond had been negotiating a further sale of the land to English businessman David Rowland (no relation to Tiny). Rowland's Monaco Group SA had agreed to buy half the land, but the sale was aborted in December 1988.

The sale to Kitool was reversed in Bond Corporation's 1988–89 accounts, on the grounds that Kitool had been unable to complete settlement. This meant that Bond Corporation had had to write $74 million out of its 1988 profit. The reversal implied that the whole transaction was unrealistic in the first place. The author has read most of the documents relating to the Kitool deal. The only logical conclusion to be drawn from them is that Kitool was at no stage a genuine arm's length buyer of the land.

The Kitool deal was originally agreed on 14 December 1987. The Canberra-based Kitool Pty Ltd was to buy from Sphinx Holdings Ltd (a Bond Corporation subsidiary based in the Cook Islands) a 49 per cent holding in another Cook Islands company, Seabrook Corporation Ltd, for $110 million. Seabrook Corporation owned 90 per cent of Seabrook SpA whose two wholly owned subsidiaries—Societa di Controllo E. Valorizzazione Immobiliare and Immobiliare Valchetta Nuova SrL—owned the Rome land.[26]

In the second leg of the deal, BCIL would buy the shares in Seabrook from Kitool on 15 July 1988—just after Bond Corporation's balance date.

The designers of at least the second leg of the deal appear to have been Willie West of Potts West Trumbull and merchant bankers Ross Grant and Bruce Watson of Jonray Holdings Ltd.[27] Grant and Watson were the only directors and shareholders of Kitool. For their work on the original deal and later variations they charged a fee of $100 000 to GPI.[28] As Kitool's only capital was two $1 shares held by Grant and Watson the entire $110 million had to be borrowed. The first $32 million was lent to Kitool by three companies, with the Bank of New Zealand (BNZ) acting as the ultimate source of funds. The three lenders were: Greater Pacific Investments (GPI), then a public company controlled by Brian Yuill, $11 million; Aldershot Ltd, a Spedley subsidiary, $11 million; and Equiticorp Australia, a member of the group controlled by Allan Hawkins of New Zealand, $10 million. The three companies warranted to the BNZ that they had made their own investigation into the 'affairs and financial condition' of Kitool.[29] The three lenders were given a first charge over all assets of Kitool; BNZ protected itself by being appointed the agent for the lenders. The agreements between all the parties were signed on 24 December 1987.

Another $20 million was raised for Kitool through a round robin with the Bisley subsidiary, Bisley Options Management Ltd. Bisley Options Management charged BCIL $20 million to procure the put and call option. On the same day—24 December 1987—Bisley Options Management made a subordinated loan of $20 million to Kitool, ranking behind the charge taken on Kitool's assets by GPI, Aldershot and Equiticorp Australia.[30]

A final $60 million was always intended to be paid by BCIL upon exercise of one of the options at the termination date of 15 July 1988. Either BCIL could call upon Kitool to sell the shares to it for $110 million or Kitool could put the shares to BCIL for the same amount. The agreements included a notice of determination relating to the put and call options. This notice clearly anticipated that one or other option would be exercised. BCIL would then pay out the final $60 million to Seabrook and repay the $32 million to GPI, Aldershot and Equiticorp Australia. Readers will note that there is a $2 million surplus over the $110 million sale price. That seems to have been fees to the various parties involved in the deal. Other fees must have been built into the transactions too, because Bisley showed a total fee of $3.7 million at the finish. The agreements also made it clear that all interest, stamp duties and other holding costs would be borne by BCIL. In practical, if not legal, terms BCIL was always the effective buyer of the Rome land from Bond Corporation.

When July 1988 arrived the deal changed somewhat. BCIL wanted to defer settlement until March 1989. This caused some shuffling, with GPI and Equiticorp Australia dropping out, to be replaced by Tulloch Lodge. Eventually BCIL did not buy the Seabrook shares. However, the deal was structured at all times so that Equiticorp, GPI, Aldershot and Tulloch Lodge did not have to outlay a dollar.

The combined impact of the Kitool and Hilton deals was to inflate Bond Corporation's 1988 profit by $154 million. Without them, Bond would not have reported $402 million earnings but something like $250 million. And despite the unreal nature of the two deals Bond Corporation's auditors, Arthur Andersen & Co, did not qualify the group's audit statement for 1988.

As soon as the 'Four Corners' program appeared, the financial press began hounding Bond Corporation and other parties involved for explanations of the two deals. They were met with a great deal of evasiveness, particularly over the ownership of Kitool. These evasions reinforced the journalists' belief that the two deals were essentially phoney. The suspicion spread that perhaps the rest of Bond Corporation was phoney too. Certainly there had been enough questionable incidents in its history.

It was in this atmosphere that the next bomb exploded. In April 1989, a month after the 'Four Corners' program, the Australian Broadcasting Tribunal (ABT) found that a number of allegations made against Bond were correct. This timebomb had been ticking for a long time as the ABT had made extensive inquiries into the allegations. Despite Bond's defences, the ABT found that: (a) Bond had paid a libel settlement of $400 000 to Queensland Premier Sir Joh Bjelke-Petersen, not because it was justified but because he believed his Queensland business interests might be damaged otherwise; (b) Bond had tried, improperly, to conceal the payment; (c) the chief executive of Bond Corporation's international media and communications division, David Aspinall, had misled the ABT in his evidence on the payout; (d) in a phone call, Bond had threatened to Leigh Hall, manager of the AMP Society's investment division, that he would use his TV stations to collect information on the AMP; and (e) that four Bond employees had deliberately deceived the ABT by providing faked tapes from WA radio stations. These allegations were central to the ABT's hearing to determine whether Bond, under Australian law, was a 'fit and proper' person to own a television station. The ABT had not, at this point, made such a determination, but its findings on the facts of the allegations left no doubt that it would.[31] On top of everything else that had been happening this was a further, serious blow to Bond's personal credibility.

The Hall episode was particularly damaging. The AMP Society, as a shareholder in the two Bell companies, had been trying to block moves by Bond to take control and seize the cash of Bell Resources. As it turned out the AMP was not only acting quite properly in the interests of its policyholders, but had correctly divined the threat Bond posed to the interests of other shareholders. Hall was very well known and respected in financial circles as an upright and conscientious executive—the epitome of the AMP—and Bond had tried to make out that he was a liar. Bond's claim fell apart when it turned out that Hall kept diary records of his telephone conversations.

Australian Ratings slashed the credit rating of Bond Corporation to CCC. 'As a highly leveraged company, the situation is considerably exacerbated in the current environment of high interest rates', the ratings bureau said. CCC signified 'poor protection levels' for lenders. Bond shares were now down to $1.10. Beckwith blamed the slump on stockbrokers selling short. Almost the only buyer in the market had been Dallhold, whose holding in Bond Corporation had now reached 58 per cent. Alan Bond unveiled plans to privatise Bond Corporation by taking it over. Turning Bond Corporation private would have enabled Bond to lock some skeletons back in the cupboard, but the plan had two insuperable obstacles: nobody would lend him the money and there were convertible bonds outstanding which would also have to be redeemed.

The next timebomb did not explode suddenly but rather slowly. For some time there had been an uneasy suspicion that Bond Corporation may have been draining cash from Bell Resources. One disturbing aspect to emerge concerning the Lonrho raid was that 76 million of the 95 million Lonrho shares had been bought by Bell Resources. This represented an investment of some $623 million by Bell Resources, undertaken without any reference to its other shareholders. What had been happening, unseen by the public, was the biggest corporate hijack in Australia's history. Bond Corporation had looted more than a billion dollars from Bell Resources. This began to come clear only when the 1988 annual report of Bell Resources—which balanced in December—became public in mid-1989.

The Brigitte Bardots

From late 1987, the Bond group suffered an increasing liquidity crisis, as more cash began flowing out of the group than came in. The group was still spending big on acquisitions at a time when banks were withdrawing funds. This net outflow was not immediately apparent to Beckwith because it was not reflected in figures provided to him by Oates. When Beckwith discovered the outflow of funds he sent a stinging memo to Oates. In this crisis, some person or persons at the top of the group decided to bridge the gap by back-to-back lending.

The full story did not emerge until years later, after South Australian investigator John Sulan had compiled his official report on the affairs of Bond Corporation, which unveiled the back-to-back loans. Within the Bond treasury they were also called internal borrowings, special funding, special financing or even 'Brigitte Bardots', from the initials BB. Companies—principally Bell Resources, J.N. Taylor Holdings, Bond Corporation International and Bond Brewing—would lend money to a third party, which would then make an identical back-to-back loan to Bond Corporation or Bond Corporation Finance (BCF). The third party received a commission on each transaction. The reader will immediately see that this was an uncommercial way of doing business for two reasons. Firstly, if Bell Resources had wanted to lend money to BCF it could have done so directly and not incurred a commission by routing the funds through a third party. Secondly, if Bell Resources lent money directly to BCF it became a creditor of BCF, which was (or should have been) a far more substantial company than the third party. If the third party were to collapse, Bell Resources might have no recourse against BCF or anyone else in the Bond group.

Control of Bond's central treasury operations seems to have been sporadic and uncoordinated, as the opening chapter of the Sulan Report makes clear.[32] However, the corporate treasurer, Robin deVries, appears to have been acting mostly on the orders of Beckwith. How much Bond knew about it is a moot point, but it is difficult to imagine that Beckwith orchestrated the entire operation without Bond's knowledge and consent.

It was Beckwith who appears to have conducted most of the discussions with Julian Hill, which led to a company named Markland House becoming the biggest conduit of all. This was a former Bond group company which had been listed under the name of Leighton Mining. In June 1987 it was reconstructed under the aegis of Hill, a former marine biologist who was trying his luck as a wheeler-dealer. Renamed Markland House, the company disposed of most of its mining assets, raised an additional $5 million capital and became an investor. Markland House remained a listed company with its home exchange and registered office in Perth and its head office in Sydney. After Black Tuesday, Markland House decided to turn away from investment and move into the provision of financial services. It acquired control of a small Perth company, Industrial and Mining Finance, and the broking firm Intersuisse. However, the principal activity of Markland House would be as a conduit for Bond. In early 1988 an agreement was reached between Bond Corporation and Markland House which enabled Bond to move a very significant volume of funds from one part of the group to another—generally to the central financing arm, Bond Corporation Finance—without revealing the flow of funds. The funds would flow through several Markland companies, but in March 1988 Markland House established a new subsidiary called Merchant Capital Ltd which would do much of the conduit work. Markland House was charging 0.5 per cent for back-to-backs done within Australia and 0.25 per cent for offshore loans. This was a good return for just shuffling paper. Markland House was at all times a financially marginal concern and no conscientious corporate treasurer could have justified a loan to it of any size. At June 1988 its shareholders' funds amounted to only $16 million and a year later it was headed for oblivion.

The biggest and worst use of Brigitte Bardots was in Bell Resources. Throughout what follows it should be remembered that Bond Corporation, through Bell Group, owned only 53 per cent of Bell Resources—40 per cent through Bell Group and the rest through other entities.[33] Yet the assets of Bell Resources (mostly cash) were dealt with as though they were wholly owned by Bond Corporation. The rights of the other shareholders in both Bells were completely disregarded. The abuse of their rights was particularly flagrant because Bell Group, both before and after it was taken over by Bond Corporation, had given undertakings to many of its bankers that neither it nor its subsidiaries would advance more than $25 million to companies outside the Bell group. In addition, Bond Corporation had agreed with the Bells' main financiers that it would ensure that Bell Resources and J.N. Taylor Holdings and their various subsidiaries would not make any loans to Bond Corporation except for short-term accommodation during the life of the financing facilities. In one case this prohibition on inter-company lending extended up to Dallhold. Having reached this agreement, Bond Corporation then drove a coach and horses through it by using Brigitte Bardots.

When Bond got control of Bell Group at the end of August 1988 Bell Resources had net tangible assets of $1.8 billion. Bell Resources was carrying considerable debt, with liabilities of more than a billion dollars, but its assets had included large parcels of shares in BHP, BHP Gold and Central Queensland Coal Associates. These investments had mostly been liquidated for cash at the time.

There is evidence that, from the day of the takeover, Bond Corporation viewed Bell Resources as a cash cow. According to Ron Nuich, a Bond accountant, two Bond Corporation treasury executives walked into Bell's treasury on the first day, with one of them saying: 'We just bought you guys out and by the way where is your chequebook, because we've got to write a cheque for $70 million today'.[34]

Money was siphoned out of Bell Resources in two stages.[35] The first began on 29 August 1988, three days after the Bond men took over the Bell Resources board and the day on which the offer for Bell Group closed. Most of the liquid funds of Bell Resources were held in its subsidiary, Weeks Investment. Between 29 August and 3 November a total of $607 million was shifted out of the Bell Resources group in back-to-back loans through Markland House. Of this, $55 million was on-lent to Dallhold and $545 million to BCF.[36] The BCF lending was not made through Markland House itself but through three controlled associate and subsidiary companies named Winnington, Septent and Merchant Capital. This was real cowboy financing. No responsible corporate treasury would have lent these amounts to these companies. Bell Resources did not even have a charge over the assets of Winnington, to which it had lent $302 million.

During the same period a parallel episode was occurring in Bell Resources' 84 per cent–owned subsidiary, J.N. Taylor Holdings. When Bond gained control of Bell Group and Bell Resources in August 1988 the net worth of Taylor Holdings was about $240 million, with most of the funds held in a subsidiary named J.N. Taylor Finance. Between early September 1988 and early 1989, around $175 million was siphoned out of the Taylor group to Bond Corporation and Dallhold through Markland House.

It is worth pointing out that Holmes à Court was on the Bell Resources board during most of this period, resigning on 21 October. Shareholders in both Bells demonstrated strong loyalty to Holmes à Court after the crash. He repaid them poorly. He sold out to Bond under conditions which gave them no right to the same price he received. As Bell Resources chairman, he did not accept the offer for shares that Bell Resources held in Bell Group. He appears to have done nothing to stop Bell Resources being milked through back-to-back loans. It should also be pointed out that Beckwith fell ill early in October and was off work for four weeks, so he could have had little to do with transactions during this period, when a substantial part of the upstreaming occurred.

Julian Hill appears to have suffered some pangs about what was happening. He told Beckwith that the loans put through Markland House were getting too big and recommended that they should be made through an off–balance sheet vehicle, mainly to help keep the gearing of Markland House within its required limits. Hill subsequently told investigators that he had been worried about the amount of the Bell Resources money moving through and had thought, 'Maybe we shouldn't be doing it'. He had raised this concern with members of staff. He said that their reaction was 'Who gives a stuff anyway? Let's keep earning the fees', and 'It's a good earner'. The $600 million shunted from Bell Resources into BCF and Dallhold must have earned nearly $2 million in fees for Markland House. And until October 1988 Markland House did not even have to offer Bell Resources any security. Hill told investigators that one reason for the back-to-backs was that Markland House records were in better state than those of Bond, which were 'in a hell of a mess'. The investigators reported drily that they saw little evidence to support this. In any case, routing inter-company loans through a third party does nothing to either lessen or improve the paperwork.

Markland House's role as a conduit from Bell Resources seems to have been almost its only profitable activity. As soon as the siphoning stopped, Markland House got the wobbles. Its shares were suspended from quotation in August 1989 when Merchant Capital was facing the appointment of a provisional liquidator. A receiver was appointed to Markland House itself in October 1989. Given the history of this company, there must be some question as to whether it was ever truly independent from the Bond group.

Some word of what was happening must have reached the NCSC. Its director Ray Schoer wrote to Bond Corporation on 2 November 1988 requesting details of the investment of Bell Resources funds, including details of any back-to-back loans made to BCF or Dallhold with those funds. This well-informed query sparked a restructuring of the loans through what became known as the Freefold facility. This was the second stage in the shift of funds from Bell Resources to Bond.

Freefold Pty Ltd was an Australian subsidiary of Weeks Resources Pty Ltd, a Victorian subsidiary of Weeks Royalties Ltd of Bermuda, which in turn was a subsidiary of Weeks Petroleum Ltd. At all times relevant to our story, the Freefold board was composed exclusively of top Bond executives. On the morning of 3 November Peter Mitchell instructed staff that Bell Resources had decided to lend money to Bond 'to acquire shares or make investments or do whatever'. The Markland House transactions were unwound in a great paper shuffle, routing the cash back to the Weeks group and Freefold and enabling Bond Corporation to respond to Schoer on 7 November, making no reference to back-to-back lending. Freefold then re-lent the money to BCF. By 18 November, a matter of days later, Freefold had lent $700 million to BCF. This was the limit which the Freefold board had placed on loans to the Bond group. So in December the Brigitte Bardots from Bell Resources through Markland House resumed.

Bond executives went to some lengths to make the Freefold loan appear a fully commercial facility. In its final form it was a 'come and go' facility to a maximum amount of $700 million, repayable no later than 21 March 1989. The interest rate specified was the sell rate for 30-day bills quoted on the BBSW page on Reuters' monitor system at or about 10 a.m. Sydney time on the first business day of each month, plus a margin of 150 basis points. An establishment fee of $1.5 million was specified. This put a professional gloss on the deal, but did nothing to ensure the repayment of the money.

By March 1989 more than a billion dollars had been pumped out of Bell Resources. It was not earmarked for any specific purposes within the Bond group, but much of the money was used to fund the Lonrho raid. The rest seems to have gone into the bottomless hole of general Bond group purposes. A later investigation by Deloitte turned up such items as a $50 million investment in Petrochemical Industries by Bell Resources on behalf of Bond Corporation. Bell Resources bought a Falcon jet for $24 million and made a net loan of $11.2 million to David Rowlands' company Monaco BV, which seems to have been written off.[37]

The question of which Bond executives were responsible for this was answered with some buck-passing. Alan Bond told investigators that in October 1988 he knew some Bell Resources monies were on deposit with Bond but did not know the total. Bond said that he first learned of the loans at the meeting where the Freefold facility was discussed, which presumably would have been in early November. He said that he was satisfied at the time that a proper return on the money was assured. Oates, however, said that certain decisions had been taken at an important conference of Bond executives held at the end of September 1988 in Hawaii. One decision was to realise Bell Resources assets and find a suitable single investment for the company. Oates told investigators that in particular the short-term advance of funds from Bell Resources to Bond was discussed in the context of the proposed acquisition of Lonrho.[38]

Little of this had become public on 31 December 1988, when the balance date of Bell Resources arrived. The Freefold facility came to the attention of the auditor, Frank Montgomery of Coopers & Lybrand. Montgomery examined the Bond Corporation accounts and consulted Arthur Andersen & Co, who were auditors of Bond Corporation, before deciding that no provision was warranted against a full recovery of the Freefold loans. This was a brave decision by both audit firms considering that only a month earlier Tiny Rowland had made the highly publicised claim that Bond Corporation was insolvent. It does not appear that the auditors of either Bell Resources or Bond Corporation uncovered the back-to-back lending which had been undertaken with Bell Resources funds before 31 December.

On 17 March 1989, four days before the loan repayment fell due, Freefold's directors extended it until 21 September in consideration for another $1.5 million fee. This extension was made five days after the 'Four Corners' exposé of Bond Corporation's 1988 inflated profit statement. Freefold's loan to Bond Corporation was $700 million, unsecured. In the circumstances, any normal lender who had that much cash out to Bond would have been trying desperately to get as much as possible back.

A few days later, on 30 March, Bond Corporation was due to repay a $400 million loan to Midland Bank of Britain. The biggest element in this was $230 million which Midland had lent Bond a year earlier to make the original 19.9 per cent purchase of Bell Group from Holmes à Court. As usual, Bond didn't have the money. Group treasury told Midland that it had not scheduled the loan for repayment, so it could not be repaid on 30 March. This brought three senior Midland executives to Perth during Easter for a 'rolling meeting' with Beckwith, Oates and other Bond executives. It was during this meeting that Midland first learned Bond had made extensive borrowings from Bell Resources. The executives, headed by Geoffrey Gilbert, saw this as a breach of Midland's loan terms. The bank considered that the value of its security for repayment, which was over Bond group shares, had been seriously eroded because the major asset of Bond group was its shareholding in Bell Resources and the major asset of Bell Resources had now become a receivable from Bond Corporation. The Midland executives were dismayed, but with true 1980s banking resilience tried to find a basis for 'an ongoing relationship'. Midland, whose loan to Bond had financed the takeover of Bell Resources, managed to extract itself. The facility was continued with further security and by July 1990 Midland had been repaid all but $30 million of the $400 million it was owed.[39] The shareholders of Bell Resources, who had suffered mightily as a result of the takeover, had no reason to be grateful to Midland.

On 28 April Freefold offered to extend the $700 million facility *limit*, provided that it received security. This was the same day that the Bell Resources accounts were released, which resulted in the loans becoming widely known. The loans by Bell Resources aroused widespread concern in financial circles, but little concern seems to have motivated the Freefold or Bell Resources boards. Although Bond Corporation's finances were looking increasingly shaky, Freefold was trying to lend it even more money than the enormous $700 million already advanced.

Eventually, Bell Resources lent a total of $1.2 billion to the Bond group. This staggering loan had to be given some vestigial respectability by finding some security for Bell Resources. At Bond Corporation Kenneth Judge, the lawyer who was Beckwith's executive assistant, was told to look through the group and find any free equity that could be used as security. As every other lender had been tightening its terms and seeking extra security already, there wasn't much left to offer Freefold. At first it was proposed to offer Freefold a number of assets, mainly receivables due from various parties such as the outstanding $60 million due from Ong for the Hilton (which had to be financed by Bond Corporation anyway) and the balance due from David Rowland on the Rome land (which was never received). Within a few days Bond staff realised that some of this security might breach covenants given under other finance facilities. The best the Bond group could do was to describe the Freefold loans as a deposit on the breweries. Bell could not get a mortgage over the actual breweries because a lending syndicate headed by the National Australia Bank had a large negative pledge facility in place. These banks ranked ahead of other creditors. The best that could be given to Bell Resources was a mortgage over the shares of Bond Brewing Holdings. But as the Hong Kong Bank already had first and second mortgages Bell Resources had to settle for a third mortgage on the shares of the company that owned the breweries. For $1.2 billion, this was not much of a security.

Worse, the asset was deteriorating. The breweries were loaded with a total debt of some $1.2 billion by the end of 1989. Under the ownership of Bond their market position had deteriorated from perhaps half the Australian market to barely 40 per cent. The breweries were barely able to service the debt they were carrying. They were a magnificent asset and cash flow business but had been poorly managed as well as overloaded with debt.

Explosions everywhere

For a larrikin who had always been a hairy operator, Bond had built an astonishingly large empire. It had reached huge proportions at a speed that defied gravity. In the process a number of weaknesses had been built into the structure. Any group that stays permanently high-geared will

229

always be vulnerable to rising interest rates. Bond Corporation's interest bill was now running at more than $1 billion a year, soaking up every dollar of its cash flow. The lenders were getting nervous, demanding repayment and setting ever tighter conditions. In the past Bond had escaped such scrapes by making big asset sales. But although he scored coups selling the Bond Centre in Hong Kong and the interest in the Compania de Telefonos de Chile, there was still too much unsaleable dead wood in his empire. And while his financial numbers had always been widely regarded as dubious, now nobody believed them any more. Borrowers who have lost credibility have lost their ability to borrow and when this occurs in a hostile market they are doomed.

It takes more than one bomb to destroy an empire the size of Bond's, but by mid-1989 he had explosions everywhere. In May a disgusted WA Government refused to pump any more money into the bottomless pit of PICL, the petrochemical venture. Bond shares slid below the $1 level for the first time since 1985. Dallhold was almost the only buyer. In June the ABT ruled that Bond was not a fit and proper person to hold a television licence. The decision was subsequently overturned on a technicality, but it underlined his loss of credibility. Bond and his empire were now in a cascade scenario, where each item of bad news seemed to trigger a further one. In July there was a glimpse of good news as BCIL, the one well-run group within Bond, paid a special 40c dividend to its shareholders. This was promptly offset by Lonrho releasing a report alleging that Bell Resources shareholders were being asked to buy Bond's breweries at inflated prices. Tiny was showing no mercy.

Bond shares slipped below 50c. In September the NCSC announced that it had reason to believe that offences may have been committed in connection both with Bond's $130 million sale in 1988 of the Emu Brewery site in Perth to FAI Insurances and the loans of $1.2 billion by Bell Resources to Bond. Bond shares slid to 27c as Bond sold out of Lonrho for a loss of $110 million. In October the SGIC exercised its option to put its 19.9 per cent of Bell Group to Bond at $2.70 a share, ten times the market price of Bell Group shares by then. Bond countered with an offer of $3.18, but on terms extended out to 2001. Then on 20 October 1989 Bond Corporation announced a loss of $980 million, the largest in Australian corporate history.

Bond Corporation was now mortally wounded. The rest of its history consisted of its efforts to stave off its inevitable death, as various creditors and equity holders moved in to try to retrieve what they could from the wreckage. In November the group issued its accounts for the year to 30 June 1989. The balance sheet is summarised in Table 6.1.

The most notable point is that, although the consolidated accounts showed net assets of $1793 million, most of this belonged to outside

Table 6.1   Bond Corporation in 1989 (all figures in $m)

TOTAL ASSETS		11 704
Less:		
Current Liabilities:		
Debt	3 630	
Other	463	
Non-Current Liabilities:		
Debt	5 624	
Other	193	
TOTAL LIABILITIES		9 911
NET ASSETS		1 793
SHAREHOLDERS' EQUITY		
Share capital and reserves	457	
Accumulated losses	(573)	
Shareholders' deficiency	(116)	
Minority interests	1 909	
SHAREHOLDERS' EQUITY		1 793

shareholders in such companies as Bell Group. Once these minority interests were stripped out Bond Corporation itself had a deficiency on shareholders' funds of $116 million. On asset backing, therefore, Bond shares had a *negative* worth of 27c a share. Gearing looked awful: debt totalled $9.2 million, or more than five times consolidated net assets. Normally a prudent ratio for an industrial company is regarded as a dollar of debt for every dollar of shareholders' funds. A massive $3.6 billion of debt was repayable within twelve months.

Another point was that the asset sales promised by Oates at the 1988 annual meeting had never happened. Debt was larger than ever. This added to the feeling that Bond was out of control.

And whereas the 1988 accounts had been unqualified by the auditors the 1989 audit report contained one of the longest qualifications ever seen, stretching over three and a half pages of small type. Terry Underwood, the partner of Arthur Andersen & Co who signed the audit report, said that the accounts had been prepared on the basis that Bond Corporation would continue as a going concern, but there was room for doubt because:

- Unaudited information subsequent to June indicated that losses were continuing on similar scale to those in 1988–89.
- Bond Corporation had undertaken a reconstruction and asset sale program but during this time it would depend on continued support from its lenders.
- Bond Corporation had invested a total of $249 million in the 49.9 per cent–owned PICL project but recovery of the investment was uncertain and depended on successful legal proceedings against the WA Government and Premier Peter Dowding.
- Bond Corporation had agreed to indemnify the SGIC against loss on its Bell Group shareholding. The current gap between the indemnity and Bell Group's market price was $167 million but, because

231

Bond Corporation was legally contesting the validity of the indemnity, no provision had been made for loss.

- Bond Corporation had invested $208 million in British Satellite Broadcasting Ltd (raised to $323 million after June) but recovery was uncertain because success would require substantial penetration of the UK market in a relatively short time frame.
- Bond Corporation was liable under a put option to repurchase the Emu Brewery site from FAI for $200 million. Bond Corporation had obtained a valuation saying that the land was worth this much but the auditors were still uncertain whether a provision for loss was necessary.
- Bond Media had its radio and television licences in the books at $1055 million with no provision for diminution if the ABT should force the sale of them.
- Bond Corporation had invested $414 million in Bond Media but had not written it down even though the market value of the holding was $79 million at 30 June and Bond Media had declared a loss of $2.8 million for 1988–89.
- Heileman had made losses for the past two fiscal periods and projected cash flow would be insufficient to satisfy its scheduled debt repayments for 1990. Nevertheless, Bond Corporation had made no provision for diminution of its $615 million investment in Heileman.
- Bell Group had revalued its publishing mastheads (primarily the *West Australian*) to $387 million, which might be an overvaluation of $125 million.
- Bond Brewing was in breach of certain covenants of its $880 million senior debt facility and the lending syndicate, headed by the NAB, had reserved its right to issue default notices.

Any one of the items upon which the auditors qualified their report would have been a serious black eye for a major company. The combined effect of a string of such qualifications was to confirm the market's worst suspicions that Bond was—for all practical purposes—broke. The overwhelming implication of the audit report was that, if Bond Corporation had written these various investments down to market value, the deficiency on shareholders' funds would have been greater. Unkind critics could still find in the accounts smaller items which the auditors had not mentioned. Total assets, for example, included 'other' assets of nearly $400 million. Of this, nearly $280 million comprised capitalised deferred expenses, mainly related to borrowings and advertising. If, say, Swan launched an advertising campaign that was expected to return benefits over three years then, instead of being expensed entirely against the profit and loss account in the year when the expense was incurred, it was spread over the next three years. A total of $55 million in deferred advertising costs was still included in 'other' assets in the 1989 accounts, and nearly $150 million in borrowing costs.

Bankruptcy and after

Dismemberment of the Bond empire now began. Kerry Packer was the first to move, announcing in December 1989 a takeover bid for Bond Media through a vehicle named Television Corporation of Australia (TCA). The deal was that Consolidated Press's $200 million preference shares would be converted to ordinary equity, Bond Media shareholders would be offered one TCA share for every ten Bond Media shares, and institutional shareholders would take up another 300 million shares and 150 million convertible notes. The bid would ultimately be successful, leaving Consolidated Press with 45 per cent of what became Nine Network Australia and leaving Bond Corporation with a holding diluted to 5 per cent.

His years chasing the America's Cup had made Bond a genuine enthusiast for yachting. On Boxing Day 1989 he escaped from all his land-based cares by skippering his latest boat—a magnificent blue and white maxi named *Drumbeat*—in the Sydney–Hobart, leading the fleet out of Sydney Heads in a spectacular start. This was an insouciant gesture because the bankers to Bond Brewing had been making threatening noises. Between 7 and 13 December the syndicate, led by the National Australia Bank, had issued notices of breaches of their loan agreement which they wanted rectified. Either because the breaches were incapable of rectification or because he had long become inured to threats from bankers or because he reckoned they would do nothing over Christmas, Bond went sailing anyway. In a short hearing before Mr Justice Beach in the Victorian Supreme Court on 29 December the banks had a receiver appointed to Bond Brewing. Bond sailed into Hobart later that day, taking line honours in the prestige race. As he tied up, his girlfriend Tracey Tyler slipped aboard. Next morning's papers plastered their front pages with photos of her whispering in Bond's ear that he was in receivership. Bond looked uncharacteristically shocked and dismayed.

It would be tedious to trace the death throes of the Bond empire from this point. There was a series of long, tortuous law cases as Bond fought his creditors in the court at every point in delaying actions that covered more than two years. On Bond Brewing, for example, Bond Corporation appealed to Mr Justice Beach to have the receiver removed, but was unsuccessful. Then Bond appealed to the Full Bench and was successful. John Spalvins of Adelaide Steamship had bought a substantial shareholding in Bell Resources and had persistently been denied information about its affairs by the Bond-controlled board. When Spalvins discovered the way Bell's money had been siphoned out he threatened to appoint a receiver. Bond did a deal with Spalvins to split control of Bell Resources, but then the NCSC also threatened to appoint a receiver. Bond abandoned control of Bell Resources and Geoff Hill, one of Australia's top corporate advisers, became its chairman.

One of Hill's first acts was the appointment of Deloitte as investigating accountants. One item to attract their attention was the management fees paid by Bell Resources. While under the control of Holmes à Court, Bell Resources had paid management fees at the rate of about $400 000 a month. Considering that Holmes à Court's genius for share trading had been entirely responsible for the massive growth of Bell Resources this was eminently justifiable. But from April 1988, when Bond took control, the management fees jumped to more than $1 million a month. In the calendar years 1988 and 1989 Bell Resources had paid a staggering $28 million in management fees to Bond Corporation and Bell Group, including $17 million in 'investment advisory fees'. As this was the period in which the management ripped a billion dollars out of Bell Resources it was really rubbing salt into the wound to charge fees as well. Deloitte investigators were bemused by the fact that they could not find any formal, written management agreement.[40] Hill would spend the next two years trying to retrieve the assets of Bell Resources that had been squandered by Bond. Bell Resources emerged with a mountain of debt and half of the former Bond Brewing, the other half going to Lion Nathan of New Zealand. Bell Resources changed its name to Australian Consolidated Investments and Bond Brewing became National Brewing Holdings.

Bond Corporation went into a scheme of arrangement under Ian Ferrier in August 1991. Renamed Southern Equities Corporation, its main asset was the lawsuit against the WA Government claiming $900 million over PICL. But with slim funds it had little chance and, at the end of 1993, the WA Government settled the claim for only $7 million. Southern Equities went into liquidation.

Tricontinental and the Hong Kong & Shanghai Bank had personal guarantees from Alan Bond and tried to recoup their losses from him, but repayments from Bond proved as elusive as ever. Dallhold Investments was put into liquidation in July 1991, but by that time it was heavily in debt. Bond fought what must have been Australia's longest delaying action against personal bankruptcy. On the grounds that he had personally guaranteed debts another syndicate of banks led by the Hong Kong & Shanghai petitioned for his bankruptcy. They were frustrated repeatedly by Bond's legal tactics before they eventually made him bankrupt in early 1992. By that time Bond held few assets in his own name. However, over the years significant assets had been acquired by his family and were held in a trust through a company named Armoy. Members of his family administered a trust of which he was the beneficiary. As long as Bond did not own the assets or control the trust, but only received benefits from it, the trust's assets could not be touched by his creditors.

Bond's trustee in bankruptcy was Melbourne accountant Robert Ramsay of Bird Cameron. He estimated that Bond had disbursed some $31 million in gifts to his family over the previous six years, but the creditors had little success in retrieving any of the money. Tricontinental and the Hong Kong & Shanghai, as the major creditors, had invested $1 million in the search for Bond's money by the end of 1992 and had retrieved only $151 000. Ramsay did, however, manage to seize Bond's personal superannuation fund, containing $2.4 million.

Ramsay and financial journalists who scrutinised Bond's personal affairs began marvelling at the generosity of a Swiss banker named Juerg Bollag. The banker, based in Zug, became known after Bond's daughter Suzanne divorced her husband Armand Leone in New Jersey. In court documents, Leone claimed that Bollag's duties had been 'traditionally to transfer money at the request of the Bond family from various Swiss bank accounts held by the Bond Company'. Bollag had provided the family with considerable assets. He had bought show horses costing a total of $US935 000 for Suzanne. A Bollag company had bought Upp Hall estate in Hertfordshire from Dallhold for £1.86 million, then leased it back to Dallhold at a peppercorn rental. Bollag paid jewellery bills of some $700 000 and legal bills of a further $350 000. Moreover, Bollag owned a house at 14 Sellwood Place in Chelsea, where Bond frequently stayed while in London.[41] When an interested cameraman for the *Sydney Morning Herald* tried to photograph Bollag emerging from the house Bollag swung his briefcase angrily, smashing the camera and lacerating the photographer's face. There was no law against a Swiss banker lavishly showering millions of dollars upon a bankrupt Australian businessman, but there was no precedent for it either.

Bond said Bollag was 'simply a generous friend'. His journalists marvelled even more at his generosity when Ramsay unearthed Swiss tax returns showing Bollag's stated income was $A180,000 a year and his substance (or worth) was only $A580,000. How Bollag was able to lavish such gifts upon the Bond family was never adequately explained by Bond, who was by then pleading mental incapacity. He claimed that during a heart operation he had suffered oxygen deprivation which had damaged his brain. Doctors testified that Bond's IQ had fallen from 150 (genius level) to 90. Bond said strokes had affected his memory and concentration. When questioned on deals he had done, Bond repeatedly said he could not remember. He particularly could not remember setting up the Jersey trust and a web of companies which Bollag was administering on his behalf. Under questioning, Bond frequently appeared listless, forgetful and on the point of breakdown, but at other times he was capable of lashing out angrily. A Queensland property developer gave evidence that Bond had negotiated a hard-headed deal to buy St Bee's island in the Whitsundays at the end of 1993. At one point he had threatened to sue the vendors. At the same time, Bond's lawyers had been telling a Perth court that Bond was so mentally distressed that he was incapable of briefing counsel. The bankruptcy proceedings were still in train as this book went to press.

The bankruptcy proceedings represented Bond's war on the civil front. On the criminal front, he was fighting to avoid convictions for alleged offences committed during the 1980s. When Peter Beckwith died of a brain tumour in July 1990 Bond was presented with a readymade scapegoat. In an interview with the *Bulletin*, he said:

> It is not entirely true that I was driving the company full throttle. Certainly that is the public's perception. But in fact I was not at the helm for much of the time. Peter Beckwith drove the company. He drove it as if it were his own business. If I made any mistake at all, it was to give him too much autonomy . . . I took my eye off the ball with Bond Corporation because I thought that I had a competent man there.[42]

Despite his fall, Bond had not been without admirers in the business community until this interview appeared. But admiration waned sharply as he was perceived as attempting to shift blame on to a dead friend. But, Bond's claim should not be entirely discounted. As noted earlier, Bond was not a detail man. Also, the man who cheerfully flung the keys of his prized Oldsmobile to a young friend might equally have been capable of tossing much of the day-to-day control of Bond Corporation to a trusted lieutenant. And insiders at Bond Corporation say that Beckwith did indeed exercise much control. But, whatever Beckwith's true share of blame, it would seem that the ultimate responsibility for the affairs of Bond Corporation has to be taken by the man whose name the company bore. Big policy decisions such as the raid on Lonrho and the St Moritz Hotel purchase were initiated by Bond with little or no input from his top executives. It seems more as though Bond made the big decisions and then left his executives to clean them up as best they could.

The first criminal charge faced by Bond was of having dishonestly induced WA businessman Brian Coppin to participate in the October 1987 rescue of Rothwells. Coppin told the court that he would not have contributed $6 million (which was immediately lost) to the rescue if he had known Bond was going to collect a $16 million fee for arranging the rescue. Bond was found guilty and sentenced to two and a half years in jail. He served 90 days at Wooroloo prison farm, during which he suffered an angina attack. Then the WA Court of Criminal Appeal quashed the conviction. At a retrial, the jury found he was not guilty. The Australian Securities Commission returned to the attack. In June 1993 Bond was charged with having failed to act honestly by not notifying the Bond Corporation board that it had the opportunity to acquire a Manet painting named 'La Promenade' at a cost substantially below market value.

By this time the prosecuting authorities were looking futile and foolish. Given the magnitude of the Bond empire and the nature of its dealings something as marginal as the Manet charge seemed an act of desperation. The law seemed to be having even more trouble with Bond than his shareholders had. As mentioned earlier, in December 1993 Bond's lawyers successfully applied for a six-month stay of proceedings on the grounds that the former tycoon was 'fragile and vulnerable' and that his mental capacities had collapsed so far under pressure that he 'would have difficulty running a corner store'. His mental incapacity was said to be such that he was unable to instruct his lawyers properly. Melbourne psychologist Timothy Watson-Munro testified that Bond had a high IQ but had lost the capacity for simple functions, as demonstrated by a loss of vocabulary and basic numeracy.[43] The onset of this malaise must have been sudden, because only four months earlier Bond's lawyers had been well enough instructed to threaten libel suits against another journalist and myself. The court was sufficiently impressed by the seriousness of Bond's ailment to postpone hearing of the Manet charge from January 1994 to July.

By late June, however, magisterial tolerance had expired. Perth magistrate Ivan Brown ordered Bond to face court. Brown said he accepted some damage had been done to Bond's brain during surgery but said the damage was 'microscopic'.

Biographies of Bond invariably list his greatest achievement as his victory in the America's Cup. It is certainly true that the historic win gave the nation a huge surge of national pride. But the price was equally huge. When *Australia II* crossed the finishing line at Newport in 1983 Bond Corporation's debts totalled around $200 million. As shareholders' funds were stated at $250 million this looked reasonable. Over the next six years the Bond group's borrowings multiplied forty-fold to $8.5 billion. Admittedly this included the borrowings of companies Bond took over—such as the Bells—but he also took over their assets. By the end of the six-year period his shareholders' funds were severely negative, making him hopelessly overgeared.

Table 6.2 sets out the position year by year, but needs to be read with some care. Bond Corporation notoriously took an optimistic view of asset values and profits, so those figures could be overstated. The most astonishing figure is the twenty-fold rise in debt over the final five years. Even allowing for the levels of debt inside companies which Bond took over

Table 6.2   Bond Corporation gearing and interest cover (a) (all figures in $m)

Year to	1984	1985	1986	1987	1988	1989
GEARING						
1. Total Assets	725	1 262	2 828	4 116	9 015	11 704
2. Debt (b)	(382)	(717)	(1 994)	(2 803)	(5 932)	(8 518)
3. Other Liabilities	(33)	(49)	(196)	(194)	(1 162)	(1 393)
4. Shareholders' Funds (c)	240	308	538	747	891	(116)
5. Gearing (2:4)	1.6:1	2.3:1	3.7:1	3.8:1	6.7:1	n.a.
INTEREST COVER						
6. Revenue	365	517	1 601	2 489	5 009	8 482
7. Pre-tax Profit (d)	18	33	136	184	326(e)	(986)
8. Net Interest Paid	(27)	(60)	(184)	(206)	(405)	(744)
9. Interest Cover $\left(\frac{7+8}{8}\right)$	1.5:1	1.6:1	1.7:1	1.9:1	1.8:1	n.a.

Notes:
(a)   Conventional group consolidated accounts
(b)   Exc. trade creditors, but including convertible bonds in 1987 and 1988
(c)   Excluding minorities
(d)   Including extraordinaries
(e)   If the Kitool and Hilton deals were taken out, 1988 profit would fall to about $176m and interest cover to 1.4:1

this is a staggering rise. If minority interests are excluded there was only a relatively modest rise in shareholders' funds between 1984 and 1988, while in 1989 they went negative. The extra debt being loaded into Bond Corporation was producing little added value for shareholders. Meanwhile the gearing ratio steadily blew out every year, making Bond Corporation an accident waiting to happen.

The pre-tax profit figure given in the table includes extraordinaries. This is fair, because Bond Corporation was essentially a trader in extraordinaries. The profits are unimpressive compared to either revenue or assets. They are even more unimpressive to the analyst who takes a more conservative view of the treatment of some items, such as capitalisation of interest and other expenses. For shareholders, the rewards were never proportionate to the risk. Despite the enormous sums they were given to play with, the men at the top of Bond Corporation could never generate decent earnings.

Bond was often called a visionary, but in pursuit of his visions he enriched himself and his coterie of directors at the expense of shareholders, and he rode roughshod over the rights of minority stakeholders in his enterprises. They paid a high price for the America's Cup.

7

Friedrich Mitty

I'm bloody sure if John Friedrich had been a German general, we'd have lost the war.

Max Eise

The National Safety Council of Australia's Victorian Division had for years been a small, sleepy outfit. In the 1980s it was transformed following the appointment of a new chief executive officer. When John Friedrich took over, the NSC's base—at West Sale in Gippsland—was a rundown aerodrome with a long runway and one hangar. Under Friedrich it became a showpiece. Recruits were trained on military lines. Most of the staff took part in training drills. They wore uniforms, with insignia to denote rank. It was a paramilitary outfit, with the emphasis on physical fitness, discipline and precision. Although the NSC was essentially a search and rescue service, its members trained like commandos. They even trained at parachute jumping, sometimes to boats in the open sea. Friedrich installed a large swimming pool for underwater training. When he decided that horses were needed for bush rescues, he built an indoor equestrian centre at West Sale. He always bought the best and latest equipment. West Sale also installed the very latest dog training facilities for police and RAAF dogs.

The NSC team were prepared to go anywhere and do anything. They saved people from drowning in Bass Strait, rescued stricken yachts, fought fires, found lost bushwalkers and went down mines. Friedrich's paramilitary team were the best in the business and performed admirable service. They were lavishly equipped, indeed overequipped. The NSC owned or leased 22 helicopters and eight aircraft, which one sceptic noted was well in excess of its needs. It had a superbly fitted out 42-metre vessel, the *Blue Nautilus*. There were a mini-submarine, four search and rescue boats and another six inflatable Zodiacs. There were six decompression chambers. There was a menagerie of highly trained search and rescue fauna, including 30 horses, nine pigeons and five dogs. The NSC owned dozens of vehicles including cars, fire trucks and a big Caterpillar snow plough. The Sale base had an eight-wheel-drive vehicle hinged in the middle that could cross swamps. The need for the vehicle was somewhat questionable because there were few swamps in the area. The electronics and computer gear was state of the art, including infra-red scanning devices.

Friedrich would seize on any new idea in search and rescue. On one occasion pigeons were reported to be able to spot Mae West jackets at sea. Almost immediately, Friedrich had pigeon coops at West Sale and an instructor from Hawaii training them.[1] Friedrich wanted excellence in everything he did. He set up highly sophisticated aerial mapping equipment at Sale. He also had a parachute maintenance unit which made the NSC's own harnesses and webbing. Maintenance of the life rafts and jackets was done in-house and Sale even had its own factory for uniforms, which were made from non-flammable cloth.

The rescue workers were highly trained and effective. Undoubtedly hundreds, possibly thousands, of people owe their lives to Friedrich's Victorian Division.

The leader of this gung-ho corps was brilliant and persuasive. He radiated self-confidence. He could talk a banker into a big loan or a shire council into a building development approval. His West Sale base was easily the most impressive of its kind in Australia, and must have ranked high by world standards. At least half a dozen other shires approached the NSC to have the base relocated to them. This gave Friedrich considerable bargaining power with Rosedale Shire Council, which covered the base. Friedrich spent several million dollars expanding the Sale base geographically. He appeared to be paranoid about having neighbours. He bought all the surrounding farms at top dollar. When one neighbour complained about aircraft noise Friedrich promptly bought him out. From humble beginnings, the NSC began selling its services internationally. Teams worked in Canada, Fiji, France, Papua New Guinea, the Solomons and Spain. Oddly, one person who never went on these overseas missions was Friedrich.

There was a magnetism about this balding, heavily bearded man in his forties. His English was fluent with only a slight German accent. He also spoke Italian and Spanish. For all his love of military style, Friedrich was not an aloof general. He mixed freely with the staff, lived with them, went on exercises with them, abseiled and flew helicopters with them. He was an inspirational leader, always enthused about new ideas or developments. He was one of the few staff who did not wear uniform, although he had one for ceremonial occasions. He turned up to the Monday executive meeting in a waterproof jacket and jeans.

But there was no disputing who was boss. Friedrich tended to surround himself with an elite group. One former training officer said:

> Friedrich had this thing where he'd come in and check out the new group of trainees and pick out one he liked—usually young and attractive—and appoint him. On one occasion, the fellow in question couldn't spell and had failed his physical, but Freddo said 'No, he stays'. They were extremely loyal to him but he more or less bought them. You have to remember these guys were linesmen and boilermakers before. Now, here they were on $40 000 a year, driving BMWs and flitting around Australia and the world with expense accounts to boot. It's no wonder they bowed and scraped to every one of Freddo's whims.[2]

The NSC employees were, after all, enjoying a pretty good life. They were a bunch of young men being trained in scuba diving, flying, skydiving, horse riding—and being well paid all the time.

Friedrich did not suffer fools, but he did not suffer logical objections either. In discussions which became argumentative Friedrich would raise his voice and drown out any objectors. This caused some dissatisfaction, but most of his 450 staff were fiercely loyal to him. He took great pride in them. In 1988 he was awarded the Medal of the Order of Australia for service to the community, particularly in the areas of industrial safety and search and rescue services. In the same year, the board of the NSC was alarmed to discover that its treasured chief executive was not on a contract and could leave them at any time. In July they agreed to a contract under which he was paid $130 000 a year.

An odd legal creature

This was the glittering empire and the gung-ho chief executive of the Victorian Division of the National Safety Council. But what actually was the National Safety Council? Nobody, including the board, ever seems to have asked this question during its dynamic growth in the 1980s. The NSC was an odd creature, structurally and legally. Most members of the public were probably under the impression that it was an arm of government. In fact, it was a private, non-profit company limited by guarantee. There were no shareholders. It had been set up in 1927 under the auspices of the Royal Automobile Club of Victoria. The NSC was a council of 41 unpaid members, nearly all of whom were nominees of voluntary organisations, private bodies such as the Chamber of Manufactures, or government departments. The size of the council membership was a severe weakness. When there are 41 people in charge, nobody is in charge. The tendency is for no individual councillor to feel a strong identity with the organisation and for each individual to believe the organisation is being looked after by someone else. The council met twice a year, giving its members little opportunity to acquaint themselves with the NSC's activities or finances, or to exercise much control. It was more like a club, containing a lot of names from *Who's Who*, and there was some prestige in being a councillor. A board of nine directors was selected from the council members.

When accountants later began trying to unravel the NSC's affairs they discovered that it was a very odd corporate creature indeed. It was a company limited by guarantee. The original guarantees had been given in the memorandum and articles of association by the founders in 1927. Insofar as the NSC ever had owners or guarantors, by 1989 they were all dead. As a charitable organisation limited by guarantee the NSC was freed from the statutory obligation to lodge accounts. Nevertheless, it still had to prepare private accounts for its financial year, which ended each 30 June. After the crash one councillor said: 'On a number of occasions, questions were asked about financial details and these were never, ever forthcoming and sort of sidestepped'.[3]

The NSC had been a relatively small-time affair for half a century after its birth in 1927. It promoted road safety, water safety, child safety and similar concerns but was not actively involved in rescue operations. Each safety area was a separate division of the Council. In 1968 Max Eise, through his interest in the coastguard, had become chairman of the water safety division. Later he gravitated to the chairmanship of the NSC. Eise was a retired businessman who had made a small fortune decades before from manufacturing copper piping. In his advancing years he had thrown himself into community affairs, becoming a Brighton councillor for twelve years, and working on such bodies as the Keep Australia Beautiful Council.

The NSC stayed a fairly cosy affair until 1977, when the State Electricity Commission of Victoria asked the NSC to tender to fill the position of safety engineer at the Loy Yang power station. The SECV wanted someone to arbitrate on safety in arguments between the unions and management. The NSC was an ideal third party to fill the slot and duly won the tender. However, the NSC did not have anyone with the skills to do the job and had to advertise. The outstanding applicant was John Friedrich. A rigorous selection process would have shown that he was neither an engineer nor John Friedrich, but the NSC saw no reason to look that hard at him.

Friedrich quickly showed himself a man of enthusiasm and ambition. He persuaded the NSC to install a gleaming red and silver fire tender. He also built the La Trobe Valley operation from a one-man job to a staff of 15 or 20 with a command centre and men stationed permanently in different parts of the valley ready for an emergency. The SECV paid for it all and the NSC realised it had found a natural leader.

The energetic Friedrich rapidly expanded his role beyond that of safety engineer. He kept having ideas for new roles for the NSC. Because the ambulance took six hours to drive to and from Sale, he suggested replacing it with a helicopter. He also used helicopters to fight fires. When a contract was offered for the inspection of sewerage outlets at Port Welshpool Friedrich urged the NSC to tender for the contract, build a boat and use divers for the inspections. Then they could also use the boat for rescue work in the treacherous Bass Strait.

John Friedrich was appointed chief executive officer of the National Safety Council of Australia (Victoria Division) in 1982. Chairman Max Eise and the rest of the board acclaimed Friedrich's ability. 'I'm bloody sure if John Friedrich had been a German general, we'd have lost the war', Eise said.[4]

There was a loose confederation of safety councils around Australia, but by 1989 Victoria was in a league of its own. The NSW body had an annual budget of about $4 million and those of Queensland and South Australia about $2 million each, but Victoria's NSC had a budget of around $80 million. It had also become a national operation, with four bases in New South Wales, two in Queensland, one each in Tasmania and South Australia and one at Tindal RAAF base near Darwin.

The files of the NSC were stuffed with letters of praise from politicians, Federal and State Cabinet Ministers, and defence chiefs. They all admired Friedrich's base and organisation. He always made sure they were impressed. In this chorus of approval there were only rare sour notes and they could usually be dismissed on the grounds of self-interest. The whistle was first blown on Friedrich in 1985 when a pilot, Bill Suhr, sent Premier John Cain a five-page letter querying how the NSC could offer services at such low prices and still be able to afford new equipment. As the Victorian Government was not financing the NSC it took little notice. Suhr died in an air crash the following year.

In 1986 another warning was sounded by Skywest Aviation, which had been beaten by NSC for a contract. A Skywest director, Bill Meeke, raised the theory that the NSC must have been funded covertly by ASIO or some other security organisation to be able to afford the level of service it provided. The allegation was put in July to Defence Minister Kim Beazley in July, who answered that the NSC was receiving no covert funding from ASIO or any other defence intelligence agency. Skywest had been on the right track but had jumped to the wrong conclusion. The funding of the NSC was indeed a scandal, but it would take nearly three more years to be uncovered. It is not unusual for disappointed tenderers to complain about successful rivals, and such complaints are usually treated warily by governments.

Any paramilitary outfit is liable to attract whispers of sinister purposes. In 1988 the Sydney *Sun-Herald* published a story claiming that the NSC had been supplied with black HALO parachutes, designed not for safety work but for secret invasions of enemy territory. The NSC was also alleged to have supplied services to the Brunei Armed Services, the Oman Government and Canadian fire-fighting firms. The article further alleged that Friedrich's version of the source of the NSC's income did not tally with its annual report; and that NSC planes were frequently used by staff for sport skydiving.[5] On the question of income, the article was getting closer to the core of the problem at the NSC.

The doubts grow

The myth began to unravel in the second half of 1988, as the NSC could not get its accounts for the year to June in order. The people most concerned were the NSC auditors, Horwath & Horwath. A significant percentage of the NSC's assets comprised rescue gear and other equipment in containers. For two years Horwath & Horwath had been trying with little success to verify the existence of the equipment. They were still not getting satisfactory answers from Friedrich and had informed the NSC board. Vague whispers began to circulate that there was a problem at the NSC. On 16 October Alex MacArthur, a former director of the Queensland Division of the NSC, told the Australian Federal Police in Brisbane that there was possible fraud at the Victorian NSC. He was advised to refer the matter to the Fraud Squad in Victoria.

In Victoria, Eise was becoming disturbed at his chief executive's lack of accountability and about the vagueness of financial records. Eise began checking further and to his horror discovered that there was even doubt about Friedrich's identity. His application for the job of NSC operations manager in 1982 stated that he had been born at Mount Davis in South Australia on 7 September 1945. There was no such place in South Australia and no record of Friedrich's birth there. On his marriage certificate Friedrich had given his date and place of birth as 7 September 1950, at Munich. Eise also noted another oddity. Throughout his career at the NSC Friedrich had refused all offers of overseas trips. Had he been afraid to apply for a passport? Eise took these facts to Victoria's Chief Commissioner of Police, Kel Glare, in October 1988. He also told Glare that there seemed to have been a fraud involving about $6000 and asked whether Friedrich might be working for the CIA. Glare said that it was not an offence to work for the CIA and told Eise to go away and get more evidence before he would investigate. Glare later defended his action, saying it was ridiculous to suggest that he should have forwarded Eise's complaints to ASIO or the Federal Police. 'We can't go around checking on every person's birth certificate', he said. 'It was not a matter for the Victoria Police then or now.'

Glare denied that he was dismissive towards Eise, but it is hard to find a better word to describe his conduct.[6] Here was the chairman of an organisation raising serious doubts about his chief executive and asking Victoria's top police officer for help. Obviously a man in Eise's position would need to be deeply concerned before being driven to such an action. Glare could at least have checked Friedrich's identity. Glare may have been lulled because he had known Friedrich since he had been inspector at Morwell in 1979. Glare had also refereed Friedrich for his Order of Australia award. Friedrich had been proposed for the award by Mick Miller, Glare's predecessor as Chief Commissioner. They were two of many people fooled by Friedrich, although there is no doubt that the impostor built a first-class rescue service.

Another person to cross Friedrich's trail at this time was the Victorian Treasurer, Rob Jolly. Jolly became aware in November 1988 that Friedrich had prepared an invoice for $1.3 million against the Department of Management and Budget. As the invoice had never been sent, there was no need to take any action. When Jolly's officers questioned Friedrich he said that it had been a dummy invoice, prepared against the day when a real one might be sent to the department. Jolly accepted this. Asked later to explain his inaction Jolly said, 'Well, I thought false invoices were just part of the game', a phrase that would return to haunt him.

With the deadlock continuing between the auditors and Friedrich towards the end of 1988, the board decided to call in an outside auditor. Eise suggested Ernst & Whinney, one of Australia's biggest accounting firms, which provided the services of David Balcombe and Graeme Richardson. Richardson was Eise's personal accountant.

At first there was no suspicion of fraud. Balcombe and Richardson were simply trying to collate the books and prepare accounting systems that would permit fast and accurate statements to be produced showing the NSC's position. It soon became apparent that Friedrich had total control of the existing system. All decisions went through him. Balcombe and Richardson started trying to trace transactions to follow how they were recorded and settled, and thus identify problems.

Going through the records, they found a computer printout showing $76 million owed by trade debtors. However, Balcombe noted that none of the debtors had made any repayments since the previous June. Further, the amount owed had since increased to $107 million. These receivables were one of the NSC's major assets and had been pledged as security for bank loans.

In early 1989 Balcombe and Richardson began routine checks of the receivables. The Victorian Department of Conservation, Forests and Land, for example, was shown as owing $3.8 million for the supply of standby equipment. When queried, the department said that it had incurred no such charges. The NSC workshop was shown as having bought 50 pumps and 35 generators. When Balcombe asked to see them, the workshop manager told him that the NSC had only one pump and three generators. Balcombe checked seven debtors who owed a total of $50 million, but all denied any liability. This was extremely worrying. The NSC's balance sheet showed net assets totalling $27 million. If $50 million of its receivables were non-existent, the organisation was deeply insolvent. Balcombe questioned Friedrich, who told him that the missing equipment was at mine sites or down the coast. For one reason or another Friedrich could never actually show it to him. By the end of February the Ernst team were becoming suspicious, because every time they tried to follow the line of a transaction Friedrich seemed to be the stumbling block. Friedrich was not answering questions. Balcombe and Richardson went back to the board, complaining that Friedrich was not cooperating. They gave the board a list of questions which they required the chief executive to answer. The key questions were about the large sums allegedly owing by government bodies. The accountants had begun to suspect that the amounts in the debtors' ledger were not receivables at all, but entries that had been made to mask large hidden borrowings.

Exasperated, the board summoned Friedrich to head office on Wednesday 15 March and ordered him to wait in an outer office while directors met in the boardroom. The board decided that Friedrich should be stood down from operations. The directors deliberately did not suspend him as chief executive officer. They merely wanted to divorce him from operational control, so that he would have no excuse for slipping down to Sale, away from the interrogation. Eise was reluctant, but bowed to the board consensus. He walked out and told Friedrich he had been stood down temporarily, so that he could help Ernst & Whinney. Eise asked Friedrich to be in the office the following Tuesday to answer questions from the accountants. Friedrich casually said, 'Okay, if that's what you want', but he must have recognised that it was the end.

Friedrich's wife Shirley had noticed for several months that he was under stress. He had been ill in October and—uncharacteristically—had been reluctant to return to work afterwards. On Friday 17 March Friedrich told Shirley at their Seaton home that he intended to resign from the NSC because 'things were going to get a little bit hot'.[7] He told her that there was a gigantic financial mess and that he was 'going to sit on a mountain and contemplate his navel'. He packed a lot of gear into his Range Rover and drove away from home at 4 p.m. on the Sunday, giving Shirley $5000 and telling her to go off somewhere and make a new life, because she wasn't going to see him again. Shirley was shattered by the news. The husband she knew had always been a strong family man, deeply devoted to her and the children. Now he was suddenly driving off. Distraught, she got the children together, packed a few bags and drove away too.

Friedrich on the run

Friedrich never kept his rendezvous with Ernst & Whinney, who by Tuesday realised the sickening fact that the accounts were a mess and the man behind them was on the run. The accountants told the board that they could not confirm the accounts. Huge sums which were in the book as amounts owing had turned out to be fictitious. The NSC was broke by millions of dollars. The auditors said it looked as though Friedrich had perpetrated a massive fraud. Several directors, including Eise, nearly cried.

After Friedrich had failed to turn up on 21 March the NSC's solicitors rang the Fraud Squad of Victoria Police, run by Detective Chief Inspector Laurie Neville. Neville immediately advised Federal Police to watch for Friedrich in case he tried to leave the country. But as Neville had no instructions, no warrant and no proof of crime all he could do was ask Federal Police to monitor Friedrich's movements, not to arrest or detain him. By the next day Neville had established that at least $20 million was missing, so the order was changed to 'arrest and detain'.

On Wednesday the 22nd the Victorian Supreme Court appointed Michael Humphris, of Ernst & Whinney, as provisional liquidator of the NSC. By that time investigators had realised that the NSC owed $103 million to the State Bank of Victoria alone, and that most of it was unsecured. The NSC's total debt appeared to be around $220 million. The SBV was the main lender. Others included the Australian Industry Development Corporation, Midland International Australia, Barclays Bank Australia, BBL Australia, HongkongBank of Australia, Bank of Tokyo Australia, Advance Bank, Kleinwort Benson Australia, CIBC Australia, Euro-Pacific Leasing, Standard Chartered Bank Australia, Bank of New York Australia, Sanwa Australia, Elders Finance, Rothschilds and the State Bank of South Australia.

Police hunting for Friedrich swarmed down to his country home on a property at Seaton, near Heyfield in Gippsland. It was a farm property with a few horses on it, but nothing ostentatious. There wasn't even a swimming pool. The study contained books in Friedrich's native German, plus thrillers by Wilbur Smith and John Le Carré. But Friedrich, his wife and children were all missing.

Investigators and police began checking Friedrich's background. Who was this mystery man who had conned Victorian society and taken the banks for so much money? They discovered that he had married Shirley on 10 February 1976 and in the following year had been appointed safety engineer at Loy Yang. The most revealing items were those the investigators did not find. Friedrich was not on the electoral roll and he had never held an Australian passport or even a driving licence. He was not a naturalised Australian, which meant he had been ineligible for the Order of Australia. Someone in Government House had slipped. The emerging pattern was of a man who had never applied for anything that would have entailed an identity check.

An Australia-wide manhunt began for Friedrich, fanned by a blaze of publicity in the media. The Victoria Police were plagued by hundreds of reports of sightings of Friedrich from all over Australia. He was reported in Darwin, Perth and Hobart, and at the bar of the Ettamogah pub outside Albury. Police raided an apartment on the Gold Coast to the alarm of a bald man inside with a slight similarity to Friedrich. He was reported in New Zealand, Fiji, Singapore, New Delhi and New York. Neville said: 'About the only place he wasn't reported was Outer Mongolia and we'd joke about that, but personally I always believed Friedrich was still in Australia'.[8]

The assets of the NSC were nearly as elusive as Friedrich. Humphris was working twenty hours a day trying to identify assets and get them under his control. 'Different people owned different things and we had to make sure that they remained in place and weren't carted away', he said.

> I mean, we'd find complications like a helicopter being owned by one company while the rotor blades on the same helicopter were owned by another. We couldn't have the company that owned the rotor blades sneaking in and reclaiming them. I had to convince all these people that it was in their best interests to leave everything on site and agree on a share of the proceeds later. We physically opened every one of the containers down there, looking for supposed assets. They were supposed to have something in them, a big build-up of them stacked one on top of the other in places, and we found out within a week or so that they were all empty. The cupboards were bare.[9]

The scam pulled by Friedrich had been basically simple. His paramilitary outfit had cost millions of dollars to run—far more than it earned in revenue. Friedrich had bridged the gap and financed his fantasies by borrowing from banks and other lenders. The lenders had provided the money on the basis of invoices for goods which had been delivered in containers. Except there were no goods. The containers had been empty.

The scam was explained by businessman John Hodges from Airport West. Hodges supplied 58 containers to Friedrich over the years. These had been used by Friedrich to raise $33 million from lenders. Of this Hodges had received about $500 000, being the value of the containers.

Hodges told the police that Friedrich had used three types of transaction. In the first type Friedrich would request that an invoice for an empty container as if it had been filled with $100 000 to $250 000 worth of equipment, telling Hodges that the equipment would be supplied by the NSC. After Hodges wrote the invoice Friedrich would give it to a lender who would advance what he thought was the full value of the container. Hodges would bank the cheque, keep the $10 000 cost of the container and pass the balance back to the NSC, which he had presumed would then buy the equipment. In the second type of deal Hodges would pay accounts on behalf of the NSC. This enabled Friedrich to use Hodges as a type of 'slush fund' to make purchases with no record appearing in the NSC accounts. One purchase made in this way was an $80 000 Porsche bought for an NSC executive. In the third type of deal, conducted towards the end of Friedrich's career as he was coming under increasing scrutiny, Friedrich held a copy of Hodges' invoice book and used it to write false invoices himself and thus raise money. Hodges said that the amounts involved in Friedrich deals had grown much larger in the final six months. In the first three years Hodges' dealings with Friedrich had totalled $21 million, but in the last six months they had amounted to $12 million. Hodges said that the NSC's dealings were funny but he had thought he was dealing with 'reputable people'.

Friedrich's manipulations went uncovered for a long time because he had made sure that he personally controlled all the financial dealings. This enabled him to run a fictitious set of books called the 'Z' accounts. These comprised a list of people and organisations who allegedly owed money to the NSC for services rendered. No invoices were ever presented for these services, which were entirely imaginary. However, by pledging these alleged debtors as security, Friedrichs increased the NSC's overdraft with the SBV from $2 million to $25 million.

There were more than 100 containers stacked around the Sale base, but only a handful contained any equipment. Friedrich had developed a system for dealing with auditors or bankers whenever they arrived on the base from Melbourne. When they wanted to check the containers Friedrich would open one or two of the full containers and show them the gear inside. If they tried to see another container Friedrich would divert them by asking if they would like a ride in a light plane or a helicopter. If they wanted to check a particular container they would be told it was away on an exercise. Friedrich would then fly them across country in a plane, point to a container well out in the bush and say that was the one. The container would be empty but the auditors would have no way of getting to it. Friedrich would never fly them to a container in a helicopter because the auditors might have asked him to land near it. Friedrich also conned the banks by offering their senior executives survival courses. Several top bankers togged out in camouflage gear and spent a few days doing NSC exercises in the Gippsland bush.

While Humphris was opening empty containers, the hunt for Friedrich continued. His white Range Rover was discovered at the St Kilda Road Travelodge by NSC security staff. Then Sydney police found Shirley's green Range Rover in the suburb of Belmore. On Good Friday, 24 March, they tracked down Shirley, who had been staying with her brother in Belmore. She was haggard and distraught. She knew very little about Friedrich's crimes. It was a great shock to her to have discovered that she had lived twelve years with her husband without really knowing who he was. Her consolation was that he was still a loving family man. While on the run, he had posted teddy bears to the children at the Belmore address.

News of Friedrich's frauds and disappearance had by now been published in Germany, where the media were naturally interested. In Munich, a businessman named Franz Zacherl was sitting at a cafe having a morning coffee when he noticed a photograph in a newspaper being read by another patron. The photo was upside down, but seemed familiar. 'Excuse me, sir', said Zacherl, 'may I?' When the photo was the right way up he identified it immediately as that of a former employee, Friedrich Johann Hohenberger. Hohenberger was a German who had embezzled about $200 000 from Zacherl's Munich road-building firm, Strassen & Teerbau, in 1974. Zacherl dug out an old photo of Hohenberger taken at a party, showing a very strong likeness to the German now wanted in Australia. Hohenberger had worked for the company as an engineering contractor, but never as a direct employee. Together with three accomplices, Hohenberger had forged invoices for earthworks, road-building and other work that had never been done and forwarded them to Strassen & Teerbau. Fake road-building orders from local authorities, using fake letterheads, had also been sent in. They came from mountain areas where few checks were made. When one executive became suspicious and demanded to see some roadworks Hohenberger brazenly showed him a magnificent new road built by a rival company. When the fraud was discovered the company launched actions against Hohenberger's accomplices, who said they had been convinced by him that everything they had done was legal. Most of the money was recovered.[10]

On the weekend the police were called in Hohenberger was vacationing in the Italian Alps. Police tried to arrest him, but Hohenberger had fled by the time they arrived. Zacherl believed he must have been tipped off by a friend. Leaving his Volkswagen behind, Hohenberger went out on the slopes that day and never returned. His bags were discovered more than a year later, indicating suicide. Apart from this, German sources were not very helpful because under German law there is a statute of limitations of ten years on crimes such as embezzlement. That meant that Hohenberger's file had been destroyed. Piecing the evidence together later, it is almost certain that Hohenberger tried to fake his death in a skiing accident in the Italian Alps in 1974. He then escaped Europe through Switzerland and went to New Zealand.

How did the fugitive Hohenberger get to Australia? On 20 January 1975 Hohenburger flew into Melbourne from New Zealand aboard Air New Zealand Flight 831, landing at 11.35 a.m. He was booked through to London via Singapore aboard Qantas Flight 1 on the 22nd. As his passport was in order he had no trouble gaining a 72-hour temporary entry visa. Immigration records showed that Hohenberger caught the flight; but almost certainly he did not. In those days, before terrorism became widespread, airport security was low. Hohenberger could easily have returned to Tullamarine Airport on the 22nd, booked his luggage aboard QF1, have his name ticked off the immigration lists—and then slip away to a toilet or into the crowd.

There can be no doubt that Friedrich was Hohenberger. The likeness in the photographs was strong. There was also a strong similarity between Hohenberger's handwriting and Friedrich's. Hohenberger's passport showed that he had been born on 7 September in Munich, the same date and place as Friedrich gave on his marriage certificate. Hohenberger's Christian names were Friedrich Johann, which translates easily to John Friedrich. The modus operandi for the Australian and German swindles was identical. And there was evidence on the negative side. Nobody in Australia ever claimed to have seen or known Friedrich here before January 1975, although his career after that date was fairly well established. The evidence was overwhelming that Hohenberger slipped out of Tullamarine on 22 January 1975 and became John Friedrich. As a final clincher, Sergeant Grinberg travelled to Germany in 1989 a few months after Friedrich's arrest in Australia. In the town of Landshut, near Munich, he tracked down Elisabeth Hohenberger, the mother of the vanished boy. When Grinberg showed her a photo of Friedrich she wept, immediately recognising it as her long lost son. He had never told her that he was still alive.

Friedrich's first job in Australia may have been with Codelfa Constructions Pty Ltd in Melbourne, which issued an unclaimed employee group certificate for the week to 31 January 1975, under the name of J. Friederitch, showing he had paid tax of $65 on earnings of $265. His first known sighting after that was at Ernabella Mission in South Australia on 8 March. Friedrich (as he now called himself) began work at the mission three days later, trying to instil some discipline into the Pukutja Aboriginals. The mission auditor got on badly with Friedrich, claiming that he had taken several unauthorised trips to Tasmania at the mission's expense. Eventually he was forced to pay for the air fares. That Easter, the mission's nursing sister, Shirley Manning, returned from holidays and met the new recruit Friedrich for the first time. They fell in love. In February 1976 they moved together to another Presbyterian mission on Mornington Island, in the Northern Territory. En route they were married in Sydney by the Reverend John Brown, who had run the Ernabella Mission. Fourteen years later he would deliver the oration at Friedrich's funeral. After a year on Mornington Island Friedrich applied for the Yallourn job with the NSC.

While Friedrich was on the run the total of NSC debts mounted. From an initial estimate of $40 million, the debt shot to $100 million and finally $236 million. This was an astonishing amount to have been lent to an organisation with such an odd structure. The NSC had virtually no equity in its assets. All the aircraft, boats and other equipment were under some form of chattel mortgage, lease, or hire purchase agreement. There was no hope of the NSC continuing as a going concern because its income could never meet the mounting interest bill on its debt. After a few days' investigation the liquidator, Michael Humphris, announced that there was no alternative but to wind up the NSC. The biggest creditor was the State Bank of Victoria, which was owed $103 million. This left the SBV redfaced, because it had not been long since the bank had actively wooed the NSC for its business. General manager Bill Moyle admitted: 'We won the business in open competition and we did market the council to acquire their business'.[11] The SBV reportedly won the main business away from the ANZ by shaving a quarter of a point off its interest rates. According to one story, when the NSC collapsed the ANZ sent the State Bank of Victoria a laconic telegram saying: 'Thanks'. The SBV was so embarrassed that its officers at first refused police requests to lay a complaint against Friedrichs. Then the SBV changed its mind and allowed police to proceed.

There was a long list of other banks who had also been fooled. The second largest creditor was the State Bank of South Australia, for $30 million. Elders Finance was owed $18 million and about a dozen other financiers were owed lesser sums, including $8.5 million to the Advance Bank.

Friedrich ran 5000 kilometres before he was caught. He was known to have shaved his beard off and bought a Ford in Albury in late March. The car was discovered abandoned on the other side of the continent, at Kalbarri, a coastal resort 500 kilometres north of Perth. He managed to run a little further yet, but police eventually arrested him on a roadside at Baldavis, about 50 kilometres south of Perth. It was a peaceful arrest.

Friedrich said he had bought a bus ticket to return to Melbourne and give himself up.

Neville flew to Perth to meet Friedrich, who immediately admitted that the Z accounts were false, that the containers had been empty and that the financiers had been deceived—and that he was responsible.[12] Friedrich was an amenable prisoner in these early days, helping detectives to understand the frauds he had committed. When the visiting detectives decided to celebrate by going out for a Chinese meal they invited Friedrich out of his cell to join them for a preliminary beer. He politely declined the beer, drinking a Coke with them instead.[13]

Shots in the dark

One story floated by Friedrich's biographer, Martin Thomas, was that the NSC was on the verge of a major expansion at the time it collapsed. Friedrich was signing million dollar contracts with a string of countries including Brunei, Canada, France, Hong Kong, Malaysia, the Netherlands and Spain. 'The prospect of many millions of dollars a year flowing to the council, and thus Australia, had passed the realm of a dream and was close to reality, and no one outside a few people knew', Thomas wrote.[14] But the NSC had only reached this eminence by living well beyond its means for years. As the NSC's liabilities exceeded its assets by more than $200 million at the time, there was no conceivable deal that could have saved it. Indeed, the loss would have been larger if the NSC had expanded.

Humphris was replaced by a new liquidator, John Perrins. He began a Section 541 hearing in the Victorian Supreme Court, before Master Evans, on 9 November 1989. Under Section 541 a liquidator has the right to conduct a wide-ranging examination into a company collapse to identify any assets which may be available to creditors. Friedrich's lawyer asked that the proceedings be held in private, because reporting of them could prejudice jurors at any future trial of Friedrich. Evans agreed, a decision which led to seventeen further court hearings over whether evidence could be published or not. Friedrich frustrated proceedings until 13 December, when it was ruled that his evidence could be made public.

At last everything came out in the open. Friedrich admitted that he had falsified invoices for about 100 containers for up to $250 000 a time. He said that he had done it to obtain money for the NSC. He admitted falsifying signatures of two council members to facilitate transactions. He admitted lying to the auditors. He admitted disguising borrowings from financiers as cash owing by debtors. He admitted that he had raised false invoices that bore no relation to reality. He admitted he had been falsifying accounts from 1986 to 1989. His home at Seaton had been bought through a $100 000 loan raised on two container accounts. The NSC regarded the $100 000 as a loan and had agreed that it would be non-repayable if he stayed with the organisation for five years. Another $31 000 worth of work on the building was provided by the NSC. Every answer by Friedrich was preceded by the words 'I object', which meant that his admissions at the Section 541 hearing could not be used in evidence at any subsequent criminal trial.[15]

Apart from the house and his salary Friedrich derived no personal gain from his frauds. But he was revealed as an autocrat who had been building his scam for years. Some of the evidence also revealed a nasty streak in Friedrich. One accountant, Teresina Farnham-Oliver, said that about nine months after she joined in 1986 she came to believe that the NSC was insolvent. She did not bother telling Friedrich because he would have been the one behind it all and there had been an 'air of intimidation' about him. The NSC's former chief accountant, Ian Mathews, said that he had resigned in January 1986 because he had no faith in the accounts Friedrich was producing. Mathews said that auditors or financiers visiting the base would be shown a full container of gear. They would then be taken a long way away, the container would be moved, and they would be shown the same container again. He had raised his suspicions with the previous financial controller, Olwyn Pratt. She became the subject of gossip about her mental condition and was forced to take leave in 1985. While she was away, Mathews was told to clear all financial records from her office.

If the evidence had been repeated before a criminal court, there would have been enough on Friedrich to put him in jail for a long sentence. His only mitigation was that he had reaped little personal gain from his frauds. The hearing adjourned for Christmas, due to recommence on 5 January.

Friedrich, released on bail, spent Christmas with his family at Seaton. The night before he was due to appear was disrupted by a dramatic incident. A few minutes after midnight someone fired several shots at the Friedrich house. According to Friedrich he had heard noises and went to the front door. Several shots were fired from the darkness about fifteen metres in front of him. He had dived for the floor and crawled to the phone, only to find that it was dead. He rang the police on a cellular phone. The family were awake, shocked but unhurt. The family dog— aged, blind and deaf—was the only one to sleep through it all. Police discovered six shell casings at the base of a palm tree just inside the front gate. They had been fired from a .45 pistol. The phone line had been severed by an axe. Friedrich said that he had seen the muzzle flashes, but not the shooter. Bullets were found embedded in and around the doorway.

The immediate suspicion was that Friedrich had fired the shots himself, but investigation showed that this was unlikely. A neighbour said he had heard the shots and then a car driving off quickly. Police noted that Friedrich was shaken and began to believe that it might have been a genuine attempt on his life. The motive for the shooting was never clear. If it were staged by Friedrich, using an accomplice, it gained him only a temporary respite from the hearing—which was going to be adjourned that day anyway. If it were the work of an outsider, it is not clear what shooting Friedrich would have accomplished. The one point which stands out is that it was not an expert attempt at killing him. Someone had simply blazed six quick shots in the dark at Friedrich, then sped off. In the absence of any clear motive for anyone involved the most likely explanation is that it was the work of a crank. For the rest of his life Friedrich said he believed he was a marked man and that someone was after him. He would later claim that a man had pointed a gun at him from a parked car and that on another occasion he had been attacked in a Queensland motel, receiving a bruised neck.

Clinical psychologist Ian Joblin, who examined Friedrich after the shooting, said Friedrich had concluded that the shooting was 'political'.[16] That conclusion makes no sense at all. It made no difference to any politician in Australia whether Friedrich was alive or dead. If by 'political' Friedrich was hinting that security agencies were after him, the claim looks even less valid. If a security agency wanted Friedrich dead, its operators would surely have made a more professional job of it than the panicky shooting at Seaton and a bruised neck in Queensland.

These incidents, or alleged incidents, gave Friedrich an excuse to start hiding. While on bail awaiting trial he behaved like a man on the run. He hid out in a terrace house in West Melbourne and then headed north. In the last eighteen months of his life he phoned Joblin 36 times, including calls from Lismore, Cooktown, Normanton and Cairns. He worked briefly in a coal mine at Lithgow and lived in a caravan in northern Queensland. For much of the time Shirley and the children were with him.

Friedrich was becoming increasingly paranoid. Joblin described a meeting with Friedrich in West Melbourne where Friedrich was agitated, almost tearful, and talking about his total inability to cope. Joblin said:

> He was, I felt, totally obsessed with 'the organisation', whatever the organisation was, and he was in a state of unorganised chaos. And this guy, if he is in a state of chaos, he's down and cannot handle it. That's just totally foreign to him. He had to have everything right, be just so. And whenever it was otherwise, out of that, then he was lost.[17]

Friedrich talked to Joblin about being a marked man by a mysterious 'they'. He also hinted at suicide. Towards the end of his life Friedrich would claim that the State Bank of South Australia had hired a hit man who had given him the choice between suicide and having his family killed. This can be dismissed as pure fantasy, if only because it would have been well beyond the SBSA's competence.

Friedrich was undoubtedly haunted by a fear that he could be extradited from Australia back to Germany to face justice for his crimes in Munich. The fear—probably like others that haunted Friedrich in his last two years—was entirely illusory. No criminal charges had ever been filed against Friedrich in Munich and the German statute of limitations had expired anyway. Friedrich did not know this, although he was aware of another danger. A change in the immigration laws was due on 18 December 1989, which he believed would render him ineligible for permanent residency. Friedrich arranged an overnight trip with his lawyer, Mark Barrett, a few days before the deadline. Barrett left Melbourne at 4 a.m. one night, picked up Friedrich at Sale and drove him up to Canberra via Cooma. There he met Canberra immigration officials and applied for permanent residency under the name of Friedrich Johann Hohenberger. The Department of Immigration issued him a work permit, but was still considering the application for permanent residency when he died.

John Perrins issued writs against the auditors, Horwarth & Horwath, claiming $263 million. This raised one of the most bizarre aspects of the entire case. Horwath & Horwath claimed that they had warned the board by qualifying the NSC accounts for both 1985–86 and 1986–87. In 1986, Horwath & Horwath auditor Price Williams qualified the accounts because he had been unable to verify some outstanding contract income.[18] The qualification in 1986–87 was more serious. The auditors had noted that the accounts included $73 million of leased and owned containerised equipment and said that they had been unable to physically identify most of the equipment because it was in inaccessible areas or with users. This should have triggered immediate concern. After all, $73 million represents a lot of rescue equipment to have lying about in containers. Horwath & Horwath's audit report for 1986–87 had gone on to say: 'Accordingly, we are not in a position to, and do not, express an opinion on either the physical existence, the valuation, or the security of these assets held by financiers'. When the audit was in progress for 1987–88, Horwath & Horwath again tried unsuccessfully to verify the existence of the rescue gear. When they were frustrated by Friedrich the auditors took their concerns to the board.

This raised the question of how nobody on the board had noticed a problem until late in 1988. The answer was a communication breakdown between the auditors and the board, combined with some elementary trickery by Friedrich. When the qualified audit report for 1986–87 had been given to Friedrich by the auditors he had simply cut out the offending paragraphs, photocopied the rest of the report (which contained standard innocuous phrases) and sent the doctored report to the banks and the board.

This was schoolboy stuff. Failure to detect it does not reflect well on either the board members or the banks' lending departments. An audit report is a stereotyped document. In the 1980s it normally began with an introduction along standard lines. It was usually addressed 'To the members of . . . ', and the first sentence would begin 'We have audited the books of . . . ' The doctored report sent in by Friedrich contained no such phrases. It began baldly:

> In our opinion, the accounts of the National Safety Council of Australia, Victoria Division. . .are properly drawn up in accordance with the provisions of the Companies (Victoria) Code so as to give a true and fair view of the state of affairs of the company and of the group as at 30th June 1987.[19]

A lazy layman flicking through the pages of an annual report could be forgiven for being fooled by such an audit statement. It is much harder to forgive the board and the banks. The statement does not conform to accounting standards. It begins with a sentence normally found towards the bottom of the audit report. The auditor's report on the accounts is one of the most important documents considered by a board each year. Directors were lax to have allowed such a truncated statement to pass unquestioned.

Nor can the auditors escape censure. Having discovered a yawning hole in the accounts, amounting to $73 million in 1987, they simply gave their findings to Friedrich and left it to him to pass them on to the board. Friedrich was at all times the person most likely to be responsible for the deficiency. It is incredible in these circumstances that the auditors should have had no effective communication with the board for two years. Under Section 285 of the Companies Code, auditors were supposed to hand their reports to the board. Also, having made a serious qualification to the NSC accounts, the auditors do not appear to have noticed that the report had been published with the qualification entirely removed.

The NSC itself was disbanded. Many of the staff were deeply aggrieved. They believed they had worked hard and created a unique organisation. They had indeed, but it had not been paid for and could not be afforded.

The State Bank of Victoria sued Friedrich and directors of the NSC. All except one of the directors settled out of court with the State Bank, agreeing to pay their own legal expenses. The exception was Max Eise, who fought the case in court, lost and was ordered to pay $97 million. This was way beyond his ability to pay. Eise eventually made his own settlement, losing his small fortune and finishing on the pension. Friedrich was also ordered to pay the bank $97 million. Friedrich was charged with 98 counts of fraud. His trial was set down for August 1991, but it would never be held.

Early on the morning of 26 July Shirley took their three children—Catherine, Timothy and Haydn—to school. Friedrich stayed in bed a little longer, then rose. He had one final secret that nobody knew about. He owned a small antique handgun: a snub-nosed .38 made in 1900 but still serviceable. He slipped the gun into his jacket pocket and went for a stroll. He walked about four kilometres to the top of Harper's Hill. Bernard Johnston, a Telecom worker and neighbouring farmer, saw Friedrich walking up the hill alone at about 9.20 a.m. From the top of the hill he would have seen a peaceful vista of the surrounding country-side—the hills, the undulations, the farms. But the peace Friedrich was seeking that morning was eternal. At the top of the hill he drew the pistol, placed the muzzle behind his left ear and shot himself dead. His body was discovered by his friend and minder, James Burcide, at 5.45 p.m.

While on the run, Friedrich wrote several letters to his wife and children. In the last of these, written to Shirley the day before he was arrested, there were indications of suicide. At one point he said: 'I think now I have arrived at the end of my useful lifetime'. At another, he said: 'Without you I would long ago have walked away into another world'. One policeman interviewed by Martin Thomas put forward the theory that Friedrich may then have been contemplating another faked death.[20]

Those who believed in conspiracy theories had a field day with Friedrich. He was variously alleged to have been a plant of the CIA and the KGB. He was supposed to have been running covert operations for ASIO. He was supposed to have run a huge money-laundering operation and to have a fortune stashed in Switzerland. There were whispers that he had been assassinated.

The most lurid story was told by 'Brian', a freelance pilot who talked to the media while Friedrich was on the run. 'Brian' alleged that he had flown Friedrich on secret missions over high security areas, including Pine Gap in Central Australia. He said that Friedrich had made many grid drawings and illustrations of what he saw; 'Brian' hinted that he was involved in espionage. The identity of 'Brian' was never revealed by the media who splashed his story, but Victoria Police later interviewed a bitter former employee of the NSC who told a similar story and claimed that Friedrich had ruined his life. On another occasion the NSC was said to have been behind an attempted counter-coup in Fiji against Brigadier Rabuka. There was never any corroboration for any of these allegations, which appear to have been entirely fictitious.

A Federal parliamentary inquiry headed by Senator Chris Schacht investigated the alleged clandestine links of Friedrich and the NSC and came up with nothing. The inquiry was incomplete when parliament was prorogued for an election in 1990 and did not resume afterwards. The most that ever emerged was that the NSC had worked in conjunction with the defence forces at times, which seems perfectly natural, and that it had provided some services to the Pine Gap base. However, NSC staff were never allowed access to the secret areas of the base. It was officially denied that there was any closer contact, and there is reason to believe the denials. There is ample evidence that Friedrich devoted his entire energies to the NSC. It is rather difficult to imagine what he could have been doing that would have been of practical use to military intelligence or ASIO. Furthermore, any closer association with either ASIO or the military would have entailed a security check—the one thing that Friedrich always took pains to avoid.

A security specialist was retained by Victoria Police to check out the rumours about the NSC. He reported that there had been a natural interaction between the NSC and the military, because they used common rescue equipment and their staff had to undergo similar training. The state-of-the-art gear of the NSC doubtless reflected Friedrich's obsession with military toys, rather than a real need for them, but even the HALO (High Altitude Low Landing) parachutes had valid rescue usage in high altitude areas. The NSC had actively sought to recruit Special Air Service troops because they had been trained to use such equipment. The NSC had also used military bases around Australia for its operations, leading to good liaison between the NSC and the military. Beyond that, the specialist's report found that allegations about the NSC were unfounded and based on pure conjecture. Protesters outside the Pine Gap base, for instance, had noticed NSC staff in their distinctive yellow uniforms going in and out of the base.

By a logical broad jump the NSC was then linked with ASIO and the CIA. While Friedrich's NSC might have been useful for commando operations, it is hard to see how it could have aided espionage or intelligence-gathering. The specialist checked every identifiable source of allegations against the NSC and found each of them had an axe to grind, either as a commercial rival or disgruntled ex-employee. None of them had any evidence to support their allegations.

The specialist's report to Victoria Police concluded:

> There were a number of individuals and agencies contacted during the NSCA VD inquiry. Allegations both of a specific and general nature were inquired into in the course of assessing the credibility of informers and information relevant to the inquiry. These allegations did not reveal any specific information that supported the various allegations put forward. I did not uncover any approaches that had been made to the NSCA VD for involvement in activities outside their field of operations. There is

no existing information of a nature that warrants further investigation by other government departments.[21]

On all the evidence, Johann Hohenberger/Friedrich was a Walter Mitty. While he appears to have pocketed some of the $200 000 swindled from Strassen & Teerbau, he made nothing except his salary and modest home from his swindles at the NSC. His objective was not money but the chance to build a paramilitary apparatus. Boats, vehicles, helicopters, planes, dogs, horses, the best of everything. A loyal corps of uniformed staff who would do his bidding. He was a boy who liked to play soldiers—or semi-soldiers anyhow. For someone who appears to have been an outstanding team leader, his grasp of reality was amazingly slight. His swindles were a straightforward kind which were bound to be discovered eventually. A more sophisticated swindler would have built more complicated defences. He believed he was in danger of extradition to face embezzlement charges, when no such charges had ever been laid and by then could not be.

It is doubtful whether Friedrich ever came to grips with legal processes. As soon as he was detected he began hinting at a plot by mysterious 'others', although his swindles had been executed entirely by himself. At times he had hinted to acquaintances that he was with the CIA, but there is no hard evidence of any such connection. More probably he was a delusionary who needed to feel important; as part of that need he created phantom enemies who were stalking him. The shots fired at the Seaton house may have been part of the masquerade. The most likely explanations are that they were the work of a crank, or that Friedrich used an accomplice. The shooter could hardly have loosed off the shots with less effect if he had tried.

Some homing instinct must have guided Friedrich to the NSC, an unconventional organisation with weak management and few financial controls. A strong personality and a weak board allowed him to build an empire on borrowed money. Only in Australia in the 1980s would his swindles have remained undetected for so long. At the inquest into Friedrich's death Joblin described him as living in a total world of fantasy, in which the NSC had supported his sense of superiority. 'I felt he was somewhat narcissistic', said Joblin. 'He seemed to live in a delusional state relating to his importance and he had to build up that organisation around him to support that mental state.' The deputy state coroner, Iain West, found that the deceased's real name was Friedrich Johann Hohenberger and that he had died by suicide.

On the day before his suicide, Hohenberger completed a manuscript entitled 'Codename Iago'. In it he claimed that he had been born in South Australia in 1931, that his father had died soon after his birth and that he had returned with his mother to Munich. There he had grown up and got an engineering degree and been recruited as an intelligence agent. He claimed to have been trained in Camp Pearce, Virginia, and to have been a CIA agent in Laos in the early 1970s. He said he would not have joined the NSC if he had 'known its true nature', hinting that it was a clandestine organisation with ASIO links and that one of its main purposes was to keep US bases safe in Australia. He claimed that an NSC helicopter with infra-red detectors was used to patrol Pine Gap and detect infiltrators at night. He said that he had been remitting part of his salary to his 'true employers'. Simultaneously, he claimed that the Federal Government had been 'giving banks the thumbs-up for loans to be pushed in our direction as a method of payment for certain services that they did not want to be seen directly paying for'.[22]

He also said that he had three names in his life: his true name, which he would not reveal; Iago, which he alleged was his codename; and his assumed name of John Friedrich. He said that he was not really Hohenberger, and hinted that he had assumed the name after reading of the real Hohenberger's death in a skiing accident.

Excerpts from the manuscript were published in the *Age* in October 1991. It was pure moonshine from start to finish. If he had been born in 1931 he would have been 60 at the time of his death, which was at least ten years too old. He was identified as Johann Hohenberger by his mother and ultimately by himself when he made a permanent residency application to the immigration authorities. Hohenberger had never been to Virginia or Laos. Hohenberger did not have time to fit in a big career in intelligence before he joined the road-building firm at the age of 22. And the loans to the NSC were mostly made by the State Bank of Victoria. Even Walter Mitty would have hesitated to claim that the SBV—of all banks in Australia—was acting under a 'thumbs-up' direction from the Federal Government. It was the very independence of the state banks from Federal control that led to some of our worst banking disasters of the 1980s.

Friedrich himself gives the game away by his choice of codename. By modern standards he had a fair knowledge of the English classics. In his manuscript he points out that Iago is 'a villain who deliberately strings together such a mass of circumstantial evidence'. He said that Iago was 'the closest thing I have to a true identity'. His last manuscript was also his last fraud. Or, if the reader wishes to be more charitable, Hohenberger wanted to close his life with what strand he could of mystery and drama. Because by that time there really wasn't much mystery left at all.

8
The wild bastard

Hooker will continue to be the Laurence Olivier of the property field. Its completeness and reliability remain. Now we will add a little Harrison Ford, a touch of Indiana Jones.

George Herscu

George Herscu is perhaps the best illustration of the mental gulf that exists between corporate cowboys and what might be called normal people. By the middle 1980s Herscu had spent half a lifetime as a property dealer and must have ranked as one of Australia's richer men, with a net worth somewhere north of $100 million. He had a vulgarly opulent house at 7 Whernside Avenue in Toorak, he was successful, he was approaching his sixties. Most people in this situation would have retired and spent the rest of their life in luxurious idleness. Instead, Herscu hocked everything he had, invested it in Hooker Corporation and sent it broke. He lost his entire fortune, including his house. His family also committed themselves heavily to Hooker shares and saw their investments wiped out. Having accumulated more wealth than he could have spent in a lifetime, he lost the lot and impoverished his family into the bargain. There is something rather heroic about folly on this scale.

But Herscu's main characteristic was always vitality. Born in Romania in 1928, he spent World War II in Nazi labour camps. After the war, he said, he spent a whole year 'dancing all night in Paris'.[1] Herscu migrated to Tasmania in 1950 as a penniless refugee and worked briefly as a storeman, but it wasn't the same as Paris. 'In Tasmania all the dogs went to bed after 6 p.m. so I joined the Arthur Murray Dance School just to get some action', he said.[2] Herscu soon decided that he would rather work for himself. He moved to Victoria, went into partnership in a milk bar, then tried a number of other small businesses with apparent success. 'I know a good business', he once told a reporter. 'I can smell it.'

His third business was a delicatessen at Reservoir. 'I went in to look and decided straight away I was going to buy', he said. 'The woman said, "Don't you even want to look in the books?", and I said, "No, I'll take it", and gave her $2500. Then I redid the shop and six months later I sold it for $5000.' Herscu had discovered property, the foundation of many a migrant's fortune in Australia. He borrowed money and started buying more shops and then small strip shopping centres in the Melbourne suburbs.[3]

In the late 1950s he teamed up with Moses (Maurice) Alter, a Polish migrant who had hit on the same formula. One day they went to look at some shops in a Forest Hills centre owned by a consortium headed by Paul Fayman. The impulsive Herscu decided that he wanted to own the whole shopping centre, so Alter and Herscu wound up in partnership with Fayman. This started a string of successful property deals and the odd diversification. In 1965 they expanded into the meat trade, buying Swift's Newport Freezing Works.

By the late 1960s Herscu had become a prominent member of what was jokingly called Melbourne's Jewish mafia. This community centred on St Kilda and East Caulfield, and featured many businessmen who were known to be wealthy but whose dealings were tantalisingly private. They tended to be clannish, preferring to deal with each other or with private companies rather than expose their financial affairs in public companies. Whenever members of the fraternity were sighted in a public company it was akin to sighting whales at sea—not a rare event, but always interesting. The WASPs who still dominated Melbourne's business community would begin speculating about how many more whales there were below and which were the biggest.

At the top of the community were the Smorgon family, who had been in Australia for generations and were widely respected for their integrity and acumen. They had displayed a remarkable ability to hold together as a family while accumulating a fortune in the meat and paper industries. For three years the Smorgons were partners with Herscu, Alter and Fayman in Newport Freezing. Some of the community were investors, such as the Libermans. Many were in the garment industry, such as Marc Besen and Joe Brender. One rising star was the young Dick Pratt, who would later become a force in the packaging industry. At the bottom of the ladder the community had its rascals, but certainly not more than the WASPs.

Most of the big deals involving members of Melbourne's Jewish community were financed to some extent by the ANZ Bank. This was the result of a deliberate drive for Jewish custom. In the late 1960s and early 1970s an ANZ officer named Rex Davidson cultivated the community, winning their trust and their considerable custom.

The taking of Hanover

Nearly all of the Jewish community invested in property, but three of the most aggressive investors proved to be Alter, Fayman and Herscu. In March 1969 this trio gained two-thirds of Allans Finance Ltd, a small public company, in a quick first-come, first-served raid. Allans had made a living financing the purchase of electrical goods, but under Herscu, Alter and Fayman was soon turned into a property dealer and developer named Hanover Holdings. Although the three Jews controlled the share register, a WASP was always chairman. The first was Alwynne Rowlands, who retired in 1971 to become Lord Mayor of Melbourne. He was succeeded by James Firebrace Hemphill, a former ANZ officer.

Hanover Holdings made a flying start in the wild nickel boom of 1970. Hanover picked up a large block of shares in a sleepy timber merchant, J.A. Terrett & Co, and sold them to a promoter named Robert Jacobson. Jacobson used Terrett as a backdoor listing for some nickel claims, renamed the company Wingellina Nickel and was dubbed 'Australia's Mr Mining' in an overexcited press release. Herscu, Alter and Fayman had the opportunity to profit from this deal, because they each received more than 300 000 options on Wingellina shares. Wingellina stock went through a rapid rise to $6, slumped back close to zero and gradually faded from view. The options were not exercised.

Hanover rode the property boom of the early 1970s exceedingly well. It was involved in a fast succession of deals which rapidly increased in size. The first deals—joint property ventures in the suburbs of Burwood and Frankston—were for hundreds of thousands of dollars, but by 1972 Hanover could buy the Eureka Stockade bar and restaurant complex in Bourke Street for $3.5 million. It then announced a $10 million office complex in South Melbourne. The finance was being provided by the ANZ and the Chase NBA Group, and to a lesser extent from retained profits. Chase NBA was partly owned by the broking firm of A.C. Goode & Co, which handled most of Hanover's share transactions and market raids.

Hanover's profits multiplied along with its deals in the early 1970s. Its operations expanded to Sydney and Surfers Paradise and it picked up half of Melbourne's Chevron Hotel from the Kornhauser family. In 1971–72 net profit leaped 137 per cent and in 1972–73 it rose a further 90 per cent, to $1.7 million. Hanover was the hottest name in property. It announced a rise in dividend and a three-for-seven bonus issue, and was planning a $48 million expansion over the next four years. At home it acquired 49 per cent of Landall Holdings, a property developer which had agreed to buy from it some housing subdivisions in the Melbourne suburbs. But Australia was already getting too small for Hanover, which was looking at property in Britain, Europe and the United States.

The property boom had its bust in mid-1974 when five big players collapsed in four months. The first was Home Units of Australia in July, followed by Mainline Corporation in August, Cambridge Credit in September, then Landall and Keith Morris in October. Shareholders who had been clamouring to get aboard fast-growing property companies a few months earlier now typically went into fast reverse and panicked to get out. Hanover did not escape the rout. It was a well-known high-flyer and was known to be exposed to Landall, which went into receivership. Worse, Hanover had already reported a 63 per cent decline in profit for the year to June 1974. Directors tried to reassure shareholders by keeping their promise to pay a 9 per cent dividend even though earnings had only been 8.5 per cent.

Hanover wrote off its Landall investment and faced another problem when the retailer Walsh's Holdings was unable to pay back-rent of $185 000. Hanover began a fire sale of its extensive property portfolio. It announced a profit of $707 000 for 1974–75, but a scrutiny of its accounts showed that this would have been a loss without a $1 million profit on a quick land sale to the Victorian Housing Commission.

While the shares were low Alter, Fayman and Herscu bought. Their combined holdings increased by 3.8 per cent in 1974–75. A rumour began circulating that the trio were going to make a takeover bid for the company. A 'don't sell' notice was issued on 25 November, the day before the annual meeting. Shareholders showed amazingly little interest. Only 25 people turned up at the meeting and not one question was asked.[4] Three weeks later Fayman, Alter and Herscu announced a bid of 85 cents a share through a company named Tallerk Pty Ltd. They already held 64.4 per cent of Hanover, of which 6 per cent had been acquired through a nominee company during the year.

The rationale for the bid was that the three men did not always agree and wanted to take full ownership of the company so that they could split it up and go their separate ways. While this may have been true, to outsiders it also looked as though they were buying it on the cheap. At 85c the bid was handsome in share market terms. Hanover stock had gone as low as 30c in the panic and hit a peak of 68c when the 'don't sell' was released. However, 85c was still a long way below net tangible asset backing, which had been stated in the 1975 accounts at $1.32 per share.

Hanover had put many of its properties on the market since balance date. The bid looked an uneven bargain because shareholders had no way of knowing what sort of offers were being made for the assets, while directors would have been fully aware. Arthur Andersen & Co issued a Part B opinion valuing the shares at 85c on the basis of earnings but refraining from making any comparison with the stated balance sheet values. Sceptics pointed out that the balance sheet—showing net assets at $1.32 a share—had been signed by Price Waterhouse as Hanover's auditors on 7 November. The Andersen opinion valuing the shares at 85c was dated 19 November—just twelve days later.

The bid created some outcry. The broking firm of Brian Randall & Co, which had arranged the original Allans takeover for Fayman, Herscu and Alter, said that it would be fairer to liquidate the company and distribute the proceeds to all the shareholders. The Australian Shareholders' Association criticised the bid. The Hanover board stepped up pressure on shareholders by announcing that while revenue had climbed in the six months to December, profit had slumped 78 per cent to $181 000. Analysts pointed out that almost all of the profit drop had been caused by a change in accounting policy which had written an extra $576 000 off interest and overheads. Hanover spooked the shareholders further by omitting interim dividend. The three men who held two-thirds of the company were putting a blowtorch to the minority holders.

Slowly and reluctantly the shareholders opted for acceptance, although liquidation would have been a fairer solution. A few months after the takeover was completed and the trio had 100 per cent control Hanover revalued its properties by $4.4 million and its accounts showed net tangible assets of $1.64 a share—nearly double the price the small shareholders had been forced to accept. The episode left a nasty taste which lingered for years.

If you've got it . . .

Herscu withdrew to private property development through his family company Hersfield Developments. He prospered, developing shopping centres in the Melbourne suburbs and south-eastern Queensland. Hersfield buildings were not always top quality but they made money. Hersfield would build a shopping centre, fill it with tenants, then push the rents up to give it a strong positive cash flow. As property prices were rising anyway during this period, this strongly increased the value of the centre. He would then borrow more money against that centre to help build another. In this way, he pyramided a number of shopping centres into a highly profitable empire. Each shopping centre was owned by a separate company and paid dividends and fees to Hersfield as the management company.

Herscu's personal net worth was increasing in bounds. He enjoyed golf and racing, becoming a member of the Victorian Amateur Turf Club. His horses included Hyperno, a solid galloper which won the 1979

Melbourne Cup. When his personal wealth was estimated at $120 million, Herscu reckoned it was more.

Herscu enjoyed and flaunted his wealth. His dress sense was colourful, often featuring blue suits and yellow ties. When holidaying at his Surfers Paradise apartment he often wore all-yellow outfits. The Whernside Avenue home was modelled on Tara from *Gone With The Wind*—a book that he said he had read ten times because he loved the romance and the wild characters. 'I asked the builder to build double of everything', he said. 'We have an inside jacuzzi and an outside jacuzzi, and the one outside is built so big, with double pipes, that when I first got in it the water lifted me right up into the air.' Herscu was extravagant and unabashed. He had three cars: a $200 000 Rolls Royce in Melbourne and Jaguars in Sydney and Queensland. 'Beautiful things like Rolls Royces and Jaguars are made for people to enjoy', he said. 'Money should be enjoyed. I love to enjoy myself. To spend money. To dance—do the cha-cha. I love people with life in them and love to live.'

He bought Hyperno on the same sort of impulse as when he bought the delicatessen. The moment he discovered Hyperno someone told him that the horse had kicked its breaker in the head. 'I love wild bastards', he said.[5] Herscu was a pretty wild bastard himself. He was always an optimist and went for his investments with wholehearted passion.

It may well have been true that he found the more sanguine temperaments of Fayman and Alter incompatible. Community gossip said that Alter thought of himself as the financial expert, Fayman considered himself the most intellectual and Herscu thought he was the one 'with balls'. According to one story, he flattened one of his shopping centres to get rid of four tenants who had been refusing to leave. Herscu denied knocking down the centre, but admitted 'taking away the fittings and stock'. In 1985, at an age when many of his contemporaries were joining the local bowls club, Herscu was still a wild bastard.

The move into Hooker

The property crashes of 1974 were followed by a second wave at the start of 1977. Two of Australia's largest finance companies, CAGA and ASL, announced big writeoffs. Then, on 10 February, the *Australian Financial Review* revealed that Hooker Corporation had a large and previously undisclosed property exposure through a string of joint venture companies.[6] Hooker shares plunged alarmingly on the disclosure, because this was a very nervous time for the property market. A few days later a third finance company, IAC, announced another batch of writeoffs, and in March Sir Paul Strasser's Parkes Development collapsed.

It was not the first time that Hooker had hit rough water. During the Menzies credit squeeze of 1961 the company, then run by its founder Les Hooker, had nearly hit the wall. It was rescued by Keith Campbell. By 1977 he had become Sir Keith Campbell and was chairman of Hooker. It was strange that he had allowed the company to stray into the same vulnerable state from which he had rescued it sixteen years earlier. The task of rescuing Hooker a second time virtually killed Campbell, who died in 1983. However, he left it in sound shape under an able managing director in Barry Glover.

By the middle of the 1980s Hooker had regained its lustre as one of Australia's foremost property companies. The land bank that had almost sunk the company in the 1970s was now valuable property and on the brink of realising a fortune for Hooker's faithful shareholders.

Between 1980 and 1985 stockholders' equity had grown from $87 million to $157 million. If special reserves were included the figure was nearly $200 million. From a skinny net profit of $8 million in 1980 earnings had risen to $34 million, and return on average capital was up from 26.7 per cent to 42.8 per cent. Hooker was in real estate in Australia and the United States, where it was prospering. It had spread into retailing (through the giftware chains Edments and Prouds), car parks, beef, and property trust management. Its agency business, L.J. Hooker, was one of the best known in Australia. And debt had been brought under control. Debt was a little high at $344 million compared to total assets of $568 million, but nothing to be alarmed about because the real estate appeared conservatively valued.

Several corporate players had already scented that Hooker was underpriced. In February 1984 Consolidated Press Holdings and TNT made a profitable foray into the stock before selling out to builders Ted Lustig and Max Moar. A year later Alan Bond dabbled in the stock and then Hooker beat off an unwelcome takeover bid by Lee Ming Tee's Sunshine Australia. Lee Ming Tee got 30 per cent, then sold 20 per cent to the New Zealand property developer, Chase Corporation.

Why Herscu should have resurfaced to bid for Hooker at this time is not entirely comprehensible. He could easily have opted for prosperous retirement, happily swinging an iron at the Cranbourne Golf Club and racing his horses. Instead, at the age of 57, he had been possessed by the scheme of building giant shopping centres in the United States and becoming a billionaire. As a vehicle for this grandiose idea, he decided to seize control of one of Australia's largest property companies.

Herscu's raid on Hooker was financed by his old banker, the ANZ, which lent him $200 million. One of his chief advisors was his lieutenant, Paul Carter. Herscu bought secretly until he had acquired a stake of 20 per cent. Under the takeover law he could not acquire more shares without making a formal bid. Then, bidding through his company GSH Finance Pty Ltd, Herscu announced in September 1985 that he was seeking a total stake of about 44 per cent at $2.44 a share. Hooker directors fought the bid on the grounds that the terms were unfair. Herscu was not going to accept more than 44 per cent of the company. If more shareholders wanted to accept, their acceptances would be scaled down pro rata. This had the potential to leave shareholders in a position that was neither fish nor fowl, being unable to get out and being left with odd lots or unmarketable parcels. The Hooker board pointed out that the higher the level of acceptance the lower the proportion of their holding the shareholders would be able to sell.

The advent of Herscu on the Hooker register had been greeted with some suspicion around the stock exchange. Old hands had not forgotten Hanover and there was some muttering about the possible fate of minority shareholders in a company controlled by Herscu. Just as he and his partners had got 100 per cent of Hanover on the cheap, Herscu was now getting control of Hooker on the cheap. The board reluctantly recommended the offer after two of the largest shareholders, James Hardie Industries and National Mutual Life, announced that they would accept. Until then, the board had been urging shareholders not to sell. In hindsight, the best course the shareholders could have taken would have been to unload all their holdings onto the market.

A lot of shareholders tried to get out. Holders of 65 per cent accepted the offer. As Herscu already held 20 per cent, he could nearly have made a full takeover. But he scaled the acceptances back so that each acceptor sold only 36.7 per cent of his or her stock. Herscu now controlled the company with his nominated 44 per cent, but the market judgement was clear. Another 41 per cent would have got out if they could and this knowledge must have unsettled at least a proportion of the last 15 per cent. But they were all trapped. No rival bidder was likely to try his arm against an entrenched 44 per cent holder so small shareholders were there until Herscu wanted to take them out, which might be never. Control premium had vanished from the stock, which promptly dropped below the bid price of $2.40.

Herscu told Hooker that five of the eight existing directors would be sacked, including the chairman, Fred Millar. Herscu marched into Hooker House in Pitt Street with his team and was kept waiting outside the closed boardroom doors while the existing directors debated. When they emerged the old directors lined up opposite Herscu's men like two football teams. Then Fred Millar shook Herscu's hand and said: 'There are now two directors. The rest of us have resigned'. Then they all walked out.[7]

One of the two remaining was Glover, who stayed on as managing director. Glover and other executives stood to collect a windfall. The change in board control had triggered an option agreement which enabled executives to take up 7.75 million shares at $1.44, or 40c below the prevailing market price. Glover stood to gain 1.25 million of them, with the rest spread between 98 other people. Ten days later Glover changed his mind and announced that he was quitting Hooker after 25 years. This announcement caused little surprise. Herscu had a well-earned reputation as a headstrong individual who insisted on getting his own way. He had become chief executive of Hooker, which meant that power had been effectively removed from Glover's hands. So Glover opened his golden parachute and baled out. Hooker's Australian general manager, Ron McGarva, and chief auctioneer, Graham Hennessey, followed him out, leaving Hooker's management looking bare at the top. Herscu appointed Carter executive director.

The old guard bequeathed one benefit to Herscu. Profit for the six months to December 1985 was up by 48 per cent. 'We got a bargain', boasted Carter, who had done much of the number-crunching before the bid. Herscu, ever the optimist, was excited by Hooker's prospects. At an investment presentation in May 1986 he told analysts:

> Now we have a new drama, and Hooker is being coached to be the leading character . . . It will have more spark. Hooker will continue to be the Laurence Olivier of the property field. Its completeness and reliability remain. Now we will add a little Harrison Ford, a touch of Indiana Jones.

Frantic expansion

Herscu was obsessed with status. When one Melbourne businessman asked him why he wanted a corporate jet, he replied: 'You know Frank Lowy's got one and John Elliott's got one, so why shouldn't I have one?'. Freed from the cautious custody of Campbell and Glover, Hooker suddenly became expansive. Hooker bid for Australia's leading whitegoods maker, Email Ltd, and tendered together with Harrahs Hotels of the United States for the casino contract at Sydney's Darling Harbour. Herscu also decided to go ahead with a $45 million office block in Lonsdale Street. The previous management had been loath to demolish the existing building on the site until they could secure tenants for the new block, believing that the block was too big to build as a speculative proposition. As the *Financial Review* perceptively observed: 'The latest move clearly shows the different philosophies between the new chief executive, Mr Herscu, and his predecessor Mr Barry Glover'.[8]

The effervescent Herscu was bubbling with delight at the prize he had won. Now he was planning huge expansions in the United States. The world was his oyster. In May 1986, within three months of taking over Hooker, he unveiled plans for a $750 million retail mall development in the States. Three huge shopping malls were to be built in Cincinatti, Denver and Tampa in conjunction with the French hypermarket group, Euromarche. Each of the malls would cover about 100 000 square metres with a quarter of the space taken by one of Euromarche's Biggs hypermarkets. The investment would be through Hooker's wholly owned US subsidiary Hooker Barnes, which also planned to take a 10 per cent interest in Hyper Shoppes Inc, whose dominant investors were Euromarche and Lazard Freres. Hooker Barnes would own and run the malls. Herscu was confident that Hooker could get 85 per cent non-recourse finance, and possibly 100 per cent, for the projects. Non-recourse finance, sometimes called project finance, is exactly what it sounds. The lender is secured only over the specific project. Non-recourse lenders on the malls would be able to seize the malls in the event of default, but would have no claim on other assets of Hooker.

It now became clear why Herscu had taken over Hooker. The mall projects had been under negotiation since March 1985: nine months before Herscu won control. Hooker had been chosen as the vehicle for the malls, apart from its own attractions. But, having won Hooker, Herscu doubled the size of the proposed malls. Herscu claimed that the investments would increase Hooker's profits tenfold.

The malls would be unlike any previously seen. They would be very large and combine shopping with entertainment. 'What I'm doing is imaginative and innovative', Herscu said.

> Our malls will be beautiful and we'll be successful. They are very big: that's the way we like it. We'll have big hypermarkets and up to five department stores with an entertainment centre attached. There'll be movie theatres, laser beam theatres, ice and roller skating rinks, health studios and fairy wheels, rides and games rooms.

This was announced on 1 May 1986. That month saw a spate of further expansionary proposals pour from Herscu. Two further Hooker housing developments were opened in California, bringing the total to nine in the States. Simultaneously, Hooker announced that it would double its building rate in Australian housing over the next eighteen months.

This frantic activity boosted the share price to $2.70. James Hardie was unloading the rest of its holding but this selling volume had been more than offset by purchases, notably by Herscu. The market would have been better advised to pause and reflect. All this expansion was going to cost money and although Hooker's profits were rising nicely, the bulk of it would have to be provided by debt at a time when interest rates were high. And Hooker had by no means been low-geared when

271

Herscu took over. But Australia was approaching the height of the 1980s boom and the mood was buoyant.

Perhaps some insiders knew that the Hooker–Harrahs consortium had won the Darling Harbour casino tender. Champagne corks popped in Hooker House when this was announced at the end of June. But an old problem was lurking to haunt Herscu. Back in 1983 an inquiry into the affairs of the Builders' Labourers Federation (BLF) had resulted in charges being laid against Herscu for bribing the union secretary, Norm Gallagher. Herscu pleaded guilty but the magistrate directed that no conviction be recorded and that he be directed to enter into a good behaviour bond.

It is hard to be too critical of Herscu over this affair. The BLF was a rogue union whose members preached Marxism but were not above using strongarm tactics on sites to demand money and benefits or to intimidate rebellious union members. The union was prepared to destroy any employer who stood up to it. Gallagher shared with Herscu many of the characteristics of a wild bastard. He had publicly gloated over the downfall of Mainline in 1974. Despite repeated instances of union thuggery, governments seemed too intimidated to take action against the BLF. Builders had no choice but to deal with the BLF and if that meant a bribe to get a building finished, then so be it. Herscu was never one to worry about legal niceties, and there is little doubt that nearly every other builder in Australia during these years did similar deals with the BLF. After years of inactivity the Federal and Victorian governments appointed a Royal Commission to inquire into the union. The inquiry, conducted by Michael Winneke, QC, discovered several instances of bribes being paid by developers. A house owned by Gallagher and his son at McLoughlin's Beach in Gippsland appeared to have been built almost entirely on the proceeds of graft. One contributor was Hersfield, supplying goods and services with an estimated value between $40 000 and $60 000. Petty cash by Herscu's standards, it must have seemed well worth paying to secure a little industrial peace.

Counsel assisting the Royal Commission, Peter O'Callaghan, compared the builders to the small shopkeepers in crime movies who paid protection money to gang bosses. Herscu told Winneke that he knew some favours were being done and that he had not wanted to know about them. Winneke found this evidence 'thoroughly unconvincing' and found that Herscu had not been telling the truth. When Herscu was convicted for paying the bribes the Chief Judge in the County Court, Judge Waldron, described him as corrupt and calculating. He may well have been, but at least he had given evidence. The BLF boycotted the Royal Commission entirely and made statements outside court accusing it of being a political tool. For this, nine BLF members were eventually fined $500 each. The only other action taken against the BLF was a four-year jail sentence imposed on Gallagher, which was overturned on appeal.

As soon as the NSW Labor Government announced that Hooker had won the casino tender the Opposition Leader, Nick Greiner, said the fact that Herscu had been challenged in the Gallagher affair was a matter of concern. Greiner's attack resulted in further inquiries. The main fact unearthed by them was that Herscu had sold 33 companies to tax scam operators a few years before who had used them in frauds known as 'bottom of the harbour' schemes. Although Herscu had never been convicted and other allegations were largely unsubstantiated, Barrie Unsworth's government decided that there was enough stigma to justify withdrawal of its approval of the casino licence. This resulted in a storm of bad publicity, mainly for the government. Greiner had further achieved his aim of destabilising the NSW Government and the casino project went into limbo. The award of this casino licence became a troubled issue for a decade afterwards as successive governments—mostly Greiner's— attempted the impossible task of finding someone with the innocence of a plaster saint who knew how to run a gambling den.[9]

Herscu's reputation suffered a little from the casino setback but Hooker's did not. Financially, Hooker was on a roll. The group posted a 56 per cent profit rise for 1985–86 and an ebullient Herscu announced that most of its future funds would be spent in the US property market. Australia had too many knockers, he said. Major developments planned by Hooker included a huge upgrading of its jewellery store chain in the States by acquiring the eleven Merksamer stores in California; the possible listing of Hooker in the States; an international Hooker property trust; expansion of the L.J. Hooker agency network through the acquisition of Colliers; and a greater exposure to commercial and industrial develop- ments in Sydney and Melbourne, with a total of $500 million on the books at balance date. The US push continued apace in October 1986 with Hooker buying a string of real estate agencies from Merrill Lynch for $US150 million.

By early 1987 Hooker's share price had reached $3.66. One major reason was buying by the AMP Society, which had been attracted by Herscu's US drive. The US expansion continued furiously in May as Hooker spent $144 million to buy the Bonwit Teller fashion chain from Campeau Corporation. This deal gave rise to one of the most revealing anecdotes about Herscu's management style. A New York executive of Hooker, Darryl Guillhot, had spent six weeks crunching numbers on Bonwit Teller and concluded that it was worth no more than $30 million to $40 million. On the day Herscu was due to arrive in New York Guillhot was waiting nervously because he was aware that this was Herscu's pet project, and the chief executive was liable to explode into a foulmouthed rage if he was crossed. Guillhot waited outside Herscu's office with the 100-page report in his hands until Herscu bustled into the office with a senior executive. Guillhot heard Herscu shouting inside, then the executive emerged and took Guillhot by the arm. 'George has had a bad flight', the executive warned as he ushered Guillhot in. 'His shoulder is hurting. He just wants to get the deal done, so don't say anything too negative.' Herscu did not read the report, nor even the three-page executive summary. He read halfway down the first page, flung it on his desk and said: 'Good . . . let's do it'.[10] So Hooker bought the chain for treble what his analyst thought it was worth. Three years later Bonwit Teller would be put into Chapter 11 bankruptcy protection after losing $30 million.

The only sour note in public at the time was in the *Wall Street Journal*, where a New York retail consultant described Herscu's shopping malls as a combination of K Mart and Disneyland. 'I just don't understand a formula that is half tourism and half shopping', said Allan Pennington. Another ominous symptom was the continuous stream of old guard Hooker executives leaving as Herscu restructured the management. Herscu was still aggressively bullish, predicting that by 1990 Hooker would be the fifth largest home builder in the United States and would have 100 jewellery stores there. The only problem the company recognised was the need to establish better perception of the group's name in the United States, where the word 'hooker' had unfortunate connotations.

Profit for 1986–87 jumped another 31 per cent to $85 million and Herscu was still committed to nonstop expansion. In Sydney, Hooker signed up to build a 30-storey office block in Pitt Street in a joint venture with the State Superannuation Board. In Melbourne, planning for Lonsdale Street was proceeding but the cost had risen to $80 million. In the United States, Hooker bid $360 million for the retail fashion chain Parisian Inc. The cost of these expansions was somewhat offset by the sale of Hooker's beef interests and the Gateway building at Circular Quay. The shares swept past $4.

Hooker then bought the New York–based department store chain, B. Altman & Co, for $140 million. This was Hooker's fourth major retail acquisition in the United States in twelve months. Meanwhile, Carter said the group expected to sell its first two malls, in Columbia and Cincinnati, during 1987–88. Carter's statement was made in the third week of October 1987, just a few days before the share market crash. By then the shares had hit their peak of $5.66.

The Cincinnati hypermall

Hooker shares were hit badly by the crash. They dived to $2 by the end of October with barely a skidmark. The crash served as a cold douche of reality for investors. Suddenly they realised that Hooker's grandiose expansions had been largely funded by debt. While Hooker's profits had been bounding upwards with the boom, few investors had considered its balance sheet. The 1987 Hooker accounts, signed off a week before the market crash, showed that total assets of $1028 million had been funded by debt which appeared to be $455 million but in truth was $160 million higher if a debt defeasance were added back. The crash had also made investors suddenly wary of property valuations in expansionary groups. The $1028 million in assets might in truth be much smaller. The shares drifted further to $1.80.

More ominous portents began gathering. One was a report that the Cincinnati mall had been only 60 per cent tenanted, and mostly by Hooker subsidiaries and associates.[11] Another was a jarring report in *Australian Business* by Professor Bob Walker that Hooker's 1987 profit had been boosted by $14 million through a piece of creative accounting called debt defeasance.[12] Hooker's defeasance had been hidden deep in the fine print of the accounts and Walker was the first to publicise it. In a tricky piece of financing aimed purely at massaging the profit and loss account, a Hooker subsidiary had borrowed $US165 million for ten years from a bank. Hooker put $US63 million of the sum into a capital-guaranteed investment whose growth would ensure the bank's repayment over the period. The Hooker subsidiary then exchanged interest obligations with a second bank and was legally released from both principal and interest obligations under the original loan. Hooker then claimed that the cash surplus of $US102 million ($A141 million) was profit realisable over ten years. However, because of hedging arrangements between the two currencies the $US102 million bore a net servicing cost of about 8 per cent a year over the ten years, amounting to $111 million.

The NCSC, spurred into an investigation by Walker's article, ruled in March 1988 that $30 million was a gain arising from interest differentials in $US and $A contracts and that the remaining $111 million of the $141 million was still a liability. The very fact that accountants could argue whether $111 million was a profit or a liability leaves a layman with the impression that the whole accountancy profession had left the planet and got lost in space. Analysts downtown skipped the whole academic debate and automatically halved the stated increase in the 1987 Hooker profit. Nor were they comforted when they realised that without the defeasance Hooker would have been in breach of its negative pledge borrowing covenants, which specified a minimum debt/equity ratio of 70/30.

In early 1988 Herscu bid $2.70 a share for the outstanding stock, trying to privatise the company. In the light of the glowing prospects he had painted for the company over the previous two years, this looked an el cheapo bid. There was a striking parallel with Hanover, where minority investors had been bought out cheaply during a temporary recession. One of the strongest campaigners against the bid was Barry Glover, who had set up an investment company named Barlile in association with David Clarke, the chairman of Macquarie Bank. Showing confidence in Glover's old company, Barlile was Hooker's second largest shareholder. Glover argued that there was more value in Hooker. A stronger warning was provided by the abrupt departure from Hooker of Glover's replacement, Paul Carter. Carter had disagreed with Herscu's growth strategy for Hooker, saying that now was the time to consolidate the company—but Herscu was still bent on expansion. This was a dramatic break for Carter, who was a friend of Herscu and had been a director of his private company, GSH Corporation. Carter was right about Hooker's growth strategy and had a more accurate perception of its future than Glover.

This was one time when long memories served investors badly. Herscu's bid was rejected by most of the minority holders and lapsed. Later they realised that they should have accepted. Hooker's problems were terminal, but it took time for their full dimensions to show. Barlile, backed by the Gertner family in Venezuela, built its stake in Hooker to 9.3 per cent by the middle of 1988. But by then Herscu had increased his own stake to 52.5 per cent.

The large easing of monetary policy by the Reserve Bank after the October 1987 crash meant that funds were relatively cheap and plentiful in early 1988. This sparked a short property boom among developers and, like all the bold riders of the 1980s, Herscu compulsively followed a trend. He plunged further into Melbourne office development and bought Kindersley House in Sydney's Bligh Street in partnership with Malcolm Edwards' Essington group. Whenever I visited Melbourne around this time I developed a hobby of counting the number of cranes visible on the CBD skyline from my taxi on the Tullamarine Freeway. The record count was eighteen and there were doubtless several more out of sight. The world had experienced the biggest ever stock market crash less than a year before and history indicated that a property sector shakeout usually follows a couple of years later. It was obvious that some, if not all, of the Melbourne CBD developers were heading for big trouble, especially after interest rates bottomed in April 1988 and began rising again.[13]

An even more visible problem for Hooker was surfacing in its fund management business. Several of the Hooker property trusts had performed dismally, despite the property boom of the mid-1980s. Hooker planned to restructure its 23 smallish trusts into three large ones. This did little to assuage investors, particularly in the Capital Growth No. 4 Trust, whose $1 units had shrunk to 40c since 1981. The trust had lost more than 60 per cent of its funds on an office unit development at Parramatta. More than 80 per cent of the unitholders demanded the removal of Permanent Trustee as trustee of the fund. After a bitter legal fight Hooker bailed out the unitholders by making a takeover bid for their units at par.

Net profit for 1987–88 was reported as static, compared to the bounding increases of prior years. Herscu said that the result had been held back by the high start-up costs of the mall developments. 'The real benefits will become apparent in the years ahead', he told investors, promising a very successful 1989 as profits from Bonwit Teller and Altman came on stream. Analysts noted that Hooker had been unable to generate any significant increase in profit despite having considerably higher sales, a worrying point. Although Hooker's revenue had risen by $577 million (more than 60 per cent), profit was up by a mere million dollars.

The half year to December was again worrying. It showed a profit rise of only 3.4 per cent, all from the Australian real estate operations. Analysts started looking harder at Hooker's accounts. In Herscu's three-year reign since taking control in 1985, the Hooker group's debt had quadrupled from $273 million to more than $1.1 billion. Gearing had risen from 173 per cent in 1985 to 255 per cent. In other words, for every $1 of funding provided by equity capital Hooker was relying on $2.55 of debt. Earnings per share over the same period had slid from 37.2 cents to 24.7 cents.

In the 1970s Hooker had suffered because of the cost of holding its big land bank, but Campbell had rightly perceived this as a great asset for the future. Herscu had largely maintained Hooker profits after the takeover by selling off some $100 million of the land bank during the mid-1980s property boom.[14] As the major costs had been incurred in prior periods this was almost pure profit. It also meant that Hooker had been living off its fat while waiting for Herscu's investments to bear fruit. The profits had largely been diverted into the greenfields mall developments in the United States.

This meant that Hooker was gambling heavily on the success of the malls: a proposition that was looking distinctly hairy by the start of 1989. Work was proceeding on malls in Cincinatti (Ohio), Denver (Colorado) and Columbia (South Carolina). Mall sites had been bought in Raleigh (North Carolina), Tampa (Florida) and Atlanta (Georgia).

The most advanced mall was Forest Fair outside Cincinnati. It had a number of faults, which were well summarised by Graeme Beaton, the US correspondent of *Australian Business*.[15] Hooker claimed to have chosen the location carefully, near the intersection of major highways: Interstate 75 to Dayton, Ohio; and Interstate 74 to Indianapolis, Indiana. The plan was to draw shoppers from a 160-kilometre radius in three states. It was literally a greenfields site, most of the neighbourhood being open pad-docks, and ten kilometres from downtown Cincinnati. Locals complained: 'Who would want to drive all the way out there?'.

The cost was estimated at $US200 million but may have been closer to $US300 million. Herscu replaced the original carpet and tiles with ones which he preferred. The balcony railings had to be tubular brass. The architects wanted a half-size carousel, but Herscu insisted on a full-size one with 30 horses. And the miniature golf course was 18 holes instead of nine. The children's sandbox was as big as a tennis court. Other entertainment included an eight-screen cinema, a baseball batting cage and bumper cars.

The mall was designed to Herscu's own taste, which tended to be glitzy. The mall was so big that the Cincinatti Bengals gridiron team could fit six fields in the longest concourse. A shopper walking the upper floor could cover three kilometres without entering any of the stores. On the bottom floor the browsing shopper could cover another 1.5 kilometres. Little chains of light bulbs blinked on and off throughout. Art work cost $US1.3 million, with a sporting motif at each entrance. A lavish opening in March 1989 had starred Herscu's favourite singer, Marie Osmond.

It looked like working at first. An estimated 70 000 people poured through the mall one weekend as the mall band played 'Tie Me Kangaroo Down, Sport'. Wallaby Bob's Pub served meat pies and wallaby-shaped fries. There were queues for the carousel and batting cage, and a couple of thousand watched the televised national children's program 'Double Dare' in the centre court. But the mall was demographically schizo-phrenic. The population near Forest Fair was predominantly Cincinnati's blue-collar workforce, who could be seen in their shorts and T-shirts in the centre court playing the arcade games and bumper cars. Mostly young families, they drank beer at Wallaby Bob's and shopped at Biggs' 2.4 hectare hypermarket, where almost everything from furniture to groceries could be bought through the 58 cash registers. So far, so good; but these were not the people the mall needed to shop at its upmarket stores.

The anchor stores in the upmarket section were mainly those owned or controlled by Hooker. The main stores were Bonwit Teller and B. Altman. Bonwit Teller's vice-chairman had resigned after his objections to the ambitious mall and Bonwit Teller's participation were overruled. Also present were the Hooker-controlled Parisian, Sakowitz and Merk-samer Jewellery. One of Herscu's largest failures had been that he could not attract non-Hooker retailers into the mall. He had ran foul of rival mall developers such as Robert Campeau, who had bought the Higbee chain and spent $US5 million to pull it out of Forest Fair, but upmarket retail chains were wary of the concept anyhow. This situation was not helped when trade creditors began refusing to supply goods to B. Altman and Bonwit Teller. Money was being siphoned out of the stores for more pressing purposes, leaving them with insufficient cash to pay for their supplies.

Unfazed, Herscu was still living the high life. When his daughter Michelle was married in June, Herscu threw a $3 million bash for 600 guests at his Toorak mansion. The gap between appearance and reality was total. Hooker shares drifted to $1.30, and Herscu announced a $1 billion asset sale to reduce gearing. Simultaneously his private company Hersfield also announced the sale of about one-third of its property assets. The big items in the Hooker sale were its three US malls, which were increasingly looking like white elephants.

A monument to greed

Hooker shares slumped to $1. The market is rarely wrong when it takes a dislike to a stock in the way it was now trashing Hooker. The real problem—not readily apparent to share market investors—was that Herscu was double-geared. He had hocked Hersfield to the hilt to buy Hooker shares. To service Hersfield's interest bill, he needed strong dividend income from the Hooker shares. In this situation, it was financial stupidity to erode Hooker's profitability. But Herscu had done precisely that by loading Hooker with debt and committing it to the enormous mall projects, from which no cash flow could arise until completion.

Herscu had dug his own grave. On 19 June it was revealed that some large credit facilities had been withdrawn. A meeting was called of Hooker's Australian and international bankers. Herscu announced that Richard Grellman of KPMG Peat Marwick had been 'invited . . . to assist management in the preparation and implementation of the business plan, with a view to a satisfactory restructuring of the company'. This fragment of financial code was decrypted instantly by the markets. Grellman—a top receiver and liquidator—was there as the company doctor and, if necessary, undertaker. The shares went down to 64 cents and it is difficult to understand the mentality of those who bought.

Grellman was not assisting, but in charge of, the asset sales. Although Herscu was still chief executive this had become a courtesy title. The role change was quickly demonstrated when the corporate jets and penthouses were offered for sale: a clear sign in any empire that the corporate cowboy had lost control. Under Barry Glover, Hooker's corporate overheads had amounted to a mere $5 million a year. Under Herscu they had ballooned to $25 million in the space of four years. Hooker possessed

279

two corporate jets—a Hawker Siddeley 125 and a Gulf Stream—and several apartments in Manhattan.

The best asset left standing was the chain of Australian real estate agencies, which were eventually sold to Richard Beck. As Beck naturally wanted to keep the L.J. Hooker name for the agency, a condition of the deal was that Hooker Corporation should change its name to Halwood Corporation. As the Hooker/Halwood liquidation dragged on for years, Beck spent considerable time objecting whenever finance writers referred to Hooker, demanding that they should call it Halwood. As Hooker was the name it had been known by for a generation and the name it had gone broke under, this was largely a forlorn effort. However, he was correct about one thing: the Australian real estate chain had always been a good business.

The US assets, which had cost so much, were generally dogs. The hypermalls had cost some $600 million and were worth maybe $400 million on the market, and then only if they were completed. Hooker had spent another $250 million on B. Altman, Bonwit Teller, Parisian and Sakowitz, and they were worth perhaps 70 per cent of that. The Merksamer jewellery group had been bought as a profitable 22-store chain, but was expanded by Herscu into an 80-store lossmaker. The US housing division lost money. In Australia, Hooker's great land bank built up by Campbell and Glover had been largely sold to finance the US investments.

Hooker's two major lenders were Westpac and the Commonwealth Bank. Their task of cleaning up the mess quickly and cleanly was greatly hindered by the fact that another 40 banks had lent money to Hooker in Australia on an unsecured basis, relying on negative pledge covenants. Any action required unanimous agreement, which was almost impossible. An even greater complication was the way Hooker had channelled the funds overseas. Typically, a loan would be raised in Australia, washed through a tax haven and lent in the United States. The chain of transactions made it exceedingly difficult to trace where each dollar had gone. Accordingly, unsecured lenders in Australia had no mechanism by which they could exercise control over assets in the United States. In addition, borrowings in America were usually secured over specific assets. Hooker's sprawling corporate empire at the end encompassed a total of 150 companies, including tax shelters in the Netherlands Antilles and Grand Cayman.

The troubles of Hooker naturally caused grave trouble upstream in Herscu's group of Hersfield companies. The ANZ led the syndicate of banks which had lent money to Hersfield. Their security was scrip in Hooker and mortgages over Hersfield's property. The banks could call upon Herscu to top up his security whenever Hooker shares went below $2.05. It was therefore no coincidence that Hersfield and Hooker had simultaneously been trying to sell properties. The fall in Hooker's share price had triggered Hersfield into selling in an attempt to raise liquidity. The ANZ Bank was concerned because first mortgages on some of Hersfield's properties were held by other syndicate members: the Australian European Finance Corporation, National Mutual Royal Bank and CIBC Australia. The ANZ bought these lenders out to improve its own security position. In July Peat Marwick reported that the Hersfield group could suffer a $25 million deficiency if its assets were not sold quickly.

Tony Hodgson and Andrew Cornell of the insolvency specialist Ferrier Hodgson & Co became receivers and managers of Hersfield. Hersfield subsidiaries had shopping centres at Waverley, Footscray, Mildura, Gladstone Park, Cranbourne, Sunshine, Labrador, Chernside Park, Monash, Sunnybank and Caboolture. Broadly they were second-ranking shopping centres with a tendency to shoddiness in the building. Once they had generated good cash flow, but now it was inadequate to pay for the high borrowings from the ANZ. Other Hersfield projects included the twin towers of the Gas and Fuel Corporation at Prince's Gate and the right to use the airspace above the Jolimont railway yards—a project that had been desultorily discussed in Melbourne for two decades. As usual with a property developer there was the occasional dog. One of the worst in Hersfield was 520 Collins Street, a second-rate building in a first-rate location. The few tenants in the 17-storey office block were soon lured away as desperate developers of bigger and newer buildings offered unbeatable terms. Hersfield directors put a value of $45 million on the building but as the property slump of the early 1990s worsened it was probably worth only a quarter of the amount. Number 520 had other problems too. When the receivers' staff were first inspecting the building one of them noticed something odd about a row of filing cabinets: the tops did not line up. A quick check showed that the floor sloped. A tennis ball placed on it would roll to the centre. The fault was rectified, but it gave the receivers little confidence in Hersfield's building expertise.

Grellman issued a statement in mid-1989 showing that shareholders' funds in Hooker were $537 million but debt totalled $1.6 billion while total liabilities were $1.9 billion. The disturbing figure in this statement was the debt total. Hooker's 1987 accounts had shown total liabilities at $510 million. The 1988 accounts had shown $1.5 billion. Now they were out to $1.6 billion. Plainly there was a strong risk that Hooker's liabilities were in excess of its assets. Hooker shares slumped to 30c, leading a rout in property stocks. Kern Corporation, which had peaked at $3.89, went below $2. Girvan, $1.65 at its height, was 25c. Pennant Holdings, once $5, was down to $1.

Grellman's reign at Hooker lasted just eighteen days. The banks had appointed him as financial adviser on 7 July when they had agreed to a

Table 8.1   Hooker statement of affairs[16] as at 26 July 1989 (all figures in $A million)

	Australia	USA	Other overseas	Total
Total assets	730.1	1 917.1	0.9	2 648.1
Total liabilities	1 279.4	852.2	47.5	2 179.1
Directors' adjustments to book values	289.0	(587.0)	—	(298.0)
Net assets	(260.3)	477.9	(46.6)	171.0
Est. accrued interest 7/89 to 12/89(a)				(127.0)
Est. trading losses 7/89 to 12/89(a)				(115.0)
Deficiency				(71.0)
(a) Provisional liquidator's estimates.				

four-month debt moratorium while Hooker sold assets and got its affairs in order. On 25 July the banks changed their minds and terminated the moratorium; John Harkness of KPMG Peat Marwick was appointed provisional liquidator. Herscu was still swinging punches, even though he had been counted out financially. 'If you look at all the problems and risks in life, you are dead and buried', he said. 'That's what I have learned.'

The estimates in Table 8.1 were prepared by three Hooker directors, Dick McCrossin, Desmond Halsted and Ronald Pearce. The figures illustrate the geographic mismatch between assets and liabilities: the bulk of the debt was raised in Australia but nearly three-quarters of the assets (by book value) were in the United States.

In Australia, Hooker's land bank was still one of its strongest assets. Housing subdivisions were being developed in Sydney and the Gold Coast. They would take years to be fully sold, but they were expected to make a profit of some $247 million. This was included in the directors' adjustment of $289 million surplus to the Australian assets. Other Australian businesses, such as Hooker's home unit developments, car parks and real estate agencies were also expected to realise surpluses. These were offset by a $32 million loss expected in the projects division, comprising the office blocks, shopping centres and industrial buildings still being completed by Hooker. The appointment of a provisional liquidator to Hooker had automatically triggered default clauses in all its major building contracts, and most projects had been put into receivership by either the mortgagees or Hooker's joint venture partner, usually Multiplex. The provisional liquidation also meant that all amounts owing under these contracts became immediately payable. This was the main reason why external liabilities had blown out to nearly $2.2 billion.

Even by the directors' relatively optimistic estimates, the United States was a disaster area. They estimated that the malls and mall sites should be written down by $100 million. Big writedowns were made in other US operations. The value of the retail stores was written down by $155 million, of which $70 million was attributed to B. Altman and nearly $40 million to Bonwit Teller. Guillhot's estimate of Bonwit Teller's worth was looking a lot more realistic than Herscu's. Herscu, incidentally, was still aggressively optimistic. He reckoned that Hooker had net assets of $650 million.

While the liquidator was struggling to sell Hooker's assets, a major slump occurred in Australian commercial property markets in the early 1990s. This left Hooker (now renamed Halwood Corporation) with a heavy deficit and the shares became worthless. The wipeout of Hooker shares was lethal for Hersfield. The Hersfield group had some $390 million in external liabilities at the time of its collapse. However, the value of its assets shrank convulsively as Hooker shares went to nothing and the property values also fell.

By now Herscu had lost all credibility and his personal life was collapsing. At the start of December 1989 FAI Insurances won a court order for Herscu to pay a $2.1 million debt owed by five of his family companies. Herscu fought the application until July 1990, then he and his wife Sheila declared themselves bankrupt with debts of more than $497 million—a record for a personal bankruptcy in Australia. One of his creditors was delicatessen owner Cyril Vincenc in Sydney's Chinatown, who had supplied tidbits for the office party Herscu had thrown on the eve of his daughter's wedding. When Herscu went bankrupt Vincenc was still owed $988. 'You know what his secretary tells me?', exclaimed Vincenc. 'That he lost more than that, so why should I worry? A stupid explanation.'[17]

At this low point in Herscu's life another misdeed returned to haunt him. In January 1990 he was again charged with bribery, this time for paying $100 000 to Russ Hinze, a former Queensland Minister for Local Government. The bribes were allegedly to resolve a dispute over pedestrian and vehicle access to Hersfield's Sunnybank shopping centre on the south side of Brisbane. Herscu pleaded not guilty in the Brisbane Magistrate's Court, but was convicted and sentenced to five years jail. Hinze was also charged over the same offence, but died before he could be brought to trial.

The community still had some sympathy for Herscu. Those who chipped in to finance his defence on the bribery charges included Dick Pratt, Frank Lowy, John Saunders and Sam Smorgon. Herscu's mansion, the Toorak replica of Tara, was sold in 1990. The furniture and even some of the fittings had been stripped out and sold to his daughter.

It should be noted that no criminal charges were ever laid against Herscu concerning Hooker and Hersfield. An Australian Securities

Commission investigation concluded that neither civil nor criminal proceedings were appropriate. Fraud was not a feature of these collapses, just misjudgement on a gargantuan scale. While in jail, Herscu suffered a heart attack. He was released in June 1993 after serving two and a half years. Herscu was bitter, claiming he was the victim of an anti-Semitic campaign orchestrated by state governments and law enforcement agencies and saying he would write a book exposing it all. This was nonsense. Herscu was jailed because he was guilty and very clumsy in hiding the fact. He still showed spirit after being released, saying: 'Of course I am very happy to be getting out of this bloody deal at last. Now I think enough is enough and I am going to get on with my life. It has been a disaster, no question about that, but I will come good again.'[18] But at 64 he was running out of steam and settled down in a modest house in Bentleigh, where he was reunited with some of the furniture from Tara.[19]

The only bright spot to emerge from the debacle was that the operational businesses in Australia—the real estate franchises, the retail chain and the car parks—were sold by Harkness with little or no loss of employment or productive capacity. The projects division was liquidated and the remainder of the land bank was subjected to a scheme of arrangement which returned dividends to creditors over the next five years.

Apart from that, the whole Hooker episode was a monument to the destructive power of greed. In 1985 Hooker had been carefully restored to health. Left alone under its then management, it would have bestowed rewards upon its patient shareholders. In 1985 Herscu had built one of the largest private development companies in Australia. If he had sold it up he could have lived out his life in luxury, surrounded by his family. Instead, he dangled fat fees in front of the ANZ and persuaded it to bankroll him into the Hooker bid. Hooker's management and directors were sacked, much of the patiently accumulated land bank was sold and the proceeds rolled up into a big ball and wagered on the US hypermall concept. When the concept failed, Hooker's remaining shareholders lost their company. Many of them had been too greedy to get out at Herscu's final bid. The banks who financed the disaster lost money on the ill-fated direction of money into the United States to finance massive expansion.

The banks had been reckless, lending huge sums to Herscu without security or even knowing where the money was going to within his empire. One banker said to the writer years later: 'The banks were dazzled by Herscu. One or two who saw trouble coming and didn't lend to him were regarded as wimps'. The non-wimp banks lost huge sums but the biggest loser was Herscu, who not only went bankrupt but took several members of his family and their home with him. Everyone involved in the Hooker affair, innocent and guilty alike, were pursued by Nemesis to their doom. And the wild bastard finished the story in a cage.

9

Qintex: the shimmering mirage

He was someone who started with nothing and he was going to try to make it. He wasn't much interested in having a mundane existence.

John Shergold

First, a disclosure. Christopher Skase was the only corporate cowboy who was a personal friend of mine. I first met him in 1972 when I took over from Des Keegan as Finance Editor of the Melbourne *Sun News-Pictorial*. Among the staff was a young man who was enthusiastic and intelligent, knew a lot about finance for his age, but was still lacking a few of the essentials of journalism. Perhaps my most enduring claim to fame will be that I taught Christopher Skase to type. You had to teach Chris something only once. He was a quick learner.

I had hardly found my desk at the 'Sun-Pic' when the *Australian Financial Review* made an offer too good to refuse, so I quit to become Melbourne Bureau Chief of the *AFR*. On the way out I did the 'Sun-Pic' one more disservice by pirating its brightest finance writer, Chris Skase. He had been working as a C Grade and I got him a B to work on the *AFR*. He was very grateful and didn't let me down. He was one of the best and brightest young staffers I ever had, with a flair for investigation and quite a tough interrogatory manner. The Melbourne bureau was a fairly close office. We went to each other's parties and knew each other's wives and families. We were friends as well as co-workers. Chris (the name he answered to, although he always preferred Christopher) had flair. He was always the best dressed person in the office—although, thinking back on the sartorial standards of Bob Gottliebsen, myself and some of the other writers of the day, that was no great achievement. He always maintained a private inner core, so that we knew little about his personal life. However, it was obvious that he was not going to spend the rest of his life as a finance journalist. He wanted to do something

285

bigger. He said at least once that he wanted to be a millionaire by the time he was 30.

Mixing with the minor entrepreneurs of the day as a finance writer gave him natural access to a career of his own: a path trodden by many finance journalists before him, including Jonathan Binns Were. Eventually Skase impressed three entrepreneurs enough to put up a little seed capital to get him started. I followed closely his first, near-disastrous takeover bid, but after that I was posted to Sydney and we drifted apart, seeing each other maybe four or five times over the next ten years. After he had built the Gold Coast and Port Douglas Mirages he threw a couple of memorable parties to open them and invited a number of his old journalistic mates along, including myself.

By that time he was running Channel 7 and was starting a breakfast business show called TV-AM which was desperately short of business knowhow. At that time I was Editor-in-Chief of *Australian Business* magazine which was desperately short of promotion. There was a natural symbiosis. I offered to put the staff of *Australian Business* at the disposal of his show to give TV-AM some talent and the magazine some publicity. I appeared regularly on the show, which lasted about two years and cured me forever of a habit of early rising. I received no money for appearing on the shows, because I was there to promote the magazine. So we helped each other a bit at a time when we needed each other.

That's about all there is to disclose, and readers can adjust for my biases as they read this chapter.

Christopher Skase was a Melbourne boy, the son of well-known 3DB announcer Charles Skase. He later told a reporter: 'I went through a period when I wanted to be a radio announcer like my father but he went to some considerable lengths to persuade me that the proprietor's lot was better than that of a disc jockey and I slowly came around to his point of view'.[1] After matriculating from Caulfield Grammar Skase spent two years working for J.B. Were. He gained valuable experience but was frustrated at not being able to move more quickly up the tree at the staid old broking firm. He bought an old Falcon and took fourteen months off touring Australia. To keep himself in cash during his odyssey he worked as a railway station sweeper, locomotive engine cleaner, postman, wharf labourer and unqualified roof repairer. He returned to Melbourne determined not to go back into stockbroking but to go into business on his own account. As a first stepping stone he joined the *Sun* and then the *AFR*.

Skase had impressed two businessmen he met. One was Peter Hutchins, a cheerfully rotund market player who ran I. & I. Securities. Another was Doug Shears, a very smart operator in the oat industry. Skase approached them with the proposition that they should put together a little seed capital and back him as a takeover raider. He wanted $100 000 but Shears and Hutchins were not prepared to put that much in, so they scouted for another partner. Hutchins' brother Barry was an accountant with Wilson Bishop Bowes & Craig, where one of the partners was John Shergold. Barry Hutchins rang Shergold, who was then managing director of Brick & Pipe Industries, where his family held a substantial interest.[2] Shergold, who had been appointed managing director of Brick & Pipe at the age of 33, was not averse to backing youth. He was also tired of Brick & Pipe being criticised for being too boring. 'We didn't have any debt and brokers were always telling us we should diversify', said Shergold. 'That was the fashion then.'

None of the bold riders started with less money than Christopher Skase. His family was not rich. Christopher's savings must have been meagre and he was in the middle of a short, unhappy first marriage. Newspaper stories generally credit him with having $15 000 when he set up in Team Securities. That would have been about his total net worth after selling out of a cottage he shared in South Yarra with his fellow writer John Byrne (who would go on to seek his fortune running a string of mining companies). Team Securities began life with $10 000 in share capital and a further $90 000 in subordinated loans. Skase subscribed $10 000, a far greater proportion of his personal wealth than that of each other partner. The original shareholdings in Team Securities were: Griffiths Bros Ltd, 35 per cent (Hutchins); Brick & Pipe Industries, 20 per cent (Shergold): Doug Shears, 20 per cent; WBB&C Nominees (Vic.) Pty Ltd, 15 per cent (nominee company of chartered accountants Wilson Bishop Bowes and Craig); Christopher Charles Skase, 10 per cent. The directors were Peter Hutchins, chairman; Christopher Skase, managing director; Doug Shears and John Shergold.

Skase's three 'big brothers' were entrepreneurs who had done plenty of small deals of their own. Between them they could provide guarantees and some finance for this young man who had impressed them with his enthusiasm and quick grasp of takeover tactics. The aim was for Team to acquire and rationalise companies which were cash poor but asset rich.

These were fledgling days for corporate cowboys. Operators such as Ron Brierley and Robert Holmes à Court were doing their first, small deals. One of their largest handicaps was finance. The banks, which would later prostitute themselves wholesale for the business of the cowboys, were in early 1975 wary about lending to them. One institution which was just starting to get its feet wet was National Mutual Life. It had formed a venture capital subsidiary named Citinational headed by a cheerfully experimental banker, Nick Dawe. At Christmas 1974 he threw a small cocktail party and invited all the fledgling movers and shakers around for a drink. The guest list included David Bardas of Sportsgirl,

Chris Box (who was into bowling alleys) and several others, all of whom were fascinated to see each other there. Normally, big institutions wouldn't let them through the front door, but here was an offshoot of the great National Mutual inviting them for drinks.

Team was formed in October 1974. In April 1975 it announced its first takeover bid. The target was The Victoria Holdings Ltd, a small listed company which owned the Victoria Hotel in Little Collins Street. Victoria Holdings was a sleepy little company which rarely traded. Issued capital was 2.4 million shares. The last sale had been at 70c. Team's bid, through a wholly owned subsidiary Team Hotels Pty Ltd, was at 85c. The largest shareholder was the National Mutual with 17 per cent of the stock. The rest of the register was split widely with the next nineteen shareholders having less than 14 per cent.

And there was a further agenda. Skase's real target was the fashionable Collins Street store Georges, whose property abutted the hotel's. 'Chris had the fanciful idea that if he bought the Victoria he could do a real estate tie up between the Victoria and Georges and eventually get both properties and businesses together', Shergold said.[3] The sheer glamour and social tone of Georges was doubtless a strong attraction for Skase. Georges was the establishment store in Melbourne. It was where Toorak shopped. Throughout his career, Skase would have a strong penchant for upmarket assets.

Skase and Dawe had obviously worked in close conjunction to plan the Victoria bid. Citinational was financier to Team for the takeover and, as soon as the bid was announced, the National Mutual accepted for its 17 per cent. As a takeover it was small beer, but financial circles were mildly impressed. At the age of 26 Skase appeared to have scored a *coup de main* in his first takeover. The Victoria Hotel was a classic undervalued asset. The company owned the freehold of the property, which was one of Melbourne's old unlicensed residential hotels. In the latest accounts it had been valued at $3.5 million, equivalent to $1.45 a share. If Team could pick up the company at 85c, and sell or redevelop the hotel, it stood to make a handsome profit. The company had posted a net profit of $213 000 in the previous year, representing 8.8c a share, so the bid was less than ten times earnings. And there was no alternative buyer in sight.

It looked like a walkover but Victoria Holdings' board, under Stuart Kennedy Blair as chairman, dug in for a siege. Blair was a tough old Scotsman, who had been orphaned at an early age and took a ferocious dislike to the outsiders trying to take over the hotel. Directors rejected the bid without giving a reason. Team stood in the market at 85c, confident that shareholders would rush to sell out. But they didn't. The bid was announced in mid-April but two months later Team had still picked up only another 34 000 shares, or a further 1.4 per cent. Frustrated,

Team requisitioned an extraordinary meeting of Victoria Holdings so that it could put its own directors on the board. At the meeting in September Skase and his colleagues at Team received a rude shock. Although they turned up at the meeting with nearly 27 per cent of the shares they were rolled easily by the incumbent board, which held proxies for 57.7 per cent. The nature of the problem now became apparent. Blair had the backing of all the little shareholders. Many of them were teetotallers from the Victorian countryside, who stayed at the Victoria when they came to the city. They liked the old hotel the way it was: cheap, friendly and dry. They sent their children to the Victoria in the hope that they would be safe from the evils of drink. They didn't trust city slickers who might change it, so they clung to the existing board.

The Team boys were now in a frustrating position. They had acquired more than a quarter of the stock in The Victoria, they had a mounting interest bill with Citinational and they couldn't get control of the company or its cash flow. 'It wasn't a bad deal', said Hutchins. 'We had bought real estate at discount to market and the company had earnings. The asset backing was there but it was going to take time to get it.'[4] Team held a board meeting at which directors decided they had to lift the offer and also to fund their company properly.

Team had to get the Victoria by attrition. In May 1976 it lifted the bid to $1 but acceptances still trickled in very slowly. Then, in July, Team had what might be called a lucky break. The Victoria announced that profit had fallen by 32 per cent and consequently dividend would be cut from five to three cents. The shares fell. Skase announced that his $1 bid would close in a few days. This stampeded some of the shareholders and lifted Team's holding to 49 per cent. Team had won control, but what at first looked like a king hit had turned into a Pyrrhic campaign. In his first takeover Skase had learned a lot of lessons. He would make very few hostile takeovers for the rest of his career. He said much later:

> Everything in round one was totally different to what the theory said it should have been. I had been sitting at the *Financial Review* working all these strategies out, reading and studying, and I was convinced when I left the *Review* in September 1974 that I knew it all . . . Victoria Holdings went not according to Hoyle . . . It went on and on. They were six very sweaty months. We did not have any money. I had a house in South Yarra. Team Securities was paying me $15 000 a year. There was nothing left at the end of the week.[5]

While waiting for the Victoria bid to come good, Team had bought 31 per cent of the tiny Tasmanian company Qintex Ltd at the end of 1975. Qintex Ltd traced its origins to a former Premier of Tasmania, Sir Phillip Fysh. He established a softgoods warehouse in Launceston and his son incorporated the business in 1920 as the public company P.O. Fysh & Co.

In 1953 it was taken over by a local retailer and became Ludbrooks Ltd. In the nickel fever of 1970 Ludbrooks expanded into tin mining in south-western Tasmania. It did poorly at mining and in 1975 it was reconstructed. The Hattam family bought the retailing business and the Ludbrooks name. The company changed its name to Qintex Ltd. Its assets were the freehold of the Launceston store, a little cash and its public listing.

Then in October 1976 Team Media Investments (a joint venture between Qintex Investments and Cleckheaton) bought 13 per cent of Victorian Broadcasting Network (VBN), which operated two Victorian provincial television stations and radio stations in Perth, Mackay and Sale. Again Skase was helped by friends. One large parcel of shares had been held by Griffith Bros. The financing was again done by Citinational. Shergold was on the boards of VBN and Cleckheaton, which was another substantial shareholder in VBN. One other important seller of VBN shares to Skase was the fledgling corporate cowboy, Robert Holmes à Court. Over the years to come, Holmes à Court and Skase frequently appeared on the same share register and on several occasions sold shares to each other. VBN was their maiden deal together.

Meanwhile, the original three musketeers of Team had been drifting apart. Peter Hutchins had sold out of Griffiths Bros, with part of the deal being that he would sell it out of Team. Doug Shears also quit so that he could concentrate on his flourishing cereals business. Shergold decided that the group should be restructured under the aegis of Brick & Pipe. The result (after a couple of intermediate stages) was that by mid-1977 Team's capital was lifted to $1.54 million, held one-third each by Brick & Pipe, Cleckheaton and VBN. The board was Shergold, Skase, and Ted Hauser and Nigel Dick from VBN. Hauser was another businessman who was impressed by Skase but Dick, according to Shergold, was suspicious of him.

The reconstruction meant the removal of several of the original shareholders. Shears and Hutchins quit and there was no longer room for Skase's tiny equity, although he remained managing director. He had a small personal shareholding in Qintex and was on the boards of Team, Qintex and VBN. The VBN board seat whetted Skase's fascination for the media. He quickly appreciated the strong cash flow of the business and was also fascinated by its glamour image.

In the next corporate play Victoria Holdings bought from Colonial Mutual 16 per cent of Skase's first target, Georges Ltd. This deal marked the first rip in what would become a parting of the ways between Skase and his backers. Shergold said:

> I remember clearly we had a board meeting to decide how much we would offer for a substantial piece of Georges and it was about $1.20.

The next Friday night I was at my beach house down at Mt Martha and I remember him ringing me. He was full and excited. He told me he had been successful in getting this shareholding, and I congratulated him. Then right at the last second of the call, almost as an afterthought, he told me he had paid more than he was authorised. The price was something like $1.45. I said: 'Why in hell are you doing that? Are you using your own money?'. He became peculiar, and said we were weak and had no guts. It was the first sign we had a problem with him, because he was never ever going to be beaten when he wanted something.[6]

The board agreed to support Skase's purchase, but then another problem arose. Again Skase hit board resistance. A crucial block of 10 per cent held by Don Trescowthick's Signet group was picked up by Federation Insurance thanks to adroit work by Peter Lawrence, a sharebroker with Roach Ward Guest. Worse, National Mutual—Skase's original backer— sold a stake to Federation. This incident fuelled a deep resentment in Skase, who saw it as the Melbourne establishment defending its own. 'Corporate and social power in Melbourne was largely concentrated in the hands of a few families', he said. 'They do not readily warm to and embrace outsiders, interlopers like myself. I may as well have been from Argentina.'[7] He would nurture this antipathy for the rest of his life.

If Skase were given to self-criticism (a non-existent phenomenon among all of the bold riders) he could equally well have blamed himself for the episode. When he first started Team he approached Lawrence and asked him to stand in the market for Victoria Holdings shares. Lawrence did so, but immediately noticed that the broker for Wallace H. Smith & Co was competing with him. This seemed odd to Lawrence, because there was usually little demand for Victoria stock. Lawrence asked Skase if he had engaged Smiths as well. It was not unusual for raiders to use more than one broker, but it was essential that they should coordinate their buying rather than operate in isolation or opposition. Skase denied strongly that he was using Smiths. What Skase did not know was that Lawrence's firm Roach Ward Guest had a common back office with Smiths. Lawrence quickly discovered that Skase had lied to him. He rang Skase, told him he had discovered the lie and said he would never work for him again.[8] By itself, the episode would not mean much. Skase had behaved foolishly but he was, after all, a young man on his first takeover raid and probably thought he was being clever. However, the episode highlighted a couple of traits that would persist in Skase's career. One was his passion for secrecy. Another was his neurosis about an establishment. Insofar as Lawrence could be called part of the Melbourne establishment, Skase could have had him on side if he had behaved correctly. Skase would later became rather neurotic, blaming other people for his troubles when in truth the architect of several of them was himself.

The first half of 1977 saw a long pause in Team's activities. The partners were apparently taking stock of their position. Team was looking rather exposed. It had liabilities of some $6 million. For this it had majority control of Victoria Holdings, large minority stakes in Qintex and VBN and a substantial holding in Georges. Shares in Victoria Holdings were looking doggy, having slumped to 54c. Team had bought into stocks at a discount to asset values, but needed to lift its earnings to service its debts and capital. Skase had gleaned some valuable experience but had scored no brilliant victories or quick riches. He was spending most of his time at the Victoria or its teetotal counterpart in Adelaide, the Grosvenor Hotel, which Team had also acquired.

Team underwent another shuffle in 1978 when the up-and-coming rag trader Abe Goldberg acquired control of Cleckheaton and discovered that it held one-third of Team. Goldberg did not dislike Team but he did dislike holding minority interests. He offered either to buy out the other Team partners or to sell to them. He was bought out by Brick & Pipe, which simultaneously bought out the VBN holding to make Team a wholly owned subsidiary of Brick & Pipe.

By the time Goldberg arrived it was becoming clear that Skase would go. Skase was on the boards of Team, Qintex, Victoria and VBN but he no longer had equity in Team, which had been his whole purpose in launching the company. His only stake was a small holding in Qintex. He was still managing director of Team, but as an employee. Shergold and the others who were providing the capital wanted him to behave like an employee, but Skase had always wanted to be on his own. The relationship with Shergold was becoming uneasy. Shergold praised Skase as a hard worker, but was unsettled by the young managing director's trait of keeping his own counsel. In the first September at Team, Shergold had invited Skase and his wife Elizabeth to a box at the football. The party enjoyed themselves and parted with a loose invitation—never taken up—for the Skases to join Shergold at Mt Martha one weekend. It was not until seven months later that Shergold learned that the Skases had divorced a few weeks after the football game. In all that time, Skase had been working in the next office to Shergold and had never mentioned the fact. Shergold was stunned by Skase's intense privacy. 'He wasn't someone who was going to tell you everything he knew', said Shergold.

A split was inevitable. It was triggered in May 1978 by an item in the Melbourne *Herald* saying that Qintex had taken a 9.9 per cent placement in the small listed company, Lustre Jewellery. Shergold was surprised, because the investment had been unauthorised, and called a board meeting for Skase to explain. 'He told us we were too slow. He wasn't going to hang around and work with people like us', said Shergold. 'By that time Team wasn't doing much so he was obviously going to do his own thing anyway. He was someone who started with nothing and he was going to try to make it. He wasn't much interested in having a mundane existence.'

Skase on his own

Skase resigned all his Team posts. At Goldberg's suggestion he was given a severance payment which he used to buy Team's 34 per cent holding in Qintex Ltd, where he was managing director. After Skase left Team he never spoke to any of its directors again. Team would become part of Brick & Pipe; over the years the investments in the Victoria and the Grosvenor would do reasonably well for the company. But they would have been too mundane to interest Skase, who was at last completely on his own.

Or not quite completely. At a Hutchins Christmas party after his divorce Skase had met Pixie Frew, wife of motelier George Frew who had founded the Commodore chain. Pixie had been raised at the right Melbourne schools without ever becoming a social snob. She was a warm-hearted, effervescent blonde in her second marriage and several years older than the young Christopher. They fell in love and Skase became her third husband. In lieu of a dowry she brought him four daughters. He treated them as his own. 'When I married Pixie the youngest was five, so I was lucky I missed all the nappy stage', he said later. 'Four teenage daughters at the age of 27 and putting together a business group is, to say the least, a challenging domestic act to balance.'[9]

When Skase took it as his own Qintex had net assets of $400 000. But half of that was a debtor who had gone into receivership after having bought the freehold of the old, rundown Ludbrooks store in Launceston. With a staff of one, and working out of his kitchen, Skase threw himself into the battle to clean up and control Qintex.[10] He cemented his control of Qintex by adopting an 'executive equity participation program' under which executives of the company took stock and options in lieu of salaries. By the start of 1979 Skase had issued himself—with shareholders' approval—800 000 10c shares paid to 1c each. This meant he had picked up another 8 per cent of the company for an outlay of $8000.

Qintex sold the Launceston freehold and looked around for acquisition targets. Skase settled on the jewellery business, where there were some small listed companies which tended to be undervalued. He took a 43 per cent stake in Lustre Jewellery, then bid for Hawke Australia. Qintex became profitable and returned to the dividend lists. It was only a 1c dividend, but that was as much as Skase had paid on deposit for 8 per cent of the company. In March 1979 he raised his sights by bidding

$4.5 million for the 126-year-old Hardy Brothers in an agreed takeover. Hardy Brothers was a luxury retailer, operating at the top of the jewellery and gift market. Part of the finance was raised by selling Qintex's remaining holding in VBN. The rest was financed by Tricontinental Corporation, still under the control of Sir Ian Potter at that stage, and by the Melbourne branch of the Commercial Bank of Australia.

The Hardy acquisition stretched the tiny Qintex balance sheet. The 1979 accounts showed that current liabilities at $4.2 million were uncomfortably larger than current assets of $3.6 million. If Qintex had followed custom and made a provision for its 1c dividend the gap would have been even larger. However, Skase took bonus shares instead of dividends. This served the double purpose of easing the strain on Qintex's balance sheet and cash flow while increasing his holding in the company. Skase was creeping towards personal control of Qintex. He issued more shares paid to 1c to executives, including himself. Qintex also made a one-for-seven cash issue underwritten by Eric J. Morgan & Co. Shares which were not applied for were allotted at the discretion of the directors. Morgans had won the underwriting because Skase had formed a friendship with a young, aggressive sharebroker named Tom Klinger. In the following year Klinger moved to McIntosh Griffin Hamson and took Skase's business with him. He would become the leading sharebroker associated with the rise of Qintex.

Qintex profits grew, but so did its appetite. It soaked up some more shares in Lustre, then made a bid for the 51 per cent it did not own. More ambitiously, it bought a 6 per cent holding back in VBN and bid unsuccessfully for another 44 per cent of the stock. In 1982 Qintex overbid Abe Goldberg in a raid on the investment company Industrial & Pastoral Holdings, with the aim of making it a vehicle for the group's real estate interests. Qintex acquired 7 per cent of Tasmania's biggest car dealer, Nettlefolds Ltd, and made a bid for the old Brisbane retailing business of Rothwells, which had turned into a cashbox. As we have seen, Laurie Connell won the battle for Rothwells.[11]

The strategy being followed by Skase was clear. He had built up a strong position in the jewellery trade, providing Qintex with cash flow. He was buying strategic stakes in companies where the share price was well under asset backing. His main problem was that his cash flow was inadequate to service his interest bill. Meanwhile, he had secured the one absolutely essential foundation stone of any entrepreneur: like Alan Bond, Robert Holmes à Court and Laurie Connell, he had control of his own company.

As a finance journalist he had been a good investigator. As an entrepreneur he tended to bridle at anyone who questioned or checked him. When Deloitte Haskins & Sells qualified the Qintex audit for 1981 they were replaced by Wallace McMullin & Smail. Skase justified the change on the basis of a tender aimed at cutting audit costs. Deloitte had held that reserves in a wholly owned shell company should have been written off against the surplus received on its sale. Qintex had thought it was not necessary because it had retained the business of the company and had sold only the shell.[12] There could have been legitimate arguments on either side. The point is that Skase did not brook criticism or interference.

Qintex continued its expansionary drive, paying $1.6 million for the Air New Zealand building in Sydney's King Street as a store for Hardy Brothers. Through Industrial & Pastoral, Qintex then picked up 19 per cent of Telecasters North Queensland (TNQ). Skase, always a strategic thinker, had picked Queensland and media as growth areas. TNQ operated television stations in Townsville and Cairns and held minority shareholdings in TV stations in Mackay, Mount Isa and Brisbane. It also operated several regional radio stations. Another asset was five acres of Townsville waterfront facing the proposed Breakwater Casino.

The TNQ board bitterly resisted the presence of Skase on the register. They complained to the Australian Broadcasting Tribunal, leading to an examination of Skase and Qintex that stretched over eight months. The main objection by the TNQ board was that Skase was an asset trader and not a long-term investor, and was therefore not a fit and proper person (in the language of the *Broadcasting and Television Act*) to have a substantial shareholding in the television group. It was certainly true that Qintex profits had been entirely made from asset sales. And Skase hardly helped his own case when he was asked what he considered 'long term' and replied that accounting standards regarded anything over one year as long term.

Skase barely swerved in his pursuit of companies, soaking up shareholdings like a sponge. He picked up a 48 per cent holding in the Queensland timber and diversified merchant Wilkinson Day & Grimes, then used that as the vehicle to buy Universal Telecasters Queensland (UTQ) which operated Channel 0 in Brisbane. The $34 million cost of UTQ was funded by Wardley Australia, the local arm of the Hong Kong & Shanghai Bank.

Skase seemed hardly to have paused for breath in his headlong acquisitions. In less than ten years he had gone from an almost penniless reporter to control of a corporate empire with gross assets of more than $100 million. He was thinking big. He talked of the UTQ acquisition as the first step in the creation of a fifth east coast media group, behind Packer, Fairfax, Herald & Weekly Times and News. He equated his purchase of Brisbane's Channel 0 with Rupert Murdoch's arrival in Sydney in the late 1950s. Sceptics thought the price of $34 million for the station too high. In a hotly contested takeover just previously, Fairfax had bought the second-rating station in Brisbane, BTQ-7, at a multiple of 32 times earnings. That was regarded as too high; but now Skase had paid 40 times earnings for the third-rating station. Skase's rationale was that Channel 0's profits were improving and that the price–earnings multiple for the 1984 financial year would be only 30. And in July TVQ-0, along with the rest of the 0/10 network in Australia, would become the exclusive telecaster of the Los Angeles Olympic Games.[13]

Under broadcasting laws at the time, Skase was allowed to hold more than 15 per cent in two television stations, but could not hold more than 5 per cent in any other station. Together with his TNQ holding, the purchase of Universal Telecasters put him in breach of the law and he had six months in which to divest a station. So Skase sold his TNQ holding down to 5 per cent.

Pausing for a moment, let us look at the accompanying diagram (Figure 9.1) which shows the structure of the Skase empire circa May 1984. Skase stood at the top of a pyramid of 48 and 51 per cent owned companies. Through his family company, Kahmea Investments, Skase controlled 48 per cent of Qintex Ltd. Qintex owned 49.9 per cent of Hardy Bros and 51 per cent of Industrial & Pastoral. Further down the chain, Industrial & Pastoral owned 50.5 per cent of PML Property Trust, 19.1 per cent of TNQ and 48.8 per cent of Wilkinson Day & Grimes, which then wholly owned UTQ. One benefit of this structure was that control could be retained at the top for relatively small outlay *if cash issues were made by the downstream companies*. In 1985 Universal Telecasters would make a $28 million issue which cost Skase nothing and recouped the bulk of his purchase price. Another 1985 issue was by Industrial & Pastoral for $16.7 million. To maintain its controlling 51 per cent equity in Industrial & Pastoral would cost Qintex Ltd less than $9 million. And Skase maintained his equity in Qintex—then up to 58 per cent—by means of Kahmea receiving 2.1 million 1c shares which would cost $4.85 to convert to fully paids. Very neat. Equity was raised in the downstream companies and the cost impact was diluted as it went back up the chain. The funding needed at the top level—by shareholders in Qintex Ltd—was very small. If Skase could not even meet that (and remember he started with virtually nothing) the board could always be persuaded to issue him partly paid shares which would maintain his equity.

The *wunderkind* kept moving. He recruited Sir Lenox Hewitt, the former secretary of the Prime Minister's Department and chairman of Qantas, to his board. When Skase ended his first ten years in charge of Qintex in 1985 the directors gave him a ten-year management contract to stay at the helm. They also issued 750 000 shares to his Kahmea Investments. The shares were only 1c paid; they would cost $3 to convert to

Figure 9.1   The Skase empire circa May 1984

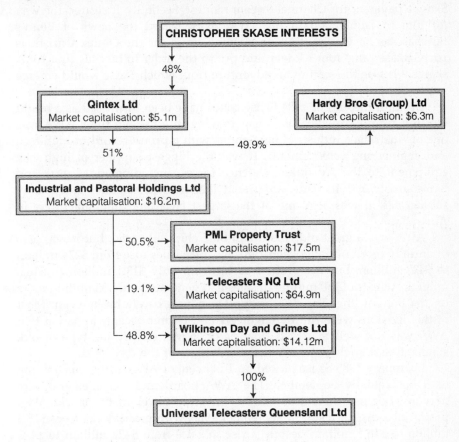

Source: *The Bulletin*, 22 May 1984

fully paids. Elsewhere in the group Industrial & Pastoral bid for Nettlefolds, in which it now held 34 per cent.

At any time Skase had a number of potential target companies under consideration. One, which seemed way out of his league, was the old electronics giant Amalgamated Wireless Australasia Ltd. He hesitated for a while because one of AWA's assets was television station QTQ-9 in Brisbane. Skase had just undergone two extensive Broadcasting Tribunal inquiries and any move that would have given him two stations in one city was bound to spark a third. But Alan Bond also wanted QTQ-9 and had twice implored AWA to sell it. A few days before Christmas 1984 Bond made an offer to good to refuse. AWA accepted, pocketing a $42 million profit on the deal which boosted the group's sagging earnings and enabled it to pay a bonus dividend that year. The deal was good news for Skase on two counts. Firstly, the price paid by Bond made Skase's payment for Channel 0 seem modest. Secondly, it cleared the way for him to launch a raid on AWA. Skase heard the news of Bond's purchase as he was putting on evening dress for the Qintex Christmas party. Skase rang Tom Klinger and put in the order to buy his first AWA shares.[14] It was the start of an adventure from which Skase would emerge intact, but only just.

Up until the end of 1984 Skase could have been dismissed as a bright kid. But from early 1985 he began moving into the big time. AWA was one of Australia's industrial blue chips, with a proud record in high-tech and engineering achievements. It was the biggest supplier of high-tech equipment to the Australian defence forces, including radar gear and Barra sonobuoys. It made equipment that tracked satellites and enemy submarines. It was also one of the largest electronics manufacturers in Australia.

AWA was a great old Australian blue-chip industrial, but it was also financially moribund. Between 1981 and 1984 sales rose from $274 million to $422 million, but net profit was up from only $13.1 million to $18.3 million. An extra $150 million in sales had generated only $5 million more on the bottom line. The fine array of products barely broke even. Most of the divisions were run by engineers and it later became apparent that AWA was not well managed financially. It was exactly the type of old, stagnant, asset-rich company that the raiders of the day loved.

In January 1985 Skase picked up 1 per cent of AWA, lifting his holding to 5 per cent by September. The AWA board and management were nervous, because there was another mystery buyer in the stock. AWA produced a dismal result in September 1985, with profit down from $18.3 million to $16.6 million despite a rise in sales from $422 million to $492 million. Then the mystery buyer was unveiled as Holmes à Court, who had acquired a further 5 per cent of AWA. It was in this atmosphere that a worried management gave an ambitious 23-year-old accountant called Andrew Koval authority to start trading foreign exchange. Koval's profits enabled AWA to rally shareholders and stave off the raiders for a while. In early 1986 Holmes à Court sold his holding to Skase, who by then had 14.9 per cent of AWA.[15]

Simultaneously, Skase began developing his ideas on property and the hotel industry. In March 1985 he paid $9 million for a 4.2 hectare site at Southport, at the northern end of Queensland's Gold Coast. Skase announced that he was going to build a 400-room international hotel on the site for $50 million. This did not evoke much attention at the time because the Gold Coast had at least five other announced international hotels being planned. But it was a quantum jump for Skase and took him on to a new plane. Instead of being a corporate raider and takeover merchant, he was planning to build something of his own. Lurking in the Qintex empire for several years had been the PML Property Trust, managed by a company named Presmarda Ltd. In July 1985, PML sacked its trustee and announced that it was going to switch direction. Previously the main assets of the trust had been Melbourne-based, mainly the Preston Markets and the Leonda reception centre at Hawthorn. Now PML said it was going to switch into the purchase and development of Queensland tourism properties. With the benefit of hindsight, this was an excellent strategy. The best move any property investor could have made in 1985 was to get out of Melbourne and into Queensland. PML raised its equity base from $20 million to $60 million to fund two resorts. One would be the Southport hotel on Main Beach. The other was a hotel projected to cost $85 million at Port Douglas in north Queensland. Qintex had already signed a letter of intent with Sheraton Pacific to operate both hotels.

The vision was great, but PML unitholders were ridden over rough-shod in the process. Through IPH, Skase controlled 54 per cent of PML's seven million units. He announced a one-for-one issue of units at $2.50. Typically for a Skase issue, the price was pitched close to the market price of $2.80. But Qintex was also granted options over ten million units at $2.50 because it would be in charge of 'project identification'. In addition, Skase announced a planned placement of 80 million units, of which Qintex would hold 50.1 per cent. The result was that PML's capital would explode from seven million units to 104 million and the equity of the existing unitholders would be greatly diluted.

During his teenage odyssey around Australia, Skase had discovered the romantic but rundown Port Douglas and its Four Mile Beach. He would later tell reporters how, with a sharp stick, he had sketched a plan on the beach sand for a resort among the coconut palms. In the event, the Port Douglas development owed a lot to the cooperation of the Queensland Government and its agencies. The Queensland Government had five parcels of freehold land on the Port Douglas coastline and had transferred them to the Queensland Tourist and Travel Corporation (QTTC) for development. The best block comprised 120 hectares of Crown land with a two-kilometre frontage on Four Mile Beach, so long and flat that it is said to have been used as an emergency airstrip in World War II. A year before the government land became available, Qintex had bought two blocks of units at Port Douglas and commissioned a pilot study on the area. When the QTTC got the land Skase offered it equity in PML Property Trust as part consideration for the land. From the start, Skase envisaged a low-rise international hotel on the site, with condominiums and a world-class golf course.[16]

This looked a serious gamble. Qintex until then had been well geared but tolerably diversified. Now it looked like putting a lot of eggs into one basket as it speculated on the future of Queensland tourism. One hotel would be in the Gold Coast, which had a plethora of hotel developments. The second would be in an area that looked impossible: nobody had ever built a first-class hotel in the Australian tropics. To get there, visitors would have to fly to Cairns Airport and find a car or bus that would take them the next 80 kilometres north to Port Douglas. It was visionary stuff and financial history is unfriendly to visionaries.

But Skase could count on a lot of local support. In August 1985 he had, in a well-publicised move, shifted the head office of his group from Melbourne to Brisbane. There need be no gainsaying that Skase genuinely believed in the future of Queensland. He had spent some time there on his working tour of Australia and he had great confidence in the future of the state. He owned one of the Brisbane television stations and was developing two hotels in the state. He had more assets in Queensland than anywhere else. Nevertheless, it was a shrewd publicity move designed to get maximum sympathy from Queenslanders. Qintex was still fairly small by Australian corporate standards, but anyone shifting head office from a major state to Queensland could be assured of a friendly welcome. Joh Bjelke-Petersen's government was particularly happy to see a thrusting entrepreneur arrive. In an interview with the *Australian Financial Review* Skase compared Queensland to California and said its growth was a long-term trend. 'If you back Qintex, you back Queensland', he said.[17]

The Melbourne boy was unrepentant about turning his back on his native city. His market forays had frequently brought him hostility from Melbourne's old-boy network. They thought he was cocky and he despised them. 'The Melbourne establishment may think what it likes but they are dying along with their city', he said. 'Look around the world and you'll find that all the cold-climate cities that based their economy on manufacturing are dying.'[18]

The Qintex empire was still frantically active as 1986 began. The Gold Coast City Council approved the plans for the Southport hotel, whose estimated cost had now risen to $75 million. Qintex kept doing other small deals. It dumped the 64 per cent stake it had accumulated in Nettlefolds, while Industrial & Pastoral Holdings acquired a one-third interest in a puzzling group called Queensland Merchant Holdings. But the big action was in AWA, where Skase bid $6.30 a share for the company in May. This bid attracted serious attention. It was the highest price AWA shareholders had seen in years, capitalising the electronics group at $360 million. The most obvious attraction to Skase was AWA's media interests, which totalled eight radio and two television stations. Three of the radio stations were in Mackay, Townsville and Cairns. In interviews, Skase said he was interested in all the defence manufacturing operations as well. Skase was bidding 21 times AWA's 1985 earnings and was determined to win, believing he perceived an undervalued situation.

Skase was wrong. AWA defended bitterly but the truth was that its manufacturing profits were going backwards. Skase eventually lifted his offer to $7 but was bought out of his stake by Capita and Pacific Assets, acting as white knights on behalf of AWA. Skase took a $13 million profit grudgingly, but he had narrowly escaped disaster. A few weeks later, AWA announced a $50 million loss due principally to foreign exchange and the company went into a tailspin from which it took six years to recover. Despite several changes of management, its great manufacturing operations seemed incapable of generating more than marginal profits. The white knights took a bath. If Skase had won AWA he would have gone broke in 1986 instead of 1989.

The luxury hotels were about to become a reality. The next problem was to finance them. The PML Property Trust, renamed Mirage Resorts Trust, was undergoing its huge capital expansion. Industrial & Pastoral, which had been capitalised at only $13 million in mid-1985, was faced with the challenge of finding nearly $100 million to maintain a 50 per cent equity in the trust. Industrial & Pastoral raised some $30 million from sales of comparatively small investments and another $30 million from a share placement in November 1985 to Qintex Ltd and institutions. The placement was handled by McIntosh. A year later I&P raised a further $35 million in a one-for-two rights issue to shareholders. The fact that so much money could be raised by such a small company is an index to the temperature of the boom by that time.

Both Mirages were magnificent resort hotels. They were low-rise buildings, brilliantly landscaped by architect Desmond Brooks. Both featured a see-through look in the foyer. As guests entered the Southport Mirage they could see straight through the picture window on the far side to the surf rolling in on Main Beach. Guests frequently halted in the middle of their arrival just to admire the view for a minute or two. The interiors were littered with objets d'art.

The Port Douglas Mirage was even more stunning. Again it was low rise with no part of the building above the height of a coconut palm. The hotel was surrounded by pools, making it appear to float on a lagoon. Several of the pools had carefully sculpted little beaches with their own sand. These safe, shallow pools were perfect for children or anyone who did not like to risk running into a sea wasp in the ocean off Four Mile Beach. Stretched on a deckchair at the water's edge, sipping a pina colada and watching the technicoloured sunbirds flitting through the tropical foliage, the whole price of the trip to Cairns and the Mirage suite seemed suddenly worthwhile. More than 110 hectares of the site were devoted to gardens and lakes. Guests could go for walks on the winding paths through the shrubbery, most of them lined with Madonna lilies. The more energetic could play a round on the 18-hole golf course designed by British and Australian Open winner Peter Thompson and which for a while boasted a three-metre crocodile on the 13th fairway.

The real money in both resorts was in the accompanying condominium development. The condominiums were built in the same tropical style as the hotels. Buyers had to undertake strict covenants to keep them clean, renovated and in the same style. The hotel undertook to service them and guaranteed a minimum annual tenancy for anyone who wanted to let their condominium. A shortage of land meant that Skase could build only 50 condomiums on the Southport site, but he had room for more than 500 at Port Douglas. Sales of condominiums would provide a cash flow while the hotels were getting started and would reduce the capital cost. And as owners required them to be serviced in future, they would provide a continuing cash flow for the hotel operator.

As if Skase did not have enough on his plate, he now invaded the United States. In December 1986 he announced the formation of Qintex America Inc, which would be capitalised at $250 million. It would invest in the same areas as Qintex: media, entertainment, leisure and property. A few weeks later Qintex America made its first investment, buying 41 per cent of Hal Roach Studios Inc for $US33.6 million. Hal Roach's main business at that time was the 'colorization' of old black and white movies. This seemed an enormous price to put on Roach, which had made losses in the previous four years and whose balance sheet disclosed assets of only $US14 million. Further, Roach had only 49.5 per cent of Colorization Inc, which was the most promising asset.

Undaunted, Qintex America plunged onward. In early February it bought 51 per cent of Princeville Development, which had the Princeville Hotel on the verdant Hawaiian island of Kauai. This was a truly exotic location. The Princeville Hotel was perched on an outcrop on one side of Hanalei Bay. The headland opposite, which could be seen from most of the hotel windows under the redesign proposed by Skase, had been chosen as the location for the mythical Bali Hai in the movie *South Pacific*. On the beach below, Mitzi Gaynor had sung 'Gonna Wash that Man Right Outa my Hair'.

Back in Brisbane Skase maintained a determinedly high profile by having his associated company Queensland Merchant Holdings sponsor the Brisbane Bears. QMH put up $550 000 to underwrite Queensland's first Australian Football Rules team until a sponsor could be found or the team floated publicly. In the tribal world of Melbourne football club loyalties Skase had been an Essendon supporter, but now he became a wholehearted Bears fan. Unfortunately, their form in the first few seasons never repaid his enthusiasm although he helped to give them a great ground at Carrara behind the Gold Coast.

In 1986 the Federal Government made a fundamental change in media ownership policy. Previously nobody had been able to own more than two television stations. Now an individual or company could own as many television stations as they liked as long as the reach did not extend beyond 60 per cent of the population. But there could be no cross-ownership of newspapers, television and radio stations. In the words of Paul Keating, they could be 'princes of print or queens of the screen'. Skase quickly decided to look for buying opportunities in television. 'We knew there would be a loose cannon somewhere, but we didn't know where', he said later.

The 'loose cannon' turned out to be Fairfax. In July 1987 Skase made his biggest purchase yet, buying the Channel 7 television stations in Brisbane, Sydney and Melbourne from John Fairfax Ltd. The deal instantly made Skase the second biggest player in Australian television. The announced price tag on the deal was $780 million, but the real value was considerably less because of a number of kickbacks negotiated by Skase, including an investment of $100 million for at least three years by Fairfax in Universal Telecasters convertible notes.[19] Skase had paid only $25 million down with another $470 million due in November. Compared with the astronomical prices paid for similar networks in the 1980s, Skase looked as though he had got a bargain. Alan Bond had bought the Channel 9s in Melbourne and Sydney from Kerry Packer for $1.05 billion and Westfield would later buy the Channel 10 network for $875 million. So Skase had bought the number two network in Australia for what seemed a good price, although it would turn out later that he too had paid too much.

Fairfax directors were glad to be quit of the television industry. They had never really been happy in it and their acquisition of Melbourne's HSV-7 in the breakup of the Herald & Weekly Times had turned into a nightmare. Under Fairfax 78 staff were sacked from HSV-7, leading to a staff walkout. Fairfax axed 'World of Sport', a three-hour Sunday show devoted to postmortems of the Saturday matches. The decision may have been correct but it outraged the show's dwindling but fanatical audience and, worse, looked like Sydney cultural imperialism. Under Fairfax HSV-7 even lost its sacred Aussie Rules football rights. Furious Melburnians turned away from the station in droves. Part of Skase's deal when he bought the network was that Fairfax had to fund the losses on HSV-7 for the first year. 'In the first few weeks we ran the station, it was losing a million a week', said Skase. 'The blood was draining out of our fingernails.'[20] Skase took a deep breath and began buying programs. The station—and the network—gradually began recovering from the alarming cash outflow.

Investors in the various listed arms of the Skase empire must have shuddered each time they read of a new acquisition. After almost every major purchase Skase would hit them with a rights issue. Industrial & Pastoral raised $35 million from shareholders in November 1986, then hit them again in July 1987 for a whopping $108 million. In twelve months, various entities in the Qintex group had raised $450 million from share-holders. Apart from the heavy rights issues that Alan Bond imposed on shareholders in his gold companies, Skase made the largest equity issues of any of the corporate cowboys. After making its 1987 share issue Industrial & Pastoral changed its name to Qintex Australia Ltd, thereby creating some confusion with its parent company Qintex Ltd.

Young man in a hurry

Who was this young man who had built an enormous empire from next to nothing in little more than a decade? He was a phenomenally hard worker. He reckoned that if he put 100 hours work into a week he could get through twenty years work in ten. He was definitely a young man in a hurry. 'You've got to give it a go', he would tell interviewers. 'You're only here once.' He had few outside interests. His working day could be anything up to fourteen hours and in one way or another he worked seven days a week. His only relaxation was swimming, but sometimes he had to hit the pool as early as 4.30 a.m. if he were flying interstate that day.

The Skases were a striking and elegant couple. Christopher was slim, olive-skinned and dark-haired, while the blonde Pixie could be both relaxed and stylish. She was a rock of support to him in a marriage that would stand great external stresses. Pixie was his business partner as well. She worked as his secretary, discussed strategies and ideas with him and added many of the stylish touches to the Mirage resorts. Pixie and Christopher were a dedicated couple, travelling everywhere together and sometimes holding hands in public. He treated her daughters as his own. Pixie's unquenchable vivacity must have been a tonic for the hard-working Christopher.

Skase was constantly moving from planes to hotels to offices to chauffeured limousines and back to planes. He read masses of material while in transit and typically conducted several meetings a day. He almost certainly took too much on board. His days tended to get out of hand. The later in the day he had an appointment the more likely it was that he would be late. (I was once MC at a Sydney lunch where Skase was to be the main speaker and present some awards. At the time we started the lunch the Skases were just taking off from Brisbane. They arrived about half an hour late, but the lunch was nevertheless a success. Skase could be an inspirational speaker and the drama of his late arrival added to the sense of occasion.) Decisions that should have been made and implemented in a day or two could stretch into weeks or months before he finally had time for them. His top half-dozen executives worked almost equally hard. Skase insisted that all homework be done and decisions taken within the group. No work was ever farmed out to merchant bankers or corporate advisors, so security was tight and executives were well informed. They all hoped to get rich on Qintex shares and options.

One of his most perceptive interviewers noted several characteristics that made Skase tick. One was total commitment, in that he had no outside interests unless barracking for the Bears could be counted. Others were: having clear and concise business objectives; emphasis on specialisation and pre-eminence in the chosen field; use of long-term strategy, which he called 'the Japanese factor'; avoiding fad industries; and a devotion to demographics, which told him where people were moving and how they were going to be spending their money.[21] It was demographics, broadly defined, that had persuaded him to move into resorts. At the Los Angeles Olympics in 1984 it first struck him that there was a trend towards a larger proportion of adults in the population, who increasingly wanted information, entertainment, travel and leisure.

The hard-driving young entrepreneur had great style. He wore a blue pinstripe suit well, usually with a pink shirt, white collar and a handkerchief spilling from the breast pocket. As he became successful he developed a penchant for big fat cigars, although they probably did his asthma no good. In Brisbane his headquarters was a luxuriously decorated penthouse at the top of Comalco House in Creek Street. The décor was ice-blue. The foyer was littered with antiquities including an Egyptian cartonage mask (circa 1300 BC), a Roman male torso and a Greek vase (circa 320 BC). The entire office was paved with vivid blue and white variegated quartzite mined in Brazil, polished in Italy and imported especially for Qintex. A receptionist answered the phones at one of two solid quartzite desks while at the other a tiny waterfall cascaded from the desktop in a soothing murmur. Skase's trappings oozed opulence, including a company yacht named *Mirage III*. The yacht's drawing room had a gilt-edged, 18th century Rapousse mirror at one end and a blue banquet table and matching silk banquette with pewter lamps from New York at the other. In one corner was a bridge table with Hermes cards and Hermes ashtrays. Christopher and Pixie flew the world in a Falcon jet formerly owned by King Hussein of Jordan. Yet beneath his exterior

Skase was a plain-living man whose idea of a good meal was a hamburger or Pixie's home cooking. There was no question that he enjoyed living and working in opulent surroundings, but at least part of their purpose was to impress the world with how far he had come and to impress financiers. A sumptuous office was almost a prerequisite for borrowing in the 1980s and none of the corporate cowboys had a better sense of style than Skase.

Nearly all the cowboys knew how to enjoy themselves, but Skase must have been the best party-giver of all. His philosophy was that he and his staff worked hard all year (they were forbidden to indulge in lunches), so he was justified in throwing a big bash at Christmas. After he moved to Queensland the parties became lavish. For Christmas 1985 he pitched a marquee alongside the Queensland Arts Centre and invited several hundred staff, associates and friends to an all-night revel with top food, wine and entertainers. In the 37-degree heat the marquee turned into a Turkish bath, but everyone enjoyed themselves enormously and only party poopers left before 2 a.m. Guests, including spouses, were flown in from Melbourne and Sydney on a chartered Boeing 727, equipped with antimacassars adorned with the 'Q' of the Qintex logo. From Brisbane Airport chauffeured limousines ferried guests to the Sheraton. Premier Joh Bjelke-Petersen—triumphant at Qintex's move to Queensland—was the guest of honour.

For the official opening of the Mirage Hotels in 1988 some 200 guests were taken by chartered jet and limousine to both the Gold Coast and Port Douglas hotels. The party lasted three days, featuring everything from a fireworks display, which came uncomfortably close to burning down the Gold Coast hotel, to scuba diving on the Low Isles off Port Douglas. Normie Rowe and Johnny Farnham sang at the dinners as those present drank unlimited supplies of 1984 St Henri. Guests returned home stunned at Skase's hospitality. His fortieth birthday party at his Hamilton home was even more impressive. Guests were driven there in limousines and offered Krug as they arrived. A marquee was pitched on the tennis court and party-goers danced on a reflective floor (gentlemen spent a lot of time looking downwards) until the early hours. The birthday toast to Skase was proposed by Robert Holmes à Court. Guests included Sally Kellerman (the original Hotlips Houlihan from *M.A.S.H.*) and George Hamilton (star of *Love at First Bite*).

All entrepreneurs need to have faith in themselves: to be convinced they are right. Skase had ferocious faith in the rightness of whatever he was doing. Perhaps only such faith could have driven him so far from such an unpromising start. He was very impatient with criticism, whether well or badly directed. From his background in journalism, Skase well knew that much of the irritating detail demanded in corporate accounts and takeover documents has been placed there in an attempt to protect investors. Those who questioned the details of Skase's affairs, however, were treated with scorn. When the Melbourne sharebroker Cortis & Carr queried the executive share allotments being made by Qintex, Skase said he was 'perplexed' at their objections. When the Victorian Corporate Affairs Commission made a string of doubtless annoying inquiries, he thundered: 'During the course of the year, the inquiries appear to have become a wide ranging fishing expedition through our corporate registers, in the hope of turning up some error to justify the inquiries'. When Deloitte qualified his accounts they were sacked as auditors. (In hindsight, Deloitte may have been better off if it had turned a blind eye to Qintex's accounts and been sacked by AWA instead.) When Australian Ratings released a critical report on Qintex in the middle of the company's joust for AWA Skase accused the agency of 'blatant bias'. Australian Ratings had questioned 'the level of subordinated equity, cashflow support, weak coverage ratio and the capacity to absorb an acquisition of the size of AWA'. These questions would certainly be justified in a few years' time.

Good concepts, shaky structure

The great share market crash of October 1987 left few visible scars on Qintex at first, but over the next two years the shares would drift inexorably downwards as the pressure of high debt and thin earnings took their toll. Fortunately, the group had disposed of many of its non-core equity holdings ahead of the crash. The investment portfolio had been $200 million at the height of the bull market, but was down to only $10 million by October 1987. Skase had even managed to sell Channel 0 in Brisbane to Darling Downs Television for $123 million. However, $98 million of the price was not due to be paid until July 1991 and Darling Downs was creaking under the weight of the acquisition.

Analysts and investors who looked at the Qintex accounts were unlikely to be reassured. Table 9.1 shows the abbreviated balance sheets and profit and loss accounts for the main operating company, Qintex Australia Ltd (QAL), through the mid-1980s.

The first point to realise in comprehending this table is that we are looking at the figures according to Qintex's treatment of them. A generally optimistic view was taken of asset values, which meant that gearing was probably somewhat higher than indicated in the table. Even so, the growth in assets was fantastic. In the short space of four years Skase took Qintex from a humble $27 million in total assets to a billion dollars. The growth was funded largely by debt. The capital base remained small

Table 9.1   Qintex Australia Ltd (all figures in $m)

BALANCE SHEET

Year to July	1983	1984	1985	1986	1987
Total assets	27	111	204	336	1 001
Debt	(4)	(46)	(103)	(191)	(516)
Other liabilities	(3)	(26)	(26)	(24)	(40)
Total liabilities	(7)	(72)	(129)	(215)	(566)
Capital	2	3	5	12	19
Reserves	11	13	37	64	115
Minorities	7	23	33	45	301
Shareholders' funds	20	39	75	121	435

PROFIT AND LOSS ACCOUNT

	1983	1984	1985	1986	1987
EBIT	0.5	0.8	4.1	9.7	41.4
Interest	(0.2)	(0.2)	(2.9)	(7.9)	(38.4)
Profit (a)	0.3	0.6	1.2	1.8	3.0
Minorities (b)	=	(1.0)	(3.9)	(4.2)	(5.4)
Profit attrib. to shareholders	0.3	(0.4)	(2.7)	(2.4)	(2.4)
Dividend	(0.6)	(0.6)	(0.9)	(1.8)	(2.2)
Retained earnings	0.4	1.1	0.9	0.1	2.2

Notes:
(a)   Stated income tax paid was negligible each year
(b)   Includes preference dividends

because Skase had to maintain control, but the biggest factor in the growth of reserves was the share premium account, which by 1987 stood at $85 million. This was genuine cash injected into the business. Skase kept capital tight but made several high-priced rights issues. The growth of minority interests is also notable. Much of the empire was controlled by bare majority holdings, so a large proportion of the consolidated assets belonged to others. What cannot be shown in the table is the even bigger empire controlled through large minority holdings. The shares in these companies, where Qintex typically held between 30 and 49 per cent, were consolidated as investments.

The most notable feature of the profit and loss accounts were the very small profits being generated on the growing asset base. This was partly because an increasing proportion of funds was being used to build the Mirages. By 1987 resorts under construction accounted for $236 million of total assets, or nearly a quarter. These were not producing any cash flow apart from a few condominium sales. Looking at the bottom line, the question arises of how QAL could afford to pay dividends. One way was by transfers from reserves, which in 1986 were tapped for $2.2 million. One could almost say that dividends were being paid from the share premium reserve. Another way was by running down retained earnings, which in 1986 fell from $893 000 to $115 000. This was an exceedingly modest level of retained earnings for a company which by then was claiming $336 million in assets and had borrowed $191 million. This is the key to understanding Qintex. Skase could never generate adequate profits on his assets, mainly because he was on a growth path. The vast sums that were pumped into Qintex were dedicated to building assets that did not produce immediate earnings. Unless they could begin producing earnings soon, the group was bound to have problems with the rising interest bill.

While the financial structure was shaky, the concepts were good. One of Skase's achievements was that he quickly welded his Channel 7s into a genuine network. Whereas Nine under Packer and Ten under Murdoch each had long-established common ownership in Sydney and Melbourne the Seven network had always been split, with the Herald & Weekly Times owning the Melbourne end and Fairfax controlling Sydney. Seven had never operated with the same unity as the other networks and the fact that television was a secondary activity for both proprietors did not help. The Fairfax empire had traditionally regarded print as its main activity and its television stations as ancillary. ATN-7 in Sydney made a small profit and BTQ-7 barely broke even, although it was Brisbane's top-rating station. HSV-7 in Melbourne had been the most parochial major city station in Australia, feeding its viewers a relentless diet of football and Australian drama. Under Fairfax it lost the footy without establishing any new image and was losing a million a week when Skase took over.

The station had also been traumatised by the fact that it had had five proprietors in seven months. (Between January and July of 1987 HSV-7 had been owned successively by the Herald & Weekly Times, Rupert Murdoch, Robert Holmes à Court, John Fairfax Ltd and Skase.) 'My first reaction was that Seven Melbourne was a bit like a car which had been pushed downhill over a number of years and had been resting fairly gingerly on the edge of a precipice', Skase said. 'Fairfax came in to rescue it and instead succeeded in pushing it over the cliff.' One TV writer who was allowed to attend a briefing of Melbourne studio staff by Skase and his media chief executive, Bob Campbell, said that for the first time in years someone had made the HSV staff feel like assets rather than liabilities.[22]

Skase and Campbell gave the network a polished look. They bought some good overseas programs but mostly they aimed at making Seven a family network and a sporting network. They gave it high Australian content, including some hypnotic soap operas. In sport, they concentrated on Australian football, golf, tennis and basketball. This was an excellent mix. Golf and football gave them good demographics with males all around Australia and basketball was rapidly catching on with young viewers. Skase shifted his network marketing headquarters to North

Sydney, which contained the highest concentration of advertising agency head offices in Australia. 'You've got to put the players where the ball is', said Skase.

Skase completed the network by buying SAS-7 in Adelaide and TVW-7 in Perth from Holmes à Court. This left him with one station too many under the media ownership laws: a problem he would never successfully address because he tried to hang on to them all for too long. He did it hoping that the Federal Government could be persuaded to lift its '60 per cent reach' rule to 75 per cent of the population. This quite arbitrary rule never made much sense. What it meant, in effect, was that nobody could own a station in each of Australia's five state capital cities but would have to leave one out, usually Adelaide. But it was nonsense, because whoever had the call sign for Seven or Ten or Nine in Adelaide would still have to take their feed from the rest of the network anyway.

Nine and Ten were lobbying quietly to have the law changed to 75 per cent, and were fairly confident of success. The Labor Government could see the sense of the television lobbyists' arguments, but the government had received much flak for allegedly bowing to the wishes of its media mates in the past and wanted to change the law without looking as though it was doing anyone a favour. Skase, in a fashion, resolved the government's problem. Ignoring warnings from the other channels that the situation was heading in the right direction and needed delicate handling, Skase went to Canberra like a conqueror. He arrived at Parliament House in a Mercedes limousine and waited in the back seat for the chauffeur to open the door under a battery of television cameras. Politicians of all parties react badly to such *hauteur*. The Federal Opposition, under John Howard, endorsed the 60 per cent barrier. The government, unwilling to make a political issue out of it, simply dropped consideration of the change. Skase returned to Brisbane, attacked the Opposition and bombarded backbenchers with faxes urging that the change be made. He dropped to the bottom of everybody's agenda and, in the process, angered Nine and Ten who saw him as upsetting the applecart.[23]

Warwick Fairfax took over John Fairfax Ltd in December 1987 and plunged instantly into a financial crisis. Although Rothwells had charged a fee of $100 million for takeover advice, it had not bedded down any of the badly needed sales of assets and Fairfax's condition deteriorated sharply in the first half of 1988. Skase was still due to pay his final tranche of $285 million on the television stations by October 1990. The new men at Fairfax offered to discount the amount if he paid immediately. In June 1988 Skase negotiated a new deal in which the final payment was reduced by about $100 million.[24] As both companies would go broke in the next few years it is hypothetical to argue who got the better of this deal. Probably the best way to view it is as a good deal for both parties. If it

Table 9.2   Qintex Australia Ltd, July 1988 (all figures in $m)

Total assets	2 381
Funded by:	
Debt	1 324
Other liabilities	331
Shareholders' funds:	
Capital	82
Reserves	408
Retained profits	28
Minorities	208
	2 381

had not been done: (a) Fairfax might well have gone into receivership earlier; (b) Skase would not have saved $100 million, which he badly needed; (c) Skase would certainly have been unable to make the payment due in 1990; and (d) Fairfax or its receiver would have had to undertake a legal fight to regain the stations. As part of the deal, Fairfax unloaded $100 million in Qintex convertible notes to Chase AMP for $55 million. That represented an immediate $45 million writedown by Fairfax, but Chase AMP would live to regret the 'bargain'.

The Qintex group's 1988 accounts, produced in October, were worrying. The balance sheet of Qintex Australia Ltd is shown in Table 9.2.

QAL reported a profit for that year of $28 million after paying interest of $87 million. QAL was carrying a frightening level of debt in relation to both assets and earnings. Skase's headlong expansion had left him with some great assets but too many of them were underperforming. The $28 million profit represented a very skinny return of just over 1 per cent on assets of $2.3 billion. Skase was in the position of an FA-18 pilot flying flat out just a few metres above the water. One hiccup and he would be in the drink. The group's interest cover was dangerously low. For every $4 it earned, $3 was going towards footing the interest bill. Or, to put it another way, a 33 per cent rise in interest rates would wipe out the profit. By the time these accounts were produced exactly such a rise was occurring. Between May 1988 and June 1989 Federal Treasurer Paul Keating pushed 90-day bill rates from 12 to 18 per cent.

Any sceptical analysis of Skase's figures made them look even worse. It was Qintex accounting policy to capitalise all development expenses until a project was completed. There could therefore be hefty expenses, including interest, which had not been charged against the profit and loss account. The ratio of shareholders' funds to external liabilities looked bad enough at $725 million to $1.65 billion. It looked even worse if minorities of $208 million were removed. And the $408 million reserves largely depended on asset valuations. The television licences were in the books at a staggering $919 million, ignoring the discounts which Skase had negotiated on the 7s. This valuation also ignored the market value of

Table 9.3   Qintex Ltd, July 1988 (parent company accounts—all figures in $m)

Investments	160
Other Assets	<u>130</u>
Total Assets	290
Funded by:	
Loans from subsidiaries	147
Convertible notes	70
Other debt	13
Provisions	1
Shareholders' funds:	
Capital	9
Reserves	41
Retained profits	<u>9</u>
	290

television stations, which was cracking by mid-1988 as it became apparent that Lowy and Bond had paid too much for Ten and Nine. But a writedown of Skase's stations to their real value would have almost wiped out the $408 million in reserves. Plainly, QAL's asset values were being written up as high as possible in order to cover the enormous debt.

Further upstream, the numbers were smaller but the ratios were even worse. Qintex Ltd owned 53 per cent of QAL. The parent company accounts of Qintex Ltd are summarised in Table 9.3.

Shareholders' funds of only $58 million were supporting debt in one form or another of $230 million. Whether this was covered by assets depended on the value of the $160 million investments. Note 32 in the Qintex Ltd accounts showed that the 53 per cent investment in QAL was valued at $158 123 000. Note 9 to the accounts read as shown in Table 9.4.

The market value of the QAL shares was more than $60 million below book value. If the investment had been written down to market, Qintex Ltd would have had a deficiency in shareholders' funds. The profit and loss account, shown in Table 9.5, was equally alarming. The parent company profit of $4.4 million was very skimpy on $290 million in assets. The profit was struck after charging $23.3 million interest. This meant that interest cover was minuscule. Revenue for the year had included $13.8 million in interest but only $3.8 million in dividends. It was vital that QAL pay higher dividends. It could only do this by generating much stronger earnings from television and the resorts.

For a while, developments looked promising. Qintex Entertainment's first mini-series in America, *Lonesome Dove*, was a runaway smash when released on CBS. In Australia, QAL sold the regional television stations at Mackay and Maryborough to Prime Television for $110 million on a three-year instalment package. However, the share market was turning increasingly bearish on television values and there were doubts whether

Table 9.4 Qintex Ltd investments, July 1988 (note 9 to the accounts)

	1988 ($000)	1987 ($000)
Shares in subsidiary companies		
— At cost	158 123	73 581
Options		
— Listed	1 395	—
Total investments (non-current)	159 518	73 581
Market value of listed investments		
— Shares	94 446	80 656
— Options	3 402	—
	97 848	80 656

Prime Television, already heavily geared, would be able to meet the payments. The market suspicions were proved correct when the Prime deal collapsed in October 1989.

But before then, Skase had stunned the market in March 1989 by selling 49 per cent of Mirage Resorts to Mitsui and Nippon Shinpan for $433 million. QAL retained 51 per cent ownership and a majority of directors on the board. Only days later, Skase sold a 38 per cent holding in Seaworld Property Trust, owner of Seaworld on the Gold Coast, to Peter Laurance's Pivot Group for $73 million. This represented a $22 million profit for Qintex, which had bought the shares from Laurance only a year before.

The markets were cheered by Skase's asset sales, which were said to be funding a large debt reduction program. But then in April he announced the biggest deal of all: the takeover of MGM/United Artists for $1.2 billion. We will not follow this deal through all its tortured convolutions. The original concept by Skase was brilliant and may even have allowed the rest of the Qintex empire to survive. In hindsight, there must be substantial doubt whether Kirk Kerkorian of MGM ever intended to go through with the deal. Perhaps it was always a chimera. Or, if you like, a mirage.

As conceived by Skase the deal would involve the formation of a

Table 9.5 Qintex Ltd (profit and loss account for 1987/88—all figures in $m)

	Group	Parent
Operating profit	25.7	4.4
Minority interest	(15.2)	—
Net profit	10.5	4.4

new public company which would contain MGM/UA and Qintex Entertainment. Qintex Entertainment would buy MGM/UA, which was 82 per cent owned by Kerkorian, for $US1 billion. Kerkorian had a strong attachment to the classic old MGM studio and its lion symbol, so he would buy that back, along with the MGM/UA television operation, for $US250 million. Of the balance, $US300 million would be funded by selling equity in Qintex America to American and Japanese investors. Another $US150 million would be available from cash in MGM/UA, and the remaining $US300 million would be wholly financed by two US banks. QAL would hold 44 per cent of Qintex America, as a vendor consideration for the stake in Qintex Entertainment which it contributed to the deal. Kerkorian had pledged to reinvest $US75 million in Qintex in a manner which was never determined. Although the deal was always referred to as a takeover of MGM, Skase did not really get MGM at all. It was a merger of Qintex Entertainment with United Artists. UA had been forced into a merger with MGM shortly before when it hit the wall because of mind-boggling cost overruns on *Heaven's Gate*: the most expensive—and possibly the worst—movie ever made.

The deal, if it was ever feasible, would have solved several problems. Skase would have got 44 per cent of a major movie house at almost no cost to Qintex. He would have shovelled the lurking and potentially lethal problems of Qintex Entertainment into a vehicle where QE might just recover. He would become a force in the world movie industry and secure valuable film stock for his Seven network. But Skase was dealing in Hollywood, where deals are rarely solid. One old Hollywood saying is: 'We gotta have a contract, or else what do we have to renegotiate?'. Kerkorian had a long history of selling MGM, buying it back and restructuring it. The Kerkorian/Skase deal was never done and the scepticism it generated further undermined the credibility of the Qintex group, which had been eroding anyway. As Kerkorian ducked and weaved and the highly publicised deal looked ever more elusive, support for QAL and its shares faded remorselessly. It was pointed out that MGM/UA had lost $US44 million the previous year and $US88 million the year before.

Typically, Skase was undaunted. He was planning a huge new Mirage resort on the Californian coast. In July 1989 Mirage Resorts was reported to have bought land at Monarch Beach, 40 miles south of Los Angeles. For a group with such global aspirations, Qintex suffered from a disturbing lack of ready cash. It was late paying licence fees for its television stations. Although QAL had produced an increased interim profit of $25 million, interest payments were still uncomfortably high at $65 million.

The Qintex group was almost certainly doomed by this point, but then came the *coup de grâce*. In August 1989 Australia's domestic airline pilots went on strike. The two domestic airlines, Australian and Ansett, were urged by the Federal Government to stand firm. The result was a long and bitter battle which lasted until March of 1990 and broke the union power of the pilots. The airlines almost stopped running in the early period of the strike. Services were chaotic. Passengers found themselves flying in uncomfortable RAAF planes or on domestic aircraft crewed by blackleg pilots from the United States or Yugoslavia. As the strike wore on the airlines became better organised, but during the early period the Australian tourist industry was hard hit. The pain was felt worst at remote destinations such as Mirage Port Douglas, where occupancy dropped to almost zero in the early period.

All three factors combined to crucify Qintex. The high interest rates of the Keating credit squeeze had made investors chary of overgeared entrepreneurs anyway and QAL's share price sagged ominously. In October 1987 the shares had been $4. They sank to $2 at the start of 1988, then drifted down to $1.50 by March 1989. After the MGM/UA bid they slid further, going below $1 in August. One item which did not help was the failure of Prime Television to raise the $110 million to buy the regional television stations.

In September 1989 the MGM/UA deal was derailed by Rupert Murdoch when he bid $1.3 billion. As the owner of 20th Century Fox, Murdoch had anti-trust problems, but the counter-bid tempted Kerkorian and created a problem Skase did not need. Skase upped the ante to $US1.5 billion and asked the backers of the original deal for more money.

The share market took the view that Skase was biting off more than he could chew. Investors ignored leaks that QAL was going to report a $50 million profit for the 1989 year and dumped the shares, pushing the price down to 40c in early October. The MGM/UA bid was aborted on 11 October, sparking a war of words as Kerkorian and Skase accused each other of acting in bad faith.

At first Skase's lenders stayed firm. After all, if the MGM/UA bid was the problem, and it had now gone away (apart from the threatened lawsuits between Kerkorian and Skase), then perhaps the group was back to square one. Then a bombshell dropped as Qintex Entertainment filed for Chapter 11 bankruptcy protection in the United States, saying that QAL had failed to provide $8 million due by the 19th to the US production group MCA Inc. The automatic question was: how come a group that had been about to take over MGM/UA for a billion and a half dollars couldn't raise a measly $8 million to pay its suppliers?

Qintex Entertainment had always been regarded as a sideshow by commentators who analysed the Qintex group. Analysts concentrated on the television network and the resorts. Qintex Entertainment was off the balance sheet, because the QAL holding was less than 50 per cent. As the

Table 9.6   The debt structure

QAL

Senior Syndicate (First charge over Seven Network, 51 per cent of Mirage Resorts and 51 per cent of Princeville)

Barclays	$115m
HongkongBank	$115m
Chase AMP	$115m
Commonwealth Bank	$100m
State Bank NSW	$75m
ANZ	$50m
Long Term Credit Bank	$50m
Bank of America	$50m
Société Générale	$30m
Sumitomo Trust	$25m
Total	$725m

$US Subordinated Facility:

DFC of New Zealand	$100m
Chase AMP	$100m

Separate QAL Facilities:

State Bank NSW	$US85m	(secured on Princeville)
First Hawaiian Bank	$US30m	

There were several other facilities, including unsecured loans and convertible notes. Trustee for the convertible noteholders, who were owed $100m., was ANZ Trustees.

QINTEX LTD

State Bank Victoria	$69.5m	(secured on 38 million QAL shares)
State Bank Victoria	$15.1m	(second charge on SEQ-8)
State Bank Victoria and BNZ	$26.5m	
HongkongBank	$19m	(first charge on SEQ-8)
State Bank NSW and HK		(secured on 46 million ordinary QAL
Bank	$19m	shares and 3 million preferentials)

KAHMEA INVESTMENTS PTY LTD

Tricontinental	$52.5m

---

investment in Qintex Entertainment did not seem large it tended to be ignored. Now lenders discovered, to their horror, the full exposure of QAL to Qintex Entertainment. The Chapter 11 shock was followed by another on 23 October when Qintex Entertainment released its accounts for April 1989. These showed assets of $US214 million funded by $US155 million in liabilities and $US63 million in shareholders' funds. Of the $US155 million liabilities, $US110 million was debt in various forms. QAL had pumped $A83 million equity and $A39 million in loans into Qintex Entertainment. Nobody in Australia had suspected that QAL's exposure to the US venture was anywhere near $132 million. Even worse, other lenders totalling nearly $US80 million ranked ahead of QAL for repayment.

The crisis in Qintex Entertainment started lenders worrying about the

Peter Bunning, managing director of Trustees Executor & Agency. AUSTRALIAN CONSOLIDATED PRESS.

A bold rider. Laurie Connell practises showjumping on Catch A King. WEST AUSTRALIAN NEWSPAPERS

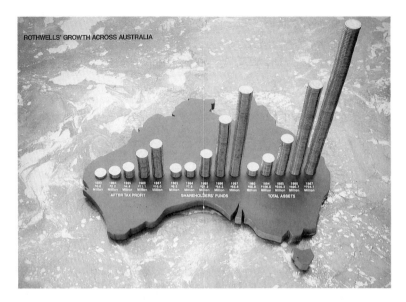

The centre spread of Rothwells' 1987 annual report used piles of gold coins to illustrate how the bank's profits, shareholders' funds and assets were soaring. It would have been closer to the truth if the coins were going downward instead of upward.

Three men in a boat, embarking on a fishing trip off WA. In the bow, facing the camera, are Laurie Connell (in the big hat), Bob Hawke and Graham Richardson. CHANNEL 7

Kevin Edwards, left, with Tony Lloyd. From being student activists with Brian Burke, they rose to become key players in his government and WA Inc. WEST AUSTRA-LIAN NEWSPAPERS

The official launch of the John Curtin Foundation. *Back row* (l. to r.): Denis Cullity (Cullity Timbers), John Horgan (chairman, WA Development Commission), Alan Bond, Laurie Connell, Ric Stowe (Griffin Coal and East-West Airlines), Sir James McCusker (Town & Country Building Society), Rod Evans (Perth city councillor and bookmaker). *Front row*: Kevin Parry, Bob Hawke, Brian Burke, John Roberts (Multiplex), and Sir Ernest Lee-Steere (Phoenix Oil & Gas). Bob Maumill said there were another hundred businessmen in the audience all straining to get into this photo. WEST AUSTRALIAN NEWSPAPERS

Right: Rocket Racer returns to scale after winning the 1987 Perth Cup, with jockey Miller aboard and led by Connell's wife Elisabeth. The horse is beginning to show signs of distress. *Below*: Only a minute after winning the Perth Cup, Rocket Racer can hardly be seen for helpers trying to hold him up. His head is below the clerk of the course's saddlecloth. WEST AUSTRALIAN NEWSPAPERS

The block cleared by Laurie Connell to build his mansion. The house was to be U-shaped with the arms extending up the sides of the block and the base across the beachfront. It would have been enormous compared to the neighbouring houses, which were quite large by normal standards. WEST AUSTRALIAN NEWSPAPERS

The triumphant press conference after Warwick Fairfax had taken over John Fairfax Ltd. Public relations advisor Marty Dougherty at left, Warwick centre and Laurie Connell right. AUSTRALIAN CONSOLIDATED PRESS

Laurie Connell announces the Rothwells' rescue in October 1987. Behind him are Alan Bond (left) and James Yonge (right). WEST AUSTRALIAN NEWSPAPERS

The young man who had it all together.
Brian Yuill in Spedley's Sydney head
office. AUSTRALIAN CONSOLIDATED PRESS

A pudgy Alan Bond with two of his chief lieutenants, Peter Beckwith on the
left and Peter Mitchell on the right. AUSTRALIAN CONSOLIDATED PRESS

Johann Hohenberger, who disappeared mysteriously in the Italian Alps when wanted for fraud in 1974. THE AGE

The man who became chief executive of the National Safety Council of Australia, Victorian Division, under the name of John Friedrich. There was no record of him in Australia before January 1975. His mother later identified Friedrich as Johann Hohenberger. THE AGE

George Herscu, jubilant and aggressive, after taking over Hooker Corporation.
KEITH BARLOW

George Herscu on his way to jail after being convicted of bribing former
Queensland Cabinet Minister Russ Hinze. AUSTRALIAN CONSOLIDATED PRESS

Christopher and Pixie Skase at the spectacular party to open the Port Douglas Mirage. RENNIE ELLIS & ASSOCIATES

Christopher and Pixie Skase on the porch of their farmhouse on Majorca. The author is at the left. Photo taken by Tony Larkins (the Skase's son-in-law). AUTHOR'S PHOTO

Cheerful rag trader and high financier, Abe Goldberg. AUSTRALIAN CONSOLI-
DATED PRESS

At the launch of Farrow Corporation (l. to r.): TV announcer Brian Naylor,
Neil Tresize (Geelong Labor MP, Minister for Sport and former Geelong
footballer), Bill Farrow and David Clarke. FARROW CORPORATION

The Adelaide Steamship board, 1986. From left, Michael Kent, John Spalvins, Ken Russell, Neil Branford and Michael Gregg. ADELAIDE STEAMSHIP

Three contenders in Sydney retailing have a friendly drink after the battle for Grace Brothers. Back to camera is Alan Bond, with John Walton centre and John Spalvins at right. AUSTRALIAN CONSOLIDATED PRESS

Ian Johns, maestro of Tricontinental, with typically aggressive mien. AUSTRALIAN CONSOLIDATED PRESS

John Spalvins opens the door of the redesigned ground floor of David Jones' main store in Sydney. AUSTRALIAN CONSOLIDATED PRESS

At the launch of Adelaide's Formula One Grand Prix, SA Premier John Bannon was at the wheel and Tim Marcus Clark looking on. At the State Bank of SA, their roles were reversed. ADELAIDE FORMULA ONE GRAND PRIX. MILTON WORDLEY

Tim Marcus Clark displays the gleaming board table in the new State Bank SA head office. The board who sat around this table presided over the loss of more than $3 billion. AUSTRALIAN CONSOLIDATED PRESS

Left: One of Australia's greatest salesmen and customer service gurus, Bob Ansett of Budget. AUSTRALIAN CONSOLIDATED PRESS *Right:* Brian Grey, founder of Compass Airlines. PAUL WRIGHT, AUSTRALIAN CONSOLIDATED PRESS

Thumbs up for Southern Cross Airlines, or Compass II. From left, Graham Tucker (director), Sir Leo Heilscher (director and former Treasurer of Queensland), Wayne Goss (Premier of Queensland), Sam Coats (chief executive) and Doug Reid (founder). AUSTRALIAN CONSOLIDATED PRESS

One of only two known photos of Chor Kian Yap, whose reign over Deposit & Investment and associated companies resulted in $150 million vanishing. AUSTRA-LIAN CONSOLIDATED PRESS

Russell Goward, the wunderkind of Westmex, in his Sydney office. AUSTRALIAN CONSOLIDATED PRESS

rest of the group. Some of them had reason to worry. The debt structure of QAL, Qintex and Kahmea is shown in Table 9.6.

Apart from the loans shown in this table, there were further loans in other companies around the empire. The most valuable assets (the Mirages and the television stations) were owned by subsidiaries of QAL. The lenders in the best position were those who were closest to the downstream assets. Better to be a lender to the subsidiary that owned the asset than to QAL; better to be a lender to QAL than to Qintex Ltd; and far better to be a lender to any of those than to Kahmea. Kahmea would have value only if Qintex Ltd could be liquidated at a surplus and that would happen only if QAL were liquidated at a surplus.

QAL had ten first-ranking lenders, known as the senior lenders. They were the top ten listed in Table 9.6. Behind them ranked some twenty unsecured lenders. The senior lenders were owed $725 million. Their attitude would determine the fate of the Qintex empire. The senior lenders met Skase on 24 October. He told them that there was a $200 million shortfall in cash flow and that an urgent injection of $40 million was needed by the Seven network so it could make overdue payments on programs. 'That information was in sharp conflict with an earlier memo from the group', said Ian Smith, who represented the Commonwealth Bank in the negotiations.[25] The lenders had every reason to be concerned. The Seven network was the cash cow for the group. It had evidently been drained of cash to such an extent that it could not pay its own suppliers. The lenders needed to know what was happening before they could extend further credit. They appointed one of Australia's top receivers, David Crawford of KPMG Peat Marwick, to investigate the group and report back. On 27 October the lenders agreed to provide $20 million in bridging finance to the Seven network, which they felt had to be supported. They also agreed to a further $25 million in standby finance, but this was later withdrawn on the objection of Barclays.

By this time another monster had surfaced. Two directors, Fred Davey and Ted Harris, had resigned over fees paid to Qintex Group Management Services. Like many large corporate groups, Qintex had created a management company to handle administration. Rather than each company in the group having its own office, fax machines, stationery, secretaries and so forth, they were provided by a management company which charged the individual companies for its services. Where the management company is wholly owned by one or more of the other companies in a group, there can be no objection to this system. It is efficient and reduces costs.

In Qintex the management company was substantially owned by Skase. This automatically created a conflict of interest. Skase was already collecting a salary as chief executive. Any management fees he collected which were over and above the management expenses appeared to be double dipping. Skase worked hard for Qintex and later said that his salary had been only $50 000 a year. It would have been far better if he had been paid a considerably larger salary in recognition of his efforts and the management company had been a wholly owned non-profit subsidiary. The fees in Qintex were huge, although it should be recognised that the bulk of them were actual costs. In the year to July 1989 fees totalled $32 million, of which $18 million was direct reimbursement of head office outgoings. The other $15 million was for general management and special projects, including a fee for negotiating the sale of 49 per cent of Mirage Resorts. Another $9.5 million was paid in fees between July and October. The National Companies and Securities Commission said that Skase should pay back about $12.5 million. Its chairman, Henry Bosch, said the payments were probably illegal.

In practice, the fees received by Skase were almost entirely committed to servicing the interest bill on his borrowings in Kahmea which in turn had been used to finance his shares in Qintex Ltd. So the benefit Skase received from the fees was not cash but the ability to maintain his 51 per cent stake in Qintex. Banks which financed a corporate cowboy's personal company in the 1980s sometimes demanded that the cowboy should have a management contract with the downstream public company so that the bank could be assured that the interest bill would be met. It is not known, however, whether an agreement of this type existed in Kahmea.

Skase was still trying to persuade the banks to accept a business plan under which he would raise $1 billion to $1.2 billion from the sale of everything except the Seven network and the management rights for the Mirages.[26] It looked unrealistic and Skase had lost credibility. The lenders had received too many nasty shocks. On 9 November the senior lenders met again. By that time the ANZ, Barclays and the Commonwealth believed that the size of the debt load would make restructuring impossible. On the 11th they received Crawford's report. Crawford, who had enjoyed some success with an informal workout of Ariadne Australia, favoured a similar workout for Qintex.

On 15 November, Qintex Entertainment dropped yet another chunk of bad news. The company announced that it expected to report a substantial loss for the year to July 1989 because the realisable value of certain assets would have to be written down following its Chapter 11 filing. The lenders were still digesting this when they met again on the 16th to discuss options. The overseas banks tended to favour a scheme of arrangement, but the Commonwealth strongly supported receivership. On the following day Skase announced his resignation as executive chairman of QAL and proposed a debt reduction plan to the banks. After he left the meeting Commonwealth Bank representatives announced that they would not support a scheme of arrangement. Barclays moved that a receiver be appointed. HongkongBank acted as agent for the syndicate. Following that meeting, Skase himself pre-empted the banks by having QAL apply to the courts for the appointment of Crawford and his Brisbane partner John Allpass as receivers of the Qintex group. Skase's tactic was to preserve the assets from a fire sale until he could implement a court-approved scheme of arrangement. This tactic did not work, as the receivership plodded on for years.

Too much dead money

Skase deserves some admiration sheerly for the distance he went in fifteen years from a \$15 000 start. At the end of the day he controlled an empire with \$2.3 billion in the books as assets. Of course the assets were overvalued and the banks had a far larger stake in the enterprise than he did, but it was nevertheless an astonishing feat which we are unlikely to see repeated for a long time. The most striking feature of his empire was the speed at which it expanded. No sooner was one takeover announced than an even bigger one would follow. The funding was through a pyramid structure, which ensured that the lion's share was financed by lenders and by cash issues to equity holders in companies at the bottom of the pyramid (which conducted the actual takeovers). The impact of the equity issues was diluted further up the chain. At the top, Skase's holding of Qintex Ltd was maintained through issues of 1c contributing shares.

The Qintex group failed because the operating companies could never generate enough earnings to service its intractably large debts. There was debt at every level of the Skase empire. There was also debt in unconsolidated entities such as Qintex Entertainment which lay outside the balance sheet. Skase's policy of headlong expansion left him with some great assets, but many were unperforming. The prime fault was that the group undertook ambitious expenditure commitments without the cash flow to service them. The group cash cow was the Seven network, which was still dragging itself out of the financial mire created by Fairfax. It was unable to cope with all Qintex's commitments.

These were very large. Princeville Mirage on Kauai was undertaking a beautiful and necessary renovation costing \$150 million. As a site for the next Mirage Skase had bought Monarch Beach in California for \$US132 million (\$A160 million). Qintex Entertainment had soaked up \$132 million and still could not pay its bills. Another \$100 million had disappeared into Queensland Merchant Holdings. Even though Qintex had not paid the full price for Monarch Beach these four projects were tying up between $400 million and $500 million, and none of them was earning a cent. Even BHP could barely have afforded to be carrying that much dead money in the middle of a credit squeeze, and Qintex was no BHP.

Queensland Merchant Holdings (QMH) was a black hole. Qintex had lent it $22 million, another $12 million had been lent by QAL and $74 million had been invested by QAL in preference and ordinary shares. QMH's major asset was an investment of $27 million in QAL shares. Other assets were loans to QAL, the subsidiary Lloyd's Ships Holdings which had built *Mirage III* and the ownership of the Brisbane Bears AFL team. Qintex's loans to QMH ranked behind advances by FAI Insurances and Bank of New Zealand, who were owed $30 million. QMH appeared to have been borrowing money from QAL to support QAL scrip on market. Ownership of QMH was deeply mysterious. QAL subsidiary IPH Equities Ltd owned 34 per cent of QMH while the other 66 per cent was owned by Imbercliff Pty Ltd. A Corporate Affairs Commission investigation failed to discover who really owned it. Qintex executive Roger Masters held 41 of Imbercliff's 100 shares, Skase held one share and another 40 were held by Jeserac Pty Ltd. There were six shares in Jeserac. Skase held one and the other five were split between three Qintex executives: Richard Capps, Peter Burden and Geoff Putland. Under questioning, Skase said he did not know if Jeserac was the beneficial owner of its shares in QMH. He didn't even know that he was chairman of Imbercliff. Masters said he held his shares beneficially for Burden, which Burden denied. Capps did not know he held shares in Jeserac.[27]

The Mackay and Maryborough TV stations were sold for $30 million to Gosford Communications, which later floated as Sunshine Television. Monarch Beach was sold for the value of the debt on it. The remaining holdings in the Port Douglas and Gold Coast Mirages were sold to Nippon Shinpan in January 1991 for $123 million. Some of the beautiful antiques which had been such a feature of the resorts' public areas were sold separately. One batch of antiques which Skase had bought for $2 million was knocked down for only $514 000. The remaining 51 per cent of the Princeville Mirage was sold to Nippon Shinpan for a net $70 million. Nippon Shinpan immediately resold the 51 per cent to Suntory. Princeville led a particularly tortured life. When Skase took it over it was a small building with only limited views of the exquisite Hanalei Bay. The old hotel was torn down and a new building was erected; landscaped and designed by Desmond Brooks. Like the Australian Mirages it had a large see-through foyer, featuring green-veined Italian marble and Corinthian columns. It was designed so that a guest walking in could see Bali Hai in the distance. Among other objets d'art the foyer featured a commissioned painting of Captain Cook, a line of 18th century throne chairs and a Louis Seize revolving clock on the reception desk. This sumptuous elegance did not suit the new owners, who decided to renovate it yet again at a cost of a further $120 million. That re-renovation was barely completed in 1992 when a hurricane swept through Kauai and demolished the hotel once more. It was re-re-renovated and opened again in late 1993.

A little addition shows that these sums did not go far enough to wipe out the debts shown in Table 9.6, where the senior lenders were owed $725 million and the next tier $200 million. The big asset left to recoup that money was the Seven network. Crawford held extensive discussions with possible buyers for Seven in a market where television profits were generally declining. The eventual solution was for the lenders to take over the network themselves as de facto owners. In May 1991 the receivers, the senior lenders and Chase AMP entered into heads of agreement which provided for the sale of the network, under terms in which the senior lenders and Chase AMP would provide equity and finance. The sale price was set at $493 million.[28] Under the restructuring the lenders agreed to provide enough money to meet Seven's cash flow needs for five years.

A new company named The Seven Network Ltd became the parent of the group, with three tiers of debt totalling $965 million supplied directly and indirectly by the senior lenders. The token capital in Seven Network was owned by Bob Campbell, managing director of Seven, 15 per cent; Ivan Deveson, former managing director of Nissan, 15 per cent; Peter Ritchie, managing director of McDonald's Australia, 15 per cent; Melbourne lawyer Michael Robinson, 15 per cent; the Seven superannuation fund, 10 per cent; and NSW State Bank, ANZ, Chase AMP, Bank of America, HongkongBank of Australia and Société Générale, 5 per cent each. The Victorian Supreme Court approved this deal, which was justified on the grounds that equity had become worthless in Seven. However, the banks now owned half the equity as well as the debt. Unsecured creditors, who were owed $686 million, lost about 98c in the dollar. Shareholders of QAL, who had owned the network (admittedly through a chain of subsidiaries), were left out in the cold in favour of new shareholders who had been selected rather arbitrarily. Seven Network was refloated as a public company in 1993.

The move to Majorca

For Skase, the mirage had faded. After he first moved to Brisbane Skase had bought two neighbouring old colonial homes in the select suburb of Hamilton. He knocked them both down to build a three-storey, colonnaded white brick house that looked like a small Italianate palace. The neo-classical lines were accentuated by a mural at the end of the swimming pool he installed alongside the house. On the far side of the pool, where the second house had formerly stood, he put in a tennis court. As 1989 drew to a close Skase sold the property for $5 million.

As with all the failed corporate cowboys, there was a call for legal vengeance on Skase. The NCSC was particularly incensed by the management fees he had charged. Qintex was gone and there was nothing he could do in Australia, where he was unemployable, so Skase went to Europe soon after the collapse. Trying to start from scratch again, he went to London for a while then discussed building a resort on the Mediterranean island of Majorca.

Skase was subpoenaed as a witness by the liquidators of Lloyd's Ships Holdings, who were inquiring into its finances. He did not appear when the case began on 19 March 1990 because he was in London suffering from severe influenza. Judge Royce Miller of the Brisbane District Court rejected an application to issue a warrant for his arrest. A week later, Skase appeared and gave evidence—his first public appearance since the collapse of Qintex. His evidence revealed that there had been an extensive dispute over *Mirage III*. The luxury boat had been built by Lloyd's but it was never clear who the buyer was supposed to be. It had never been paid for, on the grounds that it was defective. The press had always depicted *Mirage III* as Skase's personal yacht, but he used it rarely. An engineer's log showed that in 1988 Skase had used the craft for a total of sixteen days. It had also been chartered by his son-in-law, Tony Larkins. The boat had been sold to a German for $5.9 million.

When the hearing adjourned, Skase went overseas again. He kept in touch with the receivers. Allpass said that Skase had been travelling a lot but was always available for consultation. 'He's been a big help', Allpass said.[29]

Skase eventually settled at Puerto d'Andraitx (pronounced d'Ahndrutch) on the south-western tip of Majorca. He rented for $US15 000 a year an old mansion named La Noria ('The Waterwheel'). It had a swimming pool and a small farmhouse to one side. Christopher and Pixie lived in the farmhouse, which was charming. La Noria stood on about two acres of ground of which half was an orchard.

When the Lloyd's hearing resumed Skase failed to appear. He sought leave to appear a week later but this was refused. Two warrants were issued for his arrest but their execution was stayed pending appeal. He flew in a few days late on 16 September, appeared in court on the day he had originally asked for and offered 'unqualified apologies' to the judge for his absence. He explained that he was working as a consultant in Europe, a job which provided his sole source of income for the support of his family, and could lose the contract if he were absent. The contract was with Desmond Brooks, the architect formerly employed by Skase to design the Mirages. Brooks was grateful for the big contracts and fame that Skase had given him and supported the Skases for at least the first year of their exile on Majorca. While in Australia, Skase was also charged with having assaulted a Brisbane *Sunday Mail* photographer. The assault was alleged to have occurred the previous December when the photographer tried to take pictures of Skase and some friends playing tennis at Marina Mirage at Southport.

After the Lloyd's hearing the NCSC considered applying for a court order restraining Skase from leaving Australia. The application was withheld when the NCSC received an undertaking that he would return the following month for an NCSC hearing into the affairs of Qintex. Skase went back to Europe and returned to Australia on time for the NCSC hearing in October.

In May 1991 Skase returned to Australia again to defend himself on the charge of having assaulted the photographer. This visit turned into a media circus. A posse of television crews were waiting for him at Brisbane Airport. Skase handled the situation very badly. Having flown first class, he arrived with a couple of burly friends who acted as over-enthusiastic minders down to the unforgiveable sin of putting a hand over a camera lens. They forced Skase's way through the rat pack with maximum aggro, then drove off in a waiting limousine—another mistake. Hounding Skase became a media duty for the rest of his trip. (The assault charge against Skase was bogus. The assault was later admitted by Larkins.)

As Skase emerged from the first day at the Southport courthouse he was ambushed on the steps by officers of the Australian Securities Commission, who charged him with having made improper use of his position as a director by having $19 million in management fees paid to Kahmea Investments Pty Ltd. The ASC applied to the Federal Court to restrain Skase from returning overseas, but Mr Justice Pincus rejected the application on condition that Skase keep the ASC notified of his address and return when required by the courts. (In August 1992 32 more charges were laid against Skase alleging that he had acted improperly in relation to a further $7.4 million paid in fees to Kahmea.)

In July 1991 Richard Capps, the former treasurer of Qintex, was charged with a breach of Section 129 of the Companies Code, which forbade a company from financing the purchase of its own shares. The ASC alleged that QAL had paid $9.1 million to Qintex Ltd in 1989 to help that company buy QAL shares from the Superannuation Fund Investment Trust.

A little earlier, in June, Skase had declared himself bankrupt. He owed Tricontinental $52.5 million plus interest that had been lent to Kahmea. On top of that he had given personal guarantees for other Qintex group loans totalling $120 million. He declared that he owned no assets in

323

Australia or overseas apart from minor personal effects and some savings from his $7000 a month consultancy fee. Wardley and the State Bank of New South Wales had obtained a court judgement against him for $21 million owing on a personal guarantee, but it was always obvious that they and the other banks would be lucky to cover their legal fees, let alone any of the principal owing under the guarantees.

Skase's trustee in bankruptcy was Brisbane accountant Neville Pocock. He gave Skase his passport back and allowed him to leave Australia in return for a promise that he would return to the next creditors' meeting in September. While Skase was away the major banks claiming money from him became restive. In August 1991 Pocock stepped down and was replaced by Max Donnelly of Ferrier Hodgson. Donnelly demanded that Skase return but Skase said that he was too busy. Later he said that he had a bad back (from a fall down the stairs) and a pneumothorax condition (a puncturing of the lung) which prevented him from flying long distances. Donnelly applied to the Federal Court for warrants for the arrest of the Skases, but they were not granted. A judge dismissed the application on the grounds that as the warrants could not have been served in Spain they would have been of marginal utility. The ASC applied to the Federal Court to have Skase jailed for contempt of court for not honouring his undertaking to return. Mr Justice Drummond dismissed the application in January 1993.

Skase stayed in Majorca, pleading that his lungs were too bad for him to travel.

At the start of 1994 Judge Pratt of the Brisbane District Court issued a warrant for Skase's arrest. This was intended to ensure that Skase attended a court hearing into charges that he had used his position as a director to gain an advantage for himself or Kahmea through the payment of management fees. His Honour said: 'I am satisfied that for the accused no risk, whether considered severally or jointly with other risks, is of such consequence as to cause me to refuse the warrant which has been sought'. From Majorca, Skase branded the attempt to extradite him as 'attempted murder' and said the authorities would have 'blood on their hands' if he died in transit. At the time of writing, the Spanish Government had approved Skase's extradition but the move was still being fought in the courts.

The Australian media, including cartoonists and satirists, made hay with the spectacle of Skase sitting in Majorca and refusing to return. Skase was portrayed as living in luxury and defying the law. In truth, he was living plainly in a charming but small 400-year-old farmhouse. Up until the start of 1994 there had been no warrant for his extradition or even arrest. He showed no enthusiasm for returning to face an examination into his bankruptcy, but it is doubtful whether such an examination would have yielded anything significant for the banks which were his creditors. He had nothing like the $170 million they were claiming and nobody thought he had.

On Majorca with Pixie, her daughter Amanda and husband Tony Larkins, Skase was bitter and unrepentant. He said that his only error had been in not foreseeing the rise in interest rates and the unprecedented pilots' strike. In truth, Skase should take greater responsibility than that. The Qintex group had been finely stretched for years, with loans that could not be serviced by earnings. Any company in that state is vulnerable, and the longer a company is vulnerable the greater the chance that some event will occur that will kill it. Twice in the 1980s interest rates went as high as they did in 1989, although in 1989 they stayed up for a longer period.

Skase was angry about media invasion of his privacy and about reports that he had millions stashed away. When I visited him on Majorca in November 1991 he and Pixie were living frugally. He talked of making a comeback to Australia to lead QAL shareholders in a court case to recapture the Seven network. He blamed his downfall on a conspiracy involving the socialist government in Canberra and Rupert Murdoch.[30] Remarks like this indicate that the lengthy exile had distorted his view of reality. Very few political observers—and almost nobody in the Labor Party—would regard a government led by Bob Hawke and Paul Keating as seriously socialist.

Skase did have some reason to be paranoid about Murdoch. It was Murdoch who had forced up the ante on the MGM bid; it was Murdoch's *Courier-Mail* which had urged his prosecution for the alleged assault on a photographer; Murdoch and Sir Peter Abeles controlled Ansett when that airline led the fight against the pilots that wrecked the finances of the Mirages at a particularly critical time for Qintex; the Commonwealth Bank, owned by the government and whose biggest customer was Murdoch, was the most vocal of the senior lenders in refusing to extend Skase further credit in 1989. Skase can be forgiven for imagining a Murdoch-led conspiracy against him, but it is most unlikely that one existed. The prime cause of Skase's downfall was that he had borrowed far more money than he could service.

The prolonged exile in Majorca and the refusal to return to face the various hearings gave Skase probably the worst image of any of the corporate cowboys of the 1980s. While he certainly had faults it is by no means clear that he was morally the worst of the bold riders. His major asset was his stake in Qintex and his plan always was to grow rich with his company rather than at its expense. The money taken in management fees was, in this writer's view, immoral—but not illegal at the time. Almost all of it went to service Kahmea's interest bills. The hundreds of millions Skase was said to owe were on guarantees to banks which ought to have known better than to lend so much money. And, unlike many of the paper shufflers, he at least left behind a few tangible monuments in the two magnificent Mirages and a revivified Seven network. His worst flaw was that somewhere on the way up he lost touch with reality.

Several of Skase's former friends and colleagues were bitter and disillusioned afterwards. Peter Charlton's agency, Charlton & Charlton, had organised advertisements headlined 'Australians Support Qintex', when the group collapsed. Charlton was left $470 000 out of pocket for the advertisements. One of those quoted in the advertisement was television station owner Harold Mitchell, who said: 'In any business the long-term view is what's important. Qintex has the ability to grow and prosper in the long term and, I believe, should be given that opportunity'. Mitchell said that he and his wife had considered themselves close friends of Christopher and Pixie but after the crash his letters and calls went unanswered. Seven months after the collapse Mitchell said:

> At the time I honestly believed he could see things I could not. Later I believed he was simply wrong. But he had such a compelling personality and an absolute gift with words. He would have his eyes fixed on you—all the facts and details. I never felt something was wrong, not till it was all over.

Former group investment manager Stefan Borzecki, who left Qintex in 1986, said:

> He was a genius at extracting money out of people. He would understand the psychology of people—bankers, brokers, analysts—and give them exactly what they wanted to hear. He was like a snake charmer. Sometimes I'd watch him after he'd extracted what he wanted and know that next day he wouldn't even recognise the person on the street. Everything he did had a meaning and purpose. Nothing was ever accidental. It was always planned.

Borzecki left because even in 1986 he thought the relationship between share price and yield was becoming non-existent. 'I don't mind a bit of a duck and weave with the figures if you can see light at the end of the tunnel eventually', he said. 'But it was just getting darker.'[31]

Skase still attracted some loyalty from friends. Publicist Peter Sawyer, who lost money as an unsecured creditor when the group folded, stayed friendly with the Skases, sending news clippings about them to Majorca. Derryn Hinch, who lost more than $200 000 in the crash, did a fair interview with the couple on Majorca.[32] Concluding his program, Hinch said: 'I still do not distrust the man. Why feel any empathy or sympathy for him? I guess because he wasn't a billion dollar bandit. Christopher Skase tried to do something real. But he also probably believed too much in his own publicity.'

10
Abe Goldberg:
the smart one

His brief fling as one of Australia's richest people has been proved a
sham, having fooled a Who's Who *of bankers and a bar-full of pundits.*
The frenzy of deals he has engaged in over the past two years was not,
we now know, the work of a smart and self-confident investor but the
desperate gambles of a punter in search of cash flow.

Noel Bushnell

Abraham Goldberg stood only four feet ten inches and yearned to be a
lot bigger. He was a warm, likable little man, but he was never fully
accepted by leading members of Melbourne's Jewish fraternity, who had
known each other's families for generations and did not warm readily to
outsiders even of their own religion. He made a fortune in the rag trade
but was bored by it. What really gave him a charge was mixing with
bankers, brokers and corporate high-fliers. Because he had made a fortune
in textiles, and did a lot of big deals, Goldberg earned a reputation for
being one of the smartest corporate players in Australia. The truth was
that nearly every time he stepped outside the rag trade he was clobbered.
But the public, and even close associates, could only ever see part of the
picture, because Abe operated behind a confusing screen of private
companies and trusts. So the fact that he had gone broke emerged only
belatedly and shocked many financiers.

Goldberg was the classic Jewish immigrant boy made good. Before
World War II the Goldberg family had been in the textile industry in
Gawolin, Poland. After the German invasion of Poland the family had
been herded by the Nazis into a ghetto, where they feared extinction.
They bribed a farmer to hide them for a year and a half in a tiny, dark
cowshed. 'We were all packed on top of each other and lying down',
Goldberg said later. 'If one of us wanted to move, we all had to move.
When we walked out we all had to learn to walk again, like babies. There
was no light at all coming into the room except for a thin stream.'[1] One
thing he learned was the value of money. He said later that most of the
people who hid Jews during these years had done so for money.

As soon as the war ended the Goldberg family was determined to get as far from Poland as possible, so they migrated to Australia. Goldberg arrived in Melbourne in 1948, where his parents founded Parisian Knitting Mills. Goldberg's first job was on a knitting machine at his uncle's Willow Fashions, for £3/10/- a week. After a few years Goldberg and his wife Jannette set up Gold Knitting Mills in St Kilda's High Street, with a little help from his parents. He began working very long hours, from 6 a.m. to 11 p.m. He started with one employee, but in a year had built the business to twenty people. In the late 1950s Goldberg enjoyed a highly profitable joint venture, Stretch Fabrics, in partnership with Cleckheaton. He formed close friends with many of the leading figures within Melbourne's Jewish community, who between them dominated the Australian rag trade. He took over some small companies in the 1960s, aided by the prominent Melbourne lawyer, Arnold Bloch.

Like many Jewish immigrants, Goldberg found the ANZ Bank ready to lend. An ANZ lending officer, Rex Davidson, had cultivated Melbourne's Jewish community for years, believing them good risks and hard working. Davidson once said that he would rather lend money to an immigrant 'with one spinning wheel' than to a local who was 'just as likely to take off with your money down to the Carlton Football Club'.[2] After his retirement in 1977 Davidson would sit on some Goldberg boards.

By 1975 Goldberg was able to raise $8 million to take over the property developer, Hothlyn Corporation. He sold it quickly for a good profit and used the funds to raid the share market. His first major move came in early 1977 when he bought into Cleckheaton, a major handknitting concern. He also began buying shares in Bradmill Industries, one of Australia's largest textile groups. From his anonymous background in the family business Goldberg exploded into action in public companies. Together with his long-term friend Ivan Wise and Joe Brender of Katies retail chain Goldberg took over the Sydney textile importer, Isherwood & Dreyfus. By the end of 1978 Goldberg had control of Cleckheaton.

The next six years were spent doing mergers and deals in the textile industry which are fascinating to trace but irrelevant to this book. The big picture was that the Australian textile industry was being concentrated into fewer hands. After a long, tortuous battle Goldberg took over the former financier Entrad, then in 1984 finally seized control of Bradmill. With his other acquisitions, this made him the textile king of Australia. Michael Meagher, writing in the *Bulletin*, described him as the Godfather of the Australian rag trade.[3] The combined Entrad/Bradmill group had sales of around $400 million and more than 8000 employees, making it the single largest clothing and textile manufacturer and importer in the country. It was ahead of such groups as Dunlop Olympic Ltd, Bruck (Australia) Ltd, Bonds Coats Patons and Speedo Holdings.

Goldberg, through Entrad, controlled the manufacture and marketing of hosiery, men's and women's underwear, shirts, workwear, shorts, jeans and denim, knitted tops, linen and towels. Its brands were among the best known in Australia, including Pelaco and Whitmont shirts, King Gee overalls, Stubbies shorts, Actil sheets and Blues Union jeans.

Control of this empire was exercised through a complex corporate chain. As Figure 10.1 shows, the controlling company was Certosa Corporation (formerly Isherwood & Dreyfus). This was owned 45 per cent by Goldberg's Roxbury Holdings Pty Ltd, 40 per cent by Marc Besen's Marcbes Investments Pty Ltd and 15 per cent by Arnold Bloch's Legality Holdings Pty Ltd. Bloch had left his firm Arnold Bloch Liebler & Associates in 1981 to become chairman of Entrad. This move by Bloch was an indication of Goldberg's emerging strength in the textile market. Bloch was the true Godfather in Melbourne's Jewish community. Jewish businessmen would check with him before making a takeover to ensure that nobody else's interests were being compromised. He was an arbiter of disputes and would guarantee loans. For him to give up his practice to join Goldberg's board meant that Goldberg had really arrived. Goldberg was renowned for his impatience and his habit of talking over his executives, but he would always defer to Bloch in board meetings. Bloch died in 1985 and his share of the business was taken over by Goldberg and Marc Besen. Besen was a passive investor, being heavily involved in running his Sussan chain. Bloch had restrained Goldberg and channelled his energies into the successful building of a textile empire. Without Bloch, the impatient Goldberg would soon start running amok.

Following the links in Figure 10.1, Certosa wholly owned Nardis Investments Ltd (formerly Pelaco), which held 79.3 per cent of Entrad Ltd. Entrad, through the wholly owned Gibraltar Factors Pty Ltd, held 90 per cent of the Bramil Unit Trust (the other 10 per cent being owned directly by Goldberg), which held 95 per cent of Bradmill Industries Ltd. The structure was diverse in two senses. It was diverse industrially, including interests in property, retailing, tyres and American oil companies; and diverse legally, containing unit trusts as well as companies.

The second point was important. Under the then Companies Code a trust could not be consolidated as part of a group of companies. This accounting fiction disguised a reality. When an upstream company owned 100 per cent of the units in a trust its position was virtually no different from what it would be if it held all the shares in a company that owned the same assets and liabilities. Looking at the number of trusts in the Goldberg group, it becomes clear that substantial assets and liabilities could have been legally excluded from any consolidated accounts. In the euphoric 1980s such considerations went almost entirely unnoticed.[4]

Figure 10.1 The Entrad–Goldberg structure, 1984

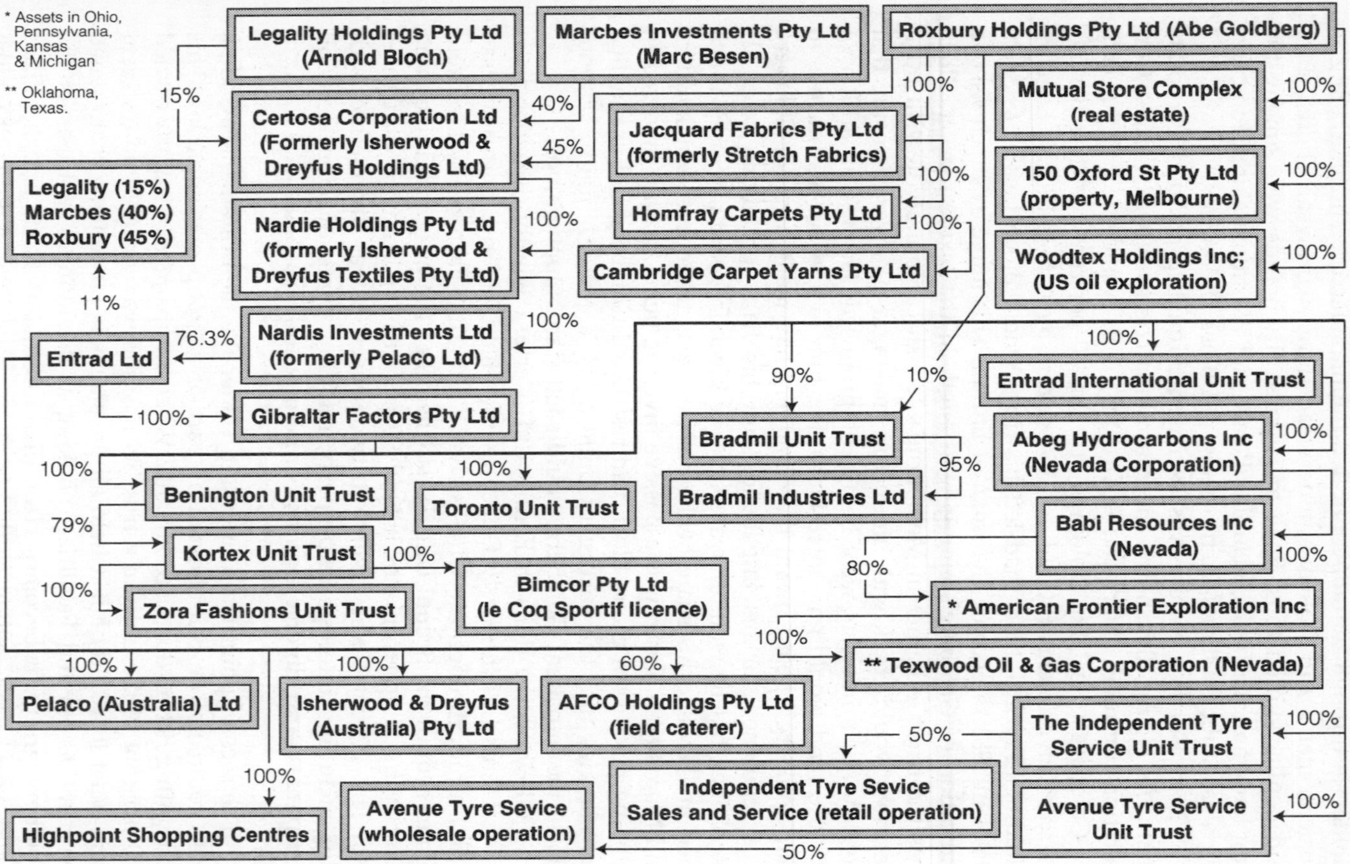

* Assets in Ohio, Pennsylvania, Kansas & Michigan.

** Oklahoma, Texas.

The Godfather had always tried to stay low profile, to the point of being the only director of Entrad who did not have his photograph in the annual report. In his early days of survival in the rag trade he had learned the virtues of being nimble. He stayed nimble all his business life, but as his deals got bigger and involved public companies his nimbleness earned him a reputation for unpredictability. He was capable of changing direction quickly and without warning if a deal was not going the way he wanted. This had caused several clashes with Australian stock exchanges and the Australian Shareholders' Association. After the Bradmill deal was completed, his net worth was estimated at $60 million. By that time he had a prestige office at the top of Collins Place and was living in Toorak. He drove a Rolls Royce.

The death of Bloch in 1985 robbed Goldberg of his most trusted advisor. One person who became increasingly important to him after then was Katy Boskovitz, an ambitious and intelligent Sydney lawyer, who had been with Entrad since 1972 (when it was a financier called Development Underwriting Ltd and run by Sir Paul Strasser). Boskovitz took on increasing responsibility within the organisation, becoming company secretary of Entrad and later a director of Linter. Another important source of advice for Goldberg was Entrad's chairman, Ron Deans.[5]

The float of Linter

March 1985 saw the public float of Linter Group Ltd. This float combined the timber business of Ralph Symonds Ltd with some textile mills formerly owned by Bradmill. The float had been arranged by what were colloquially known as 'the AFP boys'. This was a looseknit team of smart operators who had in one way or another been associated with each other through a company, Australian Farming Property Co, which became an investor and asset trader named AFP. One of them was Basil Sellers, who had taken over Ralph Symonds Ltd. Another was Peter Scanlon, who had been one of John Elliott's backroom boys when Elliott took over the sleepy old jam-maker Henry Jones IXL, the first important step on Elliott's rise to power. Two other AFP boys were John Gerahty and Robin Crawford. When Linter was launched the chairman was Gerahty, with Sellers, Scanlon and Crawford as directors. The man who was probably most responsible for bringing the deal together was Crawford. A director of Hill Samuel (later Macquarie Bank), Crawford had a long involvement with Tootal and Bradmill and it was he who had first persuaded Sellers to invest in the mills.

It was a characteristic of the AFP boys that any group they were involved in was constantly changing shape. In its first two years, Linter changed shape considerably. Forty per cent of the stock was bedded down with AFP. Linter sold its timber business and bought Steve Cosser's Broadcasting and Communications Ltd. It formed a joint venture with Entrad called Lintrad, containing King Gee overalls and industrial wear, Stubbies shorts and Bradmill Textiles, which was virtually the only Australian denim producer. Goldberg, who by then owned 54 per cent of Entrad, became chairman of Lintrad.

In 1986 Linter made a successful bid for Speedo, Australia's most famous swimwear maker. Linter funded part of the takeover by placing 9 per cent of its shares with Goldberg for $27 million. Goldberg joined the Linter board in August 1986. Then, in January 1987, Linter bought out Goldberg's half-interest in Lintrad for $27 million plus a block of shares representing another 9 per cent of Linter. This deal was done only six months after the formation of Lintrad and only five months after Goldberg had joined the Linter board.

Linter shares were around $5.70 on the market, having doubled since the float nearly three years earlier. However, investors must have found it wearying to keep track of this chameleon-like group. Large chunks of the textile industry were being shuffled around like a pack of cards and investors could never be sure what their group would look like next week. The share register was cosy, with 40 per cent of Linter having been placed to AFP and another 18 per cent to Goldberg. Figure 10.2 shows the various shuffles made by the Linter group between July 1986 and October 1987. The public shareholders were looking in through a porthole at the deals the directors were doing with each other. Nevertheless, Linter looked a strong group with good businesses. Profit for the year to March 1986 had been $7.5 million, although it was difficult to work out how much of this represented operating profit—as opposed to one-off transactions such as the sale of Ralph Symonds and the sale and leaseback of some of its textile assets.

In hindsight, Goldberg would have been better off sticking to the knitting. If he had stayed in textiles—a business he knew—he may well have stayed Godfather of the Australian rag trade and would have enjoyed good cash flow. Instead, he was flirting with the AFP boys by taking stock in Linter.

The cash from the deal helped Goldberg to restructure his empire. At the end of the restructuring the key company was Danomic Investments Ltd (the shell of the former Speedo Holdings), in which Goldberg held 47 per cent. Danomic held 49.9 per cent of Entrad, 19 per cent of Linter, 10.5 per cent of AFP, 4.5 per cent of Kerry Stokes' Oakminster Holdings, 10.2 per cent of BDC Investments (a cashbox formerly controlled by AFP which had become the vehicle for Stokes' media interests) and several other investments. There were still some textile interests in Entrad, but

Figure 10.2   The Linter shuffles

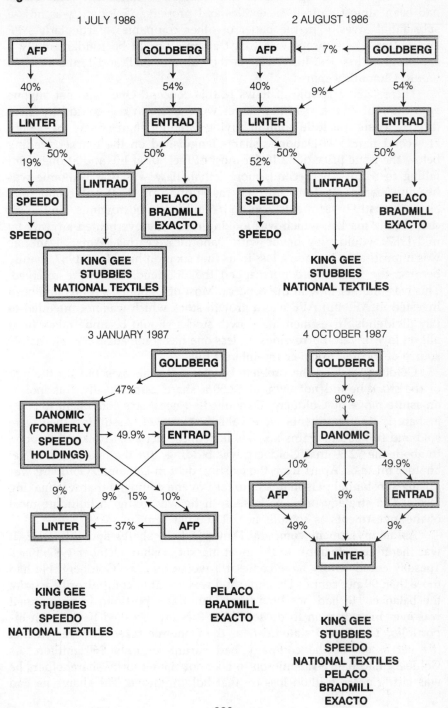

the nature of Goldberg's assets had changed significantly. Whereas he had been almost entirely in textiles and property, Goldberg was now a substantial investor in the paper of other companies, particularly AFP and Linter. The concept was that Danomic would be fundamentally a capital growth stock, like AFP. As the value of AFP and Linter rose, so would Danomic's shares.

There were a couple of flaws in this concept. One was that anyone who thought AFP and Linter shares were going to rise could buy them directly. There was little point in buying Danomic shares to get the benefit at second hand. So Danomic shares languished on the market, trading below the issue price of $2.10 for most of their brief life and at one point falling to $1.67. The second, more lethal, flaw was that Danomic was heavily geared. By June 1987 it was supporting $360 million in total assets—mostly investments—with $166 million in borrowings. Any sharp drop in the market, which was looking distinctly overheated anyway by mid-1987, would play havoc with Danomic's gearing. Worse, Danomic was unprofitable. It made a loss in its first six months to June 1987, mainly because the interest bill outstripped the dividends that were received. This was another flaw in the concept. Most of Danomic's funds had been invested in AFP but AFP was a growth stock which was not intended to pay dividends. Investment in growth stocks should be undertaken (if at all) on low or zero borrowings, unless one has some adequate alternative source of income to cover the interest bills.

Goldberg tackled the problem by making a takeover bid for the half of the stock he did not own, at $2.50 a share. Superficially, this looked an astute move by Goldberg. Danomic had net assets equivalent to $3.33 a share if its investments were valued at market. Assuming they were sold and full capital gains tax was levied, the net asset backing dropped to about the $2.50 that Goldberg was bidding. But the takeover was yet another mistake. Apart from the existing debt in Danomic, Goldberg was raising substantial personal debt to take over a company that was making losses. The strategy only made sense if he was going to liquidate most of the investments as soon as he got 100 per cent.

As an investment company Danomic held shares and little else. It was therefore vulnerable to the great market crash of October 1987. Black Tuesday could hardly have come at a worse time for Goldberg. He had more than 90 per cent of Danomic and was about to compulsorily acquire the balance. He had not liquidated Danomic's portfolio—presuming it was ever his intention to do so. Black Tuesday wreaked havoc with his portfolio. The Part B statement for the Danomic takeover revealed that the net assets of the company had shrunk to only $60 million. As Goldberg had paid $122 million to take out the minority shareholders he was facing a $60 million loss on that holding alone. The shares he had paid $2.50 for (with several Danomic shareholders protesting bitterly about the low price) now had a net asset backing of only 60c.

Danomic's biggest investments were looking horrible. Linter, which had soared to $7.50 in mid-1987, crashed to $2.13 at the end of 1988. AFP, which had been $3.50 on the dawn of Black Tuesday, collapsed to $1.90 that day and before Christmas had slid to 70c.

Three days after Black Tuesday, Linter Group announced that it had paid $67 million to buy out all of Goldberg's remaining textile interests. The deal seemed to accomplish two things for Goldberg. It got rid of $85 million debt associated with the textile interests and gave him cash to restore the damage done to Danomic by the market crash. Linter raised $12 million of the cash needed for the deal by selling four country radio stations.

Then, in March 1988, Goldberg somersaulted by making a takeover bid for Linter. Goldberg's zigzagging would have done credit to a World War II Atlantic convoy. In twenty months, he had joint-ventured Stubbies and his industrial wear with Linter, sold the other half of them to Linter, sold the rest of his textile interests to Linter and was now buying everything back again. This may have been astute footwork, but it was also possible that he simply kept changing his mind.

Again the deal was obviously done in close consultation with the AFP boys. AFP owned 49 per cent of Linter and Goldberg owned 18 per cent. In addition, Goldberg owned 19.9 per cent of AFP. Goldberg offered $3.50 cash for each Linter share, or $2.30 cash plus one share in AFP. Goldberg also announced that if Linter shareholders did not take all of Danomic's AFP shares the rest would be placed by McIntosh Hamson Hoare Govett at $1.22 each. AFP promptly announced that it would accept the cash alternative for its shares. It became clear that everyone was going to get something they wanted out of the deal. AFP was going to get cash which it needed to buttress its post-crash balance sheet. Goldberg would get his textile empire back. How much cash he outlaid depended on the number of Linter shareholders who took AFP scrip. If none of them did, the McIntosh placement would raise $105 million, covering the bulk of the $142 million Goldberg needed to pay out AFP. The net cash outlay by Goldberg to buy the 80 per cent of Linter he did not own already would be about $130 million, after allowing for the sale of his AFP shares.

The catch was the debt that would have to be raised by Goldberg. The staged sale of his textile businesses to Linter must have made him nearly debt-free by the end of 1987. Now he was plunging back in, up to his neck. In fairness, this was a fashionable tactic at the time. The share market had hit its nadir in early 1988 and high-fliers such as Peter Laurance in Pivot Group and George Herscu in Hooker were both taking the opportunity offered by the share market crash to try to privatise their companies at historically low share prices.[6]

Looking at Goldberg's deals in retrospect, it is clear that the AFP boys proved to be better judges than Goldberg. The deals always seemed to work better for them than for Goldberg. Goldberg's deals with the boys laid the cornerstone of his eventual disaster. Several of the boys finished by running companies and living the good life in London and Monaco. Goldberg finished a fugitive from the law in Poland. He was an astute enough textiler, but his judgement in investment and finance proved awful.

Goldberg's bid for Linter was part of a much bigger corporate play involving the AFP boys and including the biggest of them all: John Elliott. AFP was important to Elliott because it owned shares and options that could give it 40 per cent of his flagship, Elders IXL. At this point Elliott was in the middle of delicate negotiations with BHP, in which BHP's shareholding in Elders was to be sold for $700 million to a company called Harlin Pty Ltd—whose board was controlled by Elliott and associates, including some of the AFP boys. Under the terms of the deal Harlin had to inject $200 million capital, of which $100 million could be in Elders shares. These Elders shares were to come from AFP. But post-crash there was a danger that Elliott and the boys might lose control of AFP. The slump in AFP's share price had potentially put it in play and two of the biggest players in Australia had scented the weakness. These players were Ron Brierley of Industrial Equity and Larry Adler of FAI Insurances. They had snapped up 15 per cent of AFP's capital, creating speculation that control would change hands.

Elliott and the boys had to make AFP safe, and Goldberg was a loose cannon. Between Black Tuesday and March 1988 Goldberg had been a big supporter of AFP's share price, buying several blocks on market. This was proving to be an unrewarding exercise. He picked up much stock at $1.90 and by March the price had drifted to 90c. At that price he was facing a loss of $100 million. Worse, Goldberg was reported to have become disillusioned when he realised who some of the sellers were. By March he held 19.9 per cent of AFP and the AFP board was surprised to learn that he was discussing a joint bid for the company with Larry Adler. This would have upset the larger game, so Goldberg had to be dissuaded. This was why AFP offered Goldberg the Linter textile interests in return for the bid described above which transferred his AFP shares.[7] By having Goldberg offer his AFP shares to Linter shareholders, many of whom were in the AFP camp, or to be placed by McIntosh—Elders' house sharebroker—Elliott could be assured that most of Goldberg's block would go into friendly hands.

As shareholders of Linter began to accept Goldberg's bid, he mopped up the rest of his empire by making takeover offers for the stock he did not own in Parkston, a property company, and Entrad. The cost of this was that Goldberg's debt levels were becoming formidable. Linter's 1988 balance sheet showed that it had total assets of $536 million, but liabilities stood at $323 million. This did not include the debts owed by Danomic and the rest of the Goldberg empire including Pochette Pty Ltd, the shelf company he had used to take over Linter.

The last person to seem worried was Goldberg. He launched an unsuccessful $120 million bid for the Spotless group. Then he built his stake in the big UK group Tootal from 9.2 to 14.4 per cent and offered Tootal a £500 million merger deal. Tootal, which had defeated a hostile bid from Goldberg in 1985, rejected the proposal out of hand. By March 1989 he had 22.3 per cent of Tootal and was contemplating a takeover bid.[8] With a swag of debt already, Goldberg was seriously trying to take over a company twice his size. But in mid-May he was prised out of his holding by a rival bidder, Coats Viyella plc. Goldberg sold for £7 million above his entry price, but holding costs more than wiped out that profit.[9]

Barely a fortnight after being beaten out of Tootal, Goldberg bid $390 million for Brick & Pipe Industries. This was a wild bid, even by Goldberg's standards. Brick & Pipe was already under siege from Industrial Equity Ltd (IEL), which had bid $3.50. This valued Brick & Pipe at $340 million. The managing director of Brick & Pipe, John Shergold, was a friend of IEL's managing director, Rod Price, but did not accept the bid. 'The critics were saying it wasn't enough, but I kept thinking to myself, it's not bad', Shergold said later.[10]

> Then Abe, who I hadn't seen for years, rang up and said he wanted to see me. He came in and sat down and said he wanted to make a bid. I asked what he wanted with a brickmaking company and he said he and Jannette were tired of travelling around the world. Their friends were in Melbourne and they wanted to live here, so they wanted a business in Melbourne. He said: 'Would $4 be enough?'. I thought: 'Shit! They'll rush at him'. He said it would be a cash bid but he would only make it on the condition I stayed on to run the company. I didn't want to, because I'd seen how Abe ran companies, but on behalf of the shareholders I couldn't turn down the deal on those grounds and anyway I didn't have another job to go to. And then he told me a lie. I asked how much of the $390 million would be his and he said he would put in $250 million and borrow about another $150 million. It wasn't in my interest to talk him out of it, so he went ahead. When the bid was announced Rod Price rang me and accused me of organising a counterbid by Goldberg.

Goldberg bid $4.10, capitalising the company at $390 million, and quickly won control. The offer was financed by $150 million from CIBC Australia and $240 million from Bacharach Pty Ltd. As Bacharach was a shelf company formed only a day or two before the bid, it had obviously borrowed the money from somewhere else.[11] One of the suppliers was Melbourne businessman Dick Pratt, who controlled Regal Insurance and

Occidental Insurance. It was a crazy deal that was never going to work. Brick & Pipe's stated EBIT (earnings before interest and tax) at the time was around $39 million. The going interest rate was 20 per cent. As the bid was entirely financed on borrowings Goldberg's interest bill was $80 million. So Brick & Pipe would be operating at an immediate deficit of some $40 million a year, as long as Brick & Pipe's EBIT stayed at $39 million, which it wouldn't. The company's greatest asset was its dominance of the Victorian brick market, which depended heavily on home-building. In 1991 the number of houses built in Melbourne would fall from 38 000 to 22 000, slashing Brick & Pipe's earnings to ribbons. But by that time Goldberg was long gone.

The man who had just paid $390 million showed little interest in his acquisition. Goldberg installed Shergold as chairman and was content with just a board seat for himself. 'He was never interested in the brick company', said Shergold.

> He never went to one brick plant. To this day he has never been to a brick factory. I suggested we should go and show his head to a few plants. Instead he had a video made at great expense showing how bricks were made. He installed that in his office so he could flick it on whenever brokers or bankers walked in.

Goldberg had only a loose grip on the realities of the brick trade. He tried to cut out capital expenditure, but Shergold convinced him that it was essential. Goldberg appears to have been under the impression that Brick & Pipe was sitting on an unrealised land bank, which he suggested selling. Shergold replied: 'That's the clay! That's our lifeblood'.

Before the market could blink, Goldberg had moved on to an even bigger deal: financing a management buyout of Industrial Equity Ltd. The centrepiece of this deal was a company named Corama Pty Ltd, which would be owned 75 per cent by Goldberg and 25 per cent by IEL's two top executives, Rodney Price and Bill Loewenthal. Corama would buy 32 per cent of IEL from Brierley Investments and 19.9 per cent from Goodman Fielder Wattie at $2.40 a share. Public holders of the remaining 36 per cent were going to be asked to waive the legal requirement that Corama bid for their shares.[12] The total cost of the deal was nearly $1 billion. IEL, once a feared raider, had lately come under siege itself. Goodman Fielder had bid for the company a month earlier and John Spalvins was known to be lurking around the share register. Goldberg had given his personal guarantee for Corama's potential liabilities under the deal.

Boskovitz and Deans were alarmed by the IEL bid. They had been trying to sell Brick & Pipe assets to get the debt down and suddenly Goldberg had vaulted into an even bigger takeover. Boskovitz fell out with Goldberg and quit.

For the reasons explained in Chapter 13 the management buyout of

IEL could have been a good idea. Price and Loewenthal were planning to sell down assets quickly. They would have needed to, particularly property assets: the whole market was about to fall over a cliff. But even if the buyout was a good idea, Goldberg would have to assume debt of heroic proportions to finance it. The fact that Spalvins had become a significant shareholder meant that the Corama team had no chance of persuading a shareholders' meeting to waive their rights to accept the bid. Therefore Corama would probably have to bid $2.40 for 100 per cent of IEL—a total of $1.9 billion.

Goldberg was still a hero to his bankers. When he turned 60 in September 1989 Citibank planted a grove of trees in his honour in Israel, and flew guests from all over Australia to a birthday party in one of Melbourne's most expensive restaurants.[13]

Whispers began to circulate that all was not well with the financing. The 52 per cent bid was to have been financed by Citicorp but the ANZ, the largest financier of the rest of Goldberg's empire, suggested that the entire empire should be refinanced. Spalvins made it plain that he would force Corama would have to bid for 100 per cent. Citibank withdrew as Corama's financier and was replaced by BT Australia. Then suddenly, in October, Goldberg was trying to *sell* Brick & Pipe—just seven weeks after he had completed its takeover. Spalvins bid for IEL in November and Corama quit the battle amid a legal dispute with Brierley Investments over a $25 million deposit that Corama had paid for some of the IEL shares. Spalvins won IEL, but it was a Pyrrhic victory that killed the Adsteam group.[14]

As 1990 dawned, the rumour mill was saying that Goldberg was shaky. As his empire was almost entirely privatised there were few outside indications. But a meeting had been called with his bankers who between Christmas and New Year appointed Lindsay Maxsted, of KPMG Peat Marwick, to go over the Linter books.

A complex web

What Maxsted uncovered was one of the biggest rats' nests of the 1980s. The Goldberg empire comprised a web of companies, trusts, partnerships and individuals. Money had been shuffled around in it untraceably. The total debt was far larger than anyone had thought—to the horror of the banks—and was hopelessly in excess of the value of the assets. The Godfather of the rag trade was broke several times over. On 24 January 1990 the bankers voted to appoint receivers to Linter Group. It was the end.

Maxsted produced reports on the Goldberg family interests, on Linter Group and on Brick & Pipe. On his estimates the three entities had

Table 10.1   The Goldberg deficiency

	Assets (Realised value) ($m)	Liabilities ($)	Surplus/Deficit ($)
Goldberg Family Interests	n.a.(a)	370	(?)
Linter Group	400	1 200	(800)
Brick & Pipe	330	280	50
Total	730+	1 850	(750+)

(a)   Originally estimated at $131m. Final net value still not determined.

liabilities totalling $1.7 billion and a deficiency of $425 million. The realised deficiency would turn out to be more than double that figure. As Goldberg's private companies were wound up by more than one liquidator, and as some of the inter-company debts had not been settled by early 1994, it was not possible to put an exact figure on the actual loss. Table 10.1 gives a rough summary of the final deficiency.

Table 10.1 attempts to show the net overall position, ignoring some highly tangled inter-company debts and guarantees. Maxsted's original estimates in January 1990 were necessarily approximate for several reasons. Goldberg himself did not know his financial position to any degree of accuracy. By Christmas 1989 several of his family companies had still not prepared audited accounts for June 1989. Figures for Linter Group and Brick & Pipe were based on unaudited management accounts for October and September. This raised the question of how financiers could have lent so much money to a private group which did not have up-to-date accounts. The answer was that until then the financiers had been incredibly feckless.

As the figures began to unfold it became clear why Goldberg had bid for IEL. It was almost the only takeover play that might have generated enough profit to get him out square. It was equally clear why he had been unable to finance it. How could any financier lend another billion or so to someone in this position?

Maxsted reported that the deficit in assets had been precipitated by the share market crash of 1987.[15] In hindsight, Goldberg had almost certainly been broke since Black Tuesday. Because the group tended to be highly geared the high interest rates of 1989 had further eroded its position. The implications of this statement were sobering. For two years after becoming insolvent Goldberg had been able to make some of the biggest takeover bids in the country. In all that time financiers had not realised the depth of his troubles. True, Linter Group and Brick & Pipe were sound businesses with good cash flows. But the cash flows were quite inadequate to service the sort of debt Goldberg had raised. Also, trading profits had been diverted to fund losses in other areas, notably investments.

The accompanying Figure 10.3 is merely a skeleton outline of the Goldberg group at the time of its fall. The full group structure was so complex that it took Maxsted five A4 pages to lay it out. It included 93 companies, trusts, partnerships and individuals. Even then it did not include subsidiaries and associates of Linter, Brick & Pipe and Entrad. Gibraltar Factors Ltd was used as a clearing house for inter-group financing. It was also common for companies in the group to borrow externally and then on-lend borrowed funds to other group entities. One of the main borrowers had been a little company called Spersea Pty Ltd, which had no assets but nevertheless had raised $117 million. Bankers had been pouring money into Goldberg's empire without any idea where it was going.

Maxsted found that the main causes of the deficiency were:

- the loss taken on AFP in the 1987 crash
- losses on US operations which were later wound down
- an interest shortfall over the previous two years (i.e. the group had been paying out more in interest than it was earning)
- the loss on the attempted takeover of Tootal
- the loss on the attempted takeover of IEL

The US losses were in Entrad International Unit Trust. The other losses were spread widely throughout the group, including the loss of around $100 million on AFP. Every fixed asset in the group was subject to one or more specific mortgages. Most of the other debt had been borrowed on negative pledge. Linter Group, with its great range of textile brands, had been used to borrow money to prop up other parts of the group. Linter had raised $200 million towards the Brick & Pipe takeover. It had also raised another $270 million which had been lent throughout the group via Gibraltar Factors. The money borrowed by Spersea had been used to refinance the acquisition facility for Linter. Bacharach Pty Ltd had borrowed $150 million from CIBC and on-lent it to help finance the takeover of Brick & Pipe.[16]

As an example of what happened in Goldberg's private companies, Table 10.2 shows the position of Roxbury Holdings Pty Ltd when Goldberg's group augered in.

Roxbury's main assets were properties valued at $38.7 million, on which the ANZ Bank held mortgages totalling $19.6 million and Australian European Finance Corporation held another mortgage for $7.5 million. Tricontinental held a mortgage debenture over the rest of the company's assets for $21.9 million, so would take the remaining $12.7 million, which represented only 58c for every dollar that Tricontinental was owed. There was nothing left to cover the $86 million owed to Gibraltar Factors, the internal banker to the group.

Figure 10.3 Goldberg's empire at the fall

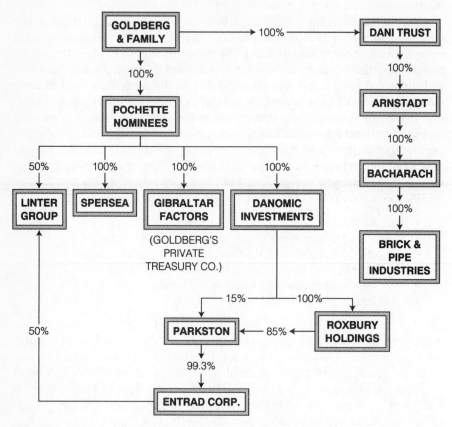

Note: This figure omits about 80 companies and trusts

This story was repeated throughout the group. Any company that had a solid asset had mortgaged it to the hilt. There was rarely anything left to cover the loans from bankers channelled through Gibraltar Factors or Spersea. The group was hopelessly unable to service its debt.

The first estimates made by Maxsted proved to be optimistic because the major assets did not realise the values Goldberg had put on them. The Linter assets were sold for only $400 million, then the funds sat on deposit while a fight ensued between creditors over their ranking. The holders of $US200 million bonds claimed that they should rank equally with negative pledge lenders totalling $A750 million. Mr Justice McClelland in the NSW Supreme Court ruled that the bondholders ranked behind the negative pledge lenders, which meant they would receive nothing. The bondholders then sued for damages, alleging fraud and deception by Linter. A New York judge ruled that the case was not in his jurisdiction, so it was taken up in Australia's Federal Court. If the bondholders succeeded in gaining equal footing with the negative pledge lenders (and if their claims for punitive damages were dismissed) all these creditors looked like receiving around 35c in the dollar.

Brick & Pipe eventually had $350 million to distribute to creditors, who fought bitterly for the money. Regal and Occidental retrieved the $55 million they had lent, but Linter (which had put $200 million into the takeover), CIBC ($150 million) and Citibank ($62 million) all took losses. After taking all these factors into account the probable final loss of Goldberg's total group was somewhere north of $750 million.

The lending to Linter was amongst the craziest of the boom. Linter's EBIT was between $60 million and $70 million. The maximum interest it could have afforded on this would have been around $40 million. At 18 per cent interest rates, this meant its maximum borrowing capacity should have been around $220 million. One can make different assumptions and come up with a different number but nobody could have totalled it to $1.2 billion, which is what the bondholders and negative pledge lenders poured into Linter. They were all looking at the group's great textile products and not its debt-servicing capacity. They were lending on the balance sheet rather than the profit and loss account. And none of them knew how many other loans had been made on the same assets. Table 10.3 shows the lenders to Linter and to Goldberg's private companies.

In the case of Westpac there was a clear absence of central control. It was bad enough that the bank itself was exposed to the Goldberg group for $105 million. But, until the group hit the wall, Westpac head office in Martin Place had no idea that Bill Acceptance and Partnership Pacific were exposed for $40 million and $15 million respectively, taking the Westpac group exposure to $160 million. Westpac immediately began trying to get its erring subsidiaries under control, but did not fully succeed with Australian Guarantee Corporation for another couple of years.

In making these loans the banks had ignored the rating services, which had repeatedly given low credit ratings to Goldberg's companies. As far back as September 1988 Moody's had rated Linter Group at BA3 for a junk bond issue. This was the issue which raised $US200 million for Linter, in addition to the amounts shown in Table 10.3. So the Goldberg group was well and truly broke.

The cash flows of the group had only been covering a fraction of the interest payable. Table 10.4 shows the cash flows, without totals because it covers different time zones for the three major groups.

For all practical purposes, the group's interest bill was outrunning its servicing capacity by $160 million a year. The Goldberg family interests and Linter Group were carrying debt way beyond their means. Goldberg

Table 10.2   Roxbury Holdings at 31 December 1989 (all figures in $m)

Assets	39.8
External liabilities	(49.0)
Owing to Gibraltar factors	(86.1)
Deficiency	(95.3)

went broke at a bad time for his creditors. Property prices were beginning to slide and the Federal Government had embarked on a tariff-slashing program which was aimed at either abolishing Australia's textile industry or making it more efficient.

Financial exile

The liquidation began. Financiers who had mortgages over Goldberg properties seized and sold them. Brick & Pipe was sold to Pioneer International for $290 million in April 1990. As some $40 million in hotels and properties were excluded from the sale, being mortgaged to various bankers, this represented $60 million less than the $390 million that Goldberg had paid for Brick & Pipe barely nine months earlier. The irony of this deal was that in 1989 Rod Price had been trying to buy Brick & Pipe for IEL. Following the takeover of IEL by Adelaide Steamship, Price had accepted a job as chief executive officer of Pioneer—and Pioneer had now bought Brick & Pipe for about the sum that Price had been offering for it in the first place. In a final irony, Price hired John Shergold as chief general manager of Pioneer's building products division, which meant that Shergold was managing Brick & Pipe again.

Speedo was sold to Pentland Industries of Britain for $47.5 million. By this time Linter was being hit by the dual impact of the recession and lower tariffs. Sales were off 11 per cent and operating profit for the year to June 1990 was down to $46 million. The rest of the Linter textile business was sold to Sara Lee for $220 million in May 1991. This was a switch for Sara Lee, which was best known in Australia for its bakery products but in 1991 was in a diversification drive.

Goldberg was made bankrupt in July 1990. Personal guarantees by Goldberg and his family totalled $202 million, including $62 million to Citibank and $55 million to Occidental. Legal claims could have doubled this figure, but it would all have been academic. By the time the bankruptcy papers were filed Goldberg had already left the country. For a man who was bankrupt he appeared able to enjoy extensive travel. He was spotted at London's Park Lane Hotel only a few months after his group had collapsed. He visited Israel and Los Angeles, then took a car trip through Budapest, Prague and Warsaw. By January 1992 he had

Table 10.3   Lenders to Goldberg and Linter (all figures in $m)

Bank	Amount lent	Borrower	Interest rate %
ABN Australia	20.0	Team Securities	
	10.0	Linter Group	19.1
	5.0	Linter Group	
AEFC	7.5	Roxbury	9.25
	2.0	Entrad Corp	19.93
	10.0	Entrad Ltd	19.93
	7.5	Entrad Ltd	19.75
	2.0	Linter Group	19.93
	1.0	Linter Group	
AMRO Australia	30.0	Linter Textiles	18.9
ANZ	25.0	Pochette	18.29
	18.0	Roxbury	8.85–10.35
	50.0	Linter Group	19.0
	5.0	Linter Group	
BA Australia	25.0	Linter Textiles	19.2
Banque Nat. Paris	20.0	Linter Textiles	18.9
Bank of New York	30.0	Linter Textiles	19.2
Bank of New Zealand	75.0	Linter Group	19.0
Bank of Tokyo	10.0	Linter Textiles	18.7
Barclays Bank Aust	25.0	Linter Textiles	19.1
	10.0	Linter Group	18.8
BCC Australia	5.0	Gibraltar	19.8
Bill Acceptance	25.0	Gibraltar	18.45
	15.0	Entrad Corp	19.52
Chase AMP	20.0	Linter Textiles	18.9
Citibank	13.5	Linter Textiles	
Commonwealth Bank	1.0	Danomic	20.5
	20.0	Linter Group	18.5
	1.5	Linter Textiles	
Credit Lyonnais	20.0	Linter Textiles	19.2
Elders	11.1	Linter Group	
HongkongBank Aust	20.0	Danomic	18.27
Nat. Mut. Royal Bank	5.0	Linter Group	
Partnership Pacific	15.0	Linter Textiles	19.1
R&I Bank WA	10.0	Linter Group	18.8
Sanwa Australia	20.0	Linter Textiles	20.2
Security Pacific	25.0	Linter Group	19.2
	3.9	Entrad Ltd	19.5
Société Générale	15.0	Linter Group	18.55
	2.0	Linter Group	
Standard Chartered	(US)4.3	Abeg Hydrocarbon	9.13
State Bank NSW	25.0	Linter Group	18.8
State Bank SA	20.0	Linter Group	19.1
State Bank Vic.	20.0	Linter Textiles	18.9
Sumitomo	50.0	Linter Group	18.42
Tricontinental	5.0	Gibraltar	
	22.0	Roxbury	20.0
	14.2	Abeg Hydrocarbon	10.13
	10.0	Entrad Ltd	19.67
	25.0	Parkston	20.0
Westpac	12.0	Entrad Corp	18.2–22.5
	14.0	Entrad Ltd	18.2–22.5
	38.75	Linter Group	19.0
	13.75	Linter Group	
	26.7	Linter Textiles	
Total	936.7		

settled permanently in his native country of Poland, which conveniently was no longer communist and had no extradition treaty with Australia. His solicitors advised the Australian authorities that he would not be returning to answer questions about his bankruptcy. The 61-year-old Goldberg had said that he had got a job as a textile industry consultant in Warsaw at less than $2000 a month after tax. However, his wife had needed extensive back surgery and he had had to hire a housekeeper, which meant that his expenses exceeded his income. As a result he could not make any contribution to his creditors. He was living on handouts from his daughters, he said.[17] A warrant was issued for his arrest but was never served because he never returned. Linter Group's QC, Allan Myers, told the Victorian Supreme Court that it was unlikely Goldberg or his son-in-law Zev Furst would return to give evidence, saying that they preferred 'to remain in the safe havens in which they now reside'. Furst was in Los Angeles.

Fairfax journalists made a spirited effort to track down Goldberg who, in court documents, had given his address as a flat in Ordynacki Street, Warsaw. Paul McGeough went to the flat; when he knocked on the door it was answered by 'a beautiful young blonde, loosely wrapped in a bathrobe'. She said that Goldberg was staying at the Marriott, Warsaw's finest hotel. The monthly salary given in his bankruptcy statement would not have lasted a week there. A phone call established that Goldberg was indeed at the Marriott, but he said he would have to check with his lawyers before giving an interview. When McGeough tried to contact Goldberg again next day he discovered that the old rag trader had checked out at 6.11 a.m. on a freezing February morning.[18] There was considerable confusion as to where Goldberg lived. Some sources said that he was based in Lodz, the centre of the Polish rag trade. But documents lodged with the Official Receiver in Melbourne showed that

Table 10.4   Estimated cash flows (all figures in $m)

	Goldberg Family Cos. Cal. 1990	Linter Group Cal. 1990	Brick & Pipe 6 mths to 30 September 1989
Rent	8.3	—	—
Dividends and interest	2.0	—	—
Total Revenue	10.3	—	—
Forecast profit		75.7	22.1
Interest	(69.1)	(177.3)	(9.5)
Tax	—	—	(8.2)
Overheads	(5.7)	(4.8)	—
Total expenses	(74.8)	—	—
Cash inflow/(outflow)	(64.5)	(106.4)	4.4

his only income was derived from Oxford International Corporation, a small export finance firm in Manhattan. The documents indicated that he was employed by Oxford, but Oxford staff said he was not employed but an associate. They said he lived in California with his wife and daughter.

Goldberg's trustee in bankruptcy claimed his Toorak mansion in Orrong Road. Two months before he declared bankruptcy Goldberg had sold the house to his daughter Deborah Furst for an alleged $US5 million. The Federal Court froze the property.

Ten warrants were issued for Goldberg's arrest, a fairly futile exercise as long as he stayed in Poland. In Australia, Boskovitz was committed on charges of furnishing false or misleading information to the Linter auditors, Price Waterhouse. Goldberg was charged with similar offences, which revolved around transactions made before Linter's balance date of 31 March in 1989. Maxsted claimed that in 1989 Elders had lent $220 million to Entrad on 29 March. Entrad had then deposited the money with Linter Group which showed the $220 million in its books as a reduction in debts owed by the Goldberg company Gibraltar Factors. The effect was to reduce the Gibraltar Factors debt from $270 million to $50 million. On the same day Linter Group bought a promissory note from Elders Finance Group for $220 million. This would seem to have closed the circle. Elders Finance had its money back and was guaranteed against loss. But the effect of the transactions was to remove $220 million of debt from Linter's books and enable it to show $220 million cash on deposit instead. The whole transaction was unwound when the promissory note matured on 12 May. Goldberg was by that time the sole shareholder of Linter, which was being funded heavily by borrowings from banks. Other transactions were also mentioned in Maxsted's claim.

Boskovitz insisted that the money was borrowed for Goldberg's bids for Tootal and IEL. Boskovitz said that Goldberg had wanted the deals done quickly and had told her to go and 'talk to the boys at Elders'. She commented: 'Mr Goldberg said, "Don't talk too much. The walls have ears".'[19] Linter Group's former chairman, Ron Deans, said that the Linter balance sheet showing $220 million cash 'was a misleading balance sheet, but only to idiots'. Maxsted sued Goldberg, Boskovitz and Elders Finance for conspiring over the transactions. Two former Linter directors, John Gerahty and David Fitzsimmons, were sued by Maxsted for up to $50 million for alleged breaches of their duties. Linter's auditors, Price Waterhouse, were also sued, for failing to detect the transactions. All the rest defended the actions but Goldberg did not. By that time his personal finances were so far under water that another adverse finding would hardly matter. And by then Goldberg was far, far away. Ashley Page, Victoria's Official Receiver and Goldberg's trustee in bankruptcy, tried to hold a court hearing in Israel, aiming to seize money alleged to be in two bank accounts at Tel Aviv. However, Goldberg was afraid to set foot in Israel in case Australian authorities seized him and extradited him, so he successfully applied for the court hearing to be transferred to Poland. When Australian bankruptcy officials interviewed him there Goldberg claimed that he had 'never personally owned a cent' because everything was in family trusts. 'I never had any beneficial interest in any assets', he said. It was finally decided to hear the case in Israel in July 1994.

As a financial exile Goldberg received only a fraction of the publicity heaped on Christopher Skase, although there were indications that he might be more rewarding to pursue. Maxsted traced a series of transactions in which $30 million had been diverted from Linter Group for Goldberg's benefit, although most of the money appeared to have been expended paying off debts or buying shares in a company called Parkston that subsequently became valueless. Maxsted believed that the result of the transactions—which went through companies in Monaco, the Cook Islands, Britain and Hong Kong—was that Linter effectively paid Goldberg $109 million for his textile interests in 1987, although he was supposed to have received only $79 million for them.[20] Even if some of these funds helped finance Goldberg after he left Australia, life as an exile was taking its toll. Witnesses who saw him in Warsaw in late 1993 said that he was looking old and haggard.

John Shergold, who knew both men, said that Christopher Skase was a hard worker who studied companies carefully before he took them over, whereas Goldberg would have been bored by such homework and was a reckless gambler in the world of high finance. What the two had in common was that they refused to be beaten in a takeover battle. And the way to win a takeover battle in the 1980s, invariably, was to raise the price. After Goldberg had won Brick & Pipe he asked Shergold why *he* hadn't taken it over. Shergold, who understood the company far better than Goldberg did, replied that even if he had had $400 million he wouldn't have spent it taking over Brick & Pipe. 'Abe's philosophy was that every government was lying about the real rate of inflation and that it was twice as high as they said', Shergold said.

> So the assets he bought today for $400 million would be worth $800 million by 1998, while the debt he owed on them would be worth nothing. In reality, the interest gap on Brick & Pipe was about $60 million a year between the $80 million he had to pay and the $22 million it would soon be earning. He was a little eager beaver and a good salesman, but I think he got bored with the textile trade. He loved going into the city and meeting important people and bankers and brokers. After he went broke I said, 'What have you done?'; and he said: 'You know me, John. I never read anything'.

11

Estate Mortgage: the giraffe who grew too high

The trust may not invest in real property.

Prospectus, Estate Mortgage Depositors Trust No. 4

If there were a prize for the most effective marketing campaign by a financial institution in the 1980s it would have to go to the Estate Mortgage trusts. Estate Mortgage advertised widely to attract depositors, but the most memorable advertisement was a television cartoon featuring a giraffe. Bending its head to ground level, the giraffe said that some investments combined low risk with low return. But investors in Estate Mortgage combined low risk with high return, the giraffe said, stretching its neck to the treetops. It was a simple hard sell, brilliantly presented. Two other cartoons featured a rhinoceros and a blue marlin, both with a simple message.

The television commercials were reinforced by a heavy advertising campaign in print and radio. In Sydney the voice of one of the nation's most influential morning broadcasters, champion Australian Rugby Union coach Alan Jones, was used to extol the virtues of Estate Mortgage. The campaigns were a resounding success. By the end of 1986, when it first began advertising on television, Estate Mortgage had $100 million under management. The first commercials were in a question and answer format, with a toll-free telephone number at the end which viewers could ring for further information. They were long advertisements, lasting 90 and 120 seconds. Estate Mortgage spent $1 million on this campaign. It was the biggest marketing campaign by any mortgage trust in Australia's history, and was so successful that Estate Mortgage's assets under management exploded to $569 million in 1987–88. By September 1988 the amount had reached $670 million, representing one-third of all money invested in mortgage trusts.

Seeing the value of advertising, Estate Mortgage spent $4 million on its next campaign, which began in 1988. This campaign used the giraffe, marlin and rhino. Depositors, enthused by the persuasive fauna, pushed Estate Mortgage's total assets to $905 million by the end of 1989. This was by far the largest amount for any mortgage trust in Australia. In comparison, Westpac had just over $500 million under management in mortgage trusts. And Estate Mortgage was planning to get even bigger, projecting that deposits could grow to $1 billion and that it would register its 100 000th depositor during 1990.

It was heady stuff for a funds group which had been small-time until the 1980s. The Estate Mortgage group had been around since 1960, but its real birth was in 1976 with the launch of its Income Trust No. 1. In 1981 it launched its Property Growth Trust No. 1 and in the following year the Investment Trust. In 1983 it launched the Depositors Trust to fund the purchase of Unilever House, which stood on Bennelong Point a few hundred metres from Sydney's famous Opera House. The Depositors Trust was partly underwritten by the Australian Bank, which guaranteed an interest payout of at least 13 per cent. The guarantee was a rolling one for only six months at a time and the rate guaranteed by the bank varied according to market, but the bank backing gave the trust security and prestige.

The Australian Bank allowed its guarantee to lapse after 1985. The reasons are informative. The managing director of the bank, Mark Johnson, was worried that the guarantee was featuring prominently in Estate Mortgage's advertisements, sometimes with what he thought was inadequate reference to the fact that it was only for the next six months. As Estate Mortgage's business was growing rapidly the guarantee had the potential to become costly, so the bank appointed one of its officers, Ralph Kelly, to make a closer check of Estate Mortgage's operations.[1] Kelly discovered that Estate Mortgage was providing a lot of construction mortgages for non-residential properties such as hotels, offices and industrial buildings. Typically, Estate Mortgage would finance a commercial project. As soon as the building was completed and tenanted, the mortgage would be sold to an institution and Estate Mortgage would use the cash to finance another similar project. Such projects naturally have a high risk at the start during the construction stage, but once they are producing rent settle down to become low-risk mortgages. Because Estate Mortgage was selling the mortgages as soon as they were producing rental, the portfolio it was holding contained a heavy element of projects at their high-risk stage.

Kelly felt that the mortgage trusts were therefore higher risk than the image they were projecting in their advertising. He also came to the conclusion that Estate Mortgage was able to charge borrowers higher rates than other mortgage trusts because it was financing borrowers who were higher risk. Kelly felt that the perception of Estate Mortgage being portrayed in the advertising was not in line with the way the group was operating. After reviewing the report the Australian Bank decided to quietly let its guarantee lapse. Estate Mortgage's mushroom growth was making it a little large for the bank by that time anyway.

It is idle to speculate, but if Burns Philp Trustee had been as alert and streetwise as the Australian Bank the Estate Mortgage disaster might have been mitigated or even avoided. The trusts could operate without a bank guarantee, but they could not have operated without a trustee.

Estate Mortgage still looked attractive to investors, even without the Australian Bank guarantee. The group chairman, Carl Davis, had a background in retail merchandising and buying with the Myer group, and in corporate administration and property development with the Scheinburg family. Davis said that the Estate Mortgage trusts invested only in first mortgages, lending no more than 66 per cent of valuation.

The structure of the trusts appeared normal. Investors bought units in the various Estate Mortgage trusts. Their cash was then invested in mortgages by the management company, Estate Mortgage Managers, under the supervision of the trustee, Burns Philp Trustee Co Ltd. Interest earned on the mortgages was distributed to the unitholders, less the management company's expenses and commissions. A typical prospectus would contain towards the front a list of questions and answers explaining the trust's structure to investors. One of the questions was 'How safe is my money?'. The following is a typical reply to the question.

> Investors' application money is paid to Burns Philp Trustee Co Ltd who holds all of the funds and securities of the trust fund in its name on behalf of the unitholders. The trustee is totally independent of the manager. Its role includes the supervision of the provisions of the trust deed and the watching over the interest of the unitholders. Authorised investments include bank deposits, government endorsed paper and registered first mortgages.
>
> A mortgage advance may exceed 66⅔% of its independent valuation only if insured by an approved mortgage insurer, and all security properties must be insured for their full insurable value at all times. The trust may not invest in real property. The trust deed limits the total raising of funds and/or borrowings of the trust fund to a maximum of 50% of its total tangible assets (value of authorised investments less income, losses (if any) and adjustments made by the audit) which is 100% of net assets. You are not lending your money to the trustee or the manager. You are purchasing units in a trust fund which you, in fact, beneficially own in part, together with all the other unitholders.

This reply, reprinted in full from a prospectus of Estate Mortgage Depositors Trust No. 4, gave a number of assurances that made it sound perfectly secure:

- The mention of Burns Philp Trustee was particularly reassuring. This was a subsidiary of one of Australia's oldest and most respected companies. Indeed, Burns Philp had a well-earned reputation for stuffiness. It was unthinkable that a trustee company bearing the name of Burns Philp might be remiss in its duties.
- The authorised investments permitted by the trust looked the most secure imaginable: government paper, bank deposits and first mortgages up to two-thirds of valuation. The trusts were forbidden from making any advances to the management company.
- The trust could not invest directly in property on its own account. This appeared to make it less risky than property trusts.
- Borrowings were limited to 50 per cent of total tangible assets. A lower percentage would have been preferable, but this limit did not appear to expose unitholders to much risk.

The management company was Estate Mortgage Managers (EMM). EMM had four directors: Carl Davis (chairman); Sydney accountant William Camphin; Richard Lew (son of Reuben Lew); and Richard Fisk. EMM was owned 39 per cent by the Rose family of Melbourne and 35 per cent by Camphin; the rest was in minor holdings including 5.8 per cent held by Richard Lew. The only shadow that might have been visible to an alert investor was the background presence of Reuben Lew, who was generally considered to be the founder of the group and remained a consultant to it. He was not entirely a reassuring figure, having previously been a bankrupt. He had been discharged in 1963 but had chosen not to become a director of EMM.

This was too faint a shadow to disturb many investors in the 1980s. Estate Mortgage enjoyed phenomenal growth. In its first year of operation its assets totalled only $12 million. They reached $82 million in 1984, $100 million by 1986 and then, as we have seen, exploded with the advertising campaigns to $905 million.

But the giraffe had been lying. Estate Mortgage was not secure, although it had spent $5 million claiming to be. In the financial markets, any security offering a higher return than its neighbours is usually accompanied by higher risk. There are few exceptions to this rule and Estate Mortgage was not one of them. If Estate Mortgage was offering higher returns to its investors it was by definition operating on a higher cost of funds than its rivals. It therefore had to lend on higher mortgage rates than its rivals to get the same profit margin, unless it could somehow operate at lower costs than they did. This may have been possible for a while, but the mortgage field was well serviced by a range of lenders such as banks and insurance companies. Borrowers would always gravitate towards the lowest rates. When this happened, Estate Mortgage would face the alternative of either allowing its business to shrink or else maintaining its returns by chasing higher risk business.

The first alternative posed considerable problems. Estate Mortgage's main selling point was that it offered higher returns. If the returns fell, investors would withdraw their money and go elsewhere. To pay them out, Estate Mortgage would have to sell its mortgages. This was possible but difficult. One of the oldest and most fundamental problems in Australian finance has been the lack of a liquid secondary market in mortgages. Normally they can only be sold at heavy discounts and sometimes they cannot be sold at all. So Estate Mortgage chose the second alternative and started chasing the lucrative fees and rates being offered by speculative construction companies. This represented a substantial change in the nature of Estate Mortgage's investments.

The construction loans

In October 1985 Estate Mortgage granted a loan facility of up to $20.65 million to PMA Development Company No. 1 Pty Ltd (PMA1). PMA1 was a company set up by Queensland developer James Remo and his wife to build a shopping centre at Southport, at the northern end of the Gold Coast. The loan is worth exploring in a little detail because it is one of the earliest known substantial construction loans made by the group and because it established a pattern which would be followed in subsequent loans.[2]

Readers will have noted, in the prospectus quoted above, the statement that 'the trust may not invest in real property'. However the PMA1 loan was dressed up legally, in essence Estate Mortgage was investing in a property development. This was in breach of the spirit, if not the letter, of Estate Mortgage's trust deeds and prospectus.

Also, the difference between investing in mortgages and investing in property developments was fundamental. When Estate Mortgage lent money on mortgage it received a stream of interest payments from the borrower. It was from this cash stream that Estate Mortgage paid its quarterly dividends to unitholders, after deducting its own expenses. A property development, however, does not normally have a cash stream until it is completed, when it may be either let or sold. Until that time the cash flows *out*, as suppliers and builders have to be paid. When a property is completed it may be sold at a big profit or a big loss.

Estate Mortgage trust deeds permitted the trusts to lend on the security of first mortgage on freehold land, provided either that the land was insured to the value of the loan or that the loan did not exceed two-thirds of the value of the land. The land valuation would become a key factor in Estate Mortgage's construction loans. A layman might think that the value of a piece of land would be the price it was worth on the market. On this basis, none of Estate Mortgage's construction deals would have been done. Instead, an estimate was made of the value of the finished construction. Then the estimated costs of construction were deducted and the residue was said to be the value of the land. It was later argued extensively in legal cases that lending on this basis was a breach of the trust deeds, which allowed loans to be made on land only on the basis of its present state and use.

It should be said that for project financing an 'on completion valuation' is not without validity, but must be used with considerable care. Obviously, an empty paddock will be worth a lot more if the Empire State is built on it. Equally obviously, the valuation depends upon a lot of assumptions such as whether the building can be fully let, what rents can be charged and whether construction costs and times can be kept under control. Any variation in any of these assumptions will have a dramatic impact on the resultant figure for the land value. In an extremely adverse case—where the building costs more to construct than its final market value—the land value can become negative.

The PMA1 loan was certainly more speculative than the type of lending contemplated by the trust deeds. It was not made on the security of a first mortgage on the property. The loan was made to carry out development. There was no ceiling on the obligation, because loans would be limited only by the anticipated value of the building to be constructed. The land was valued at $8.7 million—$100 000 more than it had just been bought for—and the valuation assumed that a development application would be obtained to build the unit block. As PMA1 was unable to meet the principal and interest payments on the loan, Estate Mortgage was taking the entire risk that the development would be successful. Interest payments would be capitalised as the project progressed and paid when it was completed and sold, which meant that it would provide no cash flow for unitholders.

There were even worse features of the loan. PMA1 agreed to pay half the profits to be derived from the deal to Welstbarrd Pty Ltd, a company whose directors and shareholders were Reuben Lew and his wife Sandra. PMA1 also agreed to pay an establishment fee of $284 750 to Estate Mortgage Financial Services Pty Ltd (EMFS) out of the proceeds of the first loan. Despite its name, Estate Mortgage Financial Services was not owned by the trusts or their unitholders. It was another Lew family company. As a final kickback PMA1 agreed to pay EMFS a monthly service fee calculated at one-twentyfourth of one per cent of the loan advance outstanding. Thus over two years the Lews would receive one per cent of the average amount which had been borrowed. These deals between the Lews and the borrower were kept secret for the next five years until Estate Mortgage collapsed. Investors knew nothing of them, nor did the trustee.

EMM, the management company which in effect was run by the Lews, recommended the PMA1 loan to Burns Philp Trustee. Burns Philp Trustee, which had no knowledge of the secret deals between PMA1 and the Lews, authorised the payment. In May 1986 the loan limit was increased to $24.6 million and in October 1986 to $30 million.

In this deal the Lews not only collected a secret commission but also skewed the risk–reward equation. The unitholders of Estate Mortgage were taking all the financial risk in the deal. If anyone was entitled to a half-interest in the profits from the project it should therefore have been the unitholders, not the Lew family. Instead, the unitholders were getting only the interest rate return on the deal. They were, unbeknownst to them, getting an interest rate return for an equity risk. And, disregarding the ethical side of the situation, the kickbacks from the loan that were being diverted to the Lews were weakening the ability of PMA1 to fund the project.

Skipping ahead of our story, PMA1 eventually defaulted on the repayments of this loan. By June 1992 the total principal owed to the trusts (nobody was bothering to count interest by then) was $33.2 million, which was not recoverable from the principals of PMA1. The unit block was worth less than the amount owing and the new trustees, liquidators John Murphy and Peter Allen from Arthur Andersen & Co, were having a hard time selling it.

This pattern was repeated in at least a dozen other construction loans made by Estate Mortgage. The trustees' statement of claim, compiled by law firm Baker & McKenzie, cited the following transactions.[3]

PMA2. The same developers formed a company named Property Development Co No. 2 Pty Ltd (PMA2), to develop a shopping centre in the Brisbane suburb of Fairfield. A loan of $14 million was approved in early 1986. PMA2 agreed to pay half the profits on the completed development to another Lew company named Yossarian Nominees Pty Ltd. PMA2 also agreed to pay EMFS $220 000 from the first loan advance.

Janmont. This loan was for redevelopment of the old Myer site in Brisbane, comprising two buildings which backed on to each other from Queen and Adelaide Streets. The developer, REMM Group, bought the buildings by tender in March 1988 for $50 million through its subsidiary Janmont Pty Ltd. A valuation commissioned by Janmont a month after the tender found the buildings were worth $80 million—an increase of 60 per cent in their value over the tender price. REMM proposed to erect a $100 million 20-storey building on the Adelaide Street frontage, connecting it through an arcade with the Queen Street building. The project was subject to finance being available. At the time REMM committed to buy this building—on terms—it had been negotiating for nearly a year to erect the new Myer Centre in Adelaide.

It is interesting to compare the chronology of the two developments. In July 1988 the SA State Government Insurance Commission and the State Bank of SA committed to the Adelaide project. In April 1989 Estate Mortgage Managers recommended a loan of up to $80 million on the Brisbane properties. Janmont, the vehicle for the loan, agreed to pay EMFS an establishment fee of $1.2 million. This meant that REMM was financing not one but two large developments in 1989 and both of them hit the wall. Janmont borrowed $40 million on the Brisbane properties but no development had begun by the time Estate Mortgage collapsed. It would seem that the money went to fund the bottomless hole of the Adelaide project.

Signature Resorts. This project was the Opal Cove resort near Coffs Harbour. Again the valuation of $10 million was well in excess of the purchase price of $5.7 million for the land. A loan of $6.66 million was made in November 1987. The facility was successively increased to $70.6 million by March 1989. Signature Resorts paid establishment fees totalling $1 059 100 to EMFS. In addition, in May 1988 Signature Resorts agreed to pay a Lew company named Bresgin Pty Ltd $600 000 in September 1989. This payment was supposed to be in consideration of Bresgin indemnifying Burns Philp Trustee against loss on the project, but the undertaking was entered into without the knowledge of the trustee company and no such indemnity was ever given.

Merall Group. Estate Mortgage made several loans to companies associated with this group to fund the construction of time-share resorts in Queensland and Victoria. The first loan was for $4.48 million in August 1985—two months before the PMA1 loan. The exposure increased to $31.8 million in September 1988 and finally to an unlimited amount in mid-1989.

These loans were not made on the security of first mortgage. The borrowers were unable to meet the principal and interest payments except out of the successful completion of the development and the sale of the time-share intervals. Murphy and Allen claimed that when the loans were made the Merall Group could not obtain funds from other sources and some of the loans might not take priority over existing second mortgagees. Another hazard was that the cost of marketing time-share intervals might consume between 40 and 50 per cent of the gross sale price. By March 1989 the loans to Merall exceeded two-thirds of the value of the securities, which was in breach of Estate Mortgage's trust deeds. By that time also, the Merall Group had a net asset deficiency of $16 million. Merall Group had agreed to pay EMFS a fee of 1.5 per cent of the first advance from Estate Mortgage.

Carlton Clock Tower. The original loan on this development in Lygon

Street, Carlton was $14.6 million in March 1987, increasing to $24 183 000 in December 1989. Murphy and Allen claimed that this loan was first made to Carlton Clock Tower Complex Pty Ltd, a recently incorporated $2 company with no assets. The assets of the guarantors were already fully encumbered. The property advanced as security had no proper street access and other lenders had priority anyhow. The valuation of $22 million was vastly in excess of the purchase price of $1.5 million, and the loan was expected to cover the cost of the land, development and interest. Also, the project had been delayed and there had been a failure to find tenants. Carlton Clock Tower agreed to pay EMFS an establishment fee of 1.5 per cent of the facility approved.

Thompson. The series of loans to Thompson Land began in June 1987 with $2.8 million lent on a site in North Melbourne. This escalated to $50 million in September 1988, by which time the security included sites in Melbourne's King and Elizabeth Streets as well. The King Street site was valued at $4 million although it had been bought for only $2.8 million, and the Elizabeth Street site was valued at $6.6 million although the price was only $4.9 million. Thompson Land agreed to pay EMM fees totalling $681 450.

Ozton. This must have been the largest single loan facility granted by Estate Mortgage. It was for the redevelopment by Malcolm Edwards' Essington Developments Ltd of the Barclays Bank and Kindersley House sites at the corner of Bligh and Hunter Streets in Sydney. The initial facility to the development vehicle Ozton Pty Ltd was $84.6 million in November 1988. Less than six months later the facility was increased to $408 million. Ozton agreed to pay EMFS $1.2 million and to pay Bresgin 30 per cent of the profits if it received the original loan. In return for the increase in the loan Ozton agreed to invest $17.2 million in Estate Mortgage units, which was a benefit for the other unitholders.

Obita. This loan facility was for the redevelopment of the former Department of Main Roads site in Sydney near Central Station. Estate Mortgage lent $24.6 million on this site in June 1989, increasing it to $27.8 million in January 1990 when the trusts were on the verge of collapse. Obita agreed to pay EMM an establishment fee of $1.5 million out of the first facility and to pay EMFS a $100 000 fee out of the increase.

These construction loans had several similarities. In each case they included a provision that EMFS would receive a monthly fee of one-twentyfourth of one per cent of the amount of the loan outstanding. Each of them was based on a valution which assumed that the project would be completed successfully. In some cases the borrowers did not even have the necessary approvals for the proposed development. In several cases the borrowers were putting no effective funds into the venture and were not in any position to put funds in. Estate Mortgage was therefore taking an equity risk for a fixed interest return. Another common feature was that all the loans failed. The list below shows the status of the deals at June 1992.[4]

PMA2. In default. $16 435 000 owing to the trusts. Amount irrecoverable from PMA2. Security properties unsold.

Janmont. In default. $40.6 million owing to the trusts. Amount irrecoverable from Janmont. Security properties unsold. Another creditor owed at least $40.1 million claiming prior-ranking security.

Signature Resorts. In default. Signature Resorts wound up in March 1991. $68.2 million owing to the trusts. Amount irrecoverable from Signature Resorts. Security properties unsold.

Merall Group. In default. Receiver and manager appointed to Merall in August 1990. $43.2 million owing to the trusts. Security properties only saleable and amount recoverable under financial restructure deed approved by Victorian Supreme Court. Loss to the trusts expected to be total.

Carlton Clock Tower. In default. $17.3 million owing to the trusts. Amount irrecoverable from Carlton Clock Tower. Security properties unsold. Another creditor owed at least $11.2 million claiming prior-ranking security.

Thompson Land. In default. Thompson Land wound up in September 1990. $26.2 million owing to the trusts. Amount irrecoverable from Thompson Land. Security properties unsold. Another creditor owed at least $6 million claiming prior-ranking security.

Ozton. In default. Ozton wound up in August 1991. $66.8 million owing to the trusts. Amount irrecoverable from Ozton. Security properties unsold. Another creditor owed at least $88.7 million claiming prior-ranking security.

Obita. In default. $26.4 million owing to the trusts. Amount irrecoverable from Obita. Security properties unsold. Another creditor owed at least $10 million claiming prior-ranking security.

One notable point from the construction loans listed above—and they are not the only ones—is that the lending tended to increase in 1988 and 1989. The Obita loan is particularly interesting because it shows that Estate Mortgage was still shovelling money out when it was at death's door.

It is not clear when Estate Mortgage first began making construction loans, but they appear to have been well established by the time Australian Bank checked the group in 1985. As the years progressed the construction loans tended to become bigger. As these loans increased in the late 1980s the trusts became progressively illiquid, because an increasing element of the interest receipts being credited in their accounts was not cash interest but capitalised interest which would only be received when the property projects were successfully sold. This reduction in real—as opposed to apparent—cash flow was masked by the rising inflow of funds from investors who had been lured into the trusts by the advertising campaigns. It was also masked by heavy borrowings. A trust could be defined as insolvent at the point where dividend distributions were being paid out of incoming capital or borrowings, rather than out of income received. This point was certainly reached sometime before Estate Mortgage's collapse. Murphy and Allen alleged in their statement of claim that Estate Mortgage could have been insolvent as early as 1986.

How the run began

Estate Mortgage's heavy advertising campaign maintained its image through these years, although there was an occasional sceptic. Moneylink Financial Planners criticised the group in November 1988 and was sued for defamation by Burns Philp Trustee. The report must have unsettled a few investment advisors, who began getting their clients out of the trusts. Redemptions of units began to exceed unit sales. So from July 1989 Estate Mortgage began to suffer a net outflow of funds, small at first but gradually growing. In the last half of 1989 $120 million was withdrawn from Estate Mortgage and sales of fresh units did not cover the withdrawals. Bain Investment Management alone withdrew $6 million.

In August 1989 Independent Funds Research (IFR) did a study of all mortgage trusts in Australia. It praised the performance of Estate Mortgage and the 'exceptional' expertise and skills it had shown in managing construction loans. However, IFR pointed out that Estate Mortgage was high risk. Other fund managers limited the total outlay on construction properties to 10–15 per cent of their portfolio. The limit imposed by Estate Mortgage was also 10–15 per cent, but on progress payments advanced. As the progress payments were only part of the completed cost of a project, this meant that Estate Mortgage's exposure to total payments could be much higher than 15 per cent of the funds under management. IFR also pointed out that Estate Mortgage was 'lending driven'. Having found a project it wanted to finance, it undertook the financing and then raised the funds by selling more units. IFR said that this introduced the additional risk that any change in economic conditions which reduced the inflow of funds could leave Estate Mortgage with insufficient funds to meet its commitments. Despite these comments IFR was, in hindsight, more generous to the company than it deserved. Two Estate Mortgage trusts were the only ones in IFR's survey to be awarded a six-star rating for their performance over the previous five years.[5]

While IFR generally praised Estate Mortgage, comments such as these reinforced the fears some investment advisors had about the trusts.

Doubts about Estate Mortgage's solvency began circulating in earnest in December 1989. On 1 February 1990 Estate Mortgage announced that audited returns for the trusts in the December quarter had ranged from 18.4 to 19.0 per cent per annum. In the year to December 1989 distributions to unitholders had exceeded $100 million for the first time. A record $60.9 million would be paid out for the December half, bringing the total for the year to $110.7 million. Announcing this, the chief executive of Estate Mortgage Managers, Richard Lew, pointed out that Estate Mortgage was one of the few investment managers that undertook a full audit before distribution as an additional protection for investors.

This might have placated investors if the dividend had actually been paid. Normally Estate Mortgage paid dividends 15 to 20 days after the end of the quarter. This time the dividend was delayed by six weeks. Investors sniffed a warning signal. (To put it in market context, the first run on Pyramid Building Society was in February 1990. The cattle were spooked and ready to stampede.) One morning a unitholder arrived at the company's Melbourne office, claiming he had been told that the Victorian Corporate Affairs Commission was going through the Estate Mortgage books. Richard Lew personally calmed him down by calling the CAC and confirming that the story was untrue.

Financial journalists started getting phone calls from Estate Mortgage's public relations firm, inviting them to lunch. A few stories appeared in the business press of a generally reassuring nature. However, they also pointed out that Estate Mortgage tended to operate at low levels of liquidity. To get its high returns, almost every dollar had to be invested.

In the panicky markets of early 1990 this was all that was needed to worry investors. Investors began to withdraw more funds from Estate Mortgage and the run became heavier as the weeks progressed. The trust deeds specified that any investors seeking to withdraw could get their money back on 21 days' notice. The management company said in the prospectus that investors could normally be paid out in seven days. But, in the first ten weeks of 1990, investors demanded the return of $100 million—which was $70 million in excess of sales—and the trusts could not find the money. In April a further $46 million had been withdrawn by the 11th, when Estate Mortgage was forced to suspend payments. The group's 60 000 investors—including those who had already applied for the return of $50 million—were told that they would be unable to withdraw money until June. The suspension had the support of the Victorian CAC, on the grounds that investors who stampeded early might damage the prospects of those who stayed in. But those who had got out were the smart ones. The rest would be frozen in for years.

The first reaction from commentators was that Estate Mortgage had fallen into the classic trap of borrowing short and lending long. This was true, but not very helpful. Call deposits are an important element in the capital base of most Australian financial institutions which invest in such long-term assets as mortgages and bonds. These include perfectly sound institutions such as savings banks. It is a fair bet that, if 10 per cent of the call depositors of any institution in Australia demanded their money back on the same day, the institution would become instantly insolvent and have to either borrow for the repayments or suspend payments, even though its underlying assets were perfectly sound. Estate Mortgage, being fully invested in mortgages, was bound to become illiquid if cash withdrawals ever substantially exceeded cash deposits. The real question was whether the assets were sound.

The basic problem was Estate Mortgage's abnormally high exposure to the construction and development market. By late 1989 it was becoming evident that trouble was looming for the property industry. The greater Estate Mortgage's exposure to uncompleted projects the greater its potential losses.

At the time of its suspension Estate had some 20 per cent of its assets in construction loans. This was too high. It was also worse than it looked, because construction loans are normally drawn down in tranches. Estate Mortgage not only had 20 per cent of its assets stuck in illiquid construction loans (many of which would prove bad) but it was committed for the undrawn component of them. As the cash squeeze on Estate Mortgage tightened progressively after mid-1989, construction companies had begun complaining about delays in progress payments. Several companies had been forced to seek alternative finance and were considering legal action. One of the biggest exposures was to Essington's Bligh Street development. Essington had received $140 million in progress payments but was now stranded for the rest.[6] Estate Mortgage had also committed itself to finance a $180 million development by Essington at Darling Harbour, of which none had been drawn. Tibor Balog's Dainford group was another with outstanding commitments from Estate Mortgage.

The construction commitments raised an ominous spectre. If construction companies were creditors of Estate Mortgage for large licks of capital, that would mean that less money could be returned to the depositors. The depositors might have to wait until the construction companies completed their projects and sold them before they could be recompensed. In the increasingly difficult commercial property market of 1990 this looked like a long wait at best. At worst, falling property values might mean a collapse of the construction companies and the Estate Mortgage depositors would never get their money back.

One solution Estate Mortgage had used in the past had been to sell all or part of a mortgage. But the secondary market in mortgages contained only a few institutional players and deals were done by private negotiation. By the start of 1990 buyers had dried up. Whether Estate Mortgage could sell its mortgages would depend upon their quality. According to the IFR survey, Estate Mortgage held a higher proportion of properties as mortgagee in possession than any other mortgage trust group. In two of the trusts around 10 per cent of the properties were held as mortgagee in possession. Estate Mortgage's director for marketing and fund-raising, Richard Fisk, said at the time that these loans were not necessarily in default. He said that Estate had been particularly active in taking control of potential problem mortgages and that this may have boosted their percentage.[7] Of course, if Estate Mortgage had been following its proclaimed practice of only lending at two-thirds of valuation, it should have had an adequate margin of safety. As they waited for more news from Estate Mortgage, investors' minds began focussing on that 'if'.

The dangers of the 'lending driven' philosophy were becoming obvious. Let us say a trust was holding $200 million in mortgages, of which $150 million had been funded by sales of units and the other $50 million by borrowing. Then suppose the management decided to fund another $20 million construction loan. The ratio of unit sales to borrowings would become $150 million to $70 million until the sales department could redress the balance by selling more units. If they did not sell more units, the trust's gearing would rise. And if the number of units fell because redemptions were outstripping sales the trust's gearing would blow out further.

The 'lending driven' approach was supported by a $200 million unsecured line of credit from a syndicate of eight banks. New loans could be made in anticipation of further funds inflow and financed from this line of credit until the money came through. The strategy relied on the public continuing to buy units. The heavy advertising campaign was therefore essential, because a continuing inflow of funds from unit sales was the lifeblood of Estate Mortgage. The trusts were vulnerable to either a reduction in their credit or a funds outflow, both of which happened in the December quarter of 1989.[8] In that quarter the line of credit was reduced to $175 million and was fully drawn. By the end of December the Income Trust No. 1, for example, had total assets of $222 million and borrowings of more than $70 million, giving it a gearing of more than 31 per cent. Interest bills were soaking up almost one-third of the income received by the trust.

The income gap revealed

For several weeks after the suspension an uneasy silence settled over the Estate Mortgage group. The managers promised to pay a distribution to unitholders for the March quarter, but it was delayed. Burns Philp Trustee said in May that funds were not yet available to pay out holders of $20 million in units who had applied for redemption before the suspension. In June Burns Philp Trustee warned that audited accounts for the March quarter indicated that unitholders would not receive a distribution for that period. The trustee company also applied to the Victorian Supreme Court to remove EMM as managers of the trusts. In court, the trustee's counsel, Dr Ian Spry, QC, said that there were 'suspected criminal actions on the part of the manager'.[9] EMM was sacked from management of the trusts on 13 June. Then the banks began pressing for liquidation of the trusts, a move that was strongly resisted by Burns Philp Trustee.

The few skerricks of news that emerged from Estate Mortgage were worrying. One was that the company had been running its trusts on an accrual basis rather than a cash basis.[10] This meant that each quarter it would calculate the distribution to unitholders on the payments it expected to receive rather than on what had actually been received. If the estimated receipts were optimistic, therefore, unitholders had been paid money that had never been earned. This practice, called 'tipping in', would obviously run into trouble if any unexpected bad debts arose. Some of the interest which had been treated as income had been capitalised on building projects and would not become payable for months or years. (In fact, much of it was never paid.) *Australian Business* revealed that the amount 'tipped in' for the September 1989 distribution had been $17 million, and in December $13 million, but in December EMM had been either unable or unwilling to make good the shortfall. Most of the December shortfall had related to bad debts where Estate Mortgage had become mortgagee in possession.

Table 11.1 shows the position of the six trusts in the March quarter of 1990. The first column shows the profit stated by each trust for the quarter. The second column shows the amount of interest included in the profit which had not actually been received. The last column shows the stated profit after deducting the unreceived interest. No wonder the March distributions were never made. Estate Mortgage would have had to pay out $5.6 million more than it had received. Worse, there was also a backlog from the December quarter of a further $14 million in unreceived interest.

On 22 June Reuben Lew was charged in the Melbourne Magistrates Court with the alleged theft of $500 000 from Burns Philp Trustee. In early July he was alleged to have received a secret commission on the PMA1 deal. Richard Lew was also charged.

Ever since the suspension KPMG Peat Marwick had been retained by Burns Philp Trustee to prepare a report on the status of the trusts. In early July their report became public. Those in the know were braced for

Table 11.1   Estate Mortgage's income gap—quarter to 31 March 1990

Trust	1 Stated net income ($000)	2 Interest not received ($000)	1 less 2 ($000)
Income Trust	9 992	14 309	(4 317)
Investment Trust	11 138	13 690	(2 552)
Depositors Trust	6 932	6 854	78
Depositors No. 2	6 607	6 215	392
Depositors No. 3	3 926	3 766	160
Depositors No. 4	5 400	4 785	615
Totals	43 995	49 619	(5 624)

a bad report because there had been a whisper for some time that things were very bad at Estate Mortgage. But to ordinary unitholders the report was a shocker. Peat Marwick's best-case outcome for the trusts was a loss of $315 million, with unitholders receiving a return of between 62c and 68c in the dollar over two to three years. The worst-case outcome was a loss of $475 million and an average return to holders of between 39c and 45c in the dollar.

Peat Marwick claimed that the poor cash position of the trusts had been concealed and that non-performing loans had not been disclosed in audited accounts and prospectuses. The report showed that operating cash requirements of the trust in the previous six months had been met by sales of units, by raising unsecured bank debt and by assigning the group's better mortgages. For an entity such as a mortgage trust, operating expenses should always be met out of income. To rely for funds for any length of time on the sales of units, increasing debt and the assignation of mortgages amounted to Estate Mortgage digging its own grave. These were stopgap measures to disguise the fundamentally unsound nature of the group's business, and must also have eroded the equity of the unitholders.

Peat's report showed that, of the total trust loan portfolio of $920 million, some $600 million—or 65 per cent—had been tied up in non-performing loans by the time of the suspension. A total of $339 million was in construction loans. The exposure of the six trusts to the construction industry varied widely, ranging from 19 per cent in the Income Trust to 71 per cent in Depositors Trust No. 4. Readers will recall that the prospectus for Trust No. 4, quoted earlier, emphasised the safety of unitholders' investments.

Unitholders were absorbing this body blow when a further threat was revealed. Macquarie Investment Management, trying to sort out the mess as an agent on behalf of the trustee, discovered that Estate Mortgage had sold put options on a number of first mortgages to third parties. As the financial pressure had grown from the increasing number of redemptions,

Estate Mortgage had begun selling its better mortgages. However, some of the buyers had been suspicious and demanded the right to put the mortgage back to Estate if there were a default. In other words, some of the cash which had been generated by sales of mortgages might have to be refunded to the buyers if there were any defaults.

Estate Mortgage was being revealed as a real can of worms. Every time investigators turned over a stone something nasty slithered out. Commentators began wondering how the trustee and the auditors had not noticed so many frauds and irregularities.[11] On 5 July Burns Philp Trustee sacked Priestley & Morris as auditors and appointed Ernst & Young. Priestley & Morris protested bitterly against the sacking, claiming that its March audit of Estate Mortgage had been heavily qualified. On another front, Melbourne chartered accountant Robert Ramsay was appointed provisional liquidator of Estate Mortgage Financial Services Ltd, one of the Lew family companies. The appointment was made by the two major creditors—Aetna Preston Securities Pty Ltd, which was owed about $16 million, and Bridgelands Pty Ltd, owed $15 million.

A meeting of investors in the six trusts was held at the Sydney Entertainment Centre on 24 July. Four thousand investors turned up, all angry at the failure of Burns Philp Trustee to detect what had been going wrong. After giving directors of the trustee company a roasting several of the unitholders threatened legal action. One point that had not escaped the unitholders was that some of the loans made by Estate Mortgage trusts had been in breach of their trust deed, which had stipulated a maximum level of two-thirds of valuation. The performance of Burns Philp Trustee had not been guaranteed by its parent, Burns, Philp & Co. Nevertheless, the share market knocked 10 per cent off the parent's share price in a week, pushing it below $3. The market was taking the view that not only was Burns Philp Trustee probably liable to the unitholders but that Burns, Philp & Co might be too.

The debate began to focus on Burns Philp Trustee. The National Companies and Securities Commission asked it to step down, which was bad enough. Worse was the confrontation which then occurred with its parent, Burns, Philp. Burns, Philp had been one of the great old family companies in Australian history, having been founded by James Burns and Robert Philp in the 1860s. It had a romantic history as an island trader, running steamships around the Pacific. By 1990 the interest of the families had been eroded to a few per cent held by the Burns family. The head of the family was David Burns, who was chairman of Burns, Philp and had a deep affection for the company's romantic tradition. The company had been changing under its toughminded Scottish managing director, Andrew Turnbull, who had steered Burns, Philp away from its marginal Pacific operations and into the food and hardware industries.

David Burns recognised the necessity for change, but had been reluctant. As friends and associates of David Burns still controlled some 30 per cent of Burns, Philp the changes Turnbull wanted were being implemented only slowly.[12]

The trustee company was a wholly owned subsidiary of Burns, Philp and nearly as old as the parent company. By 1990 it had become an outpost which David Burns and some friends had been left to run in a clubbish atmosphere. Burns Philp Trustee had a separate board of its own. One of David Burns' fellow directors there was Peter Henderson, son-in-law of Sir Robert Menzies and former secretary of the Department of Foreign Affairs. He and Burns had been best man at each other's wedding. Burns Philp Trustee had a good portfolio of trustee business. It made a contribution to the group's bottom line, while looking unexcitingly safe. So the board of Burns, Philp & Co had left it alone. (How much the parent board knew of the trustee company's affairs would later become a crucial issue in a law case.) Then Estate Mortgage collapsed and Turnbull suddenly realised that the trustee company was a potential millstone that could drag the whole group down. Burns Philp Trustee had allowed its name to be used extensively in prospectuses and advertisements as a hallmark of security for a group whose investors now looked like being wiped out. There were bound to be lawsuits alleging that Burns Philp Trustee had failed to carry out its duties with due diligence. Given the disturbing revelations that had been emerging, such lawsuits stood at least a fair chance of succeeding. If they did, the amounts involved would wipe out the trustee company's capital and investors would then come gunning after Burns, Philp for the residue. Burns, Philp had never guaranteed the trustee company, but that might not be sufficient to save it from heavy damages.

Turnbull acted vigorously to save the parent company. On 9 August he demanded that the trustee company resign immediately from the Estate Mortgage trusteeship. Burns Philp Trustee announced its retirement the following day. This turned into a legal imbroglio. Burns Philp Trustee found that it could not retire as trustee until another trustee could be found to take over. Other trustee companies were reluctant to become involved in what looked like a thankless task with potential legal liabilities. Also, if Burns Philp Trustee walked out the trusts would be left with no effective management. Since EMM's sacking, Burns Philp Trustee had been acting as de facto manager. It was the trustee's duty to appoint the manager. The NCSC wanted the trusts liquidated or placed under an administrator. However, the NCSC had no power because trusts were outside its jurisdiction. This led to a farcical position where the NCSC had to buy units in each of the busted trusts so that it could have a voice at meetings. The banks, which ranked as the major creditors ahead of unitholders, were resisting the appointment of a liquidator because they feared that a fire sale would crystallise heavy losses.

In October the situation was partly rectified when Burns, Philp appointed Global Funds Management (NSW) Ltd as the new manager of the Estate Mortgage trusts. This followed another intervention by Turnbull and the board of Burns, Philp, who had become increasingly alarmed at the threat the trustee company was posing to the rest of the group. The share price of Burns, Philp had now slid to $2.30. Turnbull, accompanied by merchant banker Mark Burrows, went to a Burns Philp Trustee meeting and demanded the resignation of the board. John Cowling, Burns, Philp's finance director, was appointed a director of the trustee company. All the former directors resigned except for David Burns, who held out for several days while ensuring that he was indemnified for legal costs. The new board immediately put Burns Philp Trustee into voluntary liquidation under Tony Sherlock of Coopers & Lybrand. Most of its $7 billion business was transferred to Permanent Trustee Co. It was only the second trustee company in Australia's history to go into liquidation, the first having been Trustees Executors & Agency Co in 1983. It was a sad end to one of Australia's oldest companies, whose motto had been 'Hands that never leave the wheel'. A month later David Burns resigned as chairman of Burns, Philp & Co. It was also a sad end for a well-meaning and personally honourable man who had tried to maintain family traditions but had great difficulty coping with the treacherous currents of the 1980s.

A slow resurrection

Global Funds Management now tried to start cleaning up the mess. The banking syndicate was demanding repayment. Global said that, if this were forced, five of the six trusts would become insolvent. Two top Sydney receivers, John Murphy and Peter Allen of Arthur Andersen & Co, were appointed trustees. Global estimated that Estate Mortgage needed to borrow an extra $140 million to complete half the construction projects in its loan portfolio. Global also claimed that breaches of the trust deed by Burns Philp Trustee had cost the trusts $575 million. Many of the so-called assets of the trusts were merely holes in the ground awaiting development. By this time the prices of commercial property had fallen badly, making most of the developments uneconomic. The value of the holes in the ground was small and in some cases negative. Inevitably there was a dispute over security. Mercantile Mutual, which had also lent money on several of the construction properties, claimed that its security over them ranked ahead of those of the banks. Murphy and Allen settled this dispute commercially by doing a rough division of properties, under which the trusts kept those that were income producing while Mercantile Mutual kept those still under construction. Mercantile Mutual also agreed to pay $30 million into the trusts two years later.

The legal manoeuvrings and disputes tended to mask the real grief caused by the collapse of Estate Mortgage. Many of the unitholders were elderly and had put a substantial portion of their savings into Estate Mortgage. Its collapse had suddenly reduced them to poverty. Some had been lured by the advertisements, some had relied on investment advisors. One of the great weaknesses of the 1980s was that investment advisors received commissions from institutions to which they directed investors' funds. This meant that there was always a temptation for an unscrupulous advisor to steer ignorant clients into whichever trust was paying the highest commissions. Several did: Estate Mortgage had always offered generous commissions to advisors.

When meetings of the unitholders were held some of the investors told harrowing stories. One widow had consulted an investment advisor who had put her entire savings into one Estate Mortgage trust. A retired couple were only slightly luckier when their advisor split their nest egg between three Estate Mortgage trusts. Even if Estate Mortgage had been as sound as it claimed this lack of diversification was imprudent to the point of criminality. In April 1991—a year after the suspension—unitholders met again to ponder their gloomy fate. They grudgingly agreed to a three-year freeze while Global tried to restore value to their holdings. They knew that some of them would be dead before they collected.

The positions of the trusts is perhaps best summarised by Table 11.2, which sets out the position of each of them at December 1990. The figures should be treated with caution because they were unaudited and Global specifically warned that they were not reliable. Some $850 million of the $920 million under management originally had been transferred between the trusts. This makes the individual numbers questionable but the totals should be in the ball park. Total assets by the end of 1990 had shrunk to $554 million, mainly because of revaluations and sales. Unitholders had invested $664 million in the group, of which half had been wiped out. The position of unitholders in Depositors Trust No. 4 was more hopeful than the rest because their interest had been guaranteed by the HongkongBank of Australia. However, the bank was contesting its liability in court.

A liquidator's hearing under Section 541 of the Companies Code was conducted in Melbourne by Master Evans. This revealed further details about how Estate Mortgage had really operated. It was in this hearing that investors learned that EMFS had been operating as a middleman between the trusts and the borrowers. EMFS had been owned by two

Table 11.2   Estate Mortgage at December 1990 (in $m—all figures unaudited)

	Investment Trust	Income Trust	Depositors Trust No. 1	Dep. Trust No. 2	Dep. Trust No. 3	Dep. Trust No. 4	Total
Total assets	126	129	90	86	53	70	554
Total liabilities	(35)	(104)	(46)	(28)	(20)	(1)	(234)
Units issued	(164)	(128)	(89)	(101)	(63)	(99)	(644)
Deficit	(73)	(103)	(45)	(43)	(30)	(30)	(324)
Unitholders' funds	91	25	44	58	33	69	320

private trust companies which in turn held their assets for Reuben and Sandra Lew's four children.

Another key company was Bresgin Pty Ltd, owned by Reuben and Sandra Lew. Bresgin was used to advance money to developers who wanted to borrow more than the limit of 66 per cent of a property's valuation. When a borrower needed, say, $800 000 on a $1 million development he could get $666 000 from the trusts and Bresgin would lend the balance.[13] Bresgin frequently took a cut of the profits on the development in return for providing the marginal finance. Sometimes the cut would be as high as 50 per cent. This was all news to ordinary investors in Estate Mortgage. The trust's advertising and prospectuses had always stated that the trusts were managed by EMM, under the (alleged) scrutiny of Burns Philp Trustee. There had never been any mention of EMFS or Bresgin. EMM had always been known to have a shareholding held by the Lew family, but there had been no disclosure that other Lew family companies were involved in the management, financing and expedition of Estate Mortgage loans—and there had certainly been no disclosure that they were taking commissions.

Bresgin had also been used to deliberately evade the requirements of the trust deed. Investors who thought they were secure because of the two-thirds limitation on loans had been deliberately deceived. Lew defended the practice of evading the limits on the grounds that it was necessary for Estate Mortgage to compete with banks and other financial institutions which had lent up to 100 per cent of valuation in the property deals of the 1980s.

Lew always denied that he controlled Estate Mortgage, but evidence at the hearing showed he had a lot of influence over its appointments. His son Richard had become chief executive. His son-in-law Jonathan Clark had become financial controller of EMFS after receiving an offer from Reuben Lew.

At one subsequent court hearing, Reuben Lew sobbed as he told the judge how he and his wife had their four children and their spouses to a family dinner every Friday night at his Toorak home. Estate Mortgage business was often discussed at these meals until 1986, when Sandra—called 'the chairlady' by Reuben—had forbidden any further reference to work at the family dinner table. The family meetings were then convened monthly on a Sunday at EMM's offices in Melbourne's William Street. Reuben said that a secretary was eventually asked to come in and record the meetings in order to prevent arguments. The sessions were often tense and sometimes took all day. The minutes indicated that Reuben Lew took the role of chairman, chiding one family member for failing to pursue a client, commenting on the capacities of a director, or forcefully recommending that another executive be asked to resign. Despite this, Lew at all times in court rejected any assertion that he took an active role in EMM business.[14]

Unitholders got an atom of revenge in October 1991 as Richard Lew and Carl Davis were convicted on charges of making false statements under Section 125 of the Companies Code. The charges related to the misleading advertisements which had claimed that Estate Mortgage was 'nice and safe'. Both men pleaded guilty. Magistrate Alistair McLean said that he regarded the breaches as serious. He sentenced Lew to eight months jail and Davis to twelve months.

It was not until November 1991—a year and a half after the suspension—that a deal was worked out between the manager and the banks. The banking syndicate was owed $175 million in principal plus $36 million in accumulated interest by the end of 1991. The banks ranked as unsecured lenders, putting them ahead of unitholders in the payout queue. The syndicate comprised HongkongBank of Australia, $40m.; Commonwealth Bank, $35m.; Barclays, $25m.; Nippon Credit, $20m.; Midland Montagu, $15m.; National Australia Bank, $15m.; State Bank NSW, $15m.; and ANZ McCaughan, $10m. For eighteen months there had been a conflict. The banks had been claiming repayment from the trusts. Global claimed that the money had actually been lent to Burns Philp Trustee, which was by then in liquidation. The banks claimed that the trusts had indemnified the trustee. Global claimed that Burns Philp Trustee had forfeited its right to indemnity by breaching the trust deed. In November the banks agreed to forfeit their $36 million interest (which was looking highly elusive anyway) and to forgo interest for another five years. They also agreed to lend a further $35 million to Estate Mortgage to help fund legal actions against third parties. In return, the trusts recognised the banks' claims and agreed to repay $175 million on terms. The unitholders, still disgruntled, agreed to the plan.

The main objections came from a dissident group led by former Indian Air Force pilot Hari Baghat, who proposed an alternative solution. Baghat had invited the Austwide property group to take over management of

Estate Mortgage. Fortunately the unitholders did not support Baghat. Austwide was in nearly as parlous a condition as Estate Mortgage, and would collapse only a few months later.

By this time the Estate Mortgage group was distributing blame as freely as it once distributed loans. The new trustees of Estate Mortgage, Allen and Murphy, sued the former auditors, Priestley & Morris. Allen and Murphy were authorised by the Australian Securities Commission to conduct a court examination of various parties, including officers of the banks and Burns Philp Trustee. Lawyers looked like making far more money out of Estate Mortgage than the unitholders ever would.

The trustee's examination unearthed a few more skeletons. The former general manager of Burns Philp Trustee, Bob Young, admitted that his company had misled the Corporate Affairs Commission over changes to trust deeds in 1987. Although the alterations had removed several safeguards for unitholders, Young had sent a routine certificate to the CAC saying that the trust deed alterations would not adversely affect the interests of unitholders. Mercantile Mutual had bought mortgages for as much as $20 million from Estate Mortgage without any written authorisation from Burns Philp Trustee. The alarm bells had first rung at Mercantile Mutual when one of its officers walked past a site in Sydney's Elizabeth Street on which it held a $20 million mortgage and discovered that the building was no longer there. It had been torn down to make way for the new Park Lane Hotel. The leading law firm Freehill Hollingdale & Page suggested that the advisory committee Burns, Philp had appointed to advise the trustee company should change minutes referring to Estate Mortgage to include the statement that the meetings were held to discuss various legal issues. By adding such words, professional legal privilege could be claimed for the minutes and—in the words of a Freehill's lawyer—'they would never see the light of day'.

The position of the trusts began to improve. The name was changed from Estate Mortgage. A new body was created called Meridian Investment Trust, which held units in the Estate Mortgage trusts which became sub-trusts. Meridian listed on the Australian Stock Exchange. As commercial property prices began getting up off the floor in early 1994 the finances looked a little brighter. Thanks to the settlement with the banks, Global and the trustees of Meridian had funds to pursue damages claims against various parties whom they alleged had contributed to the losses suffered by the Estate Mortgage trusts. The defendants included: Burns, Philp & Co; Burns Philp Trustee; Priestley & Morris; Reuben and Richard Lew; Bob Young; David Burns; Peter Henderson; Freehill Hollingdale & Page; and Peter Short, a Freehill's partner who had sat on the Burns Philp Trustee board.[15]

These damages cases took an eternity. The trustees were seeking the right to ask questions of the defendants, but the defendants appealed. The appeals went, in sequence, to the Administrative Appeals Tribunal, a Federal Court judge, a NSW Supreme Court judge, the Full Bench of the Federal Court, then the Full Bench of the Supreme Court. Both full courts threw the appeals out 3–0. Then the defendants sought a High Court appeal but were refused. All this took twelve months—in which the case had gone nowhere. By late 1993 Murphy and Allen were hoping to get it before the courts in about twelve months, but lawyers for Burns Philp Trustees were saying that they needed another three years to read all the documents produced in discovery proceedings. The trustees sought leave to proceed directly against Burns Philp Trustee's professional indemnity insurers, FAI and Lloyds. FAI and Lloyds countered by claiming that Murphy and Allen, as the new trustees of Estate Mortgage, had no standing to bring a case against them for losses suffered as a result of alleged breaches by the former trustees. If the line taken by FAI and Lloyds proved correct then the law was even more of an ass than Uriah Heep thought. If a new trustee was not the correct person to sue an old trustee for breach of duty, who was? The Victorian Supreme Court rejected the argument, finding that the new trustees had standing. Meanwhile, the 60 000 investors had still not been repaid a cent and a couple of thousand of them were already dead.

In November 1993 the law finally caught up with Reuben Lew. He was sentenced to three years jail for having improperly used his position as a company officer to gain financial advantage in the PMA1 and PMA2 deals. Judge Fricke of the Victorian Supreme Court ordered that he serve a minimum of two years. Richard Lew was sentenced to two years' jail, of which fifteen months was suspended, for similar offences. Reuben Lew was also ordered to pay $500 000 in restitution to Meridian Investment Trust. The judge also handed down a one-year suspended sentence to Brisbane valuer Tony Arnold—who had done nearly all of Estate Mortgage's valuations—for aiding and abetting Lew in breaching his duties.

The lean, balding Reuben Lew had wept at times in the court hearing, but the investors in the collapsed trusts were unmoved. 'He should have got life', was the bitter reaction of one investor quoted by the *Sydney Morning Herald*. And the law was not finished with the Lews. The liquidator of Estate Mortgage Financial Services, Robert Ramsay, launched a court action aimed at recovering $44 million from the former directors of EMFS and Reuben Lew. Ramsay also sued the auditor of EMFS, the Melbourne accounting firm of Tyshing, Price & Co. Reuben Lew declared himself bankrupt owing more than $27 million. He listed his only assets as a watch and cufflinks worth $150.

We have seen how the Lews took a percentage of the profit in nearly all of their construction deals, usually siphoned through EMFS. With this healthy flow of commissions how could EMFS have gone into liquidation? The answer is supremely ironic. At the end of 1993 Ramsay reckoned that EMFS had a deficiency of more than $50 million.[16] Some $25 million of the money siphoned from the trusts had been lent back to them in top-up loans. EMFS had lent a further $12 million to $14 million to Bresgin without security.

What the Lews had done was to siphon money out of Estate Mortgage through fees payable to their own companies via the borrowers. But the Lews believed that the borrowers were going to succeed. That is why they took equity in some of their projects. That is also why the Lews' own companies became lenders to the borrowers. If the Lews had been good judges of credit risk the schemes could well have succeeded. The Lews would have become very rich and Estate Mortgage might well have survived. The real defect of the Lews was in having a poor appreciation of credit risk and the property cycle. They were bad judges and EMFS went broke reinvesting in the same disastrous projects that would break the trusts. As liquidator, Ramsay was suing EMFS's directors—the Lews— for breach of duty. Their breach was alleged to be the act of lending the money back to the trusts. The Lews, who had deceived so many investors, also deceived themselves.

12
The great Pyramid of Farrow

The Treasurer, Rob Jolly, and the Attorney-General, Andrew McCutcheon, said today depositors' funds in the Pyramid Building Society are secure. There is no reason for people to withdraw their funds. Withdrawals are totally unnecessary and only create difficulties for customers. Rumours circulating about the society are without foundation.

Press statement, 12 February 1990

The 1989 annual report of Pyramid Building Society was aglow with the institution's achievements. It said that Pyramid had just completed the most successful year in its 30-year history. Pyramid was Victoria's largest building society and the second largest in Australia. The latest year had seen significant growth in all areas: lending, assets, profit, liquidity and capital account ratio. Net profit had risen by $8 million to more than $11 million. Chairman Ken Andrews went on to say that Pyramid was the largest division of the Australasia-wide mortgage lender, Farrow Corporation, which managed assets in excess of $2.6 billion. Farrow Corporation's net profit had soared from $4 million to more than $20 million during the year, with lending up from $657 million to $1.16 billion.

Farrow Corporation was a private company which controlled the Pyramid Building Society, Geelong Building Society and Countrywide Building Society. Bill Farrow, managing director of Pyramid and major shareholder in Farrow Corporation, said that Pyramid had grown remarkably in three decades, building expertise in providing the best in lending and investment products.[1] Farrow described Pyramid as a major provider of home finance with secured mortgage lending as its primary aim. He added:

> It also lends for residential investment properties and commercial properties, both purchase and construction . . . Strong emphasis is placed on quality properties and systems designed to ensure quality is maintained have been put in place. These include authorised valuations and borrowers meeting income/repayment ratios. Mortgage insurance is required when loans exceed certain valuation levels.

Two pages further on, he said:

Commercial and rental investment lending for a variety of property types also increased during the year. Again the emphasis was on quality. Some of the properties financed included townhouses, multi-unit residential blocks and select commercial properties. Pyramid introduced a new slogan during the year as part of a television, radio and press advertising campaign. 'For people who are money wise' best describes our customers because they really are wise to do business with Pyramid with our better investment rates, most competitive lending rates and personalised and friendly service.

Actor John Stanton had joined Pyramid during the year to provide the voice behind the radio commercials. Brian Naylor, one of Nine Network's top newsreaders, plugged Pyramid on television. Pyramid's accounts, unqualified by the auditor Day, Neilson, Jenkins & Johns, were signed off on 31 August 1989.

The report is quoted at some length to show the reassuring picture it painted of a strong, competent building society investing in quality mortgage business, mainly residential homes. Within six months of the report being signed there was a devastating run on Pyramid and before its next balance date the society had collapsed amid one of the greatest scandals of the era. Thousands of depositors suffered, the Victorian Labor Government was mortally wounded and the proud provincial city of Geelong was traumatised. Of all the corporate and financial collapses of the 1980s, the Farrow group of building societies probably hurt the most ordinary investors and had the most severe regional impact. It was made worse by the fact that the depositors had been persuaded that their money was safe. There was no way they could have told from official statements and documents that what they thought was safe was in fact high risk and bound to collapse.

After all, the three societies that made up the Farrow—Pyramid, Geelong and Countrywide—had a good long track record. Pyramid Building Society had been founded in 1959 by Vautin Andrews and Robert G. Farrow. These men were the epitome of Geelong. They were parochial in the finest sense of the word: proud of their city and motivated more by a desire to help their community than by any consideration of personal profit. Vautin Andrews became Mayor of Geelong. Bob Farrow was an accountant and, to save money in the early days when the society was started from scratch, his firm was appointed as manager of the society. Pyramid provided half of Geelong with housing loans in those early days. It operated in the traditional manner, lending money to subscribing members to buy established homes. In its infancy Pyramid's only two branches were in Geelong, but it later expanded to Belmont and Colac. It was not until the mid-1960s that Federal legislation enabled building societies to accept deposits from the public. Until that time the growth of building societies had been restricted by their limited ability to raise capital. Under the new legislation Pyramid grew quickly in the halcyon decade from the mid-1960s to the mid-1970s. Deposits grew from just under $180 000 in 1965 to $11.9 million in 1975. Total assets leaped from $400 000 to $13.6 million.

During these years Bob Farrow was plagued by ill-health. He would not retire until 1986, but his third son Bill appears to have had to take considerable responsibility from an early age and particularly after a series of severe heart attacks suffered by Bob in 1979. Bill had trained as an accountant and shown great aptitude for the business. Vautin's son Bruce was also working for the society. One of Bill Farrow's first presentations to the board, in 1970, demonstrated that the Farrow company was being paid less than a commercial rate for managing Pyramid. The society had no staff of its own and it was apparent that Bob Farrow had effectively been subsidising Pyramid. The management fees were put on a commercial footing, although the incident caused some embarrassment.

Farrow's empire expanded by taking over Pyramid's local competitor, the Geelong Building Society, in 1971. The Geelong Building Society traced its origins back to 1867. It had followed a conservative growth path until taken over by R.G. Farrow & Co. In 1984 Farrow took over the Third Extended Starr-Bowkett Building Society, which was then renamed Countrywide Building Society. It was the smallest of the three, with only two branches. Up until 1986 the three societies remained heavily focussed on their traditional area of lending on residential mortgages. But in the heady days post-deregulation Bill Farrow decided to get into the big time. In the 1986 annual report he signalled that the group intended to expand its non-home portfolio rapidly. 'The group has proved its ability to write large volumes of mortgage business', he said.

> These activities shall be funded from a combination of retail deposits, wholesale loans from the money markets and secondary mortgage markets, secured if necessary by assignment of mortgage assets . . . The group readily acknowledges the impact of deregulation and believes that no financial entity shall be able to achieve traditional wide margins . . . Further, interest spread must be significantly replaced by fee generation as margins shall continue to rapidly erode in this new era of competition in all financial markets.

With these words, Farrow had spelt out how the Farrow group would dig its own grave.

All three societies were well known locally and identified heavily with their community in Geelong and the surrounding districts. Pyramid sponsored a limited-over cricket competition and the football broadcasts on radio station 3AW. Pyramid exploited its customers' fierce loyalty to the Geelong VFL team—nicknamed the Cats—by building a large model cat wearing the team's blue and white hoops. In truth, the societies were expanding well beyond their Geelong base to become the dominant building society in Victoria and were doing increasing business outside the borders of Victoria. The group had even expanded internationally with the takeover of a building society in New Zealand. Growth in total assets is shown in Table 12.1.

Table 12.1   Growth in total assets[2]

Year	Pyramid ($m)	Geelong ($m)	Countrywide ($m)
1975	13.6	2.9	n.a.
1980	67.2	19.6	n.a.
1985	280.6	96.2	6.5
1986	378.4	112.8	38.7
1987	546.6	179.7	76.2
1988	958.8	284.7	128.7
1989	1 670.3	415.0	150.8
1990	1 836.3	328.6	124.5

Pyramid was abnormal not only for its rapid growth but also in its ownership. Most building societies around Australia were owned by hundreds or thousands of small shareholders, or by a large financial institution. Pyramid, Geelong and Countrywide were owned and managed by the Farrow family. After Bob Farrow retired in 1986, Bill Farrow took charge. He also made David Clarke a junior partner. Clarke was a local hero, having been 'best and fairest' for the Geelong footy team in 1978 and 1979. According to reports he was more aggressive and ambitious than Farrow. A friend said: 'Clarkey's the tough bloke. If you've got a staff problem, for example, Bill would say "I feel sorry for that person because they're having problems at home", whereas Clarkey would say "Well that's a whole lot of bullshit. They've done a rotten job and they've got to go" '. Unlike many footballers, Clarke had planned his post-football career carefully, moving in Geelong business circles and becoming an accountant with Price Waterhouse.[3] Clarke's family held about 20 per cent equity in Farrow Corporation for the rest of the group's life.

Farrow Corporation was building a six-storey head office—a skyscraper in Geelong terms—on Corio Bay. The two-building complex featured a grand wood-panelled foyer, attracting some criticism that the corporation grew too fast, was too slick, too good to be true. Despite all the signs of prosperity and solidity, some investors either knew or suspected that things were amiss in the Pyramid group. In early 1990 there was a sudden and damaging run as depositors withdrew their money from Pyramid.

The reasons for this run have never been established. Bill Farrow would later allege a whispering campaign by banks which were jealous of Pyramid's success. There may have been a grain of truth in this. On such skimpy anecdotal evidence as is available, the reports about Farrow do seem to have begun emanating from other financial institutions; but it may have been because the Farrow group societies were borrowing increasing amounts of money from them. Whatever the reason, Victorian investors had plenty of reason to be jittery as 1990 began. Victoria was in a state of anarchy. The MetPlan dispute, over a proposal to halve the number of workers on the tramways, had produced uproar. In the first days of January tram drivers blocked Bourke Street from end to end with their trams, then welded them to the rails. The government of Premier John Cain, which owed heavy debts to its Socialist Left faction, seemed utterly unable to cope with the situation. The spectacle of Victoria's notorious left-wing unions running the state was enough to make any small depositor shudder.

The run really began on 12 and 13 February, when a total of $31 million was withdrawn. The directors approached the Victorian Government, which decided to reassure depositors. Treasurer Rob Jolly and Attorney-General Andrew McCutcheon called a press conference on 13 February. They issued the following statement:

> The Treasurer, Rob Jolly, and the Attorney-General, Andrew McCutcheon, said today depositors' funds in the Pyramid Building Society are secure. There is no reason for people to withdraw their funds. Withdrawals are totally unnecessary and only create difficulties for customers. Rumours circulating about the society are without foundation.
>
> The ministers said that Pyramid has extensive lines of credit into the banking system and is supported by the leading national banks. The Treasurer has been assured that adequate liquidity support will be available under these arrangements.
>
> The ministers noted the statement issued by the Registrar of Building Societies [David LaFranchi] pointing out the extensive liquid assets of Pyramid Building Society and the results of the Registrar's monitoring activities. The Registrar said that Pyramid currently has liquid assets totalling in excess of $400 million.
>
> Building Societies are required to lodge detailed monthly financial reports with the Registrar. The Registrar has stated that these reports show that the society has adequate asset backing and is responsibly managed. Ongoing monitoring of the society has revealed nothing of concern.
>
> Building societies are subject to State legislation which is designed to ensure that depositors' funds are secure. They are required to lend predominantly on the security of freehold mortgages and 50 per cent of their assets must be in residential mortgages. Building societies have a secure asset base.
>
> The ministers have said that the Victorian Government will cooperate with all relevant authorities to ensure that depositors' funds are secure.

The press release got the names and titles of the ministers correct. Apart from that it is a challenge to find a single accurate statement in the release. Depositors' funds in Pyramid were not secure. There was every reason to withdraw them. The rumours had excellent foundation. Pyramid was not supported by leading banks, which had not assured the Treasurer that adequate liquidity support would be available. The Registrar had inadequate monitoring facilities and did not know the depth of Pyramid's problems. State legislation did not ensure that depositors' funds were secure and certainly did not ensure that half of Pyramid's funds were in residential mortgages. And, instead of cooperating to ensure that depositors' funds were secure, the government would try to duck its responsibilities shamefully when the time came.

Depositors were reassured by everyone involved. Jolly said that the rumour about Pyramid had been 'started presumably by someone who had a vested interest in starting it'. David Clarke said that rumours of an impending financial collapse had been circulating for the past year. Most originated with rival bankers unable to match Pyramid's interest rates, he said.[4] The run on the building society was also said to have been a mistake. On Friday 8 February the *Australian Financial Review* had run a story about an unrelated company named Pyramid Australia which was said to have an exposure to Bond Corporation. That was supposed to have sparked the run on the building society. To further reassure Pyramid depositors, Farrow Corporation sent copies of Jolly and McCutcheon's release to all 200 000 of them. The press release was accompanied by the following letter, dated 15 February 1990:

> As you may have already heard, various financial institutions, including ourselves, have been subjected to various rumours and speculation.
>
> These rumours about us are not true. We have just had the most successful 6 months in our history, posting a half-yearly profit in excess of $12 million after tax, coming on top of a 1989 profit of $22 million, after tax. In addition, January 1990 was the second-highest inflow month in our history.
>
> To reinforce our position, I have asked the government to independently confirm this position and I enclose a copy of their response.
>
> Yours sincerely,
> R.G. Farrow,
> Chairman.

Despite these reassuring statements, depositors kept withdrawing. The run on Pyramid was more damaging and lasted for longer than was revealed at the time. The run was said to have finished in the week of Jolly's statement, but it continued heavily for weeks afterwards. Between 12 and 28 February Pyramid suffered a net outflow of $134 million. The run continued into March with another net outflow of $92 million between 7 and 20 March.[5]

Eight days after the Jolly–McCutcheon statement Price Waterhouse was commissioned to report on the financial health of Farrow Corporation. Farrow Corporation was trying to restore its finances by selling $100 million of its mortgages, but by the time Price Waterhouse made a summary report to directors on 21 March the group had sold only $68 million. Price Waterhouse told directors:

> The outflows in depositors funds, together with the delays in achieving further sales of parcels of mortgages mean that Farrow needs a cash injection of $100 million urgently. Without such an injection there is a significant risk of Farrow's buiding society entities being unable to maintain sufficient liquidity to continue to lend under current building society regulations. Any major curtailment in the ability to lend could lead to a run starting again. One hundred million would restore their liquidity ratio and enable a moderate level of lending to continue. We remain firmly convinced [a warning Price Waterhouse had first made to Farrow directors on 7 March] that before any announcement of provisioning levels Farrow needs a substantial recapitalisation involving a new shareholder of high standing such as a bank or other major financial institution.

Price Waterhouse pointed out that it would take time to recruit a new shareholder and that Farrow needed the $100 million injected in cash straightaway. By any definition this was a very grave diagnosis of Farrow's situation. No fairy godmother with $100 million cash was visible or likely to be. The Price Waterhouse report was kind to management, saying that Farrow had been reasonably well run until the February stampede by depositors. The residential loan portfolio was relatively low risk with $1281 million spread across 11 400 loan accounts. The commercial loan portfolio, however, was described as medium to high risk with $1153 million spread across 1700 loan accounts. Price Waterhouse pointed out that a significant proportion of Farrow's profit was derived from application fees. This meant its profit would suffer severely if it were unable to write new loans. It was therefore critical that the building societies should be able to continue lending. Under Victorian law building societies were supposed to keep at least 12.5 per cent of their funds liquid. Any society slipping below that level was warned by the Registrar to return to it. If the level went below 7.5 per cent the Registrar had the power to appoint a liquidator or administrator. By the time Price Waterhouse reported, Pyramid's liquid funds were at 12.1 per cent, Countrywide's at 11.2 per cent and Geelong's at 6.7 per cent. Farrow was therefore trapped in a vicious circle. The societies could not lend because their liquidity levels were too low; if they didn't lend they couldn't generate profits; and if they didn't make profits their liquidity levels would come under further pressure from another run. The necessarily brief report by Price Waterhouse had flagged most of the real problems in the group, but had underestimated their size.

The February run had attracted media attention to Pyramid. Investigating journalists did not turn up any damning exposes, but they did reveal that the society was unusual in being privately owned by two families and that it had a reputation for entrepreneurial lending. During March and April Pyramid embarked on an advertising splurge to woo new depositors by offering interest rates up to two per cent above other building societies. This was a desperate attempt to get fresh money and the very size of the gap between rates offered by Pyramid and its competitors should have warned depositors. Behind the scenes, the Farrow group was trying to stave off collapse by borrowing money and selling assets. Branches were told to discourage depositors from withdrawing funds. Several financial institutions were approached to buy Pyramid assets or to inject equity into the group.

Readers have already noted the huge run on funds in February and March and may have wondered where Farrow found the cash to meet it. The answer was that between the beginning of February and the end of May the building societies raised $250 million by selling or securitising their mortgages. This move would have important ramifications. Every dollar raised by selling or assigning a mortgage was a dollar pledged to a lender who would rank ahead of the depositors if a liquidation occurred. Also, the more mortgages the societies sold to financial institutions, the more likely the institutions were to realise that the societies were in trouble. An increasing number of people in the financial world therefore began to realise that the Farrow group was in difficulties. Staff at some bank branches began warning clients against investing in Pyramid. Potter Partners, acting for Farrow, worked hard to find an equity partner, but without success. The ANZ was the only major institution to show much interest. Several heads of agreement were drafted, but the ANZ was never better than lukewarm about the deal. Managing director Will Bailey later told the ABC: 'Early in May it became evident that if we were interested we could get some more details, and at that point of time we decided we wouldn't go ahead'. Bailey said that the ANZ never got close to doing a deal. In a letter to LaFranchi Potters claimed that, as well as the ANZ, Citibank, State Bank of South Australia and the St George Building Society were also interested.

The second run

All these talks were inconclusive. To potential buyers the attraction of the societies was their branch network and deposit base. The drawback was the unknown depth of bad debts. If the Victorian Government had been prepared to guarantee the bad debts of the societies they could probably have been taken over. Bill Farrow and David Clarke offered that any consideration received by them could be held in escrow for two years and could be offset against future loan losses. This would have meant, in practice, that they would have got zero but it might also have spared them some of the consequences of a collapse. Cain and Jolly should have realised that, as the February statement had committed the government to the societies anyway, they might as well have made a virtue of a necessity and given a guarantee to the potential buyers. This could have ensured a smoother transition, fewer losses and much less panic and distress. Instead, the government prevaricated and ensured a worse disaster for themselves and the depositors. The government offered to guarantee half of any losses up to $60 million. By this time it was early June and Pyramid depositors had begun a second, terminal run on the society, taking $90 million out of the societies in May. As the run deepened, Cain reportedly made a last-ditch offer to the ANZ of a $100 million guarantee.[6] But the ANZ was no longer interested and no other buyer had emerged. By mid-June depositors had withdrawn a further $60 million and the Farrow group's societies had gone below the required liquidity levels. On 24 June 1990 the government, acting on the recommendation of LaFranchi, suspended trading by the three societies for a week and appointed accountant Ken Russell of Coopers & Lybrand as administrator.

The authorities still did not realise the depth of the Farrow group's plight. LaFranchi said the run had eroded the liquidity of the societies to the level where an independent assessment was required. Russell said his appointment was due to the 'unwarranted and long-sustained run' which had begun in February. But this was whistling in the dark. The suspension had made depositors more nervous than ever. As soon as the suspension was lifted they would rush to withdraw deposits unless they were given some very sound reason not to, such as the takeover of the societies by a big brother of undoubted strength. It was at this juncture—the day after Pyramid's suspension—that the Victorian Premier, John Cain, denied that there was any government guarantee for depositors in the three societies.

This act was both shameful and stupid. Readers are invited to re-read the statement of 13 February and draw their own conclusions. It contains no explicit guarantee but there is an overwhelming implicit one. By the words of its own ministers the government had vouched for the soundness of Pyramid and had advised depositors not to withdraw their money. The government had also undertaken to ensure that depositors' funds were secure. If any private institution had expressed similar sentiments of support it would have faced a stiff task persuading the courts that it was not a guarantor. Indeed, it is interesting to compare the Victorian Government's position with that of Burns, Philp & Co in the Estate Mortgage case.

The Jolly–McCutcheon statement morally obliged the government to guarantee depositors against loss and there must have been at least a strong argument that they were legally obliged to do so. Many a guarantee action was started in Australian courts in the 1990s on what appeared weaker grounds. It was immoral for the government not to do so. Cain's attempt to renege was also stupid because, while the government had been wrong in backing Pyramid, it could at least have salvaged some honour from the situation by acknowledging that it would underwrite depositors' losses. There are three principles here which apply to all governments at all times:

- no government should ever endorse a financial institution without first ensuring that the institution is worthy of endorsement
- if a government endorses a financial institution it should guarantee its losses
- if a government does not intend to make good such losses it should keep its mouth shut

Cain's statement unleashed a storm of denunciation. Commentators around Australia unanimously and strongly believed that Cain had acted neither wisely nor honourably. The damage to Cain increased as attention began to focus on the Victorian Government's record in the administration of building societies. After the debilitating runs on building societies in the last half of the 1970s, societies around Australia had banded together to form the National Deposit Insurance Corporation. This body had a standby credit of $100 million and laid down minimum ratios which its members should observe. Almost every worthwhile building society in Australia joined except for those in Victoria. The Victorian Government refused to participate on the grounds that it could regulate building societies itself.[7]

To this end, the government introduced and passed the *Building Societies Act* of 1986. This Act had several intrinsic defects which would later be identified in a report to the government by Norman Brady, a former chief of supervision at the Reserve Bank.[8] The main purpose of the Act was 'to provide a system of prudential regulation to ensure that deposits made with building societies by members of the public are safe'. It could well be argued that this wording by itself amounted to a guarantee of depositors in Victorian building societies. Brady pointed out that the wording also gave prudential supervision a task it could not fulfil. No system of supervision could ensure the safety of deposits. Supervision could only do its best to protect the interests of depositors. However, the Act did not give explicit authority to any particular body or person to undertake prudential supervision. The Registrar of Building Societies was entrusted with administration of the Act, but could only exercise his powers with the approval of the responsible minister. Many of the Registrar's powers were administrative and had little to do with supervision. The Registrar had wide powers to inspect documents, appoint investigators or administrators, stop societies from raising or spending funds, and direct societies to merge or to wind up. However, these powers could essentially only be used after a society had got into trouble. The aim of supervision should be to prevent it getting into trouble. Only a few areas of the Act, such as the provision of monthly returns and licensing of directors, amounted to ongoing supervision. The Act did not make it clear who the responsible minister was, the powers being split between the Treasurer and Attorney-General. The Victorian Building Societies Council had advisory powers under the Act and was responsible for administering a fund to limit losses in the event of the failure of a society.

After examining these various powers Brady concluded that the Act did not fulfil its main purpose. Having taken upon itself the responsibility of ensuring depositors' safety, the Victorian Government had framed an Act which provided inadequate supervisory powers.

The main burden of supervision fell on the Registrar, LaFranchi. As well as lacking adequate powers he lacked adequate resources. LaFranchi had been appointed Registrar in February 1989. He was also Deputy Commissioner for Corporate Affairs (at a time when various collapses had made the CAC highly active), head of the Cooperatives and Societies Division of the Corporate Affairs Department and Registrar of a number of other cooperative groups. He had a staff of 48 who were responsible for eight Acts of parliament relating to the supervision and administration of more than 250 deposit-taking institutions and 3000 cooperatives and societies. Just two staff had been allocated to monitor and supervise these last 3000.[9] A wide range of information was provided by building societies to the Registrar but lack of staff prevented proper checking, analysis and follow-up. Inspections were carried out as needed rather than regularly. The supervisors had virtually no contact with auditors of societies. Ad hoc discussions were held occasionally with management and directors, but not regularly. Brady concluded that the effective level of supervision of building societies in Victoria was minimal. 'In my view, the staff resources allocated to the Registrar are totally inadequate for him', Brady concluded.

Brady's report was commissioned by the government, which received it a month after Pyramid's collapse. The conclusions were unwelcome but should not have been surprising. LaFranchi himself had pointed out the lack of resources in a report in the previous year in which he warned that 'the likelihood of a collapse of a (building) society in Victoria is very real'. LaFranchi pointed out that although reserve funds had been built up to $20 million that amount would be insufficient to meet the loss that would be incurred if even a medium-size society were to collapse. There were nineteen societies in the state and LaFranchi believed that inspection of at least ten of them was 'becoming a matter of urgency'.[10] The total asset value of these ten was more than $3 billion.

Finally, even if the Act had given LaFranchi effective supervisory powers, even if the government had given him adequate supervisory staff and even if they had detected the weaknesses in Pyramid, there was no effective action he could have taken. Where a Registrar discovered that a building society had got into difficulties the only power the Registrar had to save it was by ordering it to merge with another society. But, following the recent transformation of the RESI Building Society into the Bank of Melbourne, Pyramid had become by far the largest building society in Victoria. Together with Geelong and Countrywide, the group had 55 per cent of the Victorian market. There was therefore no one big enough for it to be merged with. Under these circumstances there should have been a special responsibility for the authorities to monitor the Farrow group carefully. It was imperative that potential trouble be detected early, because if it were detected too late there were no practical options open to the Registrar beyond a resort to sorcery. The circumstances made it inevitable that if Pyramid got into deep trouble the Registrar would be forced to liquidate it, thereby triggering the government guarantee that was implicit in the Act.

Much of this emerged in the media in the days following Pyramid's closure. In addition it was pointed out that the Cain Government had been particularly vigorous over the years in holding down mortgage rates, presenting itself as a champion of the 'little people'. To the extent that this had prevented mortgage lenders from earning a market return on their funds, this had created yet another obligation of the government to the building societies.

Reinforcing these ethical arguments was the financial devastation that had suddenly hit Geelong. Two thousand depositors turned out in freezing rain on 27 June 1990 to demonstrate in the streets against the government. They hooted a local Labor MP who was silly enough to address them, and they supported the Mayor of Geelong, Brian Fowler, who said the Pyramid collapse should be treated as a natural disaster like the Newcastle earthquake. Cain said that it was not tenable to suggest that Victorian taxpayers 'should be called on to underwrite the activities of an organisation that's out there in the private sector . . . and I don't intend to pursue it any more'.

Having dug himself into a ghastly position, Cain kept displaying a preternatural ability to make it worse. Refusing to honour the government's obligations on Pyramid was bad enough. By broadening the argument, Cain was saying that the government would not come to the rescue of any private sector institution under the government's aegis. The result could well have been a stampede of funds out of every building society and credit union in the state. By this point Cain had managed the considerable feat of ensuring that he and his government were getting all the blame for Pyramid's collapse. It was easy—as well as true—to depict the government as dishonourable and heartless. The *Australian* interviewed Lionel Lennon, a man who had been blinded in an accident and had put the $93 000 he was awarded (his entire nest egg for life) into Pyramid. He said: 'Those same investors who the government told had safe and secure deposits are now being told "if you listened to us you were a fool" '. That was probably the most accurate summary anyone made of the government's position.

Labor backbenchers had been watching in horror as the crisis unfolded. There were 200 000 depositors in the Pyramid group, of whom only a few lived interstate. If the Victorian depositors and their families all voted against Labor at the next election the party would be annihilated. And the last faint hope of salvaging the societies died on 1 July when Russell announced that the building societies would be wound up. On the morning of 3 July Cain spoke on a Melbourne radio station, defending his decision not to bail out depositors. But he was overwhelmed at a caucus meeting a few hours later, and in the afternoon had the embarrassing task of announcing that the government would, after all, guarantee the depositors. The repayment would be made over time. All the government had achieved by its nine-day prevarication had been disgrace.

The storm that had descended on the government had given Bill Farrow the opportunity to re-emerge. Farrow was a solid, handsome 41-year-old with sound Geelong roots and a highly persuasive manner. One reporter said that he had 'a mind like a calculator'. After the February run, Farrow had worked hard to rebuild confidence in the group. He said: 'I know every loan over $1 million and I know every loan—however small—that's over 30 days'. He said that he had only fifteen loans over $1 million on watch and that he was confident about them all.[11]

After the June suspension he conceded that the second run had been damaging but said 'nevertheless, as an ongoing entity, our group is particularly viable'.[12] He claimed that there was enough money in Pyramid, Geelong and Countrywide to repay all banks and depositors within eighteen months. The return of depositors' money was only at risk if there were a fire sale. He said that reports on the high number and poor quality of the buildings societies' commercial loans were false and that other building societies had a greater proportion of commercial loans than Farrow had. Only about twenty of the company's 15 000 loans were 'of concern' and only about 2 per cent were not providing interest.[13]

This revealed yet another grave flaw in the 1986 Act. The Act provided that 50 per cent of a building society's loans should be for owner-occupied housing. It also provided that a loan should not exceed 75 per cent of the value of an owner-occupied home or 66 per cent of the value of any other property. The most disturbing aspect of the Farrow collapse had been recurrent rumours that the group had overextended itself on commercial property, which was suffering a nasty slide by the start of 1990. Around the rest of Australia building society loans on commercial property amounted to only 6 per cent of their assets. Victorian societies, however, had lent 40 per cent on commercial property, with another 20 per cent of their loans to other than owner-occupiers.[14] Despite Farrow's statement, Pyramid's spread of lending was out of whack with industry norms.

Russell's first statements about the Farrow group had been optimistic, but he soon realised a number of the problems. On 14 August, some two months after his appointment, Russell released an interim status report on the Farrow group, giving the real reason for Pyramid closing its doors in June. At the time, a secured debt for $50 million was to fall due the following week and the creditor was demanding repayment. If Pyramid had paid the debt it would have run out of cash completely within days and been forced to close its doors anyway. Russell estimated that the Farrow group had a deficiency of $250 million if its mortgages were sold at realisable values. This, too, was a long way out of whack with the statements that had been made by Farrow.

Russell pinpointed the key weakness of the group. It had attracted funds by bidding high rates for depositors. However, it could not force its lending rates much higher than its competitors, so it had to operate on tight margins between its borrowing and lending rates. In these circumstances, it made its profits from the upfront fees charged for loan applications. Russell said:

> Farrow lent on tight margins and the application fee received represented a major portion of the profit on the loan. This profit was brought to account immediately on approval of the loan, although the size of the fee did depend on the type of loan. For example, on construction loans large upfront fees were charged whereas on the traditional residential type of loan a small application fee was charged.

In the year to June 1990 the group was estimated to have paid out $12.7 million more in interest to depositors and other lenders than it had received from borrowers. The group was relying for its profit on application fees totalling $42 million. This was an essentially unhealthy position. Any deposit-taking institution must, by definition, be able to earn more interest than it pays.

Russell gave details of a report by CS First Boston and Moody's Investors Services showing that the group's $2.1 billion in mortgage loans included $200 million interest-free loans and nearly $700 million capitalised interest loans. Only $1.2 billion of the loans were required to pay current interest and, of those, about 20 per cent were more than 30 days past due. Only a minority of the group's mortgages were therefore yielding cash interest.

Tony Hodgson arrives

Up until June the attempts to refinance the societies had been attempts to find an equity partner. It was now clear that the equity of Farrow and Clarke was worth zilch. The stark alternative was that the societies had either to be sold to another financial institution or to be liquidated. In December 1990 the axe fell when Tony Hodgson of Ferrier Hodgson was appointed liquidator. Hodgson produced two reports on Pyramid, one dated 28 June 1991 and the other dated 30 June 1992. The following summary of the structure and flaws of the societies is drawn from both reports. One mitigating factor which should be borne in mind when reading it is the continuing slump in commercial property prices, which slashed Pyramid's asset values between June 1990 and June 1992. However, a property crash was foreseeable in 1989 (although perhaps not its length or severity) and Farrow can fairly be censured for leaving his small depositors so exposed to the sector. Table 12.2 shows the loans position.

Building societies in Australia had traditionally been perceived as making the major part of their loans to owner-occupiers of homes. The Building Societies Act had tried to ensure that such loans formed at least half the portfolio of any Victorian society. But, contrary to the Act, the Farrow group had lent more than two-thirds of its money on commercial and construction properties.

Table 12.3 breaks down the loan portfolios of the three societies into those which did and did not yield regular interest payments. Those that did yield interest are further divided into those which were given as security to other lenders (usually banks) and those which were unencumbered. The table shows that the group was top-heavy with loans that were not producing any cash interest. These were predominantly the commercial loans and, as we shall see later, a large proportion of them were bad. The loans that were producing cash flow were predominantly the traditional loans to homeowners. If home loans have been properly structured in the first place it is rare for homeowners to default even in

Table 12.2   Loans by type[15] (at 30 April 1991)

	Pyramid ($m)	%	Geelong ($m)	%	Country-wide ($m)	%	Total ($m)	%
Residential /Commercial	405.6	25.2	81.9	30.5	20.7	19.7	508.2	26.6
Construction	1 086.3	67.4	171.6	65.9	82.8	78.9	1 340.7	66.8
Land	119.9	7.4	15.0	5.6	1.5	1.4	136.4	6.6
Total	1 611.8	100.0	268.5	100.0	105.0	100.0	1 985.3	100.0

a recession. Loans to home owners normally produce assured cash flow, but are low-margin business because of the high unit cost of servicing. They are low margin but low risk. Loans on commercial property are high margin but high risk. Commercial property runs in cycles and the most important thing is to know when to be in and when to be out. The Farrow group seemed to believe that the property boom of the 1980s would continue forever, ignoring the share market crash of October 1987.

Instead of winding back in 1988 and 1989, Farrow had kept expanding. Looking at Pyramid, only 6.4 per cent of its loans were unencumbered and producing regular interest payments. The rest had either been given as security to other lenders or were not producing interest. Note that the security of the ordinary depositors—including those who held shares—had been diluted in two ways. Not only had the bad loans eroded their position, but a high proportion of the good loans that were left had been pledged to other lenders. The banks and other financiers who had lent money to the three societies on the security of these loans ranked ahead of depositors.

The automatic question is how a group of building societies could have got themselves into this position. The prudential requirements of the Building Societies Act had been intended to impose strict limits. Loans were supposed to be advanced primarily for homes. Loans were supposed to be adequately secured, supported by sworn valuations and mortgage insurance. The Act restricted the nature and amount of loans which could be advanced and prevented societies from making loans outside Victoria. However, the Act permitted societies to purchase mortgages on freehold or leasehold land.

The Farrow group developed an extremely complicated lending structure to exploit the Act's loopholes. A company named Farrow Mortgage Services Pty Ltd (FMS) was created to fund interstate loans. FMS had no assets of its own. Loan and security documents would be prepared in the name of FMS. At settlement the mortgage was bought by one of the societies, which thereby funded the loan. This technique outflanked the Act because the loans were ostensibly made by FMS, which was a

Table 12.3 The loan portfolios[16] at 30 April 1991

	Pyramid ($m)	%	Geelong ($m)	%	Country-wide ($m)	%	Total ($m)	%
Total loans	1 611.8	100.0	268.5	100.0	105.0	100.0	1 985.3	100.0
Comprising:								
i. Loans not providing regular cash repayments(a)								
	1 115.1	69.2	148.7	55.4	74.9	71.3	1 338.7	67.4
ii. Loans producing regular cash repayments								
– Charged to secured creditors	394.1	24.4	94.6	35.2	19.0	18.1	507.7	25.6
– Unencumbered	102.6	6.4	25.2	9.4	11.1	10.6	138.9	7.0

(a)   Including non-performing loans and loans on which interest was capitalised

company (not a building society) and therefore not subject to the Act. The technique enabled the Farrow societies not only to expand their lending operations outside Victoria but to expand into areas which were traditionally considered to be outside the domain of building societies. Loans were made to businesses operating hotels, motels, guesthouses, office buildings, caravan parks, farms, hospitals, health resorts and retirement villages both in Victoria and interstate.

The Act imposed prudential limits on the amount which could be lent on mortgage to 75 per cent of the value of an owner-occupied house or land and 66.66 per cent of the value of land in any other case. This restriction did not apply if the societies obtained mortgage insurance for at least the amount of the excess. But the Act also permitted societies to acquire assets other than mortgages provided that the total of these other assets did not exceed 6 per cent of total assets.

This 6 per cent discretion became known as the 'free tranche'. The societies used this free tranche to 'top up' loans (almost always on commercial property) above and beyond the amount which could be advanced in strict compliance with the lending limits imposed by the Act. Sometimes the free tranche was used so generously that borrowers were not required to put any of their own funds into a project.

Hodgson said that the societies' move into commercial lending had expanded dramatically from 1986 onwards, in accordance with Farrow's stated policy. The Farrow group, along with banks and other financial institutions, advanced billions of dollars on property developments. As these projects neared completion it became apparent that there were more buildings available than businesses to fill them. Values of office buildings plummeted. The societies' lending practices had left them with portfolios heavily weighted with properties which were worth far more than the

Table 12.4 Expected losses on the Mortgage portfolio

Expected losses	Pyramid ($m)	Geelong ($m)	Countrywide ($m)	Total ($m)
At 30 April 1991	481.2	56.7	26.0	563.9
At 31 October 1991	590.7	71.0	39.8	710.5
At 30 June 1992	661.7	77.4	36.7	775.8
Loss provisions as percentage of total loan portfolio	53%	41%	54%	

amounts they had lent. The problem was compounded by the fact that many of their properties were not in the prime CBD area but rather in corridors that had opened at the edge of the city. Much of the societies' portfolio was second- or third-rate property, which was less attractive to prospective tenants who were being offered bargain deals on first-class, centrally located properties. The gathering momentum of the property slump was reflected in the increase in the group's loss provisions, shown in Table 12.4.

In addition to these losses on loans, mortgages and properties there were also writedowns of investments. By the time all these were taken into account the estimated loss of the group at June 1992 was $982.8 million. By any standard, this was a disaster. A group of regional building societies had lost nearly $1 billion, representing roughly half their loan portfolio. Even after allowing for the savage slump in property prices from 1989 to 1992 this reflected exceedingly poor lending.

Hodgson was blunt. He said: 'The main cause of the failure of the societies was imprudent lending practices. In analysing the societies' historical performance, it is apparent that the societies' move away from its traditional residential based lending to larger commercial lending was, from the depositors' perspective, the societies' biggest mistake'. To implement Farrow's 1986 strategy of getting big in the commercial mortgage market the societies needed access to fresh funds. They had achieved this through four methods:

- attracting new depositors by offering interest rates 1 to 2 per cent higher than those of rival institutions
- borrowing from other financial institutions, usually banks, by pledging mortgages as security
- entering into securitisation and mortgage sale transactions
- actively marketing 'non-withdrawable investing shares' on the basis that these shares would provide depositors with a higher rate of return

In the latter case the rates offered were typically 1 to 2 per cent higher than the already high rates the societies were offering on deposits. This effectively expanded the equity capital of the group and enabled the societies to gear up by raising even more deposits. However, a number of the small investors who bought the shares were unaware of the essential difference between equity (a share) and loan funds (a deposit). They did not realise that they were no longer depositors, but owners. Hodgson said:

> At the outset of the liquidations, it became apparent that many non-withdrawable investing shareholders may have been misled by the conduct of the societies' officers to invest in shares, believing they were term deposits, without understanding that shares ranked behind depositors for dividends in the event of a liquidation. The fact that the societies paid their own staff commissions for selling these shares created a powerful incentive for staff to convince the public to invest. In some cases the societies' staff targeted existing large depositors by visiting them at home.

These methods succeeded in raising large amounts of money but resulted in the societies having a higher cost of funds than other major lenders. The societies' move into commercial lending coincided with the property market boom of the late 1980s. To enter this market the societies became aggressive lenders, known to be prepared to fund the more speculative projects. The societies were expanding into an area of lending where most of their staff had little or no experience.

A lot of the depositors' money was used to fund a few developers. A handful of borrowers accounted for the bulk of the group's losses. When the societies went into liquidation they had twelve groups of related individual and corporate borrowers holding multiple loans totalling $565 million, representing more than 20 per cent of the societies' total loan portfolio. By mid-1992 the prospective losses on these loans was around $370 million. In several cases, the depositors' money was lent recklessly.

In one case, the societies had lent $20 million for one month as part of the finance for a resort development in Queensland which was going to be refinanced. The $20 million was more than the security was worth. The refinancing never happened, the borrower defaulted and the societies became mortgagee in possession. In a second case, the group had lent more than $20 million on a twelve-storey CBD office building, based on the developer's estimate of what the completed project would be worth. The building was completed and then stood vacant with no prospect of being leased or sold. In a third case, $20 million had been lent to the developer of a CBD transport terminal and car park; the loss was estimated at $15 million. Some of these estimates were complicated by the fact that the properties were, in the depressed Victorian property market of the early 1990s, unsaleable.

The societies paid commissions to staff who introduced new lending business. By itself, this might not have been exceptionable. However, substantial commissions were paid to staff when they introduced or arranged new borrowers for loans where the original borrower had defaulted. An even worse flaw was that the same staff who were paid commissions were responsible for the management of problem loans. Hodgson said: 'It is apparent that it was in the staff's interest to rearrange problem loans, or advance further loans to existing borrowers (thereby in some instances earning additional commission) rather than taking action against defaulting borrowers'.

When the societies moved into larger scale commercial lending they began increasing profits by charging borrowers significant establishment fees when loans were approved. These fees were immediately credited as income and taken to account when calculating operating profit. Income from upfront fees and commissions grew rapidly from $4.8 million in 1986 to $42 million for the year to June 1990. However, almost none of these establishment fees were actually paid by the borrowers. They were simply added to the amount of the loan. Hodgson said that in the twelve months before the societies collapsed major borrowers were encouraged to extend the terms of their loans, which almost invariably made the size of the loans bigger. When loans were rolled over the societies charged the borrowers a rollover fee, which again was shown as a profit regardless of whether any cash was received. Of the $42 million in establishment fees shown as income in the year to June 1990, less than $3 million represented actual cash paid by borrowers. Most of the remaining $39 million was never paid. The fee income for 1990—and hence the profit—were therefore largely illusory. The same could be said of part of the reported profits for the previous year or two.

More than two-thirds of the societies' expected losses were on loans where interest was being capitalised. Much of the interest that had been capitalised was irrecoverable, although it had been reported in the societies' accounts as income This unpaid interest had therefore gone to pad the societies' reported income and hence their profits, sometimes for years. By the time the societies hit the wall, capitalised interest loans accounted for about one-third of their loan book. In many instances the societies advanced 100 per cent of the cost of a project, including establishment fees and capitalised interest. Loans on which the interest was being capitalised did not, of course, produce regular income to service the societies' borrowings from depositors and other lenders. Consequently, the Farrow group had to borrow more money to pay interest to its depositors.

As borrowers typically were not required to contribute any of their own capital, all risks associated with their projects were effectively assumed by the societies. The societies were therefore relying heavily on the estimates given by developers and their valuers of the value of the projects when completed. This left the societies heavily exposed to any fall in property values.

Any fall in value of properties below the level of the loans made by the societies should, in theory, have resulted in provisions being made for losses. In practice, the societies used various devices to avoid provisions. On certain loans the societies were given indemnities against loss by the managers (Bill Farrow, David Clarke and related entities). Any claims under the indemnities were offset against fees payable to the managers. The indemnities went as high as $6 million a year and appear to have alleviated the auditors' requirements to provide for losses on the relevant loans. In practice, the indemnities were never called upon.

Other techniques used by the societies to avoid recognition of losses included:

- converting 'interest only' and 'principal and interest loans' to 'capitalised interest' or 'interest free' loans
- reversing interest and fees charged on a loan, as distinct from writing off the interest and fees
- varying the terms and conditions of loans to extend them beyond the original expiry date
- selling the underlying property to a subsidiary company for a price sufficient to repay the defaulting loan

Often a defaulting borrower was replaced by a new borrower under favourable terms. These included:

- agreeing to make the new loan to a $2 company
- advancing funds to the new borrower on a non-recourse basis
- providing low-interest rates on the new advance; interest was typically capitalised anyway
- capitalising the establishment fee on the new loan as well
- entering into a joint venture agreement under which the societies agreed to share the losses as well as the profits
- making concessions on the terms of existing loans held by the 'new' borrowers

When arranging new borrowers to take over from defaulting borrowers the societies relinquished any rights they might have had to recover money from the defaulters. The effect of this range of practices was to disguise bad loans. In one case a borrower obtained a $10 million loan secured by second mortgages and defaulted within a month of receiving the money. An existing society borrower agreed to buy one of the security properties for an amount sufficient to repay the first mortgage on the property (held by another lender) and the second mortgage. This entailed the societies lending the 'new' borrower more than $28 million. In addition, the societies agreed to lend the new borrower $12 million secured on a property in Sydney, although the societies' valuation of that property was less than $12 million. By 1992 the societies were facing a loss of more than $25 million on the whole transaction. In another case, a loan secured by property in Queensland was rearranged on three separate occasions—after defaults—involving three different borrowers within twelve months. Whenever the societies rolled over such loans they charged establishment or rollover fees which were capitalised as part of the loan—and, of course, recognised as income.

Some of the largest losses were made in joint ventures, where the societies typically provided all the funding. The societies made handsome profits from these deals while the market was buoyant but overstayed the market and took heavy losses when property slumped. One Sydney-based development company obtained multiple loans from the societies through joint ventures. Loans to the developer, including capitalised fees and interest, totalled $100 million by the time the societies went into liquidation. Subsequent charges took the total to $130 million, but the value of the properties had fallen to only $20 million, producing a $110 million estimated loss.

The societies transferred many mortgages between themselves and made loans to each other. These practices caused a considerable tangle when they went into liquidation. Mostly, loans written by Pyramid were transferred to the smaller societies in return for cash or other loans. Hodgson said that mortgages appeared to have been transferred with little regard for the interests of the respective creditors or depositors of the societies. The number and size of these internal transactions was significant. In some cases loans were transferred three or four times in as many years. Pyramid passed a number of loans to Countrywide which resulted in losses. In December 1988 Countrywide had bought a loan from Pyramid at full value of $15 million. At the time, this loan represented nearly 10 per cent of Countrywide's total assets and more than twice its shareholders' funds. Pyramid bought the loan back as part of a larger transaction in March 1990 which involved Countrywide receiving a parcel of Pyramid's loans. The net effect of the transfers was that Pyramid had taken $15 million cash from Countrywide, which was left with a loss of $3 million on one of the Pyramid loans.

Big dollars, small investors

Hodgson instituted legal proceedings against Farrow and Clarke. He alleged that Farrow and Clarke and related entities had entered management agreements with the societies after 1 May 1986 which were void

Table 12.5 Payments to Farrow and Clarke

	1986–87 ($m)	1987–88 ($m)	1988–89 ($m)	1989–90 ($m)	Total ($m)
Management fees paid by the societies	7.2	11.8	16.5	33.2	68.7
Personal drawings of Farrow, Clarke and associates	1.0	4.0	5.9	15.4	26.3

under the Building Societies Act. On these grounds Hodgson demanded that $70 million in management fees paid to Farrow, Clarke and associates be refunded. (It should be noted that a proportion of these fees would have been for legitimate administration expenses.) Hodgson alleged that the liquidity of the societies was adversely affected by the substantial outflow of funds to Farrow and Clarke.

The staff of the societies were employed not by the societies but by R.G. Farrow & Co, which was controlled by Farrow and Clarke. By June 1990 R.G. Farrow & Co employed 680 people. The company charged the societies a management fee based on the average gross assets of the societies. The various fees and drawings of Farrow and Clarke from the societies are shown in Table 12.5.[17] More than half of the 1989–90 drawings of $26.3 million were made in the three months before the societies collapsed.

Hodgson claimed that the management agreements were void because the Building Societies Act had outlawed such agreements from 1 May 1986. The manager of the societies was R.G. Farrow & Co, which was a partnership between Farrow, Clarke and Farrow Management Pty Ltd. The deed of partnership was dated 28 April 1986, but Hodgson alleged that it had in fact been entered into after 1 May, thereby making it invalid.[18]

One entity to attract Hodgson's attention was Farrow Securities Ltd. From 1984 to the middle of 1987 Farrow Securities was directly owned and controlled by the three societies. In August and September 1987 a string of transactions resulted in ownership being transferred to interests associated with Farrow and Clarke. Soon after the change Pyramid invested $54.5 million in Farrow Securities. In 1990 dividends of more than $1.7 million were paid to Farrow and Clarke interests, of which $650 000 was paid three weeks before the societies collapsed. Just before the collapse Pyramid invested a further $16 million in Farrow Securities. Out of these funds Farrow Securities paid $1 million to R.G. Farrow & Co as management fees. The other $15 million was spent buying the companies which owned R.G. Farrow & Co from Farrow (who received $12 million) and Clarke ($3 million). As the only major asset of R.G.

Farrow & Co was the management rights to the societies, these transactions meant that Pyramid—through Farrow Securities—had paid $15 million for the right to manage itself. Hodgson launched several claims against Farrow and Clarke. They were also charged with alleged offences relating to the 'free tranche' lending. At the time of writing, Farrow and Clarke were defending all civil and criminal actions.

Farrow claimed that a senior bank executive had been the source of a rumour about Pyramid in February of that year. But on all evidence the societies had been badly run. Depositors had been wooed by the image of a strong group of societies, lending on quality assets. In truth, a large proportion of the quality assets had been mortgaged to banks. By the time two runs had sapped the group's cash reserves the assets that were left were of decidedly low quality. The group slogan 'For people who are money wise' could hardly have been less appropriate. Pyramid and its smaller sisters were vulnerable and the wisest thing that depositors could have done was get out, as many did. Farrow and Clarke's own drawings from the societies did nothing to bolster the group's strength. After the runs began Bill Farrow had a natural interest in trying to reassure depositors and potential buyers of the societies. Even so, some of the statements he made look dubious in the light of later revelations. He claimed that there were only fifteen exposures of more than $1 million that were on watch, and that he was confident about them all. This hardly squares with the dubious loans and lending practices unveiled by Russell and Hodgson or the fact that, two years later, the estimated loss on the group was nearly $1 billion. Nor does it square too well with the accelerated drawings by Farrow and Clarke in Pyramid's dying months.

Farrow and Clarke got their money out and left the depositors facing a disaster. They were rescued, after a fashion, by the Victorian Government. Depositors with balances of less than $100 were paid out in full. Other depositors were given two options by the government's agent, the State Bank of Victoria. The first was an immediate payment of 25c in the dollar. Depositors accepting this option gave the bank the right to receive 25 per cent of any distribution subsequently due to depositors. This meant that if Pyramid depositors eventually received 80c in the dollar those accepting the first option would receive 25c plus 60c. They were thus not covered in full, although they got some cash up front. Depositors accepting this offer were then given a second option of accepting a security bond for the remaining 75c. Under this bond they would receive the remaining 75c over periods ranging from two to five years. But there was a catch. The amount to be received by depositors under this option depended upon their 'guaranteed balance', which was defined as the balance of their account at 24 June 1990 less any interest paid or credited to their accounts after 30 June 1989. Many depositors claimed that it was unjust to deduct their last year of interest. As Pyramid was paying around 18 per cent in 1989–90 the differential could be substantial. Under both options, the government's offer was significantly below 100c in the dollar.

Overall, however, depositors were probably better off accepting the cheese-paring offer of the government than hoping for a big payout from the liquidation. In October 1992 Hodgson estimated that the recovery for depositors would be 51c to 53c from Pyramid, 70c to 71c from Geelong and 80c to 81c from Countrywide. These payments would be reduced by three to four cents if non-withdrawable investing shareholders were ranked with depositors rather than behind them.

The agony of the non-withdrawable shareholders dragged on interminably. In June 1992 the Full Bench of the Victorian Supreme Court found that these shareholders did rank behind the depositors. This improved the prospective payout for the depositors but meant that the non-withdrawable shareholders had lost everything. Their only remaining hope was an action taken by one of their number, Phillip Lauren, who claimed damages from the Victorian Government and various ministers for false statements which encouraged him to keep his money in Pyramid. Holders of non-withdrawable shares marched on the state parliament in September 1992 demanding that the government cover their losses. After the Cain Government fell Liberal Premier Jeff Kennett sought to join the Reserve Bank of Australia as a co-defendant in the Lauren case. The Victorian Government was now alleging that the RBA had been monitoring the Pyramid group since 1988, and that the Jolly–McCutcheon statement of February 1990 had been made on the advice of the Governor of the Reserve Bank, Bernie Fraser.[19] Fraser and the RBA denied the allegations.

The new Victorian Government showed as little conscience about the Farrow group's victims as Cain had. Kennett's Treasurer, Alan Stockdale, believed that Cain should not have made the offer to Pyramid depositors, much less help bail out the non-withdrawable shareholders.

In some respects the Farrow group's was one of the most disturbing collapses of the 1980s, because Pyramid and the other two societies had specifically targeted small investors, who became their major victims. It should be emphasised that they were not the only victims. Of nearly $1.5 billion in deposits held by the three societies almost $300 million was in deposits of $100 000 or more, whose holders could be classified as professional investors. But small to medium-size depositors provided most of Farrow group's resources—and it should not be forgotten that some large deposits were, like Lionel Lennon's, a nest egg arising from injury compensation or a legacy. Many of these unsophisticated depositors must have been persuaded by Pyramid's publicity that it was a sound institution and by the Victorian Government's posturing and legislation that they had some form of government guarantee. Neither premise was correct. By rejecting the National Insurance Deposit Corporation and passing its own Building Societies Act, the Victorian Government had given the illusion of providing protection but in reality had failed to provide either effective legislation or a watchdog with teeth. Under this illusory aegis the Farrow group enjoyed mushroom growth by crediting non-existent interest and fees as income, while luring depositors with high rates. An increasing proportion of the portfolio comprised high-risk loans to commercial developers at a time when the group should have been quitting office property. Meanwhile, the depositors' position was further eroded by the practice of using the better mortgages as security for bank borrowings and, in effect, double gearing. Every independent investigation of the societies—by Price Waterhouse, CS First Boston, Russell and Hodgson—quickly revealed major flaws which do not appear to have been evident to the Registrar. The regulatory apparatus having proved ineffective, the government then chiselled the depositors who had been relying upon it for a guarantee. It would have been better if there had been no legislation at all, thereby making it clear to depositors that they were at risk, rather than provide defective legislation then try to renege when it failed.

13

The sinking of Adelaide Steamship

[Chess] taught me you plan your moves long in advance, you consider all your options and you don't tell your opponent what you're doing.

John Spalvins

The Adelaide Steamship Company was formed in 1875 to run passengers and cargo between Melbourne and Adelaide. At its birth, Adelaide Steamship had to fight for existence in a brief but bitter rate war with the rival shipowners, particularly Howard Smith Ltd. It took five years before the shipowners came to a cartelisation agreement under which Adelaide Steamship was given the Adelaide monopoly in return for giving its bunkering business in Melbourne and certain other concessions to Howard Smith Ltd. Over the next two decades Adelaide Steamship expanded its routes to Sydney, the Queensland sugarfields and to Western Australia as the Kalgoorlie gold rush gathered momentum.[1] Adelaide Steamship flourished but it also kept a wary eye on its old rivals.

By the 1950s the business establishment of Adelaide centred on Advertiser Newspapers (although control was really vested in Melbourne's Herald & Weekly Times), the Bank of Adelaide, John Martin & Co, Elder Smith & Co, SA Brewing and Adelaide Steamship. After the 1980s had ended, the only one of these that would not have been destroyed or taken over in some form would be SA Brewing. But in the 1950s the links were close between these companies. Their directors were the doyens of Adelaide and nearly all of them were members of the Adelaide Club on North Terrace, the hub of financial power in South Australia. The power was exercised discreetly and paternalistically, but it was power nevertheless.

Firmly in the chair at Adelaide Steamship was Sir Richard Hawker, a pastoralist from Bungaree where the Hawker brothers had been the first settlers when the colony of South Australia was founded. He was, virtually by birth, a member of the Adelaide Club. His wife Frances was a

400

Rymill, another of the state's oldest families. Another director was Alfred Moxon Simpson, head of the Simpson family who held a block of shares in Adelaide Steamship. Simpson was also on the boards of the Bank of Adelaide and Elders. Yet another director was leading accountant Joe Winter, who was also on the Elders board. Adelaide Steamship was in those days a sleepy and secretive company. It operated a fleet of tugs and a couple of coastal steamers but its real strength was its investments, with significant holdings in such companies as Coal & Allied (where Sir Richard was on the board), AWA and North Australian Cement. Shareholders of Adelaide Steamship were paid an annual dividend and told little or nothing about its affairs.

In 1959 a takeover bid by H.C. Sleigh forced directors to boost dividends and reveal previously hidden reserves. As the *Bulletin*'s analyst observed:

> Until the 'new look' acquired two years ago, shareholders were given only the barest details on which to assess the value of their shares. Parent company accounts only were presented and these consistently showed profits to be just sufficient to cover dividend requirements—usually by no more than a few pounds, while large amounts were sneaked into reserves. Assets appeared in the books considerably undervalued.[2]

Under the rule of John Spalvins in the 1980s the Adsteam books would be equally opaque. It must be open to question whether shareholders in Adelaide Steamship ever had much more than the foggiest notion of what their company was doing or what their shares were worth.

The 1960 accounts were revealing in another way. The finance editor of the *Advertiser* noted: 'The broad conclusion from the new look accounts is inescapable, namely, that coastal shipping was relatively unprofitable last year'. The company's historian said that the conclusion for the Adelaide Steamship board was also inescapable: 'salvation lay in reorganisation and diversification'.[3]

The board had mustered a staunch and successful defence but the Sleigh raid had shaken them out of long complacency. The group explored alternative businesses aggressively, with little luck. It ventured into salt farming at Shark Bay; built an excellent but uneconomic ship, Troubridge, to exploit the Kangaroo Island trade; and built a shipyard at Birkenhead on Adelaide's Port River. All these ventures generated heavy losses. The old company had lost direction and there were recurrent rumours of a takeover.

Adelaide Steamship had traditionally been managed by captains who had risen through the marine industry; appointments to top management were made internally. The key man in the transformation of Adelaide Steamship would be Ken Russell, a longtime employee who became assistant general manager in 1960 and general manager in 1967. In 1973 there were important changes at the top. Sir Richard Hawker stepped down after 21 years as chairman to be replaced by James Felgate, the deputy chairman and former chief executive who had spent nearly half a century working for the company.

Under Felgate's chairmanship Russell would be the architect of Adelaide Steamship's transformation. Since 1960 he had laboured to diversify the company away from the shipping business, where earnings were always apt to be destroyed by costly strikes and other industrial disputes. Seamen and watersiders would strike over whether they were provided with Lifebuoy or Palmolive soap and whether their barrows had rubber or steel wheels. The Birkenhead shipyard had lost 100 days in 1972 through industrial disputes. Russell's drive was recognised by the fact that after becoming general manager he was appointed to the board— only the third executive to become a director. He was a toughminded, down-to-earth manager, but he also had breadth of vision.

Russell's second-in-command was Les Hancock, the deputy general manager. The third-ranking post in the managerial hierarchy was that of assistant general manager. Instead of appointing another long-serving company man, Adelaide Steamship broke with tradition in 1973 and head-hunted for the job. The choice fell on a Latvian immigrant, Janis Gunnars Spalvins.

Business was in Spalvins' blood. His father had been a businessman in Riga until the Russians took over the Baltic states. The Spalvins family were on the extermination lists of the Communist regime. His father—like many Latvians—chose the Germans against the Russians. He became a general in the Wermacht and was killed by the Russians. The eight-year-old Janis left Latvia with his grandmother. They lived in Berlin for a while, surviving the height of the Allied bombing attacks. They moved to Czechoslovakia, where Janis was reunited with his mother, who had remarried. In 1948 the family moved to Munich and in 1950 they migrated to Adelaide. Janis, brought up as a Lutheran but his education heavily disrupted by the war, was separated from the rest of the family and sent to a boarding school in Toowoomba. It was very tough on the twelve-year-old. He was in a strange country, learning a strange language, on his own and with only a patchy education. He showed enormous determination in overcoming all these obstacles to learn English and become a bright pupil.

He returned to Adelaide at the age of fourteen, matriculated and studied economics at night while working as a bank clerk and later as a cost accountant at Chrysler. At nineteen he was hired as an accountant for a small engineering company called Camelec. For a company of its size, Camelec could boast considerable talent. Spalvins' boss was John Uhrig, who was on his way to becoming the managing director of the big whitegoods maker Simpson Pope. Another staff member was Brian

Burns, who would go on to run Seppelt. Camelec was small but on the expansionary track. Over the next decade and a half it would grow from 50 employees to 1000. In hindsight, the most surprising aspect is that the ambitious Spalvins should have stayed with the company for sixteen years. The man who had risen to run Camelec's finances was impressive: tall, confident, handsome and with piercing blue eyes. Uhrig would later say: 'He was outstanding in financial matters and in asset trading. He always had the skills of a trader.'[4]

Spalvins left Camelec basically because he was frustrated by the way the board kept a rein on his financial schemes. For such an ambitious man, the stolid old Adelaide Steamship company would not have seemed the obvious alternative. But Adelaide Steamship wanted to move and wanted someone with ideas. By 1973 the Adsteam group[5] had net tangible assets of $20 million and less than $11 million in debt. Operating profit was around $2 million a year. It was an indication of the changing times in traditionally WASP Adelaide that a Latvian who still spoke only fair English would be given such a key job in Adelaide Steamship. But, apart from an undeniably brilliant business brain, Spalvins had a couple of other advantages. In 1961 he had wooed and won Cecily Rymill, a beautiful and charming girl who was the toast of the Adelaide business world. Being married into the Rymill family had never been a handicap in Adelaide, and incidentally made Spalvins an in-law of Sir Richard Hawker. And Camelec had its own links to the Adelaide establishment, notably through its chairman, Alwyn Barker (later Sir Alwyn), who was also chairman of Kelvinator Australia and—of course—a member of the Adelaide Club. Barker thought Spalvins was talented and passed the opinion to his close friend John Rymill, Spalvins' father-in-law.

Spalvins played a relatively small role in his early days at Adelaide Steamship. The company's early salvation was mainly due to its close links to one of Australia's greatest financiers, Sir Ian Potter. Sir Ian was chairman of McIlwraith McEacharn, which had a joint venture with Adelaide Steamship called Bulkships Ltd. In August 1974 Adelaide Steamship and McIlwraith each sold half of their stake to TNT, freeing up cash for Adelaide Steamship while leaving it with a substantial continuing interest in the shipping trade. Then Sir Ian, wearing another hat as chairman of Tricontinental Corporation, arranged for Adelaide Steamship to issue a $4 million convertible debenture to Tricontinental. That was a good deal for both parties. It bedded down some firm capital for Adelaide Steamship and gave Tricontinental solid earnings. Tricontinental was then being run by Sir Cecil (Peter) Looker and David Haynes as well as Potter. Its days as a harebrained financier were still some way off.

Adelaide Steamship had begun dabbling in real estate in Western Australia in partnership with one of the directors, Michael Gregg. This lifted profits to $3 million and enabled a bonus dividend to be paid in its centenary year of 1975. Then it went on the expansionary trail through a series of takeover bids. The mainspring was Russell, who had the confidence of the board and won its agreement to an acquisition strategy. Spalvins was mainly doing the backroom work, studying price–earnings ratios and cash flows. Spalvins received enormous publicity in later years, but he was not really captain of the ship until the mid-1980s. Right through the takeovers of David Jones, Tooth and Petersville Sleigh, Russell was the man in charge. Spalvins got much of the limelight in the David Jones bid, for example, but the man who took the decision and convinced the board was Russell. One other player who should be mentioned was Sydney merchant banker Geoff Hill. Hill, then at the merchant bank Commercial Continental, had been advising Adelaide Steamship before Spalvins arrived. He was responsible for much of the strategy and advice on the early takeovers.

Adelaide Steamship recognised at an early stage one of the watershed trends of the 1970s: the crumbling loyalty of institutions to corporates. Typically, Adelaide Steamship would identify an asset-rich company and acquire a stake of about 10 per cent. Then Adelaide Steamship would launch a bid, usually below asset backing per share. The target company was usually old. If the target board had enough friends they could find a white knight to buy out the raider, in which case Adelaide Steamship would retire at a profit. More often Adelaide Steamship proceeded to mop up enough shares to give it control—usually a little short of 50 per cent—then moved on to the next target. Dividends from the target company were presumed to be high enough to cover the costs of any funding. Debt was not used in the first takeovers, but later Adelaide Steamship used a mixture of unsecured borrowings and preference shares.

Adelaide Steamship's first takeover attempt was an unsuccessful bid for Moreton Central Sugar Mill Co in Queensland. Then Russell, Hill and Spalvins identified building materials as a growth area. Adelaide Steamship won the Victorian timber company VIA Ltd after a bitter contest. Next, Adelaide Steamship took Sellers Atkins and picked up a controlling interest in Duncan's Holdings. It funded all three bids from internal sources and by late 1976 had emerged as a strong player in the timber industry in New South Wales, Victoria and South Australia. Adsteam then embarked on a string of market raids on small to medium-size companies with solid assets and good cash flow. In the depressed share markets of the late 1970s Adsteam had adopted the classic strategy of a cash-rich player. It was buying shares at a discount to their real worth. Because all the companies it was taking over were profitable, Adsteam was getting a return of 15–20 per cent on the money it invested in takeovers. This meant that, although the takeovers were internally funded, Adsteam had more money for takeovers because its internal cash flow was constantly increasing.

The businesses it acquired or controlled through substantial minority shareholdings were good but eclectic. By 1980 they included Martin Wells (spectacle maker), Raynors Holdings (metal products), Abel, Lemon (commodity importer), Luke Ltd (engineering) and Clark Rubber Stores. By this time Ken Russell was managing director and Spalvins was general manager. They can take the credit for turning Adsteam into one of the most aggressive and successful takeover raiders in Australia during these years. Russell described himself as 'just a simple shipping man' and tagged Spalvins as 'our Minister for Development'.[6] They had formed one of the most formidable two-man teams in Australian business, with Hill in the shadows.

The circle of wagons

But the raider was also being stalked by its enemy of the past century, Howard Smith Ltd. In 1979 Howard Smith had raised its stake in Adelaide Steamship to just over 10 per cent. It was the sole substantial shareholder on the company's register, with 3.3 million shares. Directors of Adelaide Steamship controlled only about a quarter of a million shares, almost entirely held by Russell and Spalvins, the latter having joined the board that year. The hunters were becoming hunted. The Adelaide Steamship directors were absolutely determined to fight off their old enemy. Casting about for defensive measures, it became apparent to Russell that their traditional ally, Elders, would be unable to give much help. In the years of Adelaide Steamship's rise Elders had been in a long decline. So Adelaide Steamship looked doomed to fall to Howard Smith if it could not lift its share price and get some friendly support on the share register. (In financial jargon this is called 'drawing the wagons into a circle'—perhaps an apt metaphor for Adelaide Steamship considering that in the Wild West covered wagons were called prairie schooners.)

In November Adelaide Steamship executives put an 'insurance policy' in place by persuading shareholders to approve a generous option scheme, entitling executives to up to 3 per cent of the company. Executives who wanted to take these shares had to outlay only 10 per cent of the price; the other 90 per cent would be funded by an interest-free loan from the company. Adelaide Steamship also bought an interest in the Stannard business in Sydney, part of the consideration being a parcel of shares for the Stannard family on the basis that it would be voted in support of the existing board. In June 1980 Howard Smith moved its stake up to 13 per cent.

A fortnight later Adsteam hit the big time by taking a 19 per cent stake in the historic Sydney retailing business of David Jones. The great retailer still bore the Jones name and had Charles Lloyd Jones as its chairman. But the family's equity had dwindled to around 10 per cent and the company had become takeover prey. Ron Brierley's Industrial Equity Ltd (IEL) had rattled the family by picking up 9 per cent. In July Adsteam revealed that it held 19 per cent, secretly accumulated over several months. David Jones directors welcomed Adsteam as a white knight, offering it three board seats. In a bloodless coup Adsteam scooped up effective control of David Jones. South Australian investors, long used to having their companies raided by outsiders, were gratified to learn that an Adelaide company had won a substantial stake in one of the eastern state's best known retailers. Russell and Spalvins became local heroes. Their next step was to buy 20 per cent of the David Jones 49 per cent–owned investment offshoot, DJ's Properties. DJ's Properties in turn held a 20 per cent stake in the old Sydney brewer, Tooth & Co.

In September Adsteam raised its holding and took the reins of power by reducing the role of Charles Lloyd Jones from executive chairman to chairman. This broke a 142-year tradition of a Jones being chief executive of the upmarket retailer. Spalvins became chief executive of David Jones. The moves were greeted with dismay by blue-blooded David Jones shareholders. At the annual meeting one irate shareholder asked Spalvins whether he would know the difference between a linen sheet and a cotton sheet. Spalvins replied: 'I'm a professional manager, not a retailer'.

Meanwhile, Howard Smith had built its Adelaide Steamship holding to 17 per cent and in 1981 requested a board seat. The request was flatly rejected. Russell and Spalvins defended Adsteam by keeping a coterie of loyal shareholders together who probably represented some 30 per cent. The biggest was the Stannard family with a 6 per cent holding and a joint shipping venture with Adsteam. There were just enough wagons in the circle to keep the Indians out, but a more permanent barrier had to be found.

On another front, Brierley had returned to the fray by buying 10 per cent of Tooth. After some sparring Adsteam bought out Brierley, which meant that it now controlled 35 per cent of Tooth counting the 23 per cent held through DJ's Properties. In a separate move David Jones acquired Melbourne's fashionable Collins Street retail store, Georges Ltd. Much of the Adsteam empire was being controlled through substantial minority holdings—a point to which we shall return.

In July 1981 Russell retired as managing director to become deputy chairman of Adelaide Steamship. The chairman was Joe Winter, a conservative accountant with a good eye for figures but whose main concern was his post as deputy chairman of Elders. By now Elders was developing considerable problems of its own and would soon fall prey to the

Table 13.1   Adelaide Steamship's expansionary decade
(Consolidated accounts)

	1973 ($m)	1982 ($m)
BALANCE SHEET		
Total assets	35.6	599.4
Total liabilities	(15.1)	(239.5)
Net assets	20.5	359.9
PROFIT & LOSS ACCOUNT		
Pre-tax profit	2.3	27.7
Income tax	(0.2)	(1.8)
Birkenhead closure	(3.4)	—
Outside interests	—	(8.5)
Equity accounted profits	—	6.6
Extraordinaries	0.3	0.5
Equity accounted extras	—	30.0
Less equity share of dividends	—	0.9
Net result	(1.0)	53.6

rampaging John Elliott. The new managing director of Adelaide Steamship was Spalvins. Michael Kent, who would become Spalvins' right-hand man, was general manager, commercial, and Neil Branford was company secretary. Also in July, Spalvins moved into the chairman's seat at Tooth, where DJ's Properties now had nearly 80 per cent of the stock.

After the reshuffle the team hardly paused for breath before launching yet more takeovers. A raid on the old food technology company Mauri Brothers & Thomson was beaten off, but Adsteam chalked up a profit of $2 million in a month. Adsteam picked up 10 per cent of Metro Meat and bid for the rest, while David Jones bid for the old Melbourne retailer Buckley & Nunn. In April 1982 the restless group also bought 20 per cent of the auto parts maker, National Consolidated Ltd. This was followed in July by a raid on the petrol and coal company H.C. Sleigh Ltd.

Adelaide Steamship's accounts for the year to June 1982 were a milestone in the evolution of the group. Table 13.1 compares the figures for 1982 with those for 1973 when Spalvins joined the company.

This is amazing growth. Total assets have expanded sixteen-fold. Net assets have multiplied eighteen times and pre-tax profit thirteen times. Profit attributable to Adelaide Steamship shareholders has mushroomed from a $1 million loss to a $53 million profit. However, analysts studying the accounts were uncomfortably aware that they were not seeing the full picture. Adelaide Steamship was a conglomerate. It wholly owned Duncan's Holdings, Sellers Atkins, Martin Wells, Abel Lemon, Metro Meat, WA Realty, Raynors Holdings and much of its traditional tugs and marine towage division. But a large part of the empire was controlled through substantial minority holdings. These included:

- Luke Ltd (engineering) 48.9 per cent
- Sidney Cooke (industrial fasteners) 44.8 per cent
- Robb & Brown (building materials and timber) 35.1 per cent
- Clark Rubber (rubber stores) 48.9 per cent
- David Jones (retailer) 48.4 per cent
- DJ's Properties (investor) 42.7 per cent
- Tooth & Co (brewing) 40.8 per cent
- Clements Marshall (agricultural merchant) 19.99 per cent

These were all equity-accounted in Adelaide Steamship's 1982 accounts. For the benefit of non-accountants this needs a word of explanation. Under the law prevailing in the 1980s every group of Australian companies had to present consolidated accounts at the end of each financial year.[7] These accounts had to include the figures for all companies in which the parent held an interest of more than 50 per cent. Where the parent had a substantial holding, which was less than 50 per cent but represented control, the group had the option of equity-consolidating such companies. This meant, to take an example from the list above, that Adelaide Steamship could count as part of its consolidated assets 48.4 per cent of the assets of David Jones. Adelaide Steamship could also count as part of its consolidated profit 48.4 per cent of the profit of David Jones, net of any dividends actually paid by David Jones to Adelaide Steamship.

Equity-accounted profits from these minority-controlled companies had in 1982 accounted for $30 million of Adelaide Steamship's stated $53 million profit. These were not profits actually earned by Adelaide Steamship but had been credited to its account as part of someone else's profit. In adverse circumstances the actual cash might never find its way into Adelaide Steamship's coffers. There is thus always the danger of an illusory element in equity-accounted profits, although it was not so bad in Adelaide Steamship's case because the degree of control was fairly high.

As a defence against Howard Smith, Russell and Spalvins had meanwhile begun closing the circle of share registers. By June 1982 David Jones owned 9.2 per cent of Adelaide Steamship and Luke Ltd owned another 5.2 per cent. Other associates had also built up handy blocks of shares. Corinthian Industries, a door-making company half owned by Adelaide Steamship, had emerged with another 2 per cent. In this way the associates of Russell, Spalvins and companies in the Adsteam group now controlled some 30 per cent of Adelaide Steamship's capital. Adelaide Steamship had lifted capital through a number of share placements made just below market prices in the past year. These had apparently gone largely to associates, achieving the double effect of raising a barrier against Howard Smith while diluting Howard Smith's holding. One who could take some credit for the process to this stage was Hill, who had masterminded a few placements and issues for Adelaide Steamship.

The strategy had two disquieting aspects. The first was that if the process continued the senior executives and the board could make themselves self-perpetuating. If the David Jones board and the Adelaide Steamship board always voted their blocks of stock for each other they could become impregnable. This happened in future years as the boards appointed more common directors and the level of cross-ownership grew.

The second aspect was that the circle of holdings could inflate profits. A dividend paid by David Jones would go 48 per cent to Adelaide Steamship, enhancing its profits and enabling it to pay a higher dividend to David Jones. This was not too important a phenomenon while David Jones' holding in Adelaide Steamship was 9 per cent, but it would become important when the holding grew.

Another problem was illustrated by the phantom presence of Tooth & Co. At June 1982 Tooth was owned 40.8 per cent by Adelaide Steamship, which equity-accounted that much of the company's profits. However, another 39 per cent of Tooth was owned by DJ's Properties. As Adelaide Steamship owned 42 per cent of DJ's Properties outright (and more through David Jones) it had effective control of 80 per cent of Tooth. Yet Tooth was not consolidated into the accounts of either Adelaide Steamship or David Jones. Tooth had dominated the NSW beer market for decades but was in decline by the time Adsteam got control. Its Kent brewery on Broadway was sold to Carlton & United Breweries. All Tooth had left was a string of hotels and it was on its way to becoming an investment company.

Finally, analysts were left wondering how much the group had borrowed. The $239.5 million total liabilities of Adelaide Steamship for 1982 (Table 13.1) included $170 million in debt. These were the figures in Adelaide Steamship's consolidated accounts. If that was all there was, the ratios looked safe. But the empire of partly owned entities was potentially a perfect way of getting debt off balance sheet. If the analysts couldn't see Tooth in the Adelaide Steamship accounts, maybe there was a swag of debt they couldn't see either. And, as in many mushroom empires of the era, Adsteam's accounts were always moving. The percentage that the companies owned of each other changed continually—usually increasing. No year was ever really comparable with the previous year.

The self-perpetuating board

Spalvins revelled in the mystification he was creating. Against some stiff competition (notably from Robert Holmes à Court), Spalvins was always the most enigmatic of the corporate cowboys of his day. He once said that if any outsider ever understood the workings of his empire he would have to change them. This air of mystery was a mighty weapon for Spalvins. Standing an imposing six feet four inches, he would typically respond to a journalist's question by asking another question in riposte, accompanying it with a slight, superior smile. He was built like Superman and looked as though he understood secrets of finance denied to ordinary mortals. This undoubtedly inspired many investors—and analysts—to trust him blindly. Not that they had much choice, because the group's accounts became increasingly impenetrable. And there was no denying his intellectual brilliance. In 1989 he was one of 26 chess players in a simultaneous exhibition match with the former world champion Boris Spassky and held the grandmaster to a draw.

But the analysts who were puzzled by Spalvins' accounts were in the backrooms of the sharebrokers' offices. As the great share boom of the 1980s gathered steam it was the dealers in the front room who were reaping in money for the brokers, and they loved Spalvins. His string of takeovers had generated enormous activity and hence commissions. He was always in the market for scrip. And the group was a big issuer of scrip, making frequent placements and preference issues. By 1982 Adelaide Steamship was high on almost every broker's list of recommendations. From being a sleepy, provincial tugboat operator it had blossomed into one of Australia's top 50 listed companies, with a market capitalisation of $200 million.

Adsteam's expansion continued. It bought H.C. Sleigh—a neat piece of revenge on a company which in 1959 had tried to take over Adelaide Steamship. Sleigh had lost millions on a coal property it had bought in the United States, but on the other hand it had one of Australia's best food companies in Petersville. Adsteam then invested further in the industry by bidding for Australian Bacon and picked up 20 per cent of the old Sydney retailer, Grace Brothers. The battle for Grace Brothers became one of the epics of the 1980s with many twists and turns as Alan Bond, Adsteam and Coles Myer jockeyed for control. At one point the contenders took the takeover to the Privy Council.

The Adsteam group had become an enormous conglomerate. It was in food, retailing, property, marine towage, automotive supplies and building materials. Conglomerates usually contain the seeds of their own destruction, because top management is not capable of overseeing so many diverse industries simultaneously. But in Adsteam's case the line operations were always well managed. David Jones was regenerated as Sydney's top retailer, in class if not volume. The operations of National Consolidated and Petersville, each dealing with a multitude of products, were not harmed by Adsteam's control. Spalvins can take great personal credit for this. He spent his life on aircraft, ferrying from one company meeting to another. He always carried a briefcase and copious notes. His phenomenal powers of memory and concentration enabled him to master the minutiae of each business under Adsteam's umbrella. His head also contained price–earnings ratios, dividend yields and share prices for dozens of other companies that were current or potential targets. His grasp of detail was awesome, particularly to subordinates. It also enabled him to keep administration costs down. Adsteam's far-flung empire was run from its headquarters at 123 Greenhill Road, Unley. This was a small two-storey building on the edge of Adelaide's southern parklands, tastefully decorated with mementoes of the company's maritime past. Adsteam never moved into large or glitzy headquarters like those of some of its rivals. On Spalvins' desk was a plaque carrying Richard Nixon's famous quotation: 'If you have them by the balls, their hearts and minds will follow'.

When the 1983 accounts were unveiled it became apparent that one of Adsteam's main activities during the year had been strengthening its hold on subsidiaries. The holding in DJ's Properties had been winched up 5 per cent during the year to 47.9 per cent. Adelaide Steamship's holding in Tooth was up 2 per cent to 43 per cent but another 43.9 per cent was held by DJ's Properties. Tooth held 48.8 per cent of H.C. Sleigh and 47.2 per cent of National Consolidated. The Adelaide Steamship accounts were a web of equity-accounted interests. Profit attributable to shareholders of Adelaide Steamship was stated at $40 million in the consolidated accounts, of which $8.7 million was its equity share of associated company profits and another $9.5 million was its equity share of extraordinary profits made by associated companies. Income tax provision was nearly nil because Adelaide Steamship was deriving most of its profits in the form of dividends paid by subsidiaries and associates. The accounts were discussed at considerable length by finance writers and analysts trying to fathom what they really meant. The general tenor was praise for Spalvins, who as usual was being Delphic in response to questions.

Another straw in the wind was the retirement of Moxon Simpson as a director in July 1983, after 23 years on the Adelaide Steamship board. He was replaced by Michael Kent, who was now finance director. Whereas the old Adelaide Steamship board had never included more than one executive director—and for long periods none at all—it now had three. Ken Russell had ceased to be an executive but had been chief executive for a long time and was highly active in his role as deputy chairman. Spalvins was managing director and Kent was finance director. There were four outside directors. Winter was chairman, but Adelaide Steamship was only one of his board posts, which included Elders, Adelaide & Wallaroo Fertilisers, Bridgestone and National Commercial Union. Lynn Arnold, 69 years old, was the resident Sydney director;

Michael Gregg, 49, was the resident Perth director and a joint venturer in some WA property deals with Adsteam; Wilfred Sweetland, 70, was the resident Melbourne director.

Kent's promotion to the board marked the start of a trend. From here onwards outside directors would be replaced, if at all, by executive directors. Given Spalvins' far-reaching grasp of the details of the complex Adsteam empire, the outside directors' ability to challenge him—even if they had wanted to—was waning. And very few executives ever challenge their managing director at a board meeting. Kent's accession to the board can be taken as the approximate point at which control of the empire passed from the board to the executives. Shareholders had no reason to complain. Adsteam's profits and assets were shown to be soaring, the company's shares were rising, Adsteam was spoken of in hushed tones in financial circles and Spalvins was being acclaimed as a genius. The *Australian Financial Review* calculated that, for every $1000 invested in Adelaide Steamship in 1978, an investor would have seen the parcel appreciate to $6750 by September 1983 and received a dividend yield of 37.5 per cent. True, a few puzzled analysts were still grumbling in their backrooms but they attracted little attention in the face of success like this.

Meanwhile, Adelaide Steamship had won another victory. After a doughty ten-year defence the company had beaten off Howard Smith. At the end of 1983 Howard Smith baled out, selling its 18 per cent for $52 million. Spalvins' tactic of pulling the wagons into a circle had locked Howard Smith out of the board or any control of the company. Its only feasible way of winning the fight was by making a takeover bid—an option which had become increasingly expensive as Adelaide Steamship's share price rose. Howard Smith had become increasingly worried about Spalvins' tactics. Meanwhile depressed coal prices had weakened Howard Smith's base and increased pressure on its board to liquidate the holding and apply the cash elsewhere. Seeing off Howard Smith was a sweet triumph for the Adelaide Steamship board, particularly Ken Russell, and added to Spalvins' aura of invincibility.

The 18 per cent stake was spread around institutional holders, with BT Australia and the AMP Society taking large chunks. Four million of the shares were picked up by David Jones, raising its holding in Adelaide Steamship to 20 per cent. Not only had Adelaide Steamship seen off its old rival, but it had taken the opportunity to draw the circle of wagons even closer. The door was now shut against raiders.

Adsteam was still on the takeover trail. In early 1984 it launched bids for North Australian Cement and the old Adelaide winemaker B. Seppelt & Sons. Success in Seppelt would have put Adsteam into a dominant position in the wine industry, as it already controlled Penfolds and Kaiser

Stuhl. Adsteam got 26 per cent of Seppelt, but the winemaker defended staunchly in long and complex court proceedings. In November Adsteam sold its Seppelt holding to South Australian Brewing for a $3.5 million profit. This showed that, for all its successes, Adsteam was still not omnipotent on its home turf of Adelaide. The group also faced tough resistance in its cement takeover and eventually sold its holding in North Australian Cement to Queensland Cement & Lime for a $10 million profit.

But, while these takeovers were trudging through the courts, Adsteam had bigger fish to fry. It was quietly accumulating shares in the biggest Australian company of them all—BHP. In the last days of 1984 it was revealed that Adsteam had about 2 per cent of BHP and that Robert Holmes à Court had another 5 per cent. 'In corporate terms, 1985 will be the year of attack on BHP', *Australian Business* predicted.[8] A takeover of BHP had previously been unthinkable because of the sheer size of the target. It was also a national icon. But to the raiders of the 1980s all things were possible and BHP met all normal takeover criteria. It had an open register and its share price at $5.25 was well below its net tangible asset backing of $8.43. Holmes à Court had already launched a takeover bid for BHP in 1983, offering two shares in a company named Wigmores plus $1 cash and one of its options in return for each share in BHP. As Wigmores was capitalised at only $40 million—its prime asset being the WA franchise for Caterpillar tractors—the offer was treated with derision. When BHP's chairman, Sir James McNeill, was told of the bid he asked: 'Wig who?'. Wigmores got only 800 000 BHP shares. In 1984 Holmes à Court returned to the attack with another scrip offer. This time he offered Bell Resources shares and options in return for BHP shares. BHP blocked the bid in court, but not before Holmes à Court had picked up 7.5 million shares.

Attracted by the whiff of blood in the water, Spalvins started buying through the broking firm of Potts West Trumbull. BHP scented a raider accumulating shares and launched a Section 261 search which disclosed in late December that it was Adsteam. The great steel, minerals and oil group would have been even more alarmed if it had known that Adsteam had secretly drawn up a plan for a partial takeover bid for BHP. Adelaide Steamship continued to accumulate shares quietly, without being distracted from its core enterprises. It launched a bid for the security and fire protection business, Wormald, and in Adelaide bought the old retailer, John Martin.

Holmes à Court, having built a stake in BHP, decided in early 1985 that the US base metal giant Asarco was a more promising target. To raise cash for a raid on Asarco he would have to sell BHP but if he dumped the stock on market the price would be depressed. But it would not disturb the market—and would enhance his price—if he sold the stock

413

through the market in stock exchange–traded options. Holmes à Court began writing call options on BHP shares.[9] The options were due to expire in April 1984, when Holmes à Court would deliver the stock. As the volume of call options written by Holmes à Court increased they began to arrest the price of BHP. The market began to realise that when the call options were exercised in April they would trigger 25 million BHP on to the market, depressing the price. At Adsteam, Spalvins and Kent began to worry. They now had a holding of 30 million to 40 million BHP shares and if the price began to sag it could mean a nasty splotch of red ink in their accounts.

Kent flew to New York, where Holmes à Court was simultaneously grappling with Asarco and selling the rights to the Beatles' songs to a rising young pop star named Michael Jackson. At the end of April 1985, Kent and Holmes à Court struck a deal which would be kept secret for the next five months. Adsteam agreed to sell 70 million BHP shares to Holmes à Court in August and September of 1986 at $7.11 a share compared to a current share price of around $5.50. For the next few months, what appeared to be happening on the market was the reverse of the truth. Holmes à Court delivered his stock as options expired and appeared to be selling as his holding dwindled from 6 per cent to below five per cent. Spalvins, who had to build his holding to reach 70 million, appeared the big buyer. BHP chiefs were fairly relaxed because they felt that Spalvins was unlikely to make a takeover bid. There were even rumours that BHP might encourage a friendly bid from Spalvins to keep Holmes à Court at bay. Under the pressure of Adsteam buying, BHP shares began rising. Adsteam probably put its 70 million shares parcel together at an average price between $5.50 and $6, giving it a potential profit of $100 million. But by October the share price had gone over $8, making Holmes à Court a big winner too.

Holmes à Court was beaten back from Asarco by a variety of rough tactics and returned to the BHP market in earnest in October 1985, when he bought heavily into call options as well as buying 10 million shares at $8.50. This took him above the 10 per cent level, making him a substantial shareholder under the law as it then stood. He was forced to make a substantial-shareholder statement detailing his holdings. At last the $500 million option deal with Adsteam had to be disclosed. It caused a sensation in financial circles. Not only was it the biggest option deal in Australia's history (some would call it the biggest bet), but it presaged a serious bid for BHP.

Spalvins, interviewed by journalists, was even more Delphic than usual. He would not divulge his intentions. 'I would say it is like a chess game', he said. 'And in a chess game there are an average 33 moves. I would say we are in about move six or seven. And occasionally chess games go on much longer.' Reflecting on his own essays at chess, Spalvins said: 'It taught me you plan your moves long in advance, you consider all your options and you don't tell your opponent what you're doing'.[10] By this time Adsteam had collected 101 million BHP shares—just under 10 per cent of the company—including the 70 million optioned to Holmes à Court. In November Adsteam unloaded 22 million of its shares at $9.20 and $9.02. Spalvins said that he had turned bearish on BHP.

> BHP is a magnificent company with tremendous resources and a management team which has really improved its performance. It would be a tremendous investment at $5.50 or $6, but once you start going past that we start asking ourselves questions. I keep saying to myself that the share price has doubled and the oil price has halved.[11]

Spalvins backed his judgement and unloaded more BHP. By early 1986 Adsteam had chalked up some nice profits, but its stake was down to 66 million shares—less than it needed to honour the option deal.[12] Spalvins was becoming the share market's biggest gambler. While the market had been watching BHP, Spalvins had been buying into Westpac. In March Adsteam suddenly sold 6.5 million shares in the bank at $5.16, apparently clearing about 60c a share. Buoyed by this success, Spalvins began trading as though he felt infallible. He sold large blocks of BHP shares, confident that he could buy them back at lower prices to cover his option deal with Holmes à Court.

This was odd behaviour, because there were several factors combining at this time to put a floor under the BHP share price. Holmes à Court had made a partial takeover bid for BHP in February, offering $7.70 cash or a scrip alternative. The bid was withdrawn in March, then renewed in April. During this time BHP was trying to put together a defensive deal with John Elliott at Elders. The net effect of these manoeuvres was to keep BHP's share price firm. Thanks to issues by BHP, the exercise price of the option had now been altered to $5.93 and the number Adsteam was required to deliver had increased to 110 million. In May Holmes à Court lifted his bid to $9.20 and Adsteam accepted for half its holding. Holmes à Court's offer closed on 27 May, but the shares retreated only to around $8.80. Spalvins had chalked up big profits by selling BHP, but he was 35 million to 40 million shares short on his obligation and every share he had to buy back to deliver to Holmes à Court would be at a loss of nearly $3. The fact that the market knew Adsteam was short of stock was helping to keep the price high. And he was due to start delivering in only six weeks. Spalvins was caught by his own misjudgement and the result was a long wrangle with Holmes à Court.

Nobody would have guessed from looking at the confident Spalvins that he had just turned a triumph into a near-disaster. In September 1986 he splashed out with the most extravagant public relations gesture of his career: the Ultimate Dinner. The dinner was to mark the 150th anniversary of South Australia and was sponsored by the Adelaide Hilton and Penfolds, the winemakers. Some 400 guests attended, many being flown from interstate and accommodated at the Hilton. The tables of the Hilton's main ballroom were laden with linen, silver, candles and lavish flower arrangements. The menu was exotic. The second course was 'Pigeon Broth William Hargraves', garnished with poached quail egg, julienne of pigeon breast and flakes of 24-carat gold leaf.[13] The main course was roast loin of wild boar from Kangaroo Island. Each course was accompanied by a different wine, chosen by Penfolds' chief winemaker Don Ditter together with the great Max Shubert who created Grange Hermitage in the 1950s. The cheese course was accompanied by three wines—the Grange Hermitages of 1971, 1966 and 1955. Presiding over this magnificent repast, Spalvins had the air of a man who had just made a fortune rather than coming perilously close to losing one.

The legal wrangle with Holmes à Court was not settled until June 1987, when Spalvins delivered scrip but was 37 million BHP shares short. Adsteam paid Holmes à Court a penalty of $2.50 a share in settlement. Holmes à Court demanded another $100 million, claiming that Adsteam had more BHP shares tucked away in a subsidiary named Bettina House of Fashion. Overall, Adsteam probably made a marginal profit on its BHP play, but it was only a fraction of what the group would have collected if it had stuck to the original deal and Spalvins had not sold the stock.

While this wrangle was continuing Spalvins made yet another big market play. Unfazed by the fact that his bearishness on BHP had proved wrong, Spalvins took a massive short position on Share Price Index futures. In any given market, there are two philosophies a trader can adopt. One is to follow the prevailing trend. As no trend continues forever, the other philosophy is to try to pick the point at which the trend will turn. One of the oldest stock market adages is 'the trend is your friend'. Traders believe that if you follow the trend you will always come out ahead, even though you lose money when it turns. Picking turning points is highly lucrative if you get it right but you can lose a lot of money if you are wrong. No trader can consistently pick turning points in any market, although many have made a nice living selling books claiming they can.

When Spalvins sold the SPI heavily in late 1986 he was picking a turning point. He also tried to make the bet good by issuing a number of statements which were bearish about the market. In October he said share prices were at levels which 'could not be justified on normal business criteria'. Talking to the Australian Society of Accountants in Melbourne, he said: 'When you see dividend yields averaging three or four per cent and price-to-earnings ratios of 13 to 14 times, you just wonder how this situation can continue when interest rates are around 18 per cent'. Spalvins' main stockbroker, Brent Potts, also went on television warning that the market was overpriced.

Spalvins' diagnosis was quite correct, but the market simply wasn't listening. The All Ordinaries Index had been rising from 1100 in June 1986 and by December was 1400. In 1987 it would run screaming to a peak of 2312 in September before the sensational collapse in October. Spalvins had shorted too early and had to cover in a rising market. Adsteam lost some $18 million on the bet.

In 1987 Adsteam decided to bolster its balance sheet by making some issues. Given the cross-shareholdings in the group, an issue by one company tended to trigger issues by the rest. Adelaide Steamship, which had been trading at $14.50, announced an issue at $11.50. The shares promptly fell to that price. David Jones, which had been trading at $17, announced an issue at $13 and was slashed to $12.80. The institutional shareholders had never really understood the company and were becoming wary of Adsteam after its big SPI loss and the still unresolved BHP exposure to Holmes à Court. Spalvins' propensity for making huge bets that nobody knew about—and losing—was unsettling the market. The issues had significant shortfalls, which had to be taken up by the underwriters. When the BHP option deal with Holmes à Court was settled in June—revealing that Spalvins had badly misjudged the market—Adelaide Steamship shares took a further hammering and slid to $8.

Undaunted, Spalvins was still playing the market. In late 1986 he had accumulated large stakes in the three major listed banks. Adsteam spent $70 million buying ANZ shares to become the bank's fourth largest holder and bought smaller stakes in the National Australia Bank and Westpac. During 1987 Spalvins was building all three holdings. By September Adsteam held 2.5 per cent of the ANZ, 2.2 per cent of Westpac and 9.8 per cent of the National, where Spalvins asked for two board seats. He also began a long public agitation in an attempt to persuade banks to increase their dividend payouts. Spalvins sought permission to lift the NAB holding above the statutory limit of 10 per cent. The Treasurer, Paul Keating, allowed the Adsteam group to go to 15 per cent. The market preferred this play, and pushed Adelaide Steamship shares back above $11. The NAB directors, however, rejected Spalvins' request to join the board.

Black Tuesday—20 October 1987—wrought ferocious havoc on the entrepreneurial stocks. Adelaide Steamship was no exception, being thumped from $9.50 to $7.10. One reason for the weakness of the entrepreneurs was their holdings in other companies. So when NAB shares slumped 70c to $4.60 that naturally triggered a fall in Adsteam.

If Adsteam had been wounded by Black Tuesday, Holmes à Court was severely mauled. Bell Group shares collapsed from $9.40 to $5.50.

Bull in a bear market

Spalvins, who had been a bear in a bull market, now became a bull in a bear market. Immediately after the crash he picked up extra shares in NAB to take his holding to 14.8 per cent. All three listed banks announced good profit increases but Westpac and NAB also announced heavy rights issues, which meant that Adsteam would have to fork out more cash to maintain its equity. Spalvins was becoming a gadfly to the banks, criticising their dividend policies. He lectured them on their low payout ratios and for ignoring their shareholders. 'I support the share issues, but as the banks have expanded shareholders have been getting small returns', Spalvins said. 'Why are the banks on price–earnings ratios of between five and six times? Why are they selling at less than asset backing? I believe I have the support of shareholders on this.'[14] A few years later the Australian trading banks would be bashed into humility by their big bad-debt writeoffs, but in 1988 they were still proud institutions and resented being lectured by Spalvins. They also resented the implicit threat that he might start mustering shareholder action against them.

One point that was not overlooked was the symbiosis that had developed between Spalvins and the banks. The Adsteam group was one of the biggest borrowers in Australia, owing $500 million to the NAB alone. It was now also the NAB's largest shareholder. The NAB was lending Adsteam money to buy shares in itself. Or, to put it the other way around, the bank's largest shareholder was also one of its largest debtors. There were possible dangers in this relationship.

Spalvins was still bullish. In May 1988 he lifted his stake in the British insurance company Commercial Union to 5.2 per cent. Later he would take it to 13 per cent. Spalvins liked UK insurers, buying a 6 per cent stake in Royal Insurance as well. Then in June he went for his next big gamble, buying 11 million shares in Bell Resources. He soon held 12 per cent of the company.

This was another odd move. Bell Resources was 40 per cent owned by Bell Group. Until April 1988 Bell Group was 43 per cent owned by Holmes à Court. Then he sold two 19.9 per cent tranches simultaneously to Alan Bond and the Western Australian SGIC.[15] The National Companies and Securities Commission prodded Bond to bid for the rest of the stock in Bell Group. Bond did so in July, lifting his Bell Group holding to 68 per cent. Meanwhile, as we noted earlier, Bond Corporation had been systematically ripping more than $1 billion in liquid assets out of Bell

Resources. Spalvins' raid into Bell Resources was a greenmail attempt. Bond at that point was proposing a takeover of Bond Corporation by Bell Resources, and by acquiring a strategic stake Spalvins had put himself in a position to block the deal. He was hoping to be bought out by Bond. What he did not know was that Bell Resources' great assets had already been taken. By December 1988 Adsteam had lifted its stake in Bell Resources to 19.8 per cent.

Earlier, in October, Adsteam enjoyed another delicious piece of vengeance. Industrial Equity Ltd had mounted a raid on Howard Smith but was being forced to abandon it. Adsteam's Petersville Sleigh, which had already built up a 10.1 per cent stake in Howard Smith, snapped up a further 9.5 per cent from Industrial Equity. Now Petersville held 19.6 per cent of Adelaide Steamship's old foe. And Spalvins was planning another reprisal. Early in 1989 he began soaking up shares in Industrial Equity, the group he had jousted so often with during the takeovers of the 1980s. Industrial Equity had been dumped heavily on Black Tuesday, its shares crashing from $5.40 to $3.40. Spalvins bought big blocks of the stock.

Fleetingly, Adelaide Steamship had triumphed in all directions. The wagons had been drawn into a circle. The group had been saved. Strategic stakes had been built up in the Australian banking system and in three old enemies—Howard Smith, Bell Resources and Industrial Equity. Another ancient enemy—H.C. Sleigh—had been taken over. Spalvins and his coterie controlled the largest industrial group of companies in Australia. Victory looked to be complete.

But there were a couple of cracks in the facade. In April 1989 *Australian Business* released a report by Australian Ratings—which had frequently been critical of Adsteam—attempting to show what a true consolidation of the group's accounts looked like. The report was disturbing, showing that earnings were weaker than reported by the group and that gearing was higher.[16] Kent strongly denied the validity of the exercise, saying that debts in other companies were non-recourse to Adelaide Steamship.

A few weeks later Spalvins discovered the black hole in Bell Resources. He demanded that the billion dollars be returned. All Bell Resources had to show for the billion that had been ripped out was a third mortgage over shares in Bond Brewing. As a syndicate of banks (led by the National) had first call on the actual brewery assets, and as the first two mortgages on the shares of Bond Brewing were held by the Hong Kong & Shanghai Bank, Bell Resources' security was virtually worthless. Shares in Bell Resources began sliding as the market realised that the company had been stripped. The only hope was for Bond to somehow put the money back, but by mid-1989 the Bond empire was looking shaky at best and doomed at worst. Spalvins—now holding 19.9

per cent of Bell Resources—threatened legal action against Bond. These two incidents were in fact far graver than cracks: they were crevasses opening in the Adsteam accounts. But many analysts and bankers blithely ignored them and kept seeing Adsteam and Spalvins through rose-coloured glasses. Adsteam would sail ahead for another eighteen months before the passengers and crew realised that it had been holed below the waterline.

While Spalvins was trying to get the billion back from Bond he was still investing. He picked up 17 per cent in the electronics giant AWA, which had lost some $40 million trading foreign exchange in 1986. The sensational nature of this loss masked the fact that AWA's fundamental business was not performing well either. Spalvins and Kent went on to the board. But Spalvins' main effort now was building his stake in Industrial Equity. By July 1989 he had built up a 12 per cent holding. His rivals were two of Brierley's former lieutenants, Rod Price and Bill Loewenthal, who were planning a management buyout of Industrial Equity. They were being supported by Abe Goldberg through a company named Corama Pty Ltd. The irony in this battle was that within a year both contenders for Industrial Equity would have hit the wall themselves. The Corama group had announced a bid of $1.9 billion for Industrial Equity, but could not tie down the financing.

Spalvins raised funds by selling out of Commercial Union and part of Adsteam's bank portfolio. He raised more funds by a placement of 20 million Adelaide Steamship shares at $8.20. The shares were placed among 40 institutions by Potts West Trumbull. Adelaide Steamship also announced a one-for-four rights issue at $3 to be followed by a one-for-five bonus issue. These combined manoeuvres raised a total of more than $1 billion which Adsteam needed for its bid for Industrial Equity. In November Spalvins announced a bid of $2.30 a share for Industrial Equity. This capitalised the company at $1.7 billion. Corama, still unable to raise finance for the buyout, crumbled quickly and Adsteam took majority control of Industrial Equity and began a leisurely mopping-up exercise to take out the minorities.

The financing of the Industrial Equity bid was interesting. The bid vehicle was a company called Dextran Pty Ltd, which had $900 million equity contributed in equal parts by David Jones, Tooth and Adelaide Steamship. The three companies had funded their $300 million each by using their undrawn lines of credit from a total of about 28 banks. A further $900 million was provided by Westpac, Toronto Dominion and Bank of America, backed by guarantees from David Jones, Tooth and Adelaide Steamship to cover any shortfall in security. Thus Westpac, Toronto Dominion and Bank of America were secured but the other 25 banks ranked behind them on negative pledge. At the end of the day

Spalvins had not put up a cent of Adsteam money to finance the bid, and some of the bankers must have swallowed hard when they eventually realised their position in the syndicate.

Adelaide Steamship was standing at the pinnacle of the greatest industrial empire ever put together in Australia. The takeover of Industrial Equity made Adsteam the biggest player in the Australian food industry, as the Southern Farmers brands came under the same roof as the Petersville brands. After Coles Myer, the group also had the largest retail business in Australia. David Jones and John Martin were already in the group. Now Industrial Equity had delivered Woolworths, Flemings, Big W and Safeways Victoria. The other big item in Industrial Equity's assets was its property portfolio. It had a string of properties around Australia, the largest being the Metroplaza site in North Sydney. Industrial Equity also had a 35 per cent stake in Number One O'Connell Street, a huge office block in the heart of the Sydney CBD. Both these projects were under construction at the time. There was a string of smaller properties as well. These added to the existing property portfolio of Adsteam, in which the largest item was 244 hotels in Tooth.

While planning the rationalisation of Industrial Equity into Adsteam, Spalvins swung back to his biggest problem area—Bell Resources. Behind the scenes Spalvins had been threatening Alan Bond with legal action over the rape of Bell Resources. Then Spalvins nominated a slate of five directors, headed by himself, to be appointed to the Bell Resources board. Bond had been trying to sell a half-stake in Bond Brewing to Lion Nathan of New Zealand. Spalvins was trying to get the brewery—almost the only worthwhile asset left in the Bond empire at the time—back into Bell Resources in exchange for the billion dollars. Spalvins applied to the WA Supreme Court to put Bell Resources into receivership—a move which would have triggered an immediate claim for the $1.2 billion. Bond, whose empire was crumbling and surrounded by enemies on all sides, agreed to a deal. Bond and Spalvins would get four directors each on the Bell Resources board with Geoff Hill as independent chairman. Hill had been advising Spalvins since 1973 and Bond since 1978 and was trusted by both parties. Under pressure from the NCSC the deal was revised so that the Bell Resources board comprised two Bond representatives, two Adsteam, two independents and Hill as chairman. Adsteam had spent $180 million on its stake in Bell Resources and it was starting to look as though the whole investment was in danger.

As 1990 opened, Adelaide Steamship's share price began coming under pressure. At the end of January, Australian Ratings produced another critical report. Adsteam and associates' total debt was estimated at $4.8 billion, nearly three times the free equity of $1.7 billion. Although Australian Ratings maintained Adelaide Steamship's rating at BB+, this time the market took notice. Simultaneously, the Westmex empire of Russell Goward collapsed. A few institutions which had never understood Adsteam, and were nervous about its levels of debt, decided to get out. Shares in Adelaide Steamship, which had peaked at $7.50 in 1989, held around $6.40 through January but in the first week of February slipped suddenly to $5.20 on heavy volume. At the same time the market took a set against AWA, crunching the shares from $1.10 to 76c. AWA was a relatively minor factor in Adsteam's fortunes but the link did little to steady investors' nerves.

Spalvins, who rarely issued statements in response to market rumours, declared that the operating performance of Adelaide Steamship, Tooth, David Jones and Petersville was continuing to grow. He predicted that Adelaide Steamship's profit for the six months to December 1989 would be over $100 million and that it would pay a fully franked dividend of at least 32c a share. In February Adelaide Steamship easily beat the forecast by announcing an interim profit of $132 million. The group also announced a 'core business plan' of selling down its investment portfolio and concentrating on its main operations, particularly food and retailing. Westpac immediately snapped up one of the investments, buying Adsteam's 7.5 per cent of the ANZ for $409 million. Some of the profit on this deal was eroded when Adsteam—after a long wrangle with the Australian Taxation Office—agreed to pay $19 million retrospective tax on its BHP deal.

Adsteam was still expanding. In March 1990 one of the group's associates, Markheath Securities, bid $145 million for a UK automotive group, Camford Engineering. On the other side of the balance sheet, Adsteam raised a little cash by selling 40 Tooth hotels. But by April it still did not have full control of Industrial Equity, with an irritating 3 per cent of the shareholders still hanging out. There was also a proposal to partly disentangle the cross-shareholdings in the group.

The banks get nervous

The Adsteam group was due to negotiate new loan agreements with its bankers in August. Instead of having loan facilities with staggered maturities, Adsteam had allowed them all to mature together. This gave the banks more negotiating power. The bankers were nervous and seeking to impose more restrictive conditions. In May Westpac was becoming concerned about its position. Westpac proposed a new banking deal to Adsteam on condition that one of the bank's top analysts be allowed to inspect the Adsteam books. While Westpac was continuing its due diligence the market was growing increasingly uneasy about the group. AWA shares went below 50c, increasing Adsteam's paper loss on that group. However, a paper profit was generated by David Jones selling a block of National Bank shares to Adelaide Steamship.

By this time Westpac was getting really worried. Despite having a man inside Adsteam it still did not fully comprehend the accounts, but had uncovered the fact that the total debt levels of the group were larger than previously thought. Westpac convened a meeting of senior executives of the other three major trading banks at its Martin Place headquarters at the start of July 1990. The meeting was a dramatic affair. Counting the numbers, the four banks suddenly discovered that their combined exposure to the Adsteam group was more than $4 billion and that total debt was around $6.4 billion. This was very high compared to the group's combined shareholders' funds of around $1 billion. 'They shat blue lights', said one observer.

The banks immediately insisted that Adsteam liquidate assets more quickly. Adsteam began by unloading some National Bank and Westpac shares. The huge debt and the need for asset sales made the market uneasy. Investors were even more unnerved when newspapers reported that the group could face a further retrospective tax bill of $100 million. At the same time a detailed analysis of the group was released by Barings analyst Viktor Shvets. The report assessed the net assets of Adelaide Steamship at between $3 and $6 but said that some $3 of it was represented by future tax benefits. Shvets' valuation of Adsteam was arguable but his methodology carried weight. The annual poll of institutions conducted by *Australian Business* had twice rated Shvets as Australia's best analyst.

Finally, there was the question of dividends. By now the banks were belatedly recognising their huge losses crystallising from the 1980s and were cutting dividends. These dividends had been a big component of Adsteam's own dividend stream. The Adsteam group had always paid out a high percentage of its profits in franked dividends. If its profits were likely to fall the dividends would have to fall too. Investors who were holding Adsteam group shares would see the yields drop and also the franking credits. For all these reasons, investors began to head for the exit.

Adelaide Steamship shares, which had recovered to $5.50 in early July, slumped to $4 in a few days. David Jones went from $8.50 to $7 and Petersville Sleigh eased from $2.30 to $2.05. At a Securities Institute briefing in Sydney, Spalvins criticised Shvets' valuations and called for Adsteam to be valued on its fundamentals. Spalvins' counterattack was blunted when another broking firm, Potter Warburg, issued an analysis querying the wisdom of the Industrial Equity takeover and valuing Adelaide Steamship shares at $3.55.

This was bad enough, but then Spalvins received a mortal blow from an old rival. When taking over Industrial Equity Spalvins had dismissed Sir Ron Brierley as 'yesterday's man'. In September Brierley wrought terrible revenge by releasing his own report on Adsteam, which estimated total debt at $7 billion and shareholders' funds at $1.8 billion. The group had been reporting increasing profits throughout the 1980s, but on Brierley's analysis it had only broken even in the three years to June 1990 when adjustment was made for inter-company transactions and dividend flow. He valued Adelaide Steamship shares at $3.07.[17] Brierley may have lost control of his flagship, but yesterday's man still had enormous clout in today's share market. Nor were investors reassured a few days later when Adsteam announced that it had written off a total of $80 million on its Bell holding. Adelaide Steamship countered by announcing a profit of $220 million. Brierley said it was essentially another break-even year. The shares crashed to just over $2, their lowest level in six years. Oddly, a statement by Brierley that the shares were worth $2.87 did nothing to calm the market.

The magic of the cross-holding structure was now working at top speed in reverse. A fall in Adelaide Steamship shares automatically caused a fall in its largest shareholder, David Jones. And a fall in David Jones shares caused further weakness in Adelaide Steamship. And so on through the empire.

The falls occurred despite a large share-propping exercise. A key member of the Adsteam group, Petersville Sleigh, held a 31 per cent stake in Howard Smith. Spalvins and Kent were on the Howard Smith board. Howard Smith revealed in September that it had been a large buyer through 1989–90, spending nearly $50 million to acquire a 2.3 per cent stake in Adelaide Steamship. At that point Howard Smith had lost $37 million on the investment. Worse, Howard Smith had lent a further $60 million to three Adsteam companies. Now Howard Smith was proposing a $136 million special dividend and capital return to shareholders, of which the biggest beneficiary would be Petersville. Howard Smith shareholders—who had never been asked to approve this major investment in an associated company—were outraged. Adelaide Steamship shares fell to $1.40. Australian Ratings slashed the group rating to CCC, the second lowest possible.

The market had lost faith in Spalvins and so had the bankers. The banks were demanding asset sales and wanted executive control of the group loosened. Under pressure, Spalvins announced an eighteen-month reconstruction program in which $3 billion worth of assets would be sold. Executive control began unravelling as Spalvins and Kent resigned from the boards of Petersville and National Consolidated. The broking firm Ord Minnett released a report saying that the value of Adelaide Steamship could be negligible or even negative.

All this had been happening against the deepening of the worst recession Australia had seen in 60 years. Confidence in Spalvins and the Adsteam group went into free fall. Adsteam announced that it was going to sell its 31 per cent of Howard Smith. The Howard Smith board promptly sacked Spalvins and Kent as directors and barred them from boardroom discussions. The proposed special dividend and capital return were deferred until the Adsteam group had refunded the $60 million outstanding in loans. As the *Financial Review* pointed out, this was all laudably tough stuff from the Howard Smith directors but the time to stand up to Spalvins had been six months before.[18]

By the time the group released its annual reports in November 1990, Adelaide Steamship shares had plummeted to 50c. At least some of the plunge had been due to short selling. Sydney stockbroker René Rivkin, the market's most flamboyant operator, admitted to making a profit of $1 million by shorting Adsteam.

The bankers moved into Adsteam in an informal receivership and began trying to get agreement on restructuring. Spalvins, once the hero of the share market, was now being forced off his boards. He and Kent resigned from AWA and Tooth. At Tooth the former managing director George Haines became chief executive. In March 1991 Adelaide Steamship, David Jones, Tooth, Petersville Sleigh and National Consolidated announced losses totalling $1.28 billion. Spalvins and Kent resigned from all remaining companies, along with company secretary Neil Branford. They agreed to stay on and work on a restructuring of the group. One problem was that Spalvins and Kent had been granted a generous swag of shares in Adelaide Steamship, financed by loans from the company. Spalvins held 16 million shares—making him the second largest shareholder in Adelaide Steamship—financed by a $33 million loan. Kent had a similar but smaller deal. As part of the termination both the loans and the shareholdings were cancelled. To add to Spalvins' troubles, his wife Cecily died in April at the age of 53.

The great group put together by Russell and Spalvins was taken over by Australia's four major trading banks. As operating businesses were at the core of the group it had to be kept going. A simple fire sale would have been counterproductive. The banks devised a formula under which a large proportion of the earnings from the businesses was paid to the banks in interest. However, these payments did not meet the total interest bill. The unpaid interest was converted into instruments called PCORNS (perpetual convertible or redeemable notes). In a liquidation PCORNS ranked after debtors but before shareholders. As Adsteam companies never managed to cover their interest bill the number of PCORNS grew apace each year, which meant in effect that the banks were further crowding out the equity held by the shareholders.

Table 13.2 Adsteam group, 30 June 1993[19] (Pro forma accounts after Woolworths float. All figures in $m.)

ASSETS	
Current Assets	2 063
Non-Current Assets:	
Property, plant and equipment	638
Other	598
Total assets	3 299
LIABILITIES	
Current Liabilities:	
Creditors & borrowings	827
Provisions	88
Non-Current Liabilities:	
Creditors & borrowings	2 352
Provisions	5
Total liabilities	3 272
SHAREHOLDERS' FUNDS	
Deficiency	(211)
Outside equity interests	(176)
Accrued PCORNS	414
Equity inc. PCORNS	27

The shares of the various companies remained listed and even flickered into life occasionally as rumours swept the market of restructuring proposals. But the shareholders had been marginalised. The effective equity in the group was held by the banks, which slowly realised that they would be struggling to recoup their debts. They were dealt a further blow when the Australian Taxation Office negotiated a payment of $250 million in retrospective taxes plus the cancellation of $100 million in tax credits. Petersville Sleigh and all the great food brands were sold to Pacific Dunlop, but more cash was needed. The group's biggest remaining asset was Woolworths, which was operating brilliantly under chief executive Paul Simons. Woolworths was floated in May 1993, raising $2.4 billion for Industrial Equity (IEL). In addition, Woolworths had carried some $560 million in debt (excluding trade creditors) when it floated.

Table 13.2 summarises the pro forma balance sheet of the Adsteam economic entity after the Woolworths float. This economic entity included as controlled entities David Jones, Tooth, IEL, National Consolidated, Metro Meat, Markheath and their controlled entities. This was the most accurate way of gauging the group without double counting.

The PCORNS are shown in the table as a plus but they were really an additional liability. There was therefore little comfort in these accounts for Adelaide Steamship shareholders. Unless further asset sales could be made for considerably more than book value, or the shrunken group could generate earnings that outstripped the interest bill, the PCORNS would continue to grow and to erode the equity of the ordinary shareholders.

The Adsteam collapse was the biggest and most far reaching in Australia. This was no paper castle. Here were some of Australia's greatest businesses. Kent said that the group was the second largest employer in Australia and he may well have been right. It was a dominant player in the food and wine industries. It was the biggest rival to Coles Myer in retailing. It was the biggest shareholder in the Australian trading banks. It had substantial stakes in a number of other industries ranging from timber to automotive parts. Its stated profits had risen every year and so had its assets. Its leading spirit, John Spalvins, was widely acknowledged as a genius. How could such a group fail?

Flawed structure

Before attempting an explanation it is necessary to understand the structure of the group. The group changed shape somewhat from year to year. The overall trend was for companies to develop increasingly large shareholdings in each other. Figure 13.1 shows how the main operating companies related to each other when the group reached its final flowering in June 1990.[20] To analysts there were several disturbing features of the structure.

One was that several important companies were 'ghosts' in a conventional consolidation. Accountancy rules provided that a company did not need to be consolidated until the holding exceeded 50 per cent. Metro Meat was owned 50/50 by Adelaide Steamship and Tooth and so was not consolidated into either company's accounts. To a lay observer, this seems stupid because David Jones held 44.8 per cent of Tooth and Adelaide Steamship held another 18.7 per cent, a total of 63.5 per cent. But as Adelaide Steamship only held 49.7 per cent of David Jones directly it did not have to consolidate either David Jones or Metro Meat. The author had been told for years that there were serious problems in Metro Meat (one of Australia's largest meat companies) but nobody could ever find out because of the structure. Indeed, a structure such as this raises the automatic suspicion that it has been created deliberately to conceal the true position, particularly the debts and losses.

A second disturbing point was the lack of logic in the structure of the operating companies. Adsteam was Australia's largest food group, but the food was split between Petersville, Industrial Equity and Metro Meat. Wine interests were split between Industrial Equity and Tooth. The only single-interest companies were those such as Martin Wells, Metro Meat and Woolworths, which were wholly or jointly owned and therefore did not publish separate accounts. Companies which entered the empire with a single purpose, such as David Jones, were soon diversified so that

Figure 13.1   Adsteam group structure, September 1990

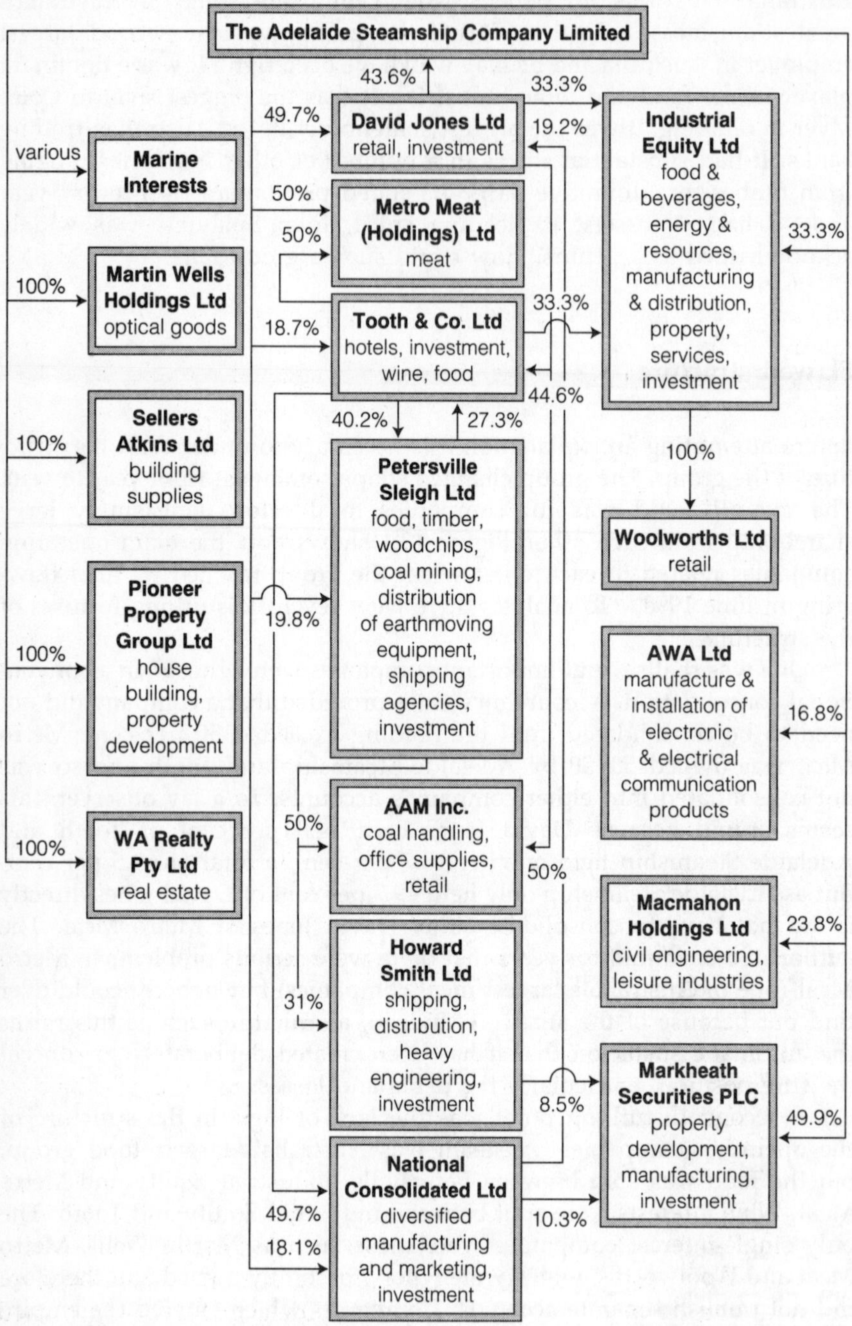

The Adelaide Steamship Company Limited

various → **Marine Interests**

49.7% — **David Jones Ltd** retail, investment — 43.6% — 33.3% — 19.2%

Industrial Equity Ltd food & beverages, energy & resources, manufacturing & distribution, property, services, investment — 33.3%

100% → **Martin Wells Holdings Ltd** optical goods

50% — **Metro Meat (Holdings) Ltd** meat

50%

18.7% — **Tooth & Co. Ltd** hotels, investment, wine, food — 33.3% — 44.6%

100% → **Sellers Atkins Ltd** building supplies

40.2% — 27.3%

Petersville Sleigh Ltd food, timber, woodchips, coal mining, distribution of earthmoving equipment, shipping agencies, investment

100% → **Pioneer Property Group Ltd** house building, property development — 19.8%

100% → **WA Realty Pty Ltd** real estate

50% — **AAM Inc.** coal handling, office supplies, retail — 50%

Woolworths Ltd retail — 100%

AWA Ltd manufacture & installation of electronic & electrical communication products — 16.8%

31% — **Howard Smith Ltd** shipping, distribution, heavy engineering, investment

Macmahon Holdings Ltd civil engineering, leisure industries — 23.8%

8.5% — **Markheath Securities PLC** property development, manufacturing, investment — 49.9%

49.7% — 18.1% — **National Consolidated Ltd** diversified manufacturing and marketing, investment — 10.3%

Note: Holdings under 5% not included

428

The sinking of Adelaide Steamship

Table 13.3   Adsteam's rising debt

| | Total Debt | | inc. Current Debt | |
Company	1989 ($m)	1990 ($m)	1989 ($m)	1990 ($m)
Petersville	618	770	99	358
National Consol.	462	622	90	158
IEL	2 372	2 418	1 284	1 340
Tooth	555	1 077	93	593
Adelaide Steamship	970	955	143	212
Total	4 977	5 842	1 509	2 661

an analyst could not tell how its retailing business was performing relative to its other interests. In the absence of any good explanation for such a Byzantine structure the automatic suspicion is that it has been created deliberately to conceal the performance of the operating businesses rather than to reveal them. In fact, the operating businesses ran very well and a large part of the credit for this can be taken by Spalvins, who worked very hard to ensure that they stayed on track.

A third disturbing point was the gearing potential. The rough rule of thumb for industrial companies such as those of the Adsteam group is that they should be about 50 per cent geared. That is, they should be funded by about $1 of debt for every $1 of equity. It's only a rough rule. If Adelaide Steamship were to gear up to 60 per cent debt that would not bother analysts much, and even a little higher would be tolerated. But if Tooth and David Jones and Petersville were all to gear up to 70 per cent it would be more worrying. And a joint venture like Metro Meat could gear up like crazy without anyone knowing because it did not appear in any public company's accounts. Borrowing levels rose remorselessly in the Adsteam group. Consider Table 13.3, showing 1989 and 1990 debt levels.

Not only was total debt rising at a time of prolonged high interest rates, but current debt was rising. This was bound to produce refinancing problems and shows why Adsteam was increasingly at the mercy of its bankers. Adsteam for years had been pyramiding debt and disguising the extent through its minority-controlled empire.

Spalvins and Kent always argued strenuously that, because the debt raised by each company in the group was non-recourse to other companies, it was misleading to aggregate the debt of all the group entities and so produce a figure for group debt. This was a legitimate argument. However if David Jones, say, were unable to cope with its debt and were to go into receivership its shares would have fallen to zero. This would have caused a big writedown (as eventually it did) in the value of Adelaide Steamship's investments because Adelaide Steamship owned 49.7 per cent of David Jones. It would also have wrought major damage

429

on the balance sheet of National Consolidated, which owned another 19.2 per cent of David Jones. The failure of any one entity in the group to meet its obligations would therefore have a domino effect throughout the rest of the group. The chain was only as strong as its weakest link and the weakest link could have been something the analysts couldn't see, such as Metro Meat or Markheath.

Strong operating businesses such as National Consolidated and Petersville of course needed debt to fund their working capital. But at some point, probably in the early days when David Jones was buying stock in Adelaide Steamship to protect it from Howard Smith, Spalvins made another discovery. If he bought shares on market in a company the share price went up. This also pushed up the market value—and hence book value—of the investment in that company. So total assets went up and so did shareholders' funds. So the impact of David Jones buying Adelaide Steamship shares was to enhance its own shareholders' funds. That in turn allowed David Jones to borrow more money to buy more shares. Spalvins and Kent had discovered the financial equivalent of perpetual motion. And they believed it. In 1987 Spalvins told Geoff Hill, quite seriously, that the only investments he could contemplate in the market at that time were in his own shares.

A profit case study: Petersville

Superficially, the results of all the Adsteam companies looked terrific. Every year the earnings were larger and the dividends were larger. The profits have not been quoted so far because I did not wish to burden the reader with numbers. However, we must now look at some of them. Let us take as an example in Table 13.4 the profit of Petersville Sleigh for the year to June 1990, stated as a healthy $122 million.

The declared net profit of $122.5 million represented a 67 per cent increase on the previous year. It also enabled a high payout ratio. But how did Petersville make the profit? Its great food brands (Peters, Birds Eye, Edgell, Herbert Adams etc.) and other operating businesses had chalked up profits totalling $98.3 million. But these earnings were entirely wiped out by the interest bill of $98.7 million. They had gone solely to service Petersville's debt. The debt had been used to finance its investments, notably its 27 per cent holding in Tooth and its 31 per cent of Howard Smith. Dividends from these investments provided the $99.6 million investment income, mainly comprising $59.1 million in dividends from Tooth and $23.9 million from Howard Smith. These accounted for nearly all of Petersville's 1990 profit, with future tax benefits and a few asset sales making up the balance. Note that the $8.3 million future tax

Table 13.4   Petersville's 1990 profit—divisional results (all figures in $m)

Food	70.6
Forestry & building supplies	21.1
Other businesses	6.6
Investment	99.6
Operating profit	197.9
Interest	(98.7)
Asset sales	18.2
Corporate overheads	(0.2)
Tax benefit	8.3
Minorities	(1.2)
Net profit	122.5
Dividends paid	(89.7)
Retained earnings	32.8

benefit did not represent real cash. A company that made a loss was entitled to carry it forward to future years and apply it as a tax deduction against future profits. But the benefit would be received only if and when Petersville made future profits against which the tax loss could be applied. Then, and only then, would it represent a real benefit to Petersville.

If the future tax benefit were eliminated the actual profit available to Petersville shareholders would come down to $114.2 millon. Of this, $89.7 million or 78 per cent was being paid out in dividends. This was a high payout ratio compared to the normal practice that only about half of available profit should be paid in dividends. This pattern was repeated in almost every Adsteam company. Funds from the actual operations of each company were wiped out by a comparable interest bill, and the reported profit comprised mostly profits from associated companies. The principle was that of the merry-go-round. The profitability of each company depended on continuation of a strong dividend flow from others. Worse, it was capable of being manipulated. The directors of Tooth could crank up Petersville's profit by raising their dividend. And vice versa— because Petersville owned 27 per cent of Tooth, which owned 40 per cent of Petersville.

Spalvins always publicly advocated high dividend payout ratios, particularly for the bank shareholdings. Instead of a company retaining profits to fund its growth, Spalvins' argument was that companies should pay out as high a proportion as possible and leave it to the shareholders to decide—through a dividend reinvestment scheme—whether to reinvest money in the company. Spalvins' argument had considerable merit, but in practice the same policy within the Adsteam company meant that each company was giving the others artificially high profits.

Let us look a little further upstream. Note that Petersville's profit depended heavily on its receipt of a $59.1 million dividend from Tooth.

Total dividends paid by Tooth in that year were $215 million. But could Tooth afford to pay that? Tooth had recorded an operating profit of $188 million plus a future tax benefit of $28 million, making a total of $216 million. So out of a total profit of $216 million Tooth paid $215 million in dividends. And of that $216 million, $28 million was a tax benefit which would not be realised until some indeterminate future date (in fact, never). Thus Tooth had paid $27 million more in dividends than it had actually earned for the year. If it had reduced dividend to a more prudent level Petersville's profit and dividend would also have fallen. And so on throughout the group.

The Petersville/Tooth example reveals the financial modus operandi of the Adsteam group, which could be roughly summarised as a three-step operation:

- At the base of the Adsteam group were several operating businesses with good earnings.
- Those earnings were mortgaged to the hilt to raise debt.
- The debt was used to finance takeovers or big share market gambles.

When stated like this the weakness of the structure is immediately clear. The group was going to be in trouble whenever (a) one of the share market gambles failed to come off, or (b) the profit flow from the core operations was substantially disrupted. It is to Spalvins' credit that he bought real businesses and ran them very well. Spalvins was a brilliant manager and decision maker in the operating businesses. However, the profit flow from the operating businesses began running into trouble in 1988 or 1989 as the deepening recession began to bite. Penny-pinching customers, for example, began deserting Petersville's great food brands in favour of generics. The group might have survived this downturn if it had been brief or if the big gambles had been winners.

The six big gambles

When it came to gambling on the markets Spalvins' luck and judgement was no better than average, although this was not apparent for some time. Basically he took six gambles: the BHP play, the bank investments, shorting the SPI, the UK insurance companies, the Bell Resources play and the Industrial Equity takeover.

The BHP play

BHP was a bad investment because Adsteam bought without having a strategy to get out. Adsteam did not have the capacity to go further with its investment and did not understand what Holmes à Court was doing. Adsteam sold the stock well enough to Holmes à Court in the original option deal and cannot be much criticised for failing to see how far BHP would run. Adsteam locked in a good profit but then saw Holmes à Court poised to make a much greater one or even take over BHP. At that point, not content to quit the game and take his chips, Spalvins shorted BHP massively. At the end of the episode he barely got out of the deal with his underpants. And while the whole play was going on it must have been an enormous distraction from the running of Adsteam's core businesses.

The banks

Spalvins did, however, satisfy himself that he could hold BHP on a neutral return, because the dividends he received were equivalent to the dividends he paid on the preference shares which he used to finance them. He used the same strategy with the banks, holding them on a negative cost of about 1 per cent and gambling on a rise in price (which would certainly go up if he could bully the banks into increasing payout ratios) or perhaps even gambling on a merger between any two of them. His belief that bank stocks were cheap was fundamentally correct but probably about two years premature. Spalvins traded bank stock so heavily between his own companies that it is difficult to work out whether he was ahead or behind at the end on his gamble. At one point, for example, David Jones sold large slabs of NAB to Adelaide Steamship. This enabled David Jones to declare a big profit and, of course, a high dividend. However, it saddled Adelaide Steamship with the same holding at higher cost. Most probably the banks were a minor disaster, because Spalvins wound up with vast corporate investments which he could not control. Also, his lectures offended both the banks and the institutions at a time when all his facilities with them were due to mature. The banks began looking harder at his debt and began deserting his share registers in 1988 and 1989.

The Share Price Index

Shorting the SPI was a gamble which failed because Spalvins got the timing wrong. The net cost appears to have been about $18 million, which was a nasty wound but not mortal.

Insurance

The UK insurance companies attracted less attention than Spalvins' other plays but they were probably his most dangerous gambles. He spent £500 million investing in Royal Insurance and Commercial Union. He got out of them largely intact but they were high risk. Spalvins was taking on the City of London in an industry where he had no experience and in companies which he did not control.

The Bell play

Bell Resources was a bad mistake. The BHP play had convinced Spalvins (against the evidence) that he was a better market player than Holmes à Court. When Holmes à Court came to grief in 1988 Spalvins had watched fascinated as Ron Brierley and Kerry Packer ran a greenmail play in Bell Resources. Alan Bond controlled Bell Group, which held 40 per cent of Bell Resources. Packer and Brierley picked up a parcel of Bell Resources shares, threatening Bond's control of the cash cow of the Bell empire. They were bought out for a nice profit. In hindsight, the shares must have been bought by someone very close to Alan Bond because the shares hit the market again quite soon. Spalvins, who was friendly with Bond at that time, bought the same block of shares through Potts West Turnbull only nine days after Packer and Brierley had sold them. To his credit, Bond actually offered on at least two occasions to take Spalvins out of Bell Resources at $2.35. The buyer would have been David Rowland of Monaco Group BV, who is mentioned in Chapter 6. But Spalvins stayed in and Bell Resources became a writeoff.

Industrial Equity

IEL could have been Spalvins' salvation. The company was being run by Rod Price and Bill Loewenthal, who were trying to take over the group through a management buyout. Woolworths was beginning its great turnaround under the genius of Paul Simons. Most of the properties in the group had been joint-ventured or presold. When Spalvins took over he told Price not to do anything because he would be exercising control from that point. This was a fateful decision, because Price and Loewenthal had put together a parcel of assets which they were planning to sell for $1.3 billion to $1.5 billion. If this sale could have been pulled off it would have left Industrial Equity with Woolworths and about $700 million debt. This would have effectively translated into about $700 million equity for Spalvins. The decision not to proceed with the asset sale as soon as he took over was probably Spalvins' worst mistake. Spalvins and Kent hung on to the assets too long before trying to sell and by that time the recession was well into its stride, the property market was collapsing and Indians were punching holes all through the Adsteam wagon train.

Adsteam is a prime example of 'financial engineering'. This was quite a vogue phrase in the 1980s. The term implied that scientific precision had been brought to financing. It was financial engineering, for example, to push debts off balance sheet, to enhance profits by equity accounting, or to show preference shares as equity when they were issued in such volume and under such terms as to actually be debt.

A generation of number crunchers, analysts and shareholders had been taught to look at the bottom line. What were the company's net tangible assets? What were its earnings per share? Were they both growing? Was its gearing at acceptable levels? If the answers to these questions were favourable you had a stock the investors would buy. Adsteam companies met all these criteria brilliantly. In any market where a company is judged by the numbers it produces on the bottom line, it is inevitable that operators will emerge who will use financial engineering— within generally accepted accounting standards—to produce numbers that the market will like. These numbers can be signed true and fair by auditors but may not bear any relationship to the health of the operating business. In Adsteam this was all done quite legally.

The men who ran Adsteam seem to have fallen into their own trap. None were more brilliant users of financial techniques, but they began to confuse the numbers they were producing with reality. Some of their manoeuvres were very clever: notably the defence against Howard Smith; the takeovers of the core businesses, from David Jones to National Consolidated; their initial use of preference shares for financing; and the way they drew the wagons into a circle. However, these successes led to a delusion of infallibility, which rarely escapes unpunished in the markets.

Spalvins and Kent, masters of their own universe, lost touch with reality. They expanded too far at a time when they should have been contracting. There were no crimes involved in the fall of Adsteam, but there was the sin of hubris.[21]

Spalvins built a large potential holding in the group, financed by interest-free loans from Adelaide Steamship. However, all the evidence is that he intended to profit *with* his shareholders and not at their expense: an important distinction that should be borne in mind throughout this book. Spalvins never took money from the group that he should not have taken and never sold assets of his own to the group. He worked tirelessly in its interests and believed that he was delivering value to its shareholders. His intentions were good, but his shareholders ultimately suffered some of the worst wipeouts of the crash. Investors in high-flying groups such as Bond Corporation or Qintex should have been tolerably aware that they were taking some degree of risk. Such stocks tended to attract professional investors and relatively few small shareholders. But ordinary investors in Adelaide Steamship, David Jones and Tooth believed that they were in fundamentally sound stocks—particularly those investors who had been there for a long time. From being high-priced stocks they collapsed to nearly zero with little or no hope of recovery. This wrought particularly heavy damage among old Adelaide and Sydney families with large Adelaide Steamship or David Jones holdings. Adelaide Steamship alone had 21 000 shareholders on its register when Spalvins resigned. A corporate cowboy who is deliberately trying to deceive the public is—for all his devices—fairly obvious. The worst disasters tend to be inflicted by people who have deceived themselves.

14

Trico: the child who went wrong

Like a desperado trying to get out of trouble on the last race at Flemington.

Director Jack Ryan's description
of Tricontinental's lending policy

Tricontinental Corporation Ltd had an impeccable birth but turned into a wayward child and came to a terrible end. It was conceived by Sir Ian Potter—one of the greatest financiers and stockbrokers in Australia's history. It must have grieved the ageing Sir Ian to see his offspring become notorious for loose financing and a byword for bad banking. When it was floated as Portfolio & Development Ltd in July 1960 its background was ultra-blueblooded. It was underwritten by Ian Potter & Co, was sponsored by the merchant bank Australian United Corporation (a Potter offshoot), and boasted Australian Guarantee Corporation as a major shareholder thereby making the Bank of New South Wales one of its indirect parents. Portfolio & Development was chaired by Sir Ian Potter.[1] The board included Colonel Hector Clayton, Sir Arthur Smithers and Robert Wilson MLC.

Portfolio & Development led a blameless life as an investment company. In 1969 it changed its name to Tricontinental Corporation Ltd as it entered merchant banking. In 1970 Sir Ian added to Tricontinental's prestige by recruiting some large foreign shareholders. Security Pacific National Bank of Los Angeles took up a 25 per cent interest, Enskilda Bank of Stockholm took 6 per cent and Gillett Brothers Discount Co of London took 5 per cent. In the following year Mitsui took a further 10 per cent. In 1978 there was a major reshuffle. Tricontinental ceased to be a public company after being taken over by a consortium of financiers. The new shareholders were State Savings Bank of Victoria (25 per cent); Rural & Industries Bank of Western Australia (25 per cent); Security Pacific (20 per cent); Mitsui Bank (13 per cent); Credit Lyonnais (13 per cent), Skandinaviska Enskilda Banka (2 per cent); and Sir Ian Potter (2 per cent).

The important shareholder in this group was the State Savings Bank of Victoria (SSBV). Since 1842, when it was incorporated as the Savings Bank of Port Phillip, the SSBV had been a savings bank confined to Victoria. Savings banking in Australia had been the preserve of government institutions until 1956, when trading banks were permitted to enter the field. As banking competition mounted in the 1970s the SSBV began to spread its wings a little. It began dabbling in lending outside its traditional housing loans and took a 20 per cent interest in the Perth-based merchant bank, Westralian International Ltd. The Tricontinental reconstruction in 1978 was really a merger with Westralian. There was considerable logic in the SSBV's participation. A shareholding in a merchant bank enabled the SSBV to escape a little from the confines of savings banking. A partnership with the respected Sir Ian Potter was highly desirable. It was equally respectable to have another state bank, the R & I, as an equal shareholder. Tricontinental had a strong Victorian base and a good geographic spread of business into every state except South Australia. Importantly, it was strong in the resource-rich state of Western Australia, which always had the potential for big deals. And, thanks to Sir Ian, the bank had good international connections.

As has already been noted, this was the era when state banks were being prodded by their governments to become more entrepreneurial. The Victorian Government of John Cain actively encouraged the SSBV to get into mainstream banking. In 1980 the bank's name was changed to State Bank of Victoria (SBV) and its lending powers were widened. The bank was corporatised, with the former SSBV commissioners replaced by a board of directors. Amendments to the Act in 1982 and 1983 would liberate it further. Dr Peter Sheehan, director general of the Victorian Department of Management and Budget from 1982 to April 1990, said later: 'The government's perception in 1982 was that the Victorian economy was depressed and that many statutory authorities and departments were performing poorly'.

The department's role was in part to lead the government's efforts to introduce an economic plan and to upgrade management performance and strategy-setting within major authorities. The Treasurer and department officials worked closely with responsible ministers and other officials in relation to authorities such as the State Electricity Commission, Board of Works, Gas & Fuel Corporation and so on. As a major state instrumentality, and one within the Treasurer's portfolio, the SBV was included in this process. The need to upgrade management performance, to review strategic directions and to analyse the banking environment and opportunities available to the SBV were stressed to the board and management of the bank.[2]

The aims of Sheehan and the Victorian Government were laudable.

Their execution, unfortunately, was execrable. The Victorian Government's attempts at capitalism would almost all end in disasters, with catastrophic financial results for the state. The biggest single disaster would be the SBV and its erring subsidiary, Tricontinental.

The SBV had been a simple savings bank for well over a century. After 1980 it had to make a fast transition into a full service bank. This transition was undertaken at a time of unprecedentedly fierce competition for banking business in Australia and also during the plunge into the uncharted waters of deregulation. A strategic plan was produced for the SBV by Merrill Lynch Capital Markets in 1983. Six months later the Victorian Treasurer, Rob Jolly, announced an economic plan for the state called 'Victoria—The Next Step', which included an expanded role for the SBV. The bank was encouraged to consolidate and expand its corporate lending and to build on its strength in the retail sector with a view to providing customers with one-stop shopping for financial services. There was strong encouragement in both the Merrill Lynch plan and Jolly's strategy for the SBV to expand overseas. A new and very experienced chief executive, Bill Moyle, was appointed in August 1984. The SBV was going places.

Tricontinental was a solid enough company when the SSBV took its stake in 1978. Sir Ian was chairman, with Geoff Redenbach as managing director. Tricontinental mostly traded in the short-term money market, underwrote issues, managed funds, gave takeover and merger advice and provided other corporate services. As usual with money market operators its balance sheet showed heavy liabilities in the form of deposits matched by corresponding assets in the form of short-dated fixed interest securities. At 30 June 1979 deposits totalled $191 million, or 92 per cent of total liabilities including shareholders' funds. This was probably quite sound because any sudden demand for a return of deposits should have been capable of being met by selling the securities or allowing them to mature. The soundness of an operation which runs on short-term or call deposits depends largely on the liquidity of its assets. Failure to observe this was one of the prime reasons for the collapse of Tricontinental.

Between 1980 and 1985 Tricontinental expanded rapidly, with total assets almost trebling from $335 million to $970 million. This was largely funded by a rise in short-term deposits from $290 million to $785 million. An increasing proportion of these deposits was 11 a.m. money; that is, deposits repayable at 11 o'clock next day. Sometimes such deposits may stay in place for weeks or even months, but they are always liable to be called and the more heavily a bank depends on them the more vulnerable it is, because it will only be able to pay out by dumping a large proportion of its assets on to the market. The heavy reliance on call money also potentially exposed Tricontinental to higher costs, because to keep its

11 a.m. deposits in place the bank would have to offer one of the most attractive interest rates each day. In 1983 Australian Ratings gave Tricontinental a Grade 4 rating—the second lowest investment rating on its table—because it had 'certain features below the industry norm'. Australian Ratings was primarily concerned about its dependence on 11 a.m. money. Redenbach dismissed the rating as 'not soundly based'.

August 1984 saw two significant steps in the deregulation of Australian banking. Licensed banks were allowed to compete with merchant banks in the short-term money markets and the restriction was removed which previously confined an Australian bank to 60 per cent ownership of a merchant bank. A few weeks later Moyle discussed the implications for the SBV with Jolly. Moyle said that both the SBV and the R & I believed they should sell their stakes in Tricontinental 'on the basis that deregulation makes the investment anachronistic'.[3] Once state banks were allowed to undertake a full range of merchant banking activities they no longer needed to own a separate merchant bank.

The foreign shareholders seemed interested in buying Tricontinental. Credit Lyonnais considered a bid, but was only lukewarm. Mitsui offered to buy Tricontinental for the value of its net tangible assets, subject to an investigation of the bank by Touche Ross. Touche Ross spent three months investigating and reported to Mitsui in February 1985. Touche Ross valued the bank at $40 million, some 16 per cent below the book value of its net tangibles at December 1984. A number of the points made in the Touche Ross report indicate that the problems which would ultimately wreck Tricontinental were already present to some degree in 1985.[4] Touche Ross noted that pre-tax profit for the December 1984 half would be only $960 000 compared to a budget of $4.8 million, and they were unable to identify a clear reason for the fall in earnings. Other points raised by Touche Ross were:

- Special arrangements were entered into with clients which had a timing effect on operating results. (It is not quite clear what was meant by this, but the implication was that profits were propped by one of a diversity of means.)
- Profits had been increased by transactions which gave rise to prepaid fees. (Such fees might not be repeatable in future years, which meant that profits could not be assured. And to the extent that upfront fees had been incorporated into the loan they might never be realised anyway.)
- A major proportion of the loan portfolio was concentrated on several major client groups (the high net worth—and high risk—individuals).
- A significant amount of total loans was provided to the Jewish community and in loans for property development.
- Information on loans was not always completely documented, which

meant that significant reliance had to be placed on senior staff (who presumably kept details in their heads).

- A number of loans had been in arrears for some time and had not been closed because of concern that action might endanger the underlying security. (The corollary implication was that Tricontinental might have underprovided for bad loans.)

After reading this report Mitsui tiptoed away from the deal. With Mitsui not bidding for Tricontinental the SBV was left in the lurch. It was feared that the Mitsui withdrawal could trigger serious problems for Tricontinental. Senior staff were likely to leave and other banks would withdraw credit facilities from Tricontinental, leading to critical funding problems.[5] From being a seller of Tricontinental, Moyle was forced to contemplate protecting the SBV's position by buying the outstanding 75 per cent of the bank.

The announcement of the SBV's purchase of Tricontinental in March 1985 was designed to give other banks and financiers the clear impression that the SBV had assumed effective ownership and control. In truth, the SBV's move was defensive and tentative. The SBV had given itself a six-month breathing space in which to explore a number of options. At one end of the range, it could buy out the other shareholders. At the other end, it could sell Tricontinental or even liquidate it.

The affairs of Tricontinental were the subject of a lengthy debate by the SBV board on 26 March. The SBV did not really need a merchant bank, but Tricontinental would offer it expansion in an area where it wanted to expand. The hazards were at least partially recognised. During the board debate Neil Smith pointed out that a couple of Tricontinental's loans were between $40 million and $100 million. He raised the frightening prospect that, if one of these loans failed, Tricontinental's capital base would be wiped out. Nevertheless, in July the SBV board decided to buy out the other shareholders for just under $30 million. Proportionately, this was a slightly lower price than Touche Ross' valuation.

The SBV board can perhaps be excused for its decision to buy Tricontinental on the grounds that its options were limited. No other serious buyer appears to have emerged and in the buoyant banking days of 1985 it would have seemed defeatist—if not downright eccentric—to liquidate a merchant bank. The SBV board can, however, be criticised for not heeding the warning signals implicit in the Touche Ross report. The subsequent Royal Commission on Tricontinental found that there was considerable uncertainty in the evidence as to how much the SBV directors knew of the report. However, it seems clear that Moyle was at least well briefed on its contents. The notes of the SBV board record that the SBV had the report, implying that it must have been available to any director who wanted to read it. There is evidence that Smith had seen it and another board member, Dr Duncan Ironmonger, had certainly seen it.[6] As Ironmonger was an outside board member, one would presume the document was available to the SBV's executive directors.

The SBV made no substantial changes to Tricontinental apart from replacing Redenbach with Jack Ryan, a veteran SBV executive who became managing director. Some extra loan provisions were made but lending policies essentially remained the same.

Having taken 100 per cent of Tricontinental, the SBV exerted little control over it. The SBV behaved from the start as though it planned to sell Tricontinental at some future date. One SBV director, Ian Renard, said:

> It seemed to me that when we came to sell it, we would have the greatest chance of selling it at all, and secondly at a good price, if we had a stand alone entity which was profitable and carried out the full range of merchant banking services. If we integrated too much of their operations into SBV's it would be very difficult to dispose of it, and I didn't want to fall into that trap.[7]

Pursuing this strategy, the SBV developed banking areas of its own which were in competition with those of Tricontinental and left Tricontinental to operate autonomously of its parent.

This SBV strategy appears to have been implicit rather than definite. Directors of both SBV and Tricontinental were fuzzy about the policy when questioned by the Royal Commission. The strategy contained one fatal flaw. It was founded on the assumption that Tricontinental was sound. The Touche Ross report had raised doubts about the very fundamentals of Tricontinental, which were not adequately pursued by the SBV board, let alone corrected. The matters raised by Touche Ross should have been addressed before letting Tricontinental go its autonomous way. Otherwise the SBV was running the risk that not only might it have difficulty selling Tricontinental in future but that Tricontinental might become—as it did—an Achilles heel to the bank itself. In particular the board should have addressed Tricontinental's problems because the SBV had raised the merchant bank's borrowing status. As Moyle said:

> Following the SBV takeover, Tricontinental could raise much more funds at lower cost because it was a more highly rated borrower. As a result, Tricontinental could expand its assets more quickly. Tricontinental's expansion did not begin because of any change of policy towards the creation of loans, but mainly because Tricontinental's credit rating improved.

The new board of Tricontinental would be:

- Sir Ian Potter, who would step down as chairman at the end of 1985.
- Neil Smith, chairman of the Gas & Fuel Corporation of Victoria and Trans Australian Airlines. These were both active chairmanships, and

the question must be raised as to how well he could concentrate on his responsibilities at Tricontinental, particularly after he succeeded Sir Ian as chairman in January 1986. Smith remained as chairman until May 1989 and must bear some responsibility for the affairs of Tricontinental in that time. He suffered a heart attack in the second half of 1985 and lost a couple of stone in weight. He told the Royal Commission: 'I regret that owing to my other business commitments and an underlying belief [that] at the proper time SBV would sell Trico, I did not consider it necessary to learn more about merchant banking'. Smith took no part in day to day management and did not attend management meetings. He was content to let Jack Ryan undertake board surveillance of the management.

- J.F. Lewin of Security Pacific, representing the former foreign banks which became preference shareholders.
- Arnold Hancock, the chairman of the SBV. Hancock was deputy chairman of Tricontinental until the end of 1985, then resigned from the board. The deputy chairmanship was taken over by Ryan.
- Jack Ryan, a senior officer of the SBV. He had filled in as acting chief executive of the SBV until Moyle was appointed in August 1984, and then served as Moyle's deputy. Ryan was managing director of Tricontinental for the remainder of 1985, after which he was succeeded by Ian Johns.
- Bill Moyle, who had 38 years experience in banking, merchant banking and finance. Before joining the SBV Moyle had been managing director of Chase-NBA Group and in 1982 and 1983 had been chairman of the Australian Merchant Bankers' Association.
- John Rawlins, an experienced banker who had been recruited by Moyle to develop the SBV's treasury operations.
- Ian Johns, then executive director of Tricontinental.
- Bruce Ziebell, another executive director of Tricontinental, and Ian Johns' right-hand man.

Ian Johns had become general manager of Tricontinental's corporate banking and financial services division in 1982. He was young, burly and aggressive. With a cheerfully ebullient manner and a shock of receding hair that exposed a large forehead, he exuded confidence. He was the archetypal thrusting new banker of the 1980s. He knew nearly all the bold riders of the day and enjoyed doing deals with them. Bruce Ziebell was an accountant who had been with Tricontinental since 1973, rising through several executive posts. He sprouted an enormous and unruly beard.

Jack Ryan had taken the managing director's role as a caretaker, expressing his desire to retire at the end of 1985. Hancock and Moyle scouted the banking field but decided that they could find nobody better than Johns to replace Ryan. Johns was young, but not abnormally so by the merchant banking standards of the 1980s, and he had fourteen years' experience in banking including four with Tricontinental. Hancock and Moyle thought him a 'hard-nosed lender', good at recovering debts.

The core reason for the whole SBV debacle is that the neither the SBV board nor its management at this point thought through the implications of the takeover of Tricontinental. Whether they intended to sell Tricontinental or operate it as a separate entity, the first step should have been to put in their own management (which they did) and undertake any cleaning up necessary inside the company. Instead, the board remained vague about its intentions with Tricontinental and failed to take any definite action. From this indecision a disaster grew.

Johns's philosophy

Power abhors a vacuum, and the vacuum at the top of Tricontinental was filled by Ian Johns. Johns was sometimes described by contemporaries and underlings as a bully boy, because he could bluster his policies through. But he also had a sharp brain, great personal drive and was perfectly at home with the markets and corporate cowboys of the 1980s. Johns was ambitious, upwardly mobile and believed he knew what to do with Tricontinental. In the absence of any policies of their own the board let Johns develop his.

Johns had already laid down his philosophy—which became Tricontinental's—in a paper to the board in November 1984. Johns had realised that competition among banks was resulting in very fine margins between borrowing and lending rates. He advocated a policy of eschewing fine-margin business. His board paper on lending strategy said:

> During the past five years, the Tricontinental group has developed a lending market niche which is well identified in the second/third ranking public companies and the private sector, where margin returns are markedly better . . . As a result of Tricontinental's developed market niche, with marketing efforts concentrated on private companies and high net worth individuals, approximately 89 per cent of total commitments are on a secured basis. The ability of Tricontinental to structure secured facilities harnessed to a higher profit return has established Tricontinental as a leader in the marketplace, and in being correctly structured and professionally managed, this type of lending has achieved a substantial track record in profitability against minimal risk and losses . . . Due to Tricontinental's prominence as a secured lender, we have been able to most substantially increase exposure levels to any one client, as the total risk element in a facility does not equate to the total amount of dollars advanced.[8]

To further exploit its market niche, Johns recommended that Tricontinental should:

- Establish credit limits for certain clients to 'demonstrate our recognition of their standing and to encourage long-term, first opportunity relationships'.
- Maintain concentration on private companies whose loyalty was reliable.
- Give clients easy access to senior people 'void of the bureaucratic processes which are characteristic of trading banks'.
- Market heavily Tricontinental's flexibility and quick decisions on lending packages.
- Develop special loan products, such as lines of credit against share portfolios.

Johns had spelled out the way in which he was going to take Tricontinental to its doom. The high net worth individuals in the second and third ranking and private companies were overwhelmingly the corporate cowboys of the day. They cheerfully paid high margins in return for access to cash. They were high risk, but Johns believed he could control the risk by lending to them on a secured basis. This proved to be fallacious, often because the security turned out to be valueless—such as Kahmea's shareholding in Qintex Ltd. Johns' recommendations were tailor-made for the cowboys. Banking red tape would be brushed aside to give them easy top-level access and quick decisions. While there was doubtless some red tape that could usefully be removed, it was important that the fundamentals of credit control should not be abandoned in the process. Johns may well have been carried away by the glamour of rubbing shoulders with the high-fliers, because their loan applications were almost invariably approved. To pursue the chapter title's metaphor of the problem child, Tricontinental was the girl who couldn't say no.

These danger signals were more difficult to see as the boom was getting into its stride in late 1984 than they would be in hindsight. In those days it was an article of faith amongst bankers that they had to maintain market share. Enormous fees could be reaped from loans to corporate cowboys. Bankers who were cautious about such loans and clients were scorned as lacking in judgement and derided as wimps. Even their sexual prowess was called into question. The herd instinct is as strong in banking as it is anywhere, and when you are in the middle of a stampede it is not easy to perceive that it is heading over the edge of a cliff. However, it should also be noted that Johns' policies had been expounded well before the SBV had decided to take over Tricontinental—indeed, they were expounded while Mitsui was still considering a bid.

As soon as he was appointed Johns set the managerial style for Tricontinental. At his first management committee meeting on 10 January 1986 he slashed the numbers attending so that the meeting would not be 'bogged down on divisional aspects'. He also said 'these meetings should be on a group basis dealing with planning for the future rather than recording the past'. The signal was *go*. Over the coming months a number of subtle flaws developed in Tricontinental's structure. Johns separated the credit analysts from the marketing and lending division. In one respect this was a good move because it meant that the credit analysts, who were supposed to vet loan applications, were independent. However, at the same time Johns had excluded the head of the credit department, Lynton Stott, from the management committee meetings because he ranked only as an assistant general manager whereas all the other divisional heads were general managers. This meant that the voice of the credit analysts was not heard at management committee meetings after May 1987, which was precisely when they were most needed.

The 1986 Three Year Plan described Tricontinental's approach to lending quite clearly: 'The lending division prides itself in marketing the concept of assessing all proposals on their own merits—no rigid guidelines are in force and this allows managers to be innovative and commercial in their approach to financing'. To take one example, there was a guideline that 100 per cent finance should not be advanced on construction projects, but it was frequently waived. Stott reckoned that 10–20 per cent of credit submissions he saw were in breach of such guidelines as existed. Credit risk evaluation never included a formal statement of the degree or nature of credit risk associated with a loan proposal. The lending and underwriting credit committee never met formally. Each credit submission was reviewed individually by managers in a 'round robin' of phone calls.

None of the interstate offices had an overall chief. Instead, there were two to four departments in each office and each of those departments reported to a chief in Melbourne. Within head office, responsibilities for corporate banking were spread between lending, credit, project finance and securities. The effect of this structure was that only Johns, as managing director, was in a position to know the full picture on any one client at any one time. The Royal Commission concluded that Johns' influence on the credit committee was unmistakeable: 'Any facility approved by him within his discretion (up to $6 million) was presented to the committee essentially for "noting" purposes. On occasions drawdown of funds occurred before the committee's receipt of the relevant credit submission'. One former credit general manager said that where Johns had approved a loan it was regarded by the credit division as a fait accompli. The Royal Commission said: 'The clear impression he received was that Mr Johns' credit submissions were to be treated differently from other submissions, not only in relation to depth of their analysis, but more particularly in relation to the speed of their processing'.[9]

Finally, Tricontinental had a misleading way of presenting its client exposures by showing only a percentage of the exposure. To give an example, Tricontinental had lent large sums to John Avram's group of companies. It had also lent $30 million to Interwest Ltd. Because Avram owned 66 per cent of Interwest, Tricontinental recorded its exposure to Avram in that company as being only $19.8 million. This was delusionary, because Tricontinental was always at risk for the full amount if either Interwest or Avram failed. Taking other partly owned subsidiaries into account, this meant that in March 1989 Tricontinental was showing its exposure to the Avram group as $113 million when in fact it totalled $194 million. All these flaws in the accounting and managerial systems remained unknown to the public for several years.

Johns' rise to the top of Tricontinental was greeted by a spate of favourable publicity in early 1986 as glowing articles about him appeared in *Australian Business*,[10] *Business Review Weekly* and the *Australian Financial Review*. Inside the group, Johns had one notable critic—the chief general manager of the new corporate and international division of the SBV, Jim McAnany. A Commonwealth Bank veteran, McAnany was not enthusiastic about Johns' selection, regarding his experience as too shallow for somebody who was expected to run a merchant bank in tough times. Johns had begun as a junior officer at the Commercial Banking Company of Sydney, then spent some years in charge of the Tricontinental's corporate lending in Brisbane before being put in charge of the merchant bank's national credit operation in Melbourne. By boom standards his experience was adequate for the top job, but McAnany took a more old-fashioned view.

One point which worried McAnany was that, from the time Tricontinental was taken over by the SBV, there had been a 'brick wall' between the officers of the two banks. Officers of the SBV never saw credit submissions of Tricontinental. Thus SBV officers had no way of knowing whether there was duplication of loans or whether Tricontinental was lending to clients whom they had judged as unacceptable. 'The policy of rigid division was vigorously maintained', McAnany said.

As soon as Tricontinental became a wholly owned subsidiary of the SBV, Australian Ratings boosted its credit rating from BBB to A+. Tricontinental used its new borrowing respectability to the hilt, doubling its borrowings from $900 million to $1.8 billion in the year to June 1986. There was a consequent doubling of assets, which attracted the attention of the Reserve Bank of Australia.

By law, the RBA was required to supervise the trading banks but had no responsibility for state banks. However, the RBA had had consultative arrangements with the SBV since 1959. Also, Tricontinental, as a financial corporation borrowing money, was required to provide information to the RBA. In April 1986 the RBA asked Moyle what impact the heavy borrowing of Tricontinental was having on the capital adequacy ratio of the SBV. Moyle said that Tricontinental's borrowings had been very large but were levelling off and the matter was under control.[11] The RBA was at this time seeking more control over the state banks. As part of this policy the SBV entered a voluntary agreement with the RBA in June 1986, agreeing that it would continue to comply with the RBA's prudential principles, including capital adequacy requirements. This fell short of RBA control. The RBA had no statutory control over Tricontinental and was relying very much on the management and board of the SBV to exercise effective oversight of their subsidiary.

The capital adequacy ratio (of capital to total balance sheet assets) was not as closely defined by the RBA then as it would be a few years later. The RBA's concern was focussed on the capital adequacy of the SBV group. If the group was not meeting minimum capital adequacy requirements—as was often the case—the approach of the RBA was to require the SBV to bring its group capital into line. There was never any thought of a direct approach to Tricontinental. A capital adequacy ratio is supposed to ensure that there is a prudent amount of capital available to a bank to absorb losses before the funds of depositors become at risk. If a banking group were to increase its assets rapidly by increasing its borrowings, obviously the proportion of total assets funded by capital would shrink. The SBV's capital adequacy tended to be below RBA requirements. The SBV was relaxed about this, claiming that it could operate on a lower ratio because it was guaranteed by the Victorian Government. This argument was never accepted by the RBA.[12]

If the SBV was relaxed about its capital adequacy, Tricontinental was blithely unconcerned. By July 1986 its capital base was $66 million. A summary of Tricontinental's client exposures presented to the board that month showed that it had exposures to fourteen clients each exceeding half its capital base and that in four of those cases the exposures each exceeded the entire capital base. Its largest exposure to a client was $190 million, or almost three times Tricontinental's capital base and 43 per cent of the entire SBV group capital base of $439 million.[13] These exposures included committed loan facilities and such off-balance sheet items as guarantees and performance bonds.

Tricontinental's profit for 1986 was 37 per cent over budget but it was still only a tiny $8.3 million, and that was before tax. Tricontinental could not pay a dividend to its new parent because the retained earnings were needed to get its balance sheet back into kilter. Back in May 1985 Tricontinental's board had imposed a maximum gearing ratio of 25:1 on the bank and a maximum potential gearing ratio (including such items as guarantees and undrawn facilities) of 35:1. Tricontinental had been unable to keep within even these generous guidelines in 1985. To help restore its capital the SBV made a subordinated loan of $15 million (which counted as Tier 2 capital) in June 1986, then agreed to forgo dividend.

Johns had backed Christopher Skase early in his career and had seen the fledgling Qintex grow exponentially. This confirmed—and may even have helped form—Johns' conviction that he would grow fastest by picking winners among the bold riders. He spelled out his philosophy plainly in Tricontinental's 1986 annual review—a public document:

> Tricontinental has a philosophy of supporting entrepreneurial starters and growing with them. When people have an idea, cash flow and potential and the idea makes sense, Tricontinental will support them . . . Tricontinental has been moving away from the pack for some time now, shifting an amount of attention toward the business of medium-sized public companies and larger private companies, with the view to cultivating the entrepreneurial spirit that will provide the greatest growth to Australia.

Johns' orientation towards the bold riders was never any secret from the public. The boards of both Tricontinental and the SBV must have been well aware of it.

One who was concerned was McAnany, who was doomed to play the role of Cassandra in the SBV tragedy. In May 1986 McAnany prepared a paper arguing that Tricontinental's exposures should be confined by its own capital base and that, if it desired to go beyond this, it should apply to the SBV for approval. Also, Tricontinental's exposures should be monitored to ensure that SBV group exposure to any single client never exceeded 20 per cent of consolidated capital. This would conform to the prevailing prudential limit imposed within the SBV. McAnany was aware that this would mean the reduction of some of Tricontinental's larger exposures. McAnany gave his paper to Moyle, expecting it to be forwarded to the board. Moyle disagreed strongly with McAnany, who later said: ' . . . we had several vigorous ongoing discussions about my proposals . . . There was ultimately a flat disagreement between us as to policy and practice'.[14] McAnany's paper was never put to the board.

Project Survival

The state of Tricontinental in 1985 and 1986 has been given at some length to establish that all the elements that would bring Tricontinental down were in place by then. It was borrowing heavily, relying on the SBV's credit rating. It could not keep within capital adequacy or gearing ratios. Johns made no secret of the fact that Tricontinental was deliberately concentrating on the high-risk end of the market. The danger signs in the loan portfolio had been outlined by Touche Ross. McAnany had called

449

for limits on group exposures. The board of Tricontinental and most, if not all, of the SBV board were aware of all these factors, and must also have known that Tricontinental's headlong growth was putting pressure on the capital adequacy of the SBV itself. But like the financial press (who had less access to key information) they were dazzled by Tricontinental's growth. Tricontinental had shot up the ladder to rank as one of Australia's five largest merchant banks by early 1986. The SBV had hitched its wagon to a star.

The essentials did not change over the next few years. In the year to June 1987 Tricontinental's stated assets rose to $2.6 billion. This rise of 32 per cent was modest compared to the previous year's 101 per cent, but was enough to propel Tricontinental to the position of largest merchant bank in Australia, from fifth the year before. Note that its assets have been described as 'stated'. The level of rediscounting mentioned in the 1987 accounts indicates that Tricontinental may have been disguising its true growth by unloading securities just before balance date, then buying them back again soon after.

Bruce Ziebell, Johns' right-hand man, told the Royal Commission that it was possible to 'window-dress' a balance sheet to be a certain size.

> You would do it for capital adequacy and gearing purposes to make sure your balance sheet looked correct. You could window-dress a bank's balance sheet fairly easily. The common way used to be by selling negotiable securities to friends, so if you balance at June and your friend balances at September, you would sell your securities to him on 29 June and buy them back on 1 July and you probably had to return a favour on 31 August for 1 September . . . That practice would set the maximum asset size.[15]

Such window-dressing—which can take several forms—makes it very difficult for an outside analyst to reconstruct the balance sheet. For the years 1987 to 1989 we will use Tricontinental's stated figures, but they should be taken with a grain of salt. The odds are that Tricontinental's pace of expansion and hence the risks it was taking were greater than admitted. It is a moot point whether the board was aware of this. They were certainly aware that Tricontinental was still lending apace. Thanks in part to McAnany's nagging of Moyle, Tricontinental was now providing periodic reviews of its large client exposures. A review in July 1987 showed that the largest exposure to a single client was $246 million, and the four largest exposures totalled $631 million. Including separate liabilities to the SBV, the four largest exposures to the SBV group totalled $734 million, which exceeded the SBV's capital base. Tricontinental was still unable—even after window-dressing—to get its gearing down to 25:1. Consequently, the SBV again agreed to receive no dividend.

After the 1987 balance date the SBV board considered a possible sale

450

or public float of Tricontinental. However, the idea was abandoned after the share market crash in October. An assessment a week after the crash showed that Tricontinental had loans secured by shares valued at $2 billion. Tricontinental's writedowns after the crash were certainly less than realistic. There were loans on shares valued at $58 million which had not traded after the crash. Another $480 million related to companies in which Tricontinental held more than 50 per cent equity and whose decline in value was supposed to be only 15 per cent, when the overall market had gone down by a quarter. The market value of the rest of the shares held as security by Tricontinental had nearly halved from $1.4 billion to $765 million.[16] These figures should be compared with the stated shareholders' funds of Tricontinental, which were $102 million at June 1987. There seems every possibility that, if Tricontinental's assets had been realistically assessed on 21 October, the directors would have discovered that its shareholders' funds had been wiped out.

After the stock market collapse Johns began having repeated heavy clashes with John Rawlins, one of Tricontinental's directors. Rawlins increasingly questioned Johns' reports, particularly about the bank's lending and security position. At the December board meeting Rawlins demanded that Johns prepare a paper showing a full list of loans in default and (in certain cases) what mining leases were proposed to be accepted as security from borrowers. In February Rawlins criticised Johns' 'cavalier attitude to doubtful debts' and complained that the board was not always fully informed. In March Rawlins expressly refused to approve two loan facilities. A few days after the March meeting Rawlins told Moyle that he would resign unless Johns' powers were restricted and he changed his attitude. Moyle said: 'You'd better go'.[17]

Behind the scenes Tricontinental's gearing was becoming a sore point with the SBV. The merchant bank's capital stood at $130 million, well short of the $400 million needed to meet RBA guidelines. Tricontinental's management said it had an 'innovative way' of raising the funds. Innovation was needed, because Moyle had bluntly told the Tricontinental board that they could not rely on the SBV for capital.

Johns responded by exploring alternative plans—a move called 'Project Survival'. This project appears to have resulted in a proposal to 'backdoor list' Tricontinental through a company called Pine Vale Investments. The project got as far as Pine Vale beginning a draft application for a banking authority in June 1988, but the application was never completed and the plan was abandoned. It was a desultory scheme, with little information being provided even to the SBV board. Then Tricontinental bought just under 10 per cent of Advance Bank, but sold again in June to collect a $6 million profit. Finally Merrill Lynch was retained to find a buyer for Tricontinental. Merrill Lynch put a valuation of $200 million to $240 million on the merchant bank, but could not find an interested buyer.

Tricontinental's image was starting to crack. Just after balance date in 1988 *Australian Business* printed a story which raised questions about Tricontinental's role in the tangled affairs of a group called MEH Ltd. MEH was originally floated as the public vehicle of showman Michael Edgley, the float being underwritten by Tricontinental. MEH had gone into mining through a subsidiary called Chariah Resources which then bought control of two gold companies, Falcon Australia Ltd and Minefields Exploration NL. This deal was strongly opposed by Edgley on several grounds, but particularly because the two companies being acquired had external liabilities of about $38 million and high overheads. One allegation, sworn in a court affidavit, was that Tricontinental had assisted MEH in the acquisition of Chariah. This raised the possibility of conflict of interest, because Tricontinental had written the independent expert's report on the acquisition. Tricontinental had later accepted MEH's 50 per cent equity in Chariah in satisfaction of debts. Then Chariah had taken control of Falcon, in which Tricontinental held 7.5 per cent of the capital. Another 3 per cent was held by a company named Xantron Pty Ltd, whose only directors turned out to be Johns and Ziebell. Approached by *Australian Business*, Ziebell said that Xantron was not owned by Tricontinental but declined to name the beneficial owners. He said it was 'sheer coincidence' that Tricontinental had been a funds provider from time to time to Falcon, Minefields, MEH and Chariah.[18]

The accounts of Tricontinental showed that it had emerged from the 1987–88 financial year almost unscathed. Total assets increased by 22 per cent, down on previous years but still creditable. Total loan commitments rose 19 per cent to just over $4 billion. This was a danger sign. The share market crash had been the clearest possible warning that the bull market was over, but Tricontinental was still lending money with both hands. This was no time to be extending further credit to the kind of high-risk borrowers in which Tricontinental specialised.

Net profit for the year was down slightly, from $26 million to $23 million. This was creditable considering that bad debt provisions had been hiked from $5.7 million to $33.9 million. In the light of later events the bad debt provisions probably should have been much higher. Equally probably, we will never know the answer because of a glaring fault in Tricontinental's computer system. The system contained no data on due dates for interest payments, which meant that the computer was unable to recognise when an interest payment was not made by a client. The system would continue to accrue interest on the loan until the accounting department had been advised otherwise.[19] So nobody knew how many

Table 14.1 Trico's biggest clients, June 1988 (all figures in $m)

Bond group	278
Lew group	263
Citistate group	255
Skase group	202
Becton group	195
Avram group	153
Goldberg group	118
	1 464

clients were no longer servicing their debts, and perhaps it was not in anybody's interest to find out.

Even without this data it should have been obvious that Tricontinental was overexposed to its biggest clients. At balance date of 1988 Tricontinental had committed facilities in excess of its own shareholders' funds to each of seven groups. In total, these seven clients accounted for 35 per cent of all of Tricontinental's committed facilities. The clients are shown in Table 14.1. The failure of any one of these clients would have put Tricontinental into severe difficulties. In the event, four of them failed (Bond, Skase, Avram and Goldberg).

The acid test for any company's accounts is to see whether anyone will pay book value for the assets. Tricontinental was now subjected to this test, because by the end of 1988 a way had finally been found of selling Tricontinental by merging it with the Australian Bank. This seemed a neat solution because, as Moyle said at the time, the Australian Bank had a banking licence without a business while Tricontinental had a business without a licence. (In truth, the Australian Bank was the sounder and more valuable of the two banks. A few years later, Tricontinental had been reduced to atoms, while the Australian Bank was wound down slowly and gracefully.)

Neil Smith formed a link between the two banks. He had been appointed chairman of the Australian Bank in February 1989. Shortly afterwards he resigned from the SBV, which had been contemplating the merger since December. However, he was still chairman of Tricontinental, which meant he chaired both banks in the proposed merger. The merger would be done in three steps. First, the SBV would take over the Australian Bank. Then the Australian Bank would take over Tricontinental. Then the merged entity would be floated publicly with the SBV retaining 10 per cent.

In reality, Tricontinental was being backlisted into the smaller Australian Bank. Tricontinental was the biggest merchant bank in Australia, with assets of $3.4 billion at book value, compared to $320 million for the Australian Bank. But by this time adverse rumours were beginning to circulate about the state of Tricontinental's loan portfolio and its true value was being severely questioned behind the scenes.

There was qualified official approval for the move. The purchase of more than 10 per cent of any licensed bank in Australia requires the permission of the Federal Treasurer. This was forthcoming, provided that the sale of Tricontinental was approved by the RBA. At the back of everybody's mind was the 'lender of last resort' convention, which effectively makes the RBA and hence the Federal Government the guarantor of deposits in any licensed bank in Australia. The RBA was a lender of last resort to the Australian Bank, but in the shaky days of late 1988 the RBA was certainly not going to extend that guarantee blindfold to Tricontinental.

The RBA demanded a submission from Johns outlining the affairs of Tricontinental. It was not until this was received, in early 1989, that officers of the RBA realised the extent to which Tricontinental was depending on short-term funding. The RBA assessed Tricontinental—without a detailed knowledge of its asset portfolio—as having an undue concentration of risk in its lending. The RBA also believed that Tricontinental's capital adequacy was below average for merchant banks.[20]

In a letter to Smith in February 1989 the RBA set out the details of its main concern, saying: 'Tricontinental's loan pattern is not acceptable for an authorised bank; it is significantly skewed towards high risks'. Before the proposed acquisition by Australian Bank, the RBA required:

- There be no exposures to any one borrower (including related entities) representing more than 30 per cent of the capital base.
- An independent due diligence investigation to identify all doubtful debts of Tricontinental, for which specific provisions should then be raised. In addition, the RBA wanted higher general provisions and an indemnity from the SBV against loss on existing loans.
- A minimum ratio of capital to risk-weighted assets of the Australian Bank of 10 per cent to recognise 'the nature of the proposed lending policy'.

The RBA also expressed concern that the float should give the merged bank a widely spread shareholding; that the bank depended too heavily on short-term funding in its present form; and that the bank should have adequate depth of management. Such conservative hurdles were far too high for Tricontinental to jump, as the RBA must have known. To take just one example, at the end of 1988 Tricontinental had thirteen clients each of whose credit facilities represented more than 27 per cent of the bank's capital. Lending to these clients increased by a staggering $552 million in the March quarter. By then Tricontinental's sixteen largest clients had facilities of $2 billion, representing more than half its total loan portfolio.

Nevertheless, there was some confidence the deal could still be done.

Two Australian Bank directors, Neil Smith and Leigh Masel (the former chairman of the National Companies and Securities Commission), said that the merged bank would be able 'to satisfy the RBA on all its prudential concerns'.[21]

Smith and Masel's belief was by no means universally held. Tricontinental was beginning to attract adverse publicity. It was known to have lent money to the failed Queensland roofing contractor Behnfeld. Then in March the NCSC staged a sensational dawn raid to arrest at their homes three alleged insider traders, who were supposed to be part of a ring of 50. The charges were never proved and the ring of 50 was always a figment of the NCSC's overheated imagination. In hindsight, the NCSC seems to have been more interested in generating publicity than investigating and evaluating the facts.[22] But in the short term it was noticed that all three who had been arrested were former employees of Tricontinental. The bank's image suffered, this time unfairly.

The proposed Australian Bank merger had attracted adverse publicity from the first day. Meanwhile, other players in the money markets began forming their own conclusions and withdrawing money from Tricontinental. As Tricontinental chronically depended on the short-term market for its funding, this was equivalent to severing its lifeline. The withdrawal of funds precipitated a liquidity crisis at the bank. Australian Ratings had already noted in January that Tricontinental's credit rating depended on its ownership by the SBV. After a public float it would become virtually a stand-alone entity, which would be a different proposition. The SBV found itself obliged to find some way of supporting Tricontinental until the merger and float could go through. In one support mechanism the SBV board in March approved the purchase of a $104 million debt owed by Qintex to Tricontinental.

Jim McAnany and Michael Leonard from SBV's corporate and international division were appointed to review Tricontinental's loan portfolio to choose suitable assets. It is a measure of the ineptitude of the SBV that this was the first time SBV staff had ever examined Tricontinental's loan portfolio. Johns objected strenuously, saying an asset sale would pick the eyes of Tricontinental's portfolio, making the bank merger more difficult. The SBV tried to stem Tricontinental's haemorrhaging deposits by issuing a letter of comfort in early April to the RBA and to banks which had funds with Tricontinental. When this did little to stop the run, the SBV told the RBA it would have to lift its own deposits with Tricontinental. Under RBA rules, loans from the SBV to Tricontinental were set at a maximum of 30 per cent of the SBV's capital base. The RBA agreed that they could temporarily rise to 40 per cent. The SBV also bought loan assets totalling $642 million from Tricontinental.

It was beginning to dawn on some SBV staff and directors that there were lurking monsters in the Tricontinental loan portfolio. At a Tricontinental board meeting on 26 April 1989 the former managing director, Jack Ryan, said that the bank's current lending policy was 'like a desperado trying to get out of trouble on the last race at Flemington'.[23] Ryan had been knocking back an increasing number of credit submissions, to the point where Johns complained: 'Don't you want us to do any business?'. Even so, Tricontinental directors approved new and increased loan facilities totalling $865 million in the first four months of 1989.

Coopers & Lybrand had been commissioned to do a due diligence investigation of Tricontinental. Their report, dated 1 May, valued Tricontinental at $90 million to $99 million, but only after some notable qualifications. One assumption was that vendor warranties as to collectability of debts would be included as part of the sale agreement. Having reviewed the loan portfolio, Coopers gave itself a huge loophole by saying that as the scope of the review was less than that required for an audit 'we express no opinion on the existence and value of the assets'. Nor did Coopers express any opinion on the accuracy of the accounting information provided by Tricontinental. A due diligence with such sweeping qualifications is hardly worth having. The Deputy Governor of the Reserve Bank, John Phillips, passed the Coopers report on to his Governor, Bob Johnston, with the note: 'Governor, I don't suggest you read this, it's hardly worth the trouble'. The independent directors of the Australian Bank were clearly of the same mind, because they insisted on warranties from the SBV before they would endorse the purchase of Tricontinental. Moyle refused on the (perfectly correct) grounds that the buyer of a financial institution should satisfy itself with a due diligence investigation rather than expect to get warranties from the vendor.

The Victorian Government was getting more accurate information from cocktail circuit gossip than from its own sources. In early May one of Australia's most respected bankers, Bill Gurry, managing director of the National Mutual Royal Bank, was speaking socially to Michael Richards from the Victorian Premier's Department. Gurry told Richards that Tricontinental was 'travelling very badly and may well have incurred considerable losses'. Richards passed the news on to Premier John Cain, who phoned Gurry and heard from him the marketplace rumours. Cain told his Treasurer, Rob Jolly, to contact Gurry, who then repeated the stories to Jolly. Cain said that a few days later Jolly came back to him 'with a glowing report from Bill Moyle about how healthy Tricontinental was and how it was in good shape'. Tricontinental's problems were dismissed as 'a hiccup'.[24]

The press were better informed. On 11 May the *Herald* ran articles by Peter Alford and Ben Hills alleging that Tricontinental had potential bad debts and that Johns and Ziebell had been involved in improper share dealings.

The RBA was now thoroughly alarmed by a spate of adverse press reports about Tricontinental. A file note by one of its senior officers on 11 May said: 'Trico's current and prospective financial position is not one that would meet the criteria for a bank. Until Trico can demonstrate that it is viable as a stand-alone operation, bank supervision would not contemplate recommending an approach from Australian Bank to purchase it. We are of the view that we should now convey this message to Australian Bank'.[25] The RBA wrote to Neil Smith expressing its concern the following day.

The *Herald* articles led to questions in the Victorian parliament. Jolly defended Tricontinental, saying: 'On May 15 I was assured by Mr Moyle (and some days later by Mr Smith) that Tricontinental did not have a significant financial problem'. Moyle had said that Tricontinental's losses were 'quite modest', compared with the bad debts of Australia's three major finance companies.[26]

Moyle was an affable man who had to that point enjoyed considerable respect in Australian banking circles. He was operating under difficulties in early May, having just sustained a severe back injury, and was working as best he could from home. He was of course concerned to see the troubled merger through and may have been out of touch with recent events.

In fact, Tricontinental had terminal financial problems and its real—as opposed to stated—losses were about to be revealed. McAnany had been picking over Tricontinental's portfolio trying to find assets worth buying. He was becoming increasingly horrified at his discoveries. On 18 May— three days after Moyle had defended Tricontinental—SBV director Ian Renard visited McAnany's office. McAnany was agitated and angry. He told Renard that the loan portfolio of Tricontinental was a disgrace. He said that a number of the loans were undersecured and poorly structured and the loan portfolio reflected badly on all responsible for it. He urged Renard not to support any SBV warranty to the Australian Bank in regard to loans. McAnany also visited Moyle at home and told him that Tricontinental's loan portfolio was so bad that the capital structure of the merged bank could be wiped out. 'SBV, being the seller, would not in market terms receive any kudos for executing such a sale', he warned. McAnany told Moyle that he was having trouble identifying large loans held by Tricontinental that conformed with the SBV's prudential standards. He warned against further asset purchases. Readers will remember that, only six months before, the SBV had assured the RBA that Tricontinental's portfolio was clean.

While McAnany was warning Renard on 18 May Bruce Rasmussen,

assistant director general (finance) of the Department of Management and Budget, had been attending a Loan Council in Canberra. He was contacted by the Corporate Affairs Commission and advised that the CAC was investigating alleged breaches of the Companies Code at Tricontinental, involving Johns. On the following day Rasmussen and his boss Dr Peter Sheehan saw Neil Smith and Max Carr in Melbourne and told them of the investigation.

Smith rang Ziebell and asked for a report on Tricontinental's bad debt exposures. Johns, Ziebell and their staff put together a report on the next day, Saturday the 20th, and presented it to Smith at 2 p.m. The report stated a worst case scenario of $64 million bad debts and said that Tricontinental still had net assets of $73 million. The report was discussed that afternoon at a meeting between Sheehan, Rasmussen, Smith, Moyle and Carr. Sheehan took the view that the SBV had no choice but to stand fully behind Tricontinental. That being the case, the sale of Tricontinental with full indemnities from the SBV was 'a most unattractive option'. The meeting agreed that: the merger between Tricontinental and Australian Bank should be aborted; Tricontinental would be integrated into the SBV, which would guarantee its liabilities; the existing Tricontinental board would resign and be replaced by a wholly SBV executive board (making Johns' position redundant); and Tricontinental would stop lending. After the meeting, which lasted a little over an hour, Sheehan told Jolly of the proposals. Jolly discussed them with Cain next morning and agreed to support the SBV's action.

That Sunday afternoon saw a special meeting of the SBV board at 2 p.m. Smith, Johns and Ziebell had been summoned to wait outside the boardroom. Inside, the first speaker was McAnany who told the board that the condition of Tricontinental's loan portfolio was serious, although he was unable to quantify the likely losses. Indeed, he did not object to the board issuing a statement saying that Tricontinental would make a profit of $4 million to $5 million for 1988–89.

Moyle was still trying to salvage the Australian Bank merger. He left the meeting at one point to phone John Phillips, who said that the Reserve Bank would accept a merger if the SBV guaranteed Tricontinental's future bad debts.

The board also decided that Johns' reputation had been too badly damaged to allow him to remain in charge. Smith was summoned into the meeting and told by Hancock that Johns would be asked to stand aside.

The board decided that the SBV should take over management of Tricontinental immediately. The bank immediately stopped all lending by Tricontinental and guaranteed its liabilities. Smith resigned as a director of Tricontinental, to be replaced by McAnany and Rawlins—the two most severe critics of Johns. Ziebell resigned. Johns' resignation was not accepted at first, as he was advised to seek legal advice. He did so, and his resignation was accepted at a board meeting on 30 May.

In July Johns was arrested and charged with insider trading, corruptly receiving secret commissions, conspiracy and demanding money with menaces. Several of the charges related to dealings in Falcon Australia. The menaces and insider trading charges were dropped in February 1990, but Johns was found guilty on the charge of having taken a secret commission. Delivering sentence in the Victorian County Court, Judge Lewis told Johns that his action fell into the highest category of criminality. 'Yours was an act of betrayal', the judge said. 'The motive was as old as time: simple unadulterated greed.'[27] Johns was sentenced to seven months' jail and ordered to pay Tricontinental $1.9 million.

The SBV board was left with the inglorious job of discovering and disclosing all the skeletons in the cupboard. In October 1989 the SBV announced a loss of nearly $200 million. Moyle said that Tricontinental, with bad debts of $374 million, had 'paid the supreme corporate penalty' for failing to properly manage its loans.

Tricontinental had ceased to conduct new business from May 1989, but bad and doubtful debts owed by clients increased as time went by, requiring provisions in the SBV group accounts of $351 million in June 1989, $1114 million in December 1989 and $1712 million in June 1990. The losses of Tricontinental had by this time undermined the SBV itself. The actual and potential losses were far too great for the SBV to absorb without the support of the Victorian Government. Just as the SBV had accepted responsibility for the obligations of Tricontinental, so the government had to accept liability to depositors of the SBV. The total amount of support provided by the Victorian Government to bail out the SBV and Tricontinental totalled $2.7 billion. A little of this was retrieved a few years later, but for practical purposes this can be regarded as the SBV/Tricontinental loss. While the SBV had some losses of its own, more than $2.1 billion of the $2.7 billion related to Tricontinental. In August 1990 the Victorian Government sold the SBV to the Commonwealth Bank. In very broad terms, Victoria got $2 billion for the SBV but had to guarantee all Tricontinental's bad debts. Joan Kirner, who by then had replaced Cain as Premier, announced a Royal Commission into Tricontinental.

Disastrous loans: a few samples

The collapse of Tricontinental and the arrest of Johns sparked sensational publicity. As bits of Tricontinental's dirty washing were dragged into the open it became apparent that the merchant bank had been the financier to almost every bad risk of the day. If it had missed one it must have been an accident. Almost every time a corporate cowboy bit the dust Tricontinental would appear amongst his list of creditors. Avram's Interwest group was one of the first, failing in January 1990. This was followed by revelations of loans to Dallhold and Qintex. Ralph Ward-Ambler, who took over as chairman of the SBV, said: 'Tricontinental had a special facility for lending to people who liked to go bankrupt'.

The usual welter of litigation followed. The biggest case was launched by the State of Victoria, in the name of Tricontinental, against Tricontinental's former auditors, KPMG Peat Marwick. In the avalanche of lawsuits against former auditors this was a particularly interesting case, because Peats had been both external and internal auditors of Tricontinental. Given the size of Tricontinental's losses, it was the biggest claim ever made against an auditor in Australia. Peats defended themselves, with executive chairman George Bennett saying that Tricontinental's fortunes turned on economic issues and the chosen policies of the directors—not on auditing issues. Peats claimed that it was no part of their duty as auditors to evaluate the adequacy, appropriateness or prudence of a board's prudential policies. The documents setting out the claim and defence, together with a counterclaim by Peats, stood nearly 30 centimetres thick. The Australian system of corporate justice had been struggling for years with the consequences of the 1980s collapses, but it now threw the sponge in completely when faced with Tricontinental. The Victorian Supreme Court told the parties to the Peats action that the case was simply too big for the court to handle. The indications were that the court case could last four years and the appeals process another four. After lengthy negotiations the parties settled out of court with Peats paying the Victorian Government $136 million—by far the largest audit negligence settlement in Australian history.[28]

Meanwhile the statement of claim on behalf of Tricontinental had shown the total fecklessness of Tricontinental's lending. The following summaries indicate the sort of business done.[29]

Kahmea, Qintex Ltd, Qintex Australia Ltd

Kahmea was the family company of Christopher Skase. It held a controlling interest in QAL, the operating company through which various assets such as the Mirage Hotels and Seven Network were controlled. Kahmea had no substantial assets other than its shareholding in Qintex Ltd and Qintex Ltd had no substantial assets other than its holding in QAL.

In November 1985 Qintex asked Tricontinental to finance QAL's acquisition of 19.9 per cent of AWA—a move which sparked a takeover struggle for the old electronics group. The original financing was based on out-of-date financials because Qintex provided accounts only for the year ended July 1984; even those showed that gearing had increased from 56 per cent to 166 per cent. In the event, QAL was overbid and the takeover did not proceed: a stroke of good fortune for the Qintex group because AWA turned out to have deep problems.

After the bid failed, QAL sold its AWA shareholding but no repayment was made. Instead the loan was left in place 'for the development of the Qintex group'. The initial loan approval had called for 1.2 times cover, meaning that Qintex had to provide $12 worth of security for every $10 borrowed. Tricontinental allowed Qintex to slip below these levels.

Tricontinental approved another loan to Qintex limited to $25 million on the basis of a credit submission stating that the facility would form part of a $75 million syndicated loan. However, the syndication did not proceed and Tricontinental assumed 100 per cent of the risk by extending a facility for the full $75 million to Qintex. It was claimed that the board had not been notified either that the syndication had failed or that Tricontinental had assumed the full risk. In the event, Qintex drew down only $69.5 million of the facility.

Tricontinental directors had laid down a condition that its exposure to the whole Qintex group could not exceed $75 million. This was soon breached, with the exposure reaching $116.5 million by February 1986. The board was not informed.

Tricontinental had a set of guidelines which laid down sound principles for lending. However, they were only guidelines and did not have the force of rules. One of them was that, where shares were taken as security, they should not exceed 5 per cent of the borrower's issued capital. Otherwise, Tricontinental risked being left holding a large unmarketable block of stock in a failing group. This guideline was breached repeatedly in 1988–89. In the case of Qintex, Tricontinental was holding 34.5 million QAL shares, or 30 per cent of QAL, as security by May 1988. The security therefore had an illusory element in that the very event of a default would lower its value and at worst make it unsaleable or worthless. This happened in other Tricontinental deals.

That May Tricontinental conducted an internal review, based on figures provided by QAL, which among other things included cash flow projections showing an estimated net cash flow deficit for the group of $28.2 milllion for the year to July 1988. The internal review showed that Qintex group borrowings at June 1988 were $960 million and QAL group borrowings totalled $225 million. Tricontinental was exposed at three levels. It had lent $79 million to a QAL subsidiary called IPH Finance Pty Ltd; it had the $69.5 million loan to Qintex; and it had lent $48 million to Kahmea. As the IPH loan was secured on QAL assets and the Kahmea and Qintex loans were secured on QAL shares, the bank had accepted basically the same security for three loans totalling nearly $200 million. In addition, Tricontinental agreed to subscribe for $25 million in unsecured notes to be issued by QAL.

Nevertheless, in July 1988 Tricontinental's directors approved a facility to QAL for a further $27 million. The only security the bank received was the proposed assignment to Tricontinental of the proceeds of a call on QAL's partly paid shares. Although the call had not been made—and never would be—directors went even further, approving another facility of $25 million to QAL in mid-December. The $27 million became a total loss and only $1.5 million was recovered from the $25 million. The Qintex loan of $69.5 million was a total loss. The $48 million loan to Kahmea was a total loss except for any amounts recovered from Skase, making that a writeoff too. The $79 million loan to QAC was another total writeoff.

Atoll Corporation Pty Ltd

The Atoll case was a relatively small but remarkably sloppy transaction involving Robert Sng, who sought a loan of $420 000 in early 1987 to buy shares in Eastern Resources of Australia. The credit risk analysis contained no information about the creditworthiness of either Atoll or Sng (who had no fixed address in Australia) or their ability to repay or service the loan. Sng sought a further $13 million in October 1987, this time to buy shares in Pelsart Resources. Atoll had already bought the shares on 24 September. Tricontinental chairman Neil Smith and director Jack Ryan approved the loan on 4 October. The credit submission ignored Sng's having defaulted on topping up security on his existing loan either to the level of the loan or the 1.2 times cover required. There was still no data on the creditworthiness of Sng, who had proved difficult to contact.

The second purchase and loan were disastrously timed. After the crash of October 1987 Pelsart shares plummeted from $1.90 to 90c. In May 1988 Sng told the bank that Atoll could not pay interest for the first six months and asked for it to be capitalised. He also made clear that neither he nor the other guarantor, named Peh, could honour their guarantees. Nevertheless, the problem loans report made by the management to the board in June and July contained favourable statements about the Atoll loans and said that no loss was envisaged. In both Atoll loans Tricontinental had been supposed to get a 20 per cent share in any profits—which Johns promised to limit to $2 million in the case of Pelsart. Instead, Tricontinental had to make a bad debt provision of $8 million.

Churchill Leisure Industries, Amaldela Pty Ltd, Rocado

Amaldela was a wholly owned subsidiary of the listed Churchill Leisure

Industries. Rocado Investment & Finance Ltd, run by Steven Matthews, held 22 per cent of Churchill (see Figure 14.1). Tricontinental lent Amaldela $4.3 million in July 1986 so that it could buy 13.3 per cent of Dutch Hotel & Casino Development Corporation NV (Dutchco), a company formed to redevelop a hotel and casino on the island of Aruba in the Netherlands Antilles. Amaldela was also to acquire the operating licence of the casino. In buying the shares and the licence, Amaldela was taking up the entitlement of Rocado which was an existing Tricontinental borrower. In November 1986 Tricontinental lent $4.4 million to Churchill Leisure for the hotel refit and the purchase of slot machines.

Given the exotic and overseas nature of this investment, one would have expected an Australian banker to insist on detailed financial projections. Tricontinental did receive cash flow forecasts (in November) but not the assumptions and information on which they were based. As Ian Johns was a director of Rocado he may have felt that he had better knowledge of the casino's prospects. If so, he was wrong because the deal turned out disastrously for Tricontinental. He resigned from the Rocado board two days after the first loan application was approved.

Both the Amaldela and Churchill loans were supposed to be refinanced within six months, but neither could be. Both had to be extended several times and were finally recognised as in default. The security was supposed to be a registered charge over the 13.3 per cent of Dutchco. Tricontinental had no independent valuation of Dutchco (which was not listed) or the casino. Immediately after Tricontinental had made the Amaldela loan, Tricontinental's solicitors advised that the Dutchco shares could not be mortgaged. To overcome this, Amaldela put the Dutchco shares into a wholly owned subsidiary of Churchill named Churchill Aruba. Tricontinental would hold first mortgage over Churchill Aruba's 2900 issued shares. Repayment of the loan was supposed to come from a share issue by Churchill. However, the issue was only ever planned to raise $5.1 million—considerably less than the total of the two loans. Simultaneously, Tricontinental had been increasing its exposure to the Rocado group which by January 1987 stood at $29 million.

In March 1987 Tricontinental received the accounts for the first seven months' operations of Churchill Aruba. This showed that its financial position was very tight: expenses of the casino were over budget and hotel occupancy was below forecast levels. The following month saw Churchill's long-promised rights issue. It was a disaster, with only 11.5 per cent acceptances.

The casino was a loser. Dutchco reported a loss of $12.7 million, which wiped out its shareholders' funds. Churchill's 1987 annual report valued Churchill Aruba at nil. The same annual report showed that Churchill had accumulated losses of $5.3 million and that Churchill's auditors,

Figure 14.1 The Rocado structure

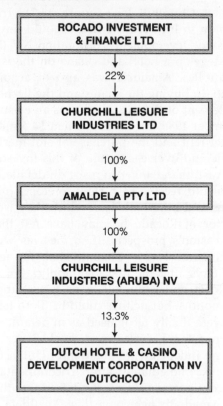

KMG Hungerford, were unable to say whether the accounts had been properly drawn up. Ultimately Tricontinental appears to have lost some $9.2 million on its Amaldela and Churchill exposure.

Rocado, Duke Securities Ltd, Direct Acceptance Corporation

In June 1986 Tricontinental had lent $19.6 million to Rocado (part of the $29 million mentioned in the previous section). Of this, $4 million was to help Rocado convert eight million rights in Direct Acceptance Corporation (DAC) into fully paid shares. A year later, the Rocado facility was in default. By that time Tricontinental had a mortgage over 25.8 million shares in DAC (representing 29.7 per cent of its capital) and 2.7 million shares in Churchill Leisure which were of little value. This was always a bad investment by Tricontinental. The main security was shares in DAC, which had not paid a dividend in three years. Its reputation in the marketplace was poor and it would ultimately go into liquidation. Any credit analysis of DAC should have foreseen this possibility.

In February 1988 it was proposed that Tricontinental would sell 16.5 million of the DAC shares to Duke Securities—realising $11.5 million which would reduce Rocado's indebtedness. This was a foolhardy move by Duke Securities, which was buying DAC shares at 61c when they were only 35c on market. The funding for Duke Securities' purchase would come from Tricontinental in the shape of a six-month loan at a concessional rate of 8 per cent interest. Buying shares way over market on borrowed money—no matter at what concessional interest rate—is an excellent way of going broke. The remaining 9.3 million DAC shares would be held by Tricontinental as a long-term investment with a book value of $6.55 million. That valued DAC shares at 70c, double the then market price. After these moves Tricontinental would be left with a writeoff of $1.55 million.

This was a case of getting out of the frying pan into the fire. Rocado would go into receivership in June 1988, which meant that Tricontinental faced the prospect of losing all or part of its investment. But making an increased investment in Duke Securities and DAC was only compounding the problem. DAC went into provisional liquidation in September 1991 and Duke Securities was part of the Duke group which collapsed in 1989. The loan to Duke Securities was supposed to be repaid in six months, but by March 1988 Duke Securities had offered to repay only $4 million of the $11.5 million facility and the rest became a two-year loan.

Simultaneously, another problem came to a head for Tricontinental. The bank had an existing loan of $20 million to Smith & Lane Holdings that was due to mature in July 1988. Smith & Lane had a 32.7 per cent shareholding in DAC. Tricontinental now arranged for those DAC shares to be sold to Duke Securities for $20 million. Again the DAC shares had been sold at well over the market price. Tricontinental's security was still the DAC shares which were continuing to slide in value, reaching 23c in August 1988—only one-third of Duke Securities' purchase price.

An audit report by Peat Marwick dated 8 December was qualified and doubted the ability of Duke Securities to continue as a going concern. This statement should have been available to Tricontinental at the time it offered Duke Securities the facility. For the year to June 1988 Duke Securities recorded a $5.9 million trading loss and its shareholders' funds showed a deficit of $7.1 million. The Duke companies collapsed the following year and the $11.5 million loan to Duke Securities was written off.

The Onion String (1983) Pty Ltd

In November 1986 New Zealand businessman Graham Hamilton applied to Tricontinental for a loan of $20.7 million to his company, Onion String, so that he could buy seven million shares in Apex Group Ltd as part of a merger between Apex and Kupe Investments Ltd. Hamilton claimed that he had a net worth of $NZ36 million (roughly $A30 million then) and that he could service the loan. Hamilton's statement showed the bulk of his worth to depend on the value of shares in his private companies, but Tricontinental made no credit check on the underlying value of those companies.

Hamilton got the loan but was unable to maintain security cover. In June 1987 he sought to refinance the loan providing cash flow forecasts—which Tricontinental never tested—to support the claim that he could service all borrowings. He also offered as security 5.8 million shares in Judge Corporation, which he said would be worth at least $NZ27 to $NZ28 each by March 1988. This was against the prevailing trend in Judge shares, which had fallen from $NZ8.50 to $NZ5.80 between January and June of 1987. Eventually, Judge shares went to nearly zero. They were part of the empire of another Kiwi corporate cowboy named Bruce Judge, who was at this point the mastermind of a tangled group under Ariadne Australia Ltd.

The collapse of Judge shares left Tricontinental with recourse only against Hamilton. His private companies and family trusts had an estimated deficiency of $NZ14.8 million by mid-1988 and he was unemployed with no source of income except the sale of his assets. Tricontinental's provision for loss was $10.4 million.

City Resources

In December 1986 it was proposed that Tricontinental lend $28 million—as part of a syndicated facility of $95 million—to the large speculative mining group City Resources, which already owed $30 million to the bank. The proposal was: City would raise $50 million by selling 33 million Elders Resources shares at $1.50 each and $30 million of the proceeds would be used to repay the original loan; $10 million would be used to repay other debts; and the remaining $10 million would service interest on the new loan from Tricontinental until the debt was refinanced by a public float. Elders Resources shares were only $1.38 at the time and City had lost $5.4 million in the year to June 1986, which did not augur well for its debt-servicing capacity.

The request for the $95 million facility was supported by a submission valuing the Australian and Papua New Guinean assets of City (mostly mining prospects) at $131.4 million. These were accepted by Tricontinental with no independent analysis. City Resources was still at the exploration stage and generating very little revenue. An exploration company is automatically a high-risk borrower and City was borrowing an unusually large amount by any explorer's standards. The proposed syndication was eventually reduced to $51 million, of which Tricontinental took $14 million and most of the remainder was taken by Elders Finance.

Then in November 1987—a month after the share market collapse—Tricontinental invested another $43 million in the syndicate. The purpose of this was to buy out the $31.3 million exposure of Elders Finance and to increase the total facility by $14 million. This was done against the background of a sliding share price for City Resources, whose shares went from $2.20 in September 1987 to 35c at March 1988. The Elders Resources shares were sold at $1.50 as planned, but Tricontinental still had to provide for a loss of $27 million on the loans.

Dallhold

The float of Bond Media in March 1987 was generally regarded as 'heavy'. Kerry Packer had wrung a high price from Alan Bond for his television interests and professionals rightly judged the float as no great bargain. Bond Corporation would hold 50 per cent of Bond Media after the float but Bond also wanted to buy 12 per cent for his family company, Dallhold Investments.

Tricontinental's exposure to Dallhold had been only $2 million. In May 1987 Dallhold borrowed a further $100 million to take up 64.5 million shares in Bond Media. This loan was always a bad idea because the Bond Media float was headed for a shortfall and the backup documentation for the loan was inadequate. The credit submission did not contain information on the total borrowings of Dallhold or the security arrangements. Nor was there any independent analysis of projected cash flow or the value of Bond Media's assets. The loan represented 100 per cent of the value of Bond Media shares, which were being floated at $1.55. The sole security for the loan was the Bond Media shares plus Alan Bond's personal guarantee.

Bond Media shares listed in June at $1.20 which meant that Tricontinental's loan was—predictably—under water from day one. The price continued weak for months, barely holding $1. When the share market collapsed on 20 October Bond Media plunged to 75c. Ten days later Dallhold tried to restructure the Tricontinental loan. The deal was that Tricontinental would maintain the $102 million facility in return for extra security. Part of the security was a second mortgage over 37 million shares in Mid-East Minerals. Another part was second mortgages over various overseas mines, including the Colosseum mine in California and the St Joe Gold group mines. These assets were part of the Bond International Group (BIG) float which was planned to raise between

$US400 million and $US500 million. The proceeds would be used to pay off Tricontinental and other bankers.

Some of these securities were none too liquid. The second mortgages ranked behind first mortgages held by HongkongBank Australia totalling $256 million. And the parcels in BIG and Mid-East Minerals represented 37 per cent and 58 per cent respectively of the issued capital of those companies. Whether Tricontinental could realise market value for these shares—presuming that the bank could get possession of them ahead of the HongkongBank—must have been dubious. By this time Tricontinental's loan facilities to the Bond group totalled $392 million, of which $285 million had been drawn.

Tricontinental conducted an internal review of the Dallhold facility in January 1988 but this appears to have been fairly meaningless. Dallhold's shares in Mid-East Minerals, for example, were valued at $4.03 each although their bid price on the share market was then 35c. In May 1988 Tricontinental agreed to a further extension of the Dallhold facility while awaiting the postponed float of BIG. Perhaps Tricontinental had little option except to wait but, even so, little credit analysis was done on this very important exposure. For instance, there had been no attempt to assess the impact of the October crash on Dallhold. Tricontinental was still operating on Dallhold's June 1987 financials. Even those were none too encouraging, with current liabilities of $194 million heavily outweighing current assets at $39 million. Tricontinental's total Bond group exposure was by mid-1988 $280 million. which amounted to three times the bank's shareholders' funds. The Dallhold loans were written off as almost total losses.

Freshening up

These are only a sample of the deals done by Tricontinental. They made similar loans to such disasters as Barrack House, Budget, Hartogen, Intellect Electronics, Interwest, Linter, Markland House, Pro-Image and Quatro. From the samples above a few points are worth making. One is that Tricontinental had a very loose approach to credit analysis for an avowed lender to the high-risk end of the market. None of the original loans listed above could have passed muster with even an apprentice credit analyst. Many of the loans were on the security of shares which were overpriced anyway and vulnerable to a downturn. Any reader patient enough to slog through the samples will have noticed another point: when the borrowers got into difficulties they could still get fresh loans or refinance them through a new borrower. In the Rocado case, for example, a bad loan to Rocado was replaced by a predictably bad loan to Duke Securities on the same security. Among bankers this process is called 'freshening up'. The Rocado loan did not have to be written down because Rocado had been replaced by Duke Securities. Several write-downs were staved off in similar fashion. This is one reason why Tricontinental's bad debt provisions in 1988 remained relatively low. They postponed the final disaster but exacerbated it.

At the end of the day, roughly half of Tricontinental's loan portfolio went bad. Tricontinental was making an increasing proportion of bad loans as it went on. An increasing proportion of them were loans that had been 'freshened up' and funded by borrowing at top interest rates on the short-term money market. The bank's crash was inevitable.

Johns bears the heaviest responsibility for the collapse. Tricontinental was structured so that he was the only executive who could see all the parts of the picture. He was involved in nearly all of the problem loans. He was an autocrat who overawed his staff, including the credit department. Much of the lending he approved can be categorised as reckless. In several cases Tricontinental lent not only to the public companies but also upstream to the private companies of cowboys, including Skase, Bond and Herscu. Johns and Tricontinental should therefore have had access to data which showed the precariousness of the personal finances of such clients, whose personal guarantees were often the security for loans to the downstream companies. In the Rocado loans, Johns had a clear conflict of interest because of his presence on the Rocado board.

All that being said, it should be remembered that Tricontinental's flaws preceded Johns' arrival in the managing director's office. Australian Ratings had pegged down the merchant bank's credit rating years before because of its perceived excessive reliance on short-term funding. Its rating subsequently rose again, not because Tricontinental's funding base improved but because it was taken over by the SBV. The Touche Ross report, which highlighted all the essential flaws that would eventually bring Tricontinental down, was written for Mitsui before Johns was appointed managing director. Johns had been general manager (lending and corporate services) since 1983, so can be assigned some responsibility for lending policy at the time of the Touche Ross report; but Redenbach was still managing director then and Tricontinental had a board headed by Sir Ian Potter.

While the board may not have known everything, they certainly knew the thrust of Johns' policies. In November 1984, before the Touche Ross report was even commissioned, Johns had presented a paper to the board advocating a policy of lending to second and third ranking companies and high net worth individuals. From this and the credit submissions they saw at every board meeting, the directors knew he was concentrating on lending to the corporate cowboys such as Bond and Skase. They

Table 14.2 Tricontinental loans in 1988/89 (all figures in $m)

Approved by general managers/credit committee	26.8
Approved by the managing director	164.1
Approved by directors	2 090.5
	2 281.4

implicitly endorsed this policy by allowing Johns to restate it in Tricontinental's 1986 annual review, which was Tricontinental's version of an annual report.

Almost all of the problem loans seem to have been endorsed by Johns, but they were also approved by the merchant bank's board. Even without the benefit of hindsight many of them should have been recognised as high-risk at the time they were made. Certainly they should have been recognised when they were 'freshened up' after October 1987. Tricontinental was still lending recklessly right up to the end of its career. The sample of cases given earlier indicates that a proportion (possibly a large proportion) of the loans in 1988–89 were renewed facilities which in some form or another masked the fact that the borrowers were unable to repay. But whether they were new loans to bad risks or 'freshened up' loans to bad risks, the board failed to recognise the problem. In the year to June 1989 Tricontinental approved new and increased lending facilities totalling $2281 million. As Table 14.2 shows, all but $191 million of these were approved by the board.

Bill Moyle was a respected banker with a wide range of personal friends in the industry. Unfortunately, he failed to heed several warning signals. He was warned about Johns and Tricontinental's policies by McAnany, but refused to take action. This may be understandable because it was not long since he had endorsed Johns' appointment. But later he also chose to ignore the warnings of Rawlins. The moral of that story is that if you are going to defend a chief executive you should first ensure that he is defensible. Otherwise you become tied to his chariot wheels.

Neil Smith played a peculiar role. He was the main dissident when the SBV proposed the takeover of Tricontinental. He pinpointed the merchant bank's problem areas but nobody listened to him. Judging by his subsequent behaviour, Smith doesn't seem to have listened to himself. As chairman of Tricontinental he allowed Johns to run the merchant bank into the ground without exercising any adequate surveillance over his managing director, despite repeated warning signals.

As usual, the auditors came in for criticism. In 1987, 1988 and 1989 KPMG Peat Marwick were the external auditors of Tricontinental, and also the internal auditors.

Going further up the chain, the SBV board was also negligent. Having acquired Tricontinental with a clear warning from Touche Ross, they should immediately have investigated the merchant bank and rectified any flaws. It is no excuse that they were planning a quick resale. They had already tried to do that with Mitsui and the sale had been aborted by Touche Ross' due diligence report. Any future sale would almost certainly (unless the SBV was very lucky) be accompanied by another due diligence report. The SBV was not in a position to sell Tricontinental unless it had done its own due diligence and knew what it was selling. It had been given clear cause for alarm. Yet the SBV board allowed Tricontinental—its utterly wayward child—to run independently and unchecked even though it was breaching the bank's own prudential guidelines, which were loose enough anyway.

15

SBSA: a fashionable bank

The story of the bank is one of a professionally aggressive and entrepreneurial chief executive without sufficient appreciation of the need for prudent banking controls and management; of an incompetent executive management happy to follow where their chief led without independent professional judgement; of a board of directors out of its depth and, on many occasions, unable or unwilling to exercise effective control; and, ultimately, of a bank that thrived on the full faith and credit of the people of South Australia.

State Auditor-General, Ken MacPherson

The Savings Bank of South Australia was formed in 1848 and the State Bank of South Australia was formed in 1896. By 1984 they had led stolidly blameless lives for 136 years and 88 years respectively. In 1984 they merged to form a new, larger State Bank of South Australia. With an expanded scope of operations and a dynamic new chief executive, the merged bank went broke within eight years.

To trace the reasons for this disaster we need to go back to the Campbell Committee, set up by Federal Treasurer John Howard in 1979 to inquire into the Australian financial system. Headed by the chairman of Hooker Corporation, Sir Keith Campbell, the committee delivered its final report in March 1981. The report recommended deregulation of the financial system. This was a worldwide trend at the time. Deregulation would be introduced in the Federal sphere in 1984 and 1985 by Paul Keating. The Campbell report recommended that, once the banking system had been deregulated to make it more competitive, there would cease to be any justification, on efficiency grounds, for continued government ownership of banks. The report recommended that, if government-owned banks were to remain, they should be 'no more fettered or subject to government interference than private sector institutions undertaking similar activities'.

The Campbell report was regarded as Holy Writ at the time. Deregulation was the buzzword of the early 1980s. The report was widely applauded by those who were anxious to break into the cosy regulated cartel of the Australian trading banks. Free market economists applauded

472

the findings and called for them to be implemented. State Premiers, eternally looking for fresh sources of revenue to pay for their expanding outlays, were delighted by the thought that their sleepy state banks could become big-time financial institutions. State governments saw a river of dividends flowing into their coffers if only the state banks would get out there and hustle. All four state banks—in Western Australia, South Australia, Victoria and New South Wales—were urged to become more entrepreneurial.

In South Australia the first obvious step was to merge the two existing banks. The merged SBSA was formed under the *State Bank of South Australia Act* of 1983. John Bannon was both Premier and Treasurer of South Australia. His young, lean face made him the most photogenic of Premiers. Behind the face was a decent, intelligent, high-minded man eager to advance the welfare of his state. Here was no ranting socialist but someone genuinely dedicated to public service. He was personally frugal, worrying about the cost of buying two spare tyres for a caravanning holiday and (while Premier) refusing to buy an air conditioner because the cost wasn't justified for a few hot days each year.[1] Thrifty South Australians identified with him and trusted him. He did a number of good things for South Australia, notably securing a Formula One Grand Prix for Adelaide. He was energetic and honest. He would have gone down in history as one of the state's best Premiers if it were not for one flaw: his failure to monitor the State Bank of South Australia. Unfortunately that one flaw turned out to be so great that it wrecked his career and forced his resignation. In essence, Bannon failed to read the signals about the way the bank was being run as long as it was paying the state dividends. Compared with some of the frauds outlined in this book Bannon's fault was slight: merely a sin of omission. But it cost his state more than three billion dollars.

The SBSA was conceived as a commercial entity, purportedly independent of government control and influence. This concept was supported by both major political parties in South Australia. However, the concept was fundamentally flawed. It failed to recognise that the bank remained a semi-government authority and therefore, in accordance with constitutional principle, was required to act in the public interest, was subject to ministerial direction, and depended on the government for its capital. As well, the state government was the ultimate guarantor. The government sought to portray the bank as a commercial entity at arm's length from the government, but in truth this was like the girl who said that she was only half pregnant. The board was appointed by the government, which also had the power to dismiss directors. The Treasurer could intervene in matters of policy or administration; he had the power to approve or reject the acquisition by the bank of an interest greater than

10 per cent in any other entity; he had the power to determine how much of the bank's profit flowed to consolidated revenue; he had the power to rearrange its finances; and he had the power to appoint an investigator. The bank's charter was to promote the balanced development of the state's economy to the maximum advantage of the people of South Australia. The bank was always a state authority and a state responsibility. The failure to recognise this was the flaw which underlay the whole disaster.

The cloudy concept of the bank as an arm's length entity resulted in the government's powers being exercised ineffectively or not at all. The moral of the story is that if you have power over something, and if you are responsible for it and are going to be blamed if it defaults, then you should exercise that power. At worst you will then be blamed for your own mistakes and not someone else's.

With the SBSA created, the crucial decision was the appointment of a chief executive. After a search the board decided on Timothy Marcus Clark, scion of an old Sydney retailing family. At the time, his credentials looked good. After getting a Harvard MBA in 1955 Clark had worked in the family retail business until the Marcus Clark stores were sold to Waltons in 1972. He then joined the Commercial Bank of Australia as general manager from 1972 until it was taken over by Westpac Banking Corporation in 1981. He took a leading role in planning the merger of the two banks and afterwards became general manager for related services (southern). Clark was assertive and ambitious. He was also a great team leader. One SA government officer said later:

> We heard that when he was in retailing he'd be the first downstairs with a chook for the person who'd sold the most fridges, or [at] the bank, with a bottle of Bollinger for the person who'd done the best business. He had very strong views and liked to lead a team . . . He was hyperactive; he could be inspiring; he was a great salesman.[2]

In some eyes there was a slight cloud over Clark. He had associated with a number of the flamboyant company promoters of the day, particularly Allan Hawkins of Equiticorp and John Elliott. Clark was an admirer of Hawkins, whom he had hired to run CBA Finance in New Zealand. When Westpac took over the Commercial Bank of Australia Hawkins led a walkout of 21 of the bank's New Zealand staff and set up his own rival business under the name of Westpac Finance. Westpac was outraged at this pirating of the name, which the bank eventually forced Hawkins to drop. Clark, still a senior officer of Westpac, raised a few eyebrows at the bank by remaining a friend of Hawkins and retaining a seat on the Equiticorp board.

Clark had aided Elliott in his takeover of Henry Jones IXL, becoming chairman afterwards. That raid also raised some eyebrows around

Melbourne because it was partly financed by General Credits, the wholly owned finance subsidiary of the CBA, which was the banker to Henry Jones. Another cloud of sorts over Clark arose from a strange and brutal incident in 1980. He was stabbed in the head and neck as he got out of his car in the driveway of his Toorak home. The attack almost killed Clark, who would bear the scars for the rest of his life. The CBA offered a $100 000 reward for information about the attacker, but the mystery remained unsolved. The attack left Clark with an understandable obsession with security. He liked houses with high walls and security television. His SBSA office had a bulletproof door.

South Australia was after an entrepreneurial banker; Clark fitted the bill. The top headhunting firm of Spencer Stuart had recommended Clark, but the report added: 'He certainly pushes hard but he will get things done, and he has got entrepreneurial flair . . . from time to time he needs a little bit of controlling but that can be supplied by the board . . . He has a very strong personality and he will quite often get his own way'. Bannon did not see this warning, but several board members did—an early sign of the communication gap between Bannon and the board. Bannon asked to meet Clark. They met on 30 November 1983, Bannon was impressed and Clark's appointment as chief executive officer and a director of the bank was confirmed. He started duty on 1 February 1984 as CEO of the two 'old banks' whose merger did not become effective until 1 July.

Even at that early point there appears to have been a grand design behind Clark's appointment. In Sydney, Nick Whitlam, as managing director of the State Bank of New South Wales, was trying to form a coalition called State Banks of Australia. Under this coalition, the SBNSW, SBV, SBSA and R & I would be able to tap into each other's retail networks to provide national facilities for their customers. Customers of the SBSA who travelled to Sydney, for example, would be able to access their account through a branch of the State Bank of NSW and even through its automatic teller machines. Later it was hoped to make the State banks uniform in operations and philosophy. As the banks were all entities of Labor governments there seemed few political difficulties, and for a while the coalition looked like working harmoniously. Whitlam organised a few meetings of the chief executives, rotating the meetings between the relevant cities. But the idea was dropped because Bill Moyle at the SBV and Clark at the SBSA had other agendas. They wanted to become big-time corporate players.

'What the state banks had was a retail network of consequence in each of these states', said Whitlam.

We could also have hooked in the Bank of Queensland and the two local banks in Tasmania. We were trying to exploit the regional franchises.

But instead, the South Australians and Victorians went mad. Tim's a nice man, but he and Bill Moyle would cooperate in name but not in fact. The state banks had something we could give each other. But they competed in the corporate area where the only people who could benefit were the corporates. Tim would always come to a meeting with a new toy, saying he'd bought a real estate company this week or a trustee company. We would think: 'Why would you buy that? What synergy is there with your business?'. And he would talk about how you needed to be a one-stop shop.[3]

From a very early stage of his appointment Clark had set his goal on expanding the SBSA into a national bank. Converted into a fervent South Australian, he was declaring that community-based regional banks could take on the big Sydney and Melbourne based banks. Such remarks by Clark were generally discounted in banking circles as pardonable patriotic rhetoric. Few realised how serious he was in his drive to expand the SBSA. If the words had been taken seriously it would have been realised that the ambitious Clark was aiming very high. The SBSA had a strong base in South Australia, but unfortunately that state was relatively poor in resources and suffered sluggish growth throughout the 1980s. The SBSA had few clients who could generate the kind of growth Clark wanted. The two most obvious—Elders and Adsteam—carried timebombs that were not obvious in 1984. Given the scarcity of big-lick local clients, Clark could only expand beyond the state's borders in search for growth. In the 1980s—probably the most competitive banking decade in our history—all the good clients had already been taken. So Clark would have to shave margins or deal with higher risk clients to get business.

Bannon warmed to Clark for two reasons. The two previous banks had been staid, little more than building societies. Clark was a whole hurricane of fresh air. He was going to take the state places. Here at last was a real livewire banker. And, like all South Australians, Bannon loathed the thought of living in a branch office state. After the takeover of the Bank of Adelaide by the ANZ in 1979, Bannon used to say that the state had been left in a financial void: its economic future was in the hands of private investors 'who would not necessarily have the interests of South Australia as their first priority'.[4]

The future being painted for the SBSA was exciting but unrealistic. No South Australian bank had ever managed the transition to national before. Nor did the SBSA have any natural advantages. Its community base was strong and loyal, but small. If the SBSA was going to embark on a highly expansionary course, it would need first-class management. If it was dealing with high-risk customers, it would need to identify problem areas quickly and accurately. If the SA Government was going to be the bank's guarantor, it would need to ensure that both these requirements were met. Instead, Bannon simply pinned his faith on Clark, as he would until the end came six years later. Bannon, in the words of Royal Commissioner Samuel Jacobs, QC, was 'dazzled' by Clark. Amongst Clark's peers—the chief executives of the big banks—he was not normally regarded as a dazzling personality.

Capital for the SBSA was provided by the government through the South Australian Financing Authority (SAFA). Clark said that the government should not be unduly concerned if the SBSA did not meet Reserve Bank capital requirements in the short term because, firstly, depositors were protected by a government guarantee, and secondly 'our risk asset portfolio is such that we do not need to have as much free capital as banks with a higher risk profile'. Under Clark the SBSA's risk profile would change radically.

SAFA had substantial advances to the SBSA in the form of concessional housing loans. When the new SBSA was created, SAFA provided capital (apparently painlessly) by converting $156 million of these loans into capital. The loans did not become equity capital (shares), however, but subordinated debt bearing a fixed interest rate of 7.4 per cent. Under Reserve Bank rules this debt could be counted as Tier 2 capital when calculating the SBSA's capital adequacy ratio.[5] The interest rate was misleadingly described as a dividend. Royal Commissioner Jacobs, in his subsequent report, said that this was a 'quite critical fallacy'. Normally a company determines the size of its profit before deciding what portion of that profit should be distributed as dividend. This fixed interest payment had to be made irrespective of the size of the profit.[6]

The Campbell report had recommended that government-owned banks be charged a fee for guarantees provided by their governments, to bring them into line with commercial practice. Bannon proposed this in a letter to the SBSA's chairman, Lew Barrett, in December 1984. Clark objected on the grounds that it was inappropriate 'for the competitive viability of the bank to be prejudiced by payment of add-on costs to an entity that is the sole beneficiary of its commercial success'. He added: 'Payment of any fee in any circumstances will add to the bank's costs at a time when pricing and margins are becoming progressively finer'. Clark's point that the government, as sole owner, would be charging a fee to itself was valid. However, his response was the first faint signal that all might not be right at the bank. Margins must have been fine indeed if they could not stand the relatively modest cost of a guarantee fee. Jacobs found it surprising that this statement did not prompt Bannon or Treasury to monitor the bank well enough to make their own assessment of the SBSA's affairs. But, despite this and many later warnings, Treasury would never monitor the bank's affairs adequately.

Further, if the bank was operating at such fine margins that it could not afford a fee for the guarantee, it raised the spectre that the guarantee might have to be called one day. But both then and later Bannon considered the possibility that the guarantee would be called as 'laughable'. He maintained this attitude almost until it happened. The chairman and Clark also arranged a regular half-hour meeting with Bannon, held about every six weeks, to brief him on what was happening at the SBSA. Treasury also sat in sometimes. It should be noted that the bank was always willing to provide information to the government (except, curiously, about executive salaries) and generally responded positively to any requests by Bannon or Treasury.

In theory there appeared to be ample safeguards, because the chief executive of the bank and his staff would be responsible to the Treasurer, the Treasury and the board. However, safeguards do not work without people who are determined to operate them. The bank provided ample data to Treasury. There was a monthly operating review (provided quarterly between June 1987 and 1990), the bank's annual profit plans, its annual strategic plans, its half-yearly reports and its annual report. Unfortunately these documents seem never to have been analysed by Treasury or the Treasurer. Probably many of them weren't even read. The bank's board would also prove ineffective. Sometimes this was due to lack of information. It was not until 1989, for example, that the board would receive regular reports of the bank's large exposures or of the compliance of those exposures with board policies. Even then the reports included only the exposures of the bank and not of the whole SBSA group.[7] Nor does the board seem to have been adequately informed of disputes with the Reserve Bank. Mostly, however, the board appears to have received voluminous information, but directors lacked either the expertise or inclination to analyse it and failed to see the warning signals.[8]

In January 1985 the board approved the SBSA's first overseas expansion. The small existing retail branch in London—described by one bank officer as 'a mail redirection and plant watering service'—would be expanded into a wholesale bank. There were two sound reasons for this decision. One was that the bank's traditional stamping grounds of South Australia and the Northern Territory offered very limited growth, so if the bank were to grow significantly it had to expand geographically. The second reason was that the SBSA needed to establish strategic overseas branches if it wished to get more business from foreign corporate clients operating in the state or from SA clients operating overseas. This was not the way that the overseas branches developed though. The London branch became heavily involved in the UK property market, and the ultimate losses made in London and New York seemed to be mainly due to gambling on the currency and interest rate markets.

Under Clark the SBSA adopted a policy of each year setting a five-year strategic plan. The first of these was unveiled in March 1985, when the board approved the SBSA's 1985–90 strategic plan. Its goal was to procure 30 per cent of the corporate and international business in the state, in addition to all other available interstate and overseas business. Clark was envisaging phenomenal growth, and nowhere would it be more startling than in the London branch which the board had approved two months earlier. Total assets of the London office were projected to grow from a mere $38 million in June 1985 to $848 million in June 1990, by which time London would represent almost 10 per cent of group assets.[9] Apart from its overseas expansion the bank also planned to cover a range of fringe banking activities through subsidiaries. This was another fashion of the mid-1980s. Financial institutions were becoming 'one-stop shops', providing a total range of financial services to their customers. The board was not uncritical of Clark's ambitious growth plan. Directors expressed concern that the SBSA was not focussing sufficiently on South Australia. They also thought Clark unrealistic in aiming for profitability as high as 70 per cent of that achieved by the major trading banks. In practice, the SBSA would expand much more rapidly than the strategic plan envisaged. The plan envisaged the SBSA group growing from assets of $4.3 billion in 1985 to $8.6 billion by 1990. In fact, assets would reach $21.1 billion that year.[10]

This was breathtaking expansion. However, profit margins would be much lower than envisaged, a matter of prime importance that was oddly always overlooked by both Treasury and Bannon.

The SBSA began to build its financial empire. In 1984 it had taken over Beneficial Finance. The next move was unplanned. The ANZ Bank was planning a takeover of the Adelaide-based Executor Trustee & Agency Co. Both the SBSA and the government thought it desirable that Executor Trustee stay in South Australian hands, so the bank outbid the ANZ. The SBSA also bought a half-interest in the Adelaide broking firm, SVB Day Porter & Co. With a trustee company and a broker, the SBSA was rapidly building its one-stop shop.

The bank's Act required the SBSA to seek the Treasurer's approval any time it bought more than 10 per cent of another entity. The Treasurer's approval had been sought, and obtained, for both the above purchases. The bank again approached the Treasurer when Beneficial Finance Corporation (BFC) acquired a half-interest in a thoroughbred financing company named Pegasus Securities Ltd. The other 50 per cent was owned by Alastair McGregor, a member of a prominent Adelaide family. The Under-Treasurer, Bert Prowse, advised the SBSA that acquisitions by subsidiaries of the SBSA fell outside the Act and therefore did not require approval. Prowse's opinion was confirmed by the bank's lawyers, which meant there was a significant loophole in the Act. Like the major trading banks, the SBSA did not guarantee its finance subsidiary. This was not really a tenable position however. If BFC were to get into trouble, it was inconceivable that the SA Government would refuse to honour its debts. And if the SA Government was the de facto guarantor of BFC, it should have had the power to monitor it under the Act. (This was one lesson which should have been burned into the consciousness of South Australian politicians. Only a few years before, the Bank of Adelaide had been brought down by its finance subsidiary, Finance Corporation of Australia.) In the event, the SBSA told Prowse that it would not seek approval for BFC acquisitions in normal trading situations, but would advise the government of any major acquisitions. BFC would become one of the SBSA's major problem areas. A lot of disasters occurred in BFC acquisitions which were hidden in corporate shelters off the SBSA's balance sheet and never reported to the government.

Adelaide's tallest building

From this history it can be seen that all the fundamental flaws which would lead to disaster in the SBSA had surfaced in the first year of its operation. Some of the danger signs were faint at the time, but all were there. Clark was going to take the bank on a course of headlong expansion, with profits unacceptably low for the size of the exposures. The Treasurer's 'hands off' policy meant that Clark was free to go his merry way. Treasury wanted a board seat but would not monitor or analyse the information it was given. The board was unable or unwilling to check Clark and any such attempt would probably have been futile because Bannon would invariably back Clark against any opposition until it was too late.

Bannon could perhaps be excused for not paying too much attention around this time, because he must have been distracted by the state election of December 1985. The SBSA Act provided that the Treasurer had to be warned in advance of increases in interest rates on housing loans. This provision may have been objectionable to a banking purist, but it was politically justifiable. Housing interest rates are so politically sensitive in Australia that no Treasurer can afford to be caught napping when they rise. In September 1985 the SBSA advised it would increase housing loans by half a per cent. Bannon asked the bank to keep the rates down and the bank obliged with a three-month freeze. ALP campaign publicity included the statement 'John Bannon acted to hold down housing interest rates'. As soon as Bannon was re-elected the rates went up again. The story demonstrates that the 'hands off' approach to the bank had its limits. If the bank was going to raise housing rates during an election campaign, the government was certainly capable of exercising its powers.

The episode was repeated in June 1987, when the SBSA deferred a housing loan increase until after the Federal election of July 1987.

The SBSA decided in November 1985 to build the State Bank Centre in King William Street—to be the tallest building in Adelaide—at a cost of $82 million. This was another phenomenon of the era. Any banker worth his salt built a head office of monumental proportions. The SA Superannuation Funds Investment Trust believed the SBSA had paid too much for the site and that the yield would be below acceptable commercial levels. Treasury reported that the project would have substantial adverse financial implications for the government until 1992. Bannon underlined his priorities by writing to the bank saying he wanted the project to have no negative effect on the returns being received by the government. The bank responded with a typically 1980s solution. It would finance the project off balance sheet through a unit trust. Funding was provided by other banks—initially by the Bank of Tokyo and later by a financing partnership comprising Westpac (60 per cent), Commonwealth Bank (30 per cent) and Beneficial Finance (10 per cent). This financing partnership leased the building to the State Bank. At the end of the lease in 1996 the financing partners were entitled to a 'compensatory payment' guaranteed by the bank, which would then own the building. The size of the payment depended upon rates of tax and interest. When this scheme was devised the 'compensatory payment' in 1996 was estimated to be $102 million, well below the projected value of the building of $150 million.[11] So the State Bank Centre went ahead: a monument to financial engineering.

At this stage, the capital adequacy ratio required by the Reserve Bank was 5 per cent. Every time the SBSA expanded its business by lending more money, its capital had to be increased pro rata. The SBSA had two fundamental ways of increasing its capital. The first was by increasing its retained earnings, which would have meant restricting dividend payout to the SA Government. The second was by the government injecting more capital. The second route was chosen, with the government continuing to convert housing loans into loan capital. Under Clark the SBSA expanded so rapidly that the government found itself having to convert its loans into capital at a much faster rate than first planned. During 1985–86 the government had to convert $50 million to loan capital, more than double the growth contemplated only a year before. The group's income-earning assets grew by 56 per cent during the year, compared to a forecast of only 28 per cent. This policy, incidentally, meant that the government was always putting more money into the bank than it got back.

This fast growth was considered healthy. A little careful analysis would have showed cause for concern. The 1985–86 year saw a growth in assets of $2.3 billion, but pre-tax profit rose only from $37 million to $41 million. Growth in assets was not being matched by growth in profit. 'There was one glaringly obvious question to be asked', Commissioner Jacobs observed.[12] 'How was this fledgling bank creating such a large niche for itself so quickly in a highly competitive and deregulated market? Was it sacrificing quality for quantity?'

The bank was also becoming increasingly unsound because of the form in which the capital was provided. The capital provided by SAFA (the Financing Authority) was really debt, because it carried a compulsory fixed interest rate, rather than equity which would carry an optional dividend requirement. This brings us to a Catch 22 at the core of the bank's failure. Every time the SBSA increased its assets substantially it had to increase its capital. Because the capital was provided by SAFA at a fixed rate of return, this meant the SBSA had to increase its reported profit in order to pay interest to SAFA. The pressure was therefore on the SBSA to turn a blind eye to bad debt provisions or anything that might reduce its stated profits. Clark would be Bannon's white-haired boy as long as he could shovel dividends back to SAFA through increased profits. Any break in that circuit—by admitting that the SBSA's assets and profits were not as good as stated—would result in a dividend cut and some loss of face for Clark with Bannon. The mechanics by which the bank's capital was provided therefore ensured that the bank would tell Bannon only the news he wanted to hear. Nor did Bannon, who put the whole structure in place, ever give any indication that he wanted to hear anything except good news.

The structure also inhibited both Treasury and SAFA from exercising too stringent monitoring over the SBSA. As the instrumentalities responsible for raising the revenue to meet Bannon's budgets, Treasury and SAFA were relying on bank dividends. For them to demand more prudent practices from the bank would be tantamount to killing the goose that laid the golden eggs. Thus the whole monitoring, capital and legislative structure of the bank was faulty.

The SBSA's London branch came under the stringent controls of the Bank of England. There the SBSA's exposure to any single entity was limited to 2 per cent of its balance sheet, for example. The board had therefore approved an alternative 'booking centre' which would be free from the London branch's constraints. So the SBSA in June 1986 had set up a Hong Kong branch to write business in London beyond the Bank of England limits. The first automatic question should have been whether it was prudent to exceed the Bank of England limits. The second automatic question should have been how this offshore expansion was going to benefit the people of South Australia. Neither question ever appears to have been asked by Treasury. Bannon welcomed the offshore expansion on the understanding that it would enhance profits, and hence dividends.

In May 1986 the SA Treasury asked Bannon for the right to have a director on the bank board. Treasury would renew this request several times in future years, but it was always resisted strongly by the board and particularly by Clark. Although Clark seems to have been quite cooperative in all other ways—at the six-weekly briefings, providing monthly operational reports and considering any submissions—he never wanted Treasury representatives on the board. Bannon always backed Clark and the board against Treasury. The story might have been different if Treasury had followed through by submitting the figures it was receiving from the bank to some critical analysis. Its case for a board seat would have been greatly strengthened if it had pointed out the frighteningly low profitability on the massive quantity of new business being generated by the bank, particularly in London. But having asked for a board seat and having been rejected, Treasury did little else. Perhaps Prowse and his senior men at Treasury felt they were in no position to rock the boat. In June 1986 Treasury had told Bannon that the state was confronted by budgetary problems and that it was important for the bank to explore the possibility of contributing more to the budget than had been projected.[13] Treasury could hardly be too critical of the bank when they were pleading to it for help.

Subtly, things were going wrong. The government was focussing entirely on dividends without looking further upstream. The implicit assumption seems to have been that the bank did not need monitoring. Yet only a few years before, in 1979, the publicly listed Bank of Adelaide had collapsed amid great scandal and public outcry. By Reserve Bank direction, it was taken over by the ANZ.[14] The reasons for the bank's failure had always been suppressed, but it was known that the rapid growth of its finance subsidiary, Finance Corporation of Australia, had been the main problem area.[15] FCA had been involved in property joint ventures, particularly in Queensland. Half a dozen years later the SA Government had its own bank expanding rapidly in areas which, on its own figures, were only marginally profitable. And the government had forsaken any right to oversee the affairs of its finance subsidiary.

Treasury remained ineffectually concerned. In September 1986 it revived the argument that the bank should pay a fee for the guarantee, suggesting a levy on certain business, including overseas transactions. The fee was to be 0.5 per cent, but lower on very low margin business. The board sought a meeting with Bannon at which it strongly resisted the proposal. The bank argued that the fee would reduce dividend income to the government and jeopardise its London operations, which were operating on low margins and would probably have to be closed.

London's net interest margins were only 0.4 per cent before allowing for staff costs, premises and other overheads. Bannon backed the board against Treasury and the guarantee fee was again shelved. The alarming feature of this episode is that nobody in the government asked why the London business—which expanded by more than 40 per cent in 1986–87—was being written at such very low margins.

The guarantor was ignoring danger signals. Commissioner Jacobs observed that ' . . . a commercial approach also requires a guarantor to understand and monitor the extent of the liability it is guaranteeing so it may ensure that the nature and degree of its risk is not altered without its knowledge and consent, if at all. The government, inappropriately, failed to do that.'[16] The danger signals were also missed by Australian Ratings, which gave the SBSA its highest credit rating: AAA for the bank on an unsecured basis and A1+ for its commercial paper.

It should also be borne in mind that criticising Clark in these years was close to heresy. He had adopted South Australia fervently. He gave countless speeches, saying that he didn't want to see bankers and lawyers getting off eastern states jets and doing jobs that could be done by Adelaide people. He moved instantly to the centre of the business community, becoming chairman of the Australian Formula One Grand Prix board after Adelaide won the right to stage the Grand Prix. He also became chairman of Australian Automotive Industries Ltd, the joint venture between General Motors Corp and Toyota Motor Corp. He was extremely sensitive to any criticism of the bank, writing letters to newspapers and frequently threatening critics with defamation writs.

The year 1986–87 saw continued physical expansion by the bank, with offices opening in Sydney, Melbourne and Queensland. During 1986–87 the SBSA also spread its financial range by establishing a wholly owned merchant bank, Ayers Finnis Ltd, and buying a half-interest in the real estate agency of Myles Pearce & Co. At June 1987 the SBSA's assets had risen from $6.3 billion to $7.9 billion. The bank and Bannon both regarded asset growth as an indicator of health and prosperity. A lay observer could also be pardoned for being happy about any entity showing strong asset growth. In a bank, however, the assets predominantly comprise loans made to clients. Growth in assets is good—indeed excellent—provided that the loans are being made to clients who will repay, and at an adequate margin over the bank's borrowing costs. The profits generated from this good business will swell retained earnings, so the bank's capital rises in proportion to its assets. But if assets are being expanded by making loans to high-risk clients, or at too low a margin over borrowing costs, the expansion is unsound.

In 1986–87 the SBSA expanded so rapidly that it needed a further injection of capital from SAFA by 30 June. The requested tranche of

$150 million was provided, again in the form of converted housing loans, but without anyone in government questioning the pace of the SBSA's growth. Pre-tax profit for 1986–87 rose from $41 million to $52 million. This was an improvement, but still a very low rate of return on assets.

Bannon *was* concerned about the low profitability. As usual, his budget needed more dividends and he requested an additional $2.3 million. Commissioner Jacobs observed:

> One has to ask why the Treasurer, having identified the relatively poor result for 1986–87, did not then take the opportunity to review in more detail the bank's affairs and to ascribe to Treasury a more substantial and specific monitoring role. Such action was really so obviously necessary as to defy a satisfactory explanation for the failure to take it . . . There were by then some reasonably potent signs of unwisdom in the collation of the bank's assets which a mildly careful look might well have identified. Of course, the primary responsibility for asking such questions lay with the board. It also apparently failed to ask them.[17]

The most concern about the expansionary pattern was registered by the Reserve Bank of Australia. In January 1987 the RBA required the SBSA to give it advance notice of any proposed exposure to a client that exceeded 30 per cent of the bank's capital base. This was a standard RBA requirement of all banks at the time. The SBSA dragged its feet, claiming the right and ability to grant loans, including quite large ones, within 24 hours and 'without any breakdown of sound analysis and credit assessment'.[18]

This was an alarming attitude on the part of the SBSA. The Reserve Bank replied that it would reply within the timeframe. On 1 June the SBSA advised the RBA that it intended to increase its total exposure to the Equiticorp group of New Zealand to $250 million, which represented 54 per cent of the bank's then capital. The RBA warned the SBSA against the exposure, saying it was imprudent because of Clark's association with the borrower. Equiticorp was a New Zealand–based company run by Allan Hawkins, whose empire had mushroomed in the wild boom of the 1980s. From the basis of a small finance company Hawkins had parlayed his ramshackle group into a player in the battle for BHP in 1986. The $250 million loan from SBSA was needed to finance an ambitious raid by Equiticorp on the big concrete group, Monier Ltd. Equiticorp's subsequent collapse would be one of the largest in New Zealand's chequered financial history. As mentioned earlier, Clark and Hawkins were longtime friends and Clark still sat on the Equiticorp board. After Equiticorp collapsed, Hawkins wrote a book criticising almost everyone except himself. One of the few to earn Hawkins' fulsome praise was Clark.[19] By that time Hawkins was broke and Clark may not have welcomed the accolade. Even in 1987 Hawkins was regarded as a fairly hairy operator.

Clark was a director of Equiticorp Holdings Ltd, the holding company of the group.

The RBA told Clark that, if the SBSA had not been a state bank, the Reserve Bank would have used its statutory powers to block the loan. The Governor, Bob Johnston, wrote to Barrett (SBSA's chairman) advising against the transaction and registering strong disapproval. But, oddly, neither the Reserve Bank nor Barrett told Treasury or Bannon of the incident.

The Equiticorp link

July 1987 saw a number of board changes. One of the founding directors of the merged bank had died and two others had retired. After three appointments the new board comprised Lew Barrett, chairman; leading Adelaide lawyer David Simmons, deputy chairman; Clark, managing director and chairman of the executive committee; Molly Byrne, a former Labor MP; William Nankivell, a director of the Southern Farmers Group; Robert Bakewell, a past chairman of the savings bank; Robert Searcy, a chartered accountant and chairman of Executor Trustee; Rodney Hartley, South Australia's Director of State Development; and Tony Summers, managing director of Bennett & Fisher (an old SA business which was headed for a collapse of its own a few years later). Bannon would still not allow Treasury a place on the board, but Treasury was doing little to help its case because it was still not monitoring or analysing the data it was receiving from the bank.

The board was chosen in line with a perceived need to have a 'balanced representative community' structure. While some community representation may well have been desirable, the SBSA was now a large bank by Australian standards and one to which the government was heavily exposed. Jacobs said:

> There was a crying need for hard-headed and diverse practical business and (if possible) banking experience at that level to enable the board at least to monitor, if not guide, the strategy of the bank, rather than leave it all to Mr Clark, whom the Treasurer himself perceived to be the driving force.[20]

After the great share market crash of October 1987 the SBSA recognised a serious change in the economic outlook. Simmons and Clark both foresaw a substantial collapse in the property market, to which BFC was heavily exposed. The SBSA's economist, Darryl Gobbett, told Clark that he feared a significant downturn in economic growth, both internationally and in Australia. Clark told the board in November that the bank was heading into very difficult times which would not correct quickly. He foresaw 'customers getting into financial difficulties, increasing non-accrual accounts, increasing bad debts and challenges in meeting our lending targets with high quality loans'. He said the bank would get many opportunities but would need to assess them conservatively. At top level, therefore, the bank's analysis and predictions could hardly have been better. But in practice its behaviour did not change.

In November the bank also conducted a review of the quality of its lending where amounts exceeded $50 000. This review highlighted a need to improve lending practices with regard to valuations, imperfect or inadequate security, poor account management and failure to classify loans as non-accrual. These were serious defects, but the review appears to have been accepted docilely by the board.

Within days of the review the board backed yet another expansion, this time into New York and the Cayman Islands. Clark justified the New York expansion on the grounds that it would create a wholesale banking operation with higher margins for corporate lending than in Australia. The Cayman Islands facility would support New York through access to lower cost funds. Clark said that, as a small operation in a large market, the SBSA could 'selectively acquire US corporate assets through existing business relationships to achieve a good return at a risk level that is attractive in relation to domestic opportunities'. It sounded good, but a little reflection should have revealed that it was absurd to suppose that a small bank could break into the highly competitive New York banking market and do business more profitably than it could at home. Commissioner Jacobs labelled the proposition 'crazy'.[21] And projections made by the SBSA itself did not bear out the proposition. The SBSA's profit plan showed that after three years the New York operation would be earning a pre-tax profit of only $3 million on assets of $750 million.

In December 1987 the SBSA played Santa Claus to Equiticorp. The bank extended a $50 million loan facility to Equiticorp (Tasman) Ltd, then bought $150 million of its receivables. The purpose of this was to fund the Equiticorp takeover of Monier. The $200 million deal appears to have been structured in this way to avoid another clash with the Reserve Bank. It was a comparatively safe deal, however, because Equiticorp quickly repaid the $150 million when Redland of the UK bought Monier's roofing division.

So the deal ended well, but not before it had raised considerable alarm among the SBSA's external solicitors in Sydney who had done the paperwork. They pointed out that there had been no legal transfer of each component of the portfolio; that no notice of assignment had been executed and served; that there had been virtually no investigation of the securities; and that documents on the assets had not been handed over before settlement. The solicitors had little time to make their own checks, but a search of one of the companies involved, Equiticorp Financial Services Ltd, had revealed it to have a debenture trust deed which required certain meetings to be held before the receivables would become available to the SBSA. The solicitors wrote to the SBSA explaining that the bank was facing a substantial risk that it might be unable to enforce security, and saying that 'normal prudential requirements' would involve the bank taking a number of steps that the bank had instructed the solicitors not to take.[22]

There was more than a little schizophrenia in the bank's behaviour. Having analysed the post-crash markets accurately and having stated the correct course of action, the SBSA was doing exactly the opposite. By early 1988 Rodney Hartley was becoming worried. The Director of State Development, he had joined the board six months before. Born in England, Hartley had begun his career as a textile chemist but had gravitated into management, holding chief executive or board positions in a number of companies. He was a director of the government-controlled Sagasco Holdings. Hartley complained both to Bannon and to the Minister for State Development, Lynn Arnold, that Clark was dismissive of the SBSA board. Hartley said the board would not and could not confront Clark and so was not really in control of the bank's affairs. Bannon and Arnold ignored these complaints. Bannon also refused, again, to give Treasury a seat on the board.

None of the supervisory systems was operational. Treasury had begun some monitoring of the SBSA but was not advising Bannon of its concerns. The Treasurer was pinning his faith on Clark and maintaining a hands-off attitude. The board, apart from Hartley, had been compliant to the managing director's wishes. The only other available supervisor was the Reserve Bank of Australia, and there had been a breakdown in that area too. The RBA had sought access to the SBSA's external auditors, which had been refused by Clark. It took more than two years for negotiations to resolve this dispute, which the board was not informed about until December 1987. The government was not told of the dispute at all. Clark claimed that as a state bank the SBSA was independent of the RBA. 'It is impossible not to view with deep suspicion the attitude of bank management, and of Mr Clark himself, on this issue', Jacobs said.[23]

In January 1988 Equiticorp Australia Ltd suggested the sale of $100 million of its receivables to the SBSA, together with a buy-back arrangement. The arrangement was planned to be similar to the sale and buy-back of receivables made by Equiticorp in the previous month. The $100 millon receivables deal was approved by the SBSA board, but the bank's legal department wrote to Equiticorp rejecting the deal on the grounds that it would place the SBSA exposure to Equiticorp over the RBA prudential limit. So Clark then suggested the deal to John Baker, the managing director of Beneficial Finance.[24]

Beneficial bought $NZ114 million worth of real estate receivables in three tranches, using a New Zealand off–balance sheet shelf company, Ravlick Holdings Ltd, for the purpose. Baker was enthusiastic about the deal, seeing it as an opportunity to buy into New Zealand without paying the large goodwill premiums that had abounded before Black Tuesday. Beneficial had looked at making a gross margin of 5 per cent and a net margin of about 3 per cent on the purchases. But the loans struck trouble almost immediately. By March 1989—barely a year after the receivables were bought—a dozen of the 40 borrowers were in receivership, liquidation or some other form of statutory management. Writeoffs totalled nearly $NZ13 million, wiping out the anticipated margin and delivering Beneficial and the SBSA group a thumping loss.[25] In a further deal, Beneficial bought Australian receivables totalling $165 million from Equiticorp. There seem to have been no losses on these. The big picture, however, is that Beneficial had pumped more than $NZ220 million ($A170 million) into Equiticorp at a time when that group was in dire need of money. And the injection of cash through Beneficial avoided RBA scrutiny.

The buying of Oceanic

The SBSA continued its reckless course in February by buying Oceanic Capital Corporation for $60 million, easily its biggest acquisition until then. To anyone who followed the financial markets the parentage of Oceanic did not inspire confidence. Oceanic was a funds management and life insurance group wholly owned by APA Holdings Ltd, part of the corporate empire of Garry Carter, a bold rider from Newcastle whose affairs had hit sticky going even before the crash. As the purchase was being made only a few months after the greatest share market crash in history there was every reason for the board to scrutinise the deal closely.

The board approved a purchase at $55 million provided that a satisfactory independent valuation was made and that $10 million was held in escrow to be paid only after consultants had found Oceanic's condition to be satisfactory. When this offer was rejected by APA the board approved the purchase at $60 million in March, although it had still not received any independent expert's report. Even without the benefit of hindsight this was a foolhardy purchase. The vendor was known to be anxious to sell and the assets had already been downvalued from $81 million to $58 million. Oceanic's profit for the year had been revised downwards from $11.2 million to $6.6 million, and that projection was made on only three months trading after the share market collapse. And, of the higher $60 million now bid by SBSA, only $2 million was held in escrow for post-takeover adjustments. APA accepted the revised bid.

On 28 April, barely a month after acquiring Oceanic, investigating actuaries reported that the assets acquired were grossly overvalued and that a reasonable price for Oceanic would have been barely half the $60 million that had been paid. This report was not given to the board. Instead, the board was told that a draft report from the actuaries had said the price was fair and reasonable. The board did not seek to see the actuaries' report. Directors had reason to be more inquisitive, because at their April board meeting they were asked to approve a loan of $38.4 million to Oceanic for the curious purpose of the 'creation of critical mass in a number of selected small unit trust products of the company'.[26] If Oceanic was worth $60 million why did it suddenly need an injection of another $38.4 million?

Years later, the report on the SBSA by the South Australian Auditor-General, Ken MacPherson, pointed out that the party which stood to gain most by the deal was Allan Hawkins' Equiticorp group. Equiticorp was under heavy financial pressure in early 1988. In a masterpiece of bad timing it had agreed on 19 October 1987 to buy 89 per cent of New Zealand Steel from the NZ Government for $NZ327 million. By March 1988 the payment date was looming.[27] Equiticorp had a secured loan to APA which it needed to be repaid, but the Carter empire's repayment ability at this point was debatable at best. MacPherson said:

> For Equiticorp Holdings, the day of cash settlement for the NZ Steel purchase was approaching; it so happened that, at all material times, the Equiticorp group was a secured creditor of APA Holdings and would receive much needed funds on the sale of the Oceanic Capital Corporation shares and the concurrent repayment of the debt due by its shareholder APA Holdings. It was very much in Equiticorp Holdings' interest for the debt owing by APA Holdings to be repaid on the due date, but this was most unlikely to happen if APA Holdings did not promptly accept the bank's offer.[28]

MacPherson pointed out that Clark was a director of Equiticorp until June 1988. He always absented himself from SBSA board discussions on transactions with Equiticorp. However, MacPherson said: ' . . . it is impossible to resist the inference that the liquidity problems then facing Equiticorp were associated with the events leading to several of the bank's transactions . . . '

In the middle of the manoeuvres with Equiticorp the SBSA board had renewed Clark's employment contract. Of all the decisions made by the board this was one of the oddest. Clark's contract was not due to expire for more than a year. In the months after Black Tuesday a bank board should have been more alert than ever to see that its chief executive knew how to handle the turbulent waters ahead. Instead, the board gave Clark a $70 000 rise to make his total package $400 000 and extended his contract until June 1992. The main opposition on the board was from Robert Bakewell who said it was time to 'cut the painter and do something else'. MacPherson said the decision to reappoint Clark was due as much as anything else to the lack of a successor within the bank. 'That this situation was allowed to arise is indicative of the fact that the board, prior to 1988, paid only casual attention to the issue of succession planning and was ill-prepared to address the matter in any structured fashion when it arose', he said.

After the Equiticorp deals Beneficial Finance hardly paused for breath before its next big project. In May the financier entered into a joint venture with Emmett Construction Group to acquire East End Market Co Ltd, which was redeveloping the old markets on the eastern fringe of the city of Adelaide. The outlay by Beneficial was more than $30 million. Bannon agreed, being anxious that the project should proceed without delay. No independent analysis was done by Treasury. The East End development would turn out to be, in Jacobs' words, 'one of the tentacles around the neck of BFC, slowly strangling it to death and materially contributing to the downfall of the other joint ventures'.[29]

By the end of 1987–88 SBSA group assets had jumped by another 40 per cent from $7.9 billion to $11 billion. This was hardly the conservative growth advocated by Clark. Treasury recognised the inconsistency, but remained passive because it thought Bannon did not want it to interfere with the bank's commercial judgement. Group pre-tax profit rose from $55.5 million to $69.5 million. While the increase in profit was welcome, the return on assets was still very low at only two-thirds of one per cent. Lending margins—the difference between the borrowing and lending rates—were as low as 0.4 per cent, which was very thin. Jacobs said: 'Mr Clark never considered not growing!'. Indeed, those who questioned expansion were heretics. When one executive in 1988 questioned the expansionary plans Clark shouted at him: 'The train is heading north. If you don't like it you can get off'. The executive was flicked from the executive committee—in practice the ruling body of the bank—as a result. Clark believed that by expanding during a recession he was being countercyclical. If it had been a short recession, as in 1961, he would have been right. But in the late 1980s the economic and financial malaise ran deep and Clark signally failed to grasp that fact. He was expanding headlong almost to his last day at the bank.

The 1987–88 profit was less good than it looked. It will be remembered that the 'capital' contributed by SAFA bore interest at a fixed rate. It was really subordinated debt rather than dividend-bearing equity. The Reserve Bank's capital adequacy requirements meant that every expansion in the SBSA's assets required a commensurate increase in its capital, and hence in its interest bill. The bank's profits in 1986–87 and 1987–88 had actually only grown by enough to service the interest on the capital increase. The state's Treasury had recognised in 1986–87 that the bank's real return on equity was virtually zero. That result was a turning point for Prowse, the Under-Treasurer, and in 1987–88 Treasury began to monitor the bank.

One of the oddest features of the SBSA's continuing headlong expansion is that Clark himself recognised the dangers. Outlining the bank's profit plan for 1988–89, Clark said: 'The bank has acquired an additional $385 million in capital to provide a platform for future growth and profitability. Our immediate ability to gear up on this additional capital is restricted by the availability of suitable quality assets and market constraints'. Yet the profit plan projected even greater growth at even lower margins. Jacobs said: 'It is as if the bank was not even paying attention to itself'.

One other growing problem was the State Bank Centre in King William Street. The original cost of $82 million had aroused the concern of Bannon, who feared—correctly—that the bank would not get as good a yield on a head office as it would by employing the same funds in its business. By the end of 1988 cost overruns in construction had blown the cost out to $120 million, and the estimated 'compensatory payment' had soared from $102 million to $160 million. As there had been no commensurate rise in rents the yield would be lower. Nevertheless, bank officers justified the cost explosion by estimating that the value of the building had risen to $236 million.[30] Clark did not tell Bannon about the cost blowout.

The omission is important. If Bannon had known, he might well have thought twice about urging the SBSA to commit to the other giant building project in the Adelaide central business district: the REMM–Myer project.

REMM–Myer and the SGIC

In mid-1987 the SBSA board had approved the 100 per cent financing of REMM's acquisition of the Centrepoint site on the corner of Rundle and Pulteney Streets. This was a key step in an even bigger development. REMM had offered the Centrepoint site to Myer as its temporary home while REMM bought and redeveloped the Myer store in the heart of Adelaide's main shopping centre, the Rundle Mall. On completion it would be leased back to Myer.

REMM (Real Estate Marketing & Management) was a group that had suddenly appeared from nowhere. Its founder and chief proprietor was Michael John Brown, a former dairy farmer who had arrived in Brisbane as a real estate salesman in 1973. REMM was a residential and commercial developer in and around Brisbane until 1985, when it hit the big time. REMM made its first move into the Brisbane CBD by buying the Barry & Roberts building in Queen Street. Work had begun on what was to be the New York Centre when Brown realised that, if he bought the adjoining Suncorp building, he could provide Myer with its first new CBD department store in 30 years. With the Brisbane Expo coming up, the planning approvals were forthcoming because the new retail centre tied in with the Queen Street Mall and the Brisbane City Council's new bus terminal below it. Myer agreed to the deal provided that REMM bought its old store on Queen and Adelaide Streets and the one in Fortitude Valley. (The financing of the old Myer store by Estate Mortgage was described in Chapter 11.)

The project was well beyond REMM's finances, but in November 1986 REMM sold the Brisbane Myer site off the plan to Chase Corporation of New Zealand, another high-flying property group that would come to a sticky end. REMM retained construction rights, project management and the right to earn 70 per cent of the profits from managing the property. This looked a good deal for REMM, which booked a $16 million profit on the sale to Chase. In turn, Chase revalued the property and sold it to an Australian subsidiary named Interchase. The Brisbane deal was the model for the Adelaide deal with Myer. The SBSA, as a banker to Chase and a member of the syndicate that financed the Brisbane Myer Centre, should have been fully informed about REMM, which completed the Brisbane project on time and within budget.

The SA Government was properly cautious at first about the Myer project in Adelaide. There was no shortage of highly placed sceptics. The project was examined by Bruce Guerin, who was head of the Department of the Premier and Cabinet (and reputedly the most powerful public servant in the state), and by Dr Barry Lindner, a senior officer in the department's major projects division. From the start REMM sought concessions or exemptions from statutory fees, claiming that the project would not be viable otherwise. Guerin and Lindner recognised this as a clear danger signal. The government charges amounted only to some $8 million in a $540 million project; if they represented a threat to its viability the whole project must have been dangerously borderline. Treasury was firmly against granting the concessions because it doubted the project's viability, saying that REMM had paid too much for the Myer site. Senior officers of the State Government Insurance Commission (SGIC) of South Australia also doubted the viability of the project, and in particular questioned the assumptions underlying the valuation.

Guerin, despite his misgivings, said: 'We have to make sure the development happens'. This attitude may partially excuse Bannon's endorsement of the project. South Australia has always been the poorest state in resources, with relatively few big projects. It would have been a big decision to let go of something the size of Myer just for a few million in government charges. But that was different from taking the next step and financing the project.

In May 1988 the project was estimated to cost $430 million, including $70 million in capitalised interest. At completion the store was supposed to have a value of $540 million. The financing proposal was that the construction cost of $430 million would be syndicated, and supported by a further $100 million standby credit provided through two letters of credit for $40 million each and a $20 million equity contribution from REMM. In hindsight, it must be open to conjecture whether REMM could have met that equity requirement. A paper to the SBSA board in May 1988 noted that REMM, in practical terms, had no net worth.

Despite this handicap the SBSA provided one of the $40 million letters of credit. This was not a high-risk proposition, because the letter of credit was only for standby finance after $430 million had first been invested in the project. Even then, the board endorsed the letter of credit cautiously, by providing that the bank's exposure would be sold down to $20 million within three months and that it would get a normal fee plus 12.5 per cent of the profit on sale following completion of construction. The board cannot be criticised for this decision. As the only bank based in Adelaide the SBSA could hardly have done less for the project.

The jarring difficulty was that the lead financing of $430 million was not tied down, and nothing would happen until it was. Bannon told Clark that he wanted the project to proceed if it was commercially feasible. Clark asked bank officers to investigate lead-financing the project. The project still had no shortage of sceptics. The general manager of the SGIC, Dennis Gerschwitz, called it 'ill-conceived' because of the limited equity participation by REMM. Dr Lindner, an enthusiast, recognised nonetheless that the initial rent would support finance costs only up to $100 million. Prowse believed that the viability of the project was 'under severe question'. But the broad picture is that Bannon wanted REMM–Myer. It was never commercially viable, but a few key players at the top of SA Inc decided that they would please Bannon and give him his project anyway.

It was the SGIC which opened the door. Until then the Commission's senior staff had been realistic in their valuations of the Myer project and had been supported by Gerschwitz. But, in a series of senior management meetings between the SGIC and the SBSA in July 1988, the SGIC attitude was reversed by its chairman, Vin Kean.[31] An Adelaide businessman with a background in the auto trade and property, Kean had built a personal fortune during the boom. He swayed Gerschwitz into supporting the project and the result was that the SGIC took two-thirds of a $485 million put option on it.[32] The SGIC seems to have wanted to help the SBSA to package a proposal that otherwise would not have been possible. It wanted to demonstrate that South Australian institutions could finance such a project. It was also taking a hell of a risk. This alone was an enormous step for the SGIC. At a proportionate value of $320 million the REMM project represented one-fifth of the SGIC's total assets. But the SGIC was having a rush of blood to the head. At about the same time it also entered into a put option for some $520 million for the redevelopment of the Commercial Bank of Australia's former head office at 333 Collins Street, Melbourne. As Treasurer, Bannon had to approve both put options. He did so on 11 August 1988.

This was a folly of some dimensions. The SGIC had just exposed itself to a total liability of more than $800 million on two properties. And it nearly became larger. At around the same time, the SGIC was seriously considering a further put option of around half a billion dollars on Sydney's Chifley Square.

The REMM put option was reckless in another respect. Until 24 hours before the final deal the put was to have been at $420 million. At the last minute it was increased to $485 million in one jump without any corresponding increase in fees. It appears that the SGIC, in conjunction with the SBSA, actually planned to be the final owner of the building. This was an unrealistically big bite for the SGIC.

A bridge too far

The SGIC put option on the REMM project was taken on 22 July. The put option meant the project now had a last-resort buyer in the SGIC (presuming the SGIC could find the cash) and thus the project was more bankable. SBSA officers drew up a proposal estimating that the project would cost $443 million, with a worst case cost of $448 million, and have a value on completion of $550 million. On this basis they proposed a two-stage financing package, the first stage being merely a bridge until the second and final stage could be put in place. The two stages were:

Stage One
- A credit facility of $120 million.
- An underwriting commitment to provide Stage Two financing to the extent of an additional $330 million. This underwriting was underpinned by the SGIC to the extent of $200 million, for which it would earn a fee of $20 000.

Stage Two
- A medium-term debt facility of $360 million.
- A construction debt facility of $90 million.
- A construction cost overrun facility financed by the SBSA's
  $40 million letter of credit, which would be the last money to be
  drawn down.

The SBSA intended to provide the Stage One credit facility of $120 million to get the project started, and to translate this into one-third of the medium-term debt facility of Stage Two when the other $240 million had been syndicated. The SBSA would then be committed for $120 million plus the $40 million letter of credit. Given the bank's intention, the proposed financing structure was flawed because it was going to be putting money into Stage One before Stage Two was bedded down. The danger was that the bank would find itself the sole financier of the project, which was never intended. This structure might have worked if there had been no time pressure on the bank. But there was strong political and bureaucratic pressure for the Myer Centre to proceed on the grounds that it would be a great project for the state. REMM was pressing to begin work.

As a last resort the SBSA had the put option, but this was not much of an escape hatch. Under the July financing proposal the put option was $120 million (one-third taken by the SBSA and two-thirds by the SGIC) plus the assumption of the $360 million medium-term debt facility. The SGIC's exposure was still enormous compared to its total assets, and there always had to be a question mark over whether it could meet its obligation without major financial disruption. Nevertheless, the SBSA board gave conditional approval to the proposal on 28 July.

The SBSA thought it could organise the syndicate in about eight weeks. This was highly optimistic considering that there was no pre-commitment from other financiers, that the syndication was for 100 per cent of cost including capitalised interest and that the bank had never managed a syndicate of this size before. (In the end the financing was not completed until September 1990 and on far worse terms for the SBSA.) In July 1988 the project was justified in a board paper which valued the completed Myer building at $553 million, based on a 7 per cent capitalisation rate and a net rental income of $38.7 million. But the project would be plagued by industrial disputes and other delays, pushing the completion cost up to $580 million compared to the original estimate of $430 million. The most perceptive comment was made by the SBSA's chief operating officer, Stephen Paddison, who said: 'We've just bet the bank on this one'. (Paddison had the best one-liners in the bank. Asked later why the government and the bank had been slow to act in the face of mounting problems, he said: 'To use a colloquialism, there was a reluctance to call one's own child ugly'.)

The SBSA was curiously desultory in trying to recruit syndicate members, making little effort in the first month. Its officers seem to have been confident that the syndication could be accomplished with little effort—an unwarrantedly complacent attitude given the angst that the project had already caused. Before the SBSA had any lenders in the bag, nonetheless, it took a further fateful step. At the end of August officers of the bank committed it to the Rundle Mall Performance Guarantee. This was an agreement between the bank, Myer Stores and REMM that if REMM failed to complete the project then the obligation to do so would be undertaken by the SBSA. 'The importance of this step should be recognised', said MacPherson.

> Its effect was that even though the bank was limited in its obligation to REMM Group to the extent of financing the project up to $500 million, its obligations to Myer Stores Ltd were not limited to that figure, and the terms of the guarantee agreement effectively committed the bank to Myer Stores Ltd in a way which was legally enforceable to provide sufficient finance for the project to be completed, notwithstanding that the cost might exceed $500 million and might well do so to a very substantial extent.[33]

The SBSA was on the hook. The start of the project had already been delayed by some tenants refusing to leave their premises and by neighbouring building owners (notably the Adelaide Club) objecting to some of the construction proposals. Now it had to proceed quickly and there was no other financier in sight. By November the SBSA had already paid $120 million towards construction costs. By February this initial outlay (purportedly the bridging facility) had risen to $170 million and there were still no other lenders to the project. Stage Two never happened in the form proposed and the financing became the bank's largest single nightmare.

Expanding into New Zealand

While the REMM disaster was getting under way the SBSA had also been expanding into New Zealand. In July 1988 the board increased the exposure limit to that country to $1 billion. Again this was despite a number of warning signs. The share market crash of October 1987 had hit the bold riders of New Zealand hard and the economic outlook was gloomy. The SBSA did not bother mentioning this move to Bannon, except to receive his approval for the takeover of Security Pacific NZ. The board paper recommending the cross-Tasman expansion painted a bright picture of growth. Board members should at least have questioned the assumptions involved given that the SBSA's own economist was forecasting a bleak future for New Zealand. The board might have tested another assumption too. Bad debt provisioning for New Zealand was to be set at 0.25 per cent. Jacobs said:

> The picture of a free-wheeling bank, without appropriate control by the board is, by this stage, almost irresistible. This is a picture that the government had not discerned, although it was clearly discernible. It is a picture which at least some members of the board by now recognised. It is a picture consistent with Mr Hartley's increasing concerns and the communication of those concerns to the government.[34]

The board was still ineffectual. It was concerned enough to ask for details of Beneficial Finance, including off–balance sheet exposures. The report, received in July, showed that Beneficial had $1.5 billion on balance sheet and another $500 million off balance sheet, including a $200 million exposure to the Equiticorp group. The board, having prodded this disclosure, took no further action. Jacobs said:

> The board, having perceived an apparently close relationship between management and Treasury, and more specifically between Mr Clark and the Treasurer, had developed a very passive approach to its role. The Treasurer, for his part, had no warrant to assume, as he did assume, that the board was performing its duties with vigour and with firm and cautious commercial judgement and direction, for by now there were ample indications to the contrary and these indications had been building up over the preceding years.[35]

Beneficial was continuing an expansion of its own. In July 1988 it established an insurance company in Singapore to insure only the risks of itself and related companies. In October it bought Campbell Capital Ltd, a Sydney-based merchant bank set up by former staff of Westpac's merchant bank, Partnership Pacific Ltd. Beneficial paid $47 million for Campbell, which had made a $2 million loss in 1987–88, on the grounds that the result would be reversed into a $2 million profit in 1988–89. Profits were forecast to treble in 1990 and 1991. However, not a cent of any profits would flow through to the distributable profits of Beneficial. In March 1989 Campbell bought 75 per cent of Ibis International Ltd, a business information service, for $3 million. A Treasury minute noted that Ibis had made a loss in the December half of 1988, that its accumulated losses were understated through selective asset revaluations, that its staff costs exceeded its revenue and that it was performing worse than others in the industry. Treasury was unhappy about the acquisition, but Prowse eventually recommended it on the grounds that he had to accept Beneficial's commercial judgement.

At the start of 1989 the SBSA hit its first public pothole. In January

Hawkins' Equiticorp group had collapsed with massive losses and the discovery that its accounts had been misleading. Clark had quit the board in the middle of 1988, but the SBSA still had a negative pledge exposure of $49 million. The SBSA immediately laid off $10 million to Beneficial. The bank estimated its likely loss at 20c in the dollar.

Cashmore's lonely crusade

State Liberal MP Jennifer Cashmore had just been appointed economic affairs shadow on the Opposition front bench. In February she received an anonymous phone tip that two out of the three officers of Beneficial who had looked at the Equiticorp deal had recommended against it. On 12 February she asked her first question in the House of Assembly regarding the SBSA. She asked whether the management of the State Bank had overruled the advice of any officer of Beneficial in approving the loan to Equiticorp and whether the bank's board had been informed of the advice. Bannon replied, properly, that he would refer the question to the bank.

Two days later Cashmore persisted, asking how much the SBSA had lent to the Equiticorp group, when it was lent and what loss the bank faced as a result of Equiticorp's collapse. Both her questions had been short, couched as straightforward requests for information about a specific loan. Bannon's response on the 14th was a long tirade. He started with a few political shots at the Liberals' recent front bench reshuffle before conceding that the SBSA, along with twenty or so banks, had an exposure to Equiticorp. He then launched a line of defence that would be used by the SBSA consistently through the next five years: he said that details of the bank's exposure to Equiticorp should be protected by the same commercial confidentiality that all its other clients enjoyed. Bannon also chose to construe Cashmore's brief questions—which were entirely limited to the propriety of the loans to Equiticorp—as an attack on the SBSA. 'It is quite extraordinary that the Opposition wants to attack it', he exclaimed.

Over the next two years Cashmore would make her parliamentary reputation as a tireless campaigner to learn the truth about the bank. She showed great fortitude in following her cause. She faced ridicule from Bannon, his minders and the Labor Party and was accused of trying to destabilise a sound institution. What she was not prepared for was similar pressure from her own side of politics. Chief executives of two of South Australia's biggest companies warned her to desist from questioning the bank's practices. Both their companies had large facilities with the SBSA. Liberal supporters also pressured her to back off. She said later:

The conspiracy of silence in South Australia was caused by several factors. One was that the SBSA was sponsoring a huge range of projects dear to the hearts of many South Australians: the arts, charity, sport, recreation and community events. Voluntary boards of all these organisations contained members of the Adelaide financial and social establishment who would not for worlds have prejudiced the wellbeing and income of those organisations.[36]

Cashmore also suffered the grave handicap of knowing little about banking and finance. She sought opinions from businessmen, accountants and even journalists on whether her questions and criticisms of the bank were soundly based. The first inside tip about Equiticorp was the only one she ever received. From then on, she merely asked questions based on what she read in the financial press about the bank and its failed customers such as Hooker and the Victorian National Safety Council. Her anonymous caller rang another three or four times, telling her that she was on the right track. 'That was a bit unnerving, because I didn't know what track I was on', she said. She never discovered his identity, but believed he was a senior officer of Beneficial.

Cashmore made a speech in April 1989 pointing out that the SA Government, as guarantor, carried the ultimate responsibility for the bank's affairs. This responsibility was not discharged by simply appointing the board: the Treasurer had to satisfy himself that the bank was conducting business soundly. She asked whether the bank's activities should be curtailed, in view of the government guarantee, and whether the bank was properly recognising its bad debts or providing for them. The government riposted with a motion condemning the Opposition for its attacks on the bank.

It would be comforting to think that Cashmore's persistence flushed out the truth about the bank. Unfortunately, it would also be untrue. Although Cashmore and the Liberals had a bitter vindication when the bank collapsed, the Opposition was instrumental neither in its collapse nor in the emergence of the truth. The bank collapsed because it was overexposed and could no longer continue. The truth was hidden from the public for two years after Cashmore's first question.

Four days after Cashmore's April 1989 speech the SBSA's deputy chairman, David Simmons, presided over a special board meeting to consider the bank's lending policies. He was becoming uneasy about the bank's management and systems. Following that meeting the SBSA gave Bannon its comments on Cashmore's speech. Commissioner Jacobs described the comments as 'deliberately evasive, if not in some respects deliberately untrue by omission'. And Clark assured Bannon at their regular meeting that there were no fundamental flaws in the bank's procedures. Jacobs said: 'The bank was now embarking on a process of disinformation by omission, a policy of keeping bad news to itself so far as it could and of offering reassurance in the face of apparently adverse situations'.[37]

In Parliament, Bannon defended Clark and the bank. In doing so he took a big further step down the road of folly. Until this point the SBSA had been a bipartisan venture supported by both sides of SA politics. By defending it Bannon made the bank a political issue. Even more fundamentally, he was defending the bank blindly without conducting his own inquiry into whether it was sound. There had been ample warning signs to give him cause for concern. He could in perfect propriety have fended off Opposition attacks while conducting an inquiry or at least a few informal, expert checks. Instead, still dazzled by Clark, he took a strong pro-bank stand. Because politicians have great difficulty in changing their position on an issue, over the next two years Bannon would become increasingly bound to the SBSA's chariot wheels.

Meanwhile, the SBSA hit a second pothole in March 1989 when the National Safety Council's Victorian division suddenly collapsed following the disappearance of its chief executive, John Friedrich (which wasn't his right name). This time the SBSA exposure was $25.8 million, apparently secured. However, the loan was based on non-existent security, Friedrich's standard asset.[38] In a fine piece of irony the SBSA issued a statement condemning the National Safety Council board for failing to control its chief executive.

Expressions of concern by directors, Treasury and Bannon were dismissed by Clark on the grounds that there was no reason to believe there were similar problems in other parts of the portfolio. This was hardly borne out by a board paper presented in April, analysing group exposures of more than $50 million to corporate borrowers. Out of a total of $4.6 billion 45 per cent was not fully secured. This paper also revealed to the board for the first time the extent of the group's non-accrual loans, at $188 million. These figures should have shown that Clark's reassurances were superficial. The figures were not provided to Treasury or Bannon.

Yet another danger signal came from across the border. In May 1989 the merchant bank Tricontinental Corporation collapsed, forcing its parent—the State Bank of Victoria—into a hasty merger with the Commonwealth Bank. The parallels between Tricontinental and the SBSA were strong, including an aggressive and absolute chief executive and an unsound drive for expansion.

The SBSA would survive another twenty months in public, but in the private world of the financial networks it lost credibility from this point. Around the boardrooms and restaurants of downtown Sydney and Melbourne it was obvious that, if Tricontinental had hit the wall, the SBSA must be in dire trouble. Although the SBSA had big exposures to Equiticorp and the National Safety Council—and was known to have exposures to other corporate cowboys—it was not provisioning adequately. Ergo, there was a strong suspicion that it was not telling the truth. If the SBSA had been a bank with public shareholders the analysts would have turned on the stock from this time and the market would have dumped the shares. As the SBSA was shielded from these forces it was allowed to run its course. There was no run on deposits because they were mostly held by the South Australian public, who were in blissful ignorance, and anyway the bank was guaranteed by the government.

The bank was lurching from bad to worse. Beneficial Finance was becoming increasingly exposed to the East End Market project as other backers withdrew. The group's exposure to New Zealand was growing like wildfire and was planned to reach $12.8 billion by 1993–94, which would by then represent one-third of total assets.

The 1989 accounts

This deteriorating position was being papered over in the accounts. The bank's monthly operating reviews showed non-accrual loans at $225 million in April 1989, rising to $246 million in May, then falling inexplicably to $190 million in June. In fact the bank was understating its level of non-accrual loans at balance date. The 1989 accounts showed yet another year of explosive growth, with assets rising to $15 billion. Pre-tax profit for the group was up to $90.8 million. Again they were underprovisioned for bad debts. The liquidators of Hawkins' failed Equiticorp group had said that the return could be anywhere between 2c and 47c in the dollar. But the SBSA had provided for a loss of only $13.6 million on the $49 million exposure. Even if Equiticorp returned the most optimistic estimate of 47c, the SBSA should have provided another $12.4 million. In addition, the bank had underprovided for its exposures to the National Safety Council and the Australis office block in Grenfell Street, Adelaide. Jacobs estimated that a further $42 million in total should have been provided against such bad debts, which would have slashed profit to around $47 million.[39]

In a letter to Clark, which the board does not seem to have seen, the auditors noted that identified risk loans now totalled $427 million and said that this should have resulted in a higher level of provisioning. They said the prevailing level was the minimum required for audit purposes but urged the bank to take a more conservative approach. The board realised that the 1989 accounts made the bank look better than it was. But the urge to please the government was still strong. Error was now reinforcing error. Jacobs said:

> The bank progressively became less than frank with the government

about its performance. To disappoint the government would be to lose face. There is little doubt that this attitude of the bank was largely directed by Mr Clark, partly because his optimism was not to be diverted or qualified by unpalatable truth, and partly because he knew by reason of his other involvements in state affairs that he had the complete confidence of the Treasurer.[40]

Treasury made its hardest pitch yet for a seat on the board, but was again rejected by Bannon at Clark's urging. This was yet another remarkable act of faith by Bannon, because the SBSA board was becoming increasingly critical of the managing director. Rodney Hartley had been complaining since 1988 about the way Clark ran the board. In 1989 David Simmons told another director, Robert Bakewell, that he thought the board was being 'snowed' on the affairs of Oceanic. Hartley wrote memos complaining about Clark to Bannon; to Lynn Arnold, the Minister for State Development; to Bruce Guerin, head of the Premier's Department; and to Paul Woodland, Bannon's economic advisor. Bannon chose to interpret Hartley's complaint as hyperbole and the result of a personality clash with Clark. When Lew Barrett retired in July 1989 Bannon installed Simmons as chairman, but took no other action on the SBSA board despite mounting evidence that the bank was headed for deep trouble. Jacobs described Bannon as living in an 'eyrie of blissful ignorance'.[41]

Pressure mounted again in state parliament, where the Leader of the Australian Democrats, Ian Gilfillan, asked a series of questions in September 1989 about the SBSA's exposure to REMM, the East End Markets, Equiticorp, Chase and other bad risks. When Gilfillan made a further statement on the subject outside parliament he was sued for defamation by the bank. Not only was the bank refusing to recognise its problems, it was issuing writs to gag anyone who questioned it. It would not be long before Gilfillan was proved perfectly justified in his concern about the bank's performance and management. But as neither he nor his party had substantial funds he was forced to make an out of court settlement. He lost several thousand dollars and was gagged by an undertaking not to speak further about the case. In the light of what was subsequently revealed this was a despicable use of defamation law by the bank.

We should never forget in this chapter that Bannon had a whole state to run, in which the SBSA was only one item (although it would turn out to be the most important). In the latter part of 1989 he was heavily distracted by the looming state election of 25 November. Bannon nearly lost office at that election, holding the mortgage belt seat of Florey by a few hundred votes. He could rule only with the support of two Independent Labor MPs, whom he rewarded by appointing them Speaker and Deputy Speaker. The election result seems to have traumatised Bannon, who hardly appeared in public until the following May. The *Sunday Mail* ran a story headlined: 'Missing: One SA Premier'.[42] During this six-month hiatus he ignored many warning calls about the SBSA.

Bannon's economic advisor, Paul Woodland, recommended in February 1990 that an independent inquiry be held into the SBSA's affairs. Bannon rejected the advice. That such an inquiry was necessary should have been apparent from the bank's own accounts. The half-year profit to December 1989 was stated at $40.7 million, but $48.7 million was paid in dividends of various kinds to the government. In fact the group was paying dividends out of capital, which was apparent from the fact that reserves fell by $8 million. Bannon took the cash and turned a Nelsonian eye to what was happening.

Jacobs castigated the accounts as misleading. The bank had managed to declare a profit of any size only by not bringing to account $35 million of bad debts, including $28 million owed by Equiticorp. The alleged profit also ignored the following bad debts and other shortcomings:

- Exposures in Britain, $4.2 million.
- Linter Group, most optimistic assessment, $6 million.
- Chase and other New Zealand exposures, $12.9 million.
- General provisions, which were under by $1.9 million.
- The SBSA had provided only $5.7 million for its $200 million exposure to Hooker Corporation, which had gone into liquidation in August. The bank's exposure included $91 million lent on the uncompleted Australis building in Grenfell Street.
- There was no provision for loss on the Eden Hotel project of Somerley Pty Ltd, on which the SBSA had an exposure of $55 million. Somerley, a joint venture between John Avram's Interwest group and property developer Alan Gostin, was building a hotel in the Melbourne CBD on the corner of Bourke and Exhibition Streets. Interwest had been put into receivership by Tricontinental in January 1990.
- The cost of financing non-accrual loans, which was said to run at about $1.4 million for each $100 million, was disregarded. As non-accruals now amounted to between $500 million and $700 million, by the bank's own count, the financing cost must have been $7 million to $9.8 million.

Any realistic assessment of these exposures would have changed SBSA's December 1989 profit into a substantial loss. The list of bad debts above does not include the off–balance sheet exposures of Beneficial Finance. On 20 February 1990 the Beneficial board had approved the financier's profit statement for the six months to December. Three days later, on 23 February the board was given a report by Price Waterhouse saying that off–balance sheet losses totalled $12.5 million, enough to wipe out the profit. At least one director said that he would not have approved the profit if he had known of the losses beforehand.

Meanwhile, the REMM syndication had been dragging. The site was plagued with industrial disputes, which by March 1990 were costing $1 million a day. The SBSA, which had said that it could put together a syndicate in eight weeks, had still not completed one. The cash provided by the bank under the so-called bridging facility had now exploded to $290 million and the estimated total cost had jumped to $600 million. The SGIC was released from its $485 million put option, which was just as well considering that it would soon be called upon to honour its $520 million put on 333 Collins Street.

The REMM financing now proposed was a lead syndicate of $360 million, which would have a first mortgage over the project. The SBSA would contribute $70 million to the lead syndicate and had an open-ended commitment to any cost above $360 million. This financing was finally put together in June 1990.

Incredibly, the bank was still expanding. Although the stockbroking industry was in obvious difficulties, and had been since October 1987, the SBSA kept acquiring brokers. In 1988 it had bought the half-share it did not already own in SVB Day Porter, and then in early 1989 it bought Cutten Pentelow to form Day Cutten. The merged firm had 35 per cent of the Adelaide equity market, but Day Porter had been operating at a loss. The rationale of this extension into broking had not been questioned. In April 1990 the SBSA bought the Sydney firm Pring Dean McNall, a subsidiary of the Standard Chartered Bank. Pring Dean was bought for the book value of its net tangible assets. The aide memoire provided by the SBSA to Treasury noted that the firm was 'marginally unprofitable'. It said that the combination of Day Cutten and Pring Dean would mean 'the immediate establishment of a profitable integrated broking platform to capitalise on an upturn in investment activity'. The move was described as countercyclical.

In May the SBSA subsidiary Oceanic Life paid $14 million to acquire Lumley Life Ltd. The justification for this was that the SBSA needed to lift the results of the poorly performing Oceanic Life. This expansion into life insurance was fought fairly hard by Treasury, which pointed out that it would be more logical to sell Oceanic and also that the move would put the SBSA into competition with the SGIC. Bannon once again came down on the side of Clark.

The same month saw the biggest acquisition ever made by the SBSA when it paid $157 million for the United Building Society. This was New Zealand's largest building society, with 84 branches. Some of United's subsidiaries were performing poorly and the price paid by the SBSA could only be justified by a very significant turnaround in the profitability of the core building society and banking businesses. United's problems were solved cosmetically at least by renaming it United Banking Group.

Table 15.1   Growth in SBSA non-accrual loans (figures in $m)

	Group	Corporate	International	BFC	Loans on Credit Watch
April 1989	225.4	88.0	55.3	70.6	
May 1989	246.1	88.0	66.1	76.8	
June 1989	190.4(1.3%)	80.6	46.1	48.5	
September 1989	348.5(2.3%)	147.3(4.0%)	n.a.	116.9	
December 1989	411.6(2.7%)	189.0(5.0%)	n.a.	106.0	1 221(7.9%)
January 1990	663.0	n.a.	n.a.	208.0	
February 1990	n.a.	n.a.	n.a.	n.a.	2 194
March 1990	638.0(3.5%)	257.0(6.9%)	n.a.	229.0	

Note: Figures in brackets show non-accrual loans as a percentage of total assets.

The SBSA had developed congenital blindness to its own problems. These expansions—none of which was financially justifiable even if the bank had been sound—were undertaken at a time when SBSA group non-accrual loans were exploding. Non-accrual loans are those on which payments of interest have not been made for three months or more. They may not be wholly or even partly bad, but it is sound banking practice to make provision for some level of loss on them. In June 1989 group non-accruals were $190.4 million (see Table 15.1) of which nearly $50 million were in Beneficial Finance. The level shot to $348 million for the group in September. There was a sharp deterioration in the group's affairs in early 1990, when group non-accruals leaped by a further 60 per cent in a month and those of Beneficial nearly doubled. Loans on credit watch are at a lower level of concern, but their size and growth between December 1989 and February 1990 were alarming. By May, when the acquisitions of Pring Dean, the United Building Society and Lumley Life were approved, it was known that non-accrual loans would probably reach $1 billion by July 1990.

All Bannon's key advisers on matters relating to the bank had operated for years under the perception that Bannon would back Clark against their criticisms. In these circumstances, advisers don't bother criticising much. Simmons, as the new chairman of the SBSA, was perceived by Bannon as a stronger man than Barrett. Simmons was privately critical of Clark, whom he thought over-optimistic, but had proved to be very diffident about attacking his sometimes fiery managing director in the boardroom. Several directors were now unhappy with Clark, notably Hartley, Searcy and Bakewell. Simmons was aware of this but did not convey their concerns to Bannon at their six-weekly meetings. It was not until July 1990, at a meeting held with Bannon to discuss the bank's probable outcome for the financial year, that Simmons told Bannon in Clark's presence that he thought the managing director was being unrealistically optimistic. Simmons' main concern, however, was that the bank might be unable to meet the dividend requirements of the government. Rather than trying to improve the bank's performance, Simmons focussed on removing the dividend requirement.[43]

As balance date approached, the SBSA resorted to financial engineering to dress up its accounts. The poorly performing assets of Beneficial Finance were to be removed to a partly owned subsidiary named Southstate Corporate Holdings Ltd. Michael Hamilton, managing director of the bank's financial services group, wrote a board paper recommending a more realistic policy. He said that only 56 per cent of Beneficial's assets were producing regular cash income and that it was suffering a massive cash shortfall.

By now the bank was falling apart everywhere. In July two hasty board meetings were convened (two, because the first did not raise a quorum) to inject $105 million into Oceanic Property Growth Trust. This was to plug a hole left by another financier withdrawing loans to the trust and to provide cash for those unitholders who were redeeming. The alternative would have been the collapse of the trust.

The 1990 accounts

The SBSA group accounts for the year to June 1990 stated a profit of $24 million. This was only reached, however, after claiming a $30 million writeback of depreciation. In operating terms the bank had made a loss, even on its own figures.

The true situation was much worse. The SBSA was not recognising bad debts. The biggest of these was the REMM project. By using increasingly artificial valuation assumptions the bank was able to pretend that the value of this project was more than the $600 million it would cost to complete. Commissioner Jacobs two years later reckoned that the bank could well have provided for a loss of $100 million. Another problem area was the Australis project. The joint venture partner, Hooker, was now in receivership with an estimated best case recovery of 56.7c in the dollar. Blanche Pty Ltd, a Hooker subsidiary, was unable to complete the Australis Centre. The estimated cost to complete the centre was $105 million, but its value at the finish could be anything from $65 million to $89 million. Given that Hooker could not make up the shortfall, the loss to the SBSA group was anywhere up to $32 million.

Beneficial Finance was a disaster area. Four days before balance date the bank board had been told that Beneficial was in dire straits because of huge exposures. Off–balance sheet assets were nearly $1 billion, some in companies the directors had never heard of, and they were making losses. Recognised non-accrual loans of Beneficial totalled $200 million. The biggest single disaster was Pegasus Leasing because the bottom had dropped out of the bloodstock market. The group's exposure to Pegasus had mushroomed from $400 000 in January 1988 to $100 million. Pegasus had carefully structured its lendings so that the only security for its advances was the horses. Customers were beginning to default in late 1990. By the start of 1991 the price of yearlings would be 40 per cent below their peak and mares would be down by as much as 90 per cent. In what was really only two years of operation, starting almost from scratch, Pegasus lost about $50 million or half the money invested in it.

The Eden Hotel on the corner of Bourke and Exhibition Streets in Melbourne was another in trouble. The joint venturer there was the Interwest group, which had collapsed in January 1990. Beneficial had a $22.5 million exposure to the $350 million project which it was developing in conjunction with the Interwest subsidiary, Somerley. The site had been bought and a large hole dug when Interwest collapsed. Worse, Beneficial did not even hold a first mortgage. The bank board approved a loan of $45.9 million in March 1990 for Beneficial to take out the first mortgage syndicate's debt and to complete the development. Ultimately, the SBSA group exposure to this development would rise to more than $100 million. No provision was made against this in the 1990 accounts, although a worst case loss of $24.2 million was already being postulated. The board appointed Price Waterhouse to carry out an urgent inquiry into Beneficial.[44]

The State Bank Centre had become a symbol of the bank's wastefulness and unreality. It towered above every other building in the city, visible for miles around. In the years ahead it would stand like a beacon as a reminder of the bank's follies. In the luxurious suites at the top it housed a treasure trove of paintings and fine wine. In eight years the bank spent nearly three quarters of a million dollars buying artworks, some of which were hung in branch and overseas offices. Another $350 000 was spent on wines which were locked in the cellar. The bottom line on the building would depend on values when the 'compensatory payment' was due in 1996, but by mid-1991 it looked like being a loss of around $60 million.[45]

One more problem that the board does not seem to have realised at this time was that black holes had developed in London and New York. These two centres by then accounted for $1.6 billion of the SBSA's assets, of which $400 million would be lost. These losses were never properly explained but much of the London loss was on property lending, which accounted for 40 per cent of the portfolio there.

The SBSA by this time was in diabolical trouble. This was recognised by at least two of the bank's senior officers: the managing director of the financial services group, Michael Hamilton, and the chief manager of group planning, Ian Kowalick. Both were painting a pessimistic picture to Treasury. Kowalick said that the level of non-accrual loans was not being reliably reported (an alarming statement given that the bank was already reporting it at around a billion dollars) and that Beneficial's off-balance sheet exposures were more extensive and worrying than even the financier's board knew.

Almost nobody believed the alleged profit which the bank claimed to have made in 1989–90. The Reserve Bank didn't believe it. At a meeting in late July 1990 Reserve Bank officers expressed concern to Hamilton on a range of issues. One was the perception by the nationally operating banks that the SBSA's published results were 'simply not believable' and that the bank clearly had a credibility problem. The Reserve Bank was also concerned about the bank's management, the rapid asset growth, Beneficial, the status of Oceanic Property Growth Trust, and the bank's exposure to the London and New Zealand property markets. Hamilton reported these concerns to Clark, but Clark never passed them on to either Bannon or the board. MacPherson observed: 'Mr Clark was, with respect to some of the bank's operations, as much concerned to limit effective Reserve Bank supervision as he was to promote it.' By this time it did not matter, because the bank was plainly doomed.

A rushed Price Waterhouse report on Beneficial was given to the bank on 30 July. It showed that, by Beneficial's own count, it had $847 million in underperforming assets which were generating insufficient cash to cover the cost of funding—or were generating no cash at all. Price Waterhouse believed that another $282 million should be added to the figure.

Simultaneously, the bank received a report from its own internal auditors on Beneficial. This report referred to some 100 entities which were not included in Beneficial's consolidated or aggregate accounts and about which little was known. The internal auditors said that Beneficial's management did not understand their own enterprise and were unable to identify divisional profitability or to accurately match assets to liabilities.

A third report on Beneficial was presented to the financier's own board by the executive director (asset management), John Malouf. This report analysed 55 clients accounting for $479 million of Beneficial's receivables. Of that group, $338 million were accounts where the committed interest obligation was not being met. Beneficial's managing director, John Baker, and the chief general manager (group management services), Eric Reichert, were abruptly sacked in early August.

In this crisis, the SBSA board was more concerned with damage control than with identifying the problems. At its meeting on 8 August the board considered the possible reaction to the release of its 1990 results. It even went to the length of providing some answers for Bannon if he were asked awkward questions. The board proposed that Bannon should say:

1. He would not seek an independent inquiry into the bank's affairs.
2. He had continuing full confidence in the board, Clark and the management.
3. The government guaranteed any liabilities of the bank.
4. The bank expected to return to a better profit position in 1990–91.
5. Both the bank and Beneficial Finance had provided fully for current exposures.

The last of these statements was wrong. The first two would have covered up the bank's incompetence and mismanagement. The third was a statement of inescapable fact. The fourth was, at best, completely unjustifiable optimism. By raising these matters the board plainly foresaw that the guarantee would be called and that there would be calls for an inquiry.

The next few months of 1990 saw a rising level of largely futile concern about the bank's affairs. Hartley tried without success to get messages to Bannon expressing his fears for the bank. Simmons and Bakewell told Bannon in October that the level of non-accrual loans had reached $1 billion and that New York and London had become trouble centres for the bank. Bannon's odd response was to take comfort in the fact that Simmons had gone overseas to check the situation personally. Bannon perceived Simmons as a 'hands on' chairman. Although both directors expressed their concerns about Clark to Bannon, nothing was done about him. Indeed, as the directors had given Clark a rise of $50 000 the previous February the board was sending very mixed signals to Bannon. The only positive steps were by Treasury, which began cashing up in anticipation of a bail-out.

Incredibly, the SBSA was *still* expanding. Its September operating review that showed that total assets had grown by 11 per cent since June to $22.3 billion. Some of these assets might more properly have been described as liabilities. A review of the United Building Society purchase, for example, had shown that the due diligence process before acquisition had been hopelessly inadequate. United needed a $130 million capital injection from SBSA almost as soon as it was taken over. The bank for months tried to hide or minimise details of its losses, even when supplying data to Bannon for answers to questions in parliament.

The bank was beginning to reorganise, but the changes were largely cosmetic. About 100 staff were axed after July and half a dozen senior executives lost their jobs at the end of November. Whether or not these moves were necessary, they utterly failed to address the bank's core problems and it must by now have been too late to avert disaster anyway. The growing and insistent criticisms from the Opposition and media were beginning to wear a little on the normally confident Clark. He spoke to Simmons about his position and Simmons said: 'When the time comes for you to go, I'll tell you to fuck off'. In context, this was a reassuring statement. But at the end Simmons and the board left the job to Bannon.

When Bannon returned in late October from an overseas trip he was told by the bank that its result for 1990–91 would be about break-even. A fortnight later the bank began talking about a $30 million to $50 million loss for the year. Treasury officials told Bannon that they were concerned at the rapid growth of the bank's non-accrual loans.

As late as December 1990 Bannon clung to the illusion that the bank's problems were manageable. The Liberal Party had been continuing to query the bank's soundness and its dealings, particularly since the collapse of Tricontinental and the State Bank of Victoria. Clark counter-attacked in a letter to Opposition Leader Dale Baker, saying the Opposition's continual questioning of the bank's management practices had caused a small run on the bank in December. 'We emphasised [in a briefing] that South Australia was totally different to Victoria and that SBSA was totally different to the SBV', wrote Clark. 'We understand that politicians often live only for the moment or until the next election, but the State Bank has a much longer-term objective of helping the economic growth and social fabric of South Australia.'

The letter completely failed to address the problem being exposed by the Liberals, which was the unknown exposures of the SBSA's off–balance sheet companies. In 1989 four off–balance sheet structures were admitted to by the bank. Now it was admitting to 58. Ultimately there would turn out to be more than 100. The bank at first said that the entities had a surplus of $83 million of assets over liabilities. A few days later the bank was forced to admit an error, saying the true position was a deficit of $31 million. The auditors—from Peat Marwick Hungerfords and Touche Ross—had noted in the 1990 accounts that they had not acted as auditors for Beneficial Finance or for a number of key subsidiaries including the Southstate group, United Banking and Ibis. Several of the off-balance sheet companies had been set up through David Simmons' law firm, Thomson Simmons & Co.[46]

One of the off–balance sheet entities was Pegasus, which had become the biggest thoroughbred financier in Australia at a time when the bottom dropped out of the bloodstock market. The joint owner, Alastair McGregor, was found dead in mid-December, apparently from suicide.

In parliament on 13 December a Liberal backbencher asked whether the bank and Tim Marcus Clark still retained Bannon's 'full and unqualified support'. Bannon replied: 'The answer to that is "Yes". I have no reason to lack confidence in those who are handling the bank's affairs'. Bannon had nailed himself to the cross once more. Amazingly, a week after giving that highly injudicious answer to parliament, Bannon went to an SBSA board meeting and urged the directors to work with Clark to solve the bank's problems. He still did not appear to have fully realised that the bank's problems were insoluble and that the writing was on the wall for Clark. By this time, however, the SBSA board had agreed that an external consultant should be appointed.

Clark's resignation

In January 1991 the board called in the US investment bank, J.P. Morgan, as an advisor. After a survey lasting only eight days Morgan's Joe Sabatini estimated that only $1.5 billion to $2 billion would be recovered from non-accrual loans totalling $2.5 billion. The board and Bannon received Morgan's report at the end of January and spent the next few days working out details of a bail-out. There was no alternative but to announce this ghastly news to the public. And Bannon was confronted with another hateful and humiliating task: Clark would have to go. Bannon called Clark into his office and told him that the directors of the SBSA believed he should resign. In his statement to the Jacobs Royal Commission Clark said: 'I asked Mr Bannon twice whether he was asking for my resignation. He replied that was not his function; he said it was between me and the board. I then asked the Premier: "John, will this help you politically if I resign?". He replied, "Yes" '.

On Sunday 10 February 1991 the SBSA announced that it had lost a billion dollars. Bannon said that the SA Government had indemnified any losses suffered by the SBSA. The Financing Authority (SAFA) would stand behind the bank with $970 million in concessional housing loans, of which $500 million had already been injected. This was the first of three bail-outs which would ultimately total more than $3 billion. Clark resigned, taking with him $830 000 in superannuation (representing his own contributions plus interest) and claiming that he had been 'set up as a scapegoat'. Part of his future was occupied giving evidence in the New Zealand case against former Equiticorp directors. Clark was given partial immunity from prosecution. His protégé Hawkins was finally sentenced to six years' jail for fraud. Three other former Equiticorp executives also received jail sentences. Hawkins was later charged by the Australian Securities Commission for alleged breaches of the Companies Code in connection with a $7.6 million option purchase scheme.

The bank was busted. Its position is shown in Table 15.2. The SBSA group accounts for 1991 showed doubtful debt provisions totalling $1733

Table 15.2   SBSA group accounts, June 1991 (all figures in $m)

PROFIT AND LOSS ACCOUNT	
Operating profit	43
Less abnormals:	
Doubtful debt provisions	(1 733)
Income tax	(132)
Other	(373)
SA Govt indemnity	2 200
Profit after abnormals	5
BALANCE SHEET	
Total assets	21 620
Total liabilities	(20 242)
Shareholders' funds	1 378

million and further abnormal losses totalling another $373 million. On top of that it had somehow managed to incur a $132 million tax bill. This would have wiped out the group's entire shareholders' funds if it had not been for the injection of $2.2 billion from the SA Government. If the injection had not been made it would have had a deficiency of some $900 million.

Of that $2.2 billion, nearly $1 billion was lost in Beneficial. Another $350 million had to be injected into the SGIC, mainly because of its put option over 333 Collins Street.

And that was not all. A year later, in August 1992, the SA Government announced that the SBSA would be divided into a 'good' and 'bad' bank, which would receive injections of $450 million and $400 million respectively. The good bank carried on under Nobby Clark, former chief executive of the National Australia Bank, as the SBSA. The bad bank comprised all the bad and doubtul assets that had to be managed. Adding the $850 million of August 1992 to the previous figures gives a total loss for the SBSA of $3.15 billion. This was even higher than the loss recorded by Tricontinental/State Bank of Victoria in a state with nearly three times the population base. Proportionately, the SBSA's was the biggest financial loss of the era. Non-accrual loans at June 1991 totalled $4.2 billion, although $2.3 billion of them were still paying some interest.

The main areas of loss have been identified in this chapter. In several cases the amounts were large but vague because they were represented by buildings which were still unsaleable in a depressed Adelaide in the early 1990s. The size of the losses also depended on whether interest and opportunity cost were taken into account. In August 1993 Colliers Jardine valued the Myer Centre at a mere $190 million, but the further $100 million loss represented by this figure was hypothetical as there was no intention of selling at that price. There were huge losses on the State Bank Centre, the Eden Hotel, the Australis building, United Building Society, Oceanic and the overseas offices.

Simmons blamed the bank's losses on the recession-induced fall in property values. 'Additionally, other management problems have become evident', he said.

> The handling of some of the group's acquisitions was not of an acceptable standard. There were in some cases shortcomings in the due diligence processes, which failed to identify faults in the acquired companies with the result that management was too slow to take effective control . . . The weaknesses that have now been exposed did not develop recently. They are a legacy of the group's entry into wholesale lending markets at a time of continually rising asset prices in the second half of the 1980s. The risk profile of the group was, in hindsight, unwise, but this was disguised by the benign economic conditions of the day. It is apparent that the board's ability to oversee the effect of management decisions has been clouded from time to time by information which, with hindsight can now been seen, was inaccurate and/or deficient.[47]

We need not quibble with Simmons' diagnosis. It is a tacit admission, however, that the board totally failed in its job of overseeing management.

The SBSA board resigned, to be replaced by a new board chaired by Nobby Clark (no relation to Timothy Marcus Clark). Nobby Clark stabilised the SBSA over the next couple of years. Ted Johnson became group managing director. Bad loans were corralled into the Group Asset Management Division (GAMD). Bannon resigned as Premier in September 1992, to be succeeded by Lynn Arnold. The 'good' bank was relaunched as Bank of South Australia Ltd, or BankSA.

The SA Government took the unusual step of appointing two inquiries into the downfall of the SBSA. In February 1991 the Auditor-General, Ken MacPherson, was appointed to find out what went wrong at the bank and why. Simultaneously, Premier Bannon announced the appointment of Samuel Jacobs, QC (formerly Mr Justice Jacobs) as a Royal Commissioner. MacPherson was to inquire into how the losses were caused. Jacobs was to inquire into the relationship and communication between the bank, the government and the board. The MacPherson inquiry was held in camera and the Jacobs inquiry was held almost entirely in public. Jacobs' first interim report was published in November 1992, which was later than scheduled but not too late considering the amount of material to be traversed.

Jacobs was heavily critical of Bannon's laxity. The report is rich in verbal shafts at Bannon; perhaps the most succinct is Jacobs saying:

> One is forced to conclude that the Treasurer was in general willing to listen to what the bank chose to tell him, or to consult with the bank at its request, but that otherwise he saw no need to know or to be consulted. There were only a few topics (such as changes to home loan interest rates) which he claimed the right to know.[48]

To a lesser extent, Jacobs also criticised directors, SA Treasury and the Reserve Bank. His criticism of Marcus Clark was relatively muted because that fell more within MacPherson's inquiry.

When attributing blame for the failure of the SBSA it must be remembered that Clark was the prime mover. He had been given the keys of the bank. It was he and his officers who made the deals, who set the expansionary pace, who shovelled money recklessly to the wheeler-dealers of the day, and who hid the truth of what they were doing by creating 100 or more off–balance sheet entities. Nobody demanded that the SBSA expand so quickly. It expanded beyond even its own ambitious strategic plan. Between 1984 and 1990 the SBSA's stated assets grew from $2.7 billion to $17.3 billion, while group assets soared from $3.1 billion to $21.1 billion. From an essentially South Australian institution it expanded so that two-thirds of its assets were located interstate and overseas. Corporate loans mushroomed to represent about 38 per cent of lending assets. The bank's funding changed as well. Wholesale funds increased from 15 per cent of total funds in 1984 to 82 per cent by 1990. This included startling growth overseas, where interest-bearing deposits totalled $2.2 billion.[49]

The Auditor-General's report was considerably delayed by litigation from directors who claimed that they were being denied natural justice and (these were the people who had presided over the loss of $3 billion) that their reputation might be harmed by his remarks. When presented to the state parliament in March 1993 MacPherson's report was critical of almost everybody involved in the bank's affairs.

> My examination of the bank's corporate lending has shown that it was poorly organised, badly managed and badly executed. Credit risk evaluation was shoddy. Corporate lending policies and procedures were not even compended into a credit policy manual until 1988, and even then contained serious omissions. The ultimate loan approval authority—the board of directors—lacked the necessary skills and experience to perform its function adequately. Senior management's emphasis was on doing the deal, and doing it quickly. The growth in loan portfolio is explained in part by the profit imperative. While the bank's budgeted asset growth was exceeded in every year, its budgeted profit was not. The bank's lending practices included taking a significant portion of its income in the form of up-front fees, part of which represented, in substance, interest on the loan. For a significant period, these up-front fees were shown as income in the year they were received. This meant the easiest way to increase profits was simply to make more loans . . . The organisational structure of the bank meant there were no internal checks or controls on the growth . . . Those departments of the bank which should have acted as internal regulators were isolated and without authority . . .
>
> Throughout this, the bank's board of directors was, for the most

part, ineffective. I have some sympathy for the bank's non-executive directors. They lacked both banking experience and, in most cases, hard-headed business acumen. They were manipulated, and not properly informed of what was going on. The information given to them was voluminous, but obscure. It took an expert and practised eye to sort the wheat from the chaff and to know what information was not there. The board lacked that. But whatever sympathy one may have for its predicament, the board of directors was the governing body of the bank, charged with responsibility to administer the bank's affairs and to control the chief executive in his performance of his management function. A reasonably prudent board—whatever its skills—would have done much more than the bank's board did. It was not beyond the capabilities of the non-executive directors to take commonsense measures and to stand no nonsense.

To be blunt, there is nothing esoteric about asking questions, seeking information, demanding explanations and extracting further details. There is nothing unduly burdensome in expecting each director, to the best of his or her ability, to insist on understanding what was laid before them, even at the risk of becoming unpopular. Both the law, and a basic sense of duty and responsibility, demand it. The non-executive directors submitted to me that they did these things. Sometimes they did. But not often enough, and not strongly enough. I have repeatedly found that the board of directors failed to adequately or properly supervise, direct and control the operations, affairs and transactions of the bank.

The Auditor-General found that Marcus Clark bore a heavy share of the blame for the bank's losses. 'He seemed oblivious to the risks he was running and ignored words of caution', said MacPherson.

Again and again, the evidence shows Mr Clark to have been impatient with opposition and easily affronted. His personality and position were such that his banking philosophy and strategies, and his attitude to particular transactions being processed by the bank, would have been known to all. It would have been a courageous member of the staff who expressed views in a manner likely to come into conflict with the wishes of such a formidable superior. There would in my opinion have permeated through the bank the aura of a domineering leader who exerted a strong influence on senior staff members.

On the senior staff, MacPherson found:

As a group, the bank's senior managers were not up to the job. Worse, they acquiesced in and abetted without any adequate expression of professional judgement, the course set for the bank. If the managers had any conception of what was required to safely manage the bank, they did not display it. Instead, they displayed a cavalier approach to the board, to the Reserve Bank and to the principles of sound business management that speaks ill of their professionalism and judgement, let alone their banking skills.[50]

In a later report MacPherson was equally caustic about Beneficial Finance, whose defects were much the same as those of the bank. He said that the old core business of Beneficial had continued to be generally well managed, but that the structured finance and projects division—created to chase new business opportunities—had operated 'beyond the pale of any reasonable principles of proper financial management'. He continued:

> It paid no attention to the basic principles of credit risk management, blithely assumed the continual availability of unlimited funding regardless of the term of its exposures or their cash flows and assumed that commercial property development was eternally and unerringly profitable. The division was run by irresponsible managers who speculated wildly in commercial property, driven by little more than thought for the next sale.

The Auditor-General also pointed out that senior executives of Beneficial were comparatively overcompensated. Managing director John Baker's total remuneration package had stood at nearly $525 000, more than double the packages for the then heads of the Commonwealth Bank and the State Banks of New South Wales and Victoria. Executives' fringe benefits had included a Gold Coast apartment equipped with a baby grand piano, the ability to take part of their remuneration in 'shadow' salary, and a range of loans. Beneficial had also developed 'paper meetings' as an alternative to board meetings. Minutes were produced of meetings that were never held.[51]

The SBSA's charter, enshrined in legislation, was 'to promote the balanced development of the state's economy to the maximum advantage of the people of South Australia'. If the SBSA were to be of any advantage to the people of South Australia the first, implicit, requirement was that it should not go broke. Yet a perfectly sound bank was driven headlong down the road to ruin from day one, with Clark at the steering wheel. The bank could serve South Australia in two ways: by supporting South Australian enterprises or by making profits outside the state. It was certainly necessary to have some presence outside the state to improve the bank's growth prospects and to offset too heavy a reliance on one economically small and resource-poor region. However, investing in loss-making ventures outside the state was entirely antithetical to the charter.

In tennis, a player who never double-faults is not trying hard enough with his second serve. Similarly, a banker who never makes a loss is being too cautious in his approach to business. So occasional losses must be expected in banking. But the SBSA's crazy spending spree almost guaranteed that it would make them. Its two biggest purchases—the United Building Society and Oceanic—were of entities outside the state. In both cases the due diligence process must have been inadequate because both

517

needed large and urgent injections of cash as soon as they were taken over.

On all evidence Clark was happy to provide data to Treasury and to brief Bannon regularly, but resented intervention from anyone who might have effectively gainsaid him. At no stage during his reign at the bank did Treasury gain a seat on the board. Several of the directors regarded him as manipulating the board and believed they had little or no effective control over him. He also partially emasculated the Reserve Bank's monitoring role. Between 1987 and 1988 he chose not to take part in annual prudential consultations and other meetings with Reserve Bank officers. When the bank was formed in 1985 the Reserve Bank sought to have regular and direct communication with the bank's auditors, but this wish was rebuffed by Clark until 1988–89. Several strictures of the Reserve Bank, particularly on the exposure to Equiticorp, were never notified to the board or to Bannon. They never saw any more of the bank than Clark wanted them to see.

The reports by Jacobs and MacPherson did not lead to any criminal action. A civil action was launched by the Bank of South Australia on 30 March 1994—the day before the statute of limitations would have expired—against Marcus Clark and seven other former directors of the bank: Lew Barrett, David Simmons, Bob Bakewell, Molly Byrne, William Nankivell, Robert Searcy and Tony Summers. FAI was joined in the action as the insurer of the former directors. The SA Attorney-General, Trevor Griffin, said the proceedings had been issued to protect the bank's position. Clark and the other directors were being sued in connection with the purchase of Oceanic Capital. At the time of writing, Clark and the directors were defending the action. The bank also launched a claim against its former auditors, KPMG Peat Marwick.

The Reserve Bank, the SBSA board and the SA Treasury all deserve some share of blame for their half-hearted and ineffectual attempts to rein in the runaway bank. However, they would have needed to be much more forceful to overcome the effect of Bannon's support for Clark.

In later correspondence with the author, Bannon sought to defend his role in the SBSA affair. He said he had defended the bank in parliament on the basis of information provided by the bank. 'In most cases it can be seen that the Opposition was fishing', he said.

> They just happened to be more right than wrong in this case. The inevitable consequence of these things being raised in such a political environment, where anything could be said without legal consequence and concern about the damage it might do to the institution, meant that I was not in a position to do much else. The only enquiry I could have held against the objections of Treasury or Bank Board would have been using Section 25 of the Act to get the Governor to appoint the Auditor-General or some other person to investigate the bank.

Bannon said that the Act had been deliberately drafted to ensure that the Treasurer of the day would keep his hands off the bank. He went on to say:

> Not only were the board's attempts to discipline the chief executive feeble but their advice to me was both feeble and totally equivocal. How on the one hand you can be concerned about the activities of your chief executive while on the other awarding him a pay increase and bonus and expressing great satisfaction in being able to extend his contract I don't know.[52]

On the equivocation of the board Bannon has a fair point. However, his other arguments are questionable. Oppositions are always fishing in some sense, but Jenny Cashmore's questions and speeches in 1989 were far more right than wrong. She had unearthed a genuine problem of the first importance, which deserved to be dealt with immediately and energetically by the government. Bannon's view of his limitations in such circumstances is deeply disturbing. He was saying, in effect, that if the Opposition discovered maladministration in the bank he had no power of inquiry short of a Section 25 investigation. That premise would never have been accepted by Premiers such as Sir Thomas Playford or Don Dunstan. Bannon could quite properly have appointed any expert he chose to inquire into specific allegations against the bank and it could have been done quickly and informally. The board would not have resisted and Clark would have been hard put to find good arguments. One is forced to conclude that Clark—who throughout refused to have a Treasury representative on the board—was a stronger personality than Bannon and that Bannon sought to avoid a confrontation. That would never have stopped Playford or Dunstan.

We should also remember that Bannon totally lacked business experience. After his schooling at the upper-class St Peter's College his career continued through university, trade unions and politics. He never ran a business or even worked in private enterprise. As a St Peter's schoolboy from a relatively poor family, Bannon was surrounded by boys from wealthy establishment families and may have credited them with some innate business ability which he lacked. One reporter said: 'Marcus Clark comes from an old, established, wealthy family that has been in business for the past 100 years. Bannon would not presume to question whatever Marcus Clark did; he would just automatically assume that he knew what he was doing'.[53]

For whatever reason, Bannon made himself a hostage to Clark. When Clark was under attack in early 1989, for example, for having an alleged conflict of interest over Equiticorp, Bannon said: 'I would like to put on record that in Marcus Clark we have one of the most active, efficient, aggressive and entrepreneurial bankers in this country and it is to South

Australia's benefit'. Bannon had been given plenty of warning signals about Clark and the SBSA but ignored them all, and Clark was unassailable as long as he had the Premier's support.

In the same year, 1989, a quick tough decision had to be taken by Bannon on the future of a development known as Marineland. He was reluctant to act and the result cost the state millions. After that, Bannon's hesitancy to act ruthlessly was dubbed by unkind critics as the 'dolphin syndrome'. No dolphin ever cost as much as the State Bank of South Australia.

16
A few quick ones

*The skill in dealing with a customer you might think is unfairly critical
of your performance or your company's product is to give them the
attention they deserve and acknowledge their point of view, and if there
is any legitimacy in their complaint you fix it.*

Bob Ansett

This book is primarily about the large corporate collapses of the 1980s.
However, some of the worst disasters for investors occurred in smaller
companies that collapsed very quickly. It is always disturbing to see a
company hit the wall after only a few years' trading. When a company
cannot even last a year from its formation or from being taken over by
new management, the picture can be very disturbing indeed. It can raise
questions about the adequacy of information given to the public at the
time of the company's formation or takeover. The 1980s were remarkable
for the number of spectacular crashes that occurred among companies
that were fledglings or only recently taken over, often with deeply
respectable backgrounds. The losses in these cases were mostly taken by
equity investors and small creditors. Such crashes occurred despite a
continual tightening of prospectus law during the 1980s. As the Compass
I and II airlines showed, such collapses were still continuing into the
1990s.

Bishopsgate

At the end of 1982 an arrogant young Greek with a thrusting, aggressive
manner walked into the Sydney offices of P & O Australia. He gave his
name as Andrew Stathis and offered to buy Bishopsgate Insurance. The
offer was attractive. Bishopsgate was a respected general insurer which
had been operating in Australia since 1965 under the aegis of the
renowned P & O shipping line. When P & O Australia was floated publicly by its British parent, Bishopsgate had become part of the Australian

521

company. P & O Australia was only too happy to sell Bishopsgate. Like many insurance companies, Bishopsgate tended to make underwriting losses and rely on investment gains to offset them. In 1981 its net loss had been $761 000, but in 1982 it had returned to a profit of $926 000. P & O had been trying to sell it for eighteen months.

Stathis told P & O that the buyer of Bishopsgate would be the commodity broker Richardson Mann, in which he held a 25 per cent interest. P & O had previously been blocked by the Foreign Investment Review Board from selling Bishopsgate to the respected UK insurer C.E. Heath, so the company welcomed an Australian buyer. The price negotiated with Stathis was $4.75 million. He paid $1 million down with the balance on terms. The ANZ Bank had given a total and unconditional guarantee for the outstanding amount. Further, Stathis was represented by the top law firm of Freehill Hollingdale & Page. P & O did not know Stathis, but the money was guaranteed and his representatives were respectable enough. P & O Australia's board agreed to the deal and contracts were exchanged on 21 January 1983.[1] The statement to the stock exchange—agreed by P & O and Stathis—said that the issued capital of Bishopsgate had been sold to Richardson Mann Corporation and interests associated with that company.

Oddly, Richardson Mann did not point out that this was an error. Bishopsgate had really been bought by Stathis. After the purchase Stathis held 1.5 million shares in Bishopsgate and a friend, Dr Enn Vilo, held 750 000. Another 500 000 were held by Shoal Investments of Hong Kong. Of Stathis' holding, 550 000 were held through a nominee company of Richardson Mann. The Estonian-born Vilo lived in Vaucluse and had a medical clinic in nearby Woollahra. The board of Bishopsgate became Kenneth Doyle (chairman), Stathis, Vilo and a Richardson Mann broker, Campbell Gorrie. Stathis and Vilo were executive directors, the other two non-executive. Doyle was a respected insurance figure, being managing director of Sten Re, the reinsurance subsidiary of Reed Stenhouse of Britain.

Bishopsgate's balance sheet at December 1982 showed total assets of $41 million. Liabilities totalled $34 million, leaving $6.6 million in stated net assets. The main assets were investments of $17.8 million and trade debtors of $16.6 million. Over the next seven months Stathis simply cashed in every liquid asset he could lay his hands on and stole the money. At the end of the day he fled Australia, having looted Bishopsgate of almost $19 million.

The ANZ may not have been so anxious to guarantee Stathis if they had known more of his lifestyle. He lived in luxurious home units around fashionable Point Piper and Toft Monks in Elizabeth Bay, but rarely rented one for more than two or three months before moving to the next. One of his landladies described him as 'a very nice chap'. This opinion was not universally shared. The 31-year-old Stathis was small, swarthy and a flashy dresser. He wore large rings, smoked fat cigars and drove a red Jaguar XJS. 'A whiz kid, hundred miles an hour and flashy', one associate said. Stathis could be cordial but could also display a thrusting, unpleasant manner and could burst into sudden rages. Louise Waterhouse, a member of one of Australia's biggest bookmaking families, said: 'He was arrogant and very demanding. If we didn't pay up to the second he'd throw a tantrum'. Stathis was a big punter at the racetrack, where he dealt only with half a dozen of the top rails bookmakers, who knew him as Andy the Greek. Later it would become apparent that the size of his wagers had risen greatly about a year before taking over Bishopsgate. For six months he was the biggest punter on the Sydney tracks. On Friday nights he used to play in a high-stakes poker game.

At about the same time that he became a big punter Stathis had also splashed into the property market. He bought property in Double Bay and Macquarie Place and was negotiating for a five-storey retail and office block on the corner of Pitt and Park Streets. Stathis struck acquaintances as boastful. 'He professed to be a whiz kid on the property scene', one bookmaker said. Another said that he also purported to be an expert on commodities. 'He was always talking about gold. He was a switched-on sort of bloke—running fast.'[2]

As a privately owned insurance company Bishopsgate had to make a quarterly report on its affairs to the Insurance Commissioner. Some big companies became dissatisfied with the service they were getting from Bishopsgate for their workers' compensation and other business, and began switching out. Those who got out included Ampol Petroleum, Sanitarium, Philips Industries and Comalco. Bishopsgate appeared to be running down its business. Its rates were uncompetitive and anyway the companies did not like Bishopsgate's new owner.[3] The commissioner became suspicious in July and began investigating reports that there was a deficiency in Bishopsgate. Stathis was holding the company's investment records in Sydney. On Thursday 4 August an inspector of the Insurance Commission named Chris Adams phoned Bishopsgate's general manager, Michael McKenna, and asked if the records had been returned to head office in Melbourne. McKenna said that Stathis still had them. Adams said he wanted to inspect the records in Melbourne the next day. McKenna phoned Stathis, who said he would be in Melbourne on the following day.

But when Adams arrived at the Bishopsgate office on Friday 5 August Stathis was not there. A young woman phoned to say that he was tied up in a Sydney court case. Adams and McKenna tried to contact Stathis in Sydney, but without success. The Insurance Commission, disturbed, issued a directive that Bishopsgate should not sell, deal or remove from Australia any assets for fourteen days. But the bird had already flown. On Thursday, before the woman had phoned, Stathis had left Australia on a Japan Airlines flight for Paris via Tokyo.

On Tuesday the 9th, Warwick Leeming of Duesbury was appointed provisional liquidator. Richardson Mann put out a statement saying that it had held Bishopsgate shares only as a nominee for Stathis. Richardson Mann itself had no investment in Bishopsgate and none of its clients' money had been lost.

Investigators tracing through Bishopsgate quickly found that Stathis had looted the company for nearly $19 million. No savings bonds could be found. Only $500 000 was left in a bank fixed deposit that Stathis had apparently been unable to convert. Other disturbing facts began coming to light. He was now identified as Andrew Stathopolous, on bail pending trial for conspiring with four others to grow an estimated $60 million worth of Indian hemp at Cowra in 1979. He had still been on bail of $20 000 when he caught the JAL flight to Tokyo. He had been bankrupted in March 1981 and the bankruptcy had been annulled the following August. But details could not be ascertained because the file on both the bankruptcy and the annulment were missing from the Villawood registry in Sydney.

Slowly, police began piecing his background together. He had been born Andreas Stathopolous in Greece in 1952 and had come to Australia with his family at the age of two. His father and mother were respected as hard-working immigrants who made considerable sacrifices to help their children. He had grown up in Blayney, where he sometimes helped out in his family's cafe. His family put him through the exclusive Cranbrook school in Sydney, where he was a prefect and chairman of the Explorers' and Adventurers' Club. When the family moved to run another cafe in Cowra Stathis had attended Cowra High School before going on to study law.

A cousin of Stathis later said that there had been a marked change when he returned to Cowra with his law degree. 'He went his own way', the cousin said. 'His father had worked so hard for him and the other children. He was a very reliable and hard-working man but when he saw how Andrew had turned out he got sick. He was very upset with him. He got sick and had a heart attack and died.'[4] Perhaps it was as well that Mr Stathopolous died in the 1970s and did not see how his son turned out. Andrew Stathis became a co-owner of one of Cowra's best motels, the Coachman (later the Town House), but did not made a success of it. He began punting seriously in Cowra, where his motel sponsored a greyhound race. He often flew to Sydney for race meetings.

In 1979 he was arrested on an illegal gambling charge and in December of that year was arrested again on the marijuana charge. Stathopolous had faced a committal hearing lasting 22 days and involving 39 exhibits. Andrew and three others were committed to stand trial, with Andrew on $20 000 bail. Mysteriously, the matter never came to trial. Indeed, the whole pursuit of this case seems to have been very lax considering that an alleged $60 million worth of marijuana had been involved. In March 1983 it was mentioned in the District Court in Sydney before Judge Foord, who waived the requirement that Stathopolous report twice a week to police as part of his bail conditions. No date had been set for his trial, despite the delay of three and a half years since committal. After Stathopolous had fled Australia, clerks in the Sydney office of the Director for Public Prosecutions could find no record of a case involving Stathopolous being listed or heard.

Stathopolous hit trouble with the Town House in Cowra. His mother Maria was made bankrupt when she could not meet a guarantee she had given Tooheys Ltd, which was owed $17 000. Mrs Stathopolous was left destitute with only a $65 a week widow's pension.

Piecing Stathopolous' career together in retrospect, it was evident that he had struck it rich before he bought Bishopsgate. From about mid-1981—a few months after his bankruptcy—Stathopolous began to display wealth ostentatiously, wearing expensive clothes and smoking Davidoff cigars. Bruce McHugh, then one of the biggest bookmakers in Australia, ran a credit check on Stathis (as he was then known) when he wanted to open an account. McHugh discovered that Stathis had bought Kyle House in Macquarie Place for $4.5 million. This was six months to a year before he bought the insurance company. His property purchases also seem to have pre-dated Bishopsgate and he already owned 25 per cent of Richardson Mann when he started negotiating with P & O. Stathis had not made a success of the Town House and it is unlikely that he could have picked up money of that dimension by gambling. Given Stathis' record before and after, the most probable explanation is that he made his pre-Bishopsgate millions in drugs.

But this was not evident on McHugh's credit check, which showed Stathis looking pretty good. He owned a valuable property, was a part owner of a commodity broker and had a business card showing him as an LIB. McHugh's business manager John Bamford said: 'Stathis bet for cash. Fairly substantial sums but not every race and not every Saturday. In the last three months he was at the course much more regularly betting big sums—$10 000 and more. He probably showed a credit on his gambling. But betting at the races was just a round of drinks to him'.

On 12 August 1983 a warrant was issued for Stathis' arrest, but he would never be seen in Australia again. About 100 000 policyholders had been caught by the collapse. Leeming arranged cover for them from

VACC Insurance. Accountants believed that at least $6.7 million of the missing money had been transferred overseas without Reserve Bank approval, which in those days was illegal. Bishopsgate was wound up, with Leeming as liquidator. P & O was still owed $500 000 of the purchase price by the ANZ, which tried to welch on the final payment. P & O pointed out that the ANZ guarantee had been 'unconditional and irrevocable'. P & O had not known Stathis and would not have sold Bishopsgate to him without the bank guarantee. The ANZ paid, reluctantly.

Leeming and the investigators began uncovering Stathis' modus operandi. Stathis never attended a board meeting and never seems to have even set foot in the company's premises. He exercised effective enough control over its money, though. Six days after taking control Stathis had the board appoint him executive director responsible for finance and investments, giving him command of the investment portfolio, which had previously been run by BT Australia. He committed 37 thefts on Bishopsgate. The first was only a fortnight after he took over, when he used $3.75 million from Bishopsgate's own funds to pay the balance of the purchase price to P & O. Over the next seven months he systematically stole $27.5 million from Bishopsgate and repaid $8.5 million of it.[5]

Bishopsgate's investments were mainly in short-term money market deposits and Commonwealth bonds. As BT investments matured they were withdrawn by Stathis and reinvested in a company named AEK Nominees. In early March Stathis diverted $4.5 million into AEK to be invested in Australian Savings bonds. A further $13 million was diverted into AEK between March and July.

Stathis lost $4.5 million playing gold and silver futures in the United States, $1 million on the Australian gold futures market and a further $250 000 on the Australian share market. A large amount of the stolen money which was transferred to the United States was channelled through the American commodity brokers, Dean Witter Reynolds. Some of these funds were later passed on, not always directly, to Stathis companies in Australia and Hong Kong. The money was moved through an intricate international web of companies, indicating that the theft was carefully planned. Of the total $19 million stolen, $5.75 million was identified as having been lost in speculations, $3.75 million was used to pay P & O, $2 million was used to buy Bishopsgate shares and the other $7.5 million was missing. The replacement of BT by AEK bothered the Insurance Commissioner and that was why the commission began investigating Bishopsgate in late June.

Stathis was a bad businessman. He lost money on the Town House. Bishopsgate would probably have lost money anyway, but under Stathis its assets were simply stolen. Even if Stathis had won money on his gold speculations, instead of losing, it is doubtful that he could have survived much longer at Bishopsgate. The Insurance Commissioner was becoming too inquisitive. The fact that there was a hole of some $6 million in the accounts made his departure inevitable.

Stathis planned his exit carefully. In the weeks before he was discovered he parcelled all his properties into companies, then sold the companies to a Filipino multimillionaire. Stathis' last Monday in Australia was 1 August, a bank holiday. With the net closing on him he went to the racetrack. Operating on behalf of a Sydney bookmaker, Stathis backed a maiden called Beau Belle at Bundama and collected $100 000. The bookmaker never saw the money. Stathis then made further bets with McHugh on credit, not parting with any of the $100 000 he was holding. He obviously intended to collect on his winnings and welch on his losses. He lost $60 000 to McHugh and gave him a cheque. McHugh banked the cheque on the Tuesday, but on Wednesday the bank rang the bookmaker to say Stathis' account had been closed. On Thursday Stathis told McHugh the cheque had been a client's and that his replacement cheque would be at Tattersalls Club—the bookies' traditional settling ground—on Friday. That phone call may well have been made from Kingsford-Smith airport, because by Friday Stathis was gone.

Kyle House was sold for $3.85 million for the benefit of Bishopsgate creditors and Stathis' companies were put into liquidation. Ultimately, creditors would receive between 25c and 30c in the dollar. Four years later, in October 1987, Stathis hit the headlines again. He had been arrested in Piraeus carrying 23 kilograms of pure heroin in a suitcase. At the same time Australian Federal Police alleged that Stathis was part of Operation Lavender, a drug syndicate which had imported $40 million worth of cannabis resin into Australia in 1984. A Greek court sentenced Stathis to jail for life on the Piraeus charges. This meant there was little point in extraditing him to Australia, so no further action was taken here. It also meant that either Stathis had lost the millions he stole from Australia in the intervening four years or else the drug trade had become his way of life.

The Cowra drug charges of 1979 left some sinister undertones. At the committal hearing it was alleged that when an arresting officer had seized metal boxes containing more than $86 000, one of Stathis' co-accused had threatened: 'If you touch any of that money, you'll end up another Mackay'. The reference was to Donald Mackay, MP, the anti-drug campaigner who was murdered in the NSW town of Griffith in 1979. There was also a report that two Sydney criminals, Stan Smith and Tony Eustace, had unsuccessfully tried to get the then NSW Attorney-General Paul Landa and High Court judge Lionel Murphy to intervene in the Stathis case.

This was heavy metal. Smith was one of Australia's most feared and notorious criminals. If any of these reports were correct Stathis had some deeply unsavoury connections. Indeed, we need not doubt that despite his parents' efforts he had turned out to be a deeply unsavoury person. One question which was never answered was how it was possible for an ex-bankrupt facing a serious drug charge to become the owner of an insurance company. Another question was how the drug charges—and all record of them—could have vanished into thin air inside the NSW court system.

Budget

At the end of 1988 investors were invited to subscribe to a prospectus issued by Budget Corporation Ltd. The sentimental attraction was powerful. There was no better marketer in Australia than Bob Ansett, the charismatic head of Budget. He had built it into the largest car rental business in Australia and had become one of Australia's best known businessmen in the process. He appeared in endless television commercials, using an easy, relaxed sales pitch with the selling line: 'Budget drives your dollar further'. Professionals were chary about investing, however, noting that after the float the 50c shares—sold for $1 each—would have net tangible asset backing of only 1c each. But Ansett's sunny personality and known dedication to his car rental customers carried the day. Subscribers invested $12.5 million in Budget Corporation.

The company hit the wall in less than a year. When any company fails this quickly, it always raises the question of whether the problems which killed it could have been known at the time the prospectus was issued. Subsequent investigations raised a lot of doubts about the Budget prospectus.

The float was promoted by Ansett and his partner Stan Hamley, whose Budget Transport Industries Pty Ltd was the ultimate holding company of Budget Corporation. Ansett and Hamley were joined on the board of Budget Corporation by Peter Nixon, a former National Party MP and a minister in Malcolm Fraser's government. Nixon said he had decided to become a director because of his respect for Ansett and because Ansett had told him the Budget business was sound.[6]

The operating company which actually rented all the cars was Budget Rent A Car System Pty Ltd (BRACS). BRACS had 29 rental outlets of its own and managed the booking system, the car fleet and the marketing for itself and 71 Australian licensees, covering 280 locations. BRACS was also the lessee of Budget's 11 000 cars. Some of the bigger licensees leased cars in their own right, but the majority sub-leased from BRACS. BRACS was owned by Budget Transport Industries, not by Budget Corporation.

Budget Corporation was floated as the owner of the intellectual property and contractual rights to the Budget rental business. Budget Corporation operated nothing. Its sole income was royalties from BRACS. Budget Corporation paid BRACS $23 million for these rights and royalties. Budget Corporation also had a five-year service agreement with Ansett, who had contracted to promote the product.

The prospectus said:

> The directors of the company do not consider that the viability of the company is dependent upon the financial condition of Budget Rent A Car. The directors believe that, in the unlikely event that Budget Rent A Car was unable to meet its management or licensee commitments to the company, the company could: (a) readily find an operator or operators to enter into licence agreements to carry on the car rental activities. . .; (b) contract with another party to provide such services to the company as Budget Rent A Car is now committed to provide.

It must be doubted whether this statement was ever accurate. A breakdown of the operating company was bound to cause trouble to the company that had to live off its royalties. Fifteen months later the liquidator of BRACS, Peter Allen, said in a report to creditors: 'A closedown of the BRACS operation would almost certainly cause the failure of Budget Corporation and a significant number of Australian licensees'. Even Ansett and Hamley changed their minds on the subject. Replying to a stock exchange query in October 1989 (only ten months after the prospectus), Budget Corporation directors said that *at the time of the prospectus* the board did not think the viability of Budget Corporation depended upon the financial condition of BRACS. The statement continued: 'Messrs Ansett and Hamley hold the view that at the present time the viability of Budget Corporation is dependent upon the financial condition of Budget Rent A Car System Pty Ltd'.

The prospectus had not given any information on the financial condition of BRACS, even though it would prove a most material factor for investors. This raised the question of whether investors would have stumped up $12 million if they had been aware of BRACS' financial condition. The answer, provided long after Budget had crashed, was that before the float at least two firms which were to have been connected with the prospectus had been denied the BRACS figures and consequently played no part in the float.

Ansett had been considering a Budget float since before the 1987 stock market crash. Originally a float of the whole Budget group was planned. Arthur Young & Co had been retained to write a valuation on the Budget name for the prospectus. Arthur Young completed the report but did not

Table 16.1   BRACS' accounts, 1981–87 (all figures in $m)

	81	82	83	84	85	86	87
PROFIT AND LOSS ACCOUNT							
EBIT	2.0	1.1	0.9	2.3	4.0	1.1	(1.5)
Net profit (loss)	0.9	(0.1)	0.0	1.0	1.3	(1.9)	(1.7)
Extraordinaries	—	(0.2)	(0.2)	0.6	—	8.2	(12.2)
BALANCE SHEET							
Total assets	9.7	12.4	14.7	21.7	33.0	41.9	32.2
Total liabilities	7.8	11.0	13.1	18.3	28.0	30.6	34.9
Net assets	1.9	1.4	1.6	3.4	5.0	11.3	(2.7)
Lease commitments	n/a	39.3	72.6	122.4	153.1	90.1	101.0

sign it off because the firm could not get access to BRACS' 1988 accounts. Then, around August 1988, Budget had decided to float only the BRACS' royalty stream and decided that it did not need the Arthur Young valuation.

When the draft prospectus was reviewed by the Australian Stock Exchange's national listing committee in October 1988, it insisted that certain passages be added about company operations. It was at the listing committee's insistence that the directors' statement was included that Budget Corporation did not depend on BRACS. Originally the underwriter was to be May Mellor Laing & Cruickshank. That firm dropped out because Budget refused to supply BRACS' accounts. Eventually the float was underwritten by Dicksons Ltd and Oakminster Ltd.

A dig through the Victorian Corporate Affairs Commission files would have uncovered the BRACS accounts up to September 1987 (which were not filed until September 1988). They are shown in Table 16.1.

Hardly an inspiring picture for investors. By assiduous publicity and price-cutting Budget had by 1988 won about half of the Australian car rental market. However, market share had been gained at the expense of the bottom line. BRACS' profit was marginal all through the 1980s and it had chalked up losses of $1.9 million and $1.7 million in 1986 and 1987. By September 1987 it had a deficiency on assets and $101 million outstanding in lease commitments. In the year to September 1988 BRACS lost a further $2.7 million. This ought to have been evident to the promoters at the time of the Budget Corporation float. Disclosure of the numbers would have given BRACS a financial black eye which even the effervescent salesmanship of Ansett would have had a hard time overcoming.

Instead, investors subscribed to the float ignorant of the BRACS numbers. The investors were exposed to a great deal of media hype about and by Ansett at the time. He released a book called *The Customer*, telling how Budget looked after its customers. Soon afterwards a biography of Ansett appeared, written by Robert Pullan and promoted by Ansett.

A few quick ones

Looking at Table 16.1, readers will note a fall in total assets in the year to September 1987. Peter Allen said later that a lot of assets were sold over a two- to three-year period to fund the operating losses of the group. 'The final sale was the float of Budget Corporation', he said. 'After that there wasn't anything of substantial value to sell to plug the losses.' Reporting this, finance journalist Noel Bushnell said: 'It seems reasonable to conclude that BRACS, at least, was in trouble at the time of the Budget Corporation float and that the money raised then failed to turn the business around. Indeed, the sale might really be seen as merely delaying the inevitable'.[7]

It must be doubted whether BRACS was in any position to divert a chunk of its revenue into Budget Corporation. If it could not, then the whole basis of the float was undermined because Budget Corporation would be devoid of income.

Budget Corporation shares were listed in January 1989. By March, newspapers were saying that Ford was refusing to supply cars to Budget. Which *part* of the Budget group was not specified, nor the reason. But the word was around that BRACS was in trouble. Ford stopped supply of cars from 9 to 16 March because of 'a commercial dispute'. Rumours of liquidity problems in the group strengthened. There was talk of a management buyout. In May the *Australian Financial Review* reported that BRACS had failed to meet $3 million in lease payments to Ford.

The directors' statement in the prospectus that BRACS could be replaced if necessary was looking more dubious than ever. BRACS was in a liquidity bind. It was unable to meet lease payments to the finance subsidiaries of the car companies, who were increasingly reluctant to supply BRACS with new cars. It was also unable to afford to pay royalties to Budget. By September 1989 BRACS owed Budget some $7.6 million in fees which it was unable to pay.

In a boardroom coup Hamley resigned and Ansett was sacked. Nixon grappled unsuccessfully with the mess for a few weeks, but there was no hope. By November Budget was insolvent and Allen was appointed as liquidator. In the first few weeks as he tackled the job he heard a word used occasionally that was unfamiliar to him. It sounded like 'snowpoes'. Thinking it was a technical term in the car rental business and not wanting to appear uninformed, Allen pulled an executive aside one day and asked what the word meant. 'Snopos?', said the executive. 'Sold but not paid out.' Allen suddenly realised what had happened. When a leased car reaches the end of its useful life to a car rental company it is sold, and the proceeds are used to discharge the amount outstanding on the lease from the finance company. Budget had been selling its cars but not paying off the leases. Apart from anything else this meant that Budget was still paying for cars it no longer owned.

In April Allen stepped down as liquidator because of a potential

531

conflict of interest and was replaced by Greg Kelly of Price Waterhouse. By that time Budget Transport Industries and BRACS had announced a $20 million loss for the year to September. The Budget name was sold and an attempt was made to relaunch the car rental business. It collapsed again in March 1992. The shell of Budget Corporation was relisted as a mining company named Titan Hills Australia and subsequently changed its name again to Keydata Corporation. Ansett was left owing $65 million as a result of personal guarantees and went bankrupt. He managed to continue a career as a public speaker for some time. Businessmen still found his thoughts on customers and marketing useful.

Hamley and Ansett were charged with making false and misleading statements in the Budget Corporation prospectus. They denied the charges and said they would mount a vigorous defence. They also defended a damages case brought by Keydata alleging breach of contract and negligence. A lawyer and an accountant who signed the prospectus were also joined in the court cases.

Compass I

Bryan Grey had always nurtured an ambition to run a major Australian airline. In the decades following World War II the domestic airlines of Australia operated as a cosy duopoly. Ansett was privately owned and Trans Australia Airlines (later Australian Airlines) was government-owned, but to the travelling public there was scant difference. Fares were identical and parallel scheduling meant that aircraft flying the same route were only five minutes apart. It was even joked that the lifts in the airlines' head offices were synchronised to go up and down together.

Things began to change in the deregulatory fervour that swept the Federal Government in the late 1980s. It was decided that the aviation industry would be deregulated from November 1990, allowing newcomers to compete with the two giants. This gave Grey the opportunity he had been thirsting after for a lifetime in aviation. He had been in Ansett, Air Nuigini, Air Vanuatu and East-West. Having retired with a handsome handout, he had settled down in his late fifties to a comfortable life on his grazing property near Hamilton, in Victoria's rich western district, when the deregulation policy was taking shape. In mid-1987 he started preparations for Compass Airlines. By the end of 1989 he had finalised leases for five wide-bodied Airbus jets.

In May 1990 the prospectus for Compass Holdings Ltd was released. Underwritten by Potter Partners, the prospectus sought $50 million from the public. This did not count $2.3 million put in by Grey in cash and payments to creditors, for which he was issued 4.6 million shares. Grey and interests associated with him received another 5.4 million shares in recognition of salaries and time devoted to Compass before the float. Grey also received 30 million options to buy further shares at the issue price of 50c.

Compass policy, spelt out in the prospectus and largely followed, was to operate five single-class aircraft between Sydney, Melbourne, Adelaide, Perth, Brisbane, Coolangatta and Cairns. 'Compass will set its pricing policy so as to achieve an acceptable level of profitability', the prospectus said. At peak and off-peak times, Compass said, it would price fares at 80 per cent of the Ansett and Australian Airlines standard economy fares. The curfew fares (9 p.m. to 7 a.m.) would be 50 per cent of standard fares. Curfew services would operate Sydney–Perth, Melbourne–Perth and Melbourne–Cairns. 'The directors believe that Ansett and Australian are limited in their ability to match the Compass fares as they are restricted in achieving significant cost reductions as a result of a number of factors affecting their operations', the prospectus said. Profit in the first year was predicted at $18 million. Subscribers to the float were offered free flight credits over ten years.

Grey was unfailingly enthusiastic about Compass. He was ebullient about its prospects and slammed its rivals and critics. He said Compass would be able to offer lower fares than the other airlines because they could not afford to discount for long. When Ord Minnett issued a warning against investing in new airlines (there were several other possible starters at the time) Grey attacked it on the grounds that 'it is subjective, does not address aviation facts logically and shows shallow depth of knowledge of the industry'. He was particularly critical of the Federal Government for its decision to grant 30-year leases on terminal space to Australian and Ansett. Under the lease terms the major airlines were compelled to provide only two gates at each terminal to newcomers. Grey claimed that this space was inadequate. But, obstacles or not, he pressed ahead. The float was oversubscribed, raising $65 million. On 1 December 1990, the opening day of deregulation, the first Compass flight took off from Brisbane to Sydney.

Very few new ventures have been received with such warmth by the Australian public. There was a rush to book seats on Compass. Several factors were at work. One was discontent with the cavalier attitude towards passengers sometimes showed by the existing duopoly. But the lower fares were a bigger factor. Passengers jumped at the chance to slice 20 per cent or more off the standard fares. The curfew routes were particularly popular. People who had never been able to afford to visit distant locations such as Cairns and Perth quickly took advantage of the Compass half-fare flights. Many people who had rarely—and sometimes never—flown before suddenly took to the skies.

The public response was all Compass could have hoped for. The airline also had a major asset in Grey's flair for promotion and public relations. He had excellent relations with the aviation press, and a fund of one-liners, usually cracks at the major airlines or the Federal Government. The image of an underdog battling the establishment won him huge public support. Unfortunately, the launch was marred by glitches. The reservation system could not handle the traffic. More than 25 000 incoming calls had not got through to reservations staff. As a result, only a handful of passengers were trickling on to the first Compass flights despite huge pent demand. One 9.15 a.m. flight between Sydney and Melbourne had only 41 passengers on a 280-seat Airbus. Peak flights were only 15 per cent occupied. Nine flights had to be cancelled. For an airline that had planned on an ambitious 75 per cent load factor, this was a disaster.

Grey hinted darkly at sabotage. He said the 25 000 calls on the fifth day of operation had been flooding in at the rate of 35 a minute which represented huge volume even for a large international airline. The rumour was spread that the Compass switchboard might have been jammed by computerised dialling. This sounds a bit far-fetched. Compass' rivals were undoubtedly prepared to play rough, but it seems more likely that Compass had simply underestimated the demand and that the system had been inadequate. Calls that did get through seemed to be genuine enough.

Compass responded by slashing fares even further. The Sydney–Perth return fare was cut to $250—barely 20 per cent of the standard economy fare of $1100. Other fares were slashed 45 to 61 per cent below standard fares. Compass had also made a misjudgement of its market. It was winning the bottom end of the travelling market, but not the business travellers. This meant it was getting poor load factors on its peak early morning and evening flights, which were primarily used by business travellers. In contrast, it was getting enormous demand for the long-haul flights, which meant it had to bring in the Sydney–Perth route four months earlier than planned.

Despite this bumpy start Compass managed to fly a creditable 62 000 passengers in its first two months with only two operating aircraft. The Melbourne–Perth and Sydney–Brisbane routes were best patronised, but Compass was struggling on the Sydney–Melbourne trunk route where it had hoped to get a better share of the traffic.

Ansett and Australian were not standing still. They had discounted down to Compass' levels on the short-haul routes. They did not attack Compass on the long-haul fares. This was a shrewd move because it meant that Compass planes were flying an inordinate amount of time on long-distance, ultra-low fare routes that could not break even. In January the airfare war stepped up another notch. Compass offered one-way Sydney–Melbourne flights for $99, compared with a standard fare of $227.

In March Compass released its report for the half year to December 1990. It had flown only in the last of these six months, and would have had heavy operational costs throughout but little cash flow so a poorish result was expected. The airline declared an operating loss of $2.7 million for the period. This figure was after crediting $3.4 million interest received from investing short term the proceeds of the public float. If this interest were subtracted, the true loss from operations appeared to be $6.1 million. This looked pretty bad for one month's flying, but undoubtedly there were several costs incurred in the start-up period. However, there were reports of further operational problems in January and February.

Compass was still battling to attract business travellers. It wooed Ansett Golden Wing members with an entrepreneurial offer. Golden Wing members who paid the equivalent of an Ansett full economy return fare for a Compass flight were promised a second return ticket to the same destination free of charge. The free ticket could be allocated to a partner for travel on the same flight. By May Compass was offering a 'recession buster' fare of $85 Sydney–Brisbane, which was $5 less than the train fare and thirteen hours faster. The major carriers hit back with fare discounts of up to 70 per cent on routes where they competed with Compass. In six months, Australia's domestic air fares had gone from being among the highest in the world to among the lowest.

The war was getting brutal. Compass discovered pollsters questioning its passengers and found that Ansett had recruited Australian National Opinion Polls to survey them. Australian Airlines, which was providing terminal space for Compass, warned its Flight Deck members that they could use valet parking only if they were flying on an Australian flight, a clear sign that some of them had been using the valet parking then flying Compass. When the Compass tug broke down at Brisbane Airport the airline asked if it could borrow one of Australian's. Australian refused, and the flight stayed stuck on the runway until the tug could be repaired. The quarterly report of News Ltd, which owned half of Ansett, indicated that that airline had lost $60 million in the first full quarter of Compass operations. That must have meant that all three airlines were operating at losses.

On top of that, Compass had a little bad luck. The plan to increase its fleet from two to four planes had to be delayed. One Airbus was held back by industrial disputes in Europe. The other fell off the assembly line and damaged its tail. Undaunted, Grey unveiled plans in July to take over Australian Airlines, which the government was planning to privatise. The plan was financially unreal but a typical piece of promotion by the audacious Grey. Then Compass opened flights to Adelaide, spreading discounting to yet another capital city. Here the argument about terminal space became so locked that Compass wound up operating out of a tin shed 100 yards away from the main terminal.

The war was covered intensively by the media, getting acres of coverage in the daily papers. As well there were full-page advertisements by all the airlines, alternating between blasts of criticism of each other and offers of new low fares. One winner was the tourist industry. The Compass-induced boom in air travel had given tourism a big kickstart in its recovery from the pilots' strike. This was particularly true for Cairns, which had suddenly become accessible at affordable fares. Other winners were the travelling public who were getting fares at what turned out to be below cost. However, the discount fares applied only on those routes flown by Compass. While the Sydney–Melbourne fare had been slashed to $85, the Kununurra–Darwin fare for roughly three-quarters of the distance was $173. But by July Compass was able to claim 21 per cent of the traffic on the routes it flew.

It should be recorded that Compass was an excellent airline. The planes were clean and good-looking. The staff were neat, friendly and efficient. As it was a no-frills airline there was no club lounge and meals on short trips were limited to a sandwich and a piece of fruit. But at the low fares prevailing this did not bother the passengers—many of whom had never flown on an aircraft before and so were unaccustomed to frills anyway. Best of all, Compass staff were deeply dedicated to the airline.

The competition was ferocious. Major corporations had begun sending staff on Compass or insisting that flight bookings for middle and junior executives be made on the cheapest available airline. Grey claimed that one major company had taken a block of 1000 tickets. On *Australian Business* we discovered that, if we needed photographs taken in Melbourne, it was cheaper to send our Sydney staff photographer on a day return trip for two or more jobs than to hire a freelance in Melbourne. The majors struck back by announcing that they would introduce 'frequent flier' plans. Clearly the majors would be able to offer better benefits than Compass. Grey promptly attacked the plans, saying: 'It's just more free tickets. Nobody wins'. As Compass must have been the biggest offerer of free tickets at the time, this was a case of the pot calling the kettle black. In August Ansett and Australian launched frequent flier plans. In September Compass hit back with a three-for-one plan. Anyone buying a full Compass Class return ticket would receive two free return tickets to the same destination.

Four things had become very clear. The first was that all three airlines must have been operating at losses. The second was that the situation could not continue. The third was that, as the airline with the smallest capital, Compass was the most vulnerable. The fourth was that Grey had been over-optimistic in believing that the major airlines would not match Compass discounts except in the short term. The air war had by this time been raging for the best part of a year and the fares were at ridiculously low levels. Grey was complaining that the majors were leading the ruinous discounting. By September that may have been correct, but in the first half of 1991 Compass had led the way.

Grey was correct in one respect. Price-cutting is good business only as long as prices do not go below the real cost of the goods or services concerned for any significant period. Any business which takes prices below cost should only do so for a clear goal which must be achievable within a short period. Driving prices below cost for a long period is probably the fastest and surest way of going broke. In trying to grab market by price-cutting, Grey had underestimated the ferocity and deter-mination of the majors. By putting fares down to ridiculous levels, and then keeping them there, Grey condemned himself to fight a Pyrrhic war in which he had to be the loser.

By mid-September Grey was feeling the heat. He predicted that cheap fares would end soon and begin to rise before the end of the year. Compass' first annual report issued in October showed that the airline was bleeding. It had made a loss of $16.6 million. That was bad enough, but the balance sheet looked tender. Total assets were stated at $140 million against liabilities of $86 million, leaving net assets at $54 million. Closer inspection showed that some $30 million of the assets comprised capitalised expenditure on route establishment, development and staff training. That $30 million was actually costs which had been incurred but not charged against profit. If they had been charged the loss would have blown to $46 million and wiped out two-thirds of Compass' capital. Accounting standards allowed such costs to be capitalised and shown as intangible assets; but they would have value only if Compass survived. If they were written off, net assets fell to $24 million and gearing looked high. Elsewhere, the accounts showed that outstanding free tickets which could be claimed against Compass had stood at $31 million at 30 June; and they had almost certainly risen in the fares war since then. Although Compass was claiming more than 12 per cent of the airline market and a load factor of 84 per cent in September, it looked vulnerable.

Far from rising, fares dived even lower. Compass pushed the Sydney–Melbourne fare down to $79 in October, only to be matched within 24 hours by Ansett and Australian. The demand was so high that the Australian branch of the International Air Transport Association nearly ran out of blank air tickets for travel agents. Compass was generating more traffic, with the number of passengers in 1991 a million higher than in 1990. The trouble was that the bulk of them were being flown at a loss. The rumours strengthened that Compass was heading for the wall.

On 29 November *BRW* magazine named Bryan Grey as Businessman of the Year. By that time his airline must have been insolvent by all but the most technical considerations. It would not last out the rest of the year.

On 18 December the crisis struck. Grey and his advisors had flown to Canberra to plead for more time to pay $3.6 million due to the Civil Aviation Authority for airport charges. Grey was arguing that Australian had provided Compass with inadequate terminal space and that he was about to launch a successful lawsuit against them for $30 million. He also claimed that Compass had operated profitably in September and October and should therefore be allowed time to pay. Federal Cabinet took a dim view of these arguments, apparently believing that the uncertainty of a lawsuit was not much of a guarantee against snowballing airport charges. John Kerin, as minister responsible for civil aviation, entered the meeting room and, before Grey had opened his mouth, said baldly: 'We have received your letter—you will get no latitude from us and as far as we are concerned you can be closed down'.[8] This was the death knell. If Compass could not pay its airport fees, the liability would fall upon the lessors of the aircraft. By rejecting Grey's plea for time, Kerin had given the lessors a strong financial incentive to repossess their planes.

That night Compass aircraft were grounded for several hours after legal representatives of the lessors tried to take physical possession of an Airbus at Tullamarine airport. Three representatives of the Polaris leasing company barged on to the 7.15 p.m. flight with the assistance of security men from TNT, which had a 50 per cent stake in Ansett. They were eventually persuaded to leave and the flights resumed.

A cash-strapped Compass pleaded with the Federal Government for time to pay its air navigation charges and landing fees. Grey went into urgent talks with financiers and warned travel agents to sell tickets only for that day's flights. On the 21st Compass collapsed, leaving thousands of passengers stranded on the eve of their Christmas holidays. There was chaos at the air terminals. The RAAF helped get some passengers home for Christmas. Ian Ferrier was appointed provisional liquidator. His biggest problem was sorting out the chaos among those passengers who had paid by credit card and still held an unused ticket. In some cases, the passenger had the right to reclaim the money from the credit card issuer but in others they did not. Payments made to travel agents were held in trust, but for the airline, not the passenger.

Compass retained amazing goodwill. A fighting fund was set up by staff—many of whom had not been paid for several weeks—and raised $4 million from the public. This was a better result than many charities experience. Compass had certainly allowed many Australians to see Australia more cheaply than they could ever have hoped. It had also provided a boost for the tourist industry, especially in Queensland, at a welcome time.

However, Compass had achieved these things while flying at a loss throughout its career. In just over one year's flying Compass had wiped out more than $60 million cash subscribed to its float. Ferrier later reckoned that its total operating losses were around $70 million. There was a deficiency of another $70 million, mostly in sums owing to unsecured creditors including all those holding unused Compass tickets. The collapse of the airline immediately triggered demands for all outstanding lease payments on the aircraft, which totalled $150 million.

Grey blamed almost everyone except himself. He blamed Ansett and Australian for cutting fares, although fare cuts had been initiated by Compass as a deliberate strategy. He blamed Australian for providing 'the worst terminal gates in the western world' for Compass passengers. Certainly the gates were small and tended to be in the worst areas of the terminals, but they were not the major factor in the aircraft's demise. To test the airline, the author once flew Sydney–Adelaide return on Compass. This involved using Compass' worst terminal, the tin shed at West Beach airport. On the return flight the passengers filed into the crowded shed and had been seated for some time when they were told there would be a delay of an hour or so. Nobody was angry. The passengers stayed seated, happily chattering like sparrows. They were going to Sydney on cheap tickets and they were grateful to Grey for the opportunity. Bad gates may have deterred some passengers, but Compass' load factor was rising despite them. Grey created a fine airline, but Compass' core problem was that it cut its prices too far. It was not good strategy for a small new player against a long-established duopoly to start a ruinous price-cutting war unless it had a big brother with deep pockets. Given the limited capital available to Compass, it was only a matter of time before the airline fell out of the sky.

Compass II

The story of Doug Reid carries at least an echo of George Herscu. Reid picked up a fortune late in his career. All he had to do was relax and enjoy himself. Instead he made a staggeringly bad investment, lost a large chunk of the money and got himself into serious trouble with the law.

Colleagues of Reid invariably described him as a nice person and honest. He was a Melburnian who had grown up in an establishment ambience, being educated at Brighton Grammar and living at Toorak. Reid spent most of his career with the petrochemical company Monsanto Australia, rising to become one of its senior executives. In 1989 he led a management buyout of Monsanto, then sold it to Consolidated Press Holdings which renamed it Chemplex. Reid collected some $25 million. He was in his mid-fifties and could have sat back and lived the rest of his life in luxury. He made a few investments, buying property in England and Europe. During the buyout, the broker handling the negotiations invited Reid to join a syndicate which was planning to set up a new airline in Australia. As Compass was hitting a few bumps at the time, Reid was at first wary about the proposition but gradually allowed himself to become convinced it was a viable proposition. So he became one of the founders of Southern Cross Airlines, and started planning Australia's next new airline.

Reid persuaded himself that it would work if he had a proper business plan. Consultants pointed to a Texas-based airline, Southwest, as a model of how a small carrier could operate profitably by using one model of aircraft and sticking to high-yield routes. Impressed, Reid sounded out a former vice-president of Southwest, Sam Coats, as potential chief executive of Southern Cross.[9]

Reid left Australia for a combined business and pleasure trip to Europe on 20 December 1991: the day Compass collapsed. On his return he was staying with some friends at Portsea and saw an ironman contest on a nearby beach. One of the first things he noticed was Compass staff collecting money. He was impressed both by their devotion to the airline and the affection it had engendered in the public.

In aviation parlance, this was Reid's point of no return. He should have retired gracefully. His wife, family and many of his friends were not enthusiastic. The spectacular collapse of Compass should have been ample warning that starting a third airline in Australia was fraught with peril, but Reid had become convinced he could do it. He decided to capitalise on the goodwill generated by Compass.

The provisional liquidator of Compass, Ian Ferrier, was only too willing to sell. When Compass collapsed at the end of 1991 the biggest creditors were the aircraft lessors. They had repossessed the Airbuses, but the world aviation market was going through a recession and planes were hard to sell or lease. The lessors were Canadian Airlines and two leasing companies, Monarch and Polaris.

Ferrier knew he would get little money for the few tangible assets of Compass and whatever cash he raised in that way would be soaked up by liquidator's fees and preferential creditors such as employees. (One of the problems was that Compass had operated so briefly that nobody had taken much leave, which meant there was a large backlog of holiday pay owing.) Ferrier's only chance of a substantial return to creditors therefore was to sell the airline as a going concern. There was no hope of getting cash for Compass, but the creditors might settle for scrip in a new airline.

Even if the new airline did not survive, the creditors would be no worse off than if Ferrier simply conducted a fire sale of the Compass assets.

Ferrier had been approached by other airline hopefuls, but Southern Cross looked the best bet. 'We looked at the prospectus and saw that it addressed the major issues which had caused the failure of Compass', said Ferrier. 'There were two reports from Arthur Andersen and Airline Economics Inc. We thought it had a fairly good board. We looked at Doug Reid and found he had just made $20-odd million in Chemplex.'[10] So creditors and shareholders of Compass accepted 40 million 50c shares in Compass at par as vendor securities for selling the Compass name to Southern Cross. Henceforth Southern Cross Airlines would be the name of the public company operating as Compass Airlines. Compass II, as it was called, came with a readymade livery, staff and reservation system. The vendor shares could not be traded for a year.

One legacy from Compass was a batch of unsecured creditors in the form of holders of unused tickets. Compass II generated goodwill by promising that unused Compass I tickets would be honoured. As the tickets were effectively a type of standby to fill otherwise empty seats, this was not an expensive promise. Another legacy from Compass I was a reservoir of goodwill from the Queensland Government, which had appreciated Bryan Grey's contribution to tourism. The government provided $2.9 million in bridging loans to Compass to be repaid from the float. Another $1.1 million loan was virtually a grant, being for 99 years and interest free, so that Compass could build a terminal at Coolangatta. Furthermore, the Queensland Government took 1.5 million shares and sub-underwrote the float. In return, Compass agreed to establish its headquarters in Brisbane.

The Southern Cross prospectus issued in April 1992 sought $50 million from the public in 100 million 50c shares. The airline's business plan was spelt out in detail. Compass II would fly not Airbuses but MD-80s from McDonnell Douglas, which Coats said would cost half as much to operate as wide-bodied twin jets. Compass II would keep down costs by contracting out such services as ground handling and catering; by using only one type of aircraft; by taking advantage of the then low leasing rates; and by keeping staff numbers small and productive. Compass II planned to remedy one important defect of Compass I by launching an executive class which would cater to business travellers. The first flights of Compass II would be along the major traffic routes of the east coast and it would only fly to Perth after increasing its fleet from five aircraft to seven. As an inducement, subscribers to the float would be able to fly one free return trip on any Compass II route.

The prospectus projected that Southern Cross would make a $7.6 million loss in the year to June 1993, and that this would turn into profits of $19.3 million in 1994 and $29.5 million in 1995. An important point was whether Southern Cross would have enough capital. Chartered accountants Arthur Andersen & Co estimated that on the projected first year loss Southern Cross would still be holding $35.5 million at June 1993, which was seen as about the critical juncture in the airline's future.

The board looked impressive. Chairman Sir Leo Heilscher had run the Queensland Treasury well during Sir Joh Bjelke-Petersen's long rule as Premier. Heilscher was seen as one of the most powerful public servants in Australia during his tenure and a reason why the Queensland economy was the best in Australia by the 1990s. Graham Tucker was probably Queensland's best known and most respected company director, with a suite of top board seats in that state. Another director was Leigh Masel, former chairman of the National Companies and Securities Commission. Managing director Coats had come to Australia with a good reputation gained in running Southwest.

Compass II also proposed to discount fares. In making fare comparisons, one of the problems was that the major airlines had discounted fares so heavily that it was by then difficult, if not meaningless, to find any standard fare. Australian and Ansett were loading their full fare economy passengers into business class, making comparisons even harder. On the Melbourne–Sydney route Compass II projected an executive class fare of $159 and Compass Class (economy) of $129. The Compass Class fare could be slashed as low as $59, however, if bought fourteen days in advance for an off-peak time.

The issue was underwritten by J.B. Were & Son. Stories appeared in mid-June that the float had been undersubscribed, but Reid said he was confident that it would be filled. The application period was extended by a fortnight but the float still reportedly fell short by 46 per cent. Reid blamed the shortfall on the news which broke during the float that Qantas was to merge with Australian Airlines. He said the public feared that this would create a mega-carrier that would easily fight off Southern Cross.

During the float Southern Cross issued a supplementary prospectus updating its profit forecasts. It still predicted a loss of $7.6 million for its first year of operation, but said that lower air navigation charges should improve its second-year profit from $11.3 million to $13.2 million.

With no Bryan Grey at the helm Compass II operated without the hype and publicity that had accompanied Compass I. Nor did it suffer the same traumas. It seemed to be operating with reasonable efficiency, but very quietly. Indeed, compared to its predecessor, Compass II was almost an invisible airline. No publicity, no promotion, no stunts, no one-liners from the chief executive. And, most noticeably, no full-page advertisements in the papers. Compass II seemed to be conserving money. In hindsight, this may well have been because it didn't have any.

At the post-float statutory meeting on 9 October the directors announced that the total cash raised had been $51.73 million, comprising $50 million from the public float and $1.73 million spent by Reid before the float, which he had taken in shares. The shares touched 50c when they listed in July, held around 45c through October and slowly drifted below 40c in January 1993. If Compass' predictions in its supplementary prospectus were correct the shares were a steal at the price. But they kept edging lower. On 1 February 2.4 million Southern Cross shares—the biggest parcel traded—were sold at 30.5c even though the prevailing price was 38c. Professional traders took this as a bear signal and wondered who the seller could have been.

Three weeks later, on 23 February, Southern Cross announced a loss of $11 million for the half-year to December. By itself this was not too bad, because the original forecast of a $7.6 million loss for the first financial year had anticipated an $11 million loss in the first half, balanced by a second-half profit of $4 million. The real alarm bells were set off in the accompanying half-year balance sheet, which showed cash of only $4.3 million. The $50 million raised in the float had nearly all vanished and there was no adequate explanation. The prospectus forecasts had predicted a cash balance of $35.5 million by June. Given that Compass II was expected to operate at a loss in the first half, the December cash balance should have been around $32 million. So more than $27 million was missing. How had Southern Cross wiped out almost its entire capital?

The directors said in the interim report that revenue had fallen 5 per cent short of budget for the half. They expected losses to continue in the second half but said that monthly losses should be significantly reduced following the introduction of an extra two aircraft in March. They tried to soothe investors' fears by announcing: 'The company has concluded a financing package of $9.2 million for its ongoing business'. Investors had plenty of reason to be alarmed. If the company had continued making losses after December the airline must have been close to insolvency. It had held together only by raising debt. The shares slid to 32c, and anyone who didn't sell must have had a a death wish. The Australian Stock Exchange queried several figures in the accounts. On 3 March directors asked for the shares to be suspended from trading.

On the following day Heilscher revealed that the $9.2 million had not been raised, saying that Southern Cross had hit a 'glitch, but no more than a glitch' with its funding. Heilscher said that he was still hoping to get funding in the next few days. But it was the end. Compass was insolvent for the second time in fifteen months. Southern Cross had lasted less than a year from the issue of its prospectus and less than eight months operationally. It was revealed the airline was nearly $500 000 in arrears with its fees payable to the Civil Aviation Authority. Richard Barber of Price Waterhouse was appointed provisional liquidator.

The great question was where the money had gone. Part of the answer was that some of it was never there. Barber made several allegations against Doug Reid in the Queensland Supreme Court. Barber said that his staff and solicitors had conducted an intensive review of agreements and associated documentation regarding deposits made with a US-based company, Apogee, as security for aircraft leases. 'I am advised by my solicitors that these agreements appear to be a sham', Barber told the court. He alleged a breach of Section 205 of the Companies Code, which forbade a company to finance the purchase of its own shares.

The allegations related to the float of Southern Cross. The $50 million issue was underwritten by J.B. Were & Son. The only two sub-underwriters named in the prospectus were the Queensland Treasurer and Apogee Finance Group Inc. A memo from Tucker, who resigned from the Southern Cross board a week before the crash, suggested that the total amount deposited with Apogee was $10 million. The implication was that Southern Cross had paid Apogee $10 million purportedly for aircraft leases or deposits, but in reality to prop up the float by subscribing for Southern Cross shares. In the Queensland Supreme Court Richard Chesterman, QC, for Barber, said it had been suggested that Apogee had held the funds as a performance bond to back an indemnity to Scandinavian Airline System (SAS) from which Southern Cross had leased three aircraft in case Southern Cross defaulted on its payments. Chesterman said that Apogee had not given SAS an indemnity. He alleged that a letter purportedly confirming the indemnity had been deemed a forgery by SAS's London solicitors.

If all this were true Southern Cross had really only raised $40 million instead of $50 million. That $10 million deficiency had been roughly made up by other funds. The Queensland Government had virtually given Compass $1.1 million. Reid had lent it $4 million as well as funding $1.7 million of its start-up costs. Another $1 million had been lent by Asia Pacific Ltd. So in theory the airline still had about $50 million. From this should be deducted float costs of $3.5 million, leaving around $46 million of which some $44 million should have been cash. Where had it gone?

In the days before it crashed Southern Cross tried desperately to find a financial saviour. It approached several institutions, but the only result was to make its troubles more widely known and to hasten the decline in its fortunes. The document used by Southern Cross in its presentation showed five unbudgeted variations which were the key to the collapse of Compass II:

1. While the operating deficit ran $4 million over budget, it was by no means the largest cause of the disaster. Compass II kept its operating losses within reasonable bounds.

2. The purchase of $9 million in spares—called 'rotables' in the trade—was to have been financed by McDonnell Douglas. But the financing deal was to have been part of the package only if Southern Cross leased new aircraft bought by a leasing company from McDonnell Douglas. When Southern Cross decided to buy second-hand aircraft the projected deal on spares was no longer available and they had to be financed separately.

3. An extra $8 million in deposits was partly to guarantee leases but a major element was understood to have been deposits with banks. When Compass I had collapsed the credit card issuers had decided that, whatever their legal position and whatever their ultimate recovery from Compass I, they had to cover the losses of their clients, the banks. Compass I having attracted primarily downmarket travellers, this meant that Bankcard took the biggest wound. The banks behind Bankcard were out of pocket by several million dollars and were determined not to repeat the experience with Compass II. The banks therefore forced Southern Cross to put up a large security deposit.

4. There were extra start-up costs of $8.8 million, comprising two elements. The first was $4 million in training and other expenses which were to have been supplied free by McDonnell Douglas. The remaining $4.8 million went in unexplained legal bills, which seem to have been exceedingly large.

5. Finally, there was $1.4 million in 'other' costs, mostly related to extra training.

If we take items two to five and add the $11 million half-year operating loss to them the total is $38 million. Subtracting that from the $44 million cash injected into Southern Cross gives us as close a clue as we are likely to get as to why it had only $4.3 million cash left by the end of December. The combined impact of these unbudgeted expenses was to leave Southern Cross with only scant cash in the till from the day it began flying. In particular there was no cash to spare for advertising and marketing, which were vital if Southern Cross were to succeed.

Items two to five, totalling $27.2 million, ought to have been reasonably foreseeable at the time the prospectus was issued. The costs associated with leasing deals were far more expensive than forecast in the prospectus. The end result was that the prospectus forecasts were materially defective because they never mentioned the enormous cash drain from such associated costs. Nor did Southern Cross at any stage tell the investing public about these costs, although it must have been aware of them at least from August, when Compass II began flying its MD aircraft. The prospectus forecast that leasing costs in the first year would run at about $US190 000 (around $A270 000). Southern Cross' internal profit and loss account showed aircraft leasing costs running at about that figure. This indicated that Southern Cross had achieved the lease deals contemplated in the prospectus but failed to reveal (or did not take into account) the material associated costs.

On 9 March Reid was arrested and charged with knowingly providing false information to the directors of Southern Cross. These charges were later dropped and replaced by 27 charges alleging breach of director's duties, insider trading and use of company funds to buy shares in itself. At the time of writing, Reid was defending himself against the charges. Barber, on behalf of Southern Cross, sued Reid for $10 million over the Apogee deal. Reid was already facing the loss of nearly $6 million which he had injected into the airline in loans and equity. The saviour of Compass had turned into its victim.

The plight of Asia Pacific Ltd provided a touch of black humour. The Perth-based Asia Pacific had been dabbling in fish farming and mining exploration before it decided to become a financier. Its first loan had been $1 million—representing half the company's assets—to Southern Cross. Asia Pacific made the loan with security on certain Southern Cross receivables and for a term of only 30 days. Unfortunately, the loan had been made on 17 February and Southern Cross would collapse before the 30 days were out. Asia Pacific would have been better off sticking to exploration, given that the WA goldfields were on the brink of a minor speculative boom. Even aquaculture would have been preferable.

The ensuing months saw a few facts emerge that made the history of Compass II clearer. It was revealed that the Queensland Government's financial institution Suncorp had provided an urgent loan of $2.7 million to Southern Cross to secure its fleet just days before the extended float closed. Had the loan not been made the default could have given J.B. Were reason to terminate the underwriting, which would have killed Southern Cross before birth. Suncorp was subsequently repaid in full with interest. A memo by Tucker showed that he had grave doubts about the $10 million loan to Apogee as early as November. He had demanded at a board meeting that independent solicitors be brought in to determine why Apogee was unable to refund the money. He had also raised the question of whether Southern Cross had financed the acquisition of its own shares.[11] Tucker said later that he had never got a satisfactory answer to his queries.

The hapless Reid, who had suffered the greatest loss in the airline, was attacked from all sides. He was charged with directing Westpac to pay the proceeds of a bill of exchange for $4.99 million into his own bank account, although the bill was paid for by Southern Cross. The giant National Mutual Life sued Reid for false and misleading conduct, claiming that it had been misled when it invested $1 million in Southern Cross shares. Westpac obtained an uncontested judgement for $8 million against Reid, who then applied for bankruptcy in the Federal Court. The embattled Reid was defending himself on half a dozen fronts.

Memos and correspondence of Reid and Apogee produced in evidence showed that they had conducted considerably detailed negotiations before the Southern Cross float. The dealings between Southern Cross and Apogee, which was 80 per cent owned by the Dutch airline KLM, apparently had two strands. One was a sub-underwriting agreement, but that agreement would lapse if there were any default by Southern Cross in a leasing deal which was also planned.[12] When Southern Cross decided to bypass Apogee and lease aircraft directly from SAS Apogee had threatened to sue, claiming damages of $US3.7 million. Reid told a court later that he regarded the claim as extortion.

In Brisbane Magistrate's Court Reid confessed to using $1 million from Southern Cross' heavily overdrawn bank account to buy the last shares in the float. He also confessed to forgery in an attempt to save his airline. He had photocopied signatures of two directors, Dame Margaret Guilfoyle and Brian Powell, and taped them to a document which he had faxed to Asia Pacific when trying to raise $1 million from it. Reid said that he knew the original documents had been signed and was just trying to expedite the deal. He said that the $4.99 million of Southern Cross' funds had been put into his Westpac account by mistake.

The story told to the court was sometimes confused but one point emerged clearly. Compass II had run out of cash by January—after less than six months of operation. Like Compass I it had been chronically undercapitalised. By the time it went into liquidation Southern Cross had unpaid debts of $27 million. If this is added to the $50 million net cash raised in the float and the loans it means that the company lost some $77 million.

Between them Compass I and Southern Cross had raised $125 million from the public and lost the lot, but it wasn't a lot by the standards of the aviation industry. During the same period Ansett spent $150 million merely upgrading its Sydney terminal. The costs of entry for a third domestic carrier would therefore seem well beyond what any grassroots company could afford for the foreseeable future—not to mention the fact that it would be a long time before investors would trust another grass-roots airline anyway. One financier, talking to the *Bulletin*, put the whole affair in perspective. 'There's only room for two and a bit players in the domestic airline industry', he said. 'And the bit is never going to make any real money.'[13]

Deposit & Investment

Deposit & Investment Company Ltd was formed in Sydney in 1882 as The New South Wales Mont de Piété Deposit and Investment Co Ltd. It dropped the first seven words from its title in 1951. The company was formed with the object of lending money at interest upon freehold or leasehold property in any of the Australasian colonies, including New Zealand, Fiji and New Caledonia.

It had a shaky period in the mid-1960s when larger financiers such as Reid Murray were going to the wall, but it recovered and from 1969 was a subsidiary of Washington H. Soul Pattinson & Co. Directors included Bill Pattinson, Washington Soul's chairman Jim Millner, and Hugh Dixson, scion of the family whose tobacco fortune founded the Dixson Gallery in the NSW State Library. John Darling and Sir John Dunlop were also on the board for a while. Deposit & Investment was deeply respectable and equally unexciting. It lent money on property, either as security for a loan or as finance for a purchaser. It also held debentures and government bonds and loan stock. It remained a small company but it would be hard to imagine a more solid one.

The shares had been delisted when the company was taken over in 1969. Henceforth it was financed primarily by debentures and notes issued to the public. Its solid record and blue-blooded board attracted a clan of small, safety-conscious investors who were happy to subscribe even though these debentures and notes were no longer listed on the stock exchange—which meant that there was no ready market for them and no stock exchange scrutiny of the company.

Nor was there any apparent reason why these investors should have worried. Deposit & Investment kept the even tenor of its ways. In the year to July 1985, for instance, it recorded a profit of $192 000. This was solid, though not much of a return on shareholders' funds of $19.1 million. The shareholders' funds represented the difference between total assets of $38 million and liabilities of $18.9 million, of which $18 million was debenture stock. Gearing was therefore less than 50 per cent, which is very conservative for a financier. The assets, as ever, were in property loans. Whereas rival financiers had plunged into overpriced commercial property Deposit & Investment had stuck mainly to housing, where the returns were traditionally safe but low.[14]

Control changed in November 1985 when Washington Soul sold Deposit & Investment to a group of Asians headed by Chor Kian Yap, a Malaysian Chinese based in Hong Kong. The old directors resigned and were replaced by a board headed by Yap. Before departing, the old board sent a circular to the debenture holders pointing out that control had changed and that they had the right to redeem their debentures early if they wished. 'We were a little concerned about this chap from Malaysia', said Millner. 'We went as far as we could legally in the circular. A great majority of the debenture holders did redeem. But then Yap wrote to them all offering higher interest rates and many of them reinvested.'[15]

After reviewing the loan and investment portfolio, the new board provided $4.2 million for doubtful debts against property-related loans made in the 1970s. This resulted in Deposit & Investment reporting a $3.6 million loss for 1985–86. The balance sheet still showed shareholders' funds at $15.5 million, but apart from $18.2 million in debentures there were also $7 million in bills and $2.7 million in unsecured deposits. This blew external liabilities out to $28.5 million and meant that shareholders' funds accounted for little more than one-third of group funds.

In addition, the annual return said that Deposit & Investment had 'embarked on fee-based activities, particularly in investment banking and mortgage banking'. The report said:

> As part of its investment banking activities the group has also made selective investments in businesses which complement the group's activities or which may become important clients of the group or which the directors are confident will generate good dividend income or capital gains.

Many of Deposit & Investment's loyal debenture holders may not even have bothered reading the report, but from habit just kept renewing their investments as they matured.

The report for the year to July 1987 was not issued until January 1988. It showed a profit of $1 million after allowing for a further doubtful debt of $470 000. Shareholders' funds were stated to have increased to $16.5 million, but external liabilities had blown out to $40 million, of which some $18.8 million was debenture stock. Directors noted that since the end of the financial year world stock markets had undergone 'a severe setback', but said they believed that no permanent diminution had occurred. Note 22 to the accounts showed that the group was carrying a loss of $3.5 million on its investments. Deposit & Investment had also bought shares in a Hong Kong company after balance date and its shares had fallen $1.5 million below cost as a result of Black Tuesday. Directors said that the $1 million profit reflected a further improvement in the trend set under the new board. They also said that there had been no material changes in the company's affairs since balance date.

The report for the year to July 1988 never emerged. By 14 February 1989 the trustee for the debenture holders, Perpetual Trustee (of which Hugh Dixson was chairman), had become alarmed. Perpetual appointed Tony Sherlock of Coopers & Lybrand as receiver, a task which was considerably complicated by the fact that Chor Kian Yap had fled Australia, never to return.

Sherlock was not the only man after Yap. Australian Securities Commission investigators also wanted to discuss Deposit & Investment with him. Deposit & Investment had made its last interest payment to debenture holders on 31 December 1988. The dividend cheques were accompanied by an invitation to subscribe to fresh debentures or unsecured deposits in Deposit & Investment. Six weeks later the company was in receivership and Yap had fled. Yap must have known at the time he invited holders to make fresh loans to the company that it would soon be unable to continue trading. This was an offence under the Companies Code, carrying civil and criminal penalties.

A report as to affairs by a subsequent board of directors in 1991 showed that under Yap, Deposit & Investment had lost some $61 million in loans and investments, leaving it with a deficiency of $51 million. To this should be added the losses in other companies raped by Yap.

At the end of 1986 Yap had taken over a second-board company, SRC Laboratories Ltd, for $10 million and turned it into an investment vehicle named Sunmark Ltd. Sunmark was to be based in Perth and to invest in property, finance and industry, mainly in Asia. In October 1987 Sunmark took a 51 per cent holding in Multivest Ltd, another Perth-based property and investment company with an Asian board.

The June 1988 accounts of Multivest showed the company in good condition, with total assets of $22 million of which $19.3 million comprised property, $1.3 million plant and equipment and the rest cash and debtors. Liabilities totalled a mere $5.6 million, of which $4.7 million was in bank bills. This left Multivest's shareholders' funds at nearly $17 million. Yap said the directors were 'delighted' to report a successful year. Completion of a housing project had left the group with 'relatively low net borrowings and quality assets to provide reliable cash flows to support its future expansion'. The directors' statement continued:

> Your directors will be actively seeking to invest in sound, profitable operations which will generate recurring cash flows and ultimately enhance the net worth of the company. Your company views the future with optimism, having established a quality asset base necessary to generate the cash flows which are required to finance its successful expansion.

That report was dated October 1988. In July 1989 Multivest shares were suspended because the company could no longer pay its debts. Creditors moved in to seize properties under mortgage. Shareholders were never given a satisfactory explanation of what had happened, although they received a partial one in the form of an expert's report by Arthur Young & Co when an offer was made for their shares in mid-1989. The report indicated that, somewhere between October 1988 and July 1989, Multivest had borrowed $12 million and put the entire amount on deposit with Sun Sovereign Ltd, a money market subsidiary of Sunmark, and had lost the lot. Sun Sovereign had lent $32 million to unidentified associated companies and was unable to recover any of it. Naturally, Sun Sovereign's losses had also pulled the rug from under Sunmark, which went into liquidation in April 1989.[16]

Sherlock, as receiver for Deposit & Investment, brought a $73 million negligence suit against the auditors, KPMG Peat Marwick, alleging negligence relating to the Deposit & Investment accounts for the year to July

1986. That was the first set of accounts presented by Yap, who was in control of Deposit & Investment for just over three years. At the time of writing, Peats were defending the action.

Yap's companies had lost an amazing amount of money in a very short period. Inter-company loans meant that there was some duplication in the figures, but the total amount lost appeared to be around $150 million. Tony Douglas-Brown of Horwath & Horwath said that Yap liked to send money through circular chains of companies in the form of inter-company loans, but in many cases it had not been possible to trace the full length of the chain or understand what had happened. The chains had involved companies based in every state of Australia as well as the British Virgin Islands, Liberia, Singapore, the United States, Britain and Hong Kong. Several of the companies could no longer be traced, especially those in Liberia.[17]

Yap had a passion for secrecy. There were only two known photographs of him. He kept most of his subordinates in the dark, giving them information only on a 'need to know' basis. Liquidators cleaning up the Sunmark files found a written instruction to the office receptionist saying that she was never to admit whether Yap was in the building, but always to give the impression that he was not. Yap had kept meticulous personal files but removed them all from his office just before the collapse. One former colleague described him as 'a wheeler dealer who paid scant attention to detail and lived on aeroplanes'. Yap had spent a lot of time outside Australia, maintaining apartments throughout the world apparently paid for from his companies' coffers. He had a home in Perth but also maintained an apartment in Mount Street (in the same block as Alan Bond). Nevertheless, when passing through Perth he would sometimes stay at the Hyatt.

He was unknown when he arrived in Australia. This was just as well for Yap, because an inquiry into his history would have disturbed investors. He had begun his career in the Kuala Lumpur offices of London brokers Lawrence Prust, where he appears to have been well regarded as long as someone kept an eye on him. However, the next two broking firms who employed him were less impressed. They were forced to take losses of millions of dollars after discretionary accounts operated by Yap were found to be owed substantial sums by holders who could not be traced. Partial restitution was made to one firm.[18]

There seems to be a pattern here. In both Malaysia and Australia Yap invested money with unknown people and it was never recovered. In neither Malaysia nor Australia could the owners of the companies trace where the money had gone. In the absence of any explanation from Yap—or even any effort by him to return—there must be strong grounds for suspicion.

The various investigators, liquidators and receivers never made any contact with Yap. He was variously reported in Hong Kong, Britain, Malaysia and Taiwan, where he reportedly held citizenship. At one point there was talk of an expedition by a former SAS officer to get him back to Australia, but nothing happened.

Duke

Kia Ora Gold Corporation was a success story. After battling around as a junior explorer it found a gold deposit at Marvel Loch, south of Southern Cross in Western Australia. Kia Ora's chairman, Harold Abbott, the former managing director of Martin Corporation, plugged away for years to develop Marvel Loch, supported by brokers and shareholders who injected some $10 million into Kia Ora. Marvel Loch turned into a producing mine. In 1987 Kia Ora sold the mine in two tranches to Mawson Pacific for $66 million, the final deal being approved on 23 September 1987. As a result Kia Ora would have net assets totalling $68 million, most of it in cash. The shares would have a cash backing of 85c each.

For a moment it looked as though the dreams of Kia Ora shareholders had come true. After years of struggle their company had found a mine and sold it at a good price. Now they could collect. Indeed, even without the benefit of hindsight, a capital return to shareholders would have been the fitting thing at this point. But it was not to be. Instead of passing the rewards of its success back to the shareholders Kia Ora bid for Western United, a Perth-based financial services group in which the Kia Ora board held a 33 per cent interest. Harold Abbott was chairman of Western United and his brother Gary was managing director. The Western United bid was announced on 13 October, barely three weeks after the sale of Marvel Loch.

Even at the time it appeared that Western United was being over-priced, which meant that Western United shareholders were getting a better deal than those in Kia Ora. The two bids offered a mixture of cash and scrip with a market value ranging from $85 million to $100 million, depending on which alternative the shareholders chose. Either way, it was a big premium on Western United's market capitalisation of $60 million. After the takeover Kia Ora had Western United in its books at $67 million (reflecting the par value of the shares issued). As Western United had reported a profit of $1.7 million in 1987 the bid represented 40 times earnings, a high multiple for a financial services group. Worse, Western United had less than $5 million in net tangible assets, which meant that Kia Ora had paid a whopping $62 million goodwill. Despite

Figure 16.1 The Duke group

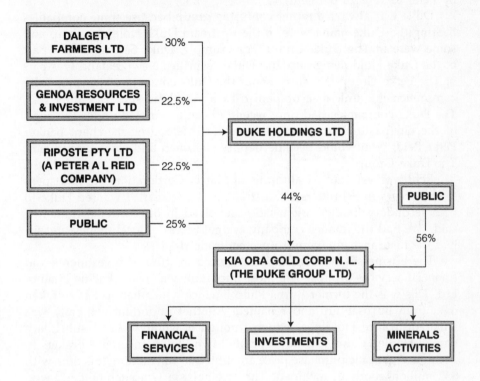

all these factors the takeover was approved by a meeting of Kia Ora shareholders. The takeover attracted little publicity because it was over-shadowed by the calamities of Black Tuesday, which happened a week after the bid was announced.[19] Western United became a wholly owned subsidiary of Kia Ora.

Hardly had the takeover been completed than it was followed by a second in May 1988, in which Kia Ora bought a group of companies from Duke Holdings Ltd. Consideration was $12.25 million cash, the issue of 59.4 million ordinary shares and the assumption by Kia Ora of Duke liabilities totalling $28 million. The share issue would give Duke a 44 per cent holding in the enlarged Kia Ora, which would then change its name to The Duke Group Ltd.

At the finish The Duke Group (Kia Ora) would be 56 per cent owned by the public, including former shareholders of Western United and the original shareholders of Kia Ora whose equity was by now greatly diluted. The other 44 per cent of The Duke Group would be owned by Duke Holdings. Duke Holdings in turn was owned by Dalgety Farmers (30 per cent); public shareholders (25 per cent); Genoa Resources &

Investment Ltd (22.5 per cent); and Riposte Pty Ltd, a company controlled by Peter Reid (22.5 per cent).

Duke was always a rather confusing group because some companies bearing the Duke name were in the upstream Duke Holdings camp and some were in The Duke Group. For example, Duke Securities was part of the Duke Holdings group, but Duke Securities New Zealand was part of The Duke Group. No story about the Duke companies was ever fully comprehensible unless accompanied by a visual aid such as Figure 16.1. The Duke companies had only recently been assembled under the aegis of the old pastoral house of Dalgety and Melbourne merchant banker Peter Reid, who would become deputy chairman and chief executive of The Duke Group.

Reid was yet another alumnus of Martin Corporation. He had spent several years in Schroders in Australia and overseas. 'I wanted Duke to be a secondary finance organisation involved in international trade', he said. 'We had the finance company, we got access to local money and we had the insurance company to protect trade risks.'[20]

The businesses sold to Kia Ora were a mixture of investments and financial services groups. The most important was Duke Pacific Finance Ltd. This was the former Burns Philp Finance which had just been taken over from Burns Philp and renamed. Another important company was Duke Insurance Holdings, which through a wholly owned subsidiary named Hadley Cannon Group operated two Lloyds insurance brokers in London. Again the purchase price amounted to $67 million, this time with $32 million goodwill included. The original Kia Ora shareholders, who had been sitting on cash of $66 million, had within eight months bought two financial service groups for more than $130 million, of which $97 million was goodwill. By any standards this was a ridiculous premium. Not the least disturbing fact was that by May, when Kia Ora was taking over the Duke assets, it had already written off $20 million of the goodwill paid for Western United.[21]

When two takeovers are made in rapid succession like this it is often difficult afterwards to work out which dog had the most fleas. The Duke Group's maiden annual report, for the year to 30 June 1988, was issued on 28 October. While the balance sheet was that of the merged Duke Group, the profit and loss account was essentially that of Kia Ora and Western United, as the Duke companies had only been part of Duke Group for a month. The group reported an operating loss of nearly $900 000. However, if goodwill writeoffs totalling $1.7 million were added back, this could have been viewed as a pre-tax profit of $788 000. As far as Kia Ora shareholders were concerned it was still a dog of a result for all the money they had outlaid. The balance sheet showed total assets of $265 million against liabilities of $188 million. This was uncomfortably

Table 16.2 The Duke values (all figures in $m)

Business	Median value
Duke Pacific Finance	18.0
Duke Finance Holdings	18.9
Hadley Cannon	12.0
Kearns Corp (34.6%)	3.4
Other	13.0
Total	65.3

high gearing at 2.5:1. Shareholders' funds were stated at $76 million, but nearly $40 million of that was represented by goodwill, making the gearing ratio look even worse. The only justification for paying high goodwill for a business is that it will be commensurately profitable. Manifestly, Western United had not justified the massive goodwill paid for it.

Whatever hope Duke had evaporated in October 1988 when Rothwells finally hit the wall. There was a flight to quality by professional investors, who withdrew deposits from second-ranking financiers such as Duke and put their money in the banks. Reid said that Duke lost $60 million in deposits in the last ten weeks of 1988. Duke liquidated assets as fast as it could to meet the run, while shareholders pumped in another $10 million in December.[22]

By early 1989 the group's bankers had insisted that an independent evaluation be made of the group by Arthur Andersen & Co. Andersen was appointed by Reid at the end of March and reported just over a month later. Andersen found that the Duke businesses which had been bought for such fancy prices were almost worthless and that the group was losing money.[23] The purchase of the Duke businesses in the previous May had been supported by an assessment by Arthur Young & Co. The median values attached to the main businesses were as shown in Table 16.2.

On these numbers—which in the Arthur Young report were presented as a range from a low estimate of $64 million to a high estimate of $68.3 million Young concluded that the $67 million price tag which had been set on the Duke businesses was fair. The $67 million included $32.3 million goodwill. Young said that the goodwill was high because Duke Finance was a business which generated high returns on assets which were very highly geared, and because the UK insurance broker Hadley Cannon was projected to earn high levels of fee income, generated by the expertise of its people rather than its balance sheet assets.

Less than a year later the group was broke. During that time several of the assets classified under 'other' in Table 16.2 had realised their book values, but Duke Pacific, Duke Finance and the holding in Kearns were worthless and Hadley Cannon was estimated to be worth around $6 million. During that year many loans were made between various subsidiaries of the group. The group bought too many underperforming assets, undertook the funding of a takeover it could not afford (Cherry Lane) and lost money in the share market.

Andersen found that Duke Pacific Finance, widely regarded as the foundation stone of the group, was insolvent. 'We believe Duke Pacific had a negative cash flow of approximately $766,000 during March 1989', Andersen reported. 'Included in calculating this amount was approximately $440 000 of loan principal reductions. If Duke Pacific's income was evaluated on a cash basis we believe the operating deficiency could be as high as $1.2 million.'

Reid said that despite the Andersen report he had almost secured a moratorium from the banks in 1989, when the group was hit by a *coup de grâce*. In May 1989 Pat Burke's Hartogen oil and mining group went to the wall, with Hartogen and its associate Genoa going into liquidation. 'Genoa was a major shareholder in Duke', said Reid. 'The banks Pat was dealing with were the same as the Duke banks and they threw their hands in the air and said: "It's all too hard". '[24]

The collapse of the Hartogen group certainly didn't help but Duke had enough problems of its own anyway. To meet the run Duke had sold its better assets. Those that were left by early 1989 included too many bad loans and investments. Indeed, it hardly seemed to have any good ones left. Duke Finance was owed $15 million by fashion house Cherry Lane. It then financed a takeover of Cherry Lane by Gerah Imports. Then Duke Finance found itself unable to pay Gerah $1.5 million, with the result that Gerah placed Duke Finance in provisional liquidation.

Duke Securities had assets with a book value of $49 million whose real worth was estimated by Andersen at between $10 million and $20 million. It invested $11 million in Direct Acceptance Corporation, a company which had been fiscally parlous for years and was headed for liquidation and scandal itself.

Large amounts disappeared into Duke Securities Ltd, a wholly owned subsidiary of Duke Holdings. On the records available, if Duke Securities ever made a good investment it was an accident. It sank $17 million into investments which were mostly worth zero by May 1989.[25] The group had spread geographically, with subsidiaries in South-East Asia, Hong Kong, New Zealand and Canada. All of them lost money. Duke Canada was rather remarkable. By May 1989 it had money owing from some thirteen customers, almost none of whom were capable of repaying in full.

Sorting out The Duke Group took a long time. There were several transactions involving other busted enterprises such as Tricontinental and Direct Acceptance. It also took a long time to sort out the rights of creditors because almost every company within The Duke Group had external creditors as well as inter-company loans. The picture was further complicated by cross-guarantees of subsidiaries to banks. The liquidator of Duke Group, Adelaide accountant John Sheahan of Sheahan Sims, estimated the group deficiency at $48 million.

Sheahan sought to recover money for creditors and shareholders by suing Arthur Young for its evaluation of the Duke businesses, claiming $175 million in damages. In the court case Tom Gray, QC, for Sheahan, claimed that Kia Ora had paid $67 million for Duke businesses worth at most $51 000. Gray claimed that Kia Ora shareholders had been given 'materially incorrect' information in the Young report. Young settled out of court for an undisclosed figure, rumoured to be around $35 million. Sheahan then went a little further back into history and launched an action against the accountancy firm of Nelson Wheeler. Sheahan sued for $100 million, alleging negligence in Nelson Wheeler's independent report which had found the bid for Western United by Kia Ora to be fair and reasonable. Nelson Wheeler defended the action. Harold Abbott, Peter Reid and another Duke director, Paul Fitzsimmons, were charged with causing Duke Group to finance dealings in its own shares. Reid and Fitzsimmons were also charged with failing to act honestly under the Companies Code. All three directors defended the charges.

Reid pleaded not guilty, but he had already been punished by the shattering of his empire and his dream of building a finance house. 'I don't think I could ever run a business again', he said. 'I have good concepts, but I'm not good at picking the right people.'[26]

Electronic Enterprises

Ken Wright's career started off on the wrong foot when the young Darling Downs accountancy graduate came to Sydney in 1969 and got a job with the construction group, Mainline Corporation. By 1974 he had risen to become assistant company secretary, but then Mainline collapsed. Wright started work on his own as a tax accountant, scoring a coup when his one-man firm acted for Bob Hope on a tour of Australia and New Zealand in 1978. The tall, slim Wright, who habitually wore dark glasses and a Zapata moustache, became starstruck by the entertainment industry. He did some lucrative work for clients in the music, movie and record industries, then branched out in 1983.[27]

Wright's corporate empire centred on two companies which had been making heavy weather of traditional industries. In 1985 he picked up just over 50 per cent of the former electrical goods group, Hecla, which had become insolvent in the 1970s, and renamed it Investment Engineering Ltd. Investment Engineering in turn controlled a former agricultural machinery group, Agmac Ltd, which had been renamed Electronic Enterprises Ltd after acquiring a chain of record and electronics stores as well as the rights for an AIDS diagnostic kit. Electronic Enterprises also ran a couple of book and record clubs. This diversification was deliberate. Wright had been deeply impressed in his youth by a story about Canadian Pacific Railways that said that CPR would have gone out of business if it had merely concentrated on running a railroad.

Electronic Enterprises had a knack of getting good publicity. In April 1985 it was one of two companies to win a Federal Government contract to supply AIDS blood-screening equipment—a market worth a total of around $2.5 million a year. The company reported a profit of $1.6 million for 1984–85 plus extraordinary profits of $2.1 million. Electronic Enterprises declared a dividend of 3.5c a share. This impressed old shareholders, who had watched Agmac register three previous years of increasing losses. As well, Electronic Enterprises announced a one-for-five bonus issue.

The performance also impressed Potter Partners analyst Roger Colman, who in September published a buy recommendation for Electronic Enterprises, saying the group was 'in the embryonic stages of substantial expansion'. The survey continued:

> As with most entrepreneurial groups, it is not a case of buying existing operations . . . but the ambition and capabilities of the man in charge—Mr K.J. Wright . . . We are satisfied that the K.J. Wright group . . . has a better than even chance of developing into an entrepreneurial group such as those of Mr Christopher Skase, Mr Bruce Judge, Mr Lee Ming Tee and others with capitalisations of around $100 million. The current capitalisation of $12 million is so small that the risk reward ratio strongly favours investment. The chance of EEP achieving a $50 or $100 million capitalisation . . . is in our opinion substantially over 50 per cent. The risk of complete bankruptcy/liquidation—from $12 million to nothing—is minor.

One result of this enthusiasm was that several of Potter's staff bought into the stock. In the undiscriminating days of 1985 it all looked pretty good. It was the height of the AIDS scare and AIDS kits were the most fashionable investment imaginable. The mushroom growth of Skase and Judge had been widely admired. Wright seemed to have turned Electronic Enterprises around and was talking about a takeover in the home entertainment business in New York. In November Electronic Enterprises announced that it was planning to float its AIDS business separately.

But the public image and the private reality were a long way apart.

Behind the scenes, directors were indignant when board meetings were cancelled in June and August due to Wright's trips overseas. Chairman David Patten objected strongly at the September board meeting, where five directors resigned to be replaced by executives. One director had to go to court to regain control of shares which he had left in Wright's trust and wished to sell. In November the board retained consultants Buckmaster Hawkey Pty Ltd to report on the company's affairs.[28]

Wright was locked in litigation with former clients. One doctor had discovered that Wright had not filed tax returns for him for three years. The doctor won a judgement for $37 000 against Wright in November. Other clients were trying to recover money entrusted to Wright for investment, including some who had invested in trusts run by his Maffra Investments for land development in north Queensland.

Simultaneously, Wright had been having a dispute with the auditors, Nygh Hopper and Partners, over his treatment of profit and loss items. The auditors were particularly concerned about a maze of transactions between Investment Engineering, Electronic Enterprises and Wright's company Clarke Bros. Holdings, all of which had occurred without the board's authorisation or knowledge. At one point Wright had lent Investment Engineering $4 million out of the group's bank account to buy shares in Electronic Enterprises.

As neither Wright nor the companies had much cash, acquisitions had largely been funded by issuing scrip. As this had diluted Wright's control he had sought board approval to be issued with 14 million options to maintain his shareholding. But at the same time he was raising money by selling shares in Investment Engineering and Electronic Enterprises. Clarke Bros. raised $1 million by selling Investment Engineering shares between May and September, but raised its holding back up to 41 per cent by underwriting a three-for-five share issue. There was doubt, however, whether Wright had actually paid for the shares taken up in the shortfall.

As December opened, the net was closing on Wright. He sold his Porsche 928, then spent 3 December in the office making a series of round robin transactions in an attempt to rectify the loan balances between Clarke, Investment Engineering and Electronic Enterprises. On 4 December he sold a beachfront block of land he had bought a year earlier, netting a $500 000 profit. The 6th saw a stormy board meeting. Buckmaster Hawkey came down on the side of the auditors. After a private meeting with Patten, Wright and his managing director Richard Sheslow resigned. Two days later Wright boarded a jet for the United States.

The whole bubble burst on 10 December, when the board announced the retirements of Wright as chief executive officer and of Richard Sheslow as managing director. As Wright had always been regarded as synonymous with Electronic Enterprises the announcement stunned the investment community. Wright, who had always been easily accessible to the financial press for positive stories about his company, was suddenly unavailable and overseas. The profit was written back to just over $1 million. The float of the AIDS kit was cancelled, along with the bonus issue and the 3.5c dividend. The shares, which had been 35c when Potter's staff were buying, were suspended because the company had failed to lodge accounts.

When the accounts were put together in January 1986 they showed more than $5 million in unauthorised loans to Wright. Buckmaster Hawkey reported that the group's financial position was dire. Instead of making a profit in 1984–85 Electronic Enterprises had lost $450 000. Worse, it had lost three times that much between July and December. The price of the shares plummeted to a few cents when suspension was lifted briefly in January, but investors were put out of their misery a month later when Electronic Enterprises was placed in receivership. A warrant was issued for Wright's arrest on charges of receiving money on false pretences, but he was never seen again. However, he did send the *Australian* a postcard from Santa Barbara.

Western Women

Late 1990 saw the corporate unveiling of Western Women Management Pty Ltd, the brainchild of an aggressive, ambitious woman named Robin Greenburg. She proclaimed that her mission was to found a finance house run by women and for women. Western Women owned all the shares of the Victoria-based First Mortgage Permanent Building Society, which was going to be renamed the First Womens Permanent Building Society and 'take account of customers' circumstances and ability to pay rather than their asset backing'. Greenburg also launched a prospectus for W & W Investments Pty Ltd to support enterprises at least 51 per cent owned by women or 'to raise money for investment in ethical industries such as alternative power sources'.

Women were attracted by the concept, but Greenburg complained that she was fighting prejudice in her efforts to set up a financial institution for ordinary people. She complained of a 'concerted effort' to stop her operating a building society and accused the bureaucracy and the media of collaborating with the financial establishment. The Registrar of Building Societies was accused because he was taking time to lift a suspension order on the First Permanent.

Greenburg was using all the right buzzwords and won some

sympathy. The 'Corporate Woman' column of the *Australian Financial Review* said:

> Imagine a bank which sympathetically helps an enterprising young woman, with a five-year business plan but little else behind her, to set up her own small business. Or a building society which offers a mortgage to a recently divorced woman—with few assets and no credit rating but a good ability to pay. For many Australian women, such examples remain exactly that—sheer imaginings. A common complaint remains that women still experience discrimination and more difficulty in obtaining finance, both for business and personal use, than men do. But, if a West Australian female financier has her way, that situation will soon end.[29]

The *AFR* conceded, however, that Greenburg had two bankruptcies behind her. She had been declared bankrupt in 1972 in New South Wales—as Robin Rickards—when Knickerbocker Pet Products of Double Bay went to the wall. A marriage later she went bankrupt again in 1983 in South Australia—as Robin Rosenbaum. She was discharged from her second bankruptcy in 1986. In a brilliant epigram, Greenburg said she had suffered from 'sexually transmitted debt . . . you get it from your husbands'.

The Australian Securities Commission was unimpressed. On 28 February 1991 it applied to the WA Supreme Court to restrain Western Women Management and its associated company Western Women Financial Management Pty Ltd from raising money from the public or selling shares to them except through a registered prospectus. The ASC also asked the court to appoint a receiver to Western Women to determine its assets. Greenburg accused the ASC of being sexist. The ASC said that it had received a lot of complaints from disgruntled investors in Western Women. Women who had deposited money with Greenburg were having trouble getting it back.

The prospectus for W & W Investments professed exemplary feminist attitudes but looked a poor investment proposition. W & W was seeking $7.5 million from the public, comprising 10 million 50c shares plus a further $2.5 million in oversubscriptions. The first problem, from a shareholder's viewpoint, was the voting structure. Control of W & W was retained by Western Women Management Trust, a trust associated with the directors and the holder of the management shares. There were 1000 management shares which cost only $500 but which would carry 60 per cent of the votes at any meeting of the company. 'This will ensure that the women behind the company's inception will remain in the position to control the future direction of the company and to provide the company with the expertise and experience to successfully achieve the company's set objectives', the prospectus said. 'The knowledge of the directors of the financial concerns of women is considered a strategic asset of the company.'

As the investors were being invited to subscribe to what was essentially a cashbox and were also being asked to abdicate control forever to a handful of self-appointed experts at the top, the financial experience of those who would run the company was crucial. However, the prospectus failed to mention Greenburg's previous bankruptcies. The prospectus also gave only vague indications of how the $7.5 million might be spent. One proviso was that no investment of more than $500 000 would be made in any company connected with the directors without the prior approval of the ordinary shareholders. This could be taken as a sign that the directors were planning significant investments in companies connected with themselves. Also the limit was on individual investments, not the total. There would be nothing to stop directors making as many $499 000 investments in their own companies as they liked. Finally, W & W Investments was not going to be listed on the stock exchange. Directors would do their best to organise a secondary market in the shares.

Against some stiff competition it remains one of the worst prospectuses I have ever read, in terms of investor protection. Committed feminists might have supported the concepts espoused by Greenburg, but only the financially suicidal could have invested in any company that gave investors so little protection.[30]

Western Women was financially dead as soon as the WA Supreme Court agreed to the ASC's request and appointed a receiver. The good news was that the receiver was a woman, Diana Newman of Bird Cameron. The bad news was that she was appointed on International Women's Day (9 March 1991). Greenburg claimed that her group had been attacked because it was not part of the system.

This claim might have found more sympathy if curious reports had not begun emerging from Perth. Documents of Western Women began appearing in strange places. A member of the Fremantle Rowing club found a plastic garbage bag, weighted with a stone, washed up on the shores of the Swan River. Inside were Western Women documents, including cancelled cheques and details of transactions. Then a bushfire started near the small country town of Gingin. Firefighters battling the blaze traced the source to a kerosene-soaked garbage bin. Although the fire had ravaged part of the surrounding countryside, enough of the bin's contents were salvaged to identify them as more Western Women documents.

In her short but active life as a financier Greenburg had managed to attract the not inconsiderable sum of $9.4 million in deposits, including $500 000 from the R & I Bank. In the final analysis some $6 million was lost. Greenburg had embezzled some $3 million of it—spent on high living, credit cards and $1 million in antiques and jewellery. Greenburg fled. Warrants were issued for her arrest, but she gave herself up three months later in Perth. Meanwhile, police had unearthed yet more Western Women documents buried in a heap of fertiliser in her garden.

In September 1992 she pleaded guilty to 49 charges of theft and arson and was sentenced to seventeen years' jail, of which fourteen were for starting the bushfire. Her only defence was that she had destroyed documents to protect investors' confidentiality. The WA Government, National Australia Bank and R & I Bank later offered $3.8 million in compensation to her depositors. Her lawyer, David Grace, tried to get Greenburg's sentence reduced. He told the WA Court of Criminal Appeal that she had a 'grossly abnormal personality' and 'saw herself as grand and invincible'. He said that her abnormal personality also explained why she was unable to express remorse for her actions.

Westmex

Of all the whiz-kids of the 1980s few were younger or whizzed to the top faster than Russell Goward. He started as an office boy in the National Library in Canberra and rose to head the research department of the financial institutions section of Treasury. The day he did his last exam in the public service he quit and went to Sydney to make money. Goward joined Hill Samuel, where he started as a statistical research officer with Will Buttrose.[31] After five years he left to join Industrial Equity Ltd, a young man on the fast track. With his attractively lean youthful face, blue eyes and mop of curly black hair Goward looked like a heart-throb, and was. His financial drive was matched by a strong physical drive. On early morning jogs around the neighbourhood he would sometimes drop in on his wife's sister and make love en route, so to speak.

Goward was a protégé of Ron Brierley, rising to be chief executive of Industrial Equity at the age of 29. But, even though IEL was one of the most active raiders, traders and greenmailers on the bourse, it was not enough for Goward, who wanted to make his own fortune. He moved out in early 1986, a few days short of his 32nd birthday, to take over Westmex Ltd. Westmex was a former exploration company that had run out of puff and was being used by Melbourne investor David Hains as a medium for dabbling in the share market. Goward placed some shares to improve its spread and had Westmex relisted in March 1986. Taking 1c paid contributing shares, Goward acquired 30 per cent of Westmex for $120 000. He owed 21c each on 12 million shares and could not trade them for five years.

In the bull market of the mid-1980s an ambitious entrepreneur with a bit of track record could usually count on some support from brokers, bankers and institutions hoping to hitch a ride on his coat-tails. Goward's record with IEL and his fast driving manner won several of them, even though his youthful cockiness turned others off. This never fazed Goward. 'If I wanted to be a nice guy I'd be a politician', he said. Westmex shares jumped from 35c to $1.10 almost solely on the fact that Goward had arrived at the boardroom. He quickly took advantage of the premium by announcing a rights issue at $1 a share to raise $19.6 million, even though this meant that he would have to chip in $6 million himself.

Goward moved quickly. By June he had taken a controlling stake in the UK oil company Charterhall plc, which then took over Pancontinental Petroleum. He took control of an Australian oil trust and the CRA subsidiary, IOL Petroleum. In yet another oil play Westmex (acting through Charterhall) took over BA Oil & Gas Management (BAOGM). In the year to June 1987 Westmex reported an operating profit of $6 million. The figure was disputed by its auditors, Mann Judd, who disagreed with Westmex policy of including 'acquisition discounts' which amounted to unrealised gains on investments.

The BAOGM takeover by Charterhall was at the centre of the dispute. BAOGM had the management rights to a company named BA Petroleum. A few days before the takeover the BAOGM board had revalued these management rights to $5 million. Then they sold BAOGM to Charterhall for the value of its tangible assets, plus $1 million for the management rights to BA Petroleum. Because these rights had been valued at $5 million, Charterhall—and hence Westmex—claimed a profit of $4 million on the deal. It needs no accountancy expertise to see the unreal nature of this alleged profit. For one thing it hadn't been realised. For another, the $5 million valuation could hardly have been regarded as realistic if a few days later the board which made the valuation was prepared to sell the asset for one-fifth of that price.

A dividend proposed by Westmex also created a problem. Its stake in Charterhall was held through a wholly owned subsidiary. Westmex proposed to revalue its holding in Charterhall to 48c a share (disregarding the fact that the market price was fluctuating around 35c at the time) and the revaluation increment could be paid to Westmex by the subsidiary as a dividend. This could be stated as a profit and a dividend could be paid to Westmex shareholders. Westmex was proposing to pay out cash although it had not received any. Mann Judd senior partner, John Biddle, said: 'It made my blood run cold to think that dividends might be paid out of a share revaluation reserve'.[32]

After a dispute with Westmex, Mann Judd agreed to resign on the condition that all relevant facts were disclosed to the National Companies and Securities Commission. The NCSC sided with the auditor, estimating that profit had been overstated by nearly $5 million. Biddle and his partners at Mann Judd deserve high praise for the firm's sacrifice of the Westmex account. Mann Judd was a second-tier accountancy firm and Westmex was one of its biggest and most promising clients. Plenty of other—and larger—accountancy firms would have been prepared to wink at optimistic accounting by such a hot, growing customer. Sadly, the Mann Judd resignation stands alone as the only known instance during the boom of an auditor being prepared to quit rather than bend principles. In October Westmex agreed to change its policy on acquisition discounts, but by then Mann Judd was gone.

Westmex continued on the expansionary trail, taking a stake in the specialist business paper supplier, Moore Business Systems. Black Tuesday wrought little apparent damage on Westmex. Goward's strategy had been to buy into businesses—mostly in oil and in office supplies—which were largely unaffected by the collapse. In March 1988 he reported a 600 per cent interim profit increase to $8 million. In June he bought the 97-year-old newsagents' cooperative ANCOL, which supplied stationery to newsagencies throughout Australia. ANCOL included the agency for Soccerpools and the courier service for the collection of Lotto coupons and instant lottery tickets. In Britain, Westmex bought a series of shoe retailers. Goward pointed out that he was in recession-proof industries.

Westmex shares, which had been 65c earlier in the year, jumped to over $1. Profit for 1987–88 was reported at $17.5 million, a rise of 75 per cent. The growth continued in December as Westmex bought a stake in the British underpants maker Corah plc. The story went out that one in every ten Englishmen now wore underpants made in a knitting mill controlled by Westmex. And Westmex kept expanding in British shoe shops and Australian stationery. In early 1989 Westmex must have been the stock most recommended, outside the top 100 companies, by Australian brokers. *Australian Business* went along with the trend, nominating Westmex as the outstanding new entrant in its listing of Australia's Top 500 companies. The nomination was in recognition of Westmex's result for 1987–88. Unfortunately, the judges were not perceptive enough to see what was going to happen to the group in the year to June 1989.[33]

Westmex kept going with bids for Australian Petroleum Fund and the Glasgow retailer A. Goldberg & Son. In August 1989 Westmex announced a 34 per cent increase in net profit to $27 million and a 6.5c dividend. The company also announced a one-for-four rights issue at 75c to fund further acquisitions. The shares stood at $1.41.

One of the attractions of Goward was that he always preached an investment philosophy along the lines of Warren Buffet. Goward claimed that he never took a salary from Westmex or even owned a company car. He said that he planned to get rich from dividends and the rise in value of Westmex shares. He worked a long seven days a week, which he did not regard as a hardship because he thought business was fun. He ran a spartan head office. As a result he won wide admiration—until the publication of Westmex's 1989 annual report, which must rank as one of the most schizophrenic financial documents of the era. The noble sentiments in the front half of the report were in total contrast to the disaster revealed in the accounts at the back. The opening pages stated the corporate objective of Westmex as:

> *To optimise long term returns to shareholders.* This will be achieved by maximising the dividends paid and the wealth created in the company through the identification, acquisition and development of well managed operating businesses in chosen industries with the potential to show outstanding returns (operating profits plus increases in business value) on the funds Westmex has invested in them—where those businesses can be acquired at an immediate discount on underlying business value and onsold when they reach their full potential.

The annual report went on to spell out the principles in greater detail. It aimed at earnings-per-share growth of 20 per cent per annum and a dividend payout ratio of 70 per cent. Westmex would always have some gearing, but felt uncomfortable if it went above 1:1 (defined as debt as a proportion of the 'true value' of shareholders' funds). New share capital would be raised only when the board was convinced that Westmex could continue to show above-average returns. Activities would be confined to Britain and Australia. Finally, the report said: 'Although we manage, our attitude is proprietary. Most senior executives have the majority of their wealth invested in Westmex and we regard other shareholders as partners in the business'.

The sentiments were impeccable. But any shareholder who kept reading on to the financial detail in the back half of the report must have received a nasty shock. Westmex's balance sheet showed total assets of $582 million against liabilities of $413 million, leaving net assets of $169 million. Of that $169 million, $70 million represented the interests of minority holders. Shareholders' funds attributable to Westmex shareholders were therefore only $99 million. Creditors and borrowings totalled $410 million, giving Westmex a debt to shareholders' funds ratio of more than 2:1, well above the 1:1 referred to earlier in this book. The balance sheet is shown in Table 16.3.

But the gearing ratio might have been academic because of the impact of intangibles on shareholders' funds. The $153 million intangibles represented goodwill on acquisition. This was the amount Westmex had paid for companies over and above the value of their net tangible assets. If this goodwill were written off, so were the shareholders' funds. Westmex actually had a deficiency of $54 million in net tangible assets. In addition, analysts looked at the 'other' assets of $107 million. The largest item there

Table 16.3   Westmex balance sheet, 30 June 1989 (all figures in $m)

ASSETS	
Current Assets	172.8
Non-Current Assets:	
Investments	82.7
Property, plant, equipment	66.4
Intangibles	153.2
Other	107.3
Total Assets	582.4
LIABILITIES	
Current Liabilities:	
Creditors & borrowings	183.8
Provisions	3.0
Non-Current Liabilities:	
Creditors & borrowings	226.7
Provisions	0.2
Total Liabilities	413.8
SHAREHOLDERS' FUNDS	
Share capital	16.6
Reserves	36.7
Retained profits	45.3
Minority interests	70.0
Net Assets	168.6

was $86 million for trade and brand names. The valuations placed on goodwill and brand names could only be justified if those businesses were earning good profits. Most of the intangibles related to the footwear and stationery businesses which had been bought during the year. The segmental results in Note 28 to the accounts showed that the stationery business had earned less than $1 million on assets of $85 million. Footwear had done better, but still earned only $7.5 million on assets of $188 million. Analysts quickly worked out that if Westmex could not generate better earnings than these it would be unable to meet its interest bill. They were also spooked by the huge goodwill which had reduced Westmex's net tangible asset backing to a negative.

Investors began dumping the stock, which slid from $1.30 in early October to $1. At the annual meeting in November Goward mysteriously criticised competitors for sabotaging the stock price, saying the under-bidders for ANCOL were 'doing a poor man's Tiny Rowlands' by ringing stockbrokers and trying to discredit the company. The shares were bashed further, sliding to 59c at the start of December. Then they were clobbered by the AMP, which sold six million shares at between 35c and 45c. Goward was both bitter and brave, claiming he was 'still 100 per cent committed to Westmex'. Goward's stake had been diluted to 25 per cent, but he had borrowed heavily to finance the shares he had taken up in rights issues and stood to be wiped out if the company collapsed. As 1990 opened, the price had gone to 25c. Much later the ASC would allege that Goward had been one of the sellers. In 1994 he was charged with making a false and misleading statement by telling investors he had not sold shares, although he had sold $5 million worth in Hong Kong. Goward denied that he had sold any shares and defended the charge.

Goward sold his personal assets. His deer farm at Mangrove went, along with his six-bedroom mansion in Sydney's leafy Wahroonga. He had spent $1.5 million on the house, including a floodlit all-weather tennis court and a solar-heated swimming pool with a pool house incorporating its own kitchen, bathroom, bedrooms, spa, sauna and gymnasium. Goward was so devoted to gardening that he had imported 200 000 earthworms and had spent $200 000 on computerised watering systems. In February ANCOL was put into receivership and a few days later Westmex followed suit. Goward was bankrupted with debts of $33 million—and divorced. His accounting had been creative, but he suffered more from it than anyone else. He retained a few friends. Former Westmex investment director Maurice Loomes provided him with some financial assistance and his wife lent him a Land Cruiser.

Goward was one of the more endearing corporate cowboys of the 1980s. His examination in bankruptcy mainly centred on cheques he had made out to his estranged wife Catherine to ensure that she had enough money to live on. He managed to bequeath her a $1.25 million house at Pymble. She did not make the best possible use of it, however, leasing the house to notorious confidence man Phillip Kingston Carver who later defaulted on the rent.

Immediately after the Westmex collapse Goward moved into a house at Mona Vale and took up gardening for six months. The curly mop was cut back and straightened out. He remarried, but his new wife Nicole then suffered the indignity of having her wedding and engagement rings confiscated by Goward's trustee in bankruptcy, accountant Hugh Wily of Armstrong Wily. Property developer John Lyons gave Russell and Nicole a few wedding gifts, including payment of food and legal bills and the setting up of a $5000 punting account at the TAB. Wily pursued Goward, claiming that he had made cheap duplicates of his wife's wedding ring and had withheld the real $5000 rings. Goward was charged with perjury for allegedly having lied to a court about the value of Nicole's rings. At the time of writing, Goward was seeking legal aid to defend the charges. In the total context of the Westmex collapse it seemed an exceedingly petty charge to bring.

17
Give or take a billion

*In times of great commercial prosperity there has been a tendency to
over-speculation on several occasions since then [the South Sea Bubble].
The success of one project generally produces others of a similar kind.
Popular imitativeness will always, in a trading nation, seize hold of such
successes, and drag a community too anxious for profits into an abyss
from which extrication is difficult.*

Charles Mackay, *Extraordinary Popular Delusions
and the Madness of Crowds*

Mackay's classic history of the South Sea Bubble, the tulip mania of
Holland and the Banque Royale was published in 1841. Despite its
popularity, the tome was totally unsuccessful in preventing the outbreak
of Britain's great railway share mania of 1845. The pattern of all those
manias—and the subsequent panics—has been the same. The prosperous
classes become persuaded of the value of some commodity, which can
be anything from nickel or tulips to property or shares. Solid profits made
by early investors in these commodities lure more investors into the
market. As the boom gathers heat, investment gives way to gambling.
Also, speculators borrow heavily in the hope of the huge profits which
can be gained by leveraging. The market prices of the commodities lose
all connection with realistic values. 'Rich people no longer bought the
flowers to keep them in their gardens, but to sell them again at cent per
cent profit', observed Mackay of the 17th century Dutch tulip craze. 'It
was seen that somebody must lose fearfully in the end. As this conviction
spread, prices fell, and never rose again. Confidence was destroyed, and
a universal panic seized upon the dealers.' And so the tulip boom ended,
and so the bold riders' boom ended, and so all future booms will end.

While Australia has seen plenty of minor booms and busts, that of
the 1980s was particularly damaging. Give or take a billion dollars, the
bold riders mentioned in this book lost around $16 billion. Table 17.1 sets
out the estimates.[1] In reading this table it should be remembered that loss
figures can be subject to wide variation. One reason is that in some cases
the wipeout of shareholders' funds has been added to the recorded losses,
while for other groups the losses shown are the liquidator's or receiver's
estimated deficiency without the shareholders' equity added back. The

table therefore understates the true position. A second reason for the variation is that in some cases the creditors continued to add interest after a group collapsed but in the real basket cases it was perceived as an academic exercise, so they didn't bother. A third reason is that liquidators' estimates of deficiencies depend on their estimates of asset values. Many of the companies in Table 17.1 held a significant proportion of their assets—or so-called assets—in property, which may have realised more or less than expected. For these and other reasons the table does not pretend to be mathematically accurate, but rather gives a global estimate of the cost of the corporate insanities of the 1980s.

If anything, the global estimate is conservative. It does not include private companies of the bold riders such as Dallhold and GPI. It would have been tedious to try to remove the double counting where the private companies had guaranteed the downstream public companies. And, as the table shows only consolidated group losses, it omits associated companies. The most notable of these was Bell Resources, which lost some $1.5 billion while under Bond Corporation control. Also, the table omits a host of collapses such as Ariadne ($640 million), Girvan Corporation ($440 million), Metrogrowth ($27 million) and the WA Teachers' Credit Union ($44 million). By any prior standards these would have ranked as large disasters, but it is a yardstick of the 1980s that space limitations crowded any detailed examination of them out of this book. Bearing these factors in mind, the total lost by the bold riders of the 1980s must have been at least $20 billion.

This was the biggest string of corporate disasters in Australian history. The companies in Table 17.1 controlled almost the entire Australian beer industry, the country's largest industrial group (Adsteam), the largest pastoral company (Elders), the second largest retail chain (Woolworths, inside Adsteam), the largest food and textile groups, the largest car renter, the largest mortgage trust group and a substantial slice of the commercial property market.

The men who ran these companies were widely admired. Some, such as Brian Yuill and Abe Goldberg, were unknown to the wider public and Chor Kian Yap tried to ensure that no photograph of him existed. But others such as Alan Bond and Bob Ansett were as well recognised as film stars—a rare phenomenon among top businessmen in Australia. Alan Bond was a national hero, rightly, when he won the America's Cup. John Elliott was seen by some as the man who would revive the Liberal Party. Some—particularly Robert Holmes à Court and John Spalvins—cultivated an enigmatic image that gave them a reputation for omniscience.

They built some new assets, such as the Port Douglas Mirage, but more often they reorganised assets which had been created by others. Some businesses may have been improved by this process, but many were

Table 17.1 What they lost

Group (a)	($m)
Adsteam (b)	2 100
Bond Corp (b)(c)	5 330
Budget	86
Compass I (d)	290
Compass II	78
Deposit & Investment (e)	100
Duke	30
Estate Mortgage (f)	700
Hooker (b)(g)	1 390
International Brewing (h)	1 530
Interwest	300
Linter (i)	750
National Safety Council (Vic.)	250
Pyramid, Geelong, Countrywide	980
Qintex (b)(j)	1 260
Rothwells	600
Spedley (k)	400
TEA	20
Western Women	6
Westmex	350
Total	16 550

(a) Estimates only, based on consolidated accounts. Bank and finance companies excluded to avoid double counting.

(b) Consolidated group losses plus previous shareholders' funds. (Most other figures in the table are receivers' or liquidators' estimates of deficiencies between assets and liabilities. Thus they do not include wipeout of previous shareholders' funds. Losses may therefore be somewhat understated.)

(c) Does not include associated companies, such as Bell Resources, where $1.5 billion was lost. Also, does not include Bond's private company Dallhold.

(d) Of this, $150 million is amounts owing on aircraft leases which crystallised as due and payable as soon as Compass I stopped flying. Bryan Grey has protested that this amount should not be included, on the grounds that the payments were supposed to have stretched over a further decade. However, it is a debt that cannot be ignored and there seems no other way of treating it in a table such as this. The other $140 million estimated as lost in Compass I comprised the $70 million equity which was wiped out plus $70 million in unused tickets which was owing when it collapsed.

(e) Includes Multivest and Sunmark.

(f) Does not include losses in Low private companies, such as $44 million in Estate Mortgage Financial Services.

(g) Does not include Hersfield losses.

(h) Formerly Harlin Holdings, the company formed by John Elliott and friends to hold the controlling interest in Elders IXL.

(i) Does not include Goldberg private companies.

(j) Does not include Skase's private company Kahmea.

(k) Of the Spedley losses $240 million was absorbed by its shareholder, ANI. The stated losses do not include Yuill's private company, GPI.

not. Anything bought by Alan Bond or Abe Goldberg was quickly loaded with debt to the Plimsoll line and sometimes beyond. In a sense, they were parasites of Australian society and finance. The savings of ordinary Australians (and quite a few from overseas) were splurged on spending sprees for their companies and themselves. They lived lavish lifestyles on other people's money and never repaid it. Their companies paid little or nothing in taxes, yet they assiduously sought favours and subsidies from governments, particularly in Western Australia.

The banks

One thing the bold riders had in common was that all of them were operating on other people's money. Apart from the two Compasses, which mainly lost equity capital, all their empires were fuelled by debt. This has been so throughout history. For two hundred years Australia has never had any shortage of corporate cowboys and all of them borrowed as much as they could.[2] What was truly remarkable about the 1980s was the willingness—even desperation—of the financial system to lend to them. Never before in our history have so many financiers—both in Australia and around the world—been so eager to lend money to bold riders. The corporate cowboys were complemented by cowboy bankers. Table 17.2 estimates the banks' losses.[3]

This table collates bank bad debt writeoffs and provisions between 1990 and 1993. As can be seen, they totalled $28 billion. This figure needs to be treated with some reservation. Even a well-run bank in prosperous times should make some bad debt provisions. Any bank that has no bad debt provisions can be fairly accused of not trying hard enough. And losses were bound to be higher than normal in the three years covered by the table, because these years also covered the longest and severest recession Australia had seen since the Great Depression. Small businesses died by the tens of thousands during these years, so loan writeoffs were going to be high for banks even if they had not exposed themselves so imprudently to the bold riders of the boom. On the other hand, the table does not take into account the huge losses suffered by such fringe banking institutions as the SA and WA State Government Insurance Commissions. After allowing for these factors a ballpark guess on what the banking and financial system lost on imprudent lending (as opposed to normal and recession-induced losses) in the 1980s would be somewhere around $20 billion.

Having reached the same ballpark figure—necessarily roughly—in both Table 17.1 and Table 17.2, it seems justifiable to count $20 billion as the cost of the decade of the bold riders.

Who bore the cost? Table 17.2 indicates that at least part of Australia's

Table 17.2 What the banks lost—net bad debt writeoffs and provisions, 1989 to 1993

Bank	($m)
Westpac	6 367
ANZ	4 690
National	3 271
State Bank SA	3 150
Commonwealth	2 976
State Bank Victoria	2 427
Bank of New Zealand	1 338
State Bank NSW	831
Citibank	713
R & I	541
HongkongBank	517
Security Pacific	326
Barclays	256
Natwest	224
Chase AMP	193
Standard Chartered	146
Lloyds	131
Bank America	90
Société Générale	50
Total	28 237

decade of excess was subsidised by foreigners. Overseas banks poured money into Australian corporate cowboys during the decade. The Australian banks were fairly wary of Alan Bond, for example, whose banking mainstay was the Hong Kong & Shanghai. Overseas banks carried a high proportion of losses. So did the state banks who were trying to muscle into the corporate market. The State Bank of Victoria and State Bank of South Australia effectively went broke and needed massive governmental rescues. Apart from the money lost by overseas banks, the bill for the bold riders was paid by Australian taxpayers (who had to bail out the profligate states of Western Australia, Victoria and South Australia); by shareholders in the banks (who saw their fortunes diminish and dividends slashed); and by the remaining creditworthy customers of banks (who were slugged mercilessly for years afterwards as the banks got their balance sheets back into order). And unsecured creditors and trade creditors were wiped out by the thousand.

Banking in the 1980s in Australia degenerated into a mad scramble to maintain market share. At the end of the day the four major trading banks managed to maintain their share overall, although the National emerged as the dominant bank and Westpac slipped a long way from its former leadership.

Were the losses avoidable? The overwhelming majority of them certainly were. The first chapter showed the process by which traditional

573

banking caution broke down in the 1980s (with the breakdown actually starting in the 1970s). The case histories detailed in this book show that the weaknesses of the corporate cowboys would in nearly all cases have soon been detected by any diligent credit check. One of the few to do so was the Australian Bank, which was alert and streetwise enough to detect early warning signals in Estate Mortgage.

The Australian Bank was really only doing what banks are supposed to do. Hardly anyone else did, and the foregoing chapters are riddled with examples. The SBSA bought Oceanic Capital for $60 million and United Building Society of New Zealand for $157 million without completing a thorough due diligence. No adequate reason was ever given for making such large purchases in such haste. The problems of both became apparent almost before the ink was dry on the cheques, with both needing large and immediate capital injections.

There are plenty of other examples. Various banks pumped a billion dollars into Qintex although its interest cover had been skinny for years. They pumped nearly another billion into Linter although there was no way its earnings could have covered the interest. The ANZ lent $2 billion to Warwick Fairfax when none of its senior management had ever met him. The State Bank of Victoria won the NSC account without realising that its main asset was fresh air in containers. Yet the Australian Bank discovered the high-risk nature of Estate Mortgage four years before Estate collapsed.

The banks were deficient in another respect too. They lent money for takeovers and projects with little consideration of whether the borrowers were capable of *managing* the enterprise. The point may be made by contrasting Rupert Murdoch with Warwick Fairfax. Murdoch was even younger than Fairfax when he took command of his first newspaper. But he was dedicated, intelligent and spent a lifetime building what became the world's largest media empire. As long as his bankers kept Murdoch's debts under some sensible control, he would always be a better bet than Warwick Fairfax, who had so little interest in his $2 billion acquisition that he rarely turned up at the building and—on his own sworn evidence—did not always read the *Sydney Morning Herald*.[4] Another example of Warwick's diffidence was provided in January 1988, just after he had taken over John Fairfax Ltd. Ron Cotton had been installed as managing director but the rest of the takeover team had disbanded. At that juncture the National Bank was threatening to withdraw a $15 million line of credit. As Fairfax did not have the funds to meet it the company was facing the threat of liquidation the next day. If Cotton could not contact Warwick and agree on an action plan the new proprietor was in danger of losing his empire within days of acquiring it. After half a dozen desperate phone calls Cotton discovered Warwick's whereabouts. He was in Papua New Guinea on a Bible mission. Cotton scrambled out of the crisis and Fairfax did not collapse for another couple of years.

The professions

The banks (whose follies were studied at length in the opening chapter) were not the only watchdogs who did not bark. If the financial community worked the way it is supposed to, outside directors would have exercised their authority over runaway chief executives; accountants and auditors would have detected and exposed the pea-and-thimble tricks in the bold riders' accounts; lawyers would have refused to endorse their thefts; merchant banks would not have lent money and imprimatur to their schemes; brokers would not have pushed their shares; fund managers would not have invested in them; and the financial press would have castigated them. Thus another truly remarkable phenomenon of the 1980s was the way in which all these professions prostituted themselves—with the odd honourable exception—to the bold riders.

Boards of directors proved ineffectual. Out of dozens of examples that could be cited from these case histories, let us consider Trustees Executor & Agency Co. In September 1980 the TEA board specifically vetoed the use of client interest-bearing deposits (CIBs) to finance property ventures. A few months later it was allowing them to be used for just that purpose. Each monthly board meeting of TEA was presented with a full report showing how the company was being led down the road to risk. The directors were fully informed but apparently still did not realise what was happening. This illustrates one of the most intractable problems in finance. To an old, moribund company the impact of a *wunderkind* is almost irresistible. If the board members have few or no ideas, if the company is in a dead-end industry, if profits are falling, if a company with a long tradition looks like going out of business, directors are highly amenable to the arrival of a bright young saviour. The directors of TEA and Adelaide Steamship would not have been human if they had not welcomed the advent of Peter Bunning and John Spalvins. Similar episodes, not recorded in this book, occurred at the old trading house of Gollin with the arrival of Keith Gale and at the old electronics group AWA with the arrival of Andy Koval as a whiz-kid forex dealer.

Old companies must be reinvigorated by transfusions of fresh blood. A company is only a paper entity. It has life and ideas only through the people who work for it. Directors of old, tottering companies would be failing in their duties if they did not seek and back bright new managers. But having recruited their saviour, the board still has a duty to control and monitor him. In too many cases in this book boards simply did not

575

know what was happening in their companies. Boards can also be intimidated by a high-powered chief executive, afraid that if they take too
strong a stand their saviour will abandon them. History tells us that any
chief executive who is so high-handed that he will resign rather than
accept proper board scrutiny—let alone control—is almost invariably too
high-handed for his or the company's good.

But, whether the companies were old or new, too many directors
simply sat impotently while massive disasters were being created. In the
words of SA Auditor-General Ken MacPherson:

> It was not beyond the capabilities of the non-executive directors to take
> commonsense measures and to stand no nonsense. To be blunt, there is
> nothing esoteric about asking questions, seeking information, demanding
> explanations and extracting further details. There is nothing unduly
> burdensome in expecting each director, to the best of his or her ability,
> to insist on understanding what was laid before them, even at the risk
> of becoming unpopular. Both the law, and a basic sense of duty and
> responsibility, demand it.[5]

Auditors also deserve a special mention. If the audit profession cannot
function any more usefully than it did in Australia in the 1980s then it
might as well be abolished. As almost every audit firm named in this
book has since been the subject of a large lawsuit it is unfortunately risky
to say much more. Hopefully, the lawsuits against auditors and their
insurers will improve the diligence of the profession in future. One of the
few to behave honourably was Mann Judd, which chose to sacrifice the
Westmex account—one of its biggest and certainly its fastest growing—
rather than endorse what it believed to be unsound accounting policies.
Sadly, but understandably, this was not followed by any great rush of
business from companies anxious to have Mann Judd audit their accounts.

In most cases greed was the explanation for the readiness of the
professions to lower their standards. Banks, directors, lawyers and
accountants were all earning fat fees from the bold riders. And the impact
of greed went further, permeating the whole business community. Bob
Maumill tells an anecdote about Yosse Goldberg in the Parmelia dining
room foaming that Gough Whitlam and his party were communists, and
dramatically impaling a steak knife into the table in his rage. Yet a few
years later Goldberg was ecstatically doing a deal with the WA Labor
Government and donating large sums to the party. Another anecdote is
about the famous John Curtin Foundation photograph showing Alan
Bond, Laurie Connell, Sir Ernest Lee-Steere and half a dozen other
businessmen with Brian Burke and Bob Hawke. 'What you can't see just
outside the camera range is another five hundred businessmen in that
room all straining to be in the photograph', said Maumill. 'If Burkie had
locked the doors and told them they each had to contribute $5000 before

they left, if they wanted to get their next zoning application or whatever considered, he would have got the money.'[6]

The role of the financial press was widely criticised. The accusation was that the financial press made heroes of the bold riders and failed to expose their shortcomings. The answer was that the performance of the press was patchy. Some journalists were far too starry-eyed, but at the other end of the scale Terry McCrann of the Melbourne *Herald*, for example, was a notable sceptic throughout. Speaking as a senior finance writer, perhaps my own observations may be useful. One substantial inhibition on journalists at all times is the law of defamation. It is a serious allegation to say that an apparently prospering company is broke or that its directors are criminals. Consider the fate of South Australia Democrat Leader Ian Gilfillan, who was sued for defamation by the State Bank of SA for raising questions about its deals. He was mulcted of several thousand dollars and gagged from discussing the bank again. The fact that his concerns subsequently proved perfectly valid did not reverse the verdict.

As long as the boom was running such criticisms as were made by the financial press were almost totally ineffective. Since 1974 I had been a critic of Bond Corporation's accounts, particularly the assumptions underlying its asset values and claimed profits. I was a voice in the wilderness. Every year the banks lent him more money, the auditors made unqualified reports and Bond's apparent success grew. This story was repeated in a dozen other groups. Take any bold rider whose empire collapsed and look at its accounts two years before. The picture will be of rising assets and rising profits. A bank which presumably should have had access to the bold rider's books will have lent him a heap of money. A top accounting firm will have verified his accounts. He will boast the services of one of Australia's leading law firms and merchant banks. An analyst for one of Australia's top broking houses will have written a glowing recommendation for the stock. Against this array of expertise it took considerable fortitude for a lone journalist to say that the emperor had no clothes. Indeed, by early 1987 I had begun to doubt my own sanity. So many people were assuring me that everything was all right, when I thought it was not, that I started wondering whether I should take up some other occupation, because I obviously didn't understand finance any more. The crash of October 1987 came as a great reassurance.

Another factor which inhibited me was that until October 1987 I did not expect the correction to be so long and severe. All previous post-war booms had been followed by a bust in which many bold riders went out of business. But there had never been a bust which had killed off all of them. Alan Bond had survived numerous crises in the 1970s and it was not beyond imagination that he could survive again; Adelaide Steamship ran large, profitable businesses; the accounts of the State Bank of Victoria and the SBSA gave no clue to their real risk exposures. Ian Johns and Russell Goward looked good enough up-and-comers to justify giving them awards. Before Black Tuesday—and perhaps even for a while afterwards—it was reasonable to suppose that some of the cowboys would survive despite the inevitable bust. In 1986 very few analysts would have predicted the collapse of John Spalvins and John Elliott. Certainly the financial press could have performed better, but nevertheless it was more critical—in public—of the cowboys than any of the professions mentioned above. After all, it is unreal to expect the financial press to be publicly critical if the directors, bankers, lawyers and accountants are not. If the rest of the professions aren't working it is a bit much to expect finance writers to save the system by themselves.

And, except when the occasional document falls off the back of a truck, financial journalists do not have the same access to inside information as the other professions. When any boom is analysed in retrospect it becomes apparent that the financial press—despite strenuous endeavours—has usually been reporting only the tip of the iceberg. The inner machinations of any given deal are likely to be considerably larger and more complex than was realised at the time. While it was always apparent, for instance, that the Bond Media float was going to be heavy, what was not apparent was how much support it finally required. The investing public would not have realised that Dallhold had borrowed $100 million from Tricontinental to finance its equity. To take another example, the balance date round robins that underlay the annual accounts of Rothwells and Spedley were invisible to outsiders.

Accounts

This leads us to the most alarming aspect of the boom, which is the length of time for which many of the cowboys' companies could appear healthy despite the fact that they were losing money. Some were technically insolvent for years without disclosing the fact. Rothwells lost money in each year from 1984 onwards, although it declared profits in each of those years. It may even be that Rothwells never made money in any year after Laurie Connell took it over in 1982. From 1984—which was as far back as Deloitte reconstructed Rothwells' accounts—Connell owed increasing amounts to the company. That was never made public either. The McCusker investigation of Rothwells concluded that the bank was facing a continuing liquidity crisis from 1985 on. Despite this, it managed to survive until late 1988.

Rothwells' comrade-in-arms, Spedley, had been window-dressing its accounts since 1982. It would appear to have been insolvent since at least

1986. Estate Mortgage, in the opinion of its joint trustee John Murphy, was insolvent from 1986. The National Safety Council's Victorian division was probably never solvent after John Friedrich started his equipment-buying spree in 1977. The notable feature of all these cases is that they seem to have been insolvent well before Black Tuesday. They would have been quite unsalvageable afterwards. Abe Goldberg most likely went broke on Black Tuesday but survived for more than another two years. In that time he took over Brick & Pipe, tried to take over Tootal and essayed one of the biggest bids in Australia's history when he offered $1.9 billion for Industrial Equity.

The Reserve Bank and the NCSC

While all this was happening the police on the beat for the banking and corporate sectors were, respectively, the Reserve Bank of Australia and the National Companies and Securities Commission. Both were operating under severe limitations.

The Reserve Bank was faced with the non sequitur of regulating a deregulated banking system. Some of the areas where the worst excesses occurred were beyond its control the most glaring example being its lack of power over the state banks. In the areas it did control there were lapses in monitoring. Spedley, to maintain its dealing licence, had to have assets which exceeded liabilities by 5 per cent. It also had to maintain a positive current ratio. It was probably in breach of both conditions for at least the last year and a half of its life. Board papers showed consistent breaches of conditions attached to the licence from 1987 on. The ratio of 105 per cent assets to liabilities went as low as 83 per cent if investments were excluded from the asset calculation, as they probably should have been in Spedley's case.[7]

Nor was the RBA working with perfect foresight in this turbulent period. It was probably right to ease interest rates in the wake of Black Tuesday to avert a money panic. However, it eased them too far and sparked a wild property boom in 1988. Interest rates were then held too high for too long in 1989, becoming a major cause of the worst recession in modern Australia. It should be remembered that the central bank was operating during this decade with considerably fewer monetary weapons than it had in the regulated environment that had lasted since World War II. Even if a fiscal Solomon had been in charge of the RBA during the 1980s he might not have been able to curb the excesses significantly.

The NCSC's chairman, Henry Bosch, frequently pointed out that he was expected to police the biggest boom in Australia's history on a budget which barely matched the subsidy paid to the Canberra bus service. Bosch had the impossible job of being the vicar of Sodom and Gomorrah. He was preaching righteousness in an atmosphere corrupted by greed. He sounded old-fashioned and looked funny because his ears stuck out. He made apparently simpleminded statements, one being that there were good and bad takeovers. He became a target of derision among the gung-ho wheeler dealers who were making paper fortunes. He did not aid his case by making a couple of mistakes. His first major investigation was into the propriety of the behaviour of one of Australia's top corporate advisors, Mark Burrows, in the 1985 Arnotts' takeover bid for Allied Mills. This venture by the NCSC boomeranged badly. Burrows was widely respected for his competence and the NCSC was not. The NCSC did not appear to know what it was doing. Burrows later became one of the Federal Government's top advisors on corporate law reform.

A worse case was the infringement of civil liberties that occurred in an outbreak of zealotry by the NCSC over insider trading. Four alleged inside traders were arrested at dawn in Melbourne and paraded before court in handcuffs as though they were jail escapees. NCSC officers bragged to the press that the accused were part of a ring of 50 inside traders who would all be swept up soon. In the event, the NCSC had inadequate evidence to justify even the arrests, let alone the convictions. All charges were subsequently dropped or dismissed, but the reputations of those arrested were ruined.[8] On the other hand, Bosch was right more often than he was given credit for at the time. His greatest triumph was forcing Bond Corporation to make a full bid for Bell Group. But he never had enough funds and the NCSC became a lame duck in the last year of its existence before being replaced by the Australian Securities Commission on 1 January 1990.

The timing of the transition was most unfortunate, coming in the midst of the biggest collapses. Several investigations suffered as a result of bureaucratic rivalry. John Sulan, the South Australian QC who had been compiling a report on Bond Corporation, was sidelined after almost completing the job and the report was finished by ASC officers. In New South Wales, prosecutions which had been prepared regarding Spedley were effectively pigeonholed as a new regime recommenced investigation of the complex deals of this group almost from scratch. A public slanging match broke out between the ASC, which was responsible for investigation, and the Department of Public Prosecutions, which was responsible for prosecution.

The legal system

This brings us to the legal system. It is difficult to believe that the legal system of any westernised country in the modern world could operate

580

as slowly, inefficiently and inequitably as that applying to the corporate world in Australia. At one extreme, Bell Resources was looted of more than a billion dollars and yet by early 1994 nobody had ever faced court as a result. At the other extreme, Russell Goward was being vigorously pursued with perjury charges for having allegedly understated the value of his wife's $5000 wedding and engagement rings. In Spedley, one could feel sympathy for Jamie Craven as a middle-ranking executive facing four charges, while all charges were dropped against Jim Beatty, who was chairman of GPI Leisure and Tulloch Lodge.

By early 1994 the number of successful criminal prosecutions had been few and mostly for small and irrelevant offences. George Herscu served a jail sentence, but it was on a bribery charge that had nothing to do with the losses sustained by his empire. No crime was involved in the collapse of Hookers, which was simply a massive misjudgement. Rothwells' company secretary Tom Hugall served a short jail sentence and was released shortly before dying of a brain tumour. Ian Johns received a short term for receiving secret commissions. Richard and Reuben Lew were convicted on one of the several deals they had made in procuring Estate Mortgage construction loans. Brian Yuill was convicted on charges relating to benefits received from Spedley. Robin Greenburg drew a stiffer sentence than the rest of them combined, but only because she had started a bushfire while attempting to burn Western Women's records. Alan Bond was facing a charge for failing to tell the Bond Corporation board that it could buy a Manet painting at a price below market. Considering the magnitude of the Bond empire, if this was the only charge worth bringing against its founder then the ASC and DPP should have dropped the case. Other cases were pending against some of the bold riders, but all were taking a long time and were going to happen years after the alleged crime, if at all.[9] Connell had been convicted, but not for anything connected with the downfall of Rothwells.

Such few convictions as were recorded were often not sustained, particularly in Western Australia. After the DPP had laboured to obtain convictions against Alan Bond, Tony Lloyd, Kevin Edwards and Aleco Vrisakis, all convictions were quashed by the WA Court of Criminal Appeal and the WA Supreme Court. But at least the West Australians had attempted a few court cases, which was more than could be said for South Australia. By early 1994 the only criminal action taken in that state had been against a minor official of the State Government Insurance Commission for allegedly padding his expense account by $10 000. The loss of $3.5 billion by the SGIC and SBSA, in contrast, had apparently not warranted any charges being laid.

The defendants fought for their lives, trying to block or upset criminal proceedings at every conceivable point. In the process they broke into several areas of little-explored legal territory. When John Elliott was facing charges involving a $66 million foreign exchange transaction with Equiticorp, his lawyers claimed that the National Crime Authority did not have the power to investigate him. That application was finally dismissed by Justice Mary Gaudron in the High Court. Bill Farrow and David Clarke sought an order from the Victorian Supreme Court prohibiting the government-appointed inspector, David Habersberger, QC, from investigating and reporting to the Victorian Government on their conduct, claiming they were denied procedural fairness in the investigations. When a magistrate committed John Avram for trial on charges relating to a $7.5 million share placement Avram appealed to the Victorian Supreme Court to review the committal. Alan Bond's lawyers won a six-month postponement of the Manet charges on the grounds that their client was under such mental stress that he was unable to brief counsel properly.

In New South Wales the Chief Judge in Equity believed that the most efficient way of hearing the tangled Spedley actions would be to appoint one judge, Mr Justice Cole, to hear all the cases. In a judgement involving Bond Brewing Mr Justice Cole found against Yuill and ANI on some counts. Yuill and ANI then successfully appealed to the Full Bench of the NSW Supreme Court to have Mr Justice Cole removed from hearing further cases in which they were defendants, on the grounds that he could be seen to be prejudiced. This seemed to create the precedent that an adverse finding by a judge reflected the prejudices of the judge rather than the guilt of the defendant—a highly questionable principle to introduce into court proceedings. After another judge disqualified himself from hearing the case the defendants tried also to remove a third, Mr Justice Rolfe. When Mr Justice Rolfe refused to step down, and won the right to try the case, the defendants took the case to arbitration, which they could have done two years earlier.

The conduct of civil proceedings was, by and large, no more efficient than that of the criminal proceedings. Typically, a receiver would be appointed by a bank which had deep enough pockets to run a professional liability action against the collapsed company's directors, auditors and lawyers—or, more accurately, against their insurers. Big civil cases between parties with deep pockets tended to develop into long sieges. The best example was the case run by John Murphy as joint trustee of Estate Mortgage. The statement of claim was against the Lews and various other parties, but the real targets were Burns, Philp (covered by a $90 million insurance policy), the auditors Priestley & Morris ($40 million insurance) and the directors ($10 million insurance). Another prime target was the leading law firm of Freehills, which had done legal work for Burns, Philp and whose partner Peter Short had been a director of Burns Philp Trustee Co.

When Murphy and his co-trustee Peter Allen sought to interrogate the parties the application was fought successively before the Administrative Appeals Tribunal, a single judge in the Federal Court, a single judge in the NSW Supreme Court, the Full Bench of the Federal Court and the Full Bench of the Supreme Court. Both full benches rejected the defendants' application 3–0. The defendants then sought leave to appeal to the High Court but were rejected. Murphy and Allen, as the 'new trustees' of Estate Mortgage, sought to join the insurance companies— C.E. Heath and FAI—directly. This was opposed by the insurance companies on the grounds that the new trustees of Estate Mortgage were not the proper plaintiffs in an action alleging breach of trust by the former trustees. If the new trustees were not the proper plaintiffs, it was worth asking who would be. By the end of 1993 a mass of documents had been unearthed by the discovery process. The lawyers for Burns, Philp said that it would take them three years to read the documents. This would have deferred the action until 1996—six years after the collapse of Estate Mortgage. Many of the investors in units in these trusts were elderly and some would die before then.

Another worrying aspect of the legal system is the way in which it was frequently used to suppress the truth. The Sulan report on Bond Corporation began with a statement that the facts should be made public. Two years later the report had still not been released by the ASC. The official report on the collapse of TEA was not released until seven years after the trustee company's collapse in 1983. For all that time investors had no clue how their money had been lost. Master Evans of the Victorian Supreme Court banned publication of evidence given by John Friedrich in the liquidator's Section 541 hearing, on the grounds that publication might prejudice jurors in a future trial. The Herald & Weekly Times fought the order through seventeen court hearings before it was able to publish Friedrich's testimony.[10] The claim of client confidentiality was used for years to suppress the names of clients who had defaulted on the SBSA and the details of their loans. Some of the data seemed likely to stay suppressed forever.

Governments

The behaviour of governments and their instrumentalities was not a pretty sight. In Western Australia, the State Government Insurance Commission refused to provide documents to the WA Inc Royal Commission— appointed by its own government—on the grounds that legal confidentiality prevented them. Later the SGIC said that a change in the filing system prevented it from providing the documents anyway.

Brian Burke wrote a letter endorsing Rothwells in such terms that a foreign investor could have been pardoned for thinking it was an instruction to use Rothwells as their agent in any dealings with the WA Government. The government's subsequent actions to save Rothwells at almost any cost went far beyond any prudent limits. The government also handed Yosse Goldberg a small fortune for warehousing Fremantle Gas when the government could have paid the same money to the company's former shareholders.

In South Australia, questioning of the State Bank was equated with treason to the state. When Jenny Cashmore first raised questions about the deals being done with Equiticorp by the SBSA and Beneficial Finance, she was heavied by local members of the business establishment who had their cosy lines of credit from the bank.[11] Tim Marcus Clark wrote to Opposition Leader John Olsen saying:

> I do ask that in any attack on the current Labor Government in your vigorous pursuit of the treasury benches you do insist on a more responsible approach on these matters likely to affect the extreme high regard that South Australians have for their bank and the complete confidence that they have in its security—a reputation the bank richly deserves.[12]

Bannon's powerful media management team worked overtime to defend the bank and to discredit the Opposition. Bannon's minders sneered at Cashmore and the State Bank threatened defamation suits against anyone who questioned it. The Leader of the SA Democrats was effectively sued and silenced. The Adelaide media, most of whom were left-leaning and supported Bannon anyway, were cajoled or threatened into silence on the issue for a long time.[13] If Bannon and his minders had shown the same assiduity investigating the bank as they had in attacking their critics, the bank's troubles would have been detected earlier and at least part of the loss might have been averted.

John Cain's attempts to renege on payment to depositors in Pyramid have already been commented on adequately. His government made finally an offer that shortchanged many depositors. Still left out in the cold were the non-withdrawable share holders. These were the investors who had paid $120 million for shares in Pyramid on slightly higher returns than were offered to depositors. Many of these investors did not understand the difference between shares and deposits. Some had been solicited at home by Farrow staff, who earned commissions on share sales. The non-withdrawable share holders were going to have their investments wiped out unless they were ranked equally with depositors. Tony Hodgson, as liquidator of the building societies, felt strongly that they should rank equally and tried to help them. He was blocked by the

Victorian Government, which fought a successful court case to dismiss their claim.

The only card left to them was the Lauren case, in which a non-withdrawable shareholder was claiming damages on the grounds of fraud by the government which had induced them to invest in Pyramid. If Lauren's case succeeded the non-withdrawable share holders would have ranked equally. Knowing that Lauren's funds were limited, the government fought an expensive delaying action. When Labor lost power the incoming Kennett Government gave the non-withdrawable shareholders no shred of comfort. Liberal Treasurer Alan Stockdale believed that Cain should never have honoured the guarantee to depositors in the first place, let alone do anything for the non-withdrawable shareholders.

The self-righteous Australian Securities Commission can be criticised for its actions in the Spedley affair, where it launched prosecutions against its own star witness, Jamie Craven. The NSW Corporate Affairs Commission would have taken a long time to discover what had happened in Spedley if it had not done a deal with Jamie Craven, offering him immunity from prosecution as long as he told the CAC everything he knew. For the ASC to subsequently charge Craven on the grounds that he had been party to a few minor alleged crimes and had no specific immunity was a dishonourable act. It was also fairly stupid, because the ASC is unlikely to get much cooperation from the Jamie Cravens of the corporate world in future.

Liquidations and receiverships

These were not always a pretty sight either. Receivers were generally appointed by the same banks who had lent far too much money to corporate cowboys and had puffed their empires way beyond bursting point. When the empires collapsed it was the banks who shouldered their way to the front of the queue for the payout. This is not to suggest that the banks acted illegally. The whole point is that the legal system enabled them to do this, and that because of the banks' size, power and knowledge they were able to exploit the system better than could trade creditors or shareholders, who were generally wiped out in each collapse.

Let's assume that a company with $100 million in assets has been financed $50 million by banks which who have negative pledge, $25 million by trade creditors and $25 million by shareholders' equity. The shareholders have a 25 per cent cushion. The value of the assets can deteriorate by that much before they are wiped out. Then the corporate cowboy who is running the company gets into difficulties and asks his banks for another $25 million. The banks, faced with the prospect of a collapse, lend him the money. Suddenly the shareholders' cushion has shrunk to 20 per cent. If the cowboy has taken a real loss of any size the cushion will be significantly less and may well have disappeared. In that eventuality—which happened in almost every collapse in the boom—the banks will effectively own the business, the shareholders will be wiped out and probably the trade creditors too.

Two of the most disturbing case histories in this respect are those of Estate Mortgage and Farrow. Estate Mortgage and Farrow specifically sought money from small and relatively unsophisticated investors. The investors were entitled to assume that the properties upon which the unit trusts and building societies were lending money were their security in the event of a liquidation. But when Estate Mortgage and Farrow got into trouble they bought time by mortgaging their prime assets to banks and other financiers. This was done without the consent or knowledge of the investors and effectively eroded their equity. The banks and financiers knew what was happening and could invest on a fully informed basis. The investors did not know what was happening. The market was unequally informed. When Estate Mortgage and Farrow collapsed investors discovered to their dismay that a host of previously unsuspected financiers were in the queue ahead of them.

As a final fail-safe, the banks sought personal guarantees from the bold riders. This made the banks the dominant figures in the bankruptcy pursuits that so enlivened Australian financial journalism in the early 1990s, and earned many an investigative reporter a fat expense account in Majorca, Poland or Zug. However, once again, the banks had fallen down on the most elementary aspect of their profession—by failing to check whether the riders actually had any assets that would make exercising the guarantees worthwhile. Abe Goldberg said in his bankruptcy interview in Poland that he had never owned an asset. Everything had been held through family trusts. A guarantee from him was worthless, which was undoubtedly why he gave them so cheerfully. At the finish he would go bankrupt for the heroic sum of $230 million. Alan Bond finished with no assets except the generosity of Juerg Bollag, whom his trustee in bankruptcy seemed unable to touch. Christopher Skase was in Majorca with very few apparent assets and a punctured lung.

But, even where banks had both the bankrupts and their assets available, they did some apparently sacrificial deals. In the process they rode roughshod over the interests of other creditors in a couple of bankruptcies. Melbourne brothers Henry and George Saade faced a deficiency of $136 million when their property and restaurant empire got into trouble in 1992. The main lender was the ANZ Bank, which had lent the brothers $70 million. At a creditors' meeting in January 1993 the brothers offered $50 000 in full settlement of their debts. The crucial creditor, the

ANZ, had developed a relationship with the Saades under which the brothers were assisting the bank in winding down their group and continuing to run their restaurants under bank limits on their drawing accounts. Under Part X of the *Bankruptcy Act* a scheme of arrangement can be approved by a creditors' meeting provided that it is supported by half the creditors by number and 75 per cent by value. At the Saades' meeting the ANZ accepted the deal. One small creditor said that she could not understand why other creditors were supporting the proposal, which would represent a return of less than half a cent in the dollar. The ANZ representative at the meeting said that he 'did not see why creditors should even have to reply'. The motion was passed.

Another example was provided by John Avram, whose major debt after the collapse of Interwest was $161 million owing to the State Bank of Victoria and Tricontinental. At a Part X meeting Avram and his wife Kathy offered $300 000 in settlement. Small creditors were surprised to discover that John's brother Peter held the proxy for Tricontinental and voted the $161 million in favour of the proposal.[14]

Management

Not one of the busted companies in this book could fairly be said to have collapsed for reasons beyond its control. All carried the seeds of their own destruction. Some were accidents waiting to happen.

The frantic activity generated by the bold riders resulted in assets being shuffled like a pack of cards. The corporate players were so engrossed in financial engineering that they may sometimes have forgotten that there were real businesses downstream that needed a little nurturing and attention. In the 1980s the actual businesses too often became poker chips. Workers at the Stubbies plant must have turned up each Monday wondering who their boss was that week as the factory's ownership rotated restlessly between Entrad, Lintrad and Linter. Some assets changed hands so often that it was amazing management and workers could function at all. The prize example was radio station 3DB in Melbourne, which in 1987 had five different owners. It began the year as a subsidiary of the Herald & Weekly Times, was taken over by News, was sold to Holmes à Court, was resold to Kerry Stokes and was finally flicked to the Lamb family. The Lambs' first action was to fire the station manager. They were lucky to have a station left.[15]

Probably only a minority of the bold riders were good business managers. Spalvins was probably the best, paying assiduous attention to the detail of Petersville, David Jones and the rest. Indeed, there was nothing wrong with the operating businesses except that Adsteam hocked them to the hilt and then used the funds to gamble. At the other end of the scale, Abe Goldberg paid a fortune for Brick & Pipe and never once bothered to visit a brick factory. Both Goldberg and Warwick Fairfax took the view that assets would appreciate with inflation, while debt would diminish. Both overlooked the need to service their debt in the interim. This was the rationale underlying the actions of all of the corporate cowboys and the reason for their downfall. Riders such as Bond, Goldberg and Skase followed this rationale to its limit, reckoning that they could afford to buy assets at almost any price. It does not take a genius to win a bidding war when your bank has given you unlimited credit and you are prepared to pay top dollar, which Bond did repeatedly. Asset price inflation in the 1970s and 1980s had made debt cheap.

But the music was bound to stop one day and only one of the bold riders recognised the coda when it was played on Black Tuesday. That was Robert Holmes à Court, who began an immediate liquidation of his empire. Another to survive was Sir Ron Brierley, who retained a keen sense of value throughout the boom. His takeovers were always of real assets at good values. More often he would accumulate a stake in his target, bid and then be bought out by another raider. Brierley 'lost' a lot of takeovers this way, but made a lot of money. Eventually Industrial Equity itself was sold for a billion dollars. By that time Brierley had moved on. He was always content to hold only a few per cent of his empire; he never lusted for glory, his reputation stayed intact and he was still doing deals when most of his peers from the 1980s were bankrupt, fighting court cases or in jail.

A few suggestions

1. The legal system

When the tulip market busted in 17th century Holland the courts refused to settle disputes over breaches of contract on the grounds that it did not take cognisance of gambling transactions. No court used this argument in Australia in the 1990s, but the Victorian Supreme Court in effect abdicated in the Tricontinental audit suit by telling the parties that it could not cope with the case and to settle it themselves. This was the extreme example, but the various court cases outlined in this book (by no means exhaustively) should be ample to demonstrate that the corporate collapses of the 1980s left a massive legal mess in the 1990s. Here we can afford to be bold. As the legal system cannot work any worse in corporate collapses than it does now, any change must be for the better.

Before considering change, let us look at what happens after a major corporate collapse. A liquidator or receiver is appointed straight away. If fraud or other criminality is suspected a special investigator will be appointed a few weeks or months later. By that time the liquidator will have established the major reasons for the company's collapse. Indeed, the reasons usually become evident within a few days, together with the existence of any crimes. Frequently, it is on the liquidator's advice to the ASC that the special investigator is appointed. The investigator can compel witnesses to give evidence, but if they seek privilege their answers cannot be used in evidence in any subsequent court case.

The official investigation and report can take a long time. MacPherson took two years on the SBSA report and Habersburger looked like taking a similar time on Farrow. Upon receipt of these reports the ASC will refer them to the DPP who will consider prosecution. Usually the DPP will ask for more evidence on specific points. Evidence that has been given under privilege will have to be established by other means. Once the DPP decides that the brief is adequate to sustain a prosecution the case will typically go before a magistrate. If the magistrate is convinced, the accused will be committed for trial to the Supreme Court. If the accused is convicted there, he or she can appeal. Anyone who has stolen a few million dollars from a company has every incentive to spend it on top legal talent. The chances of a top QC getting the case thrown out on a technicality are high. Given a moderately combative defendant and the standard delays in the court calendar, it may take five years after a collapse before a Supreme Court conviction is secured. The time may well be longer, or there may not be a conviction at all. Considering that a liquidator of average competence can work out the reasons for a corporate collapse in about five days, the legal system takes an eternity.

So, instead of the morass of disparate court actions that follow a collapse under the existing system, let us put all important corporate cases under the jurisdiction of a special tribunal presided over by an investigating judge or QC. The broad principles upon which such tribunals would work are as follows.

When a major company collapses, or when a company collapses under scandalous circumstances or holding large sums of public money, an investigation would be held. It would be carried out by a judge or QC with expert assistance from accountants and businesspeople. The purposes of the investigation would be (1) to discover the causes of the collapse and whether any crimes had been committed, and (2) to determine the claims of creditors and shareholders against the company and its directors. The investigating judge would have the power to make criminal convictions and findings of civil liability. The criminal and civil findings would be subject to normal appeal proceedings as if they had been made by a Supreme Court.

This would be a vastly more efficient procedure than the present one. By combining the investigatory and judicial functions a great deal of time and expense would be saved. By having the investigative tribunal staffed by experts we would—one hopes—be more likely to reach a just conclusion. By combining the civil and criminal jurisdictions we should eliminate the possibility of conflicting civil and criminal judgements being handed down.

Would justice be impaired? A defendant would lose the right to trial by jury, but it has long been debatable whether this is the best way to try corporate cases. We would lose some aspects of the adversarial system. But then to have two sides arguing only those facts and opinions which suit their case is a haphazard way of arriving at the truth anyway. Defendants would still have the right to legal representation and those convicted or found liable for civil penalties would retain the right of appeal. It is worth remembering when arguing about the individual's rights before the law that the individuals in these cases are not the poor, illiterate and defenceless. They are men who have been running large companies, they will often have substantial means (sometimes stolen from their investors) and they are normally represented by the top QCs and law firms in the land.

Would the tribunal be a kangaroo court? Any suggestion that would make the legal system work more quickly and certainly is usually attacked with this pejorative phrase. It is difficult to restrain the suspicion that lawyers have a vested interest in prolonging cases as far as possible, and making their outcome as uncertain as possible, so that the maximum number of lawyers can be kept in work.

I believe that such a tribunal would establish the main causes of collapse accurately and quickly. If no crime had occurred it should quickly become evident, clearing the names of those involved. As a journalist who has been investigating corporate collapses for a quarter of a century, I cannot recall a case where the liquidator's first opinion of the prime causes of a case was subsequently found to be substantially wrong. The main contribution of the official investigator's report a year or so later is usually to elaborate on the causes and highlight previously unpublicised side deals and connections. It might be said that the reputations of directors of a collapsed company could suffer from the evidence given in a public tribunal. Those reputations tend to suffer for far longer periods under the present system. In any case, we should take a robust attitude towards such claims. Too often in the case histories given in this book we have seen directors gazing on ineffectually as a substantial disaster is created. When the enterprise they were supposed to be running sinks— and takes with it several millions in shareholders' and creditors' money— it is not unreasonable that directors should suffer a little flak. That would be infinitely preferable to what happened in TEA, where shareholders had to wait seven years before the official report was released and they discovered how their money was lost.

The proposal for a tribunal of this kind is not original. It has been suggested by an English QC and a Sydney judge. It was first put forward by me in 1988 in the epilogue to *Two Centuries of Panic*.[16] The idea received absolutely no support, but the legal chaos of the 1990s has been so absolute that I feel no shame in putting it forward again. It could hardly be categorised as a reckless experiment to change the Australian legal system in these cases, as it would be difficult to conceive any alternative system working worse.

2. Widows and orphans

A point worth considering in any future corporate legislation is that all investors are not equal. No matter how we frame securities industry legislation, there will always be a race of insiders and professional investors. At the other end of the scale there will be investors who need maximum protection: they are often referred to as 'widows and orphans'. A widow who has just received a bequest or an accident victim who has just been paid out for a claim needs a safe haven for their nest egg. There is no such thing, of course, as perfect safety in investment. However, it should be possible to delineate a safety zone where widows and orphans can put their little windfall, secure in the knowledge that the custodians will not do anything rash with it. For argument's sake let us say that the nest egg should be invested in a fund or trust, comprising solely government bonds and bank bills, which cannot gear beyond 5 per cent.[17]

We need to redefine the concept of trustee securities, so that they become a haven for unsophisticated investors. Such securities will be dull and the value of the capital might be eroded slowly by inflation and fees, but they will be a roped-off area of the financial markets where unsophisticated investors can be assured that nothing sudden and disastrous can happen to their capital. Outside the ropes, by corollary, investors will know that they are at risk to some degree. It is up to them to find out how much. I also believe that the penalties should be much harsher for those who prey on the widows and orphans than for those who offend against professional investors.

3. Havens

One of our major exports in the early 1990s was former high-flying corporate cowboys. Abe Goldberg, Andy Stathis, Chor Kian Yap, Ken Wright, Yosse Goldberg and Christopher Skase all left the country for long periods when they were wanted for questioning by liquidators and the authorities. By the start of 1994 only Yosse Goldberg had returned— and all he had ever been wanted for was any additional information he could give about the Fremantle Gas deal.

We should recognise that ultimately there is very little that any legal system can do to prevent outright robbery of the type practised by Andy Stathis. Anyone who wants to hijack the liquid assets of a company (insurance companies are particularly vulnerable) and flee the country is likely to succeed, although he will be a wanted man afterwards. By the same token, there is no reason why we should be particularly tender about the legal rights of a barefaced absconder. Where it is clear someone has absconded with substantial assets and he has failed to return after a reasonable period, perhaps we should consider launching their civil and criminal hearings in absentia. If we do not, we are going to have a lot more missing cowboys.

Another major export appears to have been their money. The lifting of exchange controls as part of the deregulatory package made it easier to spirit money well beyond Australia's shores. Perhaps this aspect of deregulation improved the facility of our commerce with the United States and Japan, but it also resulted in a lot of money being routed through exotic locations such as the Dutch Antilles, Turks and Caicos, Monaco, Cayman Island, Liberia, Panama and Jersey.

In several cases money was siphoned out of Australia through companies and trusts in far tax havens where it was impossible to trace ownership. The Cook Islands, for example, has two company registers, domestic and international. Companies on the international register can only be searched with the consent of their directors. If the investigator does not know who the directors are this becomes impossible. Investigators could not trace the money trail of Chor Kian Yap because they were unable to trace some of his companies, particularly those in Liberia. There is no honest reason for any company to set up its affairs in this way. When ownership of an overseas entity cannot be placed, it is safe to conclude that it is being used for a criminal purpose—usually to defraud shareholders or the Australian Taxation Office. This is an area where we could—without any injustice—reverse the onus of proof. What I suggest is that, where a deal is routed through Jersey, Liberia, Panama or the like, the transaction would be deemed to be for a criminal purpose unless the company could prove that it was not.

4. Equity and Debt

A lender who allows a borrower to overgear the balance sheet is taking not a fixed interest risk but an equity risk. It might be worth considering whether, in certain circumstances, the lender should then rank with the equity holders in any subsequent liquidation. Any such provision should at least make lenders stop and think before they again allowed a bold rider the keys to the safe.

. . . and finally

There will always be businesses going broke or going downhill for a host of reasons beyond their control. Capitalism is a dynamic and competitive system in which some players will inevitably lose. In addition, any business can suddenly be impacted by such factors as a change in interest or tax rates, the discovery of a new material or process, a change in overseas economic conditions, or movements in commodity prices. And, of course, there will always be a percentage of incompetent owners and managers. Small businesses are notoriously vulnerable to all these currents. The bulk of them close within the first year of business, even in prosperous times. Big businesses are harder to kill. It usually takes a combination of incompetent management and high debt. To the extent that the accounting profession collaborates by agreeing to paint false pictures of health in the balance sheets, badly run companies will be able to grow larger and for longer periods and their ultimate collapses will hurt more people. The events in the Australian corporate world in the 1980s went well beyond any normal business cycle.

The insanities of the Australian corporate and banking worlds did not happen in isolation in the 1980s. Similar trends occurred in other countries. And the Australian boom was fuelled to a significant degree by foreign banks. This book has not attempted to analyse overseas events because it took long enough just to study the major local collapses. But given that there was a global madness it was inevitable that Australia would be infected to some degree.

We will also be infected by future outbreaks. The suggestions made above would go some distance towards mitigating future disasters. If we do not do something along these lines we will sooner or later run another boom and bust cycle of the same catastrophic dimensions. That is a safe prediction. If engineers never learned from history every generation of students would be condemned to reinvent the wheel. But engineers and scientists do learn from history, and so we have seen heart transplants and human beings walking on the Moon. In economics and finance, however, the human race still starts every generation with flint axes.

Appendix

SELECTIVE CHRONOLOGY

1981

March. Andrew Stathis bankrupted.

May. First & Last Hotel knocked down to build The Quay, with TEA as financier.

June. Endeavour Resources acquires 33 per cent of Northern Mining but fails to lodge substantial shareholder notice. Conduct declared unacceptable by NCSC.
DJ's Properties, controlled by Adsteam, wins control of Tooth.

July. Alan Bond bids for Swan Brewery.
John Spalvins becomes managing director of Adsteam.

November. Alan Bond takes over Swan.
Paper presented to TEA board saying serious cash deficiency looming because of amounts lent to company's property projects.

1982

January. TEA internal auditor criticises state of accounts in property area. Report not shown to board.

February. Tooth buys H.C. Sleigh, which controls Petersville.

May. Qintex removes Deloitte as auditors at extraordinary general meeting.

June. Bond Corp unloads Santos holding.

July. Alan Bond seeks Wardley backing for Norman Ross and Grace Bros takeovers. Michael Bato refuses and is sacked from Wardley.

September. Laurie Connell takes over Rothwells.

November. John Bannon wins SA state election.
Sir Robert Norman writes to Alex Ogilvy about lack of real information on TEA's property projects.

1983

January. AHA Cup at Bunbury. Danny Hobby jumps off Strike Softly.
Andrew Stathis buys Bishopsgate Insurance.

February. Brian Burke rings Connell for campaign donation.
Burke wins WA election, meets Connell a few days later for first time.

April. Spedley takes over Group Holdings.
Adsteam buys 20 per cent of National Consolidated.

May. Collapse of Trustees Executor & Agency Co after board receives Hill Samuel report telling them company has deficiency.
Bob Hawke wins Federal election.
Rothwells becomes authorised trustee.
Qintex buys Channel 0, Brisbane.

July. Michael Kent joins Adsteam board.

November. WA Government buys Northern Mining from Endeavour Resources.
Bannon meets Tim Marcus Clark, approves him as managing director of State Bank of South Australia.

December. Keating floats $A.
Alan Bond convicted on two charges of failing to lodge substantial shareholder declaration in Northern Mining from 1981.
Howard Smith sells 18 per cent stake in Adsteam.

1984

April. Dallhold acquires Winthrop Investments, including control of Mid-East Minerals and Metals Exploration.
Victorian Treasurer Rob Jolly announces expanded banking role for State Bank of Victoria.

June. Foreign exchange licences granted to 40 applicants.

July. New State Bank of South Australia begins trading.

August. Jack Walsh dies.
Bill Moyle appointed chief executive of SBV.
Insurance Commissioner investigates Bishopsgate. Stathis flees Australia.

September. SBV tries to sell its 25 per cent of Tricontinental.

November. Ian Johns outlines proposed lending policy for Tricontinental, focussing on second and third line companies.

December. Adsteam accumulates 5 per cent of BHP.
Qintex begins buying AWA shares.

1985

January. John Leard writes 'smoking gun' memo to Neil Jones at ANI.
SBSA expands London office.

February. Australian banking licences granted to sixteen foreign banks.
John Leard resigns from Spedley boards.
Touche Ross reports to Mitsui on defects in Tricontinental. Mitsui abandons plans to buy the merchant bank.
Linter Group formed by Basil Sellers, Robin Crawford, John Gerahty and Peter Scanlon.

March. George Herscu starts negotiations to build US hypermalls.
Qintex buys site for Southport Mirage.

April. Spedley group restructures following takeover of Group Holdings.
Brian Yuill takes 40 per cent of Group Holdings (GPI) which owns 20 per cent of Spedley Holdings.
Robert Holmes à Court and Michael Kent negotiate option deal on 70m. BHP shares.

May. Western Continental takes over Fremantle Gas for $24m.
Beneficial Finance (BFC) acquires Pegasus Securities.

June. Connell donates $300 000 to Burke election campaign.

July. SBV buys outstanding 75 per cent of Tricontinental.

August. Rothwells in continuing liquidity crisis from this time.
Qintex moves head office to Queensland.

September. Herscu bids for Hooker Corp.
PML Property Trust raises $40m. to fund Mirage hotels.

October. Holmes à Court buying heavily in BHP.
Estate Mortgage grants $20m. loan facility to PMA1.

November. Bond Corp takes over Castlemaine Tooheys.
Tricontinental finances Qintex acquisition of 19.9 per cent of AWA.
SBSA decides to build State Bank Centre.
Chor Kian Yap buys Deposit & Investment.

December. Herscu wins control of Hooker.
Bannon wins second election with increased majority.

1986

January. Johns appointed managing director of Tricontinental.
Holmes à Court sells 5 per cent of AWA to Qintex, giving it 14.9 per cent.

February. Burke re-elected in Western Australia.

March. Westmex relists under Russell Goward.

April. Elders buys 19 per cent of BHP in largest market raid in history, financed by Chase, Citibank and Paribas.
AFP merger with Linter.

May. Herscu unveils plans for Hooker US hypermalls.
Skase bids for AWA.
SA Treasury makes first request for SBSA board seat. Rebuffed.

June. GPI rights issue raises $40m. Yuill borrows $17m. from Spedley to maintain his holding.
SBSA sets up Hong Kong branch to write business beyond London limits.
Estate Mortgage grants $14m. facility to PMA2.
Westmex gets controlling interest in Charterhall plc.

July. Linter bids for Speedo. Linter and Entrad form Lintrad with Abe Goldberg as chairman.

August. GPI Leisure floated, raising $100m.
Abe Goldberg joins Linter board, raises holding in Lintrad to 30 per cent.
Pyramid Building Society annual report says group intends to expand non-home lending.

September. *Australia II* wins America's Cup.
SECWA buys Fremantle Gas from Western Continental for $39.6m.

October. Connell complains to WA Liberal Party about Hassell's criticisms of Fremantle Gas deal. Hassell sacked as leader.
Float of Bond Corp International Ltd (BCIL) in Hong Kong.

November. Adsteam accumulating shares in ANZ, NAB and Westpac.
REMM sells Myer Brisbane site to Chase Corp.
First TV ads for Estate Mortgage.

December. Spalvins shorts SPI.
Qintex America formed and buys 41 per cent of Hal Roach Studios.
Chor Kian Yap takes over SRC Laboratories. Renamed Sunmark.

1987

January. Rocket Racer wins Perth Cup.
Alan Bond buys Channel 9s from Kerry Packer.
BCIL lists in Hong Kong. Hong Kong Stock Exchange criticises Bond for
making statements that pushed up share price.
Linter buys out Entrad's half-interest in Lintrad. Speedo's shell renamed
Danomic with Abe Goldberg holding 49 per cent.
Reserve Bank asks SBSA for advance notice of any exposure to a client
amounting to more than 30 per cent of capital base.

February. Tulloch Lodge floated for $15m.
ANI issues $260m. convertible notes to Dirham, controlled by Westfield.

March. Bond Media floated. Dallhold subscribes $100m. to float, entirely
funded by Tricontinental.

April. Qintex buys Princeville.

June. Warwick Fairfax recruits Connell to lead John Fairfax takeover bid.
Connell raises $950 000 for ALP at Perth lunch addressed by Bob Hawke.
Spalvins settles BHP option deal with Holmes à Court.
Westmex claims $6m. profit. Disputed by Mann Judd.
TEA's Peter Bunning convicted for taking secret commissions.

July. Qintex buys Channel 7 network from Fairfax. QAL (IPH) makes
$108m. rights issue. Qintex sells out of AWA.

August. WA Teachers Credit Union loses $125+m. Taken over by R & I.
ANZ Bank lends Warwick Fairfax $2 billion to take over John Fairfax Ltd.
Dallhold buys St Joe Gold.

September. Bond Corp announces bid for Heileman for $US1.25bn.
Abe Goldberg bids for remaining shares in Danomic.

October. Equiticorp agrees to buy NZ Steel from NZ Government.
Yap's Sunmark takes 51 per cent holding in Multivest.
Linter buys remaining textile interests of Abe Goldberg.
**Biggest worldwide share market crash in history. Australian all ordi-
naries index and Dow Jones down 25 per cent in one day.**

Run on Rothwells which is in deep trouble. Rescue orchestrated by Bond, Connell and Yonge.
Run on Spedley. ANI pumps in $60m. on top of $35m. already deposited.
Spalvins increases holdings in banks.
Stathis arrested in Piraeus carrying 23kg of heroin.

November. Bond Corp shareholders ratify restraint agreement under which key executives would get $41m. for their exclusive services over five years.
Abe Goldberg heavy buyer of AFP shares.
Marcus Clark tells SBSA board that the bank is heading into difficult times, with more bad debts.

December. Bond Corp buys GMK from Poseidon for $375m.
Ong Beng Seng pays deposit on Sydney Hilton but rest of deal subject to financing. Kitool agrees to buy 49 per cent holding in Bond Corp's Rome land, with put and call options to Bond Corp International Ltd (BCIL) exercisable in July 1988. Deal financed by BNZ through GPI, Equiticorp Australia and Aldershot.
SBSA lends Equiticorp $50m. and buys $150m. of its receivables.

1988

January. BFC buys $100m. of Equiticorp receivables with buy-back arrangement.
Deposit & Investment annual report for year to June 1987 shows post–balance date losses.

February. SBSA buys Oceanic Capital for $60m.

March. Herscu tries to buy out Hooker minorities at $2.30 a share. Fails.
Abe Goldberg bids for Linter.
REMM buys old Myer site in Brisbane for $50m.

April. Holmes à Court sells 19.9 per cent of Bell Group to Bond Corp and another 19.9 per cent to SGICWA.
GPI Leisure issues $100m. convertible notes.
Bannon becomes Federal President of Australian Labor Party.
Hartley complains to Bannon and Lynn Arnold about Marcus Clark. Ignored.
SBSA approves $38m. loan to Oceanic.
REMM's old Myer site in Brisbane valued at $80m.

May. GPI Leisure borrows $100m. from Standard Chartered and buys $100m. preference shares in Spedley Holdings.
Adsteam buys 5.2 per cent of Commercial Union of Britain.

BFC finances East End Markets development.

June. Malindi (Yuill) buys Dirham for $20.4m. Yuill now has foot on potential 19 per cent of ANI.
Adsteam buys 20 per cent of Bell Resources.
Westmex buys ANCOL.
Skase renegotiates purchase of Seven network from Fairfax.
Abe Goldberg bids for Spotless.
Marcus Clark leaves Equiticorp board.

July. Connell sells half-interest in PICL for $350m. and pays same amount to Rothwells in return for $350m. of Rothwells' bad debts.
Bond Corp forced to bid $2.70 for outstanding shares in Bell Group, except for 19.9 per cent held by SGICWA.
Bond International Gold floats in US, with Dallhold holding 49 per cent.
SGICSA writes put options on Myer Centre and 333 Collins St. SBSA leads Stage 1 financing of Myer/REMM, claiming Stage 2 will be bedded down in eight weeks. SBSA buys Security Pacific NZ.

August. Bond Corp begins draining cash from Bell Resources.

September. Alan Bond buys Glympton Park for $22m. Three days later buys schooner *Jessica* for $7.8m.
Bond Corp launches raid on Lonrho, buying 20 per cent for $655m.
Budget Rent A Car System accounts for year to June 1987 filed, showing $2.7m. deficiency.

October. Rothwells collapses. Ian Ferrier appointed liquidator.
Alan Bond buys St Moritz Hotel from Donald Trump for $US180m.
Petersville buys 19.6 per cent of Howard Smith.
BFC buys Campbell Capital for $47m.
Estate Mortgage launches giraffe ads.
ASX listing committee demands changes to Budget prospectus.
Yap says directors delighted with successful 1987 year for Multivest.

November. ANI 1:4 rights issue. Yuill borrows $12m. from FAI to fund his share.
ANZ stops cashing Spedley cheques.
Tiny Rowlands claims Bond Corp insolvent.
NCSC asks whether Bell Resources is lending funds back-to-back to Bond Corp. Bond Corp unwinds back-to-backs, then relends the money through Freefold.
Moneylink criticises Estate Mortgage. Sued for defamation.

December. Tricontinental proposes merger with Australian Bank.
Budget Corp prospectus issued. Raises $12.5m.

1989

January. ANI sells Spedley stake to BT Insurance.
Neil Jones and John Maher resign from Spedley board.
Brent Potts and Willie West sell Bisley stake to GPI and resign from Bisley board.
Adsteam buying into IEL.
Abe Goldberg buys 14.4 per cent of Tootal, bids for control.
Equiticorp collapses owing $49m. to SBSA.

February. Yuill sells Dirham to ANI for $100m. Malindi pays $12.9m. to Spedley, which repays $12.9m. of borrowings from ANI. Dirham repays $10.3m. loan from GPI Leisure. GPI Leisure deposits $10.3m. with Spedley, which repays another $10.3m. of borrowings from ANI.
Jenny Cashmore raises first questions in parliament about SBSA, asking for details of exposure to Equiticorp. Paul Woodland, Bannon's economic advisor, suggests inquiry into SBSA.
Perpetual Trustee alarmed by failure of Deposit & Investment to pay dividend or prepare 1988 accounts. Tony Sherlock appointed receiver. Yap flees country.

March. National Safety Council (Victoria) discovers deficiency. Chief executive John Friedrich (Hohenberger) flees. Liquidator appointed to NSCV.
'Four Corners' program claims Bond Corp's 1988 profit inflated by Sydney Hilton and Rome land deals.
NCSC arrests alleged inside traders in dawn raid.
SBV executives appointed to review Tricontinental's loan portfolio.
QAL sells 49 per cent of Mirage Resorts to Mitsui and Nippon Shinpan for $433m.

April. RBA withdraws First Federation dealer's licence.
Spedley Securities and Holdings go into liquidation. John Harkness appointed liquidator, later joined by Peter Allen. NCSC appoints Tony Hodgson receiver of GPI and GPI Leisure.
Friedrich arrested in Western Australia.
Australian Broadcasting Tribunal finds allegations against Bond correct.
Australian Ratings reports that Adsteam earnings weaker and debt higher than previously supposed.
Bell Resources 1988 accounts released, showing loans to Bond Corp.
Skase announces proposed merger of MGM/UA and Qintex Entertainment.
Cashmore speech in SA parliament raises questions about SBSA, pointing out that SA Government is guarantor. Attacked by Bannon.
Estate Mortgage grants $80m. facility to REMM on old Myer site in Brisbane.

Yap's Sunmark goes into liquidation following losses by subsidiary Sun Sovereign.

May. WA Government refuses to pump any more money into PICL.
SBV board takes control of Tricontinental. Johns resigns. Proposed merger with Australian Bank abandoned.
Abe Goldberg sells out of Tootal.

June. Hooker announces property sell-off including head office. Banks impose moratorium on Hooker and appoint Richard Grellman as financial advisor. Herscu throws $3m. wedding party for daughter.
ABT rules Alan Bond not fit and proper person to hold a TV licence.
Abe Goldberg buys Brick & Pipe for $400m.

July. John Harkness appointed provisional liquidator of Hooker. Tony Hodgson and Andrew Cornell appointed receivers and managers of Hersfield.
Qintex buys site in California for Mirage hotel.
Abe Goldberg forms Corama with Rod Price and Bill Loewenthal, bids for IEL.
Estate Mortgage begins suffering net outflow of funds.
Multivest shares suspended because company cannot pay its debts.

August. Start of pilots' strike.
Independent Funds Research survey says Estate Mortgage high risk, but with 'exceptional' management.
Pyramid annual report says profit up from $3 to $11m.
Westmex announces profit up 34 per cent to $27m.

September. Ian Gilfillan sued for defamation for raising questions about SBSA.
Bob Ansett and Stan Hamley resign from Budget Corp board.

October. SGICWA sells Bell Group shares for 27c and sues Bond Corp for not honouring undertaking to buy them for $2.70. Bond Corp announces $980m. loss for 1988–89.
Qintex Entertainment goes into Chapter 11 bankruptcy protection. Skase in urgent talks with bankers. Skase revealed to have collected large management fees from Qintex.
Abe Goldberg trying to sell Brick & Pipe.
Westmex annual report shows $158m. in intangible assets. Investors start selling. Shares down from $1.30 to $1.

November. Adsteam takes over IEL for $1.7bn.
Skase resigns as chief executive of Qintex. Appoints David Crawford and John Allpass as receivers.

Corama bids $1.9bn. for IEL but cannot raise funding. Loses bid to Adsteam.

Bannon narrowly wins SA election.

Budget Corp insolvent. Peter Allen appointed liquidator.

December. Friedrich fraud case. Story of empty NSC containers becomes public.

AMP dumps Westmex holding. Shares down to 35c.

Skase sells Brisbane home.

Consolidated Press Holdings (CPH) announces takeover for Bond Media.

Alan Bond takes line honours in Sydney–Hobart race on *Drumbeat*. As he ties up, Bond is told NAB syndicate has put Bond Brewing into receivership.

Banks appoint Lindsay Maxsted to examine Abe Goldberg's accounts.

1990

January. Victorian tramway workers strike over MetroPlan. Trams welded to rails in Bourke Street.

John Avram's Interwest group collapses. SBSA exposure ultimately $100m.

Maxsted appointed receiver to Linter.

Run begins on Estate Mortgage.

Run begins on Pyramid.

February. Estate Mortgage announces returns of 18.4–19 per cent for December quarter.

Run on Pyramid intensifies. Rob Jolly and Andrew McCutcheon issue reassuring statement. Run continues. Price Waterhouse commissioned to report on Farrow group.

Receivers appointed to Westmex and ANCOL.

March. Pilots' strike ends.

Run continues on Estate Mortgage. Net withdrawals of $70m. in first ten weeks of 1990.

Pyramid suffers net outlfow of $92m. between 7th and 20th. Price Waterhouse reports that Farrow needs immediate injection of $100m. and major shareholder.

April. Brick & Pipe sold to Pioneer for $290m.

Estate Mortgage suspends payments.

Allen replaced as Budget liquidator by Greg Kelly.

May. Westpac appoints analyst to Adsteam.

SBSA buys United Building Society of New Zealand for $157m.

Burns Philp Trustee sacks Estate Mortgage Managers.

Talks with banks fail to find major shareholder for Farrow.
Prospectus for Compass released. Raises $65m.

June. Reuben Lew charged with receiving secret commissions.
Ken Russell appointed administrator of Farrow. John Cain denies
Victorian Government liability to Pyramid depositors. Demonstrations in
Geelong.

July. George and Sheila Herscu declared bankrupt with debts of $497m.
Peter Beckwith dies.
Four major trading banks discover their combined exposure to Adsteam
is more than $4bn.
Abe Goldberg declared bankrupt.
SBSA injects $105m. into Oceanic Property Growth Fund.
Reuben and Richard Lew charged with Estate Mortgage offences. Peat
Marwick estimates $315m. minimum loss by Estate Mortgage.
Farrow group wound up. Tony Hodgson appointed liquidator. Cain
announces bail-out of Pyramid depositors.

August. SBV and Tricontinental sold to Commonwealth Bank. Victorian
Government guarantees Tricontinental's bad debts.
SBSA reports profit of $24m. Not believed by RBA.
Russell report on Farrow group estimates $250m. loss.

September. Ron Brierley estimates Adsteam total debt at $7bn.

October. Burns Philp Trustee resigns as Estate Mortgage trustee. Global
Funds Management takes over running of Estate Mortgage, with new
trustees. Burns Philp Trustee board resigns and company put into liquidation.

December. Herscu convicted of bribing Russ Hinze. Sentenced to five
years' jail.
Bannon defends Marcus Clark in SA parliament.
First Compass flight.

1991

January. Balance of Mirages sold to Nippon Shinpan.
SBSA calls in J.P. Morgan as advisor. Morgan estimates bank losses of
$500m. to $1bn. First billion dollar bail-out of SBSA announced. Royal
Commission appointed into SBSA's affairs.

February. Marcus Clark resigns from SBSA.
ASC applies to WA Supreme Court to restrain Western Women from
raising money from public except through registered prospectus. W&W
Investments launches prospectus seeking $7.5m.

March. Adsteam, David Jones, Tooth, Petersville and National Consolidated announce losses totalling $1.28bn.
Diana Newman appointed receiver of Western Women.

April. Estate Mortgage unitholders agree to three-year freeze.

May. Banks take over Seven network.
Skase charged over management fees.
Linter sold to Sara Lee.

June. Skase declares himself bankrupt.
First Hodgson report on Farrow.

July. Friedrich suicides.
Dallhold in liquidation.

August. Bond Corp in scheme of arrangement under Ian Ferrier.
Second bail-out of SBSA, totalling $2.2bn.

September. Peak of airfares war. Compass offers two free tickets for every one bought.
Robin Greenburg of Western Women sentenced to seventeen years' jail for theft and arson.

October. Richard Lew and Carl Davis convicted over misleading Estate Mortgage advertisements.
Compass cuts Sydney–Melbourne fare to $79. Compass annual report shows loss of $16m.

November. BRW magazine names Bryan Grey of Compass as Businessman of the Year.

December. Compass collapses. Lessors repossess aircraft. Ian Ferrier appointed liquidator.

1992

January. Doug Reid negotiates purchase of Compass from Ferrier.

April. Southern Cross Airlines (Compass II) prospectus launched, seeking $50m.

June. Second Hodgson report on Farrow. Victorian Supreme Court finds non-withdrawable share holders in Pyramid rank behind depositors.
Southern Cross Airlines prospectus reported undersubscribed.

August. Further charges laid against Skase over management fees.
SBSA split into 'good' and 'bad' banks. Further bail-out of $850m. announced.

September. Bannon resigns as Premier, endorsing Lynn Arnold as successor.
Pyramid non-withdrawable share holders march on Victorian parliament.
Hodgson estimates Pyramid depositors to receive 51–53c in the dollar.
November. First report of Royal Commissioner Jacobs on SBSA tabled.

1993

February. Southern Cross announces $11m. loss for December half. Balance sheet shows only $4.3m. cash left.

March. Ian Johns sentenced to seven months' jail on secret commission charges.
Southern Cross shares suspended. Richard Barber appointed provisional liquidator.

May. Woolworths float raises $2.45bn. for IEL.

June. Herscu released from jail.
Alan Bond charged with having failed to act honestly in connection with Manet painting, 'La Promenade'.

November. Reuben and Richard Lew convicted and jailed for Estate Mortgage offences.

December. Southern Equities (formerly Bond Corp) drops PICL suit against WA Government. Goes into liquidation.
Alan Bond's lawyers successfully get six-month stay of Manet prosecution on grounds that their client's mental faculties had collapsed.

Notes

Chapter 1

1 This is the rough total of provisions made between 1989 and 1991 by the four major trading banks, the state banks and foreign banks operating in Australia. The figure is overstated to the extent that some level of provisioning would have occurred anyway in the normal course of business. Guessing what this level might have been in normal times is a hypothetical exercise, but the losses sustained by the banks because of imprudent (sometimes stupid) lending could be guessed at $20 billion.

2 For a fuller version see Trevor Sykes, *Two Centuries of Panic*, Allen & Unwin, Sydney, 1988. Chapter 9 of that book deals with the banking crisis of 1893.

3 Jennifer Kitchener, 'Banker with an adventurous streak', *Australian Business*, 27 August 1986.

4 The various bankers quoted in this chapter were all interviewed by the author in August 1990 while researching the article 'How the banks lost your money', *Australian Business*, 3.10.1990.

5 Malcolm Wilson, 'Pioneer Concrete adopts negative pledge borrowing', *Sydney Morning Herald*, 24.3.79.

6 Including the author.

7 WA Inc Royal Commission Report, para. 12.17.27.

8 WA Inc Royal Commission Report, para. 12.12.23.

9 The losses were capped at $125 million and further losses had to be absorbed by the R&I Bank. (WA Inc Royal Commission Report, para. 12.17.43.)

10 I have found no comparable period of 20 per cent plus interest rates in my researches into the financial history of Australia. I would be glad if any authority could correct me on this point.

11 The property statistics and graphs come from JLW Research, 'Australia & New Zealand Property Digest', Issue No. 22, July 1993. My thanks to Bruce Michael of Jones Lang Wootton for his assistance.

Chapter 2

1 At the 1972 annual meeting the chairman, T.L. Webb (later Sir Thomas Webb), told shareholders the company was 'ever mindful of the desirability of exploring wider avenues of business activity and services'. TEA believed it could 'make better arrangements with respect to balances standing temporarily in the accounts of our beneficiaries and clients', he said. By handling them in bulk, rather than individually, TEA could generate higher rates of interest.

2 See the National Companies and Securities Commission special investigation into affairs of The Trustees Executors & Agency Co Ltd and related corporations, henceforth referred to as the TEA Report. Five volumes of the report were tabled in the Victorian Parliament in April 1990. The reference here is to Volume IV, Part I, para. 121.

3 TEA Report IV-I, para. 18.

4 Details of the Melbourne Clinic and subsequent property deals are taken from TEA Report IV–I.

5 Gearing is also often expressed in the form of debt to equity, which strips out liabilities such as provisions for tax and long service leave. The debt/equity calculation usually also strips out trade creditors, on the grounds that they are current liabilities which should be roughly offset by current assets such as stock and trade debtors. This debt/equity ratio has been highly fashionable in recent years, but investors using it should never lose sight of the fact that the other liabilities on the balance sheet remain real and payable, and that in a liquidation some of them (tax and employee provisions) rank ahead of secured creditors such as banks.

6 See 'Commercial Property Market Cycles in the Sydney CBD', Jones Lang Wootton Research, 1990.

7 TEA Report IV–I, para. 89.

8 TEA Report IV–I, para. 102.

9 TEA Report IV–I, para. 313.

10 TEA Report IV–I, para. 323.

11 TEA Report IV–I, para. 324.

12 TEA Report IV–I, para. 477.

13 TEA Report IV–II, para. 667.

14 TEA Report IV–I, para. 121.

15 TEA Report IV–I, para. 561.

16 TEA Report IV–I, paras 25 and 195–7.

17 TEA Report IV–II, para. 572.

18 TEA Report IV–II, para. 576.

19 Arthur Young auditors were concerned about this arrangement, saying they could not recognise the sale as a transaction because of the indemnity.

20 TEA Report IV–II, paras 675–7.

21 TEA Report IV–II, para. 683.

22 TEA Report IV–I, para. 28. The full text is given in Appendix 3.

23 TEA Report IV–I, para. 34.

24 TEA Report IV–II, para. 4.1.1 (iv).

25 TEA Report IV–II, para. 4.1.2.

Chapter 3

1 John Hamilton, *Burkie*, St George Books, Perth, 1988. This book, published just after Burke's retirement and before his star began to fade, came under political attack as a subsidised hagiography. It's a lot better than that. The backgrounding of Burke's early career and political life is excellent. However the highly visible rise of WA Inc is treated skimpily and there is hardly a mention of Laurie Connell (who financed the book). And it lacks an index.
2 Terry Maher, *Bond*, William Heinemann Australia, Melbourne 1990, pp. 152–55. The book in addition contains extensive earlier references to the Santa Maria deal, which was a crucial one in Bond's middle development. This book would be considerably more helpful if it had an index.
3 Bob Gottliebsen, *National Times*, 18.11.1978.
4 Walsh died suddenly in 1984. He came into Connell's office, gave a rundown on all the projects he was then working on, went home and died a few hours later. (Connell's evidence, WA Inc Royal Commission, 8.4.1991.) For a fuller background on Walsh, see 'The empire that Jack built', *West Australian*, 20.5.1989.
5 Evidence of Bob Maumill to WA Inc Royal Commission, 14.5.1991. The correct title of the inquiry was 'Royal Commission into Commercial Activities of Government and Other Matters', but for the purposes of this book it is referred to as the WA Inc Royal Commision.
6 *Sydney Morning Herald*, 11.12.1971.
7 Interview with author, 9.10.1991.
8 Maher, *Bond*, p. 114.
9 Trevor Sykes, *Operation Dynasty*, Greenhouse Press, Melbourne, 1989, pp. 85–6. For a fuller version see 'The Sting' by Ken Acott, *West Australian*, 14.1.1989.
10 Interview with author, 8.10.1991.
11 Noel Bushnell, 'In the court of King Joh', *Australian Business*, 11.11.1987.
12 The Queensland Government does not appear to have authorised Sir Edward to place TAB deposits with Rothwells until late November 1983. See Report of the Fitzgerald Commission of Inquiry, pp. 97–8. About $6 million appears to have been placed with Rothwells out of Queensland TAB current assets of $25 million to $30 million at the time.
13 The version given here is summarised from the evidence by Connell to the WA Inc Royal Commission on 8 and 9 April 1991.
14 For an insight into the Northcote branch see 'The Northcote Branch of the ALP', a Master of Arts preliminary thesis (University of Melbourne) by Lyle Allan. Len Brush's father Keith had been Northcote branch president before him, running it in authoritarian style. Keith vehemently opposed Federal intervention in the Victorian ALP in 1970. The Hall's Head deal is described in Section 5 of the WA Inc Royal Commission Report.
15 WA Inc Royal Commission Report, para. 6.19.5. The quote from O'Hara is from para. 5.13.20.
16 John McIlwraith, 'Commission to look at Burke diamond deal', *Australian Business*, 24.4.1991.
17 Letter dated 19.9.1983. Tendered in evidence to WA Inc Royal Commission.
18 Statement to parliament by Burke, 17.11.1983. This might be taken as the definitive statement on WA Inc at its inception.

19 Hamilton, *Burkie*, pp. 149–53.
20 Colleen Ryan and Anne Lampe, 'How Laurie sank a bank', *Sydney Morning Herald*, 28.1.1989.
21 Dempster's evidence, WA Inc Royal Commission, 11.6.1991.
22 Then Deloitte, Haskin & Sells. The name was changed to Deloitte Ross Tohmatsu by the time the McCusker Report was published. To avoid confusion I have simply called it Deloitte.
23 McCusker Report, para. 1.10. The full title of this report is 'Report of Inspector on a Special Investigation into Rothwells Ltd, Part I', tabled in WA Parliament 30.8.1990.
24 All details of the July 1984 Rothwells transactions are based on details given in the Deloitte attachments to Chapter 4 of the McCusker Report.
25 Connell's evidence, WA Inc Royal Commission, 13.8.1991.
26 Hurley's evidence, WA Inc Royal Commission, 20.3.1991.
27 Connell's evidence, WA Inc Royal Commission, 9.4.1991.
28 WA Inc Royal Commission, Part I, Vol. 3, para. 10.19.12.
29 McCusker's criticisms of the 1985 audit report on Rothwells extend from p. 54 to p. 78 of the McCusker Report.
30 McCusker Report, para. 3.15. If the debts were supposed to be owed to L.R. Connell & Partners, the situation would not have been much better. A separate check of the same thirteen alleged debtors showed that they owed only $2.6 million to LRC&P.
31 McCusker Report, para. 3.18. Carter said, in evidence to McCusker: 'The market sector at which the company's lending is aimed is the entrepreneurial businessman who is looking for quick decisions in approval of advances. Quite often the security offered is insufficient to cover the advance and the interest rate charged is 2%, 3% or even 5% over the market'. By definition, there must be risk attached.
32 McCusker Report, para. 4.24.
33 Connell's evidence, WA Inc Royal Commission, 13.8.1991, p. 8727.
34 Douglas's quotes are from the McCusker Report, paras 4.33 and 4.34.
35 McCusker Report, para. 4.13.
36 McCusker Report, para. 4.43.

Chapter 4

1 McCusker Report, para. 5.7.
2 The four books are: Trevor Sykes, *Operation Dynasty*, Greenhouse Press, 1989; Vic Carroll, *The Man Who Couldn't Wait*, Heinemann, Sydney, 1990; Gavin Souter, *Heralds and Angels*, Sydney, Melbourne University Press, 1990; and James Fairfax, *My Regards To Broadway*, 1991.
3 McCusker Report, paras 5.48 and 5.49.
4 McCusker Report, para. 5.71.
5 WA Inc Royal Commission Report, para. 21.1.12.
6 WA Inc Royal Commission Report, para. 21.1.15.
7 Vrisakis's evidence, in *Anfrank Nominees & others v. Connell & others*, WA Supreme Court, July 1989 (hereinafter called Pref. Shareholders' case).
8 Yonge's evidence, Pref. Shareholders' case, 20.7.1989.
9 McCusker Report, para. 11.18.

10 Connell's evidence, Pref. Shareholders' case, 18.7.1989.
11 Parker's evidence, Pref. Shareholders' case, 21.7.1989.
12 Yonge's evidence, Pref. Shareholders' case, 25.7.89.
13 Documents from Vrisakis to Schoer, 11.12.1987 (attached to Schoer's affidavit dated 17.1.1989 in Connell v. NCSC, Supreme Court of Victoria, No. 124 of 1989).
14 McCusker Report, para. 11.4.
15 McCusker Report, paras 11.5 and 11.6.
16 McCusker Report, paras 11.15 to 11.20.
17 McCusker Report, paras 11.15 to 11.20.
18 Connell's evidence, WA Inc Royal Commission, 15.8.1991. See also WA Inc Royal Commission Report, paras 21.1.70 to 21.1.80. The Bell Group takeover is explored in more depth in the present book's chapter on Bond.
19 Berinson's evidence, WA Inc Royal Commission, 3.9.1991.
20 Hilton's evidence, WA Inc Royal Commission, 30.8.1991.
21 WA Inc Royal Commission Report, para. 21.1.68.
22 WA Inc Royal Commission Report, para. 21.1.131.
23 McCusker Report, Chapter 7.
24 Colleen Ryan and David Humphries, *Sydney Morning Herald*, 11.1.1992.
25 Ben Hills, *The Good Weekend*, 4.4.1987.
26 WA Inc Royal Commmission Report, para. 20.10.4.
27 McCusker Report, para. 2.29.
28 McCusker Report, para. 2.33.
29 WA Inc Royal Commission Report, paras 23.14.1 to 23.14.8.
30 WA Inc Royal Commission Report, para. 26.2.1.
31 WA Inc Royal Commission Report, para. 26.4.23.
32 Connell's evidence, WA Inc Royal Commission, 19.8.1991.
33 Supreme Court of Western Australia, 23.2.1993.
34 Duncan Graham, report of District Court proceedings, SMH, 7.10.1993.
35 In July 1994, Burke was convicted of having obtained $17 000 from his parliamentary travel account by false pretences. He was sentenced to two years' jail, with a non-parole period of eight months. As this book was written, Burke was appealing against the conviction.

Chapter 5

1 Some excellent early background on Yuill is given by Valerie Lawson in 'The ceaseless strife of Brian', *Sydney Morning Herald*, 4.5.1991.
2 My thanks to John Strickland and Malcolm Irving for background on the formation of steel bills. News of the advent of steel bills was broken in the *Australian Financial Review* in a story by the young Christopher Skase.
3 Bob Macfarlan, QC, for Spedley Securities' liquidator in the damages case taken by the liquidator, John Harkness, against former Spedley directors, ANI and its auditors; NSW Supreme Court, 9.6.1992.
4 Judgement of Mr Justice Rogers, *Banque Brussels Lambert S.A. v. ANI*, NSW Supreme Court, 12.12.1989.
5 Progress Report of the Special Investigation in the Affairs of Spedley Securities Ltd and Other Companies, by Glen Miller, QC. Tabled in NSW Parliament 13.11.1990. Henceforth referred to as the Miller Report.

6 Jamie Craven, interview with author, 11.12.1993.
7 Macfarlan, Spedley/ANI case, 9.6.1992.
8 See Mr Justice Rolfe's finding on admissibility, Spedley/ANI case, 14.7.1992.
9 Details of this elaborate transaction are given in the Miller Report, Section 6.
10 Valerie Lawson, 'The ceaseless strife of Brian', *SMH*, 4.5.1991.
11 ibid.
12 Miller Report, Section 8.
13 Craven's evidence, Liquidator's Section 541 hearings, 29.4.1990.
14 Craven to author, 11.12.1993.
15 Macfarlan, Spedley/ANI case, 10.6.1992. See also Maher's evidence at Section 541 hearings.
16 At June 1984, a month before the round robins, Spedley Securities had shareholders' equity of $19.6 milllion, plus a subordinated loan of $5 million, bringing total shareholders' funds to $24.6 million. The Aldershot deal and the Spedley round robin can be found in Chapter 4.
17 Evidence of Graham Launders, auditor of Spedley Holdings, to Section 541 hearings, 26.9.1990.
18 Craven's evidence, Section 541 hearings, 12.11.1990. See also Macfarlan, Spedley/ANI case 9.6.1992, and Brent Potts' evidence in Section 541 hearings.
19 McCusker Report, Chapter III and annexures.
20 Miller Report, para. 4.22.
21 Macfarlan, Spedley/ANI case, 9.6.1992.
22 Mark Skulley and Glenn Burge, *The Age*, 12.4.1989.
23 McCusker Report, paras 5.63 and 5.64.
24 Macfarlan, Spedley/ANI case, 10.6.1992.
25 ibid.
26 Maher, Section 541 hearings. Also Macfarlan, Spedley/ANI case, 10.6.1992.
27 Macfarlan, Spedley/ANI case, 10.6.1992.
28 Affidavit of William Stuart Crosby, NCSC investigator, to Victorian Supreme Court, 27.4.1989. Crosby's affidavit was based on statements made to him by Craven. The use of the name Pluteus for Baker & McKenzie shelf companies reflects a little erudite humour. Pluteus is Latin for 'shelf'.
29 Miller Report, paras 4.14 and 4.15.
30 Miller Report, Section 5.
31 Macfarlan, Spedley/ANI case, 10.6.1992.
32 McCusker Report into Rothwells, para. 20 of section entitled 'WA State Government funding of Rothwells following October 1987 share market crash'.
33 Craven to author, 11.12.1993.
34 Spedley Securities' total assets at 30 June 1988 were $595 million.
35 Macfarlan, Spedley/ANI case, 10.6.1992.
36 Crosby affidavit.
37 Craven's evidence, Liquidator's Section 541 hearings, 2.5.1990.
38 Levings' evidence, Liquidator's Section 541 hearings, 6.5.1990.
39 Craven's evidence, Section 541 hearings, 9.10.1990.
40 Jones' evidence, ANI/Spedley case, NSW Supreme Court, 6.8.1992.
41 Craven to author, 11.12.1993.
42 Bryan Frith, *The Australian*, 5.5.1989.
43 Macfarlan, Spedley/ANI case, 10.6.1992.
44 Launders' evidence, Section 541 hearings, 2.10.1990.
45 Macfarlan, Spedley/ANI case, 10.6.1992.

46 Craven's evidence, Spedley Section 541 examination, 3.12.1991.
47 Crosby affidavit.
48 Yuill's evidence, Liquidator's Section 541 hearings into Spedley, 6.4.1990.
49 Statement from Bisley Investment Corporation to ASX, 22.3.1989.
50 John Hurst, 'ASX queries Bisley on Rome property', *Australian Financial Review*, 23.3.1989.
51 *Sun-Herald*, 2.4.1989.
52 As the Spedley scandal widened, this company's name became a great embarrassment to the highly reputable Bankers' Trust, which operated as BT Australia. BT Insurance originated in the taxi business as an offshoot of Black Top Cabs and was quite unconnected with BT Australia.
53 Yuill's evidence, Liquidator's Section 541 hearings, 8.4.1990.
54 Yuill's evidence, Liquidator's Section 541 hearings, 24.5.1990.
55 *The Australian*, 15.11.1990.
56 Trevor Sykes, *The Bulletin*, 7.12.1993.

Chapter 6

1 'Inside the mind of an entrepreneur', *Australian Business*, 12.3.1986.
2 Paul Barry, *The Rise and Fall of Alan Bond*, Bantam, 1990, p. 17. An excellent book which would be more helpful if it had an index.
3 Barry, p. 27.
4 Barry, p. 37.
5 Barry, p. 44.
6 Barry, p. 48.
7 For a fuller version of the Minsec story see Trevor Sykes, *The Money Miners*, Wildcat Press, 1978, Chapters 16 and 17.
8 Affidavit of Ron Nuich, 14.12.1990. Nuich was responsible for treasury accounting, corporate accounting and corporate consolidations for the Bond group.
9 See Trevor Sykes, 'Bond's gold mines', *Australian Business*, 8.8.1990, which outlines this and several other deals in the gold companies that worked out unfavourably for shareholders.
10 Sykes, 'Bond's gold mines'.
11 Barry, pp. 108–9.
12 The Kona Kai marina and hotel at San Diego were sold back to their former owner, local property developer Bill DeLeeuw, in August 1992. DeLeeuw had sold them to Bond for $US40.5 million in 1988. He bought them back for $US13.5 million—just one-third of the price.
13 Barry, p. 62.
14 SA House of Assembly Hansard, 24.5.1979. Hudson's speech is worth reading in full for an evaluation of Bond which most commentators reached only in hindsight.
15 Terence Maher, *Bond*, William Heinemann Australia, 1990, pp. 189–92.
16 Pierpont, 'Kicked out for being right', *The Bulletin*, 12.10.1993. See also John Alexander, 'Banker quits after Bond row,' *Australian Business*, 19.8.1982.
17 Trevor Sykes, 'How the banks lost your money', *Australian Business*, 3.10.1990.
18 Behind Elders IXL, Coles Myer, Westpac, BHP, Industrial Equity, ANZ, National Australia Bank and Fletcher Challenge.

19 Alan Kohler, *Australian Financial Review*, 17.11.1989.

20 Bond Corporation 1988 annual report.

21 *The Australian*, 3.12.1993.

22 Not all Bell Group's assets remained. Bond sold the Stoll Moss theatres in London's West End to Christopher Skase, who soon sold them back to Holmes à Court.

23 In a conversation with me about a fortnight before he died, Holmes à Court denied that he knew that Bond and the SGIC were acting in concert. 'I was naive', he said—a phrase which I never thought I would hear pass his lips. I thought then and think now that he was lying.

24 Barry, pp. 228–9.

25 A range of figures could have been quoted as the profit for the group. There were the equity and conventional consolidated accounts; and the profit figure could have been quoted either before or after tax or before or after extraordinaries. The figure of $402.5 million was the conventional consolidated profit after tax but before extraordinaries. Analysts might argue that the impact of the Hilton and Rome deals should more correctly be related to the pre-tax figure of $406.5 million, but the difference does not seem worth bothering about.

26 Agreement for Sale of Shares, Seabrook Corporation Ltd, 24.12.1987.

27 Letter from Ross Grant to Brian Yuill, 23.6.1988.

28 Originally $200 000 was suggested in a memo from Bruce Watson to Brian Yuill on 7.7.1988. This was reduced to $100 000 in a memo from Ross Grant to Yuill on 15.7.1988.

29 Facility Agreement between Kitool Pty Ltd, the lenders and the Bank of New Zealand, 23.12.1987.

30 Option Attainment Agreement between Bisley Options Management Pty Ltd and Bond Corporation International Ltd, 24.12.1987.

31 Eventually, the ABT found that Bond was not a fit and proper person to own a television station. On appeal, this finding was overthrown on the grounds that only a company could own a television station. This meant that the Act under which the ABT operated was unworkable because it contained an inherent contradiction. If only companies could own television stations, then there was no point in conducting inquiries into whether individuals were fit and proper persons to own them.

32 The term 'Sulan Report' is shorthand. John Sulan, the former Corporate Affairs Commissioner for South Australia, did the prime investigatory work on the report. This was supplemented by later work by other official investigators. In its final form, the report seems to have been the work of several authors although Sulan had provided its core.

33 Bond Corporation's holding in Bell Group Ltd rose from 68 per cent in 1988 to 74.3 per cent by June 1989.

34 Affidavit of Ron Nuich, 14.12.1990.

35 Details of the milking of Bell Resources given here are taken from the Sulan Report. For further details see Trevor Sykes, 'The case against Bond,' *The Bulletin*, 25.2.1992.

36 Of the remaining $7 million, $5 million was parked with Elders Finance, $1 million with Schroders and the rest went in fees to Markland House.

37 Report of Deloitte Haskins & Sells to Geoff Hill, chairman of Bell Resources, 23.1.1990.
38 Sulan Report, cited in *The Bulletin*, 25.2.1992.
39 Sulan Report, cited in *The Bulletin*, 25.2.1992.
40 Deloitte report to Hill, 10.1.1990.
41 Charles Boag, 'Bond's Swiss money man', *ABM*, October 1992.
42 Interview with Bruce Stannard, *The Bulletin*, 4.12.1990.
43 *The Australian*, 7.12.1993.

Chapter 7

1 Martin Thomas, *The Fraud*, Pagemasters, 1991, p. 46.
2 *Sydney Morning Herald*, 13.12.1989.
3 *The Age*, 25.3.1989.
4 Thomas, *The Fraud*, p. 66.
5 Wendy Bacon, *Sun-Herald*, 2.10.1988.
6 *The Australian*, 28.3.1989. By that date, with Friedrich on the run, it was certainly a matter for the Victoria Police. See also Glare's letter to *The Australian*, 29.3.1989.
7 Thomas, *The Fraud*, p. 61.
8 Thomas, *The Fraud*, p. 37.
9 Thomas, *The Fraud*, p. 38.
10 John Hay, 'Victim recalls Munich sting', *The Australian*, 3.4.1989.
11 *Sydney Morning Herald*, 29.3.1989.
12 Thomas, *The Fraud*, p. 116.
13 Thomas, *The Fraud*, p. 124.
14 Thomas, *The Fraud*, p. 99.
15 In any subsequent criminal trial he could have been asked the same questions. If he had not then made the same admissions, his guilt would have to be proved through other evidence. The answers he had given at the 541 hearing would not have been admissible.
16 Thomas, *The Fraud*, pp. 198–9.
17 Thomas, *The Fraud*, p. 201.
18 *Australian Business*, 12.4.1989.
19 *The Australian*, 31.3.1989.
20 Thomas, *The Fraud*, p. 114.
21 Thomas, *The Fraud*, pp. 182–88.
22 See 'I, spy', *The Age*, 12.10.1991. The article was an extract from the book entitled 'Codename Iago', to have been published by William Heinemann. Richard Flanagan assisted John Friedrich in compiling the manuscript.

Chapter 8

1 Ruth Ostrow, 'George Herscu's life in the fast lane', *Australian Financial Review*, 24.3.1986.
2 Ruth Ostrow, 'The new boy network'. A valuable source of anecdotes about the corporate cowboys.
3 Ostrow, 'George Herscu's life in the fast lane'.

4 Trevor Sykes, 'Hanover shareholders show little interest in group's future', *Financial Review*, 27.11.1975.

5 Ostrow, 'The new boy network'.

6 The story was compiled by Neil Spiers, Robert Gottliebsen and myself.

7 Ben Hills, 'House of cards', *Sydney Morning Herald*, 7.12.1990. An excellent profile of Herscu.

8 Sue Angell and Pieter Bruce, 'Herscu gives Hooker development go-ahead', *Financial Review*, 23.5.1986.

9 Two years later, Unsworth apologised to Herscu over his government's decision not to proceed with the Hooker–Harrahs casino development. 'Some people may have thought that in doing so, I was reflecting adversely on the fitness of George Herscu, Hooker's chairman, to do business with the NSW Government and to be the executive chairman of a major Australian public company. I did not intend to do so as neither I nor my then government held any such view', he said.

10 Hills, 'House of Cards'.

11 Janine Perrett, 'Hooker gambles on changing US shoppers' habits', *The Australian*, 5.1.1988.

12 Bob Walker, 'Hooker's $141m book exercise', *Australian Business*, 20.1.1988. Walker was Professor of Accountancy at the University of New South Wales.

13 See Figure 1.I (Chapter 1).

14 Bruce Jacques, 'Unhappy Hooker', *Australian Business*, 12.4.1989. This article is an excellent summary of the reasons for Hooker's share price slide.

15 Graeme Beaton, 'The malling of Hooker', *Australian Business*, 9.8.1989.

16 Hooker Corporation statement of affairs, released 10.11.1989.

17 Martin Warneminde, *Australian Business*, 11.4.1990.

18 Greg Roberts, *The Bulletin*, 15.6.1993. The best account of Herscu's jail term and release.

19 Herscu's evidence at bankruptcy hearing. Reported in *The Australian*, 30.10.1990.

Chapter 9

1 Deirdre Macken, 'Young man in a hurry', *The Age*, 18.3.1986.

2 Interview with Peter Hutchins, 10.1.1994.

3 Interview with John Shergold, 10.1.1994. The property deal would have been awkward, if not unrealistic. The Victoria was divided into three properties separated by laneways. Georges was divided into two properties on opposite sides of Collins Street. The parcel of Georges land adjoining the hotel was owned by the Scots Church and leased to the store until 2006. The idea would therefore have faced considerable practical obstacles. (See Melbourne Cityscope, Map 31.)

4 Hutchins, 10.1.1994.

5 John Edwards, 'What drives the boy billionaire', *Sydney Morning Herald*, 14.11.1987.

6 Shergold, 10.1.1994.

7 Bruce Stannard, *The Bulletin*, 14.5.1985.

8 Interview with Peter Lawrence, 11.1.1994. Lawrence was a close friend of mine when I was *AFR*'s Melbourne Editor, and I introduced Skase to him.
9 Edwards, *SMH*, 14.11.1987.
10 David Haselhurst, 'Chris Skase—cub reporter to TV tycoon', *The Bulletin*, 22.5.1984.
11 See Chapter 3.
12 *AFR*, 8.6.1982.
13 Haselhurst, *The Bulletin*, 22.5.1984.
14 Robert Kennedy, 'AWA's Christmas bargain a time-bomb', *SMH*, 21.5.1986.
15 For fuller background on AWA at this time see Trevor Sykes, 'Anatomy of a $50 million loss', *The Bulletin*, 19.1.1993.
16 Christopher Webb, 'Skase looks to $500m.', *AFR*, 28.10.1985.
17 Webb, *AFR*, 28.10.1985.
18 Macken, *The Age*, 18.3.1986.
19 For full details of the deal see Trevor Sykes, *Operation Dynasty*, Greenhouse, 1989, pp. 104–7.
20 Conversation with author, 18.11.1988.
21 Paul Gardiner, 'Behind the baby blue facade', *Australian Business*, 4.11.1987.
22 Barbara Hooks, 'Skase puts his case in the network race', *The Age*, 20.2.1988.
23 Tom Burton, 'It all comes down to a matter of style', *SMH*, 29.4.1988.
24 For the full terms of this deal see Sykes, *Operation Dynasty*, pp. 276–9.
25 Conversation with author, 22.4.1993.
26 For full details of Skase's business plan see Trevor Sykes, 'Skase: what went wrong with Qintex', *Australian Business*, 15.11.1989.
27 Neil Chenoweth, 'Who owns Queensland Merchant Holdings?', *Australian Business*, 11.4.1990.
28 Affidavit of John Allpass, Supreme Court of Victoria, April 1993.
29 Jenni Hewett, 'Chris Skase: where are you?', *AFR*, 29.6.1990.
30 For a full version of Skase's defence of himself and his attacks on others see Trevor Sykes, 'Skase lashes back', *Australian Business Monthly*, December 1991.
31 Hewett, *AFR*, 29.6.1990.
32 Television interview, Channel 10, 21.4.1993.

Chapter 10

1 Ruth Ostrow, 'The new boy network'.
2 Adam Shand, 'When the money ran out', *The Australian*, 16.2.1991.
3 Michael Meagher, 'How Abe Goldberg built his rag trade empire', *The Bulletin*, 14.2.1984; an excellent article on Goldberg's empire at that point.
4 One who noticed was John Shanahan in his Accountancy column in *Australian Business*, 12.7.1989.
5 Shand, *The Australian*, 16.2.1991.
6 Shirley Skeel, 'Why companies are going private', *Australian Business*, 27.4.1988.
7 Bryan Frith, 'Elliott's part in AFP signals wider Elders play', *The Australian*, 23.3.1988.
8 *Sydney Morning Herald*, 2.3.1989.
9 Angela Mackay, 'Goldberg's "cheap exit" from Tootal', *Australian Financial Review*, 15.5.1989.
10 Interview with author, 10.1.1994 (also subsequent Shergold quotes).

11 Maureen Murrill, 'Abe's building blocks are more than bricks', *AFR*, 28.6.1989.

12 The Companies Code then required that anyone acquiring more than 19.9 per cent of a company was legally required to bid the same price for the rest, unless shareholders could be persuaded to waive the requirement. This could be done by a meeting of shareholders under Section 12(g) of the Code. It was rarely a good idea for shareholders to agree.

13 Adam Shand, 'When the money ran out', *The Australian*, 16.2.1991.

14 See Chapter 13.

15 Maxsted Report, Goldberg family interests, para. 2.10. This is not a publicly available report. The best publicly available article based on it is Noel Bushnell, 'Where did the money go, Abe?', *Australian Business*, 14.3.1990.

16 Maxsted Report, Goldberg family interests, para. 2.12.

17 Jo Chandler, 'Goldberg, $470m. down, starts again in Poland', *The Age*, 25.1.1992.

18 Paul McGeough and John Lyons, 'Elusive Goldberg plays Warsaw Concerto', *SMH*, 25.2.1992.

19 Boskovitz gave this evidence at the Section 541 hearing into Linter's liquidation. At her committal hearings she reserved her defence and elected to go straight to trial, where she said she would plead not guilty. Downing Centre Local Court proceedings, 13.9.1993.

20 Report by Lindsay Philip Maxsted to Supreme Court of Victoria when applying for orders for information to be supplied by various parties in the liquidation of Linter Group, May 1993. See also newspaper reports of Melbourne Magistrates Court hearings from August to October 1993; particularly Bill Pheasant, *AFR*, 30.8.1993.

Chapter 11

1 Interview with Mark Johnson, 18.1.1994.

2 The details of the PMA1 loan are taken from the statement of claim compiled by Baker & McKenzie for the damages case brought by the trustees of Meridian Trusts, Peter Allen and John Murphy, against Reuben Lew and others. Details of this claim were published in *The Bulletin*, 23.11.1993.

3 Trevor Sykes, *The Bulletin*, 23.11.1993.

4 Murphy and Allen statement of claim.

5 Independent Funds Research Ltd, *Australian Mortgage Trusts: Industry Review*, August 1989, pp. 311–13.

6 Annette Sampson, 'The giraffe that grew too high', *Australian Business*, 25.4.1990. This article gives an excellent summary of the weaknesses of Estate Mortgage and the causes of its collapse, only a few days after payments were suspended.

7 Sampson, *Australian Business*, 25.4.1990.

8 Sampson, *Australian Business*, 25.4.1990.

9 *Sydney Morning Herald*, 4.6.1990.

10 Peter Maher, 'Why Estate Mortgage trusts are facing losses', *Australian Business*, 27.6.1990.

11 Bryan Frith, 'Burns Philp Trustee has much to answer for', *The Australian*, 8.7.1990.
12 For a history of the slow revolution at Burns, Philp see Trevor Sykes, 'How Burns Philp hit terra firma', *Australian Business Monthly*, September 1992.
13 Bill Pheasant, 'Taking the roof off Estate Mortgage', *Australian Financial Review*, 11.9.1991.
14 Richard Sproull, 'Family business: the fall of the Lews', *The Australian*, 5.11.1993.
15 For further detail see Meridian Investment Trust information memorandum, 15.11.1993.
16 Robert Ramsay to author, 20.12.1993.

Chapter 12

1 For the founding and early history of Pyramid see A. McI. Scott, *Men, Money & Houses*, 1981.
2 From the first report of the liquidator, Tony Hodgson, 28.6.1991. pp. 10–12.
3 Gay Alcorn, 'Farrow's aggressive, ambitious partner,' *The Age*, 8.7.1990.
4 *Sydney Morning Herald*, 14.2.1990.
5 Price Waterhouse report to directors, 21.3.1990.
6 Simon Mann, *The Age*, 3.11.1990.
7 Trevor Sykes, 'From The Desk', *Australian Business*, 11.4.1990. See also Catherine Law, same edition.
8 N.J. Brady, *The Supervision of Building Societies in Victoria*. This report, commissioned by the government, was released in July 1990.
9 Brady Report, p. 7.
10 LaFranchi Report, p. 6.
11 Rowena Stretton, 'Glamour image no safe haven', *The Bulletin*, 6.3.1990.
12 *SMH*, 28.6.1990.
13 Deborah Brewster, 'Farrow says everyone can be repaid', *The Age*, 3.7.1990.
14 Alan Wood, 'Pontius Pilate won't wash, Mr Cain', *The Australian*, 26.6.1990.
15 Compiled from appendices, first Hodgson Report, 28.6.1991.
16 From first Hodgson Report, 28.6.1991, p. 5.
17 Table from Hodgson Report, 30.6.1992, p. 26.
18 Statement of claim by Pyramid Building Society and others against Robert Farrow and others; No. 2057 of 1992, Supreme Court of Victoria.
19 Majella Corrigan, *AFR*, 18.2.1993.

Chapter 13

1 For a fuller version of Adsteam's birth see John Bach, *A Maritime History of Australia*, Pan, 1976, pp. 190–7.
2 *The Bulletin*, 24.5.1962.
3 Michael Fitzgerald Page, *Fitted for the Voyage: Adelaide Steamship Co 1875–1975*, Rigby, 1975, p. 310. Ironically, this excellent history was penned just as the company was about to embark on its huge diversification. Given the lead times in publishing, the big expansions and John Spalvins are not mentioned in the book.

4 Interview with Colleen Ryan, *Sydney Morning Herald*, 27.6.1987.
5 To avoid confusion, the name 'Adsteam' is used throughout in reference to the group. 'Adelaide Steamship' refers to the parent company.
6 Peter Ward, 'The man behind DJ's raid', *The Australian*, 3.7.1980. The 'man' in the title was Russell.
7 In this book I have used the accounting terminology of the 1980s. Today the terminology has been entirely changed. The word and concept of 'group' has been replaced by 'economic entity', for example.
8 Jennifer Kitchener and Steve Elsner, 'Why the Big Australian may topple', *Australian Business*, 23.1.1985.
9 The buyer of a call option is buying an option to take the stock at a set price by a set date. The seller of a call option, known as a writer, promises to deliver the stock at the same price and date.
10 Lachlan Drummond, 'Making money the intent of the Spalvins gambit', *SMH*, 9.10.1985.
11 Trevor Sykes, 'BHP's big bear', *Australian Business*, 12.3.1986.
12 Sykes, *Australian Business*, 12.3.1986.
13 For those who are interested, I can testify that gold leaf is tasteless and has no apparent effect on the digestive system.
14 Malcolm Maiden, 'Spalvins fires off a burst at Westpac', *Australian Financial Review*, 20.5.1988.
15 See Chapters 4 and 6.
16 Trevor Sykes, 'Adsteam unmasked', *Australian Business*, 19.4.1989.
17 Share prices of Adelaide Steamship have been used as an index of the *group's* fortunes. Unless otherwise stated, readers can assume that share prices of other group members such as David Jones and Tooth rose and fell in tandem with Adelaide Steamship.
18 Alan Kohler, Chanticleer column, *AFR*, 7.11.1990.
19 From Adelaide Steamship 1993 annual report.
20 The chart is from the 1990 annual report of Adelaide Steamship. Readers should be thankful that this book has spared them the details of how the cross-holdings changed each year.
21 The ASC took a sterner view. In April 1994 it commenced proceedings in the Federal Court in the name of the Adelaide Steamship Co against Spalvins, Kent, Branford, Russell, Gregg and Adsteam's auditors Deloitte. The ASC alleged that the former directors and auditors failed to properly account for various loans and inter-company transactions in the year to June 1990, causing Adelaide Steamship's reported profit to be overstated by at least $518 million and causing $228 million in dividends to be paid when no profits were available. This was one of the odder court cases of the 1990s. The executives then running Adelaide Steamship had only limited knowledge of the court case being taken in their name and were denied access to some of the data the ASC was using.

Chapter 14

1 He had not then received his knighthood.
2 First Report of the Royal Commission into the Tricontinental Group of Companies, 30.7.1991, p. 87. This report is henceforth referred to as RC Tricon I.

3   File note, RC Tricon I, p. 114.
4   A summary of the Touche Ross report can be found in RC Tricon I, pp. 117–19.
5   Memo from Moyle to SBV board, RC Tricon I, p. 120.
6   RC Tricon I, pp. 134–5.
7   RC Tricon I, pp. 140–1.
8   RC Tricon I, pp. 105–7.
9   RC Tricon I, p. 389.
10 *Not* written by me although as executive editor of *Australian Business* at the time I was ultimately responsible. I knew Johns slightly and Tricontinental slightly less, and accepted the opinion of others about the bank until mid-1987 when I took a harder look and started becoming concerned. Unfortunately, that was just after *Australian Business* had given Tricontinental its 1987 award for Most Improved Company.
11 RC Tricon I, p. 155.
12 Capital as defined by the capital adequacy ratio is divided into two tiers. Tier 1 includes ordinary paid capital, paid non-cumulative irredeemable preference shares, retained earnings and reserves (other than asset revaluation reserves) less goodwill and other intangibles. Tier 2 includes asset revaluation reserves, general provisions for doubtful debts, hybrid debt/equity instruments and subordinated loan capital with an original maturity of at least seven years. Today the RBA requires banks to maintain a minimum of 8 per cent capital adequacy, of which at least half must be Tier 1 capital. Until August 1988, the Reserve Bank measured capital adequacy as the ratio of capital to total balance sheet assets. From August 1988, the Reserve Bank weighted assets according to risk.
13 RC Tricon I, p. 159.
14 McAnany, statement of evidence at Royal Commission, 29.1.1991, p. 7.
15 RC Tricon I, pp. 176–7.
16 RC Tricon I, pp. 218–19.
17 RC Tricon I, pp. 318–20. In his evidence Moyle denied the remark but essentially agreed with the circumstances of Rawlins' departure.
18 Debra Stirling, 'Unravelling Tricontinental', *Australian Business*, 20.7.1988.
19 RC Tricon I, p. 213.
20 RC Tricon I, p. 447.
21 Meeting of Smith and Masel with RBA on 31.3.1989. RC Tricon I, p. 260.
22 See Trevor Sykes, 'Inside out', *Australian Business*, 5.6.1991.
23 Board minutes. RC Tricon I, p. 281.
24 RC Tricon I, p. 479.
25 RC Tricon I, p. 272.
26 Memorandum by Moyle, contained in a letter by Hancock to Jolly. RC Tricon I, pp. 289–91.
27 *The Age*, 27.3.1993.
28 Press statements by Victorian Premier, Jeff Kennett, and the KPMG executive chairman, John Harkness, 25.1.1994.
29 For a fuller version of the statement of claim see Trevor Sykes, 'Tri, Tri again', *The Bulletin*, 7.7.1992. The details of these bad loans and sloppy lending practices are generally confirmed in the details of Peats' defence documents. Peats, however, claimed that the bad loans were the fault of the executives and directors of Tricontinental and not of the auditor.

Chapter 15

1 Chris Kenny, *State of Denial*, Wakefield Press, 1993. The best book on Bannon and the Bannon years. For a profile of Bannon see Chapter 5.
2 Peter Ward, 'Towering ambition', *The Australian*, 30.6.1992.
3 Interview with author, 4.1.1993.
4 Terence Maher, 'How the State Bank went south', *Australian Business*, 20.2.1991. This article is the best exposition of the SBSA's state of affairs at the time.
5 See Chapter 14 for the definition of capital adequacy.
6 Report of the Royal Commission into the State Bank of South Australia (henceforth called the Jacobs Report), p. 52.
7 Report of SA Auditor-General Ken MacPherson, Vol. III, para. 5.2.2.2.
8 MacPherson, Vol. I, para. 1.7.6.
9 MacPherson, Vol. IX, para. 19.2.5.
10 Jacobs Report, p. 61.
11 For fuller details of the ownership and financing structure, see MacPherson, Vol. XII, paras 24.9 to 24.10.2.
12 Jacobs Report, p. 74.
13 Jacobs Report, p. 81.
14 Trevor Sykes, *Two Centuries of Panic*, Allen & Unwin, 1988, pp. 501–16.
15 The reasons are still suppressed, for all practical purposes. In 1987, when writing *Two Centuries of Panic*, I applied to Samuel Jacobs—then Mr Justice Jacobs of the SA Supreme Court—to lift a suppression order imposed in 1979 on evidence which disclosed the reasons for the failure of FCA. Jacobs reserved judgement and, despite several promptings by my lawyer, never responded to the request. The episode returned to the public light when Jacobs was appointed Royal Commissioner into the failure of the SBSA. He then said that he had lifted the suppression order. If he had, he never notified either me or my legal representative. By that time *Two Centuries of Panic* had long been printed so the matter had become academic for me, but the Adelaide representative of the *Australian Financial Review* was energetic enough to apply to see the documents, with my permission. He was told they had been lost.
16 Jacobs Report, p. 101.
17 Jacobs Report, p. 117.
18 Letter from Mr K.S. Matthews, former chief general manager, group risk management, of the SBSA. Jacobs Report, pp. 124 and 126 (endnote 71).
19 Allan Hawkins and Gordon McLauchlan, *The Hawk*, Four Star Books, 1989, pp. 20–23. If you never knew anything about Equiticorp this book would not enlighten you much. Its most notable feature is a complete absence of any explanation of why Equiticorp collapsed.
20 Jacobs Report, p. 120.
21 Jacobs Report, p. 135.
22 MacPherson, Vol. VII, para. 15.4.4.2.
23 Jacobs Report, p. 123.
24 MacPherson, Vol. VII, para. 26.7.3.
25 MacPherson, Vol. XV, para. 38.2.4.
26 Jacobs Report, p. 149.
27 Actually, the NZ Government had agreed to take 92.9 million shares in Equiticorp Holdings in return for its NZ Steel shares. Auckland stockbroking

firm Buttle Wilson had simultaneously agreed to place the shares for the government for the required $NZ327 million. This purchase had been underwritten by two Hawkins-controlled companies, which in turn had been underwritten by Equiticorp. But the share market crash of Black Tuesday had wiped two-thirds of the price off Equiticorp shares, which were marked down to little over $NZ1. This blew the underwriting deal out of the water and, effectively, Equiticorp had to pay the NZ Government for the shares. For further detail see the judgement of Mr Justice Tompkins, *The Queen v. Hawkins and others*, High Court of New Zealand, T No. 240/91.

28 MacPherson, Vol. XII, para. 26.2. For the record, Oceanic Capital survived its various owners and by 1994 was operating profitably with shareholders' funds of $35 million.
29 Jacobs Report, p. 140. All references here to the East End Markets are to Beneficial's experience in the project of that name in both the Jacobs and MacPherson reports. No reference is made or intended to the project which opened in 1991–92 and is today operating on the northern side of Rundle Street under the name of East End Markets. I am informed that the modern East End Markets project is operating profitably under different ownership.
30 MacPherson, Vol. XII, paras 24.10 to 24.10.2.
31 Jacobs Report, p. 192. Jacobs rejected evidence by Kean that he had not supported the SGIC entry into the project.
32 Jacobs Report, pp. 192–4.
33 MacPherson, Vol. VI, para. 14.2.3.2.
34 Jacobs Report, p. 204.
35 Jacobs Report, p. 205.
36 Interview with Jennifer Cashmore, 19.1.1994.
37 Jacobs Report, pp. 233–5.
38 See Chapter 7.
39 Adjustment to Table 8.9 in Jacobs Report, p. 249.
40 Jacobs Report, p. 247.
41 Jacobs Report, p. 246.
42 Kenny, *State of Denial*, p. 115.
43 Jacobs Report, p. 297.
44 Terence Maher, 'How the State Bank went south', *Australian Business*, 20.2.1991.
45 MacPherson, Vol. XII, para. 24.10.4.
46 Maher, *Australian Business*, 20.2.1991.
47 Media release by SBSA, 10.2.1991.
48 Jacobs Report, p. 139.
49 MacPherson, Vol. I, para. 1.5.3.
50 MacPherson, Vol. I, paras 1.5.3–6.
51 MacPherson, Vol. XIII, paras 27.4.2.4–5.
52 Bannon to author, 20.10.1993.
53 Kenny, *State of Denial*, p. 113.

Chapter 16

1 Lenore Nicklin, 'Australia's missing tycoon', *The Bulletin*, 23.8.1983.
2 Nicklin, *The Bulletin*, 23.8.1983.

3 Maurice Mellick, 'Little joy for Bishopsgate creditors', *Australian Business*, 14.12.1983.
4 David Hirst, *The Australian*, 18.2.1984.
5 The best detailed analysis of Stathis' thefts is by Stephen Bartholomeusz, *The Age*, 15.2.1984.
6 Noel Bushnell, 'How Budget was driven to the wall', *Australian Business*, 9.5.1990.
7 Bushnell, *Australian Business*, 9.5.1990.
8 Letter from Grey to author, 29.7.1993.
9 *Sunday Age*, 16.2.1992.
10 Trevor Sykes, 'Wrong bearings from Compass', *The Bulletin*, 6.4.1993. Most of the material in the section on Compass II is taken from this article.
11 Richard Owen, *The Australian*, 26.3.1993.
12 Bryan Frith, *The Australian*, 6.4.1993.
13 Sykes, *The Bulletin*, 6.4.1993.
14 See Pierpont, *Australian Business*, 15.3.1989.
15 Interview with Millner, 7.1.1994.
16 Pierpont, *Australian Business*, 5.7.1989.
17 *Australian Financial Review*, 21.3.1990.
18 Janette Manson, '$150m. missing in Yap's paper trail', *Australian Business*, 13.6.1990.
19 Trevor Sykes, 'A takeover in hindsight', *Australian Business*, 21.12.1988.
20 Interview with Reid, 12.1.1994.
21 Notice of extraordinary general meetings and explanatory memorandum of Kia Ora Gold Corporation NL relating to the acquisition of assets of the Duke Holdings group of companies, 17.5.1988, p. 22. The writeoff is disclosed in the expert report of Arthur Young at item 16(i).
22 Interview with Reid, 12.1.1994.
23 For a fuller version of the Andersen report see Trevor Sykes, 'The hazards of Duke', *Australian Business*, 7.6.1989.
24 Interview with Reid, 12.1.1994.
25 For further details see Trevor Sykes, 'Why Duke hit the wall', *Australian Business*, 21.6.1989.
26 Interview with Reid, 12.1.1994.
27 For background see Jane Blaikie, *AFR*, 24.4.1985.
28 The best rundown on Electronic Enterprises is by Martin Peers, 'The story behind Ken Wright's fire sale', *AFR*, 7.2.1986.
29 *AFR*, 12.2.1991.
30 See Pierpont, *The Bulletin*, 27.3.1991.
31 Ken Brass 'The lone raider', *The Australian*, 3.5.1986.
32 For the definitive account see Tim Blue, 'When to blow the whistle', *Australian Business*, 21.8.1991.
33 Yes, I was one of the judges.

Chapter 17

1 Modified from *The Bulletin*, 3.8.1993.
2 Anyone who doubts this should buy a copy of *Two Centuries of Panic*. Please.

3 Modified from a table originally printed in *Australian Business Monthly*, 'How the banks lost $28 billion', October 1993.
4 Trevor Sykes, *Operation Dynasty*, Greenhouse Press, p. 295.
5 MacPherson report, Vol. 1, para. 1.5.4.
6 Conversation with Maumill, 17.12.1993.
7 Macfarlan, Spedley/ANI case, 10.6.92.
8 Trevor Sykes, 'Inside out', *Australian Business*, 5.6.1991.
9 See Trevor Sykes, 'A Few Scalps Short of a Beheading', *The Bulletin*, 7.12.1993. See also letter from ASC Chairman Alan Cameron, *Bulletin*, 21.12.1993.
10 See Martin Thomas, *The Fraud*, pp. 208–11.
11 Interview with Cashmore, 19.1.1994. See also Kenny, *State of Denial*, Wakefield Press, 1993, Chapter 2.
12 Kenny, *State of Denial*, p. 45.
13 See Kenny, *State of Denial*, Chapter 2, 'The Bannon government and the media'.
14 Richard Gluyas, 'Part exchange,' *The Australian*, 29.3.1993.
15 Charles Wright, 'Five owners in one year,' *Australian Business*, 23.12.1987.
16 See *Two Centuries of Panic*, pp. 554–5. See also 'Law needs change on corporate crashes', an article by 'Judicious' (Mr Justice Andrew Rogers), *Australian Business*, 7.1.1987.
17 The concept could be extended to trusts and funds which invest in bills endorsed or accepted by licensed trading banks, thus having 'lender of last resort' protection. The 5 per cent gearing is to cover occasional surges in redemptions.

Index

[Note: The appendix has not been indexed. The endnotes have been indexed only where they add to text.]